Far East
English-Chinese
Pinyin Dictionary

遠　　東
英漢拼音辭典

Compiled by

The Far East Book Co.,

Editorial Committee

遠東圖書公司印行
The Far East Book Co., Ltd.

Published by
The Far East Book Co., Ltd.
66-1 Chungking South Road, Section 1
Taipei, Taiwan
www.fareast.com.tw
Distributed by
US International Publishing Inc.
39 West 38th Street
New York, New York 10018
U.S.A.
www.usipusa.com
ISBN   957-612-678-9

Table of Contents
目　錄

Preface ·································· I

序文 ····································· III

Explanation of Entries ·············· IV

體例說明 ······························· VI

The Dictionary 辭典正文 ·············· 1~299

Appendices

I. Chinese Festivals 中國節日 ········· 302

II. Countries, Cities, and Regions
國家、城市、地區 ················· 303

III. Practical Daily Usage
日常實用語句 ····················· 311

IV. Hanyu Pinyin Table 漢語拼音總表 ···· 327

Preface

A good dictionary is an indispensable aid to foreign-language learning.

The Far East Book Co. has been deeply involved in the field of Chinese language learning for many years. Among our most popular publications are the *Far East Chinese-English Dictionary* (edited by the renowned linguist Dr. Liang, Shih-chiu) which has been widely used in Taiwan and abroad for several decades, and the more recent *Far East Pinyin Chinese-English Dictionary* (edited by Graduate Institute of Chinese as a Second Language Prof. Yeh, Teh-ming) and the *Far East 3,000 Chinese Character Dictionary* (edited by Chinese linguist Dr. Teng, Shou-hsin). All our dictionaries are subjected to an exhaustive editing process before publication, our final goal always being to help students learn Chinese effectively. During the recent wave of enthusiasm for Chinese language learning, has given these dictionaries an opportunity to demonstrate their value. Recently, however, we have received numerous letters from around the world asking us when we are going to publish a modern English-Chinese Pinyin Dictionary. Three years ago, in response to these requests, we began preparing such a dictionary.

The Far East English-Chinese Pinyin Dictionary is designed for Chinese language learners. A team of professional Chinese and English language editors worked closely together to design a dictionary that contains all the most useful words, along with accurate and authoritative definitions of each. There are around 12,000 English entries, each of which is followed by a clear and precise Chinese translation. Each Chinese entry is followed by its Hanyu Pinyin in order to facilitate the study of correct pronunciation. Following the Hanyu Pinyin for each Chinese definition is an English translation or hint that helps readers to distinguish the sometimes subtle differences in meaning between Chinese words. In addition, pronunciations for both mainland China and Taiwan are provided in order to meet the practical needs of students. The book also contains four appendices: Chinese Festivals; Countries, Cities and Regions; Practical Daily Usage; and a Hanyu Pinyin Table.

Producing a dictionary requires a tremendous amount of time and energy. Far East has devoted itself fully to this project, and to its larger mission of promoting Chinese language education. Our hope is that readers will be able to use this dictionary to better express themselves in Chinese, regardless of the circumstances. Despite our very best efforts, occasional omissions or oversights are unavoidable, and so we welcome the constructive feedback of language scholars as well as our readers.

Far East Editorial Committee

序 文

學習語言，實用的辭典不可或缺。

長期以來，我們熱誠投入學習中文的領域，從海內外通行數十年的「遠東漢英大辭典」（世紀語言大師梁實秋教授主編），到近幾年相當受到肯定的「遠東拼音漢英辭典」（華語文教學研究所葉德明教授主編）和「遠東漢字三千字典」（漢語語言學專家鄧守信教授主編），每一本工具書都經過千錘百鍊的查考審校所編纂而成，目的就是要有效輔助讀者正確學習中文。在這波中文學習的熱潮當中，這些工具書大大地發揮了實際的功用。同時，我們也收到很多世界各地的讀者來訊，強烈期盼能夠出版一本現代化的英漢拼音辭典。於是，我們從三年前開始展開這項計畫。

「遠東英漢拼音辭典」，是針對學習中文的人士所設計，由一群專業的中文編輯和外文編輯根據使用者的角度來精心篩選有用的詞條和恰當的詞義。我們選錄實用詞條約 12,000 個，提供簡明清晰的中文義譯，每個中文字均標明漢語拼音，以便順利讀出正確發音。最大的特色乃於中文義譯後加註英文解釋或英文提示，幫助讀者精準掌握詞義。同時，我們分別列出兩岸說法及發音上的差異，符合實際需要；並且提供四個附錄：中國節日、國家和城市、日常實用語句和漢語拼音總表等，增加實用功能。

編纂一本辭典，費時耗力，遠東秉持推廣中文的時代使命，努力投入心血，即是要方便讀者可以隨時隨地善加運用，快速且確實地找到想要表達的中文；如此，正是本辭典的最高價值了。當然，即使盡力精益求精，疏漏之處仍在所難免，尚祈專家學者及所有讀者不吝指正。

遠東編審委員會

Explanation of Entries

I. **Dictionary entries:** A total of 12,000 words have been select-
ed, with usefulness as the main criterion.

II. **Word type:** Marked in italics. For example:

arms *n.* 武器 wǔqì (weapons). – *v.* 武裝 wǔzhuāng.

III. **Chinese definition:** Each English entry is followed by concise
Chinese definitions, which are arranged based on their frequency of use. In addition, when usage in mainland China
and Taiwan differs, the mainland China usage is listed first,
followed by a slash (/) and then the Taiwanese usage.
For example:

scheme *n.* ①計畫 jìhuà (plan). ②陰謀 yīnmóu (conspiracy).
③圖表 túbiǎo (diagram). ④設計 shèjì (design). – *v.* 計畫
jìhuà (plan), 圖謀 túmóu (connive).

sauna *n.* 桑拿浴 sāngnáyù / 三溫暖 sānwēnnuǎn.

IV. **Hanyu pinyin:** In order to help readers properly pronounce
the words, each word is followed by its Hanyu Pinyin.
When pronunciation differs across the strait, the Mainland
pronunciation is listed first, followed by the Taiwanese
pronunciation. For example:

architecture *n.* 建築 jiànzhù / jiànzhú.

V. **English explanation:** In order to help readers fully grasp the
meaning of each word, a clear and precise English explanation is added whenever there are several different
meanings for the same word. There are two types of
English explanation.

The first, which is marked [( )], is the equivalent of an
English definition for that word. The second, which is
marked [⟨ ⟩], is a hint that will help readers distinguish
between the different entries for a single word. For
example:

flourish *v.* ①繁盛 fánshèng (prosper). ②興隆 xīnglóng
(thrive). ③揮動 huīdòng (wave).

IV

fresh *adj.* ①新鮮的 xīnxiān de ⟨food⟩. ②清新的 qīngxīn de ⟨air⟩. ③淡的 dàn de ⟨water⟩. ④新奇的 xīnqí de ⟨idea⟩.

VI. **Important expressions:** This dictionary contains a number of important and useful expressions, which are marked in bold and italics. For example:

shut *v.* 閉 bì, 關閉 guānbì. ~ *off* 關掉 guāndiào. ~ *up* 住口 zhùkǒu, 閉嘴 bìzuǐ.

VII. **Appendices:** There are four in total, including (1) Chinese Festivals (2) Countries, Cities and Regions (3) Practical Daily Usage (4) Hanyu Pinyin Table.

體 例 說 明

一、詞　條：本辭典收錄約一萬二千個詞條，以實用為主。

二、詞　性：以斜體標示。例如

    arms *n.* 武器 wǔqì (weapons). — *v.* 武裝 wǔzhuāng.

三、中文義譯：為確切符合讀者的實際應用需求，每個詞條均
提供重要簡明之中文義譯，按照其常用性排序，
並同時列出兩岸差異之說法，以「/」隔開，前
者為大陸說法，後者為台灣說法。例如

    scheme *n.* ①計畫 jìhuà (plan). ②陰謀 yīnmóu
(conspiracy). ③圖表 túbiǎo (diagram). ④設計 shèjì
(design). — *v.* 計畫 jìhuà (plan), 計謀 túmóu (connive).

    sauna *n.* 桑拿浴 sāngnáyù / 三溫暖 sānwēnnuǎn.

四、漢語拼音：為幫助讀者正確念出中文的發音，每個中文字
均特別加註漢語拼音，並同時列出兩岸差異之
發音，以「/」隔開，前者為大陸發音，後者為
台灣發音。例如

    architecture *n.* 建築 jiànzhù / jiànzhú.

五、英文註解：為令讀者在應用本辭典時能完全掌握正確詞
義，除單義詞條外，所有有異義詞條之中文義
譯均加註清晰可別的英文註解，有效幫助讀者
正確選用中文義譯。本字典有兩種英文註解形
式，其一是「( )」，此為相當於該中文詞義之
英文解釋；其二是「〈 〉」，此為可供區別之重
點提示。例如

    flourish *v.* ①繁盛 fánshèng (prosper). ②興隆
xīnglóng (thrive). ③揮動 huīdòng (wave).

    fresh *adj.* ①新鮮的 xīnxiān de ⟨food⟩. ②清新的
qīngxīn de ⟨air⟩. ③淡的 dàn de ⟨water⟩. ④新奇的
xīnqí de ⟨idea⟩.

六、重要短語：本辭典所選錄之重要片語，以粗斜體標示。例如

    shut *v.* 閉 bì, 關閉 guānbì. **~ off** 關掉 guāndiào.
~ up 住口 zhùkǒu, 閉嘴 bìzuǐ.

七、附　錄：四項附錄－(1)中國重要節日 (2)國家、城市、地
區 (3)日常實用語句 (4)漢語拼音總表。

A

a *indef. art.* ①一 yī (one). ②某一 mǒuyī (some).

abacus *n.* 算盤 suànpán.

abandon *v.* ①拋棄 pāoqì (desert). ②放棄 fàngqì (give up).

abate *v.* ①減少 jiǎnshǎo (reduce). ②減輕 jiǎnqīng (lighten).

abbey *n.* 修道院 xiūdàoyuàn.

abbreviate *v.* ①縮寫 suōxiě (title). ②縮短 suōduǎn (shorten).

abdicate *v.* 讓位 ràngwèi (power).

abdomen *n.* 腹部 fùbù.

abduct *v.* ①綁架 bǎngjià (kidnap). ②拐走 guǎizǒu (entice away).

abhor *v.* 憎惡 zēngwù.

abide *v.* 忍受 rěnshòu (tolerate). ~ *by* 遵守 zūnshǒu (obey).

ability *n.* 能力 nénglì.

able *adj.* 能幹的 nénggàn de, 有才能的 yǒu cáinéng de (competent).

abnormal *adj.* 反常的 fǎncháng de.

aboard *adv. & prep.* 在船上 zài chuánshang ⟨ship⟩, 在火車上 zài huǒchēshang ⟨train⟩, 在飛機上 zài fēijīshang ⟨plane⟩, 在巴士上 zài bāshìshang ⟨bus⟩.

abode *n.* 住所 zhùsuǒ.

abolish *v.* 廢除 fèichú.

abominable *adj.* 可惡的 kěwù de (hateful).

aboriginal *adj.* 原始的 yuánshǐ de. — *n.* 土著 tǔzhù.

aborigine *n.* 原住民 yuánzhùmín.

abort *v.* ①墮胎 duòtāi ⟨pregnancy⟩. ②停止 tíngzhǐ (end).

abortion *n.* 墮胎 duòtāi.

abound *v.* 充滿 chōngmǎn.

about *prep.* ①關於 guānyú (concerning). ②大約 dàyuē (approximately).

above *prep.* ①在……之上 zài...zhī shàng (higher than). ②超過 chāoguò (more than). — *adv.* 在上 zài shàng (higher up).

abrade *v.* 磨損 mósǔn.

abreast *adv.* 並肩 bìngjiān (side by side).

abridge *v.* 刪減 shānjiǎn.

abroad *adv.* 在國外 zài guówài.

abrupt *adj.* 突然的 tūrán de / túrán de.

abscess *n.* 膿腫 nóngzhǒng.

abscond *v.* 潛逃 qiántáo.

absence *n.* ①缺席 quēxí (nonattendance). ②缺乏 quēfá (lack).

absent *adj.* 缺席的 quēxí de.

absentee *n.* 缺席者 quēxízhě.

absent-minded *adj.* 心不在焉的 xīn-bú-zài-yān de.

absolute *adj.* 絕對的 juéduì de.

absolve *v.* 免除 miǎnchú (free from responsibility).

absorb *v.* 吸收 xīshōu.

absorption *n.* 吸收 xīshōu

A

(taking in). ②專注 zhuānzhù (concentration).

abstain v. ①戒除 jièchú (refrain from). ②棄投票權 qì tóupiàoquán 〈vote〉.

abstention n. ①戒除 jièchú (refraining from). ②棄投票權 qì tóupiàoquán 〈vote〉.

abstinence n. ①禁慾 jìnyù 〈sex〉. ②戒酒 jièjiǔ 〈liquor〉.

abstract adj. 抽象的 chōuxiàng de (not concrete). — v. 提煉 tíliàn (pick out). — n. 摘要 zhāiyào (summary).

absurd adj. 荒謬的 huāngmiù de.

abundance n. 豐富 fēngfù (variety), 充足 chōngzú (plenty).

abundant adj. 豐富的 fēngfù de (plentiful), 充足的 chōngzú de (more than enough).

abuse v. ①濫用 lànyòng (misuse). ②虐待 nüèdài (ill-treat). — n. 虐待 nüèdài.

abyss n. 深淵 shēnyuān.

academic adj. 學術性的 xuéshùxìng de.

academy n. ①學院 xuéyuàn (school). ②學術界 xuéshùjiè (scholarly world).

accelerate v. 加速 jiāsù.

accelerator n. 油門 yóumén 〈pedal〉, 加速器 jiāsùqì 〈device〉.

accent n. ①重音 zhòngyīn 〈mark〉. ②腔調 qiāngdiào 〈pronunciation〉.

accentuate v. ①讀重音 dú zhòngyīn (stress a syllable). ②強調 qiángdiào (stress a point).

accept v. 接受 jiēshòu.

access n. ①接近 jiējìn (approach). ②進入權利 jìnrù quánlì (right of entry). ③通路

tōnglù (way of approach).

accessory n. 配件 pèijiàn.

accident n. 意外事件 yìwài shìjiàn. by ~ 偶然 ǒurán.

acclaim n. & v. 歡呼 huānhū.

accommodate v. ①適應 shìyìng (adjust to). ②容納 róngnà (have enough space for). ③供住宿 gōng zhùsù (offer a place to live).

accommodation n. 住宿 zhùsù.

accompany v. ①陪伴 péibàn (go with). ②伴奏 bànzòu 〈music〉.

accomplice n. 共犯 gòngfàn.

accomplish v. 完成 wánchéng (complete), 實現 shíxiàn (bring about).

accomplished adj. ①熟練的 shúliàn de (skilled). ②優秀的 yōuxiù de (good at).

accord n. 給與 gěiyǔ (give). — n. 協定 xiédìng (agreement). in ~ with 與……一致 yǔ...yízhì.

accordance n. 一致 yízhì. in ~ with 依照 yīzhào.

according adj. 一致的 yízhì de. ~ to 依照 yīzhào.

accordion n. 手風琴 shǒufēngqín.

account n. ①說明 shuōmíng (explanation). ②敘述 xùshù (narrative). ③帳目 zhàngmù (bill). on ~ of 因為 yīnwèi. take into ~ 加以考慮 jiāyǐ kǎolǜ.

accountant n. 會計員 kuàijìyuán.

accredit v. 授權 shòuquán (authorize).

accumulate v. 堆積 duījī.

accuracy n. 正確性

zhèngquèxìng.

accurate *adj.* 正確的 zhèngquè de.

accusation *n.* 控告 kònggào.

accuse *v.* 指控 zhǐkòng.

accustom *v.* 習慣於 xíguàn yú.

ace *n.* ①么點 yāodiǎn 〈cards〉. ②傑出者 jiéchūzhě, 好手 hǎoshǒu (expert). — *interj.* *A~!* 太棒了！tài bàng le!

acetate *n.* 醋酸鹽 cùsuānyán.

acetone *n.* 丙酮 bǐngtóng.

acetylene *n.* 乙炔 yǐquē.

ache *n. & v.* 疼痛 téngtòng.

achieve *v.* ①完成 wánchéng (carry out). ②獲得 huòdé (gain). ③達到 dádào (reach a goal).

acid *n.* 酸 suān.

acidic *adj.* 酸性的 suānxìng de.

acknowledge *v.* 承認 chéngrèn.

acne *n.* 粉刺 fěncì.

acorn *n.* 橡實 xiàngshí.

acoustic *adj.* 聽覺的 tīngjué de.

acquaint *v.* 使熟悉 shǐ shúxī (familiarize).

acquaintance *n.* 相識者 xiāngshízhě / xiāngshìzhě.

acquainted *adj.* 認識的 rènshi de.

acquire *v.* 獲得 huòdé.

acquisition *n.* 獲得 huòdé, 習得 xídé.

acquit *v.* 宣告無罪 xuāngào wúzuì (declare innocent).

acre *n.* 英畝 yīngmǔ.

acrid *adj.* 辛辣的 xīnlà de.

acrimonious *adj.* 尖刻的 jiānkè de.

acrobat *n.* 賣藝者 màiyìzhě (tumbler).

acronym *n.* 首字母縮略語 shǒu zìmǔ suōlüèyǔ.

acrophobia *n.* 懼高症 jùgāozhèng.

across *prep.* 橫過 héngguò, 越過 yuèguò (crosswise). — *adv.* 在對面 zài duìmiàn.

act *n.* ①行為 xíngwéi (behavior). ②一幕 yí mù 〈theater〉. ③法案 fǎ'àn (law). — *v.* ①行動 xíngdòng (take action). ②表現 biǎoxiàn (represent). ③扮演 bànyǎn (play a part). ④假裝 jiǎzhuāng (pretend).

action *n.* ①行動 xíngdòng (movement). ②作用 zuòyòng (function). *take ~* 採取行動 cǎiqǔ xíngdòng.

activate *v.* 使產生活動 shǐ chǎnshēng huódòng (actuate).

active *adj.* ①積極的 jījí de, 活躍的 huóyuè de (energetic). ②主動的 zhǔdòng de (not passive). ③活動的 huódòng de (working).

activity *n.* 活動 huódòng.

actor *n.* 演員 yǎnyuán (performer).

actress *n.* 女演員 nǚ yǎnyuán.

actual *adj.* 真實的 zhēnshí de (genuine), 實際的 shíjì de (real).

actualize *v.* 實現 shíxiàn, 落實 luòshí.

acumen *n.* 敏銳 mǐnruì.

acupuncture *n.* 針灸 zhēnjiǔ.

acute *adj.* ①敏銳的 mǐnruì de 〈senses〉. ②尖銳的 jiānruì de 〈analysis〉. ③劇烈的 jùliè de (severe).

ad *n.* 廣告 guǎnggào.

A.D. *n.* 公元 gōngyuán / 西元 xīyuán.

adamant *adj.* 堅持的 jiānchí

de, 固執的 gùzhí de.

adapt v. ①適應 shìyìng (adapt). ②改編 gǎibiān ⟨a book or a play⟩.

add v. ①增加 zēngjiā (increase). ②加 jiā ⟨mathematics⟩. ~ **up** 合計 héjì.

addict v. 上癮 shàngyǐn. — n. 上癮者 shàngyǐnzhě.

addiction n. 耽溺 dānnì.

addition n. 附加物 fùjiāwù (attachment). **in ~** 此外 cǐwài.

additional adj. 附加的 fùjiā de.

address n. ①住址 zhùzhǐ ⟨location⟩. ②演講 yǎnjiǎng (speech).

adept adj. 熟練的 shúliàn de.

adequate adj. 足夠的 zúgòu de.

adhere v. ①黏著 niánzhuó (stick firmly). ②忠於 zhōng yú (abide by).

adjacent adj. 毗連的 pílián de.

adjective n. 形容詞 xíngróngcí.

adjourn v. 休會 xiūhuì.

adjust v. ①調節 tiáojié (modify). ②適應 shìyìng (adapt to).

administer v. 管理 guǎnlǐ (manage).

administration n. ①管理 guǎnlǐ (management). ②行政機關 xíngzhèng jīguān ⟨department⟩. ③行政 xíngzhèng ⟨procedure⟩. ④政府 zhèngfǔ (state leadership).

admirable adj. 可欽佩的 kě qīnpèi de.

admiral n. 海軍上將 hǎijūn shàngjiàng.

admiration n. 欽佩 qīnpèi, 讚賞 zànshǎng.

admire v. 欽佩 qīnpèi, 讚賞 zànshǎng.

admission n. ①入場許可 rùchǎng xǔkě (permission to enter). ②承認 chéngrèn (acknowledgment). ③供認 gòngrèn / gōngrèn (confession). ④入場費 rùchǎngfèi (entry fee).

admit v. ①承認 chéngrèn (acknowledge). ②供認 gòngrèn / gōngrèn (confess). ③容許入場 róngxǔ rùchǎng (let in).

admonish v. 警告 jǐnggào.

adolescence n. 青春期 qīngchūnqī / qīngchūnqí.

adopt v. ①採納 cǎinà (use). ②收養 shōuyǎng ⟨a child⟩.

adorable adj. 可愛的 kě'ài de (cute), 令人喜愛的 lìng rén xǐ'ài de (pleasing).

adore v. 崇拜 chóngbài (worship).

adorn v. 裝飾 zhuāngshì.

ADP 自動數據處理 zìdòng shùjù chǔlǐ (automatic data processing).

adrift adj. & adv. 漂流的 piāoliú de.

ADSL 非對稱式數位用戶線路 fēi duìchèngshì shùwèi yònghù xiànlù.

adult adj. 成人的 chéngrén de. — n. 成人 chéngrén.

adultery n. 通姦 tōngjiān.

advance v. ①前進 qiánjìn (move forward). ②進步 jìnbù (make progress). — n. ①前進 qiánjìn (movement). ②進步 jìnbù (progress). ③預付 yùfù (prepayment). **in ~** 預先 yùxiān.

advanced adj. ①進步的 jìnbù

de (evolved). ②先進的 xiānjìn de (newest and best). ③高級的 gāojí de ⟨level⟩.

advantage n. ①利益 lìyì (benefit). ②優勢 yōushì (supremacy). *take ~ of* 利用 lìyòng.

adventure n. ①冒險 màoxiǎn (risk). ②奇遇 qíyù (unusual event).

adverb n. 副詞 fùcí.

adversary n. 對手 duìshǒu (competitor), 仇敵 chóudí (enemy).

adverse adj. ①反對的 fǎnduì de (opposing). ②不利的 búlì de (harmful).

advertise v. 登廣告 dēng guǎnggào.

advertisement n. 廣告 guǎnggào.

advertising n. 廣告 guǎnggào. *~ agency* 廣告公司 guǎnggào gōngsī.

advice n. 勸告 quàngào, 忠告 zhōnggào / zhōnggù (counsel), 建議 jiànyì (suggestion).

advise v. ①忠告 zhōnggào / zhōnggù (counsel), 建議 jiànyì (suggest). ②通知 tōngzhī (inform).

advisor n. 顧問 gùwèn (consultant), 指導教授 zhǐdǎo jiàoshòu ⟨academics⟩.

advocate n. 提倡者 tíchàngzhě. — v. 提倡 tíchàng.

aerial adj. ①空氣的 kōngqì de (airy). ②航空的 hángkōng de (from the sky).

aerolite n. 隕石 yǔnshí.

affable adj. 和藹可親的 hé'ǎi-kě-qīn de.

affair n. ①事情 shìqing

(matter). ②戀情 liànqíng (romance).

affect v. ①影響 yǐngxiǎng (influence). ②感動 gǎndòng (move deeply).

affected adj. 假裝的 jiǎzhuāng de (pretentious).

affection n. 情愛 qíng'ài (fondness).

affectionate adj. 摯愛的 zhì'ài de.

affiliate v. 使加入 shǐ jiārù. *~ with* 與……有關係 yǔ... yǒu guānxì. — n. 關係企業 guānxi qǐyè / guānxi qìyè (related business).

affinity n. 密切關係 mìqiè guānxi (close connection). *have an ~ for* 喜好…… xǐhào....

affirm v. ①證實 zhèngshí (acknowledge). ②斷言 duànyán (assert).

affirmative n. & adj. 肯定 (的) kěndìng (de).

affix v. 固定 gùdìng (fix). — n. 詞綴 cízhuì ⟨grammar⟩.

affluence n. 富裕 fùyù.

affluent adj. 富裕的 fùyù de.

afford v. ①力足以 lì zúyǐ, 負擔得起 fùdān de qǐ ⟨money⟩. ②承受 chéngshòu ⟨effort, time, emotion, etc⟩.

affront n. & v. 侮辱 wǔrǔ / wǔrù.

afloat adj. & adv. 飄浮的 piāofú de (floating).

afraid adj. 害怕的 hàipà de (frightened), 擔心 dānxīn (concerned).

Africa 非洲 Fēizhōu.

after prep. & conj. 在……之 後 zài...zhīhòu. *~ all* 畢竟 bìjìng. — adv. 之後 zhīhòu.

A

aftermath n. 餘波 yúbō, 後果 hòuguǒ.

afternoon n. 下午 xiàwǔ.

afterward(s) adv. 後來 hòulái.

again adv. 再 zài, 又 yòu.

against prep. ①反對 fǎnduì (opposed to). ②對照 duìzhào (compared to). ③抵抗 dǐkàng (resistant to). ④靠 kào (leaning on).

age n. ①年齡 niánlíng (number of years old). ②時代 shídài (era).

agency n. ①代理商 dàilǐshāng 〈business〉. ②機關 jīguān (organization).

agenda n. 議程 yìchéng.

agent n. 代理人 dàilǐrén, 經紀人 jīngjìrén (representative).

aggravate v. ①惡化 èhuà (worsen). ②激怒 jīnù (annoy).

aggregate n. 集合 jíhé (mass).

aggression n. 侵略 qīnlüè (attack).

aggressive adj. ①攻擊的 gōngjí de / 攻擊的, 侵略的 qīnlüè de (attacking). ②積極的 jījí de 〈not passive〉.

aghast adj. 嚇呆的 xiàdāi de.

agile adj. 敏捷的 mǐnjié de.

agitate v. ①擾亂 rǎoluàn (disturb). ②搖動 jiǎodòng (shake).

ago adv. 以前 yǐqián.

agony n. 痛苦 tòngkǔ.

agrarian adj. 農地的 nóngdì de.

agree v. ①同意 tóngyì (approve). ②一致 yízhì (correspond).

agreeable adj. ①令人愉快的 lìng rén yúkuài de (pleasant).

②贊成的 zànchéng de (in favor of).

agreement n. ①一致 yízhì (consistency). ②同意 tóngyì (approval). ③協定 xiédìng (contract).

agriculture n. 農業 nóngyè.

aground adj. & adv. 擱淺的 gēqiǎn de.

ahead adv. 在前方 zài qiánfāng (in front).

aid v. 幫助 bāngzhù, 援助 yuánzhù. — n. 幫助 bāngzhù (help).

aide n. 助手 zhùshǒu (assistant).

AIDS n. 艾滋病 Àizībìng / 愛滋病 Àizībìng.

aim v. 瞄準 miáozhǔn (point). — n. ①瞄準 miáozhǔn (target). ②目的 mùdì (intention).

air n. ①空氣 kōngqì (gas). ②天空 tiānkōng (the sky).
on the ~ 廣播中 guǎngbō zhōng / 廣播中 guǎngbō zhōng. ~ *bag* 氣囊 qìnáng. ~ *bridge* 登機橋 dēngjīqiáo / 空橋 kōngqiáo. ~ *conditioner* 空調設備 kōngtiáo shèbèi.

aircraft n. 飛行器 fēixíngqì.

airline n. ①航線 hángxiàn 〈route〉. ②航空公司 hángkōng gōngsī 〈business〉.

airmail n. 航空郵件 hángkōng yóujiàn.

airplane n. 飛機 fēijī.

airport n. 飛機場 fēijīchǎng.

airsick adj. 暈機的 yùnjī de / 暈機 yūnjī de.

aisle n. 通道 tōngdào.

ajar adj. & adv. 半開的 bànkāi de.

akin adj. ①類似的 lèisì de (similar). ②近親的 jìnqīn de

(related).

alarm n. 警報 jǐngbào.
~ clock 鬧鐘 nàozhōng.

albatross n. 信天翁 xìntiānwēng.

albino n. 白化病者 báihuàbìng zhě.

album n. ①相簿 xiàngbù ⟨photographs⟩. ②唱片集 chàngpiànjí ⟨music record⟩. ③集郵冊 jíyóucè ⟨stamps⟩.

alcohol n. ①酒精 jiǔjīng ⟨chemical⟩. ②酒 jiǔ (liquor).

alcoholic n. 酒鬼 jiǔguǐ.

ale n. 麥酒 màijiǔ.

alert adj. 警覺的 jǐngjué de, 敏捷的 mǐnjié de (watchful). — n. 警報 jǐngbào ⟨alarm⟩. — v. ①發警報 fā jǐngbào, 使警戒 shǐ jǐngjiè (warn). ②通知 tōngzhī (notify).

algae n. 海藻 hǎizǎo.

algebra n. 代數 dàishù.

alias n. & adv. 別名 biémíng, 化名 huàmíng.

alibi n. 不在場證明 bú zàichǎng zhèngmíng.

alien n. ①外國人 wàiguórén (foreigner). ②外星人 wàixīngrén (extra-terrestrial).

alienate v. 使疏遠 shǐ shūyuǎn.

alight v. 下車 xià chē (get off).

align v. 排列成行 páiliè chéng háng.

alike adj. & adv. 相似的 xiāngsì de (similar), 同樣的 tóngyàng de (of the same kind).

alimony n. 贍養費 shànyǎngfèi.

alive adj. ①活的 huó de (living). ②現存的 xiàncún de (in existence).

alkali n. 鹼 jiǎn.

all adj. 全部的 quánbù de. — pron. 所有 suǒyǒu. not at ~ 毫不 háobù. — adv. 全體 quántǐ. ~ right 好 hǎo, 沒問題 méi wèntí.

Allah n. 阿拉 Ālā.

allegation n. 指控 zhǐkòng.

allege v. 宣稱 xuānchēng.

allegiance n. 忠誠 zhōngchéng.

allegory n. ①諷喻 fěngyù / fèngyù (metaphor). ②寓言 yùyán (fable).

allergic adj. 過敏的 guòmǐn de. ~ to 對……過敏 duì...guòmǐn.

allergy n. 過敏症 guòmǐnzhèng.

alleviate v. 緩和 huǎnhé, 減輕 jiǎnqīng.

alley n. 巷弄 xiàngnòng.

alliance n. 聯盟 liánméng.

allied adj. 同盟的 tóngméng de.

alligator n. 短吻鱷 duǎnwěn'è.

allocate v. 分配 fēnpèi (distribute), 撥出 bōchū (share).

allot v. 分配 fēnpèi.

allow v. ①允許 yǔnxǔ (permit). ②承認 chéngrèn (admit).

allowance n. 零用錢 língyòngqián ⟨money⟩.

alloy n. 合金 héjīn.

allude v. 暗指 ànzhǐ.

allusion n. 暗示 ànshì.

ally v. 結盟 jiéméng. — n. 盟友 méngyǒu ⟨friend⟩, 同盟 國 tóngméngguó ⟨country⟩.

almanac n. ①曆書 lìshū (calendar). ②年鑑 niánjiàn (yearbook).

almighty adj. 萬能的

A

almond n. 杏仁 xìngrén.
almost adv. ①差不多 chàbuduō (approximately). ②幾乎 jīhū (not quite).
alms n. 救濟物 jiùjìwù.
aloe n. 蘆薈 lúhuì.
aloft adj. & adv. 在高處的 zài gāochù de.
alone adj. 單獨的 dāndú de. — adv. 單單只…… dāndān zhǐ....
along prep. 沿著 yánzhe.
aloof adv. 遠離 yuǎnlí. — adj. 冷淡的 lěngdàn de, 疏遠的 shūyuǎn de.
aloud adv. 出聲 chūshēng.
alphabet n. 字母 zìmǔ.
Alps 阿爾卑斯山 Ā'ěrbēisīshān.
already adv. 已經 yǐjīng.
also adv. 而且 érqiě, 也 yě.
altar n. 祭壇 jìtán ⟨platform⟩.
alter v. 變更 biàngēng.
alternate v. 輪流 lúnliú, 交替 jiāotì. — adj. 交替的 jiāotì de.
alternative adj. ①二擇一的 èr zé yī de (choose one between two). ②另類的 lìnglèi de ⟨different⟩. ~ medicine 非傳統醫學 fēi chuántǒng yīxué.
although conj. 雖然 suīrán.
altimeter n. 高度計 gāodùjì.
altitude n. 高度 gāodù.
alto n. ①女低音 nǚ dīyīn ⟨female⟩. ②男高音 nán gāoyīn ⟨male⟩.
altogether adv. ①完全地 wánquán de (completely). ②總共 zǒnggòng (on the whole).
altruism n. 利他主義 lìtā zhǔyì.
aluminum n. 鋁 lǚ. ~ foil

鋁箔 lǚbó.
alumna n. 女校友 nǚ xiàoyǒu.
alumnus n. 男校友 nán xiàoyǒu.
always adv. ①總是 zǒngshì (at all times). ②永遠 yǒngyuǎn (forever).
am v. 是 shì.
a.m. 上午 shàngwǔ.
amass v. 積聚 jījù.
amateur n. 業餘者 yèyúzhě.
amaze v. 使吃驚 shǐ chījīng.
amazement n. 吃驚 chījīng, 驚奇 jīngqí.
amazing adj. 驚奇的 jīngqí de.
Amazon River 亞馬孫河 Yàmǎsūnhé / 亞馬遜河 Yàmǎxùnhé.
ambassador n. 大使 dàshǐ.
amber n. 琥珀 hǔpò.
ambiguity n. 曖昧 àimèi, 含糊 hánhu.
ambiguous adj. 含糊的 hánhu de, 曖昧的 àimèi de.
ambition n. 野心 yěxīn, 企圖心 qìtúxīn / qǐtúxīn.
ambitious adj. 有野心的 yǒu yěxīn de.
amble v. 漫步 mànbù.
ambulance n. 救護車 jiùhùchē.
ambush n. 埋伏 máifu.
amenable adj. 順從的 shùncóng de, 服從的 fúcóng de.
amend v. 修正 xiūzhèng.
amendment n. 修正案 xiūzhèng'àn.
amenity n. 令人舒適之事物 lìng rén shūshì zhī shìwù.
America n. ①美國 Měiguó (the U.S.). ②美洲大陸 Měizhōu Dàlù (continent).

amethyst n. 紫水晶 zǐshuǐjīng.

amiable adj. 和藹可親的 hé'ǎi-kě-qīn de.

amicable adj. 友善的 yǒushàn de.

amid prep. 在……當中 zài...dāngzhōng.

amiss adj. & adv. 有問題的 yǒu wèntí de.

ammeter n. 安培計 ānpéijì.

ammonia n. ①氨 ān ⟨gas⟩. ②氨水 ānshuǐ ⟨liquid⟩.

ammunition n. 彈藥 dànyào, 軍火 jūnhuǒ.

amnesia n. 健忘症 jiànwàngzhèng.

amnesty n. 大赦 dàshè, 特赦 tèshè.

amoeba n. 阿米巴 āmǐbā, 變形蟲 biànxíngchóng.

among prep. 在……中 zài...zhōng.

amorous adj. ①求愛的 qiú'ài de (seeking love). ②性愛的 xìng'ài de (sexual).

amount n. ①總數 zǒngshù (the total). ②數量 shùliàng (number), 分量 fènliang (quantity). — v. ①合計 héjì (add up to). ②相當於 xiāngdāng yú (be equal to).

ampere n. 安培 ānpéi.

amphetamine n. 安非他命 ānfēitāmíng.

amphibian n. 兩棲動物 liǎngqī dòngwù.

amphitheater n. ①圓形劇場 yuánxíng jùchǎng (performance arena). ②競技場 jìngjìchǎng (competitive area).

ample adj. ①高大的 gāodà de (large). ②充裕的 chōngyù de (sufficient).

amplify v. ①擴大 kuòdà (enlarge). ②加強 jiāqiáng (increase magnitude). ③誇張 kuāzhāng (exaggerate).

amputate v. 切除 qiēchú.

amulet n. 護身符 hùshēnfú.

amuse v. 娛樂 yúlè.

amusement n. 娛樂 yúlè. **~ park** 遊樂園 yóulèyuán.

amusing adj. 有趣的 yǒuqù de.

anachronism n. 時代錯誤 shídài cuòwù.

analogous adj. 相似的 xiāngsì de, 類似的 lèisì de.

analogy n. ①相似 xiāngsì (sameness). ②類推 lèituī (reason from likeness).

analysis n. 分析 fēnxī.

analyze v. 分析 fēnxī.

anarchism n. 無政府主義 wú zhèngfǔ zhǔyì.

anarchy n. ①無政府（狀態） wúzhèngfǔ (zhuàngtài) (absence of government). ②混亂 hùnluàn / hǔnluàn (disorder).

anatomy n. 解剖（學）jiěpōu (xué).

ancestor n. 祖先 zǔxiān.

anchor n. ①錨 máo (mooring). ②主播 zhǔbō ⟨media⟩. — v. 拋錨 pāomáo, 泊船 bóchuán.

ancient adj. 古代的 gǔdài de (old).

and conj. 和 hé, 及 jí.

anecdote n. 軼事 yìshì.

anemia n. 貧血 pínxuè / pínxiě.

anesthesia n. 麻醉 mázuì.

anew adv. 再 zài, 重新 chóngxīn.

angel n. 天使 tiānshǐ.

A

anger *n.* 忿怒 fènnù.

angle *n.* ①角 jiǎo 〈mathematics〉. ②角度 jiǎodù, 觀點 guāndiǎn (point of view).

Anglican *n. & adj.* 英國國教 Yīngguó Guójiào.

angry *adj.* 生氣的 shēngqì de, 忿怒的 fènnù de.

anguish *n.* 極度痛苦 jídù tòngkǔ, 苦悶 kǔmèn.

angular *adj.* 有尖角的 yǒu jiānjiǎo de (having angles).

animal *n.* 動物 dòngwù.

animate *v.* ①賦予生氣 fùyǔ shēngqì (bring to life). ②製作動畫 zhìzuò dònghuà (make cartoons). — *adj.* 生動的 shēngdòng de (alive).

animosity *n.* 仇恨 chóuhèn.

ankle *n.* 踝 huái.

annex *v.* 併吞 bìngtūn (take over). — *n.* 附屬建築 fùshǔ jiànzhù / 附屬 jiànzhú.

annihilate *v.* 殲滅 jiānmiè.

anniversary *n.* 周年 zhōunián.

annotate *v.* 註解 zhùjiě.

announce *v.* 宣告 xuāngào, 發表 fābiǎo (proclaim).

announcer *n.* 播音員 bōyīnyuán / 播報員 bōbàoyuán.

annoy *v.* ①使……煩惱 shǐ... fánnǎo (cause aggravation). ②打擾 dǎrǎo (bother). ③騷擾 sāorǎo (harass).

annoying *adj.* ①麻煩的 máfan de (bothersome). ②討厭的 tǎoyàn de (unpleasant).

annual *adj.* 年度的 niándù de.

annuity *n.* 年金 niánjīn, 養老金 yǎnglǎojīn.

annul *v.* 註銷 zhùxiāo.

anode *n.* 陽極 yángjí, 正極

zhèngjí.

anoint *v.* 塗油 túyóu.

anomalous *adj.* 例外的 lìwài de, 反常的 fǎncháng de.

anomaly *n.* 例外 lìwài, 反常 fǎncháng.

anonymous *adj.* 匿名的 nìmíng de.

anorak *n.* 防風夾克 fángfēng jiākè / 防風夾克 fángfēng jiākè.

another *adj.* ①另一的 lìng yī de (a different). ②再一個 zài yí ge (one more).

answer *n. & v.* 答覆 dáfù, 回答 huídá (reply). ~ *ing machine* 電話錄音機 diànhuà lùyīnjī / 答錄機 dálùjī.

ant *n.* 螞蟻 mǎyǐ.

antarctic *adj.* 南極的 nánjí de.

Antarctica 南極洲 Nánjízhōu.

antecedent *n.* ①先行詞 xiānxíngcí 〈grammar〉. ②前事 qiánshì 〈history〉.

antelope *n.* 羚羊 língyáng.

antenna *n.* ①觸鬚 chùxū 〈insect〉. ②天線 tiānxiàn 〈electronics〉.

anthem *n.* 聖歌 shènggē (hymn), 讚美詩 zànměishī (eulogy). *national* ~ 國歌 guógē.

anthology *n.* 詩集 shījí 〈poetry〉, 文選 wénxuǎn 〈prose〉.

anthropology *n.* 人類學 rénlèixué.

antibiotic *n.* 抗生素 kàngshēngsù.

antibody *n.* 抗體 kàngtǐ.

anticipate *v.* ①預期 yùqí / yùqí (expect). ②期待 qídài / qídài (look forward to). ③搶先 qiǎngxiān (do something first).

antidote *n.* 解毒劑 jiědújì.

antifreeze n. 防凍劑 fángdòngjì.

antiquary n. 古物專家 gǔwù zhuānjiā, 骨董商 gǔdǒngshāng.

antiquated adj. ①陳舊的 chénjiù de (out of date). ②廢棄的 fèiqì de (no longer in use).

antique n. 古董 gǔdǒng.

antiquity n. ①古代 gǔdài (distant past). ②古蹟 gǔjī (building), 古物 gǔwù ⟨objects⟩.

antisocial adj. 反社交行為的 fǎnshèjiāo xíngwéi de.

antithesis n. 對立 duìlì.

antler n. 鹿角 lùjiǎo.

antonym n. 反義字 fǎnyìzì.

anus n. 肛門 gāngmén.

anvil n. 鐵砧 tiězhēn.

anxiety n. 憂慮 yōulǜ (distress), 不安 bù'ān (concern).

anxious adj. ①不安的 bù'ān de (concerned). ②渴望的 kěwàng de (eager).

any adj. & pron. 任何 rènhé.

anybody pron. 任何人 rènhé rén.

anyhow adv. 無論如何 wúlùn rúhé.

anyone pron. 任何人 rènhé rén.

anything pron. 任何事物 rènhé shìwù.

anyway adv. 無論如何 wúlùn rúhé.

anywhere adv. 任何地方 rènhé dìfang.

aorta n. 大動脈 dàdòngmài.

apart adv. 分開地 fēnkāi de, 分離地 fēnlí de. ~ **from** 除了 ……以外 chúle……yǐwài.

apartheid n. 種族隔離制 zhǒngzú gélí zhì.

apartment n. 公寓 gōngyù.

apathy n. 冷淡 lěngdàn, 漠不關心 mò bù guānxīn.

ape n. 猿 yuán. — v. 模仿 mófǎng (imitate).

aperture n. 小孔 xiǎokǒng.

apex n. 尖頂 jiāndǐng.

aphorism n. 格言 géyán, 警語 jǐngyǔ.

apiece adv. 每個 měi ge.

apologize v. 道歉 dàoqiàn.

apology n. 道歉 dàoqiàn.

apoplexy n. 中風 zhòngfēng.

apostle n. 使徒 shítú.

apostrophe n. ①省略符號 shěnglüè fúhào ⟨can't⟩. ②所有格符號 suǒyǒugé fúhào ⟨teacher's⟩.

appall v. 使驚駭 shǐ jīnghài.

apparatus n. 儀器 yíqì.

apparel n. 衣服 yīfu.

apparent adj. ①顯然的 xiǎnrán de (obvious). ②外表的 wàibiǎo de (seeming).

apparition n. 鬼怪 guǐguài, 幽靈 yōulíng.

appeal n. & v. ①懇求 kěnqiú (ask earnestly). ②上訴 shàngsù (take a case to a higher court).

appear v. ①出現 chūxiàn (show up). ②顯得 xiǎnde (seem).

appearance n. ①出現 chūxiàn (show up). ②外觀 wàiguān (the way one looks).

appease v. 平息 píngxī / píngxí.

append v. 附加 fùjiā (add on), 增補 zēngbǔ (supplement).

appendicitis n. 盲腸炎 mángchángyán.

appendix n. ①附錄 fùlù ⟨written work⟩. ②盲腸 mángcháng ⟨medical⟩.

appetite n. ①食慾 shíyù, 胃口 wèikǒu ⟨food⟩. ②欲望

A

yùwàng (desire).

appetizer n. 開胃菜 kāiwèicài.

applaud v. ①鼓掌 gǔzhǎng (clap). ②讚許 zànxǔ (approve of).

apple n. 蘋果 píngguǒ.

appliance n. 器具 qìjù.

applicant n. 申請人 shēnqǐngrén.

application n. ①申請 shēnqǐng (request). ②申請書 shēnqǐngshū ⟨document⟩.

apply v. ①申請 shēnqǐng (ask for). ②敷塗 fūtú (rub). ③應用 yìngyòng (put into use).

appoint v. ①任命 rènmìng ⟨position⟩. ②指定 zhǐdìng ⟨time⟩.

appointment n. ①約會 yuēhuì (arrangement to meet). ②任命 rènmìng ⟨position⟩.

appreciate v. ①欣賞 xīnshǎng (enjoy). ②感激 gǎnjī (be grateful). ③重視 zhòngshì (value).

apprehend v. ①捕捉 bǔzhuō (arrest). ②了解 liǎojiě (understand).

apprehension n. 憂懼 yōujù (anxiety).

apprentice n. 學徒 xuétú.

approach v. 接近 jiējìn (come near). — n. ①接近 jiējìn (approximation). ②通路 tōnglù (access), 入口 rùkǒu (entrance). ③方法 fāngfǎ (method).

appropriate adj. 適當的 shìdàng de. — v. 佔用 zhànyòng.

approval n. ①批准 pīzhǔn (permission). ②贊成 zànchéng (agreement).

approve v. ①批准 pīzhǔn (permit). ②贊成 zànchéng (agree).

approximate adj. 大概的 dàgài de.

April n. 四月 Sìyuè.

apron n. 圍裙 wéiqún.

apt adj. ①聰敏的 cōngmǐn de (intelligent). ②適當的 shìdàng de (suitable). ③易於……的 yìyú...de (likely to).

aptitude n. 資質 zīzhì / zízhí (capability). ~ test 性向測驗 xìngxiàng cèyàn.

aquarium n. 水族館 shuǐzúguǎn.

Aquarius 水瓶座 Shuǐpíngzuò.

aquatic adj. ①水生的 shuǐshēng de (living in water). ②水中的 shuǐzhōng de (underwater).

aqueduct n. 水道 shuǐdào.

Arab n. 阿拉伯人 Ālābórén.

Arabic n. 阿拉伯語 Ālābóyǔ ⟨language⟩.

arable adj. 可耕的 kě gēng de.

arbitrary adj. ①任意的 rènyì de (random). ②專橫的 zhuānhèng de (dictatorial).

arbitrate v. 仲裁 zhòngcái, 公斷 gōngduàn.

arc n. 弧 hú (curved line).

arcade n. 騎樓 qílóu, 拱廊 gǒngláng (gallery).

arch n. 拱門 gǒngmén.

archaeology n. 考古學 kǎogǔxué.

archaic adj. ①古代的 gǔdài de (ancient). ②廢棄的 fèiqì de (no longer used). ③古文的 gǔwén de ⟨language⟩.

archbishop n. 總主教 zǒngzhǔjiào.

archer n. 射手 shèshǒu.

archipelago n. ①群島 qúndǎo (group of small

islands). ②多島之海 duō dǎo zhī hǎi (sea with many islands).

architect *n.* 建築師 jiànzhùshī / jiànzhúshī ⟨builder⟩.

architecture *n.* 建築 jiànzhù / jiànzhú.

arduous *adj.* 艱苦的 jiānkǔ de.

are *v.* 是 shì.

area *n.* ①地區 dìqū (region). ②面積 miànjī ⟨surface measure⟩.

arena *n.* 競技場 jìngjìchǎng.

argue *v.* ①爭論 zhēnglùn (quarrel). ②主張 zhǔzhāng (hold a view).

argument *n.* 爭論 zhēnglùn (disagreement).

arid *adj.* 乾旱的 gānhàn de.

Aries 白羊座 Báiyángzuò.

arise *v.* ①出現 chūxiàn (appear). ②發生 fāshēng (happen).

aristocracy *n.* ①貴族 guìzú (nobility). 貴族階級 guìzú jiējí (upper class). ②貴族政治 guìzú zhèngzhì (government by the highest social rank).

aristocrat *n.* 貴族 guìzú.

aristocratic *adj.* ①貴族的 guìzú de (of the nobility). ②高級的 gāojí de (high-class).

arithmetic *n.* 算術 suànshù.

ark *n.* 方舟 fāngzhōu.

arm *n.* 手臂 shǒubì.

arms *n.* 武器 wǔqì (weapons). — *v.* 武裝 wǔzhuāng.

armada *n.* 艦隊 jiànduì.

armament *n.* 軍備 jūnbèi.

armistice *n.* 休戰 xiūzhàn.

armor *n.* 甲冑 jiǎzhòu.

army *n.* ①軍隊 jūnduì (military). ②陸軍 lùjūn (branch of the military).

aroma *n.* 芳香 fāngxiāng.

aromatherapy *n.* 芳香療法 fāngxiāng liáofǎ.

around *adv. & prep.* ①在…… 附近 zài...fùjìn (in the neighborhood of). ②到處 dàochù (everywhere). ③大約 dàyuē (approximately).

arouse *v.* ①激發 jīfā, 引起 yǐnqǐ (incite). ②喚醒 huànxǐng (awaken).

arrange *v.* ①整理 zhěnglǐ (order). ②安排 ānpái (plan).

array *v.* ①列陣 lièzhèn (set in order). ②盛裝 shèngzhuāng (dress). — *n.* ①陣容 zhènróng (order). ②展示 zhǎnshì (display).

arrears *n.* 拖延 tuōyán, 拖欠 tuōqiàn.

arrest *v.* ①逮捕 dàibǔ (seize by law). ②阻擋 zǔdǎng (stop).

arrival *n.* 到達 dàodá.

arrive *v.* 到達 dàodá, 來臨 láilín.

arrogant *adj.* 傲慢的 àomàn de, 自大的 zìdà de.

arrow *n.* ①箭 jiàn ⟨weapon⟩. ②箭號 jiànhào ⟨sign⟩.

arsenal *n.* 兵工廠 bīnggōngchǎng.

arsenic *n.* 砷 shēn, 砒霜 pīshuāng.

arson *n.* 縱火 zònghuǒ.

art *n.* ①藝術 yìshù, 美術 měishù (creation). ②人工 réngōng (not of nature). ③技藝 jìyì (skill).

artery *n.* ①動脈 dòngmài ⟨medical⟩. ②幹道 gàndào (main road).

arthritis *n.* 關節炎 guānjiéyán.

article *n.* ①文章 wénzhāng

A

(written work). ②物件 wùjiàn (object). ③冠詞 guàncí 〈grammar〉.

articulate adj. ①清晰的 qīngxī de (clear). ②有口才的 yǒu kǒucái de (well-spoken). — v. ①清晰地發音 qīngxī de fāyīn (pronounce clearly). ②明白地表達 míngbai de biǎodá (express clearly).

artificial adj. ①人工的 réngōng de (man-made). ②做作的 zuòzuo de (insincere).

artillery n. ①大砲 dàpào (big guns). ②砲兵 pàobīng 〈corps〉.

artisan n. 技工 jìgōng.

artist n. 藝術家 yìshùjiā.

artistic adj. 藝術性的 yìshùxìng de.

as adv. 一樣 yíyàng (equally). — conj. ①當 dāng (when). ②因為 yīnwèi (because). ③像 xiàng (like). ~ if 好像 hǎoxiàng.

a.s.a.p., ASAP 儘快 jǐnkuài.

asbestos n. 石棉 shímián.

ascend v. ①攀登 pāndēng (climb). ②上升 shàngshēng (rise).

ascent n. ①攀登 pāndēng (climb). ②上升 shàngshēng (rise).

ascertain v. 確定 quèdìng.

ascribe v. ①歸因於 guīyīn yú (attribute as the cause). ②認定為 rèndìng wéi (consider to).

aseptic adj. 無菌的 wújùn de / wújùn de.

ash n. 灰 huī, 灰燼 huījìn (ember).

ashamed adj. 羞恥的 xiūchǐ de, 慚愧的 cánkuì de.

ashore adj. & adv. 在岸上 zài àn shàng.

ashtray n. 煙灰缸 yānhuīgāng.

Asia 亞洲 Yàzhōu / Yǎzhōu.

Asian adj. 亞洲的 Yàzhōu de / Yǎzhōu de. — n. 亞洲人 Yàzhōurén / Yǎzhōurén.

aside adv. 向旁邊 xiàng pángbiān (to the side), 在旁邊 zài pángbiān (on the side).

ask v. ①問 wèn, 詢問 xúnwèn (question). ②請求 qǐngqiú (request). ③邀請 yāoqǐng (invite).

askew adj. & adv. 歪斜的 wāixié de.

asleep adj. ①睡著的 shuìzháo de (sleeping). ②麻痺的 mábì de (numb).

asp n. 埃及毒蛇 āijí dúshé.

asparagus n. 蘆筍 lúsǔn.

aspect n. ①方面 fāngmiàn (side). ②外貌 wàimào, 樣子 yàngzi (appearance).

aspersion n. 誹謗 fěibàng, 中傷 zhòngshāng.

asphalt n. 瀝青 lìqīng, 柏油 bóyóu.

asphyxia n. 窒息 zhìxí / zhìxí.

aspirate v. 氣音 qìyīn.

aspiration n. 熱望 rèwàng, 抱負 bàofù (desire).

aspire v. 熱望 rèwàng, 有抱負 yǒu bàofù (desire).

aspirin n. 阿司匹林 āsīpǐlín / 阿斯匹靈 āsīpílíng.

ass n. ①驢 lǘ (donkey). ②笨蛋 bèndàn (stupid person). ③屁股 pìgu 〈part of body〉.

assail v. 攻擊 gōngjí / gōngjí.

assassin n. 刺客 cìkè.

assassinate v. 暗殺 ànshā.

assault n. & v. 突擊 tújī / túdí (attack).

assemble v. ①集會 jíhuì, 集合

jíhé (gather together). ②裝配 zhuāngpèi (put together).

assembly n. 集會 jíhuì (gathering), 會議 huìyì (meeting).

assent n. & v. 同意 tóngyì, 贊成 zànchéng.

assert v. 斷言 duànyán, 宣稱 xuānchēng (declare firmly).

assess v. 估價 gūjià.

asset n. ①資產 zīchǎn, 財產 cáichǎn (property). ②有價值物 yǒu jiàzhí wù (valuable quality or skill). **immovable ~s** 不動產 búdòngchǎn. **personal ~s** 動產 dòngchǎn.

assiduous adj. 勤勉的 qínmiǎn de (diligent).

assign v. ①分配 fēnpèi, 派派 fēnpài (allocate). ②指派 zhǐpài, 指定 zhǐdìng (appoint). ③讓渡 ràngdù (transfer).

assignment n. ①分配 fēnpèi, 分派 fēnpài (allocation). ②指派 zhǐpài, 指定 zhǐdìng (appointment). ③任務 rènwù (duty). ④作業 zuòyè (task), 功課 gōngkè (homework).

assimilate v. ①吸收 xīshōu (absorb). ②同化 tónghuà (become part of).

assist v. 幫助 bāngzhù.

assistance n. 幫助 bāngzhù.

assistant n. 助理 zhùlǐ, 助手 zhùshǒu.

associate v. 聯合 liánhé, 結交 jiéjiāo (join or connect). — n. 同伴 tóngbàn (companion), 同事 tóngshì (co-worker).

association n. ①協會 xiéhuì (committee). ②聯合 liánhé (connection).

assume v. ①假設 jiǎshè (suppose). ②擔任 dānrèn

(undertake).

assumption n. ①假設 jiǎshè (supposition). ②擔任 dānrèn (undertaking).

assurance n. ①保證 bǎozhèng (promise). ②自信 zìxìn (confidence).

assure v. ①保證 bǎozhèng (promise). ②確信 quèxìn (make certain).

asterisk n. 星號 xīnghào.

astern adv. 在船尾 zài chuánwěi ⟨of a ship⟩.

asthma n. 氣喘 qìchuǎn.

astigmatism n. 散光 sǎnguāng.

astonish v. 使驚奇 shǐ jīngqí.

astound v. 使大驚 shǐ dàjīng.

astray adj. & adv. 迷途的 mítú de.

astride adv. & prep. 跨著 kuàzhe, 騎著 qízhe.

astrology n. 占星學 zhānxīngxué.

astronaut n. 宇航員 yǔhángyuán / 太空人 tàikōngrén.

astronomy n. 天文學 tiānwénxué.

astute adj. 聰明的 cōngming de (intelligent), 敏銳的 mǐnruì de (perceptive).

asylum n. 避難所 bìnànsuǒ, 收容院 shōuróngyuàn (refuge).

at prep. 在…… zài….

atheism n. 無神論 wúshénlùn.

athlete n. 運動員 yùndòngyuán.

athletic adj. 運動的 yùndòng de.

athletics n. 體育運動 tǐyù yùndòng.

Atlantic Ocean 大西洋

Dàxīyáng.

atlas *n.* 地圖集 dìtújí.

ATM 自動提款機 zìdòng tíkuǎnjī.

atmosphere *n.* ①大氣 dàqì, 空氣 kōngqì (air). ②氛圍 fēnwéi / 氣氛 qìfēn (ambience).

atoll *n.* 環礁 huánjiāo.

atom *n.* 原子 yuánzǐ. **~ bomb** 原子彈 yuánzǐdàn.

atrocious *adj.* ①兇暴的 xiōngbào de (evil). ②糟透的 zāo tòu de (awful).

atrophy *n. & v.* 萎縮 wěisuō.

attach *v.* ①附上 fùshàng, 貼上 tiēshàng (fasten or join). ②相關聯 xiāngguānlián (connect with). ③伴隨 bànsuí (go with).

attaché *n.* 隨員 suíyuán.

attachment *n.* 附著 fùzhuó, 附件 fùjiàn (accessory).

attack *n. & v.* 攻擊 gōngjí / gōngjí.

attain *v.* 達到 dádào (reach), 得到 dédào (achieve).

attempt *n. & v.* 嘗試 chángshì, 企圖 qìtú / qìtú (try).

attend *v.* ①出席 chūxí (be present at). ②注意 zhùyì (pay attention to). ③侍奉 shìhòu (wait upon), 照顧 zhàogu (look after).

attendant *n.* 侍者 shìzhě (servant), 服務生 fúwùshēng (waiter). — *adj.* 伴隨的 bànsuí de (accompanying).

attention *n.* 注意 zhùyì.

attest *v.* 證明 zhèngmíng (proof), 宣誓 xuānshì (claim).

attic *n.* 閣樓 gélóu.

attire *n.* ①盛裝 shèngzhuāng (formal wear). ②服裝 fúzhuāng (clothing).

attitude *n.* 態度 tàidu (outlook), 姿態 zītài (position).

attorney *n.* 代理人 dàilǐrén (agent), 律師 lǜshī (lawyer).

attract *v.* 吸引 xīyǐn, 引誘 yǐnyòu.

attraction *n.* 吸引力 xīyǐnlì.

attractive *adj.* ①好看的 hǎokàn de (good-looking). ②有吸引力的 yǒu xīyǐnlì de (appealing).

attribute *v.* 歸因於 guīyīn yú. — *n.* 特質 tèzhì / tèzhí (quality).

auburn *n. & adj.* 赤褐色 chìhèsè / chìhésè.

auction *n.* 拍賣 pāimài.

audacious *adj.* ①大膽的 dàdǎn de (brave). ②無恥的 wúchǐ de (impudent).

audacity *n.* 大膽無恥 dàdǎn wúchǐ (impudence).

audible *adj.* 聽得見的 tīngdejiàn de.

audience *n.* 聽眾 tīngzhòng 〈aural〉, 觀眾 guānzhòng 〈visual〉.

audiobook *n.* 有聲書 yǒushēngshū.

audit *v.* 稽核 jīhé, 查帳 cházhàng.

audition *n. & v.* 試聽 shìtīng.

auditorium *n.* 講堂 jiǎngtáng, 集會廳 jíhuìtīng.

augment *v.* 加大 jiā dà (enlarge), 增加 zēngjiā (increase).

August *n.* 八月 Bāyuè.

aunt *n.* ①阿姨 āyí (mother's sister, woman of mother's generation). ②伯母 bómǔ (father's older brother's wife), 嬸母 shěnmǔ (father's younger brother's wife). ③舅母 jiùmǔ (mother's brother's wife). ④姑

姑 gūgu (father's sister).

auspice n. 主辦 zhǔbàn, 贊助 zànzhù (support).

auspicious adj. 吉利的 jílì de.

austere adj. ①嚴肅的 yánsù de (severe). ②樸素的 pǔsù de (simple and plain).

authentic adj. 真正的 zhēnzhèng de, 真實的 zhēnshí de.

author n. 作家 zuòjiā, 作者 zuòzhě.

authority n. ①權威 quánwēi (power). ②專家 zhuānjiā (expert). ③當權者 dāngquánzhě (one in power). ④當局 dāngjú (government).

authorize v. ①授權 shòuquán (empower). ②認可 rènkě (permit).

auto n. 汽車 qìchē.

autobiography n. 自傳 zìzhuàn.

autocracy n. 獨裁政治 dúcái zhèngzhì.

autocrat n. 獨裁者 dúcáizhě.

autograph n. 親筆簽名 qīnbǐ qiānmíng.

automatic adj. ①自動的 zìdòng de (mechanical). ②不自覺的 bú zìjué de (without thought).

automation n. 自動操作 zìdòng cáozuò.

automobile n. 汽車 qìchē.

autonomous adj. 自治的 zìzhì de. ~ *region* 自治區 zìzhìqū.

autonomy n. 自治 zìzhì.

autopsy n. 驗屍 yànshī.

autumn n. 秋季 qiūjì, 秋天 qiūtiān.

auxiliary adj. 輔助的 fǔzhù de. — n. 助動詞 zhùdòngcí.

avail v. 應用 yìngyòng, 使用 shǐyòng (use). — n. 效用 xiàoyòng.

avalanche n. 雪崩 xuěbēng.

avarice n. 貪婪 tānlán.

avenge v. 報仇 bàochóu, 報復 bàofu.

avenue n. ①大道 dàdào (wide road). ②林蔭大道 línyìn dàdào (tree-lined road).

average n. & adj. 平均 píngjūn (mean). ②一般 yìbān (normal).

avert v. 避開 bìkāi.

aviary n. 鳥舍 niǎoshè.

aviation n. 航空 hángkōng.

avid adj. ①熱心的 rèxīn de (eager). ②貪婪的 tānlán de (greedy).

avocado n. 鱷梨 èlí.

avoid v. 避免 bìmiǎn.

await v. 等候 děnghòu, 等待 děngdài.

awake v. ①醒 xíng ⟨from sleep⟩. ②覺悟 juéwù (become conscious).

award n. & v. 獎賞 jiǎngshǎng.

aware adj. 察覺的 chájué de, 有感覺的 yǒu gǎnjué de (having a sense), 知道的 zhīdào de (knowing).

away adv. ①不在 búzài (not present). ②在遠方 zài yuǎnfāng (at a distance). ③離去 líqù (separate). *right* ~ 立即 lìjí.

awe n. & v. 敬畏 jìngwèi.

awesome adj. 了不起的 liǎobuqǐ de (very great).

awful adj. ①可怕的 kěpà de (terrible). ②極壞的 jí huài de (very bad).

awhile adv. 片刻 piànkè.

awkward adj. ①笨拙地 bènzhuō de / bènzhuó de

(clumsy). ②不合用的 bù héyòng de (not good for use). ③尷尬的 gāngà de (embarrassing).

awl n. 錐子 zhuīzi.

awning n. 雨篷 yǔpéng.

ax, axe n. 斧 fǔ.

axiom n. ①公理 gōnglǐ 〈mathematics〉. ②原理 yuánlǐ (principle).

axis n. 軸 zhóu.

axle n. 輪軸 lúnzhóu.

azalea n. 杜鵑花 dùjuānhuā.

azure n. & adj. 青色 qīngsè.

B

B.A. 文學士 wénxuéshì.

babble v. ①嘮叨 láodao (chatter). ②模糊不清地說 móhu bù qīng de shuō (make unclear sounds).

baboon n. 狒狒 fèifèi.

baby n. 嬰兒 yīng'ér.

baby boom n. 嬰兒潮 yīng'ércháo.

babysitter n. 保姆 bǎomǔ.

bachelor n. ①單身漢 dānshēnhàn (unmarried man). ②學士 xuéshì (university degree).

back n. ①背部 bèibù 〈body part〉. ②背面 bèimiàn (rear of object). — v. 支持 zhīchí (support). — adj. 背後的 bèihòu de, 後面的 hòumian de (in back). — adv. ①向後 xiàng hòu, 後退 hòutuì (backward). ②在……後面 zài...hòumian (behind).

backbone n. 脊椎骨 jǐzhuīgǔ 〈animal〉.

background n. 背景 bèijǐng.

backward(s) adj. & adv. ①向後(的) xiàng hòu (de) (behind). ②落後 luòhòu (underdeveloped). ~ (s) and forward(s) 往返的 wǎngfǎn de.

backyard n. 後院 hòuyuàn.

bacon n. 燻豬肉 xūnzhūròu, 培根 péigēn.

bacteria n. 細菌 xìjūn / xìjùn.

bad adj. 壞的 huài de. too ~ 可惜 kěxī / kěxí.

badge n. 徽章 huīzhāng.

badger n. 獾 huān 〈animal〉. — v. 煩擾 fánrǎo (bother).

badly adv. ①不好 bùhǎo (not well). ②非常 fēicháng (very much).

badminton n. 羽毛球 yǔmáoqiú.

baffle v. ①使困惑 shǐ kùnhuò (puzzle). ②阻撓 zǔnáo, 妨礙 fáng'ài (prevent).

bag n. 袋 dài, 袋子 dàizi, 手提包 shǒutíbāo.

bagel n. 硬麵包 yìngmiànbāo, 培果 péiguǒ.

baggage n. 行李 xíngli.

bail n. 保釋金 bǎoshìjīn 〈money〉. — v. 保釋 bǎoshì.

bailiff n. 執行官 zhíxíngguān.

bait n. 餌 ěr. — v. ①下餌

xià'ěr 〈fishing〉. ②誘惑 yòuhuò (tempt).

bake v. 烘烤 hōngkǎo 〈oven〉.

baker n. 麵包師 miànbāoshī.

bakery n. 麵包店 miànbāodiàn.

baking powder n. 發酵粉 fājiàofěn / fāxiàofěn.

balance n. ①平衡 pínghéng (equilibrium). ②差額 chā'é (difference). ③天平 tiānpíng 〈scales〉. — v. 使平衡 shǐ pínghéng (equalize).

balcony n. ①陽臺 yángtái 〈building〉. ②樓座 lóuzuò 〈theater〉.

bald adj. 禿頭的 tūtóu de.

bale n. & v. 綑 kǔn.

ball n. ①球 qiú (sphere). ②舞會 wǔhuì (dance party). ~ game 球賽 qiúsài.

ballad n. ①情歌 qínggē 〈song〉. ②敘事詩 xùshìshī 〈poem〉.

ballast n. 壓艙物 yācāngwù.

ballerina n. 女芭蕾舞者 nǚ bālěiwǔ zhě.

ballet n. 芭蕾舞 bālěiwǔ. ~ dancer 芭蕾舞者 bālěiwǔ zhě.

balloon n. 氣球 qìqiú.

ballot n. 投票用紙 tóupiào yòng zhǐ.

ballpoint n. 圓珠筆 yuánzhūbǐ / 原子筆 yuánzǐbǐ.

balm n. ①香膏 xiānggāo 〈liquid〉. ②鎮痛劑 zhèntòngjì (comfort).

bamboo n. 竹 zhú.

ban v. 禁止 jìnzhǐ. — n. 禁令 jìnlìng.

banal adj. 乏味的 fáwèi de.

banana n. 香蕉 xiāngjiāo.

band n. ①帶 dài, 繩 shéng (strip). ②樂隊 yuèduì 〈music〉. ③一群 yì qún (group).

bandage n. 繃帶 bēngdài. — v. 縛以繃帶 fù yǐ bēngdài / fú yǐ bēngdài.

bandit n. 強盜 qiángdào, 土匪 tǔfěi.

bandy v. ①來回投擲 láihuí tóuzhí / láihuí tóuzhí (throw). ②爭論 zhēnglùn (argue).

bang n. 猛然巨響 měngrán jùxiǎng (sudden noise).

bangle n. 手鐲 shǒuzhuó 〈hand〉.

banish v. ①驅逐出境 qūzhú chūjìng (exile). ②消除 xiāochú (put away). ③擺脫 bǎituō (get rid of).

banister n. 欄杆 lángān.

banjo n. 五絃琴 wǔxiánqín.

bank n. ①銀行 yínháng (financial institution). ②岸 àn, 堤 dī / tí (embankment). ③斜坡 xiépō (slope). ~ account 銀行帳戶 yínháng zhànghù.

banker n. 銀行家 yínhángjiā.

bankrupt n. 破產者 pòchǎnzhě. — adj. 破產的 pòchǎn de.

banner n. 旗幟 qízhì.

banquet n. 宴會 yànhuì.

banter n. & v. 嘲弄 cháonòng, 開玩笑 kāi wánxiào.

banyan n. 榕樹 róngshù.

baptism n. 洗禮 xǐlǐ.

bar n. ①棒 bàng, 棍 gùn (stick). ②門閂 ménshuān 〈door〉. ③酒吧 jiǔbā (pub). — v. ①閂住 shuānzhù (block by putting a bar across). ②阻止 zǔzhǐ (prevent), 禁止 jìnzhǐ (prohibit).

barb n. 倒鉤 dàogōu.

barbarian n. 野蠻人 yěmánrén. — adj. 野蠻的 yěmán de.

B

barbarous adj. ①殘忍的 cánrěn de (cruel). ②野蠻的 yěmán de (uncivilized).

barbecue n. 烤肉 kǎoròu 〈meat〉. — v. 燒烤 shāokǎo 〈cook〉.

barber n. 理髮師 lǐfàshī / lǐfàshī.

barbershop n. 理髮店 lǐfàdiàn / lǐfǎdiàn.

bare adj. ①赤裸的 chìluǒ de (uncovered, naked). ②起碼的 qǐmǎ de (minimum). — v. 暴露 bàolù / pùlù (expose).

barely adv. 幾乎沒有 jīhū méiyǒu (hardly).

bargain n. ①交易 jiāoyì (deal). ②協議 xiéyì (agreement). ③便宜貨 piányíhuò, 廉價品 liánjiàpǐn 〈goods〉. — v. ①議價 yìjià, 殺價 shājià (haggle). ②協議 xiéyì (try to reach an agreement).

barge n. 平底貨船 píngdǐ huòchuán, 駁船 bóchuán. — v. 魯莽衝撞 lǔmǎng chōngzhuàng.

baritone n. 男中音 nánzhōngyīn.

bark n. ①狗吠聲 gǒufèishēng 〈sound〉. ②樹皮 shùpí 〈tree〉. — v. 狗吠 gǒufèi.

barley n. 大麥 dàmài.

barn n. 穀倉 gǔcāng.

barometer n. 氣壓計 qìyājì, 晴雨表 qíngyǔbiǎo.

baron n. 男爵 nánjué.

barracks n. 兵營 bīngyíng 〈for soldiers〉.

barrage n. ①猛烈砲火 měngliè pàohuǒ (heavy gunfire). ②砲轟 pàohōng 〈of speech〉.

barrel n. ①大桶 dàtǒng 〈container〉. ②槍管 qiāngguǎn 〈gun〉.

barren adj. 貧瘠的 pínjí de.

barricade n. & v. 障礙 zhàng'ài, 路障 lùzhàng.

barrier n. ①柵欄 zhàlan (fence). ②障礙 zhàng'ài (hindrance).

barrister n. 律師 lǜshī.

barter n. & v. 以物易物 yǐ-wù-yì-wù.

base n. ①根基 gēnjī (foundation). ②基地 jīdì 〈armed forces〉. ③壘 lěi 〈ball games〉. — adj. 卑鄙的 bēibǐ de (not honorable). — v. 以……為 基礎 yǐ...wéi jīchǔ. ~ **on** 基於 jīyú.

baseball n. 棒球 bàngqiú.

basement n. 地下室 dìxiàshì.

bash n. & v. 重擊 zhòngjī / zhòngjí.

bashful adj. 害羞的 hàixiū de.

basic adj. 基本的 jīběn de, 基礎的 jīchǔ de (fundamental). — n. 基礎 jīchǔ (foundation).

basically adv. 基本上 jīběnshang.

basin n. ①盆 pén 〈bowl〉. ②水坑 shuǐkēng (pool). ③流域 liúyù, 盆地 péndì 〈drainage area〉.

basis n. 基礎 jīchǔ (foundation), 根據 gēnjù (evidence). **on the ~ of...** 根據 gēnjù....

bask v. ①取暖 qǔnuǎn (enjoy warmth), 曬太陽 shài tàiyáng (sunbathe). ②陶醉 táozuì (enjoy).

basket n. 籃 lán, 籃子 lánzi.

basketball n. 籃球 lánqiú.

bass adj. 低音的 dīyīn de. — n. ①男低音 nándīyīn

(lowest male voice). ②鱸魚
lúyú 〈fish〉.

bassoon n. 巴松管
bāsōngguǎn.

bastard n. 私生子 sīshēngzǐ
(illegitimate child).

baste v. 燒烤時塗油脂
shāokǎo shí tú yóuzhī.

bastion n. 稜堡 léngbǎo.

bat n. ①棒 bàng (club), 球拍
qiúpāi 〈ball games〉. ②蝙蝠
biānfú 〈animal〉.

batch n. ①一爐 yì lú 〈food〉.
②一批 yì pī, 一群 yì qún
(group).

bath n. ①沐浴 mùyù (wash).
②澡盆 zǎopén (bathtub).
③浴室 yùshì (bathroom).

bathe v. ①沐浴 mùyù, 洗澡
xǐzǎo (take a bath). ②水洗
shuǐxǐ (wash).

bathing suit n. 泳衣 yǒngyī.

bathrobe n. 浴袍 yùpáo.

bathroom n. 浴室 yùshì.

bathtub n. 浴缸 yùgāng.

baton n. ①指揮棒 zhǐhuībàng
〈orchestra〉. ②警棍 jǐnggùn
(police).

battalion n. 營 yíng.

batter v. ①搞壞 dǎohuài (wear
out). ②連擊 liánjí / liánjí (beat).
— n. ①麵糊 miànhù / miànhú
〈mixture〉. ②打擊手 dǎjíshǒu /
dǎjíshǒu 〈ball games〉.

battery n. ①電池 diànchí
(electric cells). ②砲兵連
pàobīnglián 〈army unit〉.

battle n. ①戰爭 zhànzhēng,
戰役 zhànyì (war). ②爭鬥
zhēngdòu (fight).

battlement n. 城垛 chéngduǒ.

bauble n. 美麗但無用之飾品
měilì dàn wú yòng zhī shìpǐn
(small item of litte value).

bawl n. & v. 大喊 dàhǎn (yell),
哭叫 kūjiào (cry).

bay n. 海灣 hǎiwān (coast).
~ *window* 凸窗 tūchuāng /
túchuāng.

bayonet n. 刺刀 cìdāo.

bazaar n. 市集 shìjí
(shopping center), 傳統市場
chuántǒng shìchǎng (tradi-
tional market).

BBS 電子公告板系統 diànzǐ
gōnggàobǎn xìtǒng / 電子佈
告欄系統 diànzǐ bùgàolán
xìtǒng (Bulletin Board System).

B.C. 西元前 xīyuán qián.

be v. 是 shì.

beach n. 海灘 hǎitān (seaside),
沙灘 shātān (sandy bank).

beacon n. ①燈塔 dēngtǎ
(lighthouse). ②烽火 fēnghuǒ
(signal fire). ③信號 xìnhào
(marker).

bead n. 念珠 niànzhū.

beak n. 鳥嘴 niǎozuǐ.

beam n. ①橫樑 héngliáng
(heavy bar). ②船舷 chuánxián
〈ship〉. ③光線 guāngxiàn 〈light〉.

bean n. 豆 dòu.

bear v. ①背 bēi, 負載 fùzài
(carry). ②生產 shēngchǎn,
生育 shēngyù (give birth to).
③容忍 róngrěn (tolerate).
— n. ①熊 xióng 〈animal〉.
②空頭 kōngtóu 〈stock market〉.

beard n. 鬍鬚 húxū.

bearing n. ①舉止 jǔzhǐ, 態度
tàidu (attitude). ②關係 guānxi,
意義 yìyì (relation). ③姿態
zītài (manner).

beast n. 獸 shòu, 動物 dòngwù.

beat v. ①打 dǎ (strike). ②擊敗
jíbài / jíbài (defeat). ③規律
鼓動 guīlù gǔdòng (pulse).
— n. ①敲打 qiāodǎ 〈drum〉.

②節拍 jiépāi ⟨rhythm⟩.

beaten *adj.* 被打敗的 bèi dǎbài de ⟨defeated⟩.

beautician *n.* 美容師 měiróngshī.

beautiful *adj.* 美麗的 měilì de.

beautify *v.* 美化 měihuà.

beauty *n.* ①美 měi, 美貌 měimào ⟨prettiness⟩. ②美人 měirén ⟨pretty person⟩.

beaver *n.* 海狸 hǎilí.

because *conj.* 因為 yīnwèi.

beckon *v.* 招手示意 zhāoshǒu shìyì.

become *v.* ①變為 biànwéi (change into), 成為 chéngwéi (come to be). ②適合 shìhé, 相稱 xiāngchèn / xiāngchèng (fit).

bed *n.* ①床 chuáng ⟨furniture⟩. ②基底 jīdǐ (base).

bedding *n.* 寢具 qǐnjù.

bedlam *n.* 喧擾 xuānrǎo.

bedroom *n.* 臥房 wòfáng.

bedsore *n.* 褥瘡 rùchuāng.

bedtime *n.* 就寢時間 jiùqǐn shíjiān.

bee *n.* 蜜蜂 mìfēng.

beech *n.* 山毛櫸 shānmáojǔ.

beef *n.* 牛肉 niúròu.

beefsteak *n.* 牛排 niúpái.

beehive *n.* 蜂窩 fēngwō.

beer *n.* 啤酒 píjiǔ.

beet *n.* 甜菜 tiáncài.

beetle *n.* 甲蟲 jiǎchóng.

befall *v.* 降臨 jiànglín, 發生 fāshēng.

befit *v.* 適合 shìhé.

before *adv. & prep. & conj.* ①以前 yǐqián (in the past). ②在……之前 zài...zhīqián (earlier than). ③在……的面前 zài...de miànqián (in front of).

beforehand *adv.* 事前 shìqián.

befriend *v.* 待之如友 dài zhī rú yǒu.

beg *v.* ①懇求 kěnqiú ⟨favors⟩. ②乞討 qǐtǎo ⟨money⟩.

beggar *n.* 乞丐 qǐgài.

begin *v.* 開始 kāishǐ (start), 始於 shǐyú (originate with).

beginner *n.* ①初學者 chūxuézhě ⟨for learning⟩. ②初始者 chūshǐzhě ⟨for starting⟩.

beginning *n.* 開始 kāishǐ (start), 起源 qǐyuán (origin).

begrudge *v.* ①嫉妒 jídù (envy). ②捨不得 shěbude (give unwillingly).

behalf *n.* **on ~ of** 為了…… (的利益) wèile...(de lìyì) (in the interest of), 作……的代表 zuò...de dàibiǎo (as somebody's representative).

behave *v.* 行為 xíngwéi, 舉動 jǔdòng (act).

behavior *n.* 行為 xíngwéi (way of acting), 態度 tàidu (attitude).

behead *v.* 斬首 zhǎnshǒu.

behind *adv. & prep.* ①在後 zài hòu (in back of). ②落後 luòhòu (not progressive). ③較遲 jiàochí (late). **~ the times** 落伍 luòwǔ.

beige *n. & adj.* 棕灰色 zōnghuīsè.

being *n.* ①生命 shēngmìng (living thing). ②存在 cúnzài (existence).

belated *adj.* 誤期的 wùqí de / wùqí de, 太遲的 tài chí de (coming too late).

belch *n. & v.* 打嗝 dǎgé.

belfry *n.* 鐘樓 zhōnglóu.

belief *n.* ①信念 xìnniàn, 信仰 xìnyǎng (religious faith). ②信

任 xìnrèn, 相信 xiāngxìn
(trust).

believe v. ①相信 xiāngxìn
(trust). ②認為 rènwéi (think).

belittle v. 輕視 qīngshì, 貶低
biǎndī.

bell n. 鈴 líng, 鐘 zhōng.

bell-bottoms n. 喇叭褲
lǎbākù.

belligerent adj. ①好戰的
hàozhàn de (war-mongering).
②交戰的 jiāozhàn de (at
war). ③好鬥的 hàodòu de
(aggressive).

bellow v. ①怒吼 nùhǒu, 咆哮
páoxiāo (yell). ②吼叫 hǒujiào
〈cow〉.

belly n. ①腹部 fùbù (abdomen).
②胃 wèi (stomach).

belong v. 屬於 shǔyú, 歸於
guīyú.

belongings n. 財產 cáichǎn,
所有物 suǒyǒuwù.

beloved adj. 所愛的 suǒ'ài de.
— n. 所愛的人 suǒ'ài de rén
〈a person〉, 親愛的朋友們
qīn'ài de péngyoumen
〈address〉.

below prep. 在……之下
zài...zhī xià (in a lower
position). — adv. 在下面 zài
xiàmian (at a lower place).

belt n. ①帶 dài, 皮帶 pídài
〈clothing〉. ②傳送帶
chuánsòngdài (conveyor).

bemoan v. 慟哭 tòngkū,
悲悼 bēidào.

bemused adj. 困惑的 kùnhuò
de (perplexed).

bench n. ①長凳 chángdèng
(long seat). ②工作臺
gōngzuòtái (long worktable).

bend v. 使彎曲 shǐ wānqū
(curve). — n. ①彎曲 wānqū

(angle). ②轉彎 zhuǎnwān
(turn).

beneath adv. & prep. 在……
下 zài...xià (under).

benediction n. 祝福 zhùfú,
祝禱 zhùdǎo.

beneficial adj. 有益的 yǒuyì
de.

beneficiary n. 受益人
shòuyìrén.

benefit n. ①利益 lìyì (advantage). ②恩惠 ēnhuì (good deed).
— v. 有益於 yǒuyì yú, 對……
有利 duì...yǒulì.

benevolent adj. 慈善的
císhàn de.

benign adj. ①和藹的 hé'ǎi de
〈person〉. ②良性的 liángxìng
de 〈disease〉.

bent adj. 彎曲的 wānqū de
(not straight). — n. ①傾向
qīngxiàng (tendency). ②愛好
àihào (hobby).

bequeath v. 遺贈 yízèng /
wèizèng.

bequest n. 遺贈 yízèng /
wèizèng, 遺產 yíchǎn.

bereave v. 剝奪 bōduó.

bereaved adj. 喪親的
sàngqīn de.

bereft adj. 喪失的 sàngshī de.

beriberi n. 腳氣病 jiǎoqìbìng.

berry n. 漿果 jiāngguǒ.

berth n. ①臥舖 wòpù (place to
sleep). ②船停泊處 chuán
tíngbó chù (place to anchor).

beset v. ①圍攻 wéigōng,
包圍 bāowéi (surround and
attack). ②困擾 kùnrǎo (trouble).

beside prep. ①在旁 zài páng
(next to). ②和……比較 hé...
bǐjiào (compared to).

besides adv. & prep. 而且
érqiě, 此外 cǐwài (also).

B

besiege v. ①圍攻 wéigōng
(surround and attack). ②困擾
kùnrǎo (trouble).

best adj. 最佳的 zuì jiā de,
最好的 zuì hǎo de. ~ *man*
男儐相 nánbīnxiàng, 伴郎
bànláng. — n. 最好 zuìhǎo.
at ~ 充其量 chōngqíliàng.
make the ~ *of* 盡力而為 jìnlì
ér wéi.

bestial adj. 像野獸的 xiàng
yěshòu de (brutish).

best-known adj. 最出名的
zuì chūmíng de.

bestow v. 給予 gěiyǔ (give),
贈與 zèngyǔ (confer).

bet v. 打賭 dǎdǔ. *You* ~! 當
然！Dāngrán! — n. 賭注
dǔzhù.

betray v. ①出賣 chūmài (sell
out). ②洩露 xièlòu (disclose).

betrothed adj. 已訂婚的 yǐ
dìnghūn de.

better adj. & adv. ①更好的
gèng hǎo de (more excellent).
②較佳的 jiào jiā de ⟨illness⟩.
had ~ 最好 zuìhǎo.

between adv. & prep. 在……
之間 zài...zhī jiān.

bevel n. ①斜面 xiémiàn (surface). ②斜角 xiéjiǎo (edge).
— v. 使成斜角 shǐ chéng
xiéjiǎo.

beveled adj. 斜面的 xiémiàn
de ⟨surface⟩, 斜角的 xiéjiǎo de
⟨angle⟩.

beverage n. 飲料 yǐnliào.

bevy n. 一群 yì qún.

beware v. 留意 liúyì, 提防
dīfang / tífáng.

bewilder v. 使迷惑 shǐ míhuò.

bewitch v. ①施魔法 shǐ mófǎ,
迷惑 míhuo (work magic on).
②迷人 mírén (charm).

beyond prep. ①在……的那
邊 zài...de nàbiān (on the far
side of). ②之後 zhīhòu (after).
③超過 chāoguò (exceeding).

bias n. ①偏見 piānjiàn, 成見
chéngjiàn (prejudice). ②斜線
xiéxiàn (diagonal).

bib n. 圍兜 wéidōu.

Bible n. 聖經 Shèngjīng.

bibliography n. ①參考書目
cānkǎo shūmù (list of refer-
ences). ②書誌 shūzhì ⟨history
of books⟩. ③作品目錄 zuòpǐn
mùlù (list of writings).

bicker n. & v. 爭吵 zhēngchǎo.

bicycle n. 自行車 zìxíngchē /
腳踏車 jiǎotàchē. ~ *path* 自行
車道 zìxíngchēdào.

bid v. ①出價 chūjià (offer as a
price). ②命令 mìnglìng, 吩咐
fēnfu (command). — n. 出價
chūjià (an offered price).

biennial n. & adj. 兩年一次
liǎng nián yí cì.

bifocals n. 遠近視兩用眼鏡
yuǎn-jìnshì liǎngyòng yǎnjìng.

big adj. ①大的 dà de (large).
②重要的 zhòngyào de
(important).

bigamy n. 重婚 chónghūn.

bigot n. 頑信者 wánxìnzhě,
偏執者 piānzhízhě.

bike n. ①自行車 zìxíngchē /
腳踏車 jiǎotàchē ⟨without
motor⟩. ②輕型摩托車 qīngxíng
mótuōchē (motorbike).

bilateral adj. 兩邊的 liǎngbiān
de, 雙方的 shuāngfāng de.

bile n. 膽汁 dǎnzhī ⟨liquid⟩.

bilingual adj. 雙語的
shuāngyǔ de.

bill n. ①帳單 zhàngdān (list of
charges). ②鈔票 chāopiào
(banknote). ③廣告單

guǎnggàodān (printed notice).
④草案 cǎo'àn (draft of law).
⑤鳥嘴 niǎozuǐ (beak).

billet n. 兵營舍 bīngyíngshè
⟨soldiers⟩. – v. 安排兵舍
ānpái bīngshè.

billiards n. 枱球 táiqiú / 撞球
zhuàngqiú.

billion n. 十億 shíyì.

billow n. 巨浪 jùlàng (large
wave). – v. 洶湧 xiōngyǒng
(swell in waves). 揚起
yángqǐ (swell out).

bimbo n. 漂亮而沒有大腦的女
郎 piàoliang ér méi dànǎo de
nǚláng.

bin n. 大箱 dàxiāng.

binary adj. 雙重的
shuāngchóng de. — n.
雙子星 shuāngzǐxīng ⟨stars⟩.

bind v. ①縛 fù / fú, 捆 kǔn
(tie together). ②包紮 bāozā
(bandage). ③凝聚 níngjù (hold
together). ④約束 yuēshù
(compel).

bingo n. 賓戈 bīngē / 賓果遊
戲 bīnguǒ yóuxì.

biochemistry n. 生物化學
shēngwù huàxué, 生化
shēng-huà.

biography n. 傳記 zhuànjì.

biology n. 生物學
shēngwùxué.

birch n. 樺樹 huàshù.

bird n. 鳥 niǎo.

bird flu n. 禽流感 qínliúgǎn.

bird-strick n. 鳥擊 niǎojī /
niǎojí.

bird-watching n. 鳥類觀察
niǎolèi guānchá.

birth n. ①出生 chūshēng,
出世 chūshì, 誕生 dànshēng
(being born). ②出身 chūshēn,
家世 jiāshì (family origin).

birthday n. 生日 shēngrì.

birthmark n. 胎記 tāijì.

birthplace n. 出生地
chūshēngdì.

biscuit n. 餅乾 bǐnggān.

bisect v. 一分為二 yī fēnwéi
èr.

bisexual adj. 雌雄同體的
cíxióng tóngtǐ de (hermaphro-
dite). – n. 雙性戀
shuāngxìngliàn.

bishop n. 主教 zhǔjiào.

bison n. 野牛 yěniú.

bit n. 一小塊 yì xiǎo kuài (small
piece), 一點點 yìdiǎndiǎn
(small amount). *not a* ~ 毫不
háobù.

bitch n. ①母狗 mǔgǒu (female
dog). ②賤女人 jiànnǚrén (bad
woman).

bite v. ①咬 yǎo (act of biting).
②一口 yì kǒu (a mouthful).
③咬傷 yǎoshāng (bite wound).
– v. ①咬 yǎo, 叮 dīng (sting).
②抓緊 zhuājǐn (grip). ③刺痛
cìtòng (cause pain).

bitter adj. ①苦的 kǔ de ⟨taste⟩.
②痛苦的 tòngkǔ de
(sorrowful).

bitterness n. 苦 kǔ.

bizarre adj. 古怪的 gǔguài
de.

black adj. ①黑色的 hēisè de
⟨color⟩. 暗淡的 àndàn de
(dark). – n. ①黑色 hēisè
⟨color⟩. ②黑人 hēirén ⟨race⟩.
~ *eye* 黑眼圈 hēiyǎnquān.
~ *hole* 黑洞 hēidòng.
~ *market* 黑市 hēishì.
~ *tea* 紅茶 hóngchá.

blackboard n. 黑板 hēibǎn.

blacken v. ①變黑 biànhēi
(become black), 變暗 biàn'àn
(become dark). ②毀謗 huǐbàng

B

(speak badly of).

blackguard n. 流氓 liúmáng, 無賴 wúlài.

blackmail n. & v. 勒索 lèsuǒ, 敲詐 qiāozhà.

blackout n. ①停電 tíngdiàn (power outage). ②昏厥 hūnjué (fainting spell).

blacksmith n. 鐵匠 tiějiàng.

bladder n. 膀胱 pángguāng.

blade n. ①刀刃 dāorèn 〈knife〉. ②細葉片 xìyèpiàn 〈grass〉.

blame n. & v. 譴責 qiǎnzé, 歸咎 guījiù.

bland adj. ①無味道的 wú wèidao de (tasteless). ②枯燥 無味的 kūzào-wú-wèi de (boring).

blank n. ①空白 kòngbái 〈paper〉. ②空白 kòngbái, 空虛 kōngxū (emptiness). — adj. ①空白的 kòngbái de 〈paper〉. ②面無表情的 miàn wú biǎoqíng de (expressionless).

blanket n. 毛毯 máotǎn.

blare n. & v. 高鳴 gāomíng, 大叫 dàjiào.

blasphemy n. 褻瀆 xièdú.

blast n. ①一陣疾風 yí zhèn jífēng (violent gust of wind). ②吹奏聲 chuīzòushēng (sound of instrument). ③爆炸 bàozhà (explosion). — v. ①炸開 zhàkāi (break open by explosion). ②摧毀 cuīhuǐ (destroy).

blatant adj. 乖張的 guāizhāng de.

blaze n. 火焰 huǒyàn (fire), 強光 qiángguāng (bright light). — v. ①燃燒 ránshāo (burn). ②發強光 fā qiángguāng (shine brightly).

blazer n. 男性上衣 nánxìng shàngyī.

bleach v. 變白 biànbái, 漂白 piǎobái. — n. 漂白劑 piǎobáijì.

bleak adj. ①荒涼的 huāngliáng de (bare). ②寒冷的 hánlěng de (cold).

bleat v. 牛羊叫聲 niúyáng jiàoshēng.

bleed v. ①流血 liúxuè / liúxiě (emit blood). ②放血 fàngxuè / fàngxiě (draw blood from).

blemish n. 污點 wūdiǎn, 瑕疵 xiácī (spot). 缺點 quēdiǎn (failing). — v. 玷污 diànwū.

blend v. ①調合 tiáohé (combine). ②混合 hùnhé, 混雜 hùnzá (mix). — n. 混合（物）hùnhé (wù).

bless v. 祝福 zhùfú (wish good to).

blessing n. ①祝福 zhùfú, 祈福 qífú (grace). ②可喜的事 kě xǐ de shì (piece of luck).

blight n. 枯萎病 kūwěibìng / kūwēibìng. — v. ①使枯萎 shǐ kūwěi / shǐ kūwēi (drying up). ②摧殘 cuīcán (destroy).

blind adj. ①瞎的 xiā de (unable to see). ②盲目的 mángmù de (unaware). ~ person 盲人 mángrén. — v. ①使失明 shǐ shīmíng (make somebody unable to see). ②使盲目 shǐ mángmù (make somebody unaware).

blindfold v. 蒙住眼睛 méngzhù yǎnjing.

blink v. ①眨眼 zhǎyǎn (wink). ②閃爍 shǎnshuò (twinkle).

bliss n. 極大的幸福 jí dà de xìngfú.

blister n. 水泡 shuǐpào, 膿疱 nóngpào 〈skin〉. — v. 生水泡 shēng shuǐpào.

blitz n. 閃電戰 shǎndiànzhàn.

blizzard n. 暴風雪 bàofēngxuě.

bloc n. 集團 jítuán.

block n. ①一塊 yí kuài (a piece of). ②阻礙 zǔ'ài, 障礙 zhàng'ài (obstacle). ③街區 jiēqū (area bordered by streets). — v. ①阻塞 zǔsè (plug up). ②阻礙 zǔ'ài (obstruct).

blockade n. & v. 封鎖 fēngsuǒ.

blockage n. ①阻礙 zǔ'ài (state of being blocked). ②障礙物 zhàng'àiwù (object).

blond(e) adj. 金髮的 jīnfǎ de / jīnfà de. — n. 金髮的人 jīnfǎ de rén / jīnfà de rén.

blood n. ①血 xuè / xiě, 血液 xuèyè / xiěyì (body). ②血統 xuètǒng / xiětǒng (family relationship). ~ **bank** 血庫 xuèkù / xiěkù. ~ **group** 血型 xuèxíng / xiěxíng.

bloody adj. ①血污的 xuèwū de / xiěwū de (covered with blood). ②血腥的 xuèxīng de / xiěxīng de (wounding and killing).

bloom n. ①花 huā (flower). ②花開 huākāi (blossom). ③壯盛時期 zhuàngshèng shíqī / zhuàngshèng shíqí (the best period). — v. 花開 huākāi (produce flowers).

blossom n. 花 huā, 花叢 huācóng. — v. 開花 kāihuā.

blot n. ①污痕 wūhén, 墨跡 mòjī (stain). ②污點 wūdiǎn, 瑕疵 xiácī (blemish). — v. 沾上 墨跡 zhānshang mòjī (spoil).

blotch n. 大污漬 dà wūzì, 大斑點 dà bāndiǎn (skin, paper, material, etc).

blouse n. 罩衫 zhàoshān, 上

衣 shàngyī.

blow n. ①打 dǎ (punch). ②打擊 dǎjī / dǎjí (shock). — v. ①吹 chuī (air). ②吹動 chuīdòng, 吹掉 chuīdiào (move). ③充氣 chōngqì (fill with air). ④吹奏 chuīzòu (trumpet). ~ **up** ①爆炸 bàozhà (explode). ②發脾氣 fā píqi (get angry).

blow-dry v. 吹乾 chuīgān.

blow-dryer n. 吹風機 chuīfēngjī.

blue n. & adj. 藍色 lánsè. ~ **chip** 績優股 jìyōugǔ / jīyōugǔ. ~ **jeans** 牛仔褲 niúzǎikù.

blue-collar adj. 藍領的 lánlǐng de.

blueprint n. 藍圖 lántú.

bluff v. 虛張聲勢 xū-zhāng-shēngshì.

blunder n. 大錯 dà cuò. — v. ①犯錯 fàncuò (make a mistake). ②盲動 mángdòng (move about uncertainly).

blunt adj. ①鈍的 dùn de (not sharp). ②直率的 zhíshuài de (straightforward).

blur v. 使模糊 shǐ móhu (become unclear). — n. 模糊的事物 móhu de shìwù.

blurry adj. 模糊的 móhu de.

blurt v. 脫口而出 tuō-kǒu-ér-chū.

blush n. & v. 臉紅 liǎnhóng, 羞愧 xiūkuì.

bluster n. & v. ①狂吹 kuángchuī (blow). ②咆哮 páoxiào / páoxiāo (vent anger). ③恫嚇 dònghè (threat).

boa constrictor n. 蟒蛇 mǎngshé.

boar n. ①野豬 yězhū (wild). ②雄豬 xióngzhū (male pig).

board n. ①木板 mùbǎn (thin plank). ②理事會 lǐshìhuì, 董事會 dǒngshìhuì (committee). ③膳食 shànshí (food). — v. ①搭乘 dāchéng (get on). ②用板蓋住 yòng bǎn gàizhù (cover with). ③寄宿 jìsù (lodge).

boast v. 自誇 zìkuā, 誇耀 kuāyào, 吹牛 chuīniú.

boat n. 船 chuán, 小船 xiǎochuán.

bob v. 上下疾動 shàngxià jídòng (move up and down). — n. 短髮 duǎnfà / duǎnfǎ (hair).

bode v. 預示 yùshì, 預兆 yùzhào.

bodice n. 緊身胸衣 jǐnshēn xiōngyī.

body n. ①身體 shēntǐ, 軀體 qūtǐ (whole of a person, animal). ②軀幹 qūgàn (torso). ③主要部分 zhǔyào bùfen (the main part). ~ *language* 肢體語言 zhītǐ yǔyán.

bodyguard n. 保鑣 bǎobiāo.

bog n. 沼澤 zhǎozé.

bogey n. 高標準桿一桿 gāo biāozhǔngǎn yì gǎn.

bogus adj. 假的 jiǎ de, 偽造的 wěizào de / wèizào de.

boil n. & v. ①煮沸 zhǔfèi, 沸騰 fèiténg (heat a liquid). ②烹煮 pēngzhǔ (cook).

boiler n. 鍋爐 guōlú, 燒水器 shāoshuǐqì (device).

boisterous adj. 喧鬧的 xuānnào de (loud).

bold adj. ①大膽的 dàdǎn de (brave). ②無禮的 wúlǐ de (impudent).

bolster n. 長枕 chángzhěn, 長墊 chángdiàn.

bolt n. ①門閂 ménshuān 〈for door〉. ②螺栓 luóshuān 〈for joining parts〉. — v. ①閂住 shuānzhù (bar a door). ②逃走 táozǒu (flee). ~ *down* 囫圇吞入 húlún tūnrù (devour).

bomb n. 炸彈 zhàdàn. — v. 轟炸 hōngzhà.

bombard v. 砲轟 pàohōng.

bomber n. ①轟炸機 hōngzhàjī 〈aircraft〉. ②轟炸員 hōngzhàyuán 〈person〉.

bond n. ①束縛 shùfù / shùfú (restraint). ②契約 qìyuē (contract). ③債券 zhàiquàn 〈finance〉.

bondage n. ①奴隸 núlì (slavery). ②束縛 shùfù / shùfú (restraint).

bone n. 骨 gǔ, 骨頭 gútou.

bonfire n. 戶外升火 hùwài shēnghuǒ.

bonnet n. 軟帽 ruǎnmào 〈hat〉.

bonus n. 紅利 hónglì, 獎金 jiǎngjīn.

bony adj. 多骨的 duōgǔ de.

book n. 書 shū, 卷冊 juàncè 〈text〉. — v. ①預定 yùdìng (reserve). ②登記 dēngjì (register).

booking n. 預約 yùyuē (reservation).

bookkeeper n. 簿記員 bùjìyuán.

bookkeeping n. 簿記 bùjì.

booklet n. 小冊子 xiǎocèzi.

bookmark n. 書籤 shūqiān.

bookshelf n. 書架 shūjià, 書櫥 shūchú.

bookshop n. 書店 shūdiàn.

bookstore n. 書店 shūdiàn.

bookworm n. 書蟲 shūchóng, 書呆子 shūdāizi.

boom n. & v. ①突趨景氣 tū

qū jǐngqì / tú qū jǐngqì (time of prosperity). ②隆隆聲 lónglóngshēng (deep resonant sound).

boor n. 粗魯的人 cūlǔ de rén.

boost v. 提高 tígāo (lift), 加強 jiāqiáng (strengthen), 鼓吹 gǔchuī (promote).

boot n. 長靴 chángxuē, 靴子 xuēzi.

booth n. ①攤位 tānwèi (stall). ②小隔間 xiǎogéjiān (shed). *telephone ~* 電話間 diànhuàjiān / 電話亭 diànhuàtíng. *voting ~* 投票處 tóupiàochù.

border n. ①邊緣 biānyuán (edge). ②邊境 biānjìng, 邊界 biānjiè (frontier). — v. 接鄰 jiēlín, 連接 liánjiē.

bore v. ①鑽孔 zuānkǒng / zuǎnkǒng (drill). ②使感到 無聊 shǐ gǎndào wúliáo (make people bored).

bored adj. 感到無聊的 gǎndào wúliáo de.

boring adj. 無聊的 wúliáo de.

born adj. 天生的 tiānshēng de (natural).

borrow v. 借 jiè.

bosom n. ①胸 xiōng (breast). ②胸懷 xiōnghuái, 內心 nèixīn (heart).

boss n. 老板 lǎobǎn.

BOT 建造、運作、移轉 jiànzào yùnzuò yízhuǎn (Build Operate Transfer).

botany n. 植物學 zhíwùxué.

botch v. 拙劣地做 zhuōliè de zuò / zhuóliè de zuò.

both adj. & adv. & pron. 二者 的 èr zhě de.

bother n. & v. 麻煩 máfan, 煩擾 fánrǎo.

bottle n. 瓶 píng, 瓶子 píngzi.

bottom n. ①底 dǐ, 底部 dǐbù (lowest part). ②尾部 wěibù, 盡頭 jìntóu (ending). ③根基 gēnjī, 基礎 jīchǔ (base). ④屁股 pìgu ⟨body part⟩. *Bottoms up!* 乾杯 Gānbēi!

bough n. 大樹枝 dà shùzhī.

bounce n. & v. ①反彈 fǎntán (rebound). ②跳起 tiàoqǐ (leap suddenly).

bound adj. ①被縛的 bèifù de / bèifú de (fastened by). ②有義 務的 yǒu yìwù de (having a duty). — n. 跳躍 tiàoyuè, 彈起 tánqǐ ⟨jump⟩.

boundary n. 界線 jièxiàn, 境界 jìngjiè.

boundless adj. 無限的 wúxiàn de.

bounteous adj. 豐富的 fēngfù de (plentiful).

bounty n. ①慷慨 kāngkǎi (generosity). ②津貼 jīntiē (reward).

bouquet n. 花束 huāshù.

bourgeois n. 中產階級 zhōngchǎn jiējí.

bow n. ①鞠躬 júgōng (bend forward). ②屈服 qūfú (yield). — n. ①弓 gōng ⟨weapon⟩. ②蝶形領結 diéxíng lǐngjié (knot). ③琴弓 qíngōng ⟨for playing instruments⟩.

bowel n. 腸 cháng ⟨organ⟩.

bowl n. 碗 wǎn, 缽 bō ⟨dish⟩.

bowling n. 保齡球 bǎolíngqiú. *~ alley* 保齡球場 bǎolíngqiúchǎng.

box n. ①箱 xiāng, 盒 hé (case). ②包廂 bāoxiāng (small private room).

boxer n. 拳擊手 quánjīshǒu / quánjíshǒu.

boxing n. 拳擊 quánjí / quánjí.

B

boy n. 男孩 nánhái. ~ *scout* 童子軍 tóngzǐjūn.

boycott n. & v. 杯葛 bēigé, 抵制 dǐzhì.

boyfriend n. 男朋友 nánpéngyou.

boyhood n. 童年 tóngnián, 少年時代 shàonián shídài.

bra n. 胸罩 xiōngzhào.

brace n. ①支撐 zhīchēng, 支架 zhījià (support). ②曲柄 qūbǐng 〈tool〉. ③齒列矯正器 chǐliè jiǎozhèngqì 〈teeth〉. — v. 支撐 zhīchēng (support). ~ *yourself*, ~ *up* 振作 zhènzuò.

bracelet n. 手鐲 shǒuzhuó.

bracket n. ①方括弧 fāngkuòhú (a mark [ ]). ②托架 tuōjià (support for something).

brackish adj. 略有鹽味的 lüè yǒu yánwèi de.

brag n. & v. 自誇 zìkuā.

braid n. ①辮子 biànzi, 髮辮 fàbiàn / fǎbiàn 〈hair〉. ②穗帶 suìdài 〈clothing〉.

Braille n. 盲人點字法 Mángrén diǎnzìfǎ.

brain n. ①腦 nǎo 〈body part〉. ②智慧 zhìhuì, 智力 zhìlì (intellect). ~ *drain* 人才外流 réncái wàiliú.

braise v. 燉 dùn.

brake v. & n. 煞車 shāchē.

bramble n. 荊棘 jīngjí, 灌木 guànmù.

bran n. 糠 kāng, 麥麩 màifū.

branch n. ①樹枝 shùzhī 〈tree〉. ②支流 zhīliú (tributary), 支線 zhīxiàn (secondary line). ③分店 fēndiàn 〈chain store〉. — v. 分支 fēnzhī.

brand n. ①商標 shāngbiāo, 牌子 páizi (trademark). ②烙印 làoyìn (mark). — v. 烙印 làoyìn (mark by burning).

brandish n. & v. 揮動 huīdòng.

brandy n. 白蘭地 báilándì.

brass n. ①黃銅 huángtóng 〈alloy〉. ②銅管樂器 tóngguǎn yuèqì 〈instrument〉. ~ *band* 管樂隊 guǎnyuèduì.

bravado n. 虛張聲勢 xū-zhāng-shēngshì.

brave adj. 勇敢的 yǒnggǎn de.

bravo interj. 好！Hǎo!

brawl n. & v. 打架 dǎjià (fight).

brazen adj. ①無恥的 wúchǐ de (shameless). ②黃銅的 huángtóng de (like brass).

breach n. ①違反 wéifǎn (transgression). ②不睦 bùmù, 不和 bùhé (alienation).

bread n. 麵包 miànbāo.

breadth n. ①寬度 kuāndù (width). ②寬宏大量 kuānhóng-dàliàng (considering others). ③範圍 fànwéi (scope).

break v. ①打破 dǎpò (come to pieces). ②違反 wéifǎn (transgress). ③弄壞 nònghuài, 破壞 pòhuài (ruin). ~ *in* 打斷 dǎduàn, 介入 jièrù (interrupt). ~ *up* 脫離 tuōlí (separate).

breakdown n. ①病倒 bìngdǎo, 崩潰 bēngkuì 〈psychological〉. ②損壞 sǔnhuài, 故障 gùzhàng 〈mechanical〉.

breakfast n. 早餐 zǎocān.

breakthrough n. ①突破 tūpò / túpò (advance). ②重大發現 zhòngdà fāxiàn (new discovery).

breakup n. ①解散 jiěsàn, 瓦解 wǎjiě (collapse). ②分手

breast *n.* 胸部 xiōngbù, 乳房 rǔfáng.

breath *n.* 呼吸 hūxī.
catch one's ~ 鬆一口氣 sōng yì kǒu qì. *out of ~* 喘不過氣來 chuǎnbúguò qì lái.

breathe *v.* 呼吸 hūxī.

breed *v.* ①生育 shēngyù (give birth to). ②飼養 sìyǎng, 養育 yǎngyù (raise). — *n.* 品種 pǐnzhǒng.

breeze *n.* 微風 wēifēng / wéifēng.

brevity *n.* ①短暫 duǎnzhàn (short duration). ②簡潔 jiǎnjié, 簡短 jiǎnduǎn (concision).

brew *v.* ①釀造 niàngzào (make drinks). ②圖謀 túmóu, 醞釀 yùnniàng (be forming). — *n.* 釀造 niàngzào ⟨beer⟩.

bribe *n. & v.* 賄賂 huìlù.

brick *n.* 磚 zhuān.

bride *n.* 新娘 xīnniáng.

bridegroom *n.* 新郎 xīnláng.

bridesmaid *n.* 女儐相 nǔbīnxiàng, 伴娘 bànniáng.

bridge *n.* ①橋 qiáo (crossing). ②艦橋 jiànqiáo ⟨part of ship⟩. ③橋牌 qiáopái ⟨card game⟩. — *v.* 架橋 jiàqiáo.

bridle *n.* 馬勒 mǎlè.

brief *adj.* 簡潔的 jiǎnjié de (succinct), 簡短的 jiǎnduǎn de (short). — *n.* 摘要 zhāiyào (summary). *in ~* 簡言之 jiǎnyánzhī.

briefcase *n.* 公事包 gōngshìbāo.

bright *adj.* ①光亮的 guāngliàng de (shining). ②聰明的 cōngming de (smart).

③愉快的 yúkuài de (cheerful).

brighten *v.* ①使光亮 shǐ guāngliàng (become bright). ②使愉快 shǐ yúkuài (make cheerful).

brilliant *adj.* ①燦爛的 cànlàn de, 光輝的 guānghuī de (splendid). ②聰明的 cōngming de, 有才氣的 yǒu cáiqì de (smart).

brim *n.* 邊 biān, 邊緣 biānyuán ⟨cup, bowl⟩.

brine *n.* 鹽水 yánshuǐ.

bring *v.* 帶來 dàilái (carry). *~ about* 導致 dǎozhì. *~ up* ①養育 yǎngyù (raise). ②提到 tídào (mention).

brink *n.* 邊緣 biānyuán.

brisk *adj.* 敏捷的 mǐnjié de, 輕快的 qīngkuài de.

bristle *n.* 鬃 zōng. — *v.* 豎立 shùlì.

brittle *adj.* 脆的 cuì de, 易碎的 yìsuì de (fragile).

broad *adj.* ①寬的 kuān de (wide). ②遼闊的 liáokuò de (vast). ③廣泛的 guǎngfàn de (wide-ranging).

broadband *n.* 寬頻 kuānpín.

broadcast *v.* ①廣播 guǎngbō / guǎngbò ⟨media⟩. ②傳布 chuánbù, 散播 sànbò / sànbò (make widely known).

broaden *v.* 擴大 kuòdà.

broadside *n.* 舷側 xiáncè ⟨ship⟩.

broccoli *n.* 花椰菜 huāyēcài / huāyécài.

brochure *n.* 小冊子 xiǎocèzi.

broil *v.* 燒烤 shāokǎo.

broken *adj.* ①壞掉的 huàidiào de (no longer functional). ②破裂的 pòliè de (in pieces). ③故障的 gùzhàng de (damaged).

broker n. 經紀人 jīngjìrén.

bronchitis n. 支氣管炎 zhīqìguǎnyán.

bronze n. ①青銅 qīngtóng 〈material〉. ②青銅器 qīngtóngqì 〈artwork〉.

brooch n. 胸針 xiōngzhēn.

brood n. ①一窩孵雛 yì wō fūchú 〈bird〉. ②一家小孩 yì jiā xiǎohái 〈human〉.

brook n. 溪流 xīliú, 小河 xiǎohé. — v. 容忍 róngrěn (tolerate).

broom n. 掃帚 sàozhou.

broth n. 清湯 qīngtāng.

brother n. ①哥哥 gēge 〈elder〉. ②弟弟 dìdi 〈younger〉. ~ s 兄弟 xiōngdì 〈male siblings〉.

brotherhood n. ①兄弟關係 xiōngdì guānxi, 手足之情 shǒuzú zhī qíng (relationship of brothers). ②協會 xiéhuì, 團體 tuántǐ (association).

brow n. ①眉 méi, 眉毛 méimao (eyebrow). ②額 é (forehead).

brown n. & adj. 棕色 zōngsè. ~ sugar 紅糖 hóngtáng.

browse v. 瀏覽書籍 liúlǎn shūjí (skim).

bruise v. 瘀傷 yūshāng.

brunch n. 早午餐 zǎowǔcān.

brush n. ①刷子 shuāzi 〈implement〉. ②小衝突 xiǎo chōngtú (short fight). ③叢林 cónglín (bushes). — v. 刷 shuā (clean), 塗 tú, 擦 cā (apply to).

brusque adj. 唐突的 tángtū de / tángtú de, 粗率的 cūshuài de.

brutal adj. 野蠻的 yěmán de (barbaric), 殘忍的 cánrěn de

(cruel).

brute n. ①野獸 yěshòu (beast). ②殘暴者 cánbàozhě, bully).

bubble n. 泡沫 pàomò, 氣泡 qìpào 〈air〉. — v. 起泡 qǐpào 〈rise in〉.

bubble gum n. 泡泡糖 pàopàotáng, 口香糖 kǒuxiāngtáng.

buck n. ①雄鹿 xiónglù (male deer). ②一美元 yì měiyuán (one dollar). — v. 摔落 shuāiluò.

bucket n. 水桶 shuǐtǒng.

buckle n. 釦環 kòuhuán. — v. 扣住 kòuzhù.

bud n. ①芽 yá, 花蕾 huālěi 〈plant〉. ②哥兒們 gērmen 〈friend〉. — v. 發芽 fāyá.

Buddhism n. 佛教 Fójiào.

Buddhist n. 佛教徒 Fójiàotú.

buddy n. ①哥倆 gēliǎng, 伙伴 huǒbàn (partner). ②老兄 lǎoxiōng (fellow).

budge v. 稍微移動 shāowēi yídòng / shāowéi yídòng.

budget n. 預算 yùsuàn. — v. 編預算 biān yùsuàn.

buff n. 淺黃褐色皮革 qiǎnhuánghèsè pígé / qiǎnhuánghèsè pígé 〈leather〉. — v. 擦拭 cāshì.

buffalo n. 水牛 shuǐniú (water buffalo), 美國野牛 Měiguó yěniú (bison).

buffer n. 緩衝器 huǎnchōngqì.

buffet n. 自助餐 zìzhùcān. ~ table 餐檯 cāntái.

buffoon n. 丑角 chǒujué / chǒujiǎo, 小丑 xiǎochǒu.

bug n. 小蟲 xiǎochóng.

bugle n. 喇叭 lǎba, 軍號 jūnhào.

build v. ①建築 jiànzhù / jiànzhú, 建造 jiànzào ⟨a house etc⟩. ②建立 jiànlì ⟨a company etc⟩. ~ *up* ①累積 lěijī (accumulate). ②增加 zēngjiā (increase). ③加強 jiāqiáng (strengthen). — *n.* 身材 shēncái, 體格 tǐgé.

builder n. 建築業者 jiànzhù yèzhě / jiànzhú yèzhě ⟨build houses⟩. ②建立者 jiànlìzhě ⟨bring into development⟩.

building n. 建築物 jiànzhùwù / jiànzhúwù.

bulb n. ①球莖 qiújīng ⟨plant⟩. ②電燈泡 diàndēngpào ⟨lamp⟩.

bulge v. 膨脹 péngzhàng, 脹大 zhàngdà.

bulk n. ①體積 tǐjī ⟨volume⟩. ②大部分 dàbùfen (most).

bulky adj. 龐大笨重的 pángdà bènzhòng de.

bull n. ①公牛 gōngniú ⟨animal⟩. ②多頭 duōtóu ⟨stock market⟩.

bullet n. 子彈 zǐdàn. ~ *train* 子彈列車 zǐdàn lièchē.

bulletin n. ①告示 gàoshì, 公報 gōngbào (announcement). ②小型雜誌 xiǎoxíng zázhì (newsletter).

bullion n. 金塊 jīnkuài (gold), 銀塊 yínkuài (silver).

bully n. 惡霸 èbà. — v. 欺負 qīfu, 威脅 wēixié.

bulwark n. ①壁壘 bìlěi, 堡壘 bǎolěi (wall built for defense). ②船舷 chuánxián ⟨ship⟩.

bump v. 碰 pèng. ~ *into* 碰到 pèngdào (meet by accident).

bumper n. 保險桿 bǎoxiǎngǎn. — adj. 豐盛的 fēngshèng de.

bumpkin n. 鄉巴佬

xiāngbālǎo.

bun n. 小圓甜麵包 xiǎo yuán tián miànbāo.

bunch n. ①串 chuàn ⟨grapes⟩. ②束 shù ⟨flowers⟩. ③堆 duī ⟨objects⟩. — n. 紮成束 zāchéng shù.

bundle n. 束 shù, 捆 kǔn, 包裹 bāoguǒ. — v. 包捆 bāokǔn, 紮 zā (wrap together).

bungalow n. 平房 píngfáng (one-story house).

bungee jumping n. 蹦極跳 bèngjítiào / 高空彈跳 gāokōng tántiào.

bungle n. & v. 搞砸 gǎozá.

bunk n. ①舖位 pùwèi (bed). ②廢話 fèihuà (nonsense).

bunker n. ①沙坑 shākēng ⟨a place filled with sand⟩. ②地堡 dìbǎo (underground shelter).

bunny n. 兔寶寶 tùbǎobao (rabbit).

buoy n. 浮標 fúbiāo, 浮筒 fútǒng. — v. ①使浮起 shǐ fúqǐ (keep floating). ②支持 zhīchí (support).

burden n. 負荷 fùhè, 重擔 zhòngdàn (heavy load). — v. 給……負擔 gěi...fùdàn, 麻煩 máfan (trouble).

burdock n. 牛蒡 niúbàng.

bureau n. ①局 jú, 處 chù, 署 shǔ (government department). ②辦公處 bàngōngchù (office).

bureaucracy n. 官僚政治 guānliáo zhèngzhì.

bureaucrat n. 官方人員 guānfāng rényuán (civil servant), 官僚 guānliáo ⟨negative connotation⟩.

burglar n. 竊賊 qièzéi (housebreaker).

burial *n.* 埋葬 máizàng 〈act〉,
葬禮 zànglǐ 〈ceremony〉.

burly *adj.* 魁梧的 kuíwú de /
kuíwù de.

burn *v.* 燃燒 ránshāo, 燒焦
shāojiāo. ~ *down* 燒盡 shāojìn.

burnish *v.* 擦亮 cāliàng.

burrow *n.* 地洞 dìdòng,
洞穴 dòngxué / dòngxuè.

bursar *n.* 會計員 kuàijìyuán.

burst *n.* & *v.* 爆炸 bàozhà
(explosion).

bury *v.* ①埋葬 máizàng (put
into the ground). ②掩藏
yǎncáng (hide away).

bus *n.* 公共汽車 gōnggòng
qìchē, 巴士 bāshì.

bush *n.* 灌木 guànmù 〈plant〉.

business *n.* ①生意 shēngyi,
買賣 mǎimai (trade). ②商店
shāngdiàn (a shop), 公司
gōngsī (a firm). ③職務 zhíwù,
職責 zhízé (task).
    mind one's own ~ 不管閒事
bùguǎn xiánshì.
    none of your ~ 不關你的事
bù guān nǐ de shì, 少管閒事
shǎo guǎn xiánshì.
    ~ *card* 名片 míngpiàn.
    ~ *hours* 上班時間 shàngbān
shíjiān.

businessman/woman *n.*
商人 shāngrén, 生意人
shēngyìrén.

business park *n.* 高科技工
業園區 gāokējì gōngyè
yuánqū.

bust *n.* ①半身雕塑像 bànshēn
diāo sùxiàng (sculpture). ②胸部
xiōngbù (chest).

bustle *v.* 匆忙 cōngmáng
(hurry), 喧擾 xuānrǎo (rush
about). — *n.* 熱鬧 rènao.

busy *adj.* ①忙碌的 mánglù de

(occupied). ②熱鬧的 rènao de
(bustling).

but *conj.* 但是 dànshì, 然而
rán'ér.

butcher *n.* ①肉販 ròufàn (one
who sells meat). ②屠夫 túfū
(one who slaughters animals for
food). — *v.* 屠殺 túshā.

butler *n.* 僕役長 púyìzhǎng.

butt *n.* ①柄 bǐng 〈tools or
weapons〉. ②煙蒂 yāndì
〈cigarette〉. ③笑柄 xiàobǐng
〈person〉. — *v.* 以頭撞 yǐ tóu
zhuàng (hit with the head).

butter *n.* 奶油 nǎiyóu.
    peanut ~ 花生醬
huāshēngjiàng.

butterfly *n.* 蝴蝶 húdié.

buttock *n.* 臀 tún, 屁股 pìgu.

button *n.* 鈕扣 niǔkòu. — *v.*
扣 kòu.

buttress *n.* 扶牆 fúqiáng, 拱
壁 gǒngbì.

buxom *adj.* 豐滿的 fēngmǎn
de.

buy *v.* ①買 mǎi (purchase).
②換得 huàndé (to be
exchangeable for).

buyer *n.* 買主 mǎizhǔ,
採購者 cǎigòuzhě.

buzz *n.* 嗡嗡聲
wēngwēngshēng.

by *prep.* ①在……近旁
zài...jìnpáng (near). ②藉以
jièyǐ (by means of). ③沿著
yánzhe (along). ④經由
jīngyóu, 經過 jīngguò (past).
⑤不晚於…… bù wǎn yú...
(not later than).

bye-bye *interj.* 再會 zàihuì,
再見 zàijiàn.

bylaw *n.* ①地方法規 dìfāng
fǎguī 〈local ordinance〉. ②組織
章程 zǔzhī zhāngchéng

〈organization〉.

bypass n. 旁道 pángdào, 外環道 wàihuándào (road).

bypath n. 小路 xiǎolù.

by-product n. 副產品

byproduct 〈object〉.

bystander n. 旁觀者 pángguānzhě.

byway n. 小路 xiǎolù.

C

cab n. 出租汽車 chūzū qìchē / 計程車 jìchéngchē (taxi).

cabaret n. 歌舞表演 gēwǔ biǎoyǎn.

cabbage n. 甘藍菜 gānláncài.

cabin n. ①小屋 xiǎowū (hut). ②船艙 chuáncāng 〈ship〉. ③機艙 jīcāng 〈airplane〉.

cabinet n. ①櫥 chú, 櫃 guì 〈furniture〉. ②內閣 nèigé 〈government〉.

cable n. ①電纜 diànlǎn 〈wires〉. ②電報 diànbào 〈communication〉. ~ *car* 纜車 lǎnchē.

cactus n. 仙人掌 xiānrénzhǎng.

CAD 計算機輔助設計 jìsuànjī fǔzhù shèjì / 電腦輔助設計 diànnǎo fǔzhù shèjì (computer-aided design).

Caesarean section 剖腹生產 pōufù shēngchǎn / pǒufù shēngchǎn.

café n. ①餐廳 cāntīng (small restaurant). ②咖啡店 kāfēidiàn (coffee shop).

cafeteria n. 自助餐廳 zìzhù cāntīng.

caffeine n. 咖啡因 kāfēiyīn.

cage n. 籠 lóng. — v. 監禁 jiānjìn.

cajole v. 哄騙 hǒngpiàn.

cake n. 糕 gāo, 蛋糕 dàngāo. *a piece of* ~ 易如反掌 yì-rú-fǎnzhǎng.

calamity n. 不幸事件 búxìng shìjiàn, 災難 zāinàn.

calcium n. 鈣 gài.

calculate v. ①計算 jìsuàn (compute). ②預計 yùjì (predict).

calculation n. ①計算 jìsuàn (count). ②預計 yùjì (prediction).

calculator n. 計算機 jìsuànjī.

calculus n. 微積分學 wēijīfēnxué / wéijīfēnxué.

calendar n. 日曆 rìlì.

calf n. ①小牛 xiǎoniú (young cow). ②小腿 xiǎotuǐ (leg).

caliber n. ①口徑 kǒujìng (diameter of a bullet). ②才幹 cáigàn (quality of a person).

call v. ①喊 hǎn, 叫 jiào (cry out). ②召喚 zhàohuàn (summon). ③打電話 dǎdiànhuà (phone). n. 呼聲 hūshēng 〈voice〉. ~ *waiting* 電話插播 diànhuà chābō / diànhuà chābò.

calligraphy n. 書法 shūfǎ.

callous adj. ①起繭的 qǐjiǎn de 〈skin〉. ②無情的 wúqíng de (emotionally cold).

callow adj. 乳臭未乾 rǔxiù-wèi-gān.

callus n. 繭 jiǎn.

calm adj. ①安靜的 ānjìng de (quiet). ②寧靜的 níngjìng de (tranquil). — n. 平靜 píngjìng. — v. ①安慰 ānwèi (comfort). ②使平靜 shǐ píngjìng (quiet).

calorie n. 卡路里 kǎlùlǐ.

camel n. 駱駝 luòtuo.

camera n. 照相機 zhàoxiàngjī 〈photos〉, 攝影機 shèyǐngjī 〈video〉.

camouflage n. & v. 掩飾 yǎnshì (cover up), 偽裝 wěizhuāng / wèizhuāng (pretend).

camp n. ①露營 lùyíng (encampment). ②營地 yíngdì 〈place〉. — v. 露營 lùyíng.

campaign n. ①戰役 zhànyì (battle). ②運動 yùndòng (movement). ③競選 jìngxuǎn 〈election〉. — v. 從事運動 cóngshì yùndòng 〈movement〉, 競選 jìngxuǎn 〈election〉.

campfire n. 營火 yínghuǒ.

campus n. 校園 xiàoyuán, 校區 xiàoqū.

can aux. v. ①能 néng, 會 huì (be able). ②可以 kěyǐ (may). — n. 罐頭 guàntou 〈container〉.

canal n. 運河 yùnhé.

canary n. 金絲雀 jīnsīquè 〈bird〉. ~ yellow 淡黃色 dànhuángsè.

cancel v. 取消 qǔxiāo (abolish), 刪去 shānqù (delete).

cancer n. 癌 ái 〈disease〉.

Cancer 巨蟹座 Jùxièzuò.

candid adj. 坦白的 tǎnbái de, 正直的 zhèngzhí de.

candidate n. 候選人 hòuxuǎnrén.

candle n. 蠟燭 làzhú.

candor n. 坦白 tǎnbái (frankness).

candy n. 糖果 tángguǒ.

cane n. ①莖 jīng (stem). ②手杖 shǒuzhàng (walking stick). — v. 鞭笞 biānchī (beat).

canister n. 金屬罐 jīnshǔguàn.

canned adj. ①裝罐的 zhuāngguàn de (in a can). ②陳腔濫調的 chén-qiāng-làn-diào de (cliché).

cannibal n. 食人肉者 shí rénròu zhě.

cannon n. 大砲 dàpào, 加農砲 jiānóngpào.

canoe n. 獨木舟 dúmùzhōu. — v. 乘獨木舟 chéng dúmùzhōu.

canon n. ①教規 jiàoguī 〈church〉. ②準則 zhǔnzé (principle).

canteen n. ①水壺 shuǐhú (water container). ②福利社 fúlìshè (bar).

canvas n. ①帆布 fánbù 〈material〉. ②畫布 huàbù 〈for painting〉.

canvass n. & v. ①拉票 lāpiào 〈for votes〉. ②招徠 zhāolái 〈for clients〉. ③調查 diàochá (survey).

canyon n. 峽谷 xiágǔ.

cap n. ①便帽 biànmào (hat). ②蓋子 gàizi (lid). ③上限 shàngxiàn (limit).

capability n. 能力 nénglì.

capable adj. 有能力的 yǒu nénglì de, 能幹的 nénggàn de.

capacity n. 容量 róngliàng.

cape n. 岬 jiǎ.

capillary n. 毛細管 máoxìguǎn 〈tube〉, 微血管 wēixuèguǎn / wéixiěguǎn

(blood vessel).
capital n. ①首都 shǒudū
(chief city). ②資金 zījīn (assets).
— adj. ①主要的 zhǔyào de
(chief). ②上等的 shàngděng de
(excellent). ~ **letter** 大寫字母
dàxiě zìmǔ. ~ **punishment**
死刑 sǐxíng.
capitalism n. 資本主義
zīběn zhǔyì.
capitalize v. ①資本化
zīběnhuà (change into money).
②大寫 dàxiě (write with a
capital letter). ~ **on** 趁機利用
chènjī lìyòng.
capitulate v. 有條件投降 yǒu
tiáojiàn tóuxiáng.
caprice n. 反覆無常 fǎnfù-
wúcháng.
Capricorn 山羊座
Shānyángzuò.
capsize v. 翻覆 fānfù.
capsule n. ①膠囊 jiāonáng
⟨medicine⟩. ②太空艙
tàikōngcāng (spaceship). ③莢
jiá ⟨plants⟩.
captain n. ①隊長 duìzhǎng
⟨team⟩. ②船長 chuánzhǎng
⟨ship⟩. ③陸軍上尉 lùjūn
shàngwèi ⟨army officer⟩.
④海軍上校 hǎijūn shàngxiào
⟨naval officer⟩.
caption n. ①標題 biāotí
(heading). ②插圖說明 chātú
shuōmíng ⟨picture⟩. ③電影
字幕 diànyǐng zìmù (subtitles).
captivate v. 迷惑 míhuo.
captive n. 俘虜 fúlǔ. — adj.
被捕的 bèi bǔ de (captured).
capture n. & v. ①捕捉 bǔzhuō
(apprehension). ②占領
zhànlǐng (conquest).
car n. 車 chē, 汽車 qìchē
(automobile).

car phone n. 汽車無線電話
qìchē wúxiàn diànhuà.
caramel n. ①焦糖 jiāotáng
(burnt sugar). ②牛奶糖
niúnǎitáng ⟨candy⟩.
carat n. 克拉 kèlā.
caravan n. 商隊 shāngduì,
車隊 chēduì.
carbohydrate n. 醣 táng,
碳水化合物 tànshuǐ huàhéwù.
carbon n. 碳 tàn. ~ **paper** 複寫
紙 fùxiězhǐ.
carcass n. 動物屍體 dòngwù
shītǐ ⟨animal⟩.
carcinogen n. 致癌物
zhì'áiwù.
card n. ①卡片 kǎpiàn (stiff
paper). ②卡 kǎ ⟨member⟩.
③名片 míngpiàn (business
card). ④明信片 míngxìnpiàn
(postcard).
cardboard n. 硬紙板
yìngzhǐbǎn.
cardigan n. 羊毛衫
yángmáoshān.
cardinal adj. ①首要的
shǒuyào de, 基本的 jīběn de
(fundamental). ②鮮紅色的
xiānhóngsè de (deep scarlet).
— n. ①樞機主教 shūjī zhǔjiào
⟨Catholic church⟩. ②鮮紅色
xiānhóngsè (vermillion).
cardiogram n. 心電圖
xīndiàntú.
care n. ①照顧 zhàogu
(protection). ②憂慮 yōulù
(worry). **take ~ of** ①照顧
zhàogu ⟨people⟩. ②處理 chǔlǐ
⟨things⟩. — v. ①在乎 zàihu (feel that
something matters). ②關心
guānxīn (be concerned about).
~ **for** 喜歡 xǐhuan, 愛好 àihào
(like).

career n. ①事業 shìyè (business). ②職業 zhíyè (job). ③生涯 shēngyá (life history).

careful adj. 謹慎的 jǐnshèn de, 小心的 xiǎoxīn de.

careless adj. 粗心的 cūxīn de (negligent).

caress n. & v. 愛撫 àifǔ.

cargo n. 貨物 huòwù.

Caribbean Sea 加勒比海 Jiālèbǐhǎi.

caricature n. 諷刺漫畫 fěngcì mànhuà / fèngcì mànhuà.

carnage n. 大屠殺 dàtúshā.

carnal adj. 肉體的 ròutǐ de 〈of flesh〉, 性慾的 xìngyù de (sexual).

carnation n. 康乃馨 kāngnǎixīn.

carnival n. 嘉年華會 jiāniánhuáhuì.

carnivore n. 肉食動物 ròushí dòngwù.

carol n. 歡樂頌 huānlèsòng (song).

carp v. 吹毛求疵 chuī-máo-qiú-cī. — n. 鯉魚 lǐyú 〈fish〉.

carpenter n. 木匠 mùjiang.

carpet n. 地毯 dìtǎn. — v. 鋪地毯 pū dìtǎn.

carriage n. 四輪馬車 sì lún mǎchē.

carrier n. ①運送人 yùnsòngrén 〈person〉. ②運輸業者 yùnshū yèzhě 〈company〉. ③帶菌者 dàijùnzhě / dàijùnzhě 〈disease〉.

carrot n. 胡蘿蔔 húluóbo.

carry v. ①攜帶 xīdài (bring). ②搬運 bānyùn (convey). ③傳達 chuándá, 傳播 chuánbó / chuánbō (spread). ~ on 繼續 jìxù. ~ out 完成

wánchéng.

cart n. ①手拉車 shǒulāchē (pushcart). ②輕便貨車 qīngbiàn huòchē (small light vehicle).

cartilage n. 軟骨 ruǎngǔ.

carton n. 厚紙盒 hòu zhǐhé.

cartoon n. ①漫畫 mànhuà (drawing). ②動畫片 dònghuàpiān / 卡通影片 kǎtōng yǐngpiàn (animation).

cartridge n. ①彈藥筒 dànyàotǒng 〈ammunition〉. ②軟片捲筒 ruǎnpiàn juǎntǒng (case).

carve v. ①雕刻 diāokè (chisel). ②切 qiē (cut).

case n. ①事 shì (event), 例 lì (example), 案子 ànzi (project). ②情形 qíngxing (situation). ③案件 ànjiàn, 訴訟 sùsòng (lawsuit). ④箱 xiāng, 盒 hé (box). ~ study 個案研究 gè'àn yánjiù / gè'àn yánjiù. in any ~ 無論如何 wúlùn rúhé. in that ~ 既然如此 jìrán rúcǐ. just in ~ 萬一 wànyī.

cash v. 現金 xiànjīn. ~ register 現金出納機 xiànjīn chūnàjī / 收銀機 shōuyínjī. — v. 兌現 duìxiàn.

cashier n. 出納員 chūnàyuán.

cashmere n. 開斯米羊毛 kāisīmǐ yángmáo.

casino n. 賭場 dǔchǎng.

cask n. 桶 tǒng.

casket n. ①棺材 guāncái (coffin). ②小珠寶箱 xiǎo zhūbǎoxiāng 〈jewelry〉.

casserole n. 砂鍋 shāguō.

cassette n. 卡式匣 kǎshìxiá, 卡帶 kǎdài (tape), 錄音帶 lùyīndài 〈sound〉, 錄像帶 lùxiàngdài / 錄影帶 lùyìngdài

⟨video⟩.

cassock n. 神職長袍 shénzhí chángpáo.

cast v. ①投 tóu, 擲 zhì / zhí (throw). ②鑄造 zhùzào (mold). ③派演 pàiyǎn ⟨actor⟩. — n. ① 投 tóu, 擲 zhì / zhí (throwing). ②鑄成物 zhùchéngwù (sculpture). ③演員陣容 yǎnyuán zhènróng (group of actors).

caste n. ①世襲階級 shìxí jiējí ⟨Hinduism⟩. ②社會階級 shèhuì jiējí (social class).

castigate v. 嚴懲 yánchéng, 痛斥 tòngchì.

castle n. 城堡 chéngbǎo.

castrate v. 閹割 yāngē.

casual adj. ①偶然的 ǒurán de (accidental). ②非正式的 fēi zhèngshì de (informal).

casualty n. 傷亡者 shāngwángzhě (dead or injured person).

cat n. 貓 māo.

CAT scan 電腦斷層攝影術 diànnǎo duàncéng shèyǐngshù.

catacomb n. 陵寢 língqǐn.

catalog(ue) n. 目錄 mùlù, 型錄 xínglù.

catalyst n. 觸媒 chùméi (a agent for change), 催化劑 cuīhuàjì ⟨chemical⟩.

catapult n. ①彈弓 dàngōng (slingshot). ②彈射器 tánshèqì ⟨apparatus⟩.

cataract n. ①白內障 báinèizhàng ⟨disease⟩. ②大瀑布 dà pùbù (waterfall).

catastrophe n. 大災禍 dà zāihuò.

catch v. ①捕捉 bǔzhuō (hold). ②趕上 gǎnshàng (be in time for). ③罹患 líhuàn (become

infected with). — n. ①接球 jiēqiú ⟨ball⟩. ②捕獲物 bǔhuòwù (something caught). ③鎖鈕 suǒhuán ⟨lock⟩.

catcher n. 捕手 bǔshǒu ⟨baseball⟩.

categorical adj. ①無條件的 wú tiáojiàn de (unconditional). ②絕對的 juéduì de (absolute).

categorize v. 分類 fēnlèi.

category n. 類 lèi, 種類 zhǒnglèi.

caterpillar n. 毛蟲 máochóng.

cathedral n. 總教堂 zǒngjiàotáng, 大教堂 dàjiàotáng.

cathode n. 陰極 yīnjí.

Catholic adj. 天主教的 Tiānzhǔjiào de.

cattle n. 牛 niú.

cauliflower n. 花椰菜 huāyēcài / huāyécài.

cause n. ①原因 yuányīn, 理由 lǐyóu (reason). ②目標 mùbiāo (aim). — v. ①引起 yǐnqǐ (arouse). ②致使 zhìshǐ (compel).

causeway n. 堤道 dīdào / tídào.

caustic adj. ①腐蝕性的 fǔshíxìng de (corrosive). ②刻薄的 kèbó de (harsh).

caution n. ①小心 xiǎoxīn, 謹慎 jǐnshèn (attention). ②警告 jǐnggào (warning).

cautious adj. 小心的 xiǎoxīn de, 謹慎的 jǐnshèn de.

cavalry n. 騎兵隊 qíbīngduì / jíbīngduì.

cave n. 洞穴 dòngxué / dòngxuè, 山洞 shāndòng. — v. 陷落 xiànluò. ~ in 塌陷 tāxiàn.

C

cavern *n.* 巨穴 jùxué / jùxuè.

caviar *n.* 魚子醬 yúzǐjiàng.

cavity *n.* ①洞 dòng, 凹處 āochù (hole). ②蛀牙 zhùyá ⟨teeth⟩.

cayenne pepper *n.* 辣椒 làjiāo.

CD 光盤 guāngpán / 光碟 guāngdié (compact disc).

CD-ROM 唯讀光盤 wéidú guāngpán / 唯讀光碟 wéidú guāngdié (compact disc read-only memory).

cease *v.* 停止 tíngzhǐ, 終止 zhōngzhǐ.

cedar *n.* 西洋杉 xīyángshān.

ceiling *n.* ①天花板 tiānhuābǎn ⟨of a room⟩. ②最高限度 zuì gāo xiàndù (highest limit).

celebrate *v.* ①慶祝 qìngzhù (commemorate). ②稱讚 chēngzàn (praise).

celebration *n.* ①慶祝 qìngzhù ⟨act⟩. ②慶祝活動 qìngzhù huódòng, 慶典 qìngdiǎn ⟨occasion⟩.

celebrity *n.* ①名人 míngrén (famous person). ②名譽 míngyù (fame).

celery *n.* 芹菜 qíncài.

celestial *adj.* 天空的 tiānkōng de, 天上的 tiānshang de.

celibate *n.* 獨身者 dúshēnzhě. — *adj.* 獨身的 dúshēn de.

cell *n.* ①小室 xiǎo shì (small room). ②小囚房 xiǎo qiúfáng ⟨prison⟩. ③細胞 xìbāo ⟨biology⟩.

cellar *n.* 地下室 dìxiàshì, 地窖 dìjiào.

cello *n.* 大提琴 dàtíqín.

cellphone *n.* 行動電話 xíngdòng diànhuà.

cellular *adj.* 細胞狀的 xìbāozhuàng de. **~ phone** 行動電話 xíngdòng diànhuà.

Celsius *adj.* 攝氏的 Shèshì de.

cement *n.* 士敏土 shìmǐntǔ / 水泥 shuǐní.

cemetery *n.* 墓地 mùdì.

censor *n.* 檢查員 jiǎncháyuán. — *v.* 檢查 jiǎnchá.

censure *n. & v.* 非難 fēinàn, 譴責 qiǎnzé.

census *n.* 戶口調查 hùkǒu diàochá.

cent *n.* 分 fēn.

centenarian *n.* 百歲人瑞 bǎisuì rénruì.

centenary *n.* 百年紀念 bǎinián jìniàn (100th anniversary).

center *n.* 中心 zhōngxīn, 中央 zhōngyāng.

centigrade *adj.* 攝氏的 shèshì de.

centimeter *n.* 公分 gōngfēn.

centipede *n.* 蜈蚣 wúgōng.

central *adj.* ①中心的 zhōngxīn de, 中央的 zhōngyāng de (at the center). ②主要的 zhǔyào de (main).

centralize *v.* 集中 jízhōng.

centrifugal *adj.* 離心的 líxīn de.

century *n.* 世紀 shìjì.

ceramic *adj.* 陶器的 táoqì de, 製陶的 zhìtáo de.

cereal *n.* ①穀類 gǔlèi (grain). ②穀類食品 gǔlèi shípǐn (food made from grain).

ceremony *n.* 典禮 diǎnlǐ, 儀式 yíshì.

certain *adj.* ①確信的 quèxìn de (sure). ②某 mǒu (one), 某些 mǒuxiē (some). ③確實的 quèshí de (absolute). *make ~* 確定 quèdìng.

certainly adv. ①確定地 quèdìng de (absolutely), 的確 díquè (really). ②當然 dāngrán (of course).

certainty n. ①確實 quèshí (assurance). ②既成事實 jìchéng shìshí (a fact).

certificate n. 證明書 zhèngmíngshū.

certify v. 證明 zhèngmíng (prove).

chafe n. & v. 擦傷 cāshāng, 擦痛 cātòng.

chaff n. 穀殼 gǔké, 糠 kāng.

chain n. ①鏈 liàn (link). ②一連串 yìliánchuàn, 一系列 yíxìliè (series). ~ store 連鎖店 liánsuǒdiàn. — v. 以鏈鎖住 yǐ liàn suǒzhù.

chair n. ①椅子 yǐzi ⟨furniture⟩. ②主席席位 zhǔxí xíwèi, 主委 zhǔwěi ⟨position⟩.

chairman n. 主席 zhǔxí.

chairperson n. 主席 zhǔxí.

chalk n. 粉筆 fěnbǐ. — v. 用粉筆寫 yòng fěnbǐ xiě.

challenge n. & v. 挑戰 tiǎozhàn.

chamber n. ①房間 fángjiān, 寢室 qǐnshì ⟨room⟩. ②議事廳 yìshìtīng, 議會 yìhuì ⟨government building⟩. ~ music 室內樂 shìnèiyuè.

chameleon n. 變色龍 biànsèlóng, 蜥蜴 xìyì.

champagne n. 香檳酒 xiāngbīnjiǔ.

champion n. ①冠軍 guànjūn (winner). ②擁護者 yōnghùzhě / yǒnghùzhě (backer). — v. 擁護 yōnghù / yǒnghù.

chance n. ①機會 jīhuì (opportunity). ②冒險 màoxiǎn (risk). by ~ 偶然地 ǒurán de. — adj.

偶然的 ǒurán de.

chancellor n. ①首相 shǒuxiàng, 總理 zǒnglǐ (prime minister). ②大臣 dàchén (official of high rank).

change v. ①改變 gǎibiàn (vary). ②更換 gēnghuàn (alter). ③兌換 duìhuàn (exchange). ④轉換 zhuǎnhuàn (shift). — n. ①變化 biànhuà (alteration). ②零錢 língqián (coins).

changeable adj. 易變的 yìbiàn de (easy to change), 可變的 kěbiàn de (unsettled).

channel n. ①海峽 hǎixiá (waterway). ②河床 héchuáng (bed of a river). ③航道 hángdào, 運河 yùnhé (canal). ④頻道 píndào (station). ⑤途徑 tújìng, 管道 guǎndào (means).

chant n. ①聖歌 shènggē ⟨religion⟩. ②口號 kǒuhào (slogan).

chaos n. 混亂 hùnluàn / hǔnluàn, 失序 shīxù.

chap v. 皺裂 zhòuliè. — n. 傢伙 jiāhuo, 小伙子 xiǎohuǒzi.

chapel n. 禮拜堂 lǐbàitáng.

chaplain n. ①牧師 mùshi (priest). ②教誨師 jiàohuìshī / jiàohuìshī ⟨prison⟩.

chapter n. ①章 zhāng, 篇 piān (part). ②段落 duànluò (period).

char v. 燒焦 shāojiāo.

character n. ①特性 tèxìng, 特徵 tèzhēng (distinctiveness). ②性格 xìnggé, 品性 pǐnxìng (personality). ③角色 juésè (role). ④文字 wénzì (letter).

characteristic adj. 典型的 diǎnxíng de. — n. 特徵

C

tèzhēng,特質 tèzhì / tèzhì.

charade *n.* 猜字遊戲 cāizì yóuxì.

charcoal *n.* 木炭 mùtàn.

charge *n. & v.* ①索價 suǒjià (asking for price). ②控告 kònggào, 指控 zhǐkòng (accusation). ③充電 chōngdiàn (putting electricity into). ④突擊 tújī / tújí (attack).

chariot *n.* 雙輪戰車 shuānglún zhànchē.

charisma *n.* 魅力 mèilì.

charity *n.* ①博愛 bó'ài, 慈悲 cíbēi (kindness). ②慈善團體 císhàn tuántǐ, 慈善機構 císhàn jīgòu (organization).

charlatan *n.* ①江湖郎中 jiānghú lángzhōng, 庸醫 yōngyī (quack). ②騙子 piànzi (cheat).

charm *n.* ①魅力 mèilì, 魔力 mólì (attractiveness). ②咒語 zhòuyǔ, 魔咒 mózhòu ⟨magic⟩. — *v.* ①迷住 mízhù (attract). ②施魔咒 shī mózhòu (use magic on).

charming *adj.* 迷人的 mírén de.

chart *n.* ①圖表 túbiǎo (diagram). ②航海圖 hánghǎitú (map of sea). — *v.* 製圖 zhìtú (map).

charter *n.* ①特許狀 tèxǔzhuàng ⟨license⟩. ②憲章 xiànzhāng (document). — *v.* 包租 bāozū (rent).

chase *n. & v.* ①追捕 zhuībǔ, 追趕 zhuīgǎn (running after). ②追 zhuī, 追求 zhuīqiú (pursuit).

chasm *n.* 裂痕 lièhén.

chassis *n.* 底盤 dípán.

chaste *adj.* 貞節的 zhēnjié de,

純潔的 chúnjié de.

chasten *v.* ①懲戒 chéngjiè (punish). ②抑制 yìzhì (constrain).

chastise *v.* 懲罰 chéngfá.

chastity *n.* 純潔 chúnjié, 貞潔 zhēnjié.

chat *n. & v.* 閒談 xiántán.

chat room *n.* 聊天室 liáotiānshì.

chateau *n.* 城堡 chéngbǎo.

chatter *n. & v.* ①喋喋不休 diédié-bù-xiū (talking quickly). ②啁啾 zhōujiū ⟨sounds of birds⟩.

chauffeur *n.* 司機 sījī.

chauvinism *n.* 沙文主義 shāwén zhǔyì.

cheap *adj.* ①便宜的 piányi de (inexpensive). ②廉價的 liánjià de (worthless).

cheat *v.* ①欺騙 qīpiàn (deceive). ②作弊 zuòbì ⟨test⟩. — *n.* 騙子 piànzi (con man).

check *v.* ①檢查 jiǎnchá, 核對 héduì (examine). ②阻止 zǔzhǐ, 抑制 yìzhì (block). ~ *in* 辦理登記 bànlǐ dēngjì. ~ *out* 結帳離去 jiézhàng líqù. — *n.* ①阻止 zǔzhǐ (stop). ②支票 zhīpiào ⟨for payment⟩. ③方格花式 fānggé huāshì ⟨pattern⟩. ④帳單 zhàngdān (bill), 收據 shōujù (receipt).

checked *adj.* 有格子的 yǒu gézi de.

checkmate *v.* 將死 jiāngsǐ, 攻王棋 gōng wángqí ⟨chess⟩.

cheek *n.* 頰 jiá, 面頰 miànjiá.

cheer *n.* ①喝采 hècǎi (applause). ②喜悅 xǐyuè, 愉快 yúkuài (happiness). — *v.* 歡呼 huānhū, 喝采 hècǎi (applaud).

cheerful *adj.* 快樂的 kuàilè de, 高興的 gāoxìng de.

cheese n. 乳酪 rǔlào, 起司 qǐsī.

chef n. 主廚 zhǔchú.

chemical adj. 化學的 huàxué de. — n. 化學藥品 huàxué yàopǐn.

chemical weapon n. 化學武器 huàxué wǔqì.

chemist n. 化學家 huàxuéjiā.

chemistry n. 化學 huàxué.

cheque n. 支票 zhīpiào.

cherish v. ①珍惜 zhēnxí / zhēnxí (care for tenderly). ②懷著 huáizhe (remember tenderly).

cherry n. ①櫻桃 yīngtáo 〈fruit〉. ②櫻桃樹 yīngtáoshù 〈tree〉.

chess n. 西洋棋 xīyángqí.

chest n. ①胸部 xiōngbù (breast). ②箱子 xiāngzi (box).

chestnut n. ①栗樹 lìshù 〈tree〉. ②栗褐色 lìhèsè / lìhésè (brown). ③栗子 lìzi 〈nut〉.

chew v. 咀嚼 jǔjué. ~ **ing gum** 口香糖 kǒuxiāngtáng.

chic n. & adj. 高雅 gāoyǎ.

chick n. ①雛雞 chújī (chicken). ②女孩子 nǚháizi (girl).

chicken n. ①雞 jī 〈animal〉. ②雞肉 jīròu 〈meat〉. ~ **pox** 水痘 shuǐdòu.

chicory n. 菊苣 jújù.

chief n. 領袖 lǐngxiù, 首領 shǒulǐng. — adj. 主要的 zhǔyào de.

chiefly adv. 主要地 zhǔyào de, 首要地 shǒuyào de.

chieftain n. 酋長 qiúzhǎng.

child n. ①小孩 xiǎohái (young person). ②子女 zǐnǚ (son and daughter).

childhood n. 童年 tóngnián.

childish adj. 幼稚的 yòuzhì de (immature), 孩子氣的

chill n. ①寒意 hányì, 寒冷 hánlěng (coldness). ②寒慄 hánlì (shivering). — v. 使寒冷 shǐ hánlěng (make cold).

chilly adj. ①寒冷的 hánlěng de (cold). ②冷淡的 lěngdàn de (aloof).

chime n. 一套樂鐘 yí tào yuèzhōng. — v. 鳴鐘 míng zhōng (ring).

chimney n. ①煙囪 yāncōng (smokestack). ②玻璃燈罩 bōli dēngzhào (glass tube).

chimpanzee n. 黑猩猩 hēixīngxīng.

chin n. 下頜 xiàhàn, 下巴 xiàba.

china n. 瓷器 cíqì.

Chinatown n. 中國城 Zhōngguóchéng, 唐人街 Tángrénjiē.

Chinese n. & adj. ①中國人 Zhōngguórén 〈people〉. ②中文 Zhōngwén 〈language〉.

chip n. ①碎片 suìpiàn, 木屑 mùxiè (small piece). ②缺口 quēkǒu (crack). ③芯片 xīnpiàn, 晶片 jīngpiàn 〈computer〉. — v. ①切成薄片 qiēchéng bópiàn (cut). ②碎裂 suìliè (break).

chirp n. & v. ①吱喳叫 zhīzhājiào, 唧唧聲 jījīshēng / jíjīshēng.

chisel n. 鑿子 záozi. — v. 鑿刻 záokè.

chivalry n. 騎士制度 qíshì zhìdù, 騎士精神 qíshì jīngshén.

chlorine n. 氯 lǜ.

chocolate n. 巧克力 qiǎokèlì.

choice n. 選擇 xuǎnzé.

choir n. 唱詩班 chàngshībān.

choke v. ①使窒息 shǐ zhìxí / shǐ zhìxí (throttle). ②窒息 zhìxí /

C

zhìxí (be unable to breathe).
③阻塞 zǔsè (block).

cholera n. 霍亂 huòluàn.

cholesterol n. 膽固醇 dǎngùchún.

choose v. 選擇 xuǎnzé, 挑選 tiāoxuǎn.

chop v. 砍 kǎn, 切 qiē. — n. 圖章 túzhāng (seal).

choppy adj. 波浪起伏的 bōlàng qǐfú de.

chopstick n. 筷子 kuàizi.

choral adj. 合唱團的 héchàngtuán de, 唱詩班的 chàngshībān de.

chord n. 和弦 héxián.

chore n. 雜務 záwù, 零工 línggōng.

choreography n. 舞蹈術 wǔdǎoshù / wǔdàoshù.

chorus n. 合唱團 héchàngtuán. — v. 合頌 hésòng.

Christ n. 基督 Jīdū.

christen v. 施洗禮 shīxǐlǐ.

Christian adj. 基督教的 Jīdūjiào de. — n. 基督徒 Jīdūtú.

Christianity n. 基督教 Jīdūjiào.

Christmas n. 聖誕節 Shèngdànjié.

chromium n. 鉻 gè.

chromosome n. 染色體 rǎnsètǐ.

chronic adj. 慢性的 mànxìng de, 長期的 chángqī de / chángqí de.

chronicle n. 編年史 biānniánshǐ, 年代記 niándàijì.

chronology n. ①年表 niánbiǎo ⟨list⟩. ②年代學 niándàixué ⟨science⟩.

chrysalis n. 蛹 yǒng ⟨pupa⟩.

chrysanthemum n. 菊花 júhuā.

chubby adj. 圓胖的 yuánpàng de.

chuck v. ①拋擲 pāozhì / pāozhí (throw). ②輕撫 qīngfǔ (touch).

chuckle n. & v. 低聲輕笑 dīshēng qīngxiào.

chum n. 密友 mìyǒu.

chump n. ①厚木塊 hòu mùkuài ⟨wood⟩. ②傻瓜 shǎguā (fool).

chunk n. 厚塊 hòukuài.

church n. ①教堂 jiàotáng ⟨building⟩. ②禮拜 lǐbài (service).

churn n. 攪乳器 jiǎorǔqì. — v. 攪拌 jiǎobàn.

chute n. ①斜槽 xiécáo (sloped passage). ②急流 jíliú (rapid fall of water).

cigar n. 雪茄煙 xuějiāyān.

cigarette n. 香煙 xiāngyān.

cinder n. ①煤渣 méizhā ⟨coal⟩. ②餘燼 yújìn ⟨ash⟩.

cinema n. ①電影院 diànyǐngyuàn (theater). ②電影 diànyǐng (films).

cinnamon n. 肉桂 ròuguì.

cipher n. ①零 líng (zero). ②不重要者 bú zhòngyào zhě (nobody). ③暗號 ànhào, 密碼 mìmǎ (code). — v. 譯成暗號 yìchéng ànhào.

circle n. ①圓 yuán ⟨shape⟩. ②週期 zhōuqī / zhōuqí, 循環 xúnhuán (a chain of events). — v. ①繞行 ràoxíng (move around). ②環繞 huánrào (encircle).

circuit n. ①巡迴 xúnhuí (journey). ②電路 diànlù ⟨electricity⟩.

circular *adj.* ①圓的 yuán de
(round). ②循環的 xúnhuán de
(cyclic). — *n.* 傳單 chuándān.

circulate *v.* ①循環 xúnhuán
⟨move⟩. ②傳布 chuánbù
(publicize).

circulation *n.* ①循環
xúnhuán ⟨movement⟩. ②傳布
chuánbù (broadcasting). ③銷
路 xiāolù, 發行量 fāxíngliàng
(distribution).

circumcise *v.* 割包皮 gē
bāopí.

circumference *n.* 圓周
yuánzhōu.

circumnavigate *v.* 環遊
huányóu.

circumstance *n.* 情形
qíngxíng, 情況 qíngkuàng.

circus *n.* 馬戲團 mǎxìtuán.

cistern *n.* 水槽 shuǐcáo, 貯水
池 zhùshuǐchí / zhǔshuǐchí
(tank).

cite *v.* ①引用 yǐnyòng, 引述
yǐnshù (quote). ②引證
yǐnzhèng (refer to as proof).

citizen *n.* ①公民 gōngmín
⟨country⟩. ②市民 shìmín ⟨city⟩.

city *n.* 城市 chéngshì, 都市
dūshì.

city hall *n.* 市政廳
shìzhèngtīng, 市政府
shìzhèngfǔ.

civic *adj.* 市民的 shìmín de
⟨city⟩, 公民的 gōngmín de
⟨country⟩.

civil *adj.* ①公民的 gōngmín
de, 市民的 shìmín de (commu-
nal). ②平民的 píngmín de
(civilian). ③禮貌的 lǐmào de
(polite).

civilian *n.* 平民 píngmín.

civilization *n.* 文明 wénmíng.

civilize *v.* 教化 jiàohuà, 開化

kāihuà.

claim *n. & v.* 聲稱
shēngchēng, 主張 zhǔzhāng
(say), 要求 yāoqiú, 請求
qǐngqiú (ask for).

clairvoyant *n.* 透視者
tòushìzhě. — *adj.* 有透視力
yǒu tòushìlì de (perceptive).

clam *n.* 蛤 gé, 蚌 bàng.

clamber *n. & v.* 攀登
pāndēng.

clammy *adj.* 濕冷黏糊的
shīlěng niánhu de.

clamor *n. & v.* 叫囂 jiàoxiāo,
喧鬧 xuānnào.

clamp *n.* 鉗子 qiánzi, 夾子
jiāzi / jiázi. — *v.* 用鉗子夾住
yòng qiánzi jiāzhù / yòng
qiánzi jiázhù.

clan *n.* 宗族 zōngzú (group),
部落 bùluò (tribe).

clandestine *adj.* 祕密的 mìmì
de (secret), 暗中的 ànzhōng
de (hidden).

clang *n.* 叮噹聲 dīngdāngshēng.
— *v.* 發叮噹聲 fā
dīngdāngshēng.

clap *n.* 轟聲 hōngshēng. — *v.*
拍手 pāishǒu, 鼓掌 gǔzhǎng
(applaud).

claret *n.* 紅葡萄酒 hóngpútáo
jiǔ.

clarify *v.* 澄清 chéngqīng
(clear up), 闡明 chǎnmíng
(expound).

clarinet *n.* 豎笛 shùdí.

clarity *n.* 清晰 qīngxī, 澄清
chéngqīng.

clash *n. & v.* ①衝突 chōngtū /
chōngtú (conflict). ②撞擊聲
zhuàngjíshēng / zhuàngjíshēng
⟨sound⟩.

clasp *n.* ①釦子 kòuzi, 鉤子
gōuzi (buckle). ②緊握 jǐnwò,

緊抱 jǐnbào (firm hold). — v.
①緊握 jǐnwò (grasp). ②緊抱
jǐnbào (hold). ③釦住 kòuzhù,
鉤住 gōuzhù (fasten).

class n. ①班 bān (group). ②課
kè (lesson). ③類 lèi, 種類
zhǒnglèi (category). ④階級
jiējí (status).

classic adj. ①古典的 gǔdiǎn
de (classical). ②經典的 jīngdiǎn
de (time-honored). — n. 一流
作品 yīliú zuòpǐn (masterpiece).

classical adj. 古典的 gǔdiǎn
de, 古典派的 gǔdiǎnpài de.
~ music 古典音樂 gǔdiǎn
yīnyuè.

classify v. 分類 fēnlèi
(categorize), 分等級 fēn děngjí
(break into levels).

classmate n. 同學 tóngxué.

classroom n. 教室 jiàoshì.

clatter n. & v. 嗶啦聲
pīpāshēng, 嘩啦聲
huālāshēng.

clause n. ①條款 tiáokuǎn
(provision). ②子句 zǐjù
⟨grammar⟩.

claw n. 爪 zhuǎ. — v. 用爪撕
yòng zhuǎ sī.

clay n. 黏土 niántǔ.

clean adj. ①乾淨的 gānjìng de,
清潔的 qīngjié de (not dirty).
②清白的 qīngbái de (pure).
— v. 清潔 qīngjié, 打掃 dǎsǎo.

cleaning n. 清潔 qīngjié, 打
掃 dǎsǎo.

cleanse v. 使清潔 shǐ qīngjié,
使純潔 shǐ chúnjié.

clear adj. ①清楚的 qīngchu
de, 清晰的 qīngxī de,
明白的 míngbái de (unambigu-
ous). ②明亮的 míngliàng de
(bright). ③晴朗的 qínglǎng de
(cloudless). — v. 清除 qīngchú.

清理 qīnglǐ.

clearing n. 開墾地 kāikěndì
⟨land⟩. ~ house 票據交換所
piàojù jiāohuànsuǒ.

clearly adv. ①清楚地 qīngchu
de (distinctly). ②顯然地
xiǎnrán de (evidently).

cleave v. 劈開 pīkāi, 裂開
lièkāi (split).

clef n. 譜號 pǔhào.

clemency n. 仁慈 réncí.

clergy n. 牧師 mùshi, 教士
jiàoshì.

clergyman n. 牧師 mùshi, 教
士 jiàoshì.

clerical adj. ①牧師的 mùshi
de ⟨clergy⟩. ②書記的 shūjì de
(secretarial).

clerk n. ①辦事員 bànshìyuán
⟨office⟩. ②店員 diànyuán
⟨shop⟩.

clever adj. ①聰明的 cōngming
de (intelligent). ②靈巧的
língqiǎo de (skillful).

cliché n. 陳腔濫調 chén-
qiāng-làn-diào.

click n. & v. 滴答聲 dīdāshēng.

client n. ①顧客 gùkè, 客戶
kèhù ⟨business⟩. ②委託人
wěituōrén ⟨law⟩.

clientele n. 顧客 gùkè.

cliff n. 懸崖 xuányá / xuányái.

climate n. 氣候 qìhòu.

climax n. ①頂點 dǐngdiǎn, 極
點 jídiǎn (high point). ②高潮
gāocháo (best part).

climb v. 攀登 pāndēng, 攀爬
pānpá.

cling v. ①緊抱 jǐnbào (hold).
②緊貼著 jǐntiēzhe (stick).

clinic n. 診所 zhěnsuǒ.

clinician n. 臨床醫生
línchuáng yīshēng.

clink n. 叮噹聲 dīngdāngshēng.

clip v. 剪剪 jiǎn, 修剪 xiūjiǎn
(cut). — n. 夾子 jiāzi / jiázi
(fastener).

clique n. 派系 pàixì.

cloak n. 斗篷 dǒupeng
(clothing). — v. 遮蓋 zhēgài,
掩蓋 yǎngài.

cloakroom n. 衣帽間
yīmàojiān.

clock n. 時鐘 shízhōng.
around the ~ 二十四小時連續
地 èrshísì xiǎoshí liánxù de.

clockwise adj. & adv. 順時針
方向的 shùnshízhēn
fāngxiàng de.

clod n. 土塊 tǔkuài, 泥塊
níkuài.

clog n. 木屐 mùjī. — v. 塞住
sāizhù (block).

cloister n. 修道院 xiūdàoyuàn
(monastery). — v. 隱居 yǐnjū.

close v. ①關 guān, 閉 bì (shut).
②結束 jiéshù (end). — adj.
①接近的 jiējìn de (near).
②親近的 qīnjìn de, 親密的
qīnmì de (dear).

closed adj. 關閉的 guānbì de.

closely adv. ①緊密地 jǐnmì de
(carefully). ②接近地 jiējìn de
(nearly).

closet n. 櫥櫃 chúguì.

closure n. ①關閉 guānbì
(shut). ②終止 zhōngzhǐ (end).

clot n. 凝塊 níngkuài. — v. 凝
結 níngjié.

cloth n. 布 bù, 布塊 bùkuài.

clothes n. 衣服 yīfú.

clothing n. 衣服 yīfú.

cloud n. 雲 yún.

cloudless adj. 無雲的 wú yún
de, 晴朗的 qínglǎng de.

cloudy adj. ①有雲的 yǒu yún
de, 陰天的 yīntiān de (sunless).
②朦朧的 ménglóng de, 晦暗

的 huìàn de (blurred).

clover n. 苜蓿 mùxu / mùsù.

clown n. 丑角 chǒujué /
chǒujiǎo, 小丑 xiǎochǒu
〈circus〉.

club n. ①俱樂部 jùlèbù
〈society〉. ②梅花 méihuā
〈cards〉.

cluck n. & v. 咯咯聲
gēgēshēng.

clue n. 線索 xiànsuǒ.

clump n. 草叢 cǎocóng 〈grass〉,
樹叢 shùcóng 〈trees〉.

clumsy adj. 笨拙的 bènzhuō
de / bènzhuó de.

cluster n. 串 chuàn, 簇 cù. — v.
群聚 qúnjù, 叢生 cóngshēng.

clutch v. 抓牢 zhuāláo. — n. ①
緊抓 jǐnzhuā (grasp). ②離合器
líhéqì 〈machine〉.

clutches n. 緊握 jǐnwò (grasp).

clutter v. 弄亂 nòngluàn, 亂
堆 luànduī. — n. 混亂 hùnluàn
/ hǔnluàn.

coach n. ①四輪馬車 sì lún
mǎchē 〈horse-drawn〉. ②客車廂
kèchēxiāng (railway carriage).
③教練 jiàoliàn (trainer). — v.
訓練 xùnliàn, 指導 zhǐdǎo /
zhǐdào.

coagulate v. 凝結 níngjié.

coal n. 煤 méi, 煤炭 méitàn.
~ *mine* 煤礦 méikuàng.

coalesce v. 聯合 liánhé, 結合
jiéhé.

coalition n. ①聯合 liánhé
(combination). ②聯盟
liánméng (alliance).

coarse adj. ①粗糙的 cūcāo
de (rough). ②粗劣的 cūliè de
(low quality). ③粗俗的 cūsú
de (boorish).

coast n. 海岸 hǎi'àn, 沿海地區
yánhǎi dìqū. — v. ①滑行

huáxíng (slide). ②沿岸航行
yán àn hángxíng 〈sail〉.
coat n. 外衣 wàiyī, 外套
wàitào. — v. 塗覆 túfù.
coating n. 被覆層 pīfùcéng.
coax v. 勸哄 quànhǒng.
cobblestone n. 圓石塊
yuánshíkuài, 鵝卵石 éluǎnshí.
cobra n. 眼鏡蛇 yǎnjìngshé.
cobweb n. 蜘蛛網 zhīzhūwǎng.
cocaine n. 可卡因 kěkǎyīn /
古柯鹼 gǔkējiǎn.
cock n. ①公雞 gōngjī (rooster).
②雄鳥 xióngniǎo (male bird).
— v. ①豎起 shùqǐ (turn upwards).
②扣扳機 kòu bānjī 〈gun〉.
cockpit n. 駕駛艙 jiàshǐcāng.
cockroach n. 蟑螂
zhāngláng.
cockscomb n. 雞冠 jīguān.
cocktail n. 雞尾酒 jīwěijiǔ.
cocoa n. 可可粉 kěkěfěn.
coconut n. 椰子 yēzi / yézi.
cocoon n. 蠶繭 cánjiǎn.
cod n. 鱈魚 xuěyú.
coddle v. 溺愛 nì'ài (pamper).
code n. ①法典 fǎdiǎn, 法規
fǎguī 〈law〉. ②規則 guīzé
(rules). ③密碼 mìmǎ (secret signs).
coed n. 女生 nǚshēng.
coerce v. 強迫 qiǎngpò.
coexist v. 共存 gòngcún.
coffee n. 咖啡 kāfēi.
coffer n. 保險箱
bǎoxiǎnxiāng.
coffin n. 棺材 guāncái, 柩 jiù.
cog n. 輪齒 lúnchǐ.
cognac n. 白蘭地酒
báilándìjiǔ, 干邑酒 gānyìjiǔ.
cohabit v. 同居 tóngjū.
cohere v. ①黏著 niánzhuó
(stick). ②連貫 liánguàn
(remain united).

coherent adj. ①一貫的
yíguàn de (consistent). ②清楚
的 qīngchu de (clear).
cohesion n. ①附著 fùzhuó, 黏
著 niánzhuó (sticking). ②凝聚
níngjù, 團結 tuánjié 〈people〉.
③凝結 níngjié 〈objects〉.
coil v. 盤繞 pánrào (wind),
捲起 juǎnqǐ (roll). — n. ①卷
juǎn (roll). ②線圈 xiànquān
〈electric wire〉.
coin n. 硬幣 yìngbì, 銅板
tóngbǎn. — v. ①鑄 (硬幣) zhù
(yìngbì) (mint). ②創造
chuàngzào (invent).
coincide v. ①同時發生
tóngshí fāshēng (happen at the
same time). ②符合 fúhé, 一致
yízhì (be in agreement).
coincidence n. 巧合 qiǎohé
(accident).
coke n. 焦炭 jiāotàn.
cold adj. ①寒冷的 hánlěng de
(chilly). ②冷漠的 lěngmò de
(unemotional). — n. ①寒冷
hánlěng 〈weather〉. ②感冒
gǎnmào (sickness). catch a ~
著涼 zháoliáng, 感冒 gǎnmào.
cold-blooded adj. ①冷血的
lěngxuè de / lěngxiě de
〈biology〉. ②殘忍的 cánrěn de,
無情的 wúqíng de (cruel).
collaborate v. ①合作 hézuò
(work together). ②通敵 tōngdí
(aid the enemy).
collapse n. & v. 倒塌 dǎotā
(fall down), 崩潰 bēngkuì
(come to ruin).
collar n. ①衣領 yīlǐng
〈clothes〉. ②項圈 xiàngquān
〈animals〉.
colleague n. 同事 tóngshì, 同
僚 tóngliáo.
collect v. 收集 shōují, 蒐集

sōují (gather together).

collection n. ①蒐集品 sōujípǐn, 收藏品 shōucángpǐn ⟨objects⟩. ②收集 shōují ⟨act of collecting⟩.

collective adj. 集體的 jítǐ de, 共有的 gòngyǒu de.

college n. 學院 xuéyuàn, 大學 dàxué.

collide v. ①碰撞 pèngzhuàng ⟨strike together⟩. ②衝突 chōngtū / chōngtú, 抵觸 dǐchù ⟨be opposed⟩.

collision n. ①相撞 xiāngzhuàng ⟨crash⟩. ②衝突 chōngtū / chōngtú, 抵觸 dǐchù ⟨conflict⟩.

colloquial adj. 口語的 kǒuyǔ de, 會話的 huìhuà de.

cologne n. 科隆香水 kēlóng xiāngshuǐ / 古龍水 gǔlóngshuǐ.

colon n. ①冒號 màohào ⟨punctuation⟩. ②結腸 jiécháng ⟨intestine⟩.

colonel n. 上校 shàngxiào.

colonial adj. 殖民地的 zhímíndì de.

colonist n. 殖民者 zhímínzhě.

colonnade n. 柱廊 zhùláng.

colony n. ①殖民地 zhímíndì ⟨area⟩. ②殖民 zhímín, 移民群 體 yímín qúntǐ ⟨people⟩.

color n. 顏色 yánsè. — v. 染色 rǎnsè ⟨dye⟩, 著色 zhuósè ⟨paint⟩.

colorful adj. 鮮艷的 xiānyàn de, 多彩的 duōcǎi de ⟨full of color⟩.

colossal adj. 巨大的 jùdà de.

colt n. 小雄馬 xiǎo xióngmǎ.

column n. ①圓柱 yuánzhù ⟨pillar⟩. ②專欄 zhuānlán ⟨article⟩.

columnist n. 專欄作家

zhuānlán zuòjiā.

coma n. 昏迷 hūnmí.

comb n. 梳子 shūzi. — v. 梳髮 shūfà.

combat n. & v. 戰鬥 zhàndòu.

combatant adj. 戰鬥的 zhàndòu de. — n. 戰鬥員 zhàndòuyuán.

combination n. 聯合 liánhé, 合併 hébìng.

combine v. 聯合 liánhé, 結合 jiéhé.

combustible adj. 易燃的 yìrán de.

combustion n. 燃燒 ránshāo.

come v. ①來 lái ⟨move towards⟩. ②到 dào, 到達 dàodá ⟨arrive⟩. ~ *about* 發生 fāshēng ⟨occur⟩. ~ *across* 偶然遇到 ǒurán yùdào ⟨happen upon⟩. ~ *back* 回來 huílái. ~ *from* 來自 láizì.

comedian n. 喜劇演員 xìjù yǎnyuán ⟨actor⟩, 丑角 chǒujué / chǒujiǎo ⟨comic⟩.

comedy n. 喜劇 xǐjù.

comet n. 彗星 huìxīng.

comfort v. 安慰 ānwèi ⟨console⟩. — n. 舒適 shūshì ⟨amenity⟩.

comfortable adj. 舒服的 shūfu de, 舒適的 shūshì de.

comic adj. ①喜劇的 xǐjù de ⟨comedy⟩. ②滑稽的 huáji de ⟨funny⟩.

coming n. 到來 dàolái ⟨arrival⟩. — adj. 即將到來的 jíjiāng dàolái de ⟨upcoming⟩.

comma n. 逗點 dòudiǎn.

command n. & v. ①命令 mìnglìng, 指揮 zhǐhuī ⟨order⟩. ②控制 kòngzhì ⟨control⟩.

commander n. ①司令官 sīlìngguān, 指揮官 zhǐhuīguān ⟨commanding officer⟩. ②海軍

中校 hǎijūn zhōngxiào 〈navy〉.
commandment *n.* 戒律 jièlǜ.
commando *n.* 突擊隊 tūjíduì / tújíduì.
commemorate *v.* 紀念 jìniàn, 慶祝 qìngzhù.
commence *v.* 開始 kāishǐ.
commend *v.* 稱讚 chēngzàn, 讚揚 zànyáng.
comment *n. & v.* ①說法 shuōfǎ (remark). ②批評 pīpíng, 評論 pínglùn (criticism). ③評註 píngzhù, 註釋 zhùshì (annotation).
commentary *n.* 註解 zhùjiě (explanatory notes).
commerce *n.* 商業 shāngyè, 貿易 màoyì.
commercial *adj.* 商業的 shāngyè de. — *n.* 廣告 guǎnggào.
commiserate *v.* 同情 tóngqíng, 憐憫 liánmǐn.
commission *n.* ①委員會 wěiyuánhuì (committee). ②佣金 yòngjīn 〈sales〉. — *v.* 委託 wěituō, 委任 wěirèn (give authority to).
commit *v.* ①犯(罪) fàn (zuì) 〈crime〉, 犯(錯) fàn (cuò) 〈error〉. ②委託 wěituō, 交付 jiāofù (entrust).
committee *n.* 委員會 wěiyuánhuì.
commodity *n.* 商品 shāngpǐn, 物品 wùpǐn.
common *adj.* ①共同的 gòngtóng de, 公共的 gònggòng de (public). ②普通的 pǔtōng de (ordinary). ③常見的 chángjiàn de (usual).
commonly *adv.* 普通地 pǔtōng de, 一般地 yìbān de.
commonplace *adj.* 平凡的 píngfán de.
commonwealth *n.* 聯邦 liánbāng (confederation), 共和國 gònghéguó (republic).
commotion *n.* 暴動 bàodòng.
communal *adj.* 公用的 gōngyòng de, 公有的 gōngyǒu de.
commune *v.* ①與……親近 yǔ...qīnjìn (be in close touch with). ②密談 mìtán (talk with in an intimate way). — *n.* 公社 gōngshè (community).
communicate *v.* ①傳達 chuándá, 傳送 chuánsòng (convey). ②溝通 gōutōng, 通訊 tōngxùn (exchange information). ③傳染 chuánrǎn (infect).
communication *n.* ①傳達 chuándá (transmission). ②溝通 gōutōng (exchange).
communion *n.* ①聖餐 shèngcān 〈Christian ritual〉. ②交流 jiāoliú (exchange).
communiqué *n.* 公報 gōngbào.
communism *n.* 共產主義 gòngchǎn zhǔyì.
community *n.* ①住宅小區 zhùzhái xiǎo qū / 社區 shèqū (neighborhood). ②團體 tuántǐ (group). ③共有 gòngyǒu (sharing).
commute *v.* ①通勤 tōngqín (travel). ②折算 zhésuàn (exchange). ③減輕 jiǎnqīng (lighten).
compact *adj.* ①塞緊的 sāijǐn de, 緊密的 jǐnmì de (closely packed). ②簡潔的 jiǎnjié de, 簡明的 jiǎnmíng de (brief). — *n.* ①契約 qìyuē (agreement). ②小型汽車 xiǎoxíng qìchē

(small car). ③小粉盒 xiǎo fěnhé 〈container〉. ~ **disc** 激光唱片 jīguāng chàngpiàn / 雷射唱片 léishè chàngpiàn. ~ **disc player** 激光唱機 jīguāng chàngjī / 雷射唱盤 léishè chàngpán.

companion n. 同件 tóngbàn, 伙伴 huǒbàn.

companionship n. 友誼 yǒuyì / yǒuyí, 交情 jiāoqíng.

company n. ①公司 gōngsī 〈business〉. ②訪客 fǎngkè, 賓客 bīnkè (visitors). ③陪伴 péibàn, 同件 tóngbàn (companion). ④友誼 yǒuyì / yǒuyí (fellowship). ⑤一群 yì qún, 一隊 yí duì (group).

comparable adj. 可比較的 kě bǐjiào de (similar), 可比擬的 kě bǐnǐ de (as good as).

comparative adj. 比較的 bǐjiào de. — n. 比較級 bǐjiàojí.

compare v. ①比較 bǐjiào (contrast). ②比擬 bǐnǐ, 比喻 bǐyù (draw a parallel).

comparison n. 比較 bǐjiào.

compartment n. 小隔間 xiǎo géjiān (small room), 車室 chēshì (carriage).

compass n. 指南針 zhǐnánzhēn, 羅盤 luópán. — v. 繞行 ràoxíng.

compassion n. 同情 tóngqíng.

compatible adj. 相容的 xiāngróng de, 符合的 fúhé de.

compatriot n. 同胞 tóngbāo.

compel v. 迫使 pòshǐ.

compensate v. 賠償 péicháng, 補償 bǔcháng.

compensation n. 賠償 péicháng, 補償 bǔcháng.

compete v. ①競爭 jìngzhēng

〈business〉. ②比賽 bǐsài 〈contest〉.

competence n. 能力 nénglì.

competent adj. 能幹的 nénggàn de (capable), 勝任的 shèngrèn de / shēngrèn de (sufficiently skilled).

competition n. ①競爭 jìngzhēng 〈rivalry〉. ②比賽 bǐsài (contest).

competitor n. 競爭者 jìngzhēngzhě, 敵手 díshǒu.

compilation n. 編輯 biānjí, 編纂 biānzuǎn.

compile v. 編纂 biānzuǎn, 編輯 biānjí.

complain v. 抱怨 bàoyuàn.

complaint n. ①抱怨 bàoyuàn (grievance). ②疾病 jíbìng (illness).

complement n. ①補充物 bǔchōngwù (supplement). ②足量 zúliàng, 全數 quánshù (aggregate). — v. 補充 bǔchōng.

complete adj. 完整的 wánzhěng de, 完全的 wánquán de. — v. 完成 wánchéng (finish).

completely adv. 完全地 wánquán de.

completion n. 完成 wánchéng.

complex adj. ①複雜的 fùzá de (complicated). ②合成的 héchéng de (compound).

complexion n. ①面色 miànsè, 膚色 fūsè (skin coloring), 外觀 wàiguān (appearance). ②形勢 xíngshì (character).

compliance n. 順從 shùncóng.

complicate v. 使複雜 shǐ fùzá, 使麻煩 shǐ máfan.

complicated adj. 複雜的 fùzá de.

complicity n. 共犯 gòngfàn, 同謀 tóngmóu.

compliment n. & v. 讚美 zànměi (praise), 恭維 gōngwei (flattery).

comply v. 順從 shùncóng, 遵從 zūncóng.

component adj. 組成的 zǔchéng de. — n. 成分 chéngfèn (ingredient), 因素 yīnsù (factor).

compose v. ①組成 zǔchéng, 構成 gòuchéng (constitute). ②著作 zhùzuò, 創作 chuàngzuò (create).

composer n. 作曲家 zuòqǔjiā.

composite adj. 混合的 hùnhé de. — n. 合成物 héchéngwù.

composition n. ①成分 chéngfèn (contents). ②著作 zhùzuò, 作品 zuòpǐn (piece). ③作文 zuòwén (essay).

compositor n. 排字工人 páizì gōngrén.

composure n. 鎮靜 zhènjìng.

compound adj. 合成的 héchéng de, 複合的 fùhé de. — n. 複合物 fùhéwù, 混合物 hùnhéwù (combination). — v. 組成 zǔchéng, 合成 héchéng.

comprehend v. 了解 liǎojiě (understand), 領悟 lǐngwù (realize).

comprehensible adj. 可理解的 kě lǐjiě de.

comprehensive adj. 廣泛的 guǎngfàn de, 全面的 quánmiàn de.

compress v. 壓縮 yāsuō (press together). — n. 壓布 yābù, 繃帶 bēngdài.

comprise v. ①包括 bāokuò,

包含 bāohán (include). ②組成 zǔchéng, 構成 gòuchéng (constitute).

compromise v. ①妥協 tuǒxié, 和解 héjiě (make concession). ②危及 wēijí / wéijí (threaten), 連累 liánlěi / liánlèi (discredit). — n. 妥協 tuǒxié, 和解 héjiě.

compulsion n. 強迫 qiǎngpò, 強制 qiángzhì / qiǎngzhì.

compulsory adj. 強制的 qiángzhì de / qiǎngzhì de, 義務的 yìwù de (obligatory).

compunction n. 良心的責備 liángxīn de zébèi, 懊悔 àohuǐ.

computer n. 計算機 jìsuànjī / 電腦 diànnǎo. ~ graphics 電腦繪圖 diànnǎo huìtú. ~ screen 電腦屏幕 diànnǎo píngmù / 電腦螢幕 diànnǎo yíngmú. ~ virus 電腦病毒 diànnǎo bìngdú.

comrade n. ①同伴 tóngbàn, 朋友 péngyou (companion). ②同志 tóngzhì ⟨of a political party⟩.

con n. & adv. 反對 fǎnduì (against). — v. 欺騙 qīpiàn (trick). pros and ~s 正反兩面 zhèngfǎn liǎngmiàn.

concave adj. 凹的 āo de, 凹面的 āomiàn de.

conceal v. 隱藏 yǐncáng, 隱匿 yǐnnì.

concede v. ①承認 chéngrèn (admit). ②讓與 ràngyǔ (give in), 讓步 ràngbù (yield), 容許 róngxǔ (allow).

conceit n. 自負 zìfù, 自大 zìdà.

conceive v. ①懷孕 huáiyùn (become pregnant). ②構思 gòusī (think of).

concentrate v. ①專心 zhuānxīn (be attentive). ②集中

jízhōng (accumulate). ③濃縮 nóngsuō (condense).

concentration n. ①專心 zhuānxīn (attention). ②集中 jízhōng (gathering). ~ *camp* 集 中營 jízhōngyíng.

concept n. 概念 gàiniàn.

conception n. ①概念 gàiniàn (concept). ②構思 gòusī, 構想 gòuxiǎng (idea).

concern v. ①與……有關 yǔ...yǒuguān (related to). ②關 心 guānxīn (care about), 注意 zhùyì (notice). ③擔心 dānxīn, 憂慮 yōulǜ (worry about). — n. ①關心 guānxīn (care). ②企業 qìyè / qǐyè, 事業 shìyè (business). ③擔心 dānxīn, 憂慮 yōulǜ (anxiety). ④關心的事 guānxīn de shì (affair).

concert n. 音樂會 yīnyuèhuì, 演奏會 yǎnzòuhuì.

concerto n. 協奏曲 xiézòuqǔ.

concession n. ①讓步 ràngbù (yielding). ②特許權 tèxǔquán (special right).

conciliate v. ①調解 tiáojiě (mediate). ②撫慰 fǔwèi (soothe).

concise adj. 簡明的 jiǎnmíng de, 簡潔的 jiǎnjié de.

conclude v. ①終結 zhōngjié, 結束 jiéshù (end). ②作出結論 zuòchū jiélùn (make judgment).

conclusion n. ①終結 zhōngjié, 結束 jiéshù (end). ②結論 jiélùn (judgment).

concoct v. ①調製 tiáozhì (make by mixing). ②編造 biānzào, 虛構 xūgòu (invent).

concord n. 和諧 héxié, 協調 xiétiáo.

concourse n. ①匯集 huìjí (crowd). ②大廳 ⟨building⟩.

concrete adj. 具體的 jùtǐ de. — n. 混凝土 hùnníngtǔ. — v. 鋪混凝土 pū hùnníngtǔ.

concur v. ①同意 tóngyì (agree). ②同時發生 tóngshí fāshēng (happen at the same time).

condemn v. ①譴責 qiǎnzé, 責難 zénàn (blame). ②宣告有 罪 xuāngào yǒu zuì (convict).

condense v. ①濃縮 nóngsuō (reduce). ②使簡潔 shǐ jiǎnjié, 簡述 jiǎnshù (abbreviate). ③凝 結 níngjié (become liquid).

condescend v. 屈尊 qūzūn, 俯就 fǔjiù.

condition n. ①狀況 zhuàngkuàng, 情形 qíngxing (state). ②條件 tiáojiàn (stipulation). ③健康情形 jiànkāng qíngxing (health). ④身分地位 shēnfen dìwèi (position in society).

condolence n. 慰問 wèiwèn, 弔唁 diàoyàn.

condom n. 避孕套 bìyùntào / 保險套 bǎoxiǎntào.

condone v. 寬恕 kuānshù, 饒 恕 ráoshù.

conduct n. ①行為 xíngwéi, 品 行 pǐnxíng / pǐnxìng (behavior). ②處理 chǔlǐ、經營 jīngyíng (management). — v. ①引導 yǐndǎo, 指引 zhǐyǐn (lead). ②指揮 zhǐhuī (be in charge of).

conductor n. ①車掌 chēzhǎng、售票員 shòupiàoyuán ⟨bus or tram⟩. ②指揮 zhǐhuī ⟨orchestra⟩. ③導體 dǎotǐ ⟨electricity⟩.

cone n. ①圓錐形 yuánzhuīxíng ⟨shape⟩. ②毬果 qiúguǒ ⟨tree⟩.

confection n. 糖果 tángguǒ, 蜜餞 mìjiàn.

confederacy *n.* 聯盟 liánméng, 邦聯 bānglián (alliance).

confederate *adj.* 同盟的 tóngméng de, 聯盟的 liánméng de. — *n.* ①同盟 tóngméng, 聯盟 liánméng (ally). ②同謀 tóngmóu, 共犯 gòngfàn (accomplice).

confer *v.* ①賜予 cìyǔ, 授予 shòuyǔ (give). ②商量 shāngliang (consult).

conference *n.* 會談 huìtán, 會議 huìyì.

confess *v.* ①承認 chéngrèn, 供認 gòngrèn (admit). ②懺悔 chànhuǐ (tell one's sins).

confession *n.* ①供認 gòngrèn (admission), 承認 chéngrèn (acknowledgment). ②懺悔 chànhuǐ (repentance).

confetti *n.* 五彩碎紙 wǔcǎi suìzhǐ.

confidant *n.* 密友 mìyǒu, 知己 zhījǐ.

confide *v.* 傾訴 qīngsù (tell).

confidence *n.* ①信賴 xìnlài (trust). ②自信 zìxìn (assurance).

confident *adj.* 自信的 zìxìn de, 肯定的 kěndìng de.

confidential *adj.* 機密的 jīmì de (secret).

confine *v.* ①監禁 jiānjìn (cage). ②限制 xiànzhì (restrict).

confines *n.* 疆界 jiāngjiè.

confirm *v.* ①證實 zhèngshí (give proof of). ②確認 quèrèn (verify).

confiscate *v.* 沒收 mòshōu, 充公 chōnggōng.

conflict *n. & v.* ①爭鬥 zhēngdòu (fight). ②衝突 chōngtú / chōngtú (disagreement).

conform *v.* 順應 shùnyìng.

confound *v.* ①使困惑 shǐ kùnhuò, 使迷惑 shǐ míhuo (confuse and amaze). ②混淆 hùnyáo / hǔnyáo (mix up).

confront *v.* 面對 miànduì, 面臨 miànlín.

Confucius *n.* 孔子 Kǒngzǐ.

confuse *v.* ①使困惑 shǐ kùnhuò (baffle). ②使混亂 shǐ hùnluàn / shǐ hǔnluàn (cause disorder). ③混淆 hùnyáo / hǔnyáo (fail to distinguish).

confusion *n.* ①困惑 kùnhuò (perplexity). ②混亂 hùnluàn / hǔnluàn (disorder).

congeal *v.* 凍結 dòngjié, 凝結 níngjié.

congenial *adj.* 意氣相投的 yìqì-xiāngtóu de.

congenital *adj.* 天生的 tiānshēng de, 先天的 xiāntiān de.

conglomerate *v.* 使成團形 shǐ chéng tuánxíng. — *adj.* 集聚的 jíjù de. — *n.* ①集成物 jíchéngwù (material). ②企業集團 qǐyè jítuán / qìyè jítuán (large business firm).

congratulate *v.* 慶賀 qìnghè, 祝賀 zhùhè.

congratulation *n.* ①賀詞 hècí ⟨words⟩. ②祝賀 zhùhè ⟨expression of joy⟩.

congregate *v.* 集合 jíhé, 聚集 jùjí.

congress *n.* ①會議 huìyì (meeting). ②國會 guóhuì, 議會 yìhuì (law-making body).

Congress *n.* 美國國會 Měiguó guóhuì.

congruent *adj.* ①一致的 yízhì de (agreeable). ②全等的 quánděng de (equal size and shape).

congruous *adj.* 適合的 shìhé de, 調合的 tiáohé de.

conifer *n.* 針葉樹 zhēnyèshù.

conjecture *n. & v.* 推測 tuīcè, 猜想 cāixiǎng.

conjugal *adj.* 婚姻的 hūnyīn de, 夫妻的 fūqī de.

conjugate *v.* 列出 (動詞) 變化 lièchū (dòngcí) biànhuà ⟨grammar⟩.

conjunction *n.* ①連接詞 liánjiēcí ⟨grammar⟩. ②連結 liánjié (connection).

conjunctivitis *n.* 結膜炎 jiémóyán / jiémòyán.

conjure *v.* ①變魔術 biàn móshù (do magic). ②施魔法 shī mófǎ (bewitch).

connect *v.* ①連接 liánjiē (join). ②聯想 liánxiǎng (associate).

connection *n.* ①連接 liánjiē (contact). ②關係 guānxi (relation).

connive *v.* 縱容 zòngróng, 默許 mòxǔ.

connoisseur *n.* 鑑賞家 jiànshǎngjiā.

connotation *n.* 暗示 ànshì, 意味 yìwèi.

conquer *v.* 擊敗 jíbài / jíbài, 征服 zhēngfú.

conquest *n.* ①征服 zhēngfú (conquering). ②戰利品 zhànlìpǐn (booty). ③佔領地 zhànlǐngdì (conquered territory).

conscience *n.* 良心 liángxīn.

conscientious *adj.* 有良心的 yǒu liángxīn de, 認真的 rènzhēn de, 盡責的 jìnzé de.

conscious *adj.* 察覺的 chájué de, 有意識的 yǒu yìshì de / yǒu yìshì de.

conscript *adj.* 徵召入伍的

zhēngzhào rùwǔ de. — *n.* 徵兵 zhēngbīng, 徵召 zhēngzhào.

consecrate *v.* 奉為神聖 fèngwéi shénshèng, 奉獻 fèngxiàn.

consecutive *adj.* 連續的 liánxù de.

consensus *n.* 共識 gòngshí / gòngshì.

consent *n. & v.* 同意 tóngyì, 答應 dāying.

consequence *n.* ①結果 jiéguǒ (result), 後果 hòuguǒ (aftermath). ②影響 yǐngxiǎng (effect).

consequent *adj.* 因而發生的 yīn'ér fāshēng de (resulting).

consequential *adj.* 因而發生的 yīn'ér fāshēng de (resulting).

consequently *adv.* 因此 yīncǐ, 所以 suǒyǐ.

conservation *n.* 保護 bǎohù, 保存 bǎocún.

conservative *adj.* 保守的 bǎoshǒu de. — *n.* 保守者 bǎoshǒuzhě, 保守派 bǎoshǒupài.

conservatory *n.* 溫室 wēnshì (greenhouse).

conserve *v.* ①保存 bǎocún (preserve). ②節約 jiéyuē (save). — *n.* 蜜餞 mìjiàn.

consider *v.* ①考慮 kǎolǜ, 思考 sīkǎo (think about). ②顧慮 gùlǜ, 顧及 gùjí (take into account). ③認為 rènwéi, 視為 shìwéi (regard as).

considerable *adj.* ①可觀的 kěguān de (worthy of note). ②相當大的 xiāngdāng dà de (large). ③相當多的 xiāngdāng duō de (many).

considerate *adj.* 體諒的 tǐliang de, 體貼的 tǐtiē de.

consideration n. ①考慮 kǎolǜ, 思考 sīkǎo (deliberation). ②體諒 tǐliang, 顧慮 gùlǜ (being considerate).

considering prep. 就……而論 jiù……ér lùn.

consign v. ①移交 yíjiāo (hand over). ②委託 wěituō (commit). ③寄運 jìyùn (send).

consist v. ~ of 由……組成 yóu...zǔchéng, 包括 bāokuò.

consistency n. ①一致 yízhì, 一貫 yíguàn (coherence). ②濃度 nóngdù (degree of firmness).

consistent adj. 前後一貫的 qiánhòu yíguàn de (invariable), 一致的 yízhì de (compatible).

consolation n. ①安慰 ānwèi (comfort). ②安慰物 ānwèiwù (something which consoles).

console v. 安慰 ānwèi.

consolidate v. ①鞏固 gǒnggù, 強化 qiánghuà (strengthen). ②合併 hébìng (combine).

consonant n. 子音 zǐyīn. — adj. 和諧的 héxié de, 協調的 xiétiáo de.

consort n. 配偶 pèiǒu.

conspicuous adj. ①顯著的 xiǎnzhù de, 明顯的 míngxiǎn de (obvious). ②引起注目的 yǐnqǐ zhùmù de (inciting attention).

conspiracy n. 陰謀 yīnmóu.

conspire v. 共謀 gòngmóu, 陰謀 yīnmóu (plan secretly to do wrong).

constable n. 警察 jǐngchá.

constant adj. ①不斷的 búduàn de (continuous). ②不變的 búbiàn de, 永恆的 yǒnghéng de (eternal).

constellation n. 星座 xīngzuò.

consternation n. 驚愕 jīng'è, 驚惶失措 jīnghuáng-shīcuò.

constipation n. 便祕 biànmì.

constituency n. 選民 xuǎnmín.

constituent adj. 組成的 zǔchéng de, 構成的 gòuchéng de (component). — n. ①成分 chéngfèn, 要素 yàosù (ingredient). ②選民 xuǎnmín (voter).

constitute v. ①構成 gòuchéng, 組成 zǔchéng (compose). ②設立 shèlì, 成立 chénglì (establish).

constitution n. ①憲法 xiànfǎ 〈law〉. ②體格 tǐgé (health). ③構成 gòuchéng, 組織 zǔzhī (structure).

constitutional adj. 憲法的 xiànfǎ de.

constrain v. ①強制 qiángzhì / qiángzhì, 強迫 qiǎngpò (force). ②束縛 shùfù / shùfú, 抑制 yìzhì (restrain).

constrict v. 壓縮 yāsuō, 收縮 shōusuō.

construct v. 構造 gòuzào, 建造 jiànzào.

construction n. ①建造 jiànzào, 構造 gòuzào (act of constructing). ②建築物 jiànzhùwù / jiànzhúwù (building). ~ site 工地 gōngdì.

consul n. 領事 lǐngshì.

consult v. ①請教 qǐngjiào, 諮詢 zīxún (ask for information or advice). ②查閱 cháyuè (look up). ③商量 shāngliang (discuss).

consultant n. 顧問 gùwèn.

consultation n. ①請教 qǐngjiào, 諮詢 zīxún (asking

for advice). ②商議 shāngyì
(discussion).

consume v. ①消耗 xiāohào
(use up). ②吃光 chīguāng
(devour). ③燒毀 shāohuǐ
(destroy by fire).

consumer n. 消費者
xiāofèizhě.

consummate v. 完成
wánchéng. — adj. 完全的
wánquán de.

consumption n. ①消耗
xiāohào (using up). ②消耗
量 xiāohàoliàng (amount
consumed).

contact n. ①聯繫 liánxì, 聯絡
liánluò (being in touch). ②聯絡
人 liánluòrén (person to get in
touch with).~s 關係 guānxi
(connections). come in ~ with 接
觸 jiēchù. ~ lenses 隱形眼鏡
yǐnxíng yǎnjìng. — v. 跟……
聯絡 gēn...liánluò.

contagion n. 接觸傳染 jiēchù
chuánrǎn.

contain v. ①包含 bāohán, 容
納 róngnà (hold). ②控制
kòngzhì, 抑制 yìzhì (control).

contaminate v. 沾污 zhānwū
(pollute), 弄髒 nòngzāng
(make dirty).

contemplate v. ①注視
zhùshì (gaze). ②沈思 chénsī,
默想 mòxiǎng (consider). ③預
期 yùqí / yùqí, 打算 dǎsuan
(intend).

contemporary n. & adj. 同
時代 tóng shídài.

contempt n. 輕視 qīngshì, 輕
蔑 qīngmiè.

contend v. 爭鬥 zhēngdòu,
競爭 jìngzhēng.

content v. 使滿足 shǐ mǎnzú.
— adj. 滿足的 mǎnzú de.

— n. 內容 nèiróng (what's
inside).

contention n. ①爭論
zhēnglùn (argument). ②主張
zhǔzhāng, 論點 lùndiǎn (view).

contentment n. 滿足 mǎnzú.

contest n. 競爭 jìngzhēng, 比
賽 bǐsài (competition). — v.
爭論 zhēnglùn (argue).

context n. 上下文
shàngxiàwén.

continent n. 大陸 dàlù
(mainland), 洲 zhōu ⟨land⟩.

continental adj. 大陸的 dàlù
de.

contingent n. 分遣隊
fēnqiǎndùi (group). — adj.
視情況而定的 shì qíngkuàng
ér dìng de (depending on).

continual adj. 連續的 liánxù
de, 不斷的 búduàn de.

continue v. ①繼續 jìxù (go on).
②持續 chíxù (remain). ③再繼
續 zài jìxù, 恢復 huīfù (restart).

continuous adj. 不斷的
búduàn de (uninterrupted), 連
續的 liánxù de (connected).

contort v. 扭歪 niǔwāi (twist),
歪曲 wāiqū (bend).

contour n. 輪廓 lúnkuò
(shape), 外形 wàixíng (outline).

contraband n. 違禁品
wéijìnpǐn ⟨goods⟩.

contract v. ①收縮 shōusuō,
縮小 suōxiǎo (condense). ②訂
約 dìngyuē (sign an agreement).
③感染 gǎnrǎn (become infected by). — n. 合同 hétong, 契約
qìyuē (agreement).

contradict v. ①反駁 fǎnbó
(speak against). ②抵觸 dǐchù
(be contrary to).

contradiction n. 矛盾
máodùn.

contralto *n.* 女低音 nǚ dīyīn.

contraption *n.* 新奇玩意 xīnqí wányì.

contrary *adj.* ①相反的 xiāngfǎn de (contradictory). ②逆向的 nìxiàng de (adverse). ③倔強的 juéjiàng de, 剛愎的 gāngbì de (stubborn).

contrast *n.* ①對比 duìbǐ, 對照 duìzhào (comparison). ②差別 chābié (difference). — *v.* ①對比 duìbǐ, 對照 duìzhào (compare). ②分別 fēnbié (differentiate).

contribute *v.* ①捐助 juānzhù (donate). ②促成 cùchéng, 有助於 yǒu zhù (assist). ③提供 tígōng (provide).

contribution *n.* ①捐助 juānzhù, 貢獻 gòngxiàn (donation). ②捐助物 juānzhùwù (donated goods).

contrive *v.* ①發明 fāmíng, 設計 shèjì (invent). ②設法 shèfǎ, 圖謀 túmóu (plan).

control *n.* ①控制 kòngzhì, 操縱 cāozòng (rule). ②抑制 yìzhì, 克制 kèzhì (restrain). ③管理 guǎnlǐ, 支配 zhīpèi (administer). ④核對 héduì (check).

controversy *n.* 爭論 zhēnglùn.

convalesce *v.* 病後康復 bìng hòu kāngfù.

convene *v.* 集會 jíhuì, 召集 zhàojí.

convenience *n.* ①方便 fāngbiàn, 便利 biànlì (being convenient). ②便利的事物 biànlì de shìwù (amenity).

convenient *adj.* 方便的 fāngbiàn de, 便利的 biànlì de.

convent *n.* 修道院 xiūdàoyuàn.

convention *n.* ①集會 jíhuì, 會議 huìyì (assembly). ②條約 tiáoyuē, 協定 xiédìng (agreement). ③慣例 guànlì, 習俗 xísú (custom).

conventional *adj.* 傳統的 chuántǒng de, 慣例的 guànlì de (customary).

converge *v.* 集中於一點 jízhōng yú yì diǎn, 匯合 huìhé (meet at a point).

conversation *n.* 會話 huìhuà.

converse *v.* 談話 tánhuà (talk). — *adj.* 倒轉的 dàozhuǎn de, 相反的 xiāngfǎn de (opposite).

conversion *n.* ①變換 biànhuàn (change). ②信仰改變 xìnyǎng gǎibiàn, 皈依 guīyī (change of beliefs).

convert *v.* ①轉變 zhuǎnbiàn, 變換 biànhuàn (change). ②改變信仰 gǎibiàn xìnyǎng, 皈依 guīyī (change beliefs).

convex *adj.* 凸狀的 tūzhuàng de / túzhuàng de.

convey *v.* ①運送 yùnsòng, 運輸 yùnshū (carry). ②傳達 chuándá (communicate).

convict *v.* 宣判有罪 xuānpàn yǒuzuì. — *n.* 罪犯 zuìfàn.

conviction *n.* ①堅信 jiānxìn (assurance). ②信念 xìnniàn (belief). ③定罪 dìngzuì (act of convicting).

convince *v.* 說服 shuōfú / shuìfú, 使信服 shǐ xìnfú.

convocation *n.* 召集 zhàojí, 集會 jíhuì.

convoy *v.* 護送 hùsòng, 護衛 hùwèi. — *n.* ①護送 hùsòng ⟨act⟩. ②護送隊 hùsòngduì ⟨group⟩.

convulse *v.* ①劇烈震動 jùliè

zhèndòng (shake). ②痙攣 jìngluán / jīngluán ⟨illness⟩.

coo n. 咕咕聲 gūgūshēng.

cook n. 廚師 chúshī. — v. 烹調 pēngtiáo, 煮 zhǔ.

cookie n. 餅乾 bǐnggān.

cooking n. 烹調 pēngtiáo.

cool adj. ①涼的 liáng de (moderately cold). ②冷靜的 lěngjìng de (calm). ③冷淡的 lěngdàn de (aloof). ④酷 kù (trendy). — v. 使變涼 shǐ biàn liáng (make cool). **~ down** 使冷靜 shǐ lěngjìng, 使平靜 shǐ píngjìng (calm).

coop n. 雞舍 jīshè, 雞籠 jīlóng.

coop up v. 關入籠內 guānrù lóng nèi.

co-op n. 合作社 hézuòshè.

cooperate v. 合作 hézuò.

cooperation n. 合作 hézuò.

cooperative adj. 合作的 hézuò de. — n. 合作社 hézuòshè.

coordinate adj. 同等的 tóngděng de (equal), 對等的 duìděng de ⟨grammar⟩. — n. ①同等的人或物 tóngděng de rén huò wù ⟨people or things⟩. ②座標 zuòbiāo ⟨map⟩. — v. ①調和 tiáohé, 協調 xiétiáo ⟨go together⟩. ②安排 ānpái (arrange).

cop n. 警察 jǐngchá ⟨officer⟩.

cope v. 對付 duìfu, 應付 yìngfu. **~ with** 應付 yìngfu, 處理 chǔlǐ.

copious adj. 豐富的 fēngfù de.

copper n. ①銅 tóng ⟨metal⟩. ②銅幣 tóngbì ⟨coin⟩.

copse n. 矮樹叢 ǎishùcóng.

copy n. ①複本 fùběn, 複製品 fùzhìpǐn (duplicate). ②一冊 yí cè, 一本 yì běn (volume). — v.

①抄寫 chāoxiě (make a copy of). ②模仿 mófǎng (imitate).

copyright n. 版權 bǎnquán, 著作權 zhùzuòquán.

coral n. 珊瑚 shānhú ⟨object⟩. 珊瑚色 shānhúsè ⟨color⟩. — adj. 珊瑚製的 shānhú zhì de. **~ reef** 珊瑚礁 shānhújiāo.

cord n. ①細繩 xìshéng ⟨string⟩. ②小電線 xiǎo diànxiàn ⟨cable⟩. ③腱 jiàn, 索狀組織 suǒzhuàng zǔzhī ⟨body part⟩.

cordial n. 甘露酒 gānlùjiǔ. — adj. 客氣的 kèqi de (polite), 熱心的 rèxīn de (enthusiastic).

cordon n. 警戒線 jǐngjièxiàn, 哨兵線 shàobīngxiàn ⟨military⟩.

corduroy n. 燈心絨 dēngxīnróng.

core n. ①果核 guǒhé ⟨fruit⟩. ②核心 héxīn (center).

cork n. ①軟木 ruǎnmù ⟨wood⟩. ②軟木塞 ruǎnmùsāi (plug).

corn n. ①玉米 yùmǐ (maize). ②雞眼 jīyǎn (skin problem). **~ chip** 玉米片 yùmǐpiàn.

cornea n. 眼角膜 yǎnjiǎomó / yǎnjiǎomò.

corner n. ①角 jiǎo (angle). ②角落 jiǎoluò (nook). ③轉角處 zhuǎnjiǎochù (turn).

cornet n. 短號 duǎnhào.

coronary adj. 冠狀的 guānzhuàng de / guànzhuàng de. — n. 心臟病發作 xīnzàngbìng fāzuò (heart attack).

coronation n. 加冕禮 jiāmiǎnlǐ.

coroner n. 法醫 fǎyī, 驗屍官 yànshīguān.

coronet n. 冠冕 guānmiǎn (crown).

C

corporal *adj.* 肉體的 ròutǐ de.
— *n.* 下士 xiàshì.

corporate *adj.* ①法人的 fǎrén de, 社團的 shètuán de 〈business〉. ②團體的 tuántǐ de, 共有的 gòngyǒu de (collective).

corporation *n.* ①法人 fǎrén, 法人團體 fǎrén tuántǐ (organization). ②市政當局 shìzhèng dāngjú (local government). ③股份有限公司 gǔfèn yǒuxiàn gōngsī (company).

corps *n.* ①部隊 bùduì 〈army〉. ②軍團 jūntuán (divisions of military force).

corpse *n.* 屍體 shītǐ.

corpuscle *n.* 血球 xuèqiú / xiěqiú.

correct *adj.* ①對的 duì de (right), 正確的 zhèngquè de (accurate). ②適當的 shìdàng de (appropriate).

correction *n.* 改正 gǎizhèng, 修正 xiūzhèng.

correlate *v.* 相關連 xiāngguānlián.

correspond *v.* ①與……一致 yǔ...yízhì (harmonize). ②通信 tōngxìn (exchange letters). ③相似 xiāngsì, 相當 xiāngdāng (be similar).

correspondence *n.* ①通信 tōngxìn (letter-writing). ②符合 fúhé, 一致 yízhì (agreement).

correspondent *n.* ①通信者 tōngxìnzhě (one who exchanges letters). ②通訊員 tōngxùnyuán, 記者 jìzhě (reporter).

corridor *n.* 走廊 zǒuláng, 迴廊 huíláng.

corroborate *v.* 證實 zhèngshí.

corrode *v.* 腐蝕 fǔshí, 侵蝕 qīnshí.

corrugate *v.* 起皺紋 qǐ zhòuwén.

corrupt *adj.* ①貪污的 tānwū de (bribable). ②腐敗的 fǔbài de (rotten). ③不潔的 bùjié de (impure). — *v.* ①賄賂 huìlù (bribe). ②腐化 fǔhuà (make corrupt).

corset *n.* 束腹 shùfù.

cosmetic *n.* 化粧品 huàzhuāngpǐn. — *adj.* 化粧用的 huàzhuāng yòng de.

cosmic *adj.* 宇宙的 yǔzhòu de.

cosmonaut *n.* 宇航員 yǔhángyuán / 太空人 tàikōngrén.

cosmopolitan *adj.* ①世界性的 shìjièxìng de (from all over the world), 世界主義的 shìjiè zhǔyì de 〈doctrine〉.

cosmos *n.* 宇宙 yǔzhòu.

cost *n.* ①費用 fèiyòng (expenditure). ②價格 jiàgé (price). — *v.* ①價值 jiàzhí (be valued at). ②花費 huāfèi (expend).

costume *n.* ①服裝 fúzhuāng (clothes). ②舞臺裝 wǔtáizhuāng 〈actor〉.

cosy *adj.* 溫暖舒適的 wēnnuǎn shūshì de.

cot *n.* 嬰兒床 yīng'érchuáng.

cottage *n.* 小屋 xiǎowū, 村舍 cūnshè.

cotton *n.* 棉 mián, 棉花 miánhuā.

couch *n.* ①長沙發 chángshāfā (sofa). ②臥椅 wòyǐ (a bed-like seat). — *v.* 表達 biǎodá (express).

cougar *n.* 美洲獅 měizhōushī.

cough *v.* 咳嗽 késou.

council n. ①會議 huìyì (assembly). ②委員會 wěiyuánhuì (committee). *city* ~ 市議會 shìyìhuì.

counsel n. ①建議 jiànyì, 勸告 quàngào (advice). ②商量 shāngliang, 商議 shāngyì (consultation). ③律師 lùshī, 法律顧問 fǎlù gùwèn (lawyer). — v. 建議 jiànyì, 勸告 quàngào.

counselor n. 顧問 gùwèn (consultant).

count v. ①數 shǔ (name the numbers). ②算 suàn (add up). ③考慮在內 kǎolù zàinèi, 包括 bāokuò (include). ④有價值 yǒu jiàzhí, 有意義 yǒu yìyì (be important). ~ *down* 倒讀秒 dàodúmiǎo, 倒數計秒 dàoshǔ jìmiǎo / 倒數計時 dàoshǔ jìshí.

countable adj. 可數的 kěshǔ de.

countenance n. 面容 miànróng (appearance), 表情 biǎoqíng (expression).

counter n. ①櫃臺 guìtái ⟨desk⟩. ②籌碼 chóumǎ ⟨chip⟩. — adj. & adv. 相反的 xiāngfǎn de.

counteract v. 抵消 dǐxiāo.

counterbalance n. ①平衡錘 pínghéngchuí ⟨weight⟩. ②平衡力 pínghénglì ⟨force⟩. — v. 使平衡 shǐ pínghéng.

counterfeit adj. 贗造的 yànzào de, 假冒的 jiǎmào de. — n. 贗品 yànpǐn, 偽造品 wěizàopǐn / wèizàopǐn.

counterfoil n. 存根 cúngēn, 存據 cúnjù.

countermand v. 撤回 chèhuí, 取消 qǔxiāo.

counterpart n. 相對的人 xiāngduì de rén ⟨person⟩, 相對的物 xiāngduì de wù ⟨thing⟩.

countersign v. 連署 liánshǔ / liánshù, 副署 fùshǔ / fùshù.

countless adj. 無數的 wúshù de.

country n. ①國家 guójiā (nation). ②鄉村 xiāngcūn (countryside).

countryman n. ①同胞 tóngbāo (compatriot). ②鄉下人 xiāngxiàrén ⟨countryside⟩.

countryside n. 鄉間 xiāngjiān, 鄉下 xiāngxia.

county n. 郡 jùn, 縣 xiàn.

coup n. ①政變 zhèngbiàn ⟨political takeover⟩. ②奏效的策略 zòuxiào de cèlüè (achievement).

couple n. ①一對 yí duì (a pair). ②夫婦 fūfù (husband and wife). ③情侶 qínglǚ (lovers). — v. 連接 liánjiē (join).

couplet n. 對句 duìjù, 對聯 duìlián.

coupon n. 優待券 yōudàiquàn.

courage n. 勇氣 yǒngqì, 膽量 dǎnliàng.

courier n. 信差 xìnchāi, 快遞員 kuàidìyuán (messenger).

course n. ①過程 guòchéng, 進程 jìnchéng (process). ②路線 lùxiàn (path). ③課程 kèchéng (curriculum). ④高爾夫球場 gāo'ěrfū qiúchǎng ⟨golf⟩. ⑤一道菜 yí dào cài (meal). — v. 運行 yùnxíng, 流動 liúdòng (flow).

court n. ①法院 fǎyuàn, 法庭 fǎtíng ⟨law⟩. ②宮廷 gōngtíng, 朝廷 cháotíng (palace). ③庭院 tíngyuàn (courtyard). ④球場 qiúchǎng ⟨ball games⟩. — v.

①討好 tǎohǎo, 奉承
fèngchéng (ingratiate). ②求愛
qiúʾài, 追求 zhuīqiú (try to win
someone's affections).

courteous *adj.* 有禮貌的 yǒu
lǐmào de, 謙恭的 qiāngōng de.

courtesy *n.* 禮貌 lǐmào, 謙恭
qiāngōng (good manners).

courtier *n.* 朝臣 cháochén.

court-martial *n.* 軍事法庭
jūnshì fǎtíng. — *v.* 以軍法審
判 yǐ jūnfǎ shěnpàn.

courtship *n.* 求愛 qiúʾài, 求愛
時期 qiúʾài shíqí / qiúʾài shíqí.

courtyard *n.* 庭院 tíngyuàn.

cousin *n.* ①堂哥 tánggē
(father's brother's son, elder),
堂弟 tángdì (father's brother's
son, younger). ②堂姊 tángjiě
(father's brother's daughter,
elder), 堂妹 tángmèi (father's
brother's daughter, younger).
③表哥 biǎogē (father's sister's
son, elder; mother's brother or
sister's son, elder), 表弟 biǎodì
(father's sister's son, younger;
mother's brother or sister's son,
younger). ④表姊 biǎojiě
(father's sister's daughter, elder;
mother's brother or sister's
daughter, elder), 表妹 biǎomèi
(father's sister's daughter,
younger; mother's brother or
sister's daughter, younger).

cove *n.* 小海灣 xiǎo hǎiwān.

cover *v.* ①蓋 gài, 覆蓋 fùgài
(overlay). ②足夠涵蓋 zúgòu
hángài (be enough for). ③包括
bāokuò (contain). ④掩護
yǎnhù (protect). — *n.* ①遮蓋物
zhēgàiwù (covering). ②封面
fēngmiàn (for papers or a
book). ③蓋子 gàizi (cap).

cover story *n.* 封面故事

fēngmiàn gùshi.

covert *adj.* 暗地的 àndì de.

cow *n.* 牛 niú, 母牛 mǔniú.

coward *n.* 懦夫 nuòfū. — *adj.*
膽怯的 dǎnqiè de / dǎnquè de.

cower *v.* 畏縮 wèisuō.

coy *adj.* 靦腆的 miǎntian de,
忸怩的 niǔní de.

CPR 心肺復甦術 Xīnfèi
Fùsūshù (cardiopulmonary
resuscitation).

crab *n.* 蟹 xiè, 蟹肉 xièròu.

crack *n.* ①裂縫 lièfèng (split).
②噼啪聲 pīpāshēng ⟨sound⟩.
— *v.* ①發爆裂聲 fā bàolièshēng
(make sound). ②破裂 pòliè, 裂
開 lièkāi (break). ③解開 jiěkāi,
解答 jiědá (solve).

cracker *n.* 薄脆餅乾 bócuì
bǐnggān (biscuit). *fire* ~ 鞭炮
biānpào.

crackle *v.* 發噼啪聲
fā pīpāshēng. — *n.* 爆裂聲
bàolièshēng.

crackpot *n.* 狂想者
kuángxiǎngzhě.

cradle *n.* ①搖籃 yáolán (small
bed for a baby). ②發源地
fāyuándì (place of origin).

craft *n.* ①手藝 shǒuyì, 手工藝
shǒugōngyì (skilled work).
②技術 jìshù, 技巧 jìqiǎo
(skill). ③船 chuán (boat), 飛機
fēijī (airplane), 太空船
tàikōngchuán (spaceship).

craftsman *n.* 工匠 gōngjiàng.

crag *n.* 峭壁 qiàobì, 危岩
wēiyán / wéiyán.

cram *v.* ①填塞 tiánsè, 塞滿
sāimǎn (fill). ②強記應考
qiángjì yìngkǎo (study).
~ *school* 補習班 bǔxíbān.

cramp *n.* 抽筋 chōujīn, 痙攣
jìngluán / jìngluán.

cranberry *n.* 小紅莓 xiǎohóngméi, 蔓越莓 mànyuèméi.

crane *n.* ①鶴 hè ⟨bird⟩. ②起重機 qǐzhòngjī ⟨machine⟩.

cranium *n.* 頭蓋骨 tóugàigǔ.

crank *n.* ①曲柄 qūbǐng ⟨apparatus⟩. ②易怒者 yìnùzhě ⟨bad-tempered⟩, 古怪者 gǔguàizhě ⟨nut⟩.

crash *n.* ①墜毀 zhuìhuǐ, 猛撞 měngzhuàng ⟨collision⟩. ②崩潰 bēngkuì, 垮臺 kuǎtái ⟨collapse⟩. ③猛然轟聲 měngrán hōng shēng ⟨sound⟩. — *v.* ①撞毀 zhuànghuǐ, 墜毀 zhuìhuǐ ⟨collide⟩. ②猛撞 měngzhuàng, 碰撞 pèngzhuàng ⟨strike⟩. ③破產 pòchǎn, 崩潰 bēngkuì ⟨come to ruin⟩.

crass *adj.* ①粗俗的 cūsú de, 粗魯的 cūlǔ de ⟨coarse⟩. ②愚蠢的 yúchǔn de ⟨stupid⟩.

crate *n.* 板條箱 bǎntiáoxiāng.

crater *n.* 火山口 huǒshānkǒu ⟨mouth of a volcano⟩. ②彈坑 dànkēng ⟨hole made by a bomb⟩.

cravat *n.* 領結 lǐngjié.

crave *v.* 渴望 kěwàng ⟨desire⟩, 懇求 kěnqiú ⟨beg for⟩.

crawl *n. & v.* 爬行 páxíng, 爬 pá ⟨creep⟩. ②徐行 xúxíng ⟨moving slowly⟩.

crayfish *n.* 小龍蝦 xiǎolóngxiā.

crayon *n.* 蠟筆 làbǐ.

craze *n.* 狂熱 kuángrè.

crazy *adj.* ①瘋狂的 fēngkuáng de ⟨mad⟩. ②狂熱的 kuángrè de ⟨excited⟩.

creak *v.* 發喀吱聲 fā kāzīshēng. — *n.* 喀吱聲 kāzīshēng.

cream *n.* ①乳脂 rǔzhī ⟨milk⟩.

②乳霜 rǔshuāng ⟨ointment⟩. ③精華 jīnghuá ⟨best part⟩.

crease *n.* 摺痕 zhéhén, 皺摺 zhòuzhé. — *v.* 弄皺 nòngzhuá.

create *v.* 創造 chuàngzào, 創作 chuàngzuò ⟨make⟩, 製造 zhìzào ⟨produce⟩.

creation *n.* 創造 chuàngzào, 創作 chuàngzuò, 創造物 chuàngzàowù.

creative *adj.* 有創造力的 yǒu chuàngzàolì de.

creator *n.* ①創造者 chuàngzàozhě ⟨maker⟩. ②上帝 Shàngdì ⟨God⟩.

creature *n.* ①生物 shēngwù ⟨living being⟩. ②人 rén ⟨person⟩. ③動物 dòngwù ⟨animal⟩.

credentials *n.* ①資歷 zīlì ⟨professional background⟩. ②證明書 zhèngmíngshū ⟨documentation⟩.

credible *adj.* 可信的 kěxìn de, 可靠的 kěkào de.

credit *n.* ①信用 xìnyòng ⟨financial⟩. ②學分 xuéfēn ⟨school⟩. ③相信 xiāngxìn, 信任 xìnrèn ⟨trust⟩. ④名譽 míngyù, 名望 míngwàng ⟨reputation⟩. — *v.* ①相信 xiāngxìn, 信賴 xìnlài ⟨trust⟩. ②帶來榮譽 dàilái róngyù ⟨bring about honor⟩. ③把……記入貸方 bǎ...jìrù dàifāng ⟨monetary account⟩. ~ *card* 信用卡 xìnyòngkǎ.

creditor *n.* 債權人 zhàiquánrén, 貸方 dàifāng.

creed *n.* 教條 jiàotiáo, 信條 xìntiáo.

creek *n.* 小溪 xiǎoxī.

creep *n. & v.* 爬行 páxíng ⟨crawl⟩, 緩慢移動 huǎnmàn yídòng ⟨moving slowly⟩.

creeper *n.* 爬蟲 páchóng.

爬行動物 páxíng dòngwù.

creepy adj. 毛骨悚然的
máogǔ-sǒngrán de.

cremate v. 火葬 huǒzàng.

crepe n. 縐紗 zhòushā (fabric
with a wrinkled surface).
~ *paper* 縐紋紙 zhòuwénzhǐ.

crescendo adv. 漸強的
jiànqiáng de, 漸響的
jiànxiǎng de.

crescent n. 新月形 xīnyuèxíng.
— adj. 新月形的 xīnyuèxíng de.
~ *moon* 新月 xīnyuè.

cress n. 水芹 shuǐqín.

crest n. ①鳥冠 niǎoguān (comb).
②山頂 shāndǐng (apex). ③飾
章 shìzhāng (badge).

crevasse n. 裂縫 lièfèng.

crevice n. 裂縫 lièfèng, 罅隙
xiàxì.

crew n. ①工作人員 gōngzuò
rényuán (workers). ②水手
shuǐshǒu ⟨ship⟩. ③組員 jīyuán
⟨airplane⟩.

crib n. 嬰兒床 yīng'érchuáng
(baby's bed). — v. 剽竊 piāoqiè /
piàoqiè, 抄襲 chāoxí (copy).

cricket n. ①蟋蟀 xīshuài
⟨insect⟩. ②板球 bǎnqiú ⟨game⟩.

crime n. 罪 zuì, 罪行 zuìxíng.

criminal n. 犯罪者 fànzuìzhě,
犯人 fànrén. — adj. 犯罪的
fànzuì de, 犯法的 fànfǎ de.

crimson n. & adj. 深紅色
shēnhóngsè.

cringe n. & v. ①畏縮 wèisuō
(flinch). ②奉承 fèngchéng, 諂
媚 chǎnmèi (toady).

crinkle v. 縐 zhòu (produce
crinkles). — n. 縐紋 zhòuwén
(wrinkle).

cripple n. 殘障者
cánzhàngzhě. — v. 使殘廢
shǐ cánfèi.

crisis n. ①危機 wēijī / wéijī
(time of great danger). ②轉折
點 zhuǎnzhédiǎn / 轉捩點
zhuǎnlièdiǎn (turning-point).

crisp adj. ①脆的 cuì de
(crunchy). ②乾冷的 gānlěng
de (cold and dry). ③清新的
qīngxīn de (fresh).

crisscross adj. 十字形的
shízìxíng de. — v. 成十字形
chéng shízìxíng.

criterion n. ①標準 biāozhǔn,
規範 guīfàn (standard). ②條件
tiáojiàn (condition).

critic n. 評論家 pínglùnjiā
⟨person⟩.

critical adj. ①批評的 pīpíng
de (criticizing). ②吹毛求疵的
chuīmáo-qiúcī de (fault-finding).
③有判斷力的 yǒu pànduànlì
de (analytical). ④危急的 wēijí
de / wéijí de (in crisis), 關鍵性
的 guānjiànxìng de (at a
turning point).

criticism n. 批評 pīpíng.

criticize v. 批評 pīpíng (find
fault), 責難 zénàn (blame).

croak n. 嘶啞聲 sīyǎshēng.
— v. 嘶啞 sīyǎ.

crock n. ①瓦罐 wǎguàn (pot).
②碎瓦片 suìwǎpiàn (broken
pieces). ③廢話 fèihuà
(nonsense).

crockery n. 陶器 táoqì, 瓦器
wǎqì.

crocodile n. 鱷魚 èyú.

crocus n. 番紅花 fānhónghuā.

crook n. ①惡棍 ègùn, 流氓
liúmáng (criminal). ②騙子
piànzi (cheat). ③彎柄手杖
wānbǐng shǒuzhàng (stick).

crooked adj. 彎曲的 wānqū
de (bent).

crop n. ①農作物 nóngzuòwù

(agricultural plants). ②收成 shōuchéng (harvest). — v. ①吃草 chīcǎo, 啃嚙 kěnniè (bite off). ②剪短 jiǎnduǎn (cut).

croquet n. 槌球遊戲 chuíqiú yóuxì.

cross n. ①十字形 shízìxíng 〈shape〉. ②十字架 shízìjià (an upright post). — v. 橫越過 héngyuèguò, 穿過 chuānguò (go across). — adj. ①橫的 héng de, 橫過的 héngguò de (passing across). ②易怒的 yì nù de, 壞脾氣的 huài píqi de (bad-tempered).

crossbow n. 石弓 shígōng.

crossbreed v. 雜交 zájiāo. — n. 雜種 zázhǒng, 混種 hùnzhǒng.

cross-country adj. 越野的 yuèyě de.

cross-examine v. 盤問 pánwèn.

crossing n. ①平交道 píngjiāodào 〈railway〉. ②十字路口 shízì lùkǒu (intersection).

cross-legged adj. & adv. 盤著腿的 pánzhe tuǐ de, 翹著腿的 qiàozhe tuǐ de.

crossroad n. 十字路口 shízì lùkǒu, 交叉路 jiāochālù.

crouch n. & v. 蹲伏 dūnfú.

crow v. ①雞叫 jījiào 〈rooster〉. ②自鳴得意 zìmíng-déyì (boast). — n. ①烏鴉 wūyā 〈bird〉. ②雞叫 jījiào 〈cock〉.

crowbar n. 鐵橇 tiěqiāo, 橇棍 qiāogùn.

crowd n. 群眾 qúnzhòng, 人群 rénqún. — v. 擠滿 jǐmǎn, 擁擠 yōngjǐ / yǒngjǐ.

crowded adj. 擁擠的 yōngjǐ de / yǒngjǐ de.

crown n. ①王冠 wángguān,

皇冠 huángguān (headwear). ②頂部 dǐngbù (apex). — v. ①加冕 jiāmiǎn (enthrone). ②加榮譽於 jiā róngyù yú (reward with).

crucial adj. 決定性的 juédìngxìng de, 極重要的 jí zhòngyào de.

crucifix n. 耶穌受難像 Yēsū shòunàn xiàng.

crude adj. ①未提煉的 wèi tíliàn de, 未加工的 wèi jiāgōng de (natural state). ②粗魯的 cūlǔ de (rude). ③粗劣的 cūliè de (amateurish).

cruel adj. 殘忍的 cánrěn de, 殘酷的 cánkù de.

cruelty n. 殘酷 cánkù.

cruise n. & v. 巡航 xúnháng.

crumb n. 麵包屑 miànbāoxiè 〈bread〉.

crumble v. 弄碎 nòngsuì.

crumple v. 變皺 biànzhòu, 壓皺 yāzhòu.

crunch v. 嘎扎地響 gāzhá de xiǎng.

crusade n. ①C~s 十字軍 shízìjūn (the Crusade). ②改革運動 gǎigé yùndòng (reform movement).

crush v. 壓碎 yāsuì, 壓壞 yāhuài.

crust n. ①麵包皮 miànbāopí 〈bread〉. ②地殼 dìké 〈earth〉.

crustacean n. 甲殼類動物 jiǎkélèi dòngwù.

crusty adj. ①有硬殼的 yǒu yìngké de (having a hard crust). ②粗暴的 cūbào de, 易怒的 yìnù de (grumpy).

crutch n. 拐杖 guǎizhàng.

crux n. 問題徵結 wèntí zhēngjié.

cry v. ①喊叫 hǎnjiào (yell). ②哭

泣 kūqì (weep). ③叫 jiào, 啼 tí ⟨animal⟩.

crypt n. 地下墓穴 dìxià mùxué / dìxià mùxuè.

crystal n. 水晶 shuǐjīng. — adj. 水晶製的 shuǐjīng zhì de.

cub n. ①幼獸 yòushòu (young animal). ②小伙子 xiǎohuǒzi, 年輕人 niánqīngrén (young man). ③生手 shēngshǒu, 學徒 xuétú (novice).

cube n. 立方體 lìfāngtǐ.

cubicle n. 小寢室 xiǎo qǐnshì.

cuckoo n. 布穀鳥 bùgǔniǎo.

cucumber n. 胡瓜 húguā, 黃瓜 huángguā.

cud n. 反芻的食物 fǎnchú de shíwù.

cuddle v. 愛撫 àifǔ, 撫抱 fǔbào.

cudgel n. 短棒 duǎnbàng. — v. 以棍棒打 yǐ gùnbàng dǎ.

cue n. 提示 tíshì, 暗示 ànshì.

cuff n. 袖口 xiùkǒu.

cuisine n. 烹飪 pēngrèn (cooking).

culminate v. 達到頂點 dádào dǐngdiǎn.

culprit n. 犯人 fànrén, 罪人 zuìrén.

cult n. ①教派 jiàopài ⟨religious⟩. ②崇拜 chóngbài (worship).

cultivate v. ①耕種 gēngzhòng (farm). ②培養 péiyǎng (foster), 栽培 zāipéi, 養殖 yǎngzhí (grow).

cultural adj. 文化的 wénhuà de, 人文的 rénwén de.

culture v. ①文化 wénhuà (art). ②文明 wénmíng (civilization). ③教養 jiàoyǎng (education).

culvert n. 排水溝 páishuǐgōu,

下水道 xiàshuǐdào.

cunning adj. 狡猾的 jiǎohuá de.

cup n. ①杯 bēi, 杯子 bēizi ⟨container⟩. ②獎杯 jiǎngbēi ⟨prize⟩.

cupboard n. 碗櫥 wǎnchú.

cur n. ①惡犬 èquǎn ⟨dog⟩. ②無賴 wúlài, 下流的人 xiàliú de rén ⟨man⟩.

curable adj. 可治療的 kě zhìliáo de.

curative adj. 有療效的 yǒu liáoxiào de.

curator n. 展覽負責人 zhǎnlǎn fùzérén.

curb n. ①人行道 rénxíngdào (sidewalk). ②邊欄 biānlán (edge). ③抑制 yìzhì (restrain). — v. 抑制 yìzhì (restraint).

curd n. 凝乳 níngrǔ.

curdle v. ①凝結 níngjié (form curds). ②變質 biànzhì / biànzhí (spoil).

cure v. 醫治 yīzhì, 治癒 zhìyù. — n. 治療 zhìliáo ⟨act⟩, 療法 liáofǎ ⟨method⟩.

cured adj. 痊癒的 quányù de.

curfew n. 宵禁 xiāojìn.

curiosity n. 好奇心 hàoqíxīn, 好奇 hàoqí.

curious adj. ①好奇的 hàoqí de (inquisitive). ②奇怪的 qíguài de (strange).

curl v. 捲曲 juǎnqū. — n. ①捲曲 juǎnqū ⟨shape⟩. ②捲髮 juǎnfà / juǎnfǎ ⟨hair⟩.

currant n. 小葡萄乾 xiǎo pútáogān.

currency n. ①通貨 tōnghuò, 貨幣 huòbì (money). ②流通 liútōng, 通用 tōngyòng (popular use).

current n. ①水流 shuǐliú

〈water〉. ②氣流 qìliú〈air〉. ③電流 diànliú〈electricity〉. — adj. ①流通的 liútōng de, 通行的 tōngxíng de〈widespread〉. ②現行的 xiànxíng de〈in effect〉. ③流行的 liúxíng de〈fashionable〉.

curriculum n. 課程 kèchéng.

curry n. 咖哩 gālí / gálí, 咖哩食品 gālí shípǐn / gálí shípǐn. ~ *favor* 拍馬屁 pāi mǎpì, 諂媚 chǎnmèi.

curse v. 詛咒 zǔzhòu, 咒罵 zhòumà. — n. ①詛咒 zǔzhòu, 咒罵 zhòumà〈words〉. ②禍源 huòyuán, 禍根 huògēn〈cause of misfortune〉.

cursor n. 光標 guāngbiāo / 游標 yóubiāo〈computer〉.

curt adj. 草率無禮的 cǎoshuài wúlǐ de.

curtail v. 縮短 suōduǎn〈shorten〉.

curtain n. ①窗帘 chuānglián〈window〉. ②帳幕 zhàngmù, 帷幕 wéimù〈stage〉.

curtsy n. 屈膝禮 qūxīlǐ.

curve n. 曲線 qūxiàn〈line〉, 彎曲 wānqū〈bend〉. — v. 彎曲 wānqū.

cushion n. 墊子 diànzi, 坐墊 zuòdiàn〈pillow〉.

custard n. 牛奶蛋糕 niúnǎi dàngāo〈cake〉, 布丁 bùdīng〈pudding〉.

custody n. ①監護 jiānhù〈guardianship〉. ②監禁 jiānjìn〈captivity〉. ③保管 bǎoguǎn, 保護 bǎohù〈care〉.

custom n. ①風俗 fēngsú, 習俗 xísú, 慣例 guànlì〈convention〉. ②關稅 guānshuì〈import duties〉.

customary adj. 習慣的 xíguàn de〈habitual〉, 習俗的 xísú de〈traditional〉.

customer n. 顧客 gùkè.

customs n. ①海關 hǎiguān〈government institution〉. ②關稅 guānshuì〈taxes〉.

cut v. ①割 gē〈sever〉, 切 qiē〈slice〉, 剪 jiǎn〈clip〉. ②縮減 suōjiǎn〈abbreviate〉. ~ *in* 中斷 zhōngduàn. ~ *and paste* 剪貼 jiāntiē.

cute adj. 可愛的 kě'ài de.

cutlet n. 薄肉片 bóròupiàn.

cutter n. ①切割器具 qiēgē qìjù〈tool〉. ②小汽艇 xiǎo qìtǐng〈vessel〉.

cutthroat n. 兇手 xiōngshǒu, 謀殺者 móushāzhě. — adj. 兇狠的 xiōnghěn de, 殘暴的 cánbào de〈ruthless〉.

cutting n. 剪報 jiǎnbào. — adj. 尖刻的 jiānkè de, 鋒利的 fēnglì de.

cuttlefish n. 烏賊 wūzéi, 墨魚 mòyú.

cybercafé n. 網路咖啡店 wǎnglù kāfēidiàn, 網吧 wǎngbā / 網咖 wǎngkā.

cyberspace n. 網絡世界 wǎngluò shìjiè / 網路世界 wǎnglù shìjiè.

cycle n. 周期 zhōuqī / zhōuqí, 循環 xúnhuán〈series〉. — v. 騎腳踏車 qí jiǎotàchē〈ride a bicycle〉.

cyclone n. 旋風 xuànfēng, 颶風 jùfēng〈hurricane〉.

cylinder n. ①圓筒 yuántǒng〈a hollow tube〉. ②汽缸 qìgāng〈piston〉.

cymbal n. 鈸 bá.

cynic n. 憤世嫉俗者 fènshì-jísú zhě.

cynical *adj.* ①譏笑的 jīxiào de, 諷刺的 fěngcì de / fèngcì de (sarcastic). ②憤世嫉俗的 fènshì-jísú de (world-weary).

cypress *n.* 柏樹 bóshù.

czar *n.* 沙皇 shāhuáng (tsar).

D

dab *v.* 塗敷 túfū. — *n.* ①輕拍 qīngpāi (pat). ②少量 shǎoliàng (small amount).

dabble *v.* 涉獵 shèliè (be involved in).

dad *n.* 爸爸 bàba.

daddy *n.* 爸爸 bàba.

daffodil *n.* 黃水仙 huángshuǐxiān.

dagger *n.* 短劍 duǎnjiàn, 匕首 bǐshǒu ⟨knife⟩.

daily *adj. & adv.* 每日的 měirì de, 日常的 rìcháng de. — *n.* 日報 rìbào.

dainty *adj.* ①高雅的 gāoyǎ de (delicate). ②講究的 jiǎngjiu de (choosy).

dairy *n.* ①乳品廠 rǔpǐnchǎng ⟨factory⟩. ②酪農場 làonóngchǎng / luònóngchǎng ⟨farm⟩. ③乳品店 rǔpǐndiàn ⟨store⟩. — *adj.* 牛奶的 niúnǎi de.

dais *n.* 壇 tán, 高臺 gāotái.

daisy *n.* 雛菊 chújú.

dale *n.* 山谷 shāngǔ.

dam *n.* 水壩 shuǐbà. — *v.* ①築水壩 zhù shuǐbà / zhú shuǐbà (close off a river). ②阻止 zǔzhǐ (block).

damage *n. & v.* 損害 sǔnhài (injury), 損失 sǔnshī (loss).

dame *n.* 夫人 fūrén.

damn *n. & v.* 咒罵 zhòumà (curse). — *interj.* 該死! Gāisǐ!

damp *adj.* 潮濕的 cháoshī de. — *n.* 濕氣 shīqì.

dampen *v.* ①使潮濕 shǐ cháoshī (make damp). ②使沮喪 shǐ jǔsàng (make sad).

dance *v.* 跳舞 tiàowǔ. — *n.* 跳舞 tiàowǔ, 舞蹈 wǔdǎo / wǔdào. ~ **hall** 舞廳 wǔtīng.

dancing *n.* 跳舞 tiàowǔ.

dandelion *n.* 蒲公英 púgōngyīng.

dandruff *n.* 頭皮屑 tóupíxiè.

danger *n.* 危險 wēixiǎn / wéixiǎn.

dangerous *adj.* 危險的 wēixiǎn de / wéixiǎn de.

dangle *v.* 搖擺 yáobǎi, 搖晃 yáohuang (hang loosely).

dank *adj.* 陰濕的 yīnshī de.

dare *v.* ①敢 gǎn, 膽敢 dǎngǎn (be brave enough to). ②激 jī (challenge).

daring *n. & adj.* 勇敢 yǒnggǎn, 大膽 dàdǎn.

dark *adj.* 黑暗的 hēi'àn de (without light). ~ **horse** 黑馬 hēimǎ. — *n.* 黑暗 hēi'àn (darkness).

darken *v.* 使黑暗 shǐ hēi'àn.

darkroom *n.* 暗房 ànfáng.

darling *n.* 親愛的人 qīn'ài de rén. — *adj.* 親愛的 qīn'ài de

dart n. 鏢槍 biāoqiāng. — v. 急衝 jíchōng, 突進 tūjìn / tújìn (rush).

dash v. ①擲 zhì / zhí, 猛擲 měngzhì / měngzhí (throw violently). ②猛撞 měngzhuàng (rush into). ③使挫敗 shǐ cuòbài (discourage). — n. ①突進 tūjìn / tújìn (sprint). ②少量 shǎoliàng (small amount). ③破折號 pòzhéhào (mark).

dashboard n. 儀表板 yíbiǎobǎn.

data n. 資料 zīliào. ~ base 數據庫 shùjùkù / 資料庫 zīliàokù.

date n. ①日期 rìqí / rìqí (day). ②約會 yuēhuì (appointment). ③棗子 zǎozi 〈fruit〉. out of ~ 過時的 guòshí de. — v. 記載日期 jìzǎi rìqí / jìzǎi rìqí.

daughter n. 女兒 nǚ'ér.

daughter-in-law n. 兒媳婦 érxífu.

daunt v. 使畏懼 shǐ wèijù, 使氣餒 shǐ qìněi (dismay).

dawdle v. 浪費光陰 làngfèi guāngyīn, 閒蕩 xiándàng.

dawn n. ①黎明 límíng (daybreak). ②開端 kāiduān (beginning). — v. 破曉 pòxiǎo.

day n. 白天 báitiān (daytime), 一天 yì tiān (one day).

daybreak n. 破曉 pòxiǎo, 黎明 límíng.

daydream n. 白日夢 báirìmèng, 幻想 huànxiǎng. — v. 作白日夢 zuò báirìmèng.

daylight n. ①日光 rìguāng (light of day). ②白晝 báizhòu (daytime).

daytime n. 白天 báitiān, 白晝 báizhòu.

daze v. 使暈眩 shǐ yùnxuàn /

shǐ yūnxuàn, 使眩惑 shǐ xuànhuò.

dazzle v. 使目眩 shǐ mùxuàn, 使眩惑 shǐ xuànhuò. — n. 眩目強光 xuànmù qiángguāng.

dead adj. ①死的 sǐ de, 無生命的 wú shēngmìng de (not alive). ②麻木的 mámù de (numb). ③失靈的 shīlíng de, 無效的 wúxiào de (not working). ④無生氣的 wú shēngqì de (boring). — n. 死人 sǐrén.

deaden v. 使減弱 shǐ jiǎnruò.

deadline n. 最後期限 zuìhòu qíxiàn, 截止時間 jiézhǐ shíjiān, 截止日期 jiézhǐ rìqí / jiézhǐ rìqí.

deadlock n. 僵局 jiāngjú (standstill).

deadly adj. 致命的 zhìmìng de 〈fatal〉. — adv. 如死地 rú sǐ de 〈like death〉.

deaf adj. 聾的 lóng de.

deal v. ①分配 fēnpèi (give out). ②發牌 fāpái (allot cards). — n. ①交易 jiāoyì 〈business〉. ②量 liàng, 份量 fènliàng (amount). ③發牌 fāpái 〈card〉. a great ~ of 大量的 dàliàng de.

dealer n. ①商人 shāngrén (trader). ②發牌者 fāpáizhě (a person who deals cards).

dean n. ①院長 yuànzhǎng, 系主任 xìzhǔrèn 〈university〉. ②主持牧師 zhǔchí mùshi 〈clergy〉.

dear adj. ①親愛的 qīn'ài de (much loved). ②昂貴的 ánguì de (expensive). — n. 親愛的人 qīn'ài de rén.

dearth n. 缺乏 quēfá, 缺少 quēshǎo (scarcity).

death n. 死亡 sǐwáng.

debase v. 降低 jiàngdī (lower value), 貶低 biǎndī (degrade).

debate n. & v. 討論 tǎolùn, 辯論 biànlùn (argue about).

debauch v. 使墮落 shǐ duòluò, 使放蕩 shǐ fàngdàng (behave badly).

debauchery n. 放蕩 fàngdàng.

debilitate v. 使衰弱 shǐ shuāiruò.

debit n. 借方 jièfāng. — v. 登入借方 dēngrù jièfāng.

debris n. ①瓦礫 wǎlì (remains). ②垃圾 lājī / lèsè (garbage).

debt n. ①債務 zhàiwù, 負債 fùzhài (money owed). ②恩情 ēnqíng (gratitude).

debut n. ①初進社界 chū jìn shèjiāojiè (young person). ②初次登台 chūcì dēngtái (actor).

decade n. 十年 shí nián.

decadence n. 衰落 shuāiluò, 頹廢 tuífèi.

decaf n. 不含咖啡因的咖啡 bù hán kāfēiyīn de kāfēi.

decant v. 慢慢倒出 mànman dàochū (pour).

decapitate v. 斬首 zhǎnshǒu, 砍頭 kǎntóu.

decay n. & v. ①腐敗 fǔbài, 腐爛 fǔlàn (rot). ②衰弱 shuāiruò, 衰落 shuāiluò (go bad).

decease n. 死亡 sǐwáng.

deceased n. 死者 sǐzhě.

deceit n. 欺騙 qīpiàn, 詐騙 zhàpiàn.

deceive v. 欺騙 qīpiàn, 詐騙 zhàpiàn.

decelerate v. 減速 jiǎnsù, 減緩 jiǎnhuǎn.

December n. 十二月 Shí'èryuè.

decency n. 合宜 héyí, 得體 détǐ.

deception n. 欺騙 qīpiàn, 詐騙 zhàpiàn.

decibel n. 分貝 fēnbèi 〈physics〉.

decide v. 決定 juédìng.

deciduous adj. 落葉的 luòyè de 〈plant〉.

decimal adj. 十進的 shíjìn de. — n. ①十進位制 shíjìnwèizhì 〈system〉. ②小數點 xiǎoshùdiǎn 〈point〉.

decimate v. 大量毀滅 dàliàng huǐmiè.

decipher v. 解碼 jiěmǎ, 解謎 jiěmí.

decision n. ①決定 juédìng (choice). ②判決 pànjué (judgment).

deck n. 甲板 jiǎbǎn 〈floor〉.

declaration n. 宣言 xuānyán, 聲明 shēngmíng.

declare v. ①公告 gōnggào, 宣告 xuāngào (announce). ②聲明 shēngmíng, 聲稱 shēngchēng (assert). ③申報 shēnbào 〈Customs〉.

decline v. ①謝絕 xièjué (refuse). ②衰落 shuāiluò, 衰微 shuāiwēi / shuāiwéi (become weaker). — n. 衰落 shuāiluò, 衰弱 shuāiruò.

decode v. 解碼 jiěmǎ.

decompose v. ①分解 fēnjiě 〈into parts〉. ②腐爛 fǔlàn (decay).

decontaminate v. ①消除污染 xiāochú wūrǎn (clean). ②消毒 xiāodú (disinfect).

decorate v. ①裝飾 zhuāngshì, 布置 bùzhì (beautify). ②授勳 shòuxūn (honor).

decoration n. ①裝飾 zhuāngshì (decorating). ②裝飾品 zhuāngshìpǐn (adornment).

③勳章 xūnzhāng (medal).

decoy n. 誘餌 yòu'ěr (bait). — v. 引誘 yǐnyòu.

decrease n. & v. 減少 jiǎnshǎo.

decree n. ①法令 fǎlìng, 政令 zhènglìng (law). ②判決 pànjué (judgment). — v. 頒令 bānlìng, 規定 guīdìng.

decrepit adj. 衰老的 shuāilǎo de.

dedicate v. 奉獻 fèngxiàn, 貢獻 gòngxiàn (devote).

deduce v. 推論 tuīlùn, 演繹 yǎnyì (reach a conclusion).

deduct v. 扣除 kòuchú (take off), 減除 jiǎnchú (reduce).

deduction n. ①扣除 kòuchú ⟨taxes⟩. ②扣除額 kòuchú'é (amount deducted). ③推論 tuīlùn ⟨logic⟩.

deed n. ①行為 xíngwéi (behavior), 事蹟 shìjì (act). ②契約 qìyuē, 契書 qìshū (contract).

deep adj. ①深的 shēn de (not shallow). ②深刻的 shēnkè de (profound). ③專心的 zhuānxīn de (concentrating). ④深奧的 shēn'ào de (abstruse). ⑤濃厚的 nónghòu de (thick). ⑥深的 shēn de, 濃的 nóng de ⟨color⟩. ⑦低沉的 dīchén de ⟨voice⟩. — adv. 深深地 shēnshēn de.

deepen v. 加深 jiāshēn, 變深 biànshēn.

deer n. 鹿 lù.

deface v. 毀傷 huǐshāng (harm), 損毀 sǔnhuǐ (spoil the surface).

defame v. 誹謗 fěibàng, 中傷 zhòngshāng.

default n. & v. ①不履行 bù lǚxíng ⟨contract⟩. ②不還債 bù huánzhài ⟨debt⟩.

defeat n. & v. ①擊敗 jībài / jíbài (beating). ②受挫 shòucuò, 失敗 shībài (frustration).

defect n. 缺點 quēdiǎn, 缺陷 quēxiàn, 短處 duǎnchù.

defective adj. 有缺點的 yǒu quēdiǎn de (imperfect), 不健全的 bú jiànquán de (incomplete).

defend v. ①防禦 fángyù, 保護 bǎohù (protect). ②辯護 biànhù (justify).

defendant n. 被告 bèigào.

defense n. ①防禦 fángyù (protection). ②辯護 biànhù (justification).

defensive adj. ①防禦的 fángyù de (protective). ②辯解的 biànjiě de (apologetic).

defer v. ①延緩 yánhuǎn, 延期 yánqī / yánqí (delay). ②遵從 zūncóng (obey).

defiance n. ①違抗 wéikàng (disobedience). ②挑戰 tiǎozhàn (challenge).

deficient adj. 不足的 bùzú de, 缺乏的 quēfá de (lacking).

deficit n. 赤字 chìzì ⟨budget⟩, 不足額 bù zú'é ⟨amount⟩.

defile v. ①弄髒 nòngzāng (make dirty). ②玷污 diànwū (make impure).

define v. ①下定義 xià dìngyì (name), 闡釋 chǎnshì (explain). ②立界限 lì jièxiàn ⟨boundary⟩.

definite adj. ①明確的 míngquè de, 確定的 quèdìng de (set). ②清楚的 qīngchu de, 清晰的 qīngxī de (clear).

definition n. ①定義 dìngyì (explanation). ②清晰度 qīngxīdù (clarity).

definitive adj. ①最後的

zuìhòu de, 確定的 quèdìng de
(final). ②權威性的 quánwēixìng
de (authoritative).

deflate v. 放出空氣 fàngchū
kōngqì (let out air).

deflation n. 通貨緊縮
tōnghuò jǐnsuō.

deflect v. 使偏斜 shǐ piānxié,
使轉向 shǐ zhuǎnxiàng.

deform v. ①使變形 shǐ
biànxíng (put out of shape).
②使殘廢 shǐ cánfèi (distort).

deformed adj. 畸形 jīxíng.

defraud v. 騙取 piànqǔ, 詐取
zhàqǔ.

defrost v. 除冰 chúbīng, 除霜
chúshuāng (remove ice).

deft adj. 靈巧的 língqiǎo de
(skillful), 熟練的 shúliàn de
(practiced).

defunct adj. ①死的 sǐ de
(dead). ②不存在的 bù cúnzài
de (no longer existing).

defy v. ①公然反抗 gōngrán
fǎnkàng (resist openly). ②不服
從 bù fúcóng, 違抗 wéikàng
(disobey). ③挑 tiǎo, 激 jī
(challenge).

degenerate v. ①退步 tuìbù,
墮落 duòluò (deteriorate). ②退
化 tuìhuà (biological phenomena).

degrade v. 降級 jiàngjí
(demote).

degree n. ①程度 chéngdù, 等
級 děngjí (level). ②度 dù, 度數
dùshù (unit of measurement).
③階級 jiējí, 地位 dìwèi (rank).
④學位 xuéwèi (university).

dehydrate v. 脫水 tuōshuǐ, 使
乾燥 shǐ gānzào.

deign v. 屈尊 qūzūn, 俯就
fǔjiù.

deity n. ①神性 shénxìng
(divine nature). ②神 shén

(spirit).

dejected adj. 沮喪的 jǔsàng de.

delay v. ①耽擱 dānge, 延遲
yánchí (make late). ②延期
yánqī / yánqí (put off).

delectable adj. ①令人愉快的
lìng rén yúkuài de (delightful).
②可口的 kěkǒu de (delicious).

delegate n. 代表 dàibiǎo. — v.
①委派……為代表 wěipài...
wéi dàibiǎo (appoint). ②委託
wěituō (entrust).

delegation n. 代表團
dàibiǎotuán (group).

delete v. 刪除 shānchú, 去除
qùchú.

deliberate adj. ①故意的 gùyì
de (intentional). ②深思熟慮的
shēnsī-shúlǜ de (carefully con-
sidered). ③從容不迫的
cōngróng-bú-pò de (unhurried
and cautious). — v. 考慮 kǎolǜ.

delicacy n. ①精緻 jīngzhì, 優
美 yōuměi (daintiness). ②微妙
wēimiào / wéimiào (subtlety).
③靈敏 língmǐn (sensitivity).
④美食 měishí, 佳餚 jiāyáo
(good food).

delicate adj. ①易損的 yìsǔn
de, 脆弱的 cuìruò de (easily
broken). ②微妙的 wēimiào de /
wéimiào de, 靈巧的 língqiǎo
de (sensitive). ③精密的 jīngmì
de (precise).

delicious adj. 美味的 měiwèi
de, 好吃的 hǎochī de.

delight n. 欣喜 xīnxǐ, 愉快
yúkuài (joy). — v. 使愉快 shǐ
yúkuài.

delighted adj. 愉快的 yúkuài
de.

delightful adj. 令人愉快的
lìng rén yúkuài de (very
pleasant).

delinquent adj. 失職的 shīzhí de (failing to perform a duty). — n. 犯罪少年 fànzuì shàonián.

delirious adj. 狂亂的 kuángluàn de (wild), 狂言 囈語的 kuángyán yìyǔ de (incoherent).

delirium n. 精神錯亂 jīngshén cuòluàn, 囈語 yìyǔ.

deliver v. ①遞送 dìsòng (hand over). ②陳述 chénshù, 發表 fābiǎo (speech).

delivery n. ①遞送 dìsòng (delivering). ②演說技巧 yǎnshuō jìqiǎo (skill in giving a speech). ③分娩 fēnmiǎn (childbirth).

Delta n. 希臘字母 Xīlà zìmǔ (Greek letter).

delta n. 三角洲 sānjiǎozhōu (mouth of a river).

delude v. 欺騙 qīpiàn (cheat), 迷惑 míhuo (confuse).

deluge n. ①大水災 dà shuǐzāi (great flood). ②大量湧至 dàliàng yǒng zhì (coming in a heavy rush).

delusion n. 幻想 huànxiǎng (false belief).

deluxe adj. 豪華的 háohuá de.

delve v. 鑽研 zuānyán (search deeply).

demand n. & v. ①要求 yāoqiú (request). ②需求 xūqiú, 需要 xūyào (need).

demarcate v. 定界線 dìng jièxiàn, 劃界 huàjiè (mark the limits of).

demeanor n. 行為 xíngwéi (behavior), 態度 tàidu (attitude).

demented adj. 瘋狂的 fēngkuáng de, 發狂的 fākuáng de (crazy).

democracy n. ①民主主義 mínzhǔ zhǔyì (idea). ②民主政治 mínzhǔ zhèngzhì (system). ③民主國家 mínzhǔ guójiā (nation).

democrat n. ①民主主義者 mínzhǔ zhǔyì zhě (advocate). ②民主黨人 mínzhǔdǎng rén (party member).

demolish v. ①拆除 chāichú, 破壞 pòhuài (destroy). ②推翻 tuīfān (tear down).

demon n. 惡魔 èmó.

demonstrate v. ①示範 shìfàn (show). ②證明 zhèngmíng (prove). ③表明 biǎomíng (make known). ④示威 shìwēi (oppose publicly).

demonstrative adj. 感情流露的 gǎnqíng liúlù de (showing feelings openly).

demoralize v. 使士氣低落 shǐ shìqì dīluò (dishearten).

demure adj. ①假正經的 jiǎzhèngjing de (pretending to be shy). ②嚴謹的 yánjǐn de, 端莊的 duānzhuāng de (serious).

denial n. ①否認 fǒurèn (not admitting). ②拒絕 jùjué (refusal).

denomination n. ①名稱 míngchēng (name). ②單位 dānwèi (unit). ③宗派 zōngpài, 派別 pàibié (religious sect).

denominator n. 分母 fēnmǔ.

denote v. 表示 biǎoshì (express), 意謂 yìwèi (hint at).

denounce v. 指責 zhǐzé, 譴責 qiǎnzé (blame).

dense adj. ①濃密的 nóngmì de (liquid or air). ②稠密的 chóumì de (people). ③愚鈍的 yúdùn de (stupid).

density n. ①密度 mìdù (physics). ②濃密 nóngmì

⟨consistency⟩.

dent n. 凹陷 āoxiàn, 凹痕 āohén. — v. 使凹陷 shǐ āoxiàn.

dental adj. 牙齒的 yáchǐ de.

dentist n. 牙醫 yáyī.

denunciation n. ①譴責 qiǎnzé (reproval). ②告發 gàofā (declaring untrue).

deny v. ①否認 fǒurèn (declare untrue). ②拒絕 jùjué (refuse).

deodorant n. 防臭劑 fángchòujì.

depart v. 出發 chūfā (start out), 離開 líkāi (leave).

department n. ①部門 bùmén (division). ②系 xì, 科 kē ⟨university⟩. ~ **store** 百貨公司 bǎihuò gōngsī.

departure n. 出發 chūfā, 離去 líqù (the act of leaving).

depend v. ①依賴 yīlài, 依靠 yīkào (rely on). ②信賴 xìnlài (trust).

dependence n. ①依賴 yīlài, 依靠 yīkào (reliance). ②信賴 xìnlài, 信任 xìnrèn (trust).

dependent adj. ①依賴的 yīlài de (depending). ②視……而定 shì...ér dìng, 取決於…… qǔjué yú... (conditional on). — n. 眷屬 juànshǔ, 被扶養人 bèi fúyǎngrén (relative).

depict v. 描繪 miáohuì (describe), 描寫 miáoxiě (capture).

deplete v. ①用盡 yòngjìn, 耗盡 hàojìn (use up). ②使空虛 shǐ kōngxū (weaken).

deplore v. 悲痛 bēitòng, 哀嘆 āitàn.

deport v. 驅逐出境 qūzhú chū jìng.

depose v. 罷黜 bàchù, 免職 miǎnzhí (dethrone). ②作證

zuòzhèng (give evidence).

deposit v. ①存放 cúnfàng, 置放 zhìfàng (place). ②儲存 chǔcún / chúcún, 存入 cúnrù (save). ③淤積 yūjī, 沈澱 chéndiàn (precipitate). ④付定金 fù dìngjīn (pay down payment). — n. ①沈澱物 chéndiànwù (precipitate). ②定金 dìngjīn, 押金 yājīn (down payment). ③存款 cúnkuǎn (savings).

depot n. ①倉庫 cāngkù, 庫房 kùfáng (storehouse). ②火車站 huǒchēzhàn ⟨train⟩, 公車站 gōngchēzhàn ⟨bus⟩.

depraved adj. 墮落的 duòluò de, 敗壞的 bàihuài de.

depreciate v. 貶值 biǎnzhí (fall in value).

depress v. ①使沮喪 shǐ jǔsàng (discourage). ②使蕭條 shǐ xiāotiáo (make less active).

depression n. ①憂鬱 yōuyù, 沮喪 jǔsàng (dejection). ②不景氣 bù jǐngqì, 蕭條 xiāotiáo (decline). ③窪穴 wāxué / wāxuè, 坑 kēng (indentation). ④憂鬱症 yōuyùzhèng ⟨disease⟩. ⑤低氣壓 dī qìyā (low pressure).

deprive v. 剝奪 bōduó, 使喪失 shǐ sàngshī (take away from).

deprived adj. ①貧困的 pínkùn de (poor). ②被剝奪的 bèi bōduó de (be taken away).

depth n. 深 shēn, 深度 shēndù.

deputy n. 代理人 dàilǐrén, 代表 dàibiǎo.

derail v. 使出軌 shǐ chūguǐ.

derivation n. ①起源 qǐyuán, 由來 yóulái (origin). ②字源 zìyuán (origin of a word).

D

derive v. ①獲得 huòdé, 得到 dédào (get). ②源於 yuányú, 引出 yǐnchū (originate from).

descend v. 下降 xiàjiàng, 落下 luòxià (go down).

descent n. ①斜坡 xiépō (decline). ②血統 xuètǒng / xiětǒng (ancestry).

describe v. ①敘述 xùshù (depict). ②描寫 miáoxiě, 描繪 miáohuì (portray).

description n. 敘述 xùshù, 描述 miáoshù (depiction).

desecrate v. 褻瀆 xièdú, 污辱 wūrù / wūrù.

desegregate v. 取消種族隔離 qǔxiāo zhǒngzú gélí.

desert n. & adj. 沙漠 shāmò. — v. ①放棄 fàngqì, 拋棄 pāoqì (abandon). ②潛逃 qiántáo (run away from).

deserve v. 應得 yīngdé, 應受 yīngshòu.

design n. ①設計 shèjì ⟨drawing⟩. ②圖案 tú'àn (pattern). ③目的 mùdì, 企圖 qìtú / qìtú (intention). — v. ①設計 shèjì (draw). ②打算 dǎsuan, 計畫 jìhuà (plan).

designate v. ①指示 zhǐshì, 指明 zhǐmíng (point out). ②指派 zhǐpài, 指定 zhǐdìng (appoint).

desirable adj. 合意的 héyì de, 渴望的 kěwàng de.

desire v. ①想要 xiǎngyào, 渴望 kěwàng (wish). ②要求 yāoqiú, 請求 qǐngqiú (request).

desk n. 書桌 shūzhuō.

desolate adj. ①荒蕪的 huāngwú de, 荒廢的 huāngfèi de (deserted). ②孤寂的 gūjì de / gūjí de (friendless). — v. ①使荒涼 shǐ huāngliáng (make desolate). ②使孤寂 shǐ gūjì /

shǐ gūjí (make lonely).

despair n. & v. 失望 shīwàng, 絕望 juéwàng.

desperate adj. ①絕望的 juéwàng de (hopeless). ②危急的 wēijí de / wéijí de, 嚴重的 yánzhòng de (serious).

despise v. 輕視 qīngshì, 蔑視 mièshì.

despite prep. 不管 bùguǎn, 儘管 jǐnguǎn.

despot n. 獨裁者 dúcáizhě, 暴君 bàojūn.

dessert n. 甜點 tiándiǎn.

destination n. 目的地 mùdìdì.

destiny n. 命運 mìngyùn.

destitute adj. 貧困的 pínkùn de.

destroy v. 破壞 pòhuài, 毀壞 huǐhuài (ruin).

destruction n. 破壞 pòhuài, 毀壞 huǐhuài.

detach v. 分開 fēnkāi, 解開 jiěkāi.

detail n. 細節 xìjié, 詳情 xiángqíng.

detain v. ①耽誤 dānwù, 耽擱 dāngē (keep waiting). ②拘留 jūliú (hold in custody).

detect v. 發現 fāxiàn, 查出 cháchū.

detective n. 偵探 zhēntàn.

detention n. 拘留 jūliú, 留置 liúzhì.

deter v. 阻止 zǔzhǐ, 阻嚇 zǔhè.

detergent n. 清潔劑 qīngjiéjì.

deteriorate v. 變壞 biànhuài, 惡化 èhuà.

determination n. 決心 juéxīn, 決定 juédìng (firm intention).

determine v. 決定 juédìng, 下決心 xià juéxīn.

determined adj. 堅決的 jiānjué de.

deterrent adj. 阻礙的 zǔ'ài de. — n. 阻礙物 zǔ'àiwù.

detest v. 憎惡 zēngwù, 痛恨 tònghèn.

dethrone v. 廢黜 fèichù, 罷黜 bàchù.

detonate v. 爆炸 bàozhà, 爆裂 bàoliè.

detour n. 迂迴道 yūhuídào.

detract v. 減損 jiǎnsǔn.

detriment n. 損害 sǔnhài, 傷害 shānghài.

devastate v. 使荒廢 shǐ huāngfèi.

develop v. ①發展 fāzhǎn (grow), 培育 péiyù (nurture). ②開發 kāifā (make use of). ③沖洗 chōngxǐ (film).

developed adj. 已發展的 yǐ fāzhǎn de. ~ *countries* 發達國家 fādá guójiā / 已開發國家 yǐ kāifā guójiā.

development n. 發展 fāzhǎn (growth), 開發 kāifā (potential).

deviate v. 偏離 piānlí.

device n. ①裝置 zhuāngzhì, 設備 shèbèi (apparatus). ②策略 cèlüè, 詭計 guǐjì (gimmick).

devil n. 惡魔 èmó, 魔鬼 móguǐ.

devious adj. ①迂迴的 yūhuí de (circuitous). ②不誠實的 bù chéngshí de (deceitful).

devise v. 設計 shèjì, 策畫 cèhuà, 發明 fāmíng (plan or invent).

devote v. 奉獻於 fèngxiàn yú, 專心於 zhuānxīn yú.

devoted adj. 忠實的 zhōngshí de.

devotion n. ①奉獻 fèngxiàn, 致力 zhìlì (contribution). ②熱愛 rè'ài (strong love).

devour v. ①狼吞虎嚥 lángtūn-hǔyàn (eat). ②毀滅 huǐmiè (destroy).

devout adj. 虔敬的 qiánjìng de, 忠誠的 zhōngchéng de.

dew n. 露 lù, 露珠 lùzhū.

diabetes n. 糖尿病 tángniàobìng.

diabolic adj. 惡魔的 èmó de, 兇殘的 xiōngcán de.

diagnose v. 診斷 zhěnduàn.

diagonal n. & adj. ①對角線 duìjiǎoxiàn (line). ②斜紋 xiéwén (pattern).

diagram n. 圖解 tújiě.

dial n. ①針盤 zhēnpán (marked face). ②號碼盤 hàomǎpán (phone). — v. 撥電話 bō diànhuà.

dialect n. 方言 fāngyán.

dialogue n. 對話 duìhuà.

diameter n. 直徑 zhíjìng.

diamond n. ①鑽石 zuànshí (stone). ②菱形 língxíng (shape). ③方塊 fāngkuài (cards).

diaper n. 尿布 niàobù.

diarrhea n. 腹瀉 fùxiè, 拉肚子 lā dùzi.

diary n. 日記 rìjì.

dice n. 骰子 shǎizi.

dictate v. ①口述 kǒushù (read). ②命令 mìnglìng (give orders).

dictation n. ①口述 kǒushù (reading). ②聽寫 tīngxiě (write down another's speech).

dictator n. 獨裁者 dúcáizhě.

dictionary n. 字典 zìdiǎn, 辭典 cídiǎn.

die v. ①死 sǐ, 死亡 sǐwáng (pass away). ②枯萎 kūwěi / kūwēi (wither).

diesel n. 柴油 cháiyóu.

diet n. 飲食 yǐnshí, 食物 shíwù (food). — v. 節食 jiéshí.

differ v. ①相異 xiāngyì, 不同 bù tóng (be different). ②意見相左 yìjiàn xiāngzuǒ, 不合 bùhé (disagree).

difference n. ①差別 chābié, 差異 chāyì, 不同 bù tóng (discrepancy). ②意見相左 yìjiàn xiāngzuǒ, 不合 bùhé (disagreement).

different adj. 不同的 bù tóng de, 相異的 xiāngyì de.

differentiate v. 區分 qūfēn, 辨別 biànbié.

difficult adj. 困難的 kùnnán de (hard), 費力的 fèilì de (tiring).

difficulty n. 困難 kùnnán.

diffuse v. 擴散 kuòsàn, 廣布 guǎngbù. — adj. ①散布的 sànbù de, 擴散的 kuòsàn de (spread out). ②冗長的 rǒngcháng de (using too many words).

dig v. 挖掘 wājué, 挖 wā (burrow). ②戳 chuō, 刺 cì (poke). — n. 戳 chuō, 刺 cì.

digest v. ①消化 xiāohuà 〈food〉. ②了解 liǎojiě 〈information〉.

digestion n. 消化力 xiāohuàlì.

digit n. ①數字 shùzì (number). ②手指 shǒuzhǐ (finger). ③足趾 zúzhǐ (toe).

dignified adj. 高貴的 gāoguì de, 尊嚴的 zūnyán de.

dignity n. ①高貴 gāoguì, 高尚 gāoshàng (nobleness). ②威嚴 wēiyán, 尊嚴 zūnyán (calm stateliness).

digress v. 離題 lítí.

dike n. ①堤 dī / tí (embankment),

水壩 shuǐbà (dam). ②溝 gōu, 渠 qú (ditch).

dilapidated adj. 倒塌的 dǎotā de, 殘破的 cánpò de.

dilate v. 使膨脹 shǐ péngzhàng, 使擴大 shǐ kuòdà (enlarge).

dilemma n. 進退兩難 jìn-tuì-liǎng-nán.

diligence n. 勤勉 qínmiǎn, 勤奮 qínfèn.

dilute v. 稀釋 xīshì, 沖淡 chōngdàn. — adj. 稀釋的 xīshì de, 淡的 dàn de.

dim adj. 微暗的 wēi'àn de / wéi'àn de (not bright), 模糊的 móhu de (not clear). — v. 使暗淡 shǐ àndàn.

dime n. 一角硬幣 yìjiǎo yìngbì.

dimension n. 尺寸 chǐcùn, 大小 dàxiǎo.

diminish v. 減少 jiǎnshǎo, 縮小 suōxiǎo.

diminutive adj. 小的 xiǎo de, 特別小的 tèbié xiǎo de.

dimple n. 酒渦 jiǔwō. — v. 出現酒渦 chūxiàn jiǔwō.

din n. 喧嘩聲 xuānhuáshēng, 嘈雜聲 cáozáshēng. — v. 喧嘩 xuānhuá, 吵鬧 chǎonào.

dine v. 用餐 yòngcān, 吃飯 chīfàn.

dinghy n. 小艇 xiǎotǐng.

dingy adj. 骯髒的 āngzāng de.

dining room n. 飯廳 fàntīng.

Dinky n. 丁克族 Dīngkèzú / 頂克族 Dǐngkèzú.

dinner n. ①晚餐 wǎncān (evening meal). ②宴會 yànhuì, 餐宴 cānyàn (banquet).

dinosaur n. 恐龍 kǒnglóng.

diocese n. 教區 jiàoqū.

D

dip v. ①沾 zhān (douse). ②掬
取 jū / jú, 汲取 jíqǔ (put and take
out). ③下降 xiàjiàng, 下沈
xiàchén (descend). — n. 斜坡
xiépō (slope).

diploma n. 文憑 wénpíng, 畢
業證書 bìyè zhèngshū.

diplomacy n. ①外交 wàijiāo
〈international relations〉. ②外交
手腕 wàijiāo shǒuwàn
(diplomatic skill).

diplomat n. 外交官
wàijiāoguān.

diplomatic adj. ①外交的
wàijiāo de (of diplomacy).
②有外交手腕的 yǒu wàijiāo
shǒuwàn de (tactful).

dire adj. ①可怕的 kěpà de
(terrible). ②迫切的 pòqiè de
(urgent).

direct v. ①指示 zhǐshì, 指引
zhǐyǐn (guide). ②指導 zhǐdǎo /
zhǐdào, 管理 guǎnlǐ (administer). — adj. ①直的 zhí de
(straight). ②直接的 zhíjiē de
(straightforward).

direction n. ①方向 fāngxiàng
(way). ②指導 zhǐdǎo / zhǐdào,
指示 zhǐshì (guidance).

directly adv. 直接地 zhíjiē de.

director n. ①指導者
zhǐdǎozhě / zhídàozhě
(leader). ②董事 dǒngshì
〈business〉. ③導演 dǎoyǎn
〈movies〉.

directory n. 通訊錄 tōngxùnlù
(a book of names).

dirt n. ①泥土 nítǔ (soil). ②污垢
wūgòu (unclean matter). ③閒話
xiánhuà, 八卦 bāguà (gossip).

dirty adj. 髒的 zāng de, 不潔
的 bù jié de. ~ **trick** 卑鄙的行
為 bēibǐ de xíngwéi. — v.
弄髒 nòngzāng.

disability n. 無能力 wú
nénglì 〈law〉.

disable v. 使無能 shǐ wúnéng,
使殘廢 shǐ cánfèi (make
incapable).

disadvantage n. ①不利 búlì
(unfavorable condition). ②缺點
quēdiǎn (weakness).

disagree v. 不同意 bù tóngyì,
意見不合 yìjiàn bù hé.

disappear v. 消失 xiāoshī.

disappoint v. 使失望 shǐ
shīwàng.

disappointment n. 失望
shīwàng.

disapproval n. 反對 fǎnduì,
不贊成 bú zànchéng.

disapprove v. 不准許 bù
zhǔnxǔ.

disarm v. 繳械 jiǎoxiè, 解除
武裝 jiěchú wǔzhuāng.

disarray n. 雜亂 záluàn, 無秩
序 wú zhìxù.

disaster n. 災禍 zāihuò, 大災
難 dà zāinàn.

disband v. 解散 jiěsàn.

disbelieve v. 不相信 bù
xiāngxìn, 懷疑 huáiyí.

discard v. 拋棄 pāoqì, 放棄
fàngqì.

discern v. 察覺 chájué
(discover), 辨識 biànshí /
biànshì (distinguish).

discharge n. & v. ①排出
páichū (send out). ②發射 fāshè
〈guns〉. ③解雇 jiěgù, 開除
kāichú 〈employees〉. ④釋放
shìfàng (let off). ⑤卸貨 xièhuò
(unload). ⑥執行 zhíxíng 〈of
one's duty〉. ⑦償還 chánghuán
〈of one's debts〉.

disciple n. 門徒 méntú, 弟子
dìzǐ.

discipline n. ①紀律 jìlǜ

(order). ②訓練 xùnliàn (training). — v. ①訓練 xùnliàn
(train). ②懲罰 chéngfá (punish).

disclaim v. 否認 fǒurèn.

disclose v. 揭發 jiēfā (reveal),
洩露 xièlòu (make known).

disco n. 迪斯科舞廳 dísīkē
wǔtīng / 迪斯可舞廳 dísīkě
wǔtīng.

discolor v. (使) 變色 (shǐ)
biànsè, (使) 褪色 (shǐ)
tuìsè / (shǐ) tùnsè.

discomfort n. 不舒適 bù
shūshì, 不安 bù'ān.

disconcert v. ①使不安
shǐ bù'ān (feel anxiety). ②擾亂
rǎoluàn (upset).

disconnect v. 使分離 shǐ
fēnlí, 切斷 qiēduàn.

disconsolate adj. 憂悶的
yōumèn de, 哀傷的 āishāng de.

discontent n. 不滿 bùmǎn.

discontinue v. 停止 tíngzhǐ,
終止 zhōngzhǐ.

discord n. ①不一致 bù yízhì
(disagreement). ②爭論
zhēnglùn (argument). ③不和諧
bù héxié ⟨sound⟩.

discordant adj. 不和諧的 bù
héxié de, 嘈雜的 cáozá de.

discount v. 打折扣 dǎ zhékòu,
貼現 tiēxiàn. — n. 折扣
zhékòu, 減價 jiǎnjià.

discourage v. ①使氣餒 shǐ
qìněi, 使沮喪 shǐ jǔsàng (dishearten). ②勸阻 quànzǔ (deter).

discourteous adj. 失禮的
shīlǐ de, 粗魯的 cūlǔ de.

discover v. 發現 fāxiàn.

discovery n. 發現 fāxiàn.

discredit v. ①使玷辱 shǐ
diànrǔ / shǐ jùdrùn, 使不名譽
shǐ bù míngyù (defame). ②懷

疑 huáiyí, 不信任 bú xìnrèn
(disbelieve). — n. ①恥辱 chǐrǔ
/ chǐrǔ, 不名譽 bù míngyù
(disgrace). ②不信任 bú xìnrèn
(loss of belief).

discreet adj. 謹慎的 jǐnshèn
de, 慎重的 shènzhòng de.

discretion n. ①謹慎 jǐnshèn
(being discreet). ②自由選擇
zìyóu xuǎnzé, 自由決定 zìyóu
juédìng (freedom to act).

discriminate v. ①區別
qūbié, 辨別 biànbié (distinguish). ②歧視 qíshì, 差別待遇
chābié dàiyù (be biased).

discus n. 鐵餅 tiěbǐng.

discuss v. 討論 tǎolùn, 議論
yìlùn.

discussion n. 討論 tǎolùn, 議
論 yìlùn.

disdain n. & v. 輕視 qīngshì,
輕蔑 qīngmiè.

disease n. 疾病 jíbìng.

disembark v. 登岸 dēng'àn, 登
陸 dēnglù.

disengage v. ①釋放 shìfàng,
解脫 jiětuō (release). ②使解開
shǐ jiěkāi, 使脫離 shǐ tuōlí
(loosen).

disentangle v. ①解開 jiěkāi
(unknot). ②鬆開 sōngkāi
(release).

disfigure v. 毀容 huǐróng, 損
毀外觀 sǔnhuǐ wàiguān.

disgrace n. & v. 不名譽 bù
míngyù, 丟臉 diūliǎn, 恥辱
chǐrǔ / chǐrǔ.

disgruntled adj. 不高興的
bù gāoxìng de, 不滿的
bùmǎn de.

disguise n. & v. 假裝
jiǎzhuāng, 偽裝 wěizhuāng /
wěizhuāng.

disgust n. 厭惡 yànwù, 憎惡

zēngwù. — v. 使厭惡 shǐ
yànwù.

disgusting adj. 令人厭惡的
lìng rén yànwù de, 令人作嘔
的 lìng rén zuò'ǒu de.

dish n. ①碟 dié, 盤 pán (plate).
②食物 shíwù, 菜餚 càiyáo
(food).

dishearten v. 使沮喪 shǐ
jǔsàng, 使氣餒 shǐ qìněi.

disheveled adj. 蓬亂的
péngluàn de.

dishonest adj. 不誠實的 bù
chéngshí de.

dishonor n. 不名譽 bù
míngyù, 恥辱 chǐrù / chǐrù.
— v. ①侮辱 wǔrù / wǔrù, 使蒙
羞 shǐ méngxiū (disgrace).
②拒付 jùfù (bank).

disillusion n. & v. 醒悟
xǐngwù.

disinfect v. 消毒 xiāodú, 殺菌
shājūn / shājùn.

disinfectant n. 消毒劑
xiāodújì.

disinherit v. 剝奪繼承權
bōduó jìchéngquán.

disintegrate v. 崩潰 bēngkuì
(collapse), 瓦解 wǎjiě (lose
unity).

disinterested adj. 公正的
gōngzhèng de (impartial).

disk n. ①圓盤 yuánpán (flat
plate). ②磁盤 cípán / 磁碟片
cídiépiàn (computer).
~ drive 磁盤驅動器 cípán
qūdòngqì / 磁碟機 cídiéjī
(computer).

dislike n. & v. 嫌惡 xiánwù,
厭惡 yànwù.

dislocate v. 使脫臼 shǐ tuōjiù
(bone).

dislodge v. 逐出 zhúchū
(remove), 移出 yíchū (move).

disloyal adj. 不忠的 bù zhōng
de, 不貞的 bù zhēn de, 背叛
的 bèipàn de.

dismal adj. 憂鬱的 yōuyù de,
愁悶的 chóumèn de.

dismantle v. 拆除 chāichú,
拆卸 chāixiè.

dismay n. & v. 驚慌
jīnghuāng, 恐懼 kǒngjù (fear),
沮喪 jǔsàng (hopelessness).

dismember v. ①肢解 zhījiě
(cut apart). ②瓜分 guāfēn, 分
割 fēngē (divide up).

dismiss v. ①解散 jiěsàn (let
go). ②解僱 jiěgù, 開除 kāichú
(fire). ③撇開 piēkāi (put away).

dismount v. 下馬 xiàmǎ (get
down).

disobey v. 違抗 wéikàng, 不
服從 bù fúcóng.

disorder n. ①混亂 hùnluàn /
hùnluàn, 紊亂 wěnluàn /
wènluàn (confusion). ②騷動
sāodòng, 騷亂 sāoluàn (riot).
③疾病 jíbìng (disease).

disorganize v. 破壞 pòhuài,
擾亂 rǎoluàn.

disown v. 否認有關係 fǒurèn
yǒu guānxì.

dispatch v. ①發送 fāsòng
(send off). ②一下子就完成
(工作) yíxiàzi jiù wánchéng
(gōngzuò) (finish quickly).
③處決 chǔjué (kill). — n. ①打
發 dǎfā (dispatching), 發 fā
(sending). ②電訊 diànxùn
(message).

dispel v. 驅散 qūsàn.

dispense v. ①施予 shīyǔ
(give), 分配 fēnpèi (allocate).
②配藥 pèiyào (medicine).

disperse v. 使分散 shǐ
fēnsàn, 使解散 shǐ jiěsàn.
— v. 分散 fēnsàn, 散開 sànkāi.

displace v. 取代 qǔdài，替代 tìdài，置換 zhìhuàn (replace).

display n. & v. ①陳列 chénliè，展示 zhǎnshì (show).②顯露 xiǎnlù，表現 biǎoxiàn (become visible).

displease v. 惹……生氣 rě... shēngqì，使不悅 shǐ bú yuè.

disposable adj. 用後可丟棄 的 yòng hòu kě diūqì de. ~ *chopsticks* 衛生筷 wèishēngkuài / 免洗筷 miǎnxǐkuài.

disposal n. 安排 ānpái，處置 chǔzhì.

dispose v. ①處理 chǔlǐ，處置 chǔzhì (deal with).②佈置 bùzhì，安排 ānpái (arrange).

dispossess v. 強奪 qiángduó，霸佔 bàzhàn.

disprove v. 駁斥 bóchì，反證 fǎnzhèng.

dispute n. & v. ①爭論 zhēnglùn，爭吵 zhēngchǎo (argument). ②反駁 fǎnbó (disagreement).

disqualify v. 取消資格 qǔxiāo zīgé.

disregard n. & v. 忽視 hūshì，不理 bù lǐ.

disrepair n. 失修 shīxiū.

disrepute n. 不名譽 bù míngyù，壞名聲 huài míngshēng.

disrespect n. 不敬 bújìng，無禮 wúlǐ.

disrupt v. ①分裂 fēnliè，瓦解 wǎjiě (break up).②中斷 zhōngduàn (disturb).

dissatisfy v. 使不滿 shǐ bùmǎn.

dissect v. ①解剖 jiěpōu / jiěpǒu (cut up).②詳細研究 xiángxì yánjiū / xiángxì yánjiù，剖析 pōuxī / pǒuxī (analyze).

disseminate v. 傳播 chuánbō / chuánbò，散布 sànbù.

dissent n. & v. 反對 fǎnduì，有異議 yǒu yìyì.

dissertation n. 論文 lùnwén.

dissociate v. 分離 fēnlí，分開 fēnkāi.

dissolve v. ①溶解 róngjiě (become liquid).②解散 jiěsàn，解除 jiěchú (break up).

dissuade v. 勸阻 quànzǔ.

distance n. 距離 jùlí. ~ *learning* 遙距教學 yáojù jiāoxué / 遠距教學 yuǎnjù jiāoxué.

distant adj. ①遙遠的 yáoyuǎn de (far).②冷淡的 lěngdàn de，疏遠的 shūyuǎn de (aloof).

distaste n. 嫌惡 xiánwù，憎厭 zēngyàn.

distill v. 蒸餾 zhēngliú / zhēngliù.

distinct adj. ①清楚的 qīngchu de，清晰的 qīngxī de (clear).②分別的 fēnbié de，不同的 bù tóng de (different).

distinction n. ①區別 qūbié，差別 chābié (difference).②優越 yōuyuè，卓越 zhuōyuè / zhuóyuè (excellence).③特徵 tèzhēng，特性 tèxìng (quality of being unusual).

distinguish v. ①區別 qūbié，辨別 biànbié (differentiate).②看出來 kànchūlái (recognize).

distinguished adj. 著名的 zhùmíng de (well known)，卓越的 zhuōyuè de / zhuóyuè (excellent).

distort v. ①使變形 shǐ biànxíng，扭曲 niǔqū (twist). ②曲解 qūjiě，歪曲 wāiqū (falsify).

distract v. ①使分心 shǐ

D

D

fēnxīn (divide attention). ②使
心煩 shǐ xīnfán, 使困擾 shǐ
kùnrǎo (trouble).
distraught *adj.* 精神錯亂的
jīngshén cuòluàn de.
distress *n.* 痛苦 tòngkǔ, 憂傷
yōushāng (anguish). — *v.* 使
痛苦 shǐ tòngkǔ, 使苦惱 shǐ
kǔnǎo.
distribute *v.* ①分發 fēnfā, 分
配 fēnpèi (allocate). ②散布
sànbù, 分布 fēnbù (spread out).
distribution *n.* ①分發 fēnfā,
分配 fēnpèi (allocation).
②散布 sànbù, 分布 fēnbù
(spreading).
district *n.* 地區 dìqū, 區域
qūyù.
distrust *n.* & *v.* 不信任 bú
xìnrèn, 懷疑 huáiyí.
disturb *v.* ①打擾 dǎrǎo,
騷擾 sāorǎo (bother). ②弄亂
nòngluàn, 擾亂 rǎoluàn
(disorder).
ditch *n.* 壕溝 háogōu, 溝渠
gōuqú. — *v.* ①挖壕溝 wā
háogōu (make a ditch). ②丟棄
diūqì, 捨棄 shěqì (abandon).
ditto *n.* 同上 tóngshàng, 同前
tóngqián.
ditty *n.* 小曲 xiǎoqǔ, 歌謠
gēyáo.
dive *n.* & *v.* ①俯衝 fǔchōng,
驟降 zhòujiàng / zòujiàng (go
down steeply and speedily). ②跳
水 tiàoshuǐ ⟨water⟩.
diver *n.* 潛水者 qiánshuǐzhě.
diverge *v.* ①分岔 fēnchà
⟨roads⟩. ②分歧 fēnqí ⟨opinions⟩.
diverse *adj.* 不同的 bù tóng
de (different), 多元化的
duōyuánhuà de (varied).
diversify *v.* 多樣化
duōyànghuà.

diversion *n.* ①娛樂 yúlè, 消
遣 xiāoqiǎn (amusement). ②轉
移 zhuǎnyí, 轉向 zhuǎnxiàng
(turning).
divert *v.* ①使轉向 shǐ
zhuǎnxiàng (change direction).
②消遣 xiāoqiǎn, 娛樂 yúlè
(amuse).
divide *v.* ①分開 fēnkāi,
劃分 huàfēn (separate). ②分配
fēnpèi (allocate). ③除 chú
⟨mathematics⟩. ④分類 fēnlèi
(categorize).
dividend *n.* ①股息 gǔxī / gǔxí
⟨stocks⟩. ②被除數 bèichúshù
⟨mathematics⟩.
divine *adj.* ①神的 shén de
(God-like). ②極好的 jí hǎo de
(excellent).
divinity *n.* ①神性 shénxìng
(state of being divine). ②神學
shénxué (religious studies).
division *n.* ①分配 fēnpèi, 劃
分 huàfēn (allocation). ②不和
bùhé (disagreement). ③分界線
fēnjièxiàn (boundary). ④部門
bùmén, 組 zǔ (department).
⑤除法 chúfǎ ⟨mathematics⟩.
divorce *n.* & *v.* ①離婚 líhūn
(ending of a marriage). ②分離
fēnlí, 分裂 fēnliè (separation).
divulge *v.* 洩露 xièlòu.
DIY 自己動手做 zìjǐ dòngshǒu
zuò.
dizzy *adj.* 暈眩的 yùnxuàn de /
yūnxuàn de, 頭昏眼花的
tóuhūn-yǎnhuā de.
do *v.* ①做 zuò (carry out). ②完
成 wánchéng (finish).
docile *adj.* 溫順的 wēnshùn
de, 馴良的 xùnliáng de /
xúnliáng de.
dock *n.* 船塢 chuánwù, 碼頭
mǎtou.

doctor n. ①醫生 yīshēng
‹medical›. ②博士 bóshì
(Ph.D.).

doctrine n. 教條 jiàotiáo,
教義 jiàoyì ‹religion›,學說
xuéshuō (theory).

document n. 文件 wénjiàn,
公文 gōngwén (paper),證件
zhèngjiàn (proof).

documentary adj. 文件的
wénjiàn de. — n. 紀錄片
jìlùpiàn.

dodge n. & v. 躲閃 duǒkāi,閃
避 shǎnbì.

doe n. ①雌鹿 cílù ‹deer›. ②雌
兔 cítù ‹rabbit›.

dog n. 狗 gǒu,犬 quǎn.

dogged adj. 頑強的 wánqiáng
de,固執的 gùzhí de.

dogma n. 教條 jiàotiáo,教義
jiàoyì (belief).

dole v. 救濟 jiùjì,布施 bùshī.
— n. ①救濟 jiùjì,布施 bùshī
(giving out). ②救濟品 jiùjìpǐn,
布施物 bùshīwù (something
doled out).

doll n. 洋娃娃 yángwáwa,玩
偶 wán'ǒu.

dollar n. 元 yuán,圓 yuán.

dolphin n. 海豚 hǎitún.

domain n. ①領土 lǐngtǔ,版圖
bǎntú (territory). ②領域
lǐngyù,範圍 fànwéi (sphere).

dome n. 圓頂 yuándǐng,圓蓋
yuángài.

domestic adj. ①家庭的 jiātíng
de (family). ②國內的 guónèi
de (native). ③人工飼養的
réngōng sìyǎng de (not wild).

dominant adj. ①支配的
zhīpèi de (dominating). ②較強
的 jiào qiáng de (stronger).

dominate v. 統治 tǒngzhì,
支配 zhīpèi (control).

domineer v. 擅權 shànquán,
跋扈 báhù.

dominion n. ①統治權
tǒngzhìquán,支配權
zhīpèiquán (authority). ②領土
lǐngtǔ,版圖 bǎntú (territory).

domino n. ⟨pl.⟩ 骨牌 gǔpái
‹game›. ~ effect 多米諾效應
duōmǐnuò xiàoyìng / 骨牌效應
gǔpái xiàoyìng.

donate v. 捐贈 juānzèng.

donkey n. 驢 lǘ.

donor n. 捐贈者 juānzèngzhě.

doom n. ①命運 mìngyùn,
註定 zhùdìng (fate). ②死亡
sǐwáng,劫數 jiéshù (death).

door n. 門 mén,戶 hù (gate).

doorstep n. 門階 ménjiē.

doorway n. 門口 ménkǒu,出
入口 chūrùkǒu.

dope n. ①麻藥 máyào,大麻
dàmá (marijuana). ②笨蛋
bèndàn (idiot). — v. 下麻藥
xià máyào.

dormant adj. ①冬眠的
dōngmián de (sleeping). ②潛
伏的 qiánfú de (inactive).

dormitory n. 宿舍 sùshè.

dosage n. 劑量 jìliàng.

dose n. 一劑 yí jì,一服 yì fú.

dossier n. 檔案 dàng'àn /
dǎng'àn.

dot n. 小點 xiǎodiǎn.

double adj. 雙倍的 shuāngbèi
de,加倍的 jiābèi de (twice as
much). ~ bed 雙人床
shuāngrénchuáng. — n. 兩倍
liǎng bèi. — v. 使加倍 shǐ
jiābèi.

doubt v. 懷疑 huáiyí.

doubtless adv. 無疑地 wúyí de.

dough n. 生麵糰 shēng
miàntuán.

dove n. 鴿子 gēzi (pigeon).

D

dowager n. 富孀 fùshuāng (rich widow).

down adv. & prep. ①往下地 wǎng xià de (from high to low). ②在下面 zài xiàmian (in a lower position). — adj. ①向下的 xiàng xià de (from high to low). ②消沈的 xiāochén de (depressed).

downcast adj. 沮喪的 jǔsàng de (depressed).

downfall n. 衰敗 shuāibài (ruin).

downgrade v. 降級 jiàngjí.

download n. 下載 xiàzài 〈computer〉.

downpour n. 大雨 dàyǔ.

downright adj. ①率直的 shuàizhí de (frank). ②完全的 wánquán de (thorough).

downsize v. 小型化 xiǎoxínghuà, 縮小 suōxiǎo.

downstairs adj. & adv. 樓下 的 lóuxià de. — n. 樓下 lóuxià.

downtown n. & adj. 鬧區 nàoqū, 商業區 shāngyèqū.

downward adj. & adv. 向下 的 xiàng xià de, 下降的 xiàjiàng de.

dowry n. 嫁妝 jiàzhuāng.

doze n. & v. 小睡 xiǎoshuì, 打 瞌睡 dǎ kēshuì.

dozen n. 一打 yì dá.

drab n. & adj. ①單調 dāndiào (dull). ②土褐色 tǔhèsè / tǔhèsè 〈color〉.

draft n. ①草稿 cǎogǎo (rough version). ②匯票 huìpiào 〈bank〉. ~ beer 扎啤 zhāpí / 生啤酒 shēngpíjiǔ. — v. ①草擬 cǎonǐ, 起草 qǐcǎo, 畫草圖 huà cǎotú (outline). ②徵募 zhēngmù (conscript).

drag v. 拖曳 tuōyè / tuōyì, 拉

lā (pull along). ~ out 拖延 tuōyán.

dragon n. 龍 lóng.

dragonfly n. 蜻蜓 qīngtíng.

drain v. ①排乾 páigān, 排水 páishuǐ (dry out). ②消耗 xiāohào (consume). — n. ①排 水管 páishuǐguǎn (pipe), 下水 道 xiàshuǐdào (ditch). ②消耗 xiāohào (use up).

drama n. 戲劇 xìjù (play), 劇 本 jùběn (script).

drastic adj. 猛烈的 měngliè de, 徹底的 chèdǐ de.

draw v. ①拉 lā, 曳 yè / yì (drag). ②吸引 xīyǐn (attract). ③畫 huà, 描繪 miáohuì 〈art〉.

drawback n. 缺點 quēdiǎn.

drawer n. 抽屜 chōuti.

drawing n. 繪圖 huìtú 〈art〉, 製 圖 zhìtú 〈technical〉.

dread n. & v. 畏懼 wèijù, 害怕 hàipà.

dreadful adj. ①可怕的 kěpà de (terrible). ②令人討厭的 lìng rén tǎoyàn de (unpleasant).

dream n. 夢 mèng. — v. 做夢 zuòmèng, 夢想 mèngxiǎng.

dreary adj. 陰鬱的 yīnyù de (depressing), 沈悶的 chénmèn de (dull).

dress n. 服裝 fúzhuāng, 衣服 yīfu. — v. 穿衣服 chuān yīfu (put clothes on). ~ up 打扮 dǎbàn.

dressing n. ①繃帶 bēngdài (bandage). ②調味料 tiáowèiliào, 調味醬 tiáowèijiàng (topping).

dressmaker n. 裁縫師 cáifengshī.

dribble v. ①滴下 dīxià (drip), 垂涎 chuíxián (drool). ②運球

yùnqiú〈ball〉.

drier n. ①烘乾機 hōnggānjī
〈machine〉. ②乾燥劑 gānzàojì
〈chemical〉.

drift n. ①吹積 chuījī
(accumulation). ②大意 dàyì
(gist).

drill n. ①練習 liànxí, 訓練
xùnliàn (exercise). ②鑽子
zuànzi〈tool〉. — v. ①練習
liànxí, 訓練 xùnliàn (exercise).
②鑽 zuān, 鑽孔 zuānkǒng
(penetrate).

drink v. ①喝 hē, 飲 yǐn
(swallow). ②飲酒 yǐnjiǔ
〈alcohol〉. — n. ①飲料 yǐnliào
(beverage). ②酒 jiǔ (alcoholic
drinks).

drip v. 滴落 dīluò, 滴下 dīxià.

drive v. ①開車 kāichē (operate
a vehicle). ②迫使 pòshǐ, 驅使
qūshǐ (compel). ③驅逐 qūzhú,
趕 gǎn (force to go away).
— n. ①駕車出遊 jiàchē
chūyóu, 開車兜風 kāichē
dōufēng (journey). ②精力
jīnglì, 力量 lìliang (energy).

driver n. 駕駛 jiàshǐ.
~'s license 駕駛執照 jiàshǐ
zhízhào.

drizzle v. 下毛毛雨 xià
máomaoyǔ. — n. 毛毛雨
máomaoyǔ.

drone n. ①雄蜂 xióngfēng
(male bee). ②嗡嗡聲
wēngwēngshēng〈sound〉.

droop v. ①低垂 dīchuí (bend).
②枯萎 kūwěi / kūwēi〈flowers〉.

drop n. ①滴 dī, 水滴 shuǐdī,
雨滴 yǔdī (drip). ②下降
xiàjiàng, 落下 luòxià (fall).
— v. ①滴下 dīxià, 落下 luòxià
(fall). ②下降 xiàjiàng, 下跌
xiàdié / xiàdié (lower). ③開除

kāichú, 退學 tuìxué (eliminate).
④放棄 fàngqì, 拋棄 pāoqì
(abandon).

drought n. 旱災 hànzāi.

drown v. ①溺斃 nìbì, 淹死
yānsǐ (die in water). ②氾濫
fànlàn (flood). ③淹沒 yānmò,
蓋過 gàiguò (be louder than).

drowsy adj. 想睡的 xiǎng
shuì de, 昏昏欲睡的 hūnhūn-
yùshuì de.

drudge n. 做苦工者 zuò
kǔgōng zhě. — v. 做苦工 zuò
kǔgōng.

drug n. ①藥物 yàowù, 藥 yào
(medicine). ②麻醉藥
mázuìyào (narcotic).

druggie n. 毒癮者 dúyǐnzhě.

drugstore n. 藥房 yàofáng
(pharmacy), 雜貨店 záhuòdiàn
(variety store).

drum n. 鼓 gǔ. — v. 擊鼓 jī gǔ /
jí gǔ, 打鼓 dǎ gǔ.

drumbeat n. 鼓聲 gǔshēng.

drunk adj. 醉的 zuì de, 酒醉
的 jiǔzuì de (tipsy). — n. 酒醉
者 jiǔzuìzhě.

drunkard n. 醉漢 zuìhàn, 酒
鬼 jiǔguǐ.

drunken adj. 酒醉的 jiǔzuì de.

dry adj. ①乾的 gān de, 乾燥
的 gānzào de (without water).
②無甜味的 wú tiánwèi de (not
sweet). ③枯燥的 kūzào de
(boring). — v. 使乾燥 shǐ
gānzào, 弄乾 nònggān.

dual adj. 二重的 èrchóng de,
雙重的 shuāngchóng de.

dub v. ①取綽號 qǔ chuòhào
(give a nickname). ②重新配音
chóngxīn pèiyīn (re-record).

dubious adj. ①懷疑的 huáiyí
de (doubtful). ②可疑的 kěyí
de (suspect).

duchess n. 公爵夫人 gōngjué fūrén.

duck n. 鴨子 yāzi.

duct n. 輸送管 shūsòngguǎn, 導管 dǎoguǎn.

dud n. & adj. 不中用 bù zhōngyòng / bú zhòngyòng, 無用 wúyòng.

due adj. ①應付給的 yīng fùgěi de (owing). ②適當的 shìdàng de (proper). ③到期的 dàoqí de / dàoqí de (expired). — n. ①應得物 yīngdéwù (deserts). ②(pl.) 費用 fèiyòng, 應付款 yīngfùkuǎn (fees).

duel n. & v. 決鬥 juédòu.

duet n. 二重奏 èrchóngzòu ⟨music⟩.

duke n. 公爵 gōngjué.

dull adj. ①晦暗的 huì'àn de (dim). ②陰沈的 yīnchén de (cloudy). ③遲鈍的 chídùn de, 笨的 bèn de (stupid). ④鈍的 dùn de, 不銳利的 bú ruìlì de (unsharpened). ⑤乏味的 fáwèi de, 無聊的 wúliáo de (boring). — v. 變鈍 biàndùn, 使遲鈍 shǐ chídùn.

dumb adj. ①啞的 yǎ de (unable to speak). ②沈默的 chénmò de, 無言的 wúyán de (silent). ③笨的 bèn de (stupid).

dumbfound v. 使啞然 shǐ yǎrán, 使驚愕 shǐ jīng'è.

dummy n. ①人像模型 rénxiàng móxíng ⟨figure⟩. ②笨蛋 bèndàn (idiot).

dump v. ①傾倒 qīngdào, 丟棄 diūqì (discard). ②傾銷 qīngxiāo (sell at low prices).

dumpling n. 蒸煮麵糰 zhēngzhǔ miàntuán ⟨dough⟩, 水餃 shuǐjiǎo ⟨Chinese food⟩.

dumpy adj. ①矮胖的 ǎipàng de (short and fat). ②破爛骯髒的 pòlàn āngzāng de (shabby and dingy).

dunce n. 遲鈍者 chídùnzhě, 蠢材 chǔncái.

dune n. 沙丘 shāqiū.

dungeon n. 地牢 dìláo ⟨prison⟩.

dupe v. 欺騙 qīpiàn. — n. 受騙者 shòupiànzhě.

duplicate adj. 複製的 fùzhì de (exactly like another). — n. 複製品 fùzhìpǐn, 副本 fùběn. — v. 複製 fùzhì, 複寫 fùxiě (copy exactly).

durable adj. 耐久的 nàijiǔ de, 耐用的 nàiyòng de.

duration n. 持續期間 chíxù qījiān / chíxù qíjiān.

duress n. 強迫 qiǎngpò, 脅迫 xiépò (coercion).

during prep. 在⋯⋯期間 zài ...qījiān / zài...qíjiān.

dusk n. 黃昏 huánghūn, 傍晚 bàngwǎn / bāngwǎn. — adj. 昏暗的 hūn'àn de.

dusky adj. 微暗的 wēi'àn de / wéi'àn de, 略黑的 lüèhēi de (darkish).

dust n. 灰塵 huīchén. — v. ①拂去灰塵 fúqù huīchén (remove dust from). ②撒粉於 sǎfěn yú (sprinkle powder on).

dusty adj. 多灰塵的 duō huīchén de (covered with dust).

Dutch adj. 荷蘭的 Hélán de. go ~ 各付各的 gè fù gè de. — n. 荷蘭人 Hélánrén.

duty n. ①義務 yìwù, 責任 zérèn (responsibility). ②職責 zhízé (task). ③稅 shuì (tax).

DVD 數字式多功能光盤 shùzìshì duō gōngnéng guāngpán, 數碼影碟 shùmǎ yǐngdié / 數位多功能影音光

碟 shùwèi duō gōngnéng yíngyīn guāngdié (Digital Versatile Disc).

dwarf n. 侏儒 zhūrú (midget). — adj. 矮小的 ǎixiǎo de.

dwell v. 居住 jūzhù. ~ **on** 細想 xìxiǎng, 詳述 xiángshù.

dwelling n. 住宅 zhùzhái (house).

dwindle v. 減少 jiǎnshǎo, 縮減 suōjiǎn.

dye n. 染料 rǎnliào. — v. 染 rǎn, 染色 rǎnsè.

dynamic adj. ①動力的 dònglì de ⟨physics⟩. ②精力充沛的 jīnglì chōngpèi de, 有動力的 yǒu dònglì de (energetic).

dynamite n. 炸藥 zhàyào.

dynasty n. 朝代 cháodài, 王朝 wángcháo.

dysentery n. 痢疾 lìjí.

E

E

each adj. 每 měi, 每個 měi ge. — pron. 各自 gèzì, 每個 měi ge.

eager adj. ①熱切的 rèqiè de (enthusiastic). ②渴望的 kěwàng de (hopeful).

eagle n. 鷹 yīng.

ear n. ①耳 ěr, 耳朵 ěrduo ⟨organ⟩. ②聽覺 tīngjué, 聽力 tīnglì (hearing).

earl n. 伯爵 bójué.

Earl Grey tea 伯爵茶 Bójuéchá.

early adv. 早 zǎo. — adj. 早 zǎo (before the expected time), 初期的 chūqī de / chūqí de ⟨a period of time⟩.

earn v. ①賺 zhuàn (gain). ②博得 bódé, 獲得 huòdé (win).

earnest adj. ①認真的 rènzhēn de (conscientious). ②誠摯的 chéngzhì de (honest).

earnings n. 賺的錢 zhuàn de qián, 收入 shōurù (income), 工資 gōngzī (wages).

earphone n. 耳機 ěrjī.

earring n. 耳環 ěrhuán.

earth n. ① E~ 地球 dìqiú ⟨planet⟩. ②陸地 lùdì, 大地 dàdì (land). ③泥土 nítǔ (soil).

earthenware n. 陶器 táoqì.

earthquake n. 地震 dìzhèn.

earthworm n. 蚯蚓 qiūyǐn.

ease n. ①舒適 shūshì, 安逸 ānyì (comfort). ②輕易 qīngyì, 不費力 bú fèilì (easiness). at ~ 自在 zìzài. with ~ 不費力 bú fèilì. — v. ①減輕 jiǎnqīng, 減緩 jiǎnhuǎn (lessen). ②放鬆 fàngsōng (relax). ③使舒適 shǐ shūshì, 使安心 shǐ ānxīn (put at ease).

easel n. 畫架 huàjià.

easily adv. 容易地 róngyì de.

east n. ①東 dōng ⟨direction⟩. ②東方 dōngfāng (eastern region). ③東邊 dōngbiān, 東部 dōngbù (eastern part). Far E~ 遠東 Yuǎndōng. Middle E~ 中東 Zhōngdōng. — adv. 東 dōng,

E

向東 xiàng dōng, 往東 wǎng dōng. — adj.①東 dōng (of the east).②東方的 dōngfāng de (of the eastern region).③東部的 dōngbù de (of the eastern part).

Easter n. 復活節 Fùhuójié.

eastern adj. 東方的 dōngfāng de. ~ hemisphere 東半球 dōngbànqiú.

eastward adj. & adv. 向東的 xiàng dōng de.

easy adj.①容易的 róngyì de (effortless).②輕鬆的 qīngsōng de, 舒服的 shūfu de (comfortable). take it ~ 放輕鬆 fàng qīngsōng.

easygoing adj. 隨和的 suíhe de.

eat v. 吃 chī.

eatable adj. 可吃的 kě chī de.

eaves n. 屋簷 wūyán.

eavesdrop v. 偷聽 tōutīng.

ebb n. & v.①退潮 tuìcháo (flow back).②衰退 shuāituì (weaken).

ebony n. 烏木 wūmù, 黑檀 hēitán ⟨plant⟩. — adj. 烏黑的 wūhēi de ⟨color⟩.

eccentric adj. 反常的 fǎncháng de (unusual), 古怪的 gǔguài de (strange). — n. 古怪的人 gǔguài de rén ⟨person⟩.

echo n. 回聲 huíshēng, 回音 huíyīn. — v. 發出回音 fāchū huíyīn (resound).

eclipse n.①日蝕 rìshí ⟨solar⟩, 月蝕 yuèshí ⟨lunar⟩.②瑕掩 xiáyǎn ⟨fame⟩.

ecology n.①生態 shēngtài (ecosystem).②生態學 shēngtàixué ⟨science⟩.

economic adj.①經濟的 jīngjì de (having to do with economy).

②經濟學的 jīngjìxué de (of economics).

economical adj. 經濟的 jīngjì de, 儉約的 jiǎnyuē de.

economics n. 經濟學 jīngjìxué.

economize v. 節約 jiéyuē.

economy n. 經濟 jīngjì (economic affairs). ~ class 經濟艙 jīngjìcāng.

ecstasy n.①狂喜 kuángxǐ (joy).②E~ ⟨一種⟩迷幻藥 (yì zhǒng) míhuànyào (an illegal drug).

eddy n. 漩渦 xuánwō (whirlpool). — v. 迴旋 huíxuán.

edge n.①邊緣 biānyuán (periphery).②邊境 biānjìng (boundary).③刀刃 dāorèn ⟨blade⟩. — v.①加邊 jiābiān (fringe).②側進 cèjìn (side).

edible adj. 可食的 kě shí de.

edit v. 編輯 biānjí, 校訂 jiàodìng.

edition n. 版本 bǎnběn.

editor n. 編者 biānzhě, 編輯 biānjí.

editorial adj. 編輯的 biānjí de. — n. 社論 shèlùn.

educate v. 教育 jiàoyù, 教 jiāo.

education n. 教育 jiàoyù.

eel n. 鰻魚 mányú, 鱔魚 shànyú.

eerie, eery adj. 陰森可怕的 yīnsēn kěpà de.

effect n.①影響 yǐngxiǎng, 效果 xiàoguǒ (result).②印象 yìnxiàng, 感覺 gǎnjué (impression).

effective adj. 有效的 yǒuxiào de (serves its purpose), 生效的 shēngxiào de (goes into effect).

effeminate adj. 娘娘腔的 niángniangqiāng de.

effervesce v. 冒泡沫 mào pàomò.

efficiency n. 效率 xiàolǜ.

efficient adj. 有效率的 yǒu xiàolǜ de.

effigy n. 肖像 xiàoxiàng.

effort n. ①努力 nǔlì (hard work). ②成果 chéngguǒ (accomplishment).

e.g. 例如 lìrú.

egg n. 蛋 dàn.

egghead n. 書呆子 shūdāizi.

eggplant n. 茄子 qiézi.

eggshell n. 蛋殼 dànké.

ego n. 自我 zìwǒ.

egocentric adj. 自我中心的 zìwǒ zhōngxīn de, 利己主義的 lìjǐ zhǔyì de.

egoism n. 自我主義 zìwǒ zhǔyì, 利己主義 lìjǐ zhǔyì.

egotism n. 自負 zìfù, 自我吹噓 zìwǒ chuīxū.

eight n. & adj. 八 bā.

eighteen n. & adj. 十八 shíbā.

eighteenth n. & adj. 第十八 dì-shíbā.

eighth n. & adj. 第八 dì-bā.

eightieth n. & adj. 第八十 dì-bāshí.

eighty n. & adj. 八十 bāshí.

either adj & pron. 二者之一的 èr zhě zhī yī de (one of two choices), 任一的 rènyì de (any). — conj. ~ ...or... 不是… …就是 búshì…jiùshì…. — adv. 也 (不) yě (bù).

eject v. ①逐出 zhúchū, 放逐 fàngzhú (exile). ②發射 fāshè, 放出 fàngchū (discharge). ③退出 tuìchū (disk, tape).

elaborate adj. 精心製造的 jīngxīn zhìzào de (complicated).

— v. 詳盡說明 xiángjìn shuōmíng.

elapse v. 逝去 shìqù.

elastic adj. 有彈性的 yǒu tánxìng de (flexible). — n. 鬆緊帶 sōngjǐndài, 橡皮筋 xiàngpíjīn.

elbow n. 手肘 shǒuzhǒu ⟨arm⟩.

elder adj. 年長的 niánzhǎng de, 年紀較大的 niánjì jiào dà de. — n. 年長者 niánzhǎngzhě, 前輩 qiánbèi.

eldest adj. 最年長的 zuì niánzhǎng de.

elect v. ①選舉 xuǎnjǔ, 選舉 xuǎnxǔ (vote for). ②選擇 xuǎnzé (choose).

election n. 選舉 xuǎnjǔ.

elector n. 選舉人 xuǎnjǔrén.

electorate n. 選民 xuǎnmín ⟨people⟩, 選舉團 xuǎnjǔtuán ⟨committee⟩.

electric adj. 電的 diàn de. ~ *power* 電力 diànlì.

electrical adj. 電的 diàn de.

electricity n. 電 diàn, 電流 diànliú.

electrocute v. ①施以電刑 shī yǐ diànxíng ⟨put to death⟩. ②觸電致死 chùdiàn zhìsǐ ⟨kill accidentally⟩.

electrolysis n. 電解 diànjiě.

electromagnet n. 電磁石 diàncíshí.

electron n. 電子 diànzǐ.

electronic adj. 電子的 diànzǐ de. ~ *publishing* 電子出版 diànzǐ chūbǎn. ~ *shopping* 電子購物 diànzǐ gòuwù. ~ *transfer* 電子轉帳 diànzǐ zhuǎnzhàng.

electronics n. ①電子工業 diànzǐ gōngyè ⟨industry⟩.

②電子工程學 diànzǐ gōngchéngxué (the study of electronics).

electroplate *n. & v.* 電鍍 diàndù.

electrotherapy *n.* 電療 diànliáo.

elegant *adj.* 優雅的 yōuyǎ de, 高雅的 gāoyǎ de.

elegy *n.* 輓歌 wǎngē.

element *n.* ①要素 yàosù, 成分 chéngfèn (part). ②元素 yuánsù (substance).

elementary *adj.* 初步的 chūbù de (beginning level), 基本的 jīběn de (basic). ~ *school* 小學 xiǎoxué.

elephant *n.* 象 xiàng.

elevate *v.* 舉起 jǔqǐ, 提高 tígāo.

elevation *n.* ①上升 shàngshēng, 提高 tígāo (act of elevating). ②高度 gāodù (height), 海拔 hǎibá (height above sea level).

elevator *n.* 電梯 diàntī ⟨passenger⟩, 升降機 shēngjiàngjī ⟨freight⟩.

eleven *n. & adj.* 十一 shíyī.

eleventh *n. & adj.* 第十一 dì-shíyī.

elicit *v.* 誘出 yòuchū, 引出 yǐnchū.

eligible *adj.* 合格的 hégé de.

eliminate *v.* ①除去 chúqù, 消除 xiāochú (remove). ②消滅 xiāomiè (wipe out), 幹掉 gàndiào (kill).

elite *n.* 精英 jīngyīng, 傑出人物 jiéchū rénwù.

elk *n.* 麋鹿 mílù.

ellipse *n.* 橢圓 tuǒyuán ⟨mathematics⟩.

elm *n.* 榆樹 yúshù.

elongate *v.* 延長 yáncháng, 延伸 yánshēn.

elope *v.* 私奔 sībēn.

eloquent *adj.* 雄辯的 xióngbiàn de, 口若懸河的 kǒu-ruò-xuán-hé de.

El Niño *n.* 厄爾尼諾現象 È'ěrnínuò xiànxiàng / 聖嬰現象 shèngyīng xiànxiàng.

else *adj.* 別的 bié de, 其他的 qítā de. — *adv.* ①此外 cǐwài (in addition). ②否則 fǒuzé (otherwise).

elsewhere *adv.* 在別處 zài biéchù.

elude *v.* 逃避 táobì, 躲避 duǒbì (escape from).

emaciated *adj.* 消瘦的 xiāoshòu de (thin), 憔悴的 qiáocuì de (feeble).

e-mail *n.* 電子信函 diànzǐ xìnhán / 電子郵件 diànzǐ yóujiàn (electronic mail).

emancipate *v.* 解放 jiěfàng.

embalm *v.* 使屍體防腐 shǐ shītǐ fángfǔ.

embargo *n. & v.* 禁運 jìnyùn.

embark *v.* ①乘船 chéngchuán (board a ship). ②著手 zhuóshǒu (start).

embarrass *v.* 使困窘 shǐ kùnjiǒng, 使尷尬 shǐ gāngà.

embarrassing *adj.* 困窘的 kùnjiǒng de, 尷尬的 gāngà de.

embarrassment *n.* 困窘 kùnjiǒng, 尷尬 gāngà.

embassy *n.* 大使館 dàshǐguǎn.

embellish *v.* 裝飾 zhuāngshì (adorn), 美化 měihuà (beautify).

ember *n.* 餘燼 yújìn.

embezzle *v.* 盜用 dàoyòng, 侵吞 qīntūn.

emblem n. ①象徵 xiàngzhēng (symbol). ②紋章 wénzhāng, 徽章 huīzhāng (badge).

embody v. 具體表現 jùtǐ biǎoxiàn (exemplify), 使具體化 shǐ jùtǐhuà (make physical).

embrace v. ①擁抱 yōngbào / yǒngbào (hold). ②接受 jiēshòu (accept). ③包含 bāohán (include). — n. 擁抱 yōngbào / yǒngbào.

embroider v. 刺繡 cìxiù.

embryo n. ①胚胎 pēitāi ⟨animals⟩. ②胚芽 pēiyá ⟨plants⟩.

emend v. 校訂 jiàodìng, 修正 xiūzhèng.

emerald n. ①翡翠 fěicuì ⟨stone⟩. ②翠綠色 cuìlǜsè ⟨color⟩.

emerge v. ①出現 chūxiàn, 露出 lòuchū (come out). ②顯露 xiǎnlù (become known).

emergency n. 緊急事件 jǐnjí shìjiàn. ~ room 急診室 jízhěnshì.

emigrant n. 移民 yímín.

emigrate v. 移民 yímín.

eminent adj. ①聞名的 wénmíng de (famous). ②顯著的 xiǎnzhù de (noticeable). ③優良的 yōuliáng de (excellent).

emission n. ①放射物 fàngshèwù (particle). ②放射 fàngshè (release).

emit v. 放射 fàngshè.

emotion n. 情緒 qíngxù, 感情 gǎnqíng.

emotional adj. ①感動的 gǎndòng de (moved). ②情緒的 qíngxù de (prone to overreaction).

emperor n. 皇帝 huángdì.

emphasis n. ①強調 qiángdiào (stress). ②加重語氣 jiāzhòng yǔqì ⟨pronunciation⟩.

emphasize v. ①強調 qiángdiào (stress). ②重讀 zhòngdú ⟨pronunciation⟩.

emphatic adj. ①強調的 qiángdiào de (using emphasis). ②堅持的 jiānchí de (insistent).

empire n. 帝國 dìguó.

empirical adj. ①憑經驗的 píng jīngyàn de (based in experience). ②經驗主義的 jīngyàn zhǔyì de (provable through experimentation).

employ v. ①雇用 gùyòng (hire). ②使用 shǐyòng (make use of).

employee n. 受雇者 shòugùzhě, 雇員 gùyuán.

employer n. 雇主 gùzhǔ.

employment n. ①職業 zhíyè (occupation). ②受雇 shòugù, 就業 jiùyè (the fact of being hired).

empress n. 皇后 huánghòu, 女皇 nǚhuáng.

empty adj. 空的 kōng de. — v. 變空 biàn kōng.

emulate v. ①努力趕上 nǔlì gǎnshàng (try to do as well as). ②仿效 fǎngxiào (admire and seek to copy).

emulsion n. 乳狀液 rǔzhuàngyè, 乳劑 rǔjì.

enable v. 使能夠 shǐ nénggòu (release).

enamel n. 瓷釉 cíyòu, 琺瑯 fàláng. — v. 塗瓷釉 tú cíyòu.

enchant v. ①使沉醉 shǐ mízuì (lure). ②施魔法於 shǐ mófǎ yú (use magic on).

encircle v. 環繞 huánrào, 包圍 bāowéi.

enclose v. ①圍起 wéiqǐ (surround). ②附寄 fùjì (put inside).

encore interj. 再表演一次 zài biǎoyǎn yí cì.

encounter n. & v. ①邂逅 xièhòu / xiègòu, 碰到 pèngdào (meeting unexpectedly). ②遭遇 zāoyù (being faced by).

encourage v. 鼓勵 gǔlì.

encouragement n. 鼓勵 gǔlì.

encroach v. 侵占 qīnzhàn.

encyclopedia n. 百科全書 bǎikē quánshū.

end n. ①盡頭 jìntóu, 末端 mòduān (last part). ②結局 jiéjú, 結束 jiéshù (cessation). ③目的 mùdì (aim). ④死亡 sǐwáng (death). — v. 結束 jiéshù, 終止 zhōngzhǐ.

endanger v. 使危險 shǐ wēixiǎn / shǐ wéixiǎn, 危及 wēijí / wéijí.

endear v. 使受鍾愛 shǐ shòu zhōng'ài.

endeavor n. & v. 努力 nǔlì, 盡力 jìnlì.

endemic adj. 地方性的 dìfāngxìng de (native). — n. 地方性疾病 dìfāngxìng jíbìng 〈disease〉.

ending n. 終止 zhōngzhǐ, 結局 jiéjú.

endless adj. 無盡的 wújìn de.

endorse v. ①認可 rènkě, 贊同 zàntóng (approve). ②簽署 qiānshǔ / qiānshù (sign).

endow v. 捐贈 juānzèng (donate).

endurance n. ①忍耐 rěnnài (forbearance). ②忍受力 rěnshòulì (tolerance).

endure v. 忍耐 rěnnài (bear), 忍受 rěnshòu (tolerate).

enemy n. 敵人 dírén.

energetic adj. ①精力充沛的 jīnglì chōngpèi de (high-spirited). ②積極的 jījí de (active).

energy n. ①精力 jīnglì, 活力 huólì (liveliness). ②能量 néngliàng (power).

enforce v. ①執行 zhíxíng (carry out). ②強迫 qiǎngpò, 強制 qiángzhì (force). ③增強 zēngqiáng (reinforce).

engage v. ①雇用 gùyòng (employ). ②忙於 máng yú (occupy). ③允諾 yǔnnuò, 保證 bǎozhèng (promise). ④與……交戰 yǔ...jiāozhàn (fight with).

engaged adj. ①已訂婚的 yǐ dìnghūn de (betrothed). ②被占用的 bèi zhànyòng de (being used). ③忙碌的 mánglù de (busy).

engagement n. ①訂婚 dìnghūn (betrothal). ②約會 yuēhuì (appointment). ③交戰 jiāozhàn (battle).

engine n. 引擎 yǐnqíng.

engineer n. 工程師 gōngchéngshī.

engineering n. 工程學 gōngchéngxué.

English n. & adj. ①英國人 Yīngguórén 〈people〉. ②英語 Yīngyǔ, 英文 Yīngwén 〈language〉.

engrave v. 雕刻 diāokè.

engross v. 使全神貫注 shǐ quánshén-guànzhù (occupy).

engulf v. 吞噬 tūnshì, 吞入 tūnrù.

enigma n. 謎 mí.

enjoy v. 享受 xiǎngshòu, 欣賞

xīnshǎng.

enlarge v. 擴大 kuòdà.

enlighten v. 啓發 qǐfā, 開導 kāidǎo (instruct).

enlist v. ①使入伍 shǐ rùwǔ, 徵募 zhēngmù (conscript). ②獲得 huòdé, 取得 qǔdé (obtain).

enormous adj. 極大的 jí dà de, 巨大的 jùdà de.

enough adj. & adv. 足夠的 zúgòu de. — interj. 夠了！ Gòu le!

enquire v. 詢問 xúnwèn.

enrich v. ①使充實 shǐ chōngshí (improve). ②使富足 shǐ fùzú (make rich).

enroll v. 登記 dēngjì.

ensign n. ①旗 qí (flag). ②海軍少尉 hǎijūn shàowèi ⟨navy⟩.

enslave v. 奴役 núyì.

ensue v. 隨後發生 suíhòu fāshēng.

ensure v. 保證 bǎozhèng, 確保 quèbǎo.

entail v. 使必須 shǐ bìxū (necessitate).

entangle v. 使糾纏 shǐ jiūchán, 牽連 qiānlián.

enter v. ①進入 jìnrù (come in). ②參加 cānjiā (engage in).

enterprise n. ①企業 qǐyè / qìyè, 事業 shìyè (business). ②進取心 jìnqǔxīn (willingness to do difficult things).

entertain v. ①娛樂 yúlè (amuse). ②招待 zhāodài (give a party).

entertainment n. 娛樂 yúlè.

enthrall v. 迷住 mízhù, 迷惑 míhuò.

enthusiasm n. 熱心 rèxīn, 熱衷 rèzhōng.

enthusiastic adj. 熱心的 rèxīn de, 熱衷的 rèzhōng de.

entice v. 誘惑 yòuhuò, 慫恿 sǒngyǒng.

entire adj. 整個的 zhěnggè de, 全部的 quánbù de.

entirely adv. 全部地 quánbù de, 完全地 wánquán de (completely).

entitle v. ①定名為 dìngmíng wéi (name). ②使有權利 shǐ yǒu quánlì (empower).

entity n. 實體 shítǐ.

entrails n. 內臟 nèizàng.

entrance n. ①入口 rùkǒu (place where one enters), 門口 ménkǒu (doorway). ②進入 jìnrù (the act of entering).

entreat v. 懇求 kěnqiú.

entrenched adj. 確立的 quèlì de, 根深蒂固的 gēn-shēn-dì-gù de (firmly established).

entrepreneur n. 企業家 qǐyèjiā / qìyèjiā.

entrust v. 委託 wěituō, 託付 tuōfù.

entry n. ①進入 jìnrù (entering), 入口 rùkǒu (entrance). ②條目 tiáomù (item). ③參賽者 cānsàizhě (competitor).

enumerate v. ①列舉 lièjǔ (list one by one). ②數 shǔ (count).

enunciate v. ①發音 fāyīn (pronounce). ②很清楚地表達 hěn qīngchu de biǎodá (express clearly).

envelop v. 包圍 bāowéi (surround), 籠罩 lǒngzhào (permeate).

envelope n. 信封 xìnfēng.

enviable adj. 令人羨慕的 lìng rén xiànmù de.

envious adj. 羨慕的 xiànmù de.

environment n. 環境 huánjìng.

E

environmental *adj.* ①環境的 huánjìng de (having to do with the environment). ②環保的 huánbǎo de (environmentalist).

environmentalism *n.* 環保主義 huánbǎo zhǔyì (theory), 環保意識 huánbǎo yìshí / huánbǎo yìshì (awareness).

envisage *v.* 想像 xiǎngxiàng, 設想 shèxiǎng (imagine).

envoy *n.* 使者 shǐzhě, 特使 tèshǐ, 公使 gōngshǐ.

envy *n. & v.* 羨慕 xiànmù.

enzyme *n.* 酵素 jiàosù / xiàosù.

epic *n.* 史詩 shǐshī.

epidemic *n.* 傳染病 chuánrǎnbìng. — *adj.* 流行性的 liúxíngxìng de.

epilepsy *n.* 癲癇症 diānxiánzhèng.

epilogue *n.* ①結尾 jiéwěi (a literary work). ②收場白 shōuchǎngbái (a play).

episode *n.* 插曲 chāqǔ.

epitaph *n.* 墓誌銘 mùzhìmíng.

epithet *n.* 稱號 chēnghào.

epitome *n.* 縮影 suōyǐng.

epoch *n.* 紀元 jìyuán, 時代 shídài.

EQ 情緒智商 qíngxù zhìshāng / 情緒商數 qíngxù shāngshù (emotional quotient).

equal *adj.* 相等的 xiāngděng de, 平等的 píngděng de. — *n.* 對手 duìshǒu. — *v.* 等於 děngyú.

equality *n.* 相等 xiāngděng, 平等 píngděng.

equally *adv.* 相等地 xiāngděng de, 同樣地 tóngyàng de.

equate *v.* 視為相等 shìwéi xiāngděng.

equation *n.* 等式 děngshì, 方

程式 fāngchéngshì.

equator *n.* 赤道 chìdào.

equestrian *adj.* 騎馬的 qímǎ de.

equilibrium *n.* 平衡 pínghéng, 均衡 jūnhéng.

equinox *n.* 春分 chūnfēn (spring), 秋分 qiūfēn (autumn).

equip *v.* 裝備 zhuāngbèi.

equipment *n.* 設備 shèbèi, 裝備 zhuāngbèi.

equity *n.* 公平 gōngping, 公正 gōngzhèng.

equivalent *adj.* 同等的 tóngděng de.

equivocal *adj.* 模稜兩可的 mó-léng-liǎng-kě de.

ER 急診室 jízhěnshì (emergency room).

era *n.* 時代 shídài, 紀元 jìyuán.

eradicate *v.* 根除 gēnchú, 消滅 xiāomiè.

erase *v.* 擦掉 cādiào, 抹去 mǒqù.

eraser *n.* 橡皮擦 xiàngpícā.

erect *adj.* 直立的 zhílì de. — *v.* ①建築 jiànzhù / jiànzhú, 建立 jiànlì (build). ②豎立 shùlì (stand upright).

erode *v.* 侵蝕 qīnshí, 腐蝕 fǔshí.

erotic *adj.* 性愛的 xìng'ài de, 情色的 qíngsè de.

err *v.* 犯錯 fàncuò.

errand *n.* 差事 chāishì.

erratic *adj.* ①乖僻的 guāipì de, 古怪的 gǔguài de (eccentric). ②反覆無常的 fǎnfù-wúcháng de (changeable without reason).

error *n.* ①錯誤 cuòwù, 過失 guòshī (mistake). ②誤差 wùchā (mathematics).

erudite *adj.* 博學的 bóxué de.

erupt v. 爆發 bàofā.

escalate v. 逐漸上升 zhújiàn shàngshēng.

escalator n. 滾梯 gǔntī, 自動扶梯 zìdòng fútī / 手扶梯 shǒufútī.

escapade n. 恣意作為 zìyì zuòwéi.

escape v. ①逃脫 táotuō, 逃走 táozǒu (flee). ②漏出 lòuchū (leak). ③逃避 táobì (avoid).

escarpment n. 懸崖 xuányá / xuányái, 絕壁 juébì.

escort n. ①護花使者 hùhuā shǐzhě (date). ②護送者 hùsòngzhě (guard). ③護衛隊 hùwèiduì (entourage). — v. 護送 hùsòng.

Eskimo n. 愛斯基摩人 Àisījīmórén.

esophagus n. 食道 shídào.

esoteric adj. 奧祕的 àomì de.

especially adv. 尤其是 yóuqí shì.

espionage n. 間諜活動 jiàndié huódòng.

essay n. 文章 wénzhāng.

essence n. 本質 běnzhì / běnzhí (nature), 精髓 jīngsuǐ (key part).

essential adj. ①必要的 bìyào de (necessary). ②本質的 běnzhì de / běnzhí de (basic).

establish v. ①建立 jiànlì, 設立 shèlì (set up). ②確立 quèlì, 確定 quèdìng (confirm).

establishment n. ①建立 jiànlì (creation). ②組織 zǔzhī, 機構 jīgòu (organization).

estate n. ①房地產 fángdìchǎn (real estate). ②財產 cáichǎn (belongings). ③遺產 yíchǎn (inheritance).

esteem v. 尊敬 zūnjìng, 尊重 zūnzhòng (respect). — n. 尊重 zūnzhòng, 尊敬 zūnjìng.

estimate n. & v. 估計 gūjì, 評估 pínggū.

estuary n. 入海口 rùhǎikǒu.

et cetera adv. 等等 děngděng (etc.).

etch v. 蝕刻 shíkè.

eternal adj. 永恆的 yǒnghéng de, 永遠的 yǒngyuǎn de (lasting), 不變的 búbiàn de (unchanging).

eternity n. ①永恆 yǒnghéng (infinity). ②來生 láishēng (the afterlife).

ether n. 醚 mí.

ethical adj. 倫理的 lúnlǐ de (having to do with ethics), 道德的 dàodé de (moral).

ethics n. 道德學 dàodéxué, 倫理學 lúnlíxué.

ethnic adj. 種族的 zhǒngzú de, 人種的 rénzhǒng de.

etiquette n. 禮節 lǐjié, 禮儀 lǐyí.

etymology n. 語源 yǔyuán, 語源學 yǔyuánxué.

EU 歐盟 Ōuméng (European Union).

eucalyptus n. 桉樹 ānshù, 尤加利樹 yóujiālìshù.

eunuch n. 太監 tàijiàn, 閹人 yānrén.

euphemism n. 委婉語 wěiwǎnyǔ.

Euro n. 歐元 Ōuyuán.

Europe 歐洲 Ōuzhōu.

European adj. 歐洲的 Ōuzhōu de. — n. 歐洲人 Ōuzhōurén.

euthanasia n. 慈悲殺人 cíbēi shārén, 尊嚴死 zūnyánsǐ / 安樂死 ānlèsǐ.

evacuate v. ①撤離 chèlí (withdraw from). ②疏散

shūsàn (remove from).

evade v. ①逃避 táobì (escape from). 躲避 duǒbì (hide from). ②規避 guībì (avoid).

evaluate v. 評價 píngjià, 估計 gūjì.

evangelic adj. 福音的 fúyīn de.

evangelist n. 傳福音者 chuán fúyīn zhě.

evaporate v. 蒸發 zhēngfā.

eve n. 前夕 qiánxī / qiánxì.

even adj. ①平坦的 píngtǎn de (flat). ②均勻的 jūnyún de, 規律的 guīlǜ de (regular). ③相等的 xiāngděng de (equal). ④沈穩的 chénwěn de (calm). ⑤偶數的 ǒushù de ⟨number⟩. — v. ①使平坦 shǐ píngtǎn (flatten). ②使相等 shǐ xiāngděng (equalize). — adv. 甚至 shènzhì, 即使 jíshǐ, 連 lián. ~ if 就算是 jiùsuàn shì, 即使 jíshǐ. ~ so 雖然如此 suīrán rúcǐ.

evening n. 傍晚 bàngwǎn / bāngwǎn, 晚間 wǎnjiān.

event n. ①事件 shìjiàn (affair). ②項目 xiàngmù ⟨sports⟩.

eventual adj. 結果的 jiéguǒ de, 最後的 zuìhòu de.

eventually adv. 最後 zuìhòu, 終於 zhōngyú.

ever adv. ①曾經 céngjīng (once). ②始終 shǐzhōng, 從來 cónglái (at all times). ~ since 自從 zìcóng. for ~ 永遠 yǒngyuǎn.

evergreen adj. 常綠的 chánglǜ de, 長青的 chángqīng de.

everlasting adj. 永遠的 yǒngyuǎn de, 永恆的 yǒnghéng de.

evermore adv. 永久 yǒngjiǔ.

every adj. ①每 měi, 每一 měi yī (each). ②所有的 suǒyǒu de (all).

everybody pron. 每個人 měi ge rén.

everyday adj. 日常的 rìcháng de.

everything pron. 每件事物 měi jiàn shìwù.

everywhere adv. 到處 dàochù, 每個地方 měi ge dìfang.

evict v. 逐出 zhúchū (force out).

evidence n. 證據 zhèngjù (proof), 跡象 jìxiàng / jīxiàng (sign).

evident adj. 明顯的 míngxiǎn de, 顯然的 xiǎnrán de.

evidently adv. 顯然地 xiǎnrán de.

evil adj. 邪惡的 xié'è de, 罪惡的 zuì'è de. — n. 邪惡 xié'è, 罪惡 zuì'è.

evocative adj. 喚起的 huànqǐ de.

evoke v. 喚起 huànqǐ, 引起 yǐnqǐ.

evolution n. ①進化 jìnhuà, 發展 fāzhǎn (development). ②進化論 jìnhuàlùn (theory of evolution).

evolve v. 進化 jìnhuà, 展開 zhǎnkāi.

ewe n. 母羊 mǔyáng.

exact adj. 正確的 zhèngquè de, 精確的 jīngquè de (precise). — v. 強行索取 qiángxíng suǒqǔ (press for).

exactly adv. ①正確地 zhèngquè de, 精確地 jīngquè de (precisely). ②正好 zhènghǎo, 剛好 gānghǎo (just).

exaggerate v. 誇張

kuāzhāng, 誇大 kuādà.

exam n. 考試 kǎoshì.

examination n. ①檢查 jiǎnchá (an act of examining). ②考試 kǎoshì (test). ③審問 shěnwèn (questioning).

examine v. ①檢查 jiǎnchá (look at closely). ②考試 kǎoshì (test). ③審問 shěnwèn (question).

examiner n. 主考者 zhǔkǎozhě, 考官 kǎoguān.

example n. ①例子 lìzi, 實例 shílì (instance). ②樣本 yàngběn (sample). **for ~** 例如 lìrú, 比如 bǐrú, 譬如說 pìrú shuō, 比方說 bǐfāng shuō.

exasperate v. 激怒 jīnù (annoy).

excavate v. 挖掘 wājué, 挖出 wāchū.

exceed v. 超過 chāoguò, 超出 chāochū.

excel v. ①擅長於 shàncháng yú (be good at). ②優於 yōuyú, 勝過 shèngguò (be better than).

excellence n. 傑出 jiéchū, 卓越 zhuōyuè / zhuóyuè.

excellent adj. 卓越的 zhuōyuè de / zhuóyuè de, 極好的 jí hǎo de, 優秀的 yōuxiù de.

except prep. 除……之外 chú ...zhīwài.

exception n. 例外 lìwài.

exceptional adj. 特別的 tèbié de, 突出的 tūchū de / túchū de.

excerpt n. 摘錄 zhāilù.

excess n. 超過 chāoguò, 過度 guòdù. **in ~ of** 超過 chāoguò.

excessively adv. 過度 guòdù.

exchange v. 交換 jiāohuàn, 調換 diàohuàn. — n. ①交換

jiāohuàn (replacement). ②交易 jiāoyì (bargain). ②兌換 duìhuàn ⟨money⟩. ②交易所 jiāoyìsuǒ ⟨place⟩. **~ rate** 匯率 huìlǜ.

exchequer n. 國庫 guókù.

excise n. 國產稅 guóchǎnshuì ⟨tax⟩. — v. 割除 gēchú (cut out), 刪除 shānchú (remove).

excite v. ①使興奮 shǐ xīngfèn, 使激動 shǐ jīdòng (stimulate). ②引起 yǐnqǐ (incite).

excited adj. 興奮的 xīngfèn de, 激動的 jīdòng de.

excitement n. 興奮 xīngfèn, 刺激 cìjī.

exciting adj. 令人興奮的 lìng rén xīngfèn de.

exclaim v. 呼喊 hūhǎn, 驚叫 jīngjiào.

exclamation n. 呼喊 hūhǎn, 驚叫 jīngjiào. **~ mark** 驚嘆號 jīngtànhào.

exclude v. ①排斥 páichì (discriminate against). ②拒絕 jùjué (reject). ③排除 páichú (remove).

exclusion n. ①排斥 páichì (discrimination). ②排除 páichú (removal).

exclusive adj. ①限制嚴格的 xiànzhì yángé de (limited). ②高級的 gāojí de (classy). ③排他性的 páitāxìng de (rejecting outsiders).

excommunicate v. 逐出教會 zhúchū jiàohuì.

excrement n. 排泄物 páixièwù, 糞便 fènbiàn.

excrete v. 排泄 páixiè.

excursion n. 遠足 yuǎnzú, 短程旅行 duǎnchéng lǚxíng.

excuse v. ①原諒 yuánliàng (forgive). ②免責 miǎnzé, 免刑 miǎnxíng (absolve). — n. 藉口 jièkǒu, 託辭 tuōcí.

execute v. ①執行 zhíxíng, 實施 shíshī (carry out). ②處決 chǔjué (put to death). ③使生效 shǐ shēngxiào ⟨contract⟩.

execution n. ①執行 zhíxíng, 實施 shíshī (carrying out). ②處死 chǔsǐ (putting to death). ③簽章生效 qiānzhāng shēngxiào ⟨contract⟩.

executive adj. ①執行的 zhíxíng de, 實行的 shíxíng de (being executed). ②行政的 xíngzhèng de (administrative). — n. ①行政官 xíngzhèngguān (administrator). ②經理 jīnglǐ, 主管 zhǔguǎn (manager).

executor n. 遺囑執行人 yízhǔ zhíxíngrén.

exemplify v. 舉例說明 jǔlì shuōmíng, 作為實例 zuòwéi shílì.

exempt v. 免除 miǎnchú, 豁免 huòmiǎn. — adj. 被免除的 bèi miǎnchú de.

exercise n. ①運動 yùndòng (sport). ②練習 liànxí (practice). ③習題 xítí, 作業 zuòyè (homework). ④演習 yǎnxí (training). ⑤運用 yùnyòng (use). — v. ①運動 yùndòng (work out). ②訓練 xùnliàn (train).

exert v. 運用 yùnyòng (use).

exhale v. 呼出 hūchū.

exhaust v. 用盡 yòngjìn, 耗盡 hàojìn (use up). — n. 廢氣 fèiqì ⟨gas⟩.

exhausted adj. 精疲力盡的 jīng-pí-lì-jìn de.

exhaustion n. ①疲憊不堪 píbèi bùkān (tiredness). ②耗盡 hàojìn (using up).

exhibit v. ①展覽 zhǎnlǎn, 陳列 chénliè (display). ②表現

biǎoxiàn, 顯示 xiǎnshì (demonstrate). — n. 展覽品 zhǎnlǎnpǐn.

exhibition n. ①展覽 zhǎnlǎn (exhibit). ②展覽會 zhǎnlǎnhuì (show). ③表現 biǎoxiàn (demonstration).

exhilarate v. 使高興 shǐ gāoxìng, 使興奮 shǐ xīngfèn.

exhort v. 力勸 lìquàn, 勸告 quàngào.

exile v. 放逐 fàngzhú. — n. ①放逐 fàngzhú (being in exile). ②被放逐者 bèi fàngzhú zhě (person who is exiled).

exist v. ①存在 cúnzài (be). ②生存 shēngcún (live).

existence n. ①存在 cúnzài (being). ②生存 shēngcún (living).

exit n. ①出口 chūkǒu (way out). ②離去 líqù (departure). ③退場 tuìchǎng ⟨theater⟩. — v. 出去 chūqu, 退出 tuìchū.

exit poll 票站調查 piàozhàn diàochá / 選情調查 xuǎnqíng diàochá.

exonerate v. 免罪 miǎnzuì, 免責 miǎnzé.

exorbitant adj. 過多的 guòduō de, 過分的 guòfèn de.

exorcize v. 驅邪 qūxié.

exotic adj. ①外國的 wàiguó de, 異國的 yìguó de (foreign). ②珍奇的 zhēnqí de, 奇異的 qíyì de (strange).

expand v. ①擴張 kuòzhāng, 擴大 kuòdà (broaden). ②展開 zhǎnkāi, 擴展 kuòzhǎn (spread out).

expanse n. 廣闊 guǎngkuò.

expansion n. 擴張 kuòzhāng, 擴大 kuòdà.

expatriate v. ①放逐國外 fàngzhú guówài (exile). ②移居國外 yíjū guówài (live abroad). — n. ①流亡者 liúwángzhě (person who is exiled). ②移居國外者 yíjū guówài zhě (one who resides abroad).

expect v. ①預期 yùqī / yùqí (anticipate), 期待 qīdài / qídài (hope for). ②要求 yāoqiú (demand). ③認為 rènwéi (believe).

expectation n. 預期 yùqī / yùqí (anticipation), 期望 qīwàng / qíwàng, 期待 qīdài / qídài (hope).

expedient n. 權宜之計 quányí zhī jì. — adj. 有用的 yǒuyòng de (useful), 有效的 yǒuxiào de (effective).

expedition n. ①遠征 yuǎnzhēng, 探險 tànxiǎn (voyage). ②遠征隊 yuǎnzhēngduì (voyagers).

expel v. 驅逐 qūzhú.

expend v. 花費 huāfèi.

expenditure n. 花費 huāfèi, 開支 kāizhī.

expense n. 花費 huāfèi, 支出 zhīchū.

expensive adj. 貴的 guì de, 昂貴的 ángguì de.

experience n. & v. 經驗 jīngyàn, 經歷 jīnglì.

experienced adj. 有經驗的 yǒu jīngyàn de.

experiment n. & v. 實驗 shíyàn, 試驗 shìyàn.

expert n. 專家 zhuānjiā. — adj. 老練的 lǎoliàn de, 熟練的 shúliàn de.

expertise n. 專門技術 zhuānmén jìshù.

expire v. ①到期 dàoqī / dàoqí, 期滿 qīmǎn / qímǎn (become invalid). ②死亡 sǐwáng (die).

explain v. ①解釋 jiěshì, 說明 shuōmíng (clarify). ②辯解 biànjiě (justify).

explanation n. ①解釋 jiěshì, 說明 shuōmíng (clarification). ②辯解 biànjiě (justification).

explicit adj. 明確的 míngquè de, 清楚的 qīngchu de.

explode v. ①爆炸 bàozhà (blow up). ②推翻 tuīfān (destroy).

exploit n. ①英勇行為 yīngyǒng xíngwéi (brave actions). ②功績 gōngjì / gōngjī (contribution). — v. ①利用 lìyòng (use something), 開發 kāifā (develop an area). ②剝削 bōxuē / bōxuè (take advantage of).

exploration n. ①探險 tànxiǎn (adventure), 探測 tàncè (probe). ②探討 tàntǎo (examination).

explore v. ①探測 tàncè (probe), 探險 tànxiǎn (adventure). ②探討 tàntǎo (examine).

explosion n. 爆發 bàofā, 爆炸 bàozhà.

explosive adj. 爆炸的 bàozhà de. — n. 爆炸物 bàozhàwù, 炸藥 zhàyào.

export v. 輸出 shūchū, 出口 chūkǒu. — n. ①輸出 shūchū, 出口 chūkǒu (exporting). ②輸出品 shūchūpǐn (exported product).

expose v. ①暴露 bàolù / pùlù (reveal). ②揭穿 jiēchuān (bring to light). ③曝光 pùguāng (come to light). ④顯露 xiǎnlù (show). ⑤接觸 jiēchù (come in contact).

⑥展覽 zhǎnlǎn, 陳列 chénliè (display).

exposition n. ①博覽會 bólǎnhuì, 展覽會 zhǎnlǎnhuì (exhibition). ②說明 shuōmíng (explanation).

exposure n. ①暴露 bàolù / pùlù (uncovering). ②揭穿 jiēchuān (being revealed). ③曝光 pùguāng ⟨film⟩. ④展覽 zhǎnlǎn (displaying).

expound v. 詳述 xiángshù, 詳加說明 xiángjiā shuōmíng.

express v. ①表達 biǎodá, 表示 biǎoshì (convey). ②速遞 sùdì / 快遞 kuàidì (express delivery). — adj. ①清楚的 qīngchu de, 明確的 míngquè de (explicit). ②快速的 kuàisù de (fast). — n. 快車 kuàichē.

expression n. ①表達 biǎodá, 表示 biǎoshì (way of conveying). ②措辭 cuòcí (phrase). ③表情 biǎoqíng (facial expression).

expulsion n. 驅逐 qūzhú.

exquisite adj. ①精緻的 jīngzhì de (fine), 優美的 yōuměi de (beautiful). ②劇烈的 jùliè de (severe). ③敏銳的 mǐnruì de (keen).

extend v. ①延長 yáncháng (prolong), 延期 yánqī / yánqí (postpone). ②擴大 kuòdà (enlarge). ③伸展 shēnzhǎn, 伸長 shēncháng (stretch out).

extension n. ①延長 yáncháng, 伸展 shēnzhǎn (prolongation). ②擴充 kuòchōng (addition). ③延期 yánqī / yánqí (postponement).

extensive adj. 廣闊的 guǎngkuò de, 廣泛的 guǎngfàn de.

extent n. ①程度 chéngdù (degree). ②長度 chángdù (length), 範圍 fànwéi (scope).

exterior n. & adj. 外部 wàibù (outer part), 外表 wàibiǎo (appearance).

exterminate v. 消滅 xiāomiè.

external adj. ①外面的 wàimian de, 外部的 wàibù de (outside). ②外來的 wàilái de (not inherent). ③外國的 wàiguó de (foreign).

extinct adj. ①熄滅的 xímiè de / xímiè de (extinguished). ②滅種的 mièzhǒng de (died out).

extinguish v. ①熄滅 xímiè / xímiè (put out). ②消滅 xiāomiè (exterminate).

extort v. 勒索 lèsuǒ, 敲詐 qiāozhà.

extra adj. 額外的 éwài de.

extract v. ①拔取 báqǔ (take out). ②引述 yǐnshù, 摘錄 zhāilù (quote). ③榨取 zhàqǔ (obtain by crushing). — n. ①濃汁 nóngzhī, 提取物 tíqǔwù (liquid extracted). ②引語 yǐnyǔ, 摘錄 zhāilù (citation).

extraordinary adj. 特別的 tèbié de.

extravagance n. ①奢侈 shēchǐ (luxury). ②浪費 làngfèi (wastefulness). ③放縱 fàngzòng (over-indulgence).

extravagant adj. ①奢侈的 shēchǐ de (luxurious). ②浪費的 làngfèi de (wasteful). ③過分的 guòfèn de (excessive).

extreme adj. ①極度的 jídù de, 極端的 jíduān de (utmost). ②盡頭的 jìntóu de, 最遠的 zuì yuǎn de (farthest). ③偏激的 piānjī de (exaggerated).

— *n*. 末端 mòduān, 極端 jíduān.

extremely *adv*. ①非常 fēicháng (very). ②極端地 jíduān de (too).

extremity *n*. ①末端 mòduān (end). ②極度 jídù (extreme degree).

exuberant *adj*. ①充滿活力的 chōngmǎn huólì de (excited). ②茂盛的 màoshèng de (luxuriant).

exude *v*. 滲出 shènchū, 流出 liúchū (flow out).

eye *n*. ①眼睛 yǎnjing ⟨body part⟩. ②眼光 yǎnguāng (taste). *an ~ for an* ～ 以牙還牙 yǐ-yá-huán-yá.

eyeball *n*. 眼球 yǎnqiú.

eyebrow *n*. 眉毛 méimao.

eyelash *n*. 睫毛 jiémáo.

eyelid *n*. 眼瞼 yǎnjiǎn.

eyesight *n*. 視力 shìlì.

F

fable *n*. 寓言 yùyán.

fabric *n*. 織物 zhīwù.

fabricate *v*. ①建造 jiànzào (construct). ②捏造 niēzào (lie), 虛構 xūgòu (invent).

fabulous *adj*. ①極好的 jí hǎo de (excellent). ②驚人的 jīngrén de (unbelievable).

facade *n*. ①假象 jiǎxiàng (pretense). ②建物正面 jiànwù zhèngmiàn (front of building).

face *n*. ①臉 liǎn ⟨body part⟩. ②表面 biǎomiàn (surface), 面 miàn (facet). ③表情 biǎoqíng (expression). ④面子 miànzi (pride). *lose* ～ 丟臉 diūliǎn. — *v*. ①面向…… miàn xiàng... (be across from). ②面對 miànduì (confront), 面臨 miànlín (encounter). ～ *-off* 對抗 duìkàng.

facet *n*. ①小平面 xiǎo píngmiàn, 面 miàn (side). ②方面 fāngmiàn (aspect).

facetious *adj*. 輕浮的 qīngfú de, 愛開不當玩笑的 ài kāi búdàng wánxiào de.

facial *adj*. 面部的 miànbù de, 臉部的 liǎnbù de. — *n*. 做臉 zuòliǎn.

facile *adj*. ①輕而易舉的 qīng-ér-yì-jǔ (easily done). ②膚淺的 fūqiǎn de (superficial).

facilitate *v*. 使便利 shǐ biànlì.

facility *n*. ①設備 shèbèi (equipment). ②容易 róngyì (ease). ③才能 cáinéng (ability).

facsimile *n*. ①模擬 mónǐ, 複製 fùzhì (copy). ②傳真 chuánzhēn (fax).

fact *n*. 事實 shìshí, 真相 zhēnxiàng. *in* ～ 其實 qíshí.

faction *n*. 派系 pàixì, 小派別 xiǎo pàibié.

factional *adj*. 派系的 pàixì de.

factor *n*. ①因素 yīnsù (component). ②因數 yīnshù ⟨mathematics⟩.

factory n. 工廠 gōngchǎng, 製造處 zhìzàochù.

factual adj. 事實的 shìshí de.

faculty n. ①才能 cáinéng, 能力 nénglì (ability). ②全體教職員 quántǐ jiàozhíyuán 〈group〉.

fade v. ①褪色 tuìsè / tùnsè (lose color). ②凋萎 diāowěi / diāowěi, 衰落 shuāiluò (wither).

Fahrenheit n. 華氏溫度計 Huáshì wēndùjì.

fail v. ①失敗 shībài (be unsuccessful). ②不足 bù zú (be insufficient). ③不及格 bù jígé (not fulfill standard). ④使失望 shǐ shīwàng (disappoint).

failing n. 缺點 quēdiǎn.

failure n. ①失敗 shībài (the fact of failing). ②失敗者 shībàizhě 〈person〉.

faint adj. ①模糊不清的 móhu bù qīng de (unclear). ②昏暈的 hūnyūn de (dizzy). — n. & v. 昏厥 hūnjué.

fair adj. ①公平的 gōngping de, 正直的 zhèngzhí de (just). ②美好的 měihǎo de (fine). ③晴朗的 qínglǎng de 〈weather〉. — n. ①市集 shìjí (market). ②博覽會 bólǎnhuì (exhibition).

fairly adv. ①公平地 gōngping de (justly). ②相當地 xiāngdāng de (rather).

fairy n. 小仙子 xiǎo xiānzǐ. ~ tale 童話故事 tónghuà gùshì.

faith n. ①信任 xìnrèn, 相信 xiāngxìn (trust). ②信仰 xìnyǎng (religious belief).

faithful adj. ①忠實的 zhōngshí de (loyal), 誠信的 chéngxìn de (honest).

fake n. ①贗品 yànpǐn, 偽造品 wěizàopǐn / wèizàopǐn (dupli-

cate). ②騙子 piànzi (cheat). — v. 偽造 wěizào / wèizào (forge), 假裝 jiǎzhuāng (pretend). — adj. 假的 jiǎ de.

falcon n. 獵鷹 lièyīng.

fall v. ①落下 luòxià, 倒下 dǎoxià (drop). ②下降 xiàjiàng (decrease). ③陷落 xiànluò (surrender). ④墮落 duòluò (degenerate). ~ apart 崩潰 bēngkuì. ~ asleep 睡著 shuìzháo. ~ for ①聽信 tīngxìn (be fooled). ②迷戀 míliàn (fall in love). ~ in love 愛上 àishang. ~ out with... 跟……吵架 gēn... chǎojià. ~ through 失敗 shībài. — n. 秋季 qiūjì, 秋天 qiūtiān.

fallacy n. 錯誤 cuòwù, 謬見 miùjiàn.

fallen adj. ①落下的 luòxià de (down). ②死亡的 sǐwáng de (dead).

fallible adj. 會犯錯的 huì fàncuò de.

fallow n. & adj. 休耕 xiūgēng.

false adj. ①假的 jiǎ de (untrue). ②錯的 cuò de (erroneous).

falsify v. 偽造 wěizào / wèizào.

falter v. 蹣跚 pánshān (stagger).

fame n. 名氣 míngqì, 聲譽 shēngyù.

familiar adj. ①認識的 rènshi de (acquainted). ②熟悉的 shúxí de (close). ③親密的 qīnmì de (intimate). ④常見的 chángjiàn de (common).

family n. 家庭 jiātíng (household), 家人 jiārén (relatives).

famine n. 饑荒 jīhuang.

famish v. 挨餓 āi'è / ái'è.

famous adj. 有名的 yǒumíng de, 著名的 zhùmíng de.

fan n. ①風扇 fēngshàn (blower). ②迷 mí (enthusiast).

fanatic n. 狂熱者 kuángrèzhě.

fanciful adj. 異想天開的 yì-xiǎng-tiān-kāi de.

fancy n. ①想像力 xiǎngxiànglì (imagination). ②看法 kànfa, 念頭 niàntou (idea). — v. ①想像 xiǎngxiàng (imagine). ②喜歡 xǐhuan (like). — adj. ①精選的 jīngxuǎn de (elaborate). ②花俏的 huāqiào de (not plain).

fang n. 尖牙 jiānyá.

fantabulous adj. 棒極了的 bàng jí le de.

fantastic adj. ①奇特的 qítè de (strange). ②很棒的 hěn bàng de (excellent). ③幻想的 huànxiǎng de (imaginary).

fantasy n. 想像 xiǎngxiàng, 幻想 huànxiǎng.

far adj. 遠的 yuǎn de (distant). — adv. 久遠地 jiǔyuǎn de (remotely). so ~ 到目前為止 dào mùqián wéizhǐ. *the F- East* 遠東 Yuǎndōng.

faraway adj. 久遠的 jiǔyuǎn de.

farce n. 鬧劇 nàojù 〈play〉.

fare n. ①票價 piàojià, 車費 chēfèi (ticket price). ②食物 shíwù (food).

farewell interj. 再會 zàihuì! — adj. 告別的 gàobié de.

farm n. 農田 nóngtián, 農場 nóngchǎng. — v. 耕田 gēngtián.

farmer n. 農夫 nóngfū.

farmhouse n. 農舍 nóngshè.

farther adj. 較遠的 jiào yuǎn de (more distant). — adv. 較遠地 jiào yuǎn de (further).

farthest adj. & adv. 最遠的 zuì yuǎn de.

fascinate v. ①使著迷 shǐ zháomí (charm). ②蠱惑 gǔhuò (bewitch).

Fascism n. 法西斯主義 Fǎxīsī zhǔyì.

fashion n. ①流行 liúxíng (popularity). ②時髦 shímào (style). ③作風 zuòfēng (manner).

fashionable adj. 時髦的 shímào de (stylish), 流行的 liúxíng de (popular).

fast adj. ①快的 kuài de (quick). ②牢固的 láogù de (attached). ③耐久的 nàijiǔ de (lasting). ~ *lane* 快車道 kuàichēdào. ~ *track* 捷徑 jiéjìng.

fasten v. 繫牢 jìláo (attach).

fast-food adj. 速食的 sùshí de.

fastidious adj. 吹毛求疵的 chuī-máo-qiú-cī de, 講究細節的 jiǎngjiu xìjié de.

fat adj. 肥的 féi de (obese), 胖的 pàng de (plump). — n. 脂肪 zhīfáng 〈biology〉, 肥肉 féiròu (fatty meat). ~ *farm* 減肥中心 jiǎnféi zhōngxīn.

fatal adj. 致命的 zhìmìng de.

fatalism n. 宿命論 sùmìnglùn.

fatality n. ①災禍 zāihuò (accident). ②死亡 sǐwáng (death). ③宿命 sùmìng (fate).

fate n. ①命運 mìngyùn (destiny). ②結局 jiéjú (end).

father n. 父親 fùqīn, 爸爸 bàba.

Father's Day 父親節 Fùqīnjié.

father-in-law n. 公公 gōnggong (husband's father), 岳父 yuèfù (wife's father).

fatigue n. 疲勞 píláo. — v. 使疲勞 shǐ píláo.

F

fatuous adj. 愚昧的 yúmèi de (stupid).

faucet n. 水龍頭 shuǐlóngtóu.

fault n. ①缺點 quēdiǎn (defect). ②錯誤 cuòwù, 過失 guòshī (error). ③斷層 duàncéng 〈geology〉. — v. 責怪 zéguài (blame).

favor n. & v. ①贊成 zànchéng (approval). ②偏愛 piān'ài (preference). *do... a ~* 幫…… (一個) 忙 bāng...(yí ge) máng.

favorable adj. ①贊成的 zànchéng de (approving). ②良好的 liánghǎo de (good).

favorite adj. 最喜愛的 zuì xǐ'ài de. — n. 最愛 zuì ài.

fawn v. 巴結 bājie, 奉承 fèngcheng (flatter).

fax n. & v. 傳真 chuánzhēn. *~ machine* 傳真機 chuánzhēnjī.

fear n. 懼怕 jùpà, 恐懼感 kǒngjùgǎn.

fearful adj. ①害怕的 hàipà de (afraid). ②可怕的 kěpà de (frightening).

fearless adj. 無畏的 wúwèi de.

feasible adj. ①可行的 kěxíng de (possible). ②適宜的 shìyí de (suitable).

feasibility n. 可行性 kěxíngxìng.

feast n. ①宴會 yànhuì (meal). ②節慶 jiéqìng (festival).

feat n. 功績 gōngjì / gōngjī.

feather n. 羽毛 yǔmáo.

feature n. ①面貌 miànmào 〈face〉. ②特徵 tèzhēng, 特色 tèsè (characteristic). ③特寫 tèxiě 〈article〉.

February n. 二月 Èryuè.

federal adj. 聯邦的 liánbāng de.

fee n. 費 fèi.

feeble adj. 微弱的 wēiruò de / wéiruò de.

feed v. 餵食 wèishí, 飼養 sìyǎng (nourish).

feedback n. 反饋 fǎnkuì / 回饋 huíkuì.

feel v. ①感覺 gǎnjué, 覺得 juéde (consider). ②觸摸 chùmō (touch), 感覺到 gǎnjué dào (experience).

feeler n. 觸角 chùjiǎo, 觸鬚 chùxū (antenna).

feeling n. ①感覺 gǎnjué (awareness). ②感情 gǎnqíng (passion). ③情緒 qíngxù (emotion). ④感受力 gǎnshòulì (responsiveness).

feet n. 腳 jiǎo.

feint n. & v. 佯攻 yánggōng (pretended attack).

feline adj. 似貓的 sì māo de (like a cat). — n. 貓科動物 māokē dòngwù.

fellow n. ①人 rén, 傢伙 jiāhuo (man). ②同伴 tóngbàn (companion), 同事 tóngshì (co-worker).

fellowship n. ①交情 jiāoqíng (companionship). ②補助金 bǔzhùjīn (grant). ③會 huì, 團體 tuántǐ (group). ④會員資格 huìyuán zīgé (membership).

female n. 女性 nǚxìng 〈human〉, 雌性 cíxìng 〈animal〉. — adj. 女性的 nǚxìng de 〈human〉, 雌的 cí de 〈animal〉.

feminine adj. ①女性化的 nǚxìnghuà de 〈women〉. ②陰性的 yīnxìng de 〈linguistics〉.

feminism n. 女性主義 nǚxìng zhǔyì, 女權主義 nǚquán zhǔyì, 男女平等主義 nánnǚ píngděng zhǔyì.

fen *n.* 沼澤 zhǎozé.

fence *n.* 柵欄 zhàlan, 籬笆 líba.

fencing *n.* 劍術 jiànshù.

fender *n.* 擋泥板 dǎngníbǎn.

feng shui *n.* 風水 fēngshuǐ.

ferment *v.* 發酵 fājiào / fāxiào, 醞釀 yùnniàng.

fern *n.* 羊齒植物 yángchǐ zhíwù.

ferocious *adj.* 兇猛的 xiōngměng de.

ferret *n.* 雪貂 xuědiāo ⟨animal⟩. — *v.* 搜索 sōusuǒ ⟨search for⟩.

ferry *n.* 渡船 dùchuán ⟨ferry-boat⟩. — *v.* 運送 yùnsòng.

fertile *adj.* 肥沃的 féiwò de, 多產的 duōchǎn de ⟨productive⟩.

fertilize *v.* 施肥 shīféi ⟨soil⟩.

fertilizer *n.* 肥料 féiliào.

fervent *adj.* 熱情的 rèqíng de, 熱烈的 rèliè de.

fervor *n.* 熱情 rèqíng, 熱烈 rèliè.

fester *v.* 化膿 huànóng, 潰爛 kuìlàn.

festival *n.* 節日 jiérì, 慶典 qìngdiǎn.

fetch *v.* ①取來 qǔlái ⟨bring⟩. ②售得 shòudé ⟨sell for⟩. ③接來 jiēlái ⟨people⟩.

fetid *adj.* 惡臭的 èchòu de.

fetish *n.* ①滿足性慾之物 mǎnzú xìngyù zhī wù ⟨in psychology⟩. ②受崇拜之神物 shòu chóngbài zhī shénwù ⟨magical figurine⟩.

fetter *n. & v.* ①腳鐐 jiǎoliào / jiǎoliào ⟨chain⟩. ②束縛 shùfù / shùfú ⟨restraint⟩.

feud *n.* 世仇 shìchóu, 不和

bùhé.

feudal *adj.* 封建的 fēngjiàn de.

feudalism *n.* 封建主義 fēngjiàn zhǔyì.

fever *n.* ①發燒 fāshāo ⟨high temperature⟩. ②熱病 rèbìng ⟨disease⟩. ③狂熱 kuángrè ⟨excited state⟩.

few *n. & pron.* 很少 hěn shǎo, 幾個 jǐge, 一些 yìxiē.

fiancé *n.* 未婚夫 wèihūnfū.

fiancée *n.* 未婚妻 wèihūnqī.

fib *n.* 小謊 xiǎohuǎng.

fiber *n.* 纖維 xiānwéi.

fickle *adj.* 多變的 duōbiàn de.

fiction *n.* ①虛構故事 xūgòu gùshì ⟨story⟩. ②小說 xiǎoshuō ⟨novel⟩.

fiddle *n.* 小提琴 xiǎotíqín.

fidelity *n.* 忠誠 zhōngchéng ⟨loyalty⟩.

fidget *v.* 坐立不安 zuò-lì-bù'ān.

field *n.* ①田地 tiándì, 田野 tiányě ⟨land⟩. ②領域 lǐngyù ⟨domain⟩. ③場地 chǎngdì ⟨area⟩.

fiend *n.* 惡魔 èmó ⟨devil⟩.

fierce *adj.* 兇猛的 xiōngměng de.

fiery *adj.* ①燃燒的 ránshāo de ⟨flaming⟩. ②暴躁的 bàozào de, 激怒的 jīnù de ⟨angry⟩.

fifteen *n. & adj.* 十五 shíwǔ.

fifteenth *n. & adj.* 第十五 dì-shíwǔ.

fifth *n. & adj.* 第五 dì-wǔ.

fiftieth *n. & adj.* 第五十 dì-wǔshí.

fifty *n. & adj.* 五十 wǔshí.

fig *n.* 無花果 wúhuāguǒ ⟨plant⟩.

fight *v.* ①吵架 chǎojià ⟨quarrel⟩. ②打架 dǎjià ⟨battle⟩. ③打

F

仗 dǎzhàng, 與……戰爭 yǔ...zhànzhēng (be at war with). ④抗爭 kàngzhēng (oppose). ~ *for...* 為……奮鬥 wèi... fèndòu.

fighter *n.* ①拳擊手 quánjīshǒu / quánjíshǒu (boxer). ②鬥士 dòushì, 戰士 zhànshì ⟨person⟩. ③戰鬥機 zhàndòujī ⟨aircraft⟩.

figment *n.* 虛構之事 xūgòu zhī shì.

figurative *adj.* 比喻的 bǐyù de.

figure *n.* ①數字 shùzì (numeral). ②身材 shēncái (body shape). ③人物 rénwù (person). ④圖形 túxíng, 圖表 túbiǎo (diagram). — *v.* ①認為 rènwéi (think), 覺得 juéde (feel). ②扮演 bànyǎn (play a role). ~ *out* 了解 liǎojiě (understand). *It* ~ *s!* 難怪 Nánguài!

filament *n.* ①線 xiàn (thread). ②燈絲 dēngsī (wire in bulb).

file *n.* ①卷宗 juànzōng, 檔案 dàng'àn / dǎng'àn (folder). ②銼刀 cuòdāo ⟨tool⟩. — *v.* 歸檔 guīdàng / guīdǎng.

fill *v.* ①充滿 chōngmǎn, 裝滿 zhuāngmǎn (make full). ②遞補 dìbǔ ⟨position⟩. ③供應 gōngyìng (supply). ~ *in,* ~ *out* 填寫 tiánxiě.

film *n.* ①膠捲 jiāojuǎn / 軟片 ruǎnpiàn ⟨photography⟩. ②電影 diànyǐng (movie). ③薄層 báocéng / bócéng (layer).

film-maker *n.* 電影製作人 diànyǐng zhìzuòrén.

filter *n.* 過濾器 guòlǜqì.

filth *n.* 污穢 wūhuì.

fin *n.* 鰭 qí.

final *adj.* 最後的 zuìhòu de.

— *n.* 期末考試 qīmò kǎoshì / qímò kǎoshì (end-of-term test), 決賽 juésài (competition).

finally *adv.* 最後 zuìhòu (at the end), 終於 zhōngyú (at last).

finance *n.* 財政 cáizhèng ⟨economic regulations⟩, 財務 cáiwù ⟨wealth⟩, 金融 jīnróng (having to do with money). *Ministry of F~* 財政部 Cáizhèngbù.

finances *n.* 財務 cáiwù (wealth), 經濟情況 jīngjì qíngkuàng (economic situation).

financial *adj.* 財政的 cáizhèng de, 財務的 cáiwù de.

find *v.* ①找到 zhǎodào (seek out). ②發現 fāxiàn (discover). ③發覺 fājué (observe), 得知 dézhī (learn).

fine *adj.* ①美好的 měihǎo de (beautiful). ②精巧的 jīngqiǎo de (delicate). ③安好的 ānhǎo de (well). ④晴朗的 qínglǎng de ⟨weather⟩. ⑤細的 xì de (slender). — *n.* 罰金 fájīn. — *v.* 處以罰金 chǔyǐ fájīn, 罰款 fákuǎn.

finery *n.* 華服 huáfú.

finger *n.* 手指 shǒuzhǐ.

fingerprint *n.* 指紋 zhǐwén.

finish *n. & v.* 結束 jiéshù (end), 完成 wánchéng (completion).

finite *adj.* 有限的 yǒuxiàn de.

fir *n.* 樅樹 cōngshù.

fire *n.* ①火 huǒ (flame). ②火災 huǒzāi ⟨calamity⟩. ③爐火 lúhuǒ (in fireplace). ~ *door* 防火門 fánghuǒmén. ~ *engine* 消防車 xiāofángchē. ~ *extinguisher* 滅火器 mièhuǒqì. ~ *hydrant* 消防栓 xiāofángshuān.

— *v.* ①射擊 shèjī / shèjí, 開槍

kāiqiāng (shoot). ②解雇 jiěgù (dismiss). ③縱火 zònghuǒ (set on fire).

firecracker n. 爆竹 bàozhú, 鞭炮 biānpào.

firefighter n. 消防隊員 xiāofáng duìyuán.

firefly n. 螢火蟲 yínghuǒchóng.

fireman n. 消防隊員 xiāofáng duìyuán.

fireplace n. 壁爐 bìlú.

fireproof adj. 防火的 fánghuǒ de.

fireworks n. 煙火 yānhuǒ.

firm adj. 穩固的 jiāngù de, 堅定的 jiāndìng de (rigid). — n. 商店 shāngdiàn (store), 公司 gōngsī (company).

first adj. 第一的 dì-yī de, 最初的 zuìchū de (initial). ~ name 名 míng. ~ person 第一人稱 dì-yī rénchēng. — n. 第一個 dì-yī ge (initial), 第一名 dì-yī míng (contest). — adv. 首先 shǒuxiān, 第一 dì-yī. ~ of all 首先 shǒuxiān. at ~ 當初 dāngchū, 最初 zuìchū.

first-class adj. 頭等的 tóuděng de.

fiscal adj. 財政的 cáizhèng de.

fish n. 魚 yú ⟨animal⟩, 魚肉 yúròu ⟨meat⟩. — v. 釣魚 diàoyú, 捕魚 bǔyú.

fisherman n. 漁夫 yúfū ⟨job⟩, 釣客 diàokè ⟨fun⟩.

fishing n. 釣魚 diàoyú, 捕魚 bǔyú.

fission n. 分裂 fēnliè.

fist n. 拳 quán, 拳頭 quántou.

fit v. 適合 shìhé, 適合於 shìhé yú. — adj. 適宜的 shìyí de, 合適的 héshì de (suitable). 適當的 shìdàng de, 對的

duì de (proper). ③健康的 jiànkāng de (healthy).

fitting adj. 適當的 shìdàng de, 適合的 shìhé de. — n. ①試穿 shìchuān ⟨clothing⟩. ②配件 pèijiàn, 裝備 zhuāngbèi (small standardized part).

five n. & adj. 五 wǔ.

fix v. ①修理 xiūlǐ (repair). ②固定 gùdìng (regularize). ③確定 quèdìng, 決定 juédìng (determine). ④使牢固 shǐ láogù (secure).

fixed adj. 牢固的 láogù de (secure), 固定的 gùdìng de (regular).

fizz n. & v. 嘶嘶聲 sīsīshēng.

flabby adj. 鬆軟的 sōngruǎn de, 鬆弛的 sōngchí de.

flag n. 旗 qí, 旗子 qízi.

flagpole n. 旗桿 qígān.

flagrant adj. ①窮兇極惡的 qióng-xiōng-jí-è de (very bad). ②無恥的 wúchǐ de (shameless).

flair n. 特色 tèsè (style).

flake n. 薄片 báopiàn / báopiàn. — v. 成片剝落 chéngpiàn bōluò.

flamboyant adj. ①燦爛的 cànlàn de (colorful). ②炫耀的 xuànyào de (showy).

flame n. 火焰 huǒyàn. — v. 發出火焰 fāchū huǒyàn (flare up), 燃燒 ránshāo (burn).

flamingo n. 火鶴 huǒhè ⟨bird⟩.

flank n. ①側面 cèmiàn (side). ②側腹 cèfù ⟨body part⟩.

flannel n. 法蘭絨 fǎlánróng.

flap v. 拍打 pāidǎ, 撲拍 pūpāi, 鼓翼 gǔyì.

flare n. & v. 火焰搖曳 huǒyàn yáoyè / huǒyàn yáoyì (flame), 閃光 shǎnguāng (flicker).

flash n. ①閃光 shǎnguāng,

閃爍 shǎnshuò (glare).
②閃光燈 shǎnguāngdēng
⟨photograph⟩. — v. ①閃光
shǎnguāng (flicker). ②突然出
現 tūrán chūxiàn / túrán
chūxiàn,閃現 shǎnxiàn
(appear suddenly).

flashback n. 倒敘 dàoxù.

flashlight n. 手電筒
shǒudiàntǒng.

flask n. 扁瓶 biǎnpíng
(flat bottle).

flat adj. ①平的 píng de,平坦
的 píngtǎn de (level). ②單調
的 dāndiào de (dull). ③扁的
biǎn de (with little thickness).
④無氣的 wú qì de ⟨tire⟩. — n.
公寓 gōngyù,樓房 lóufáng
(apartment).

flatten v. (使)平坦 (shǐ)
píngtǎn,變平 biànpíng.

flatter v. 諂媚 chǎnmèi,取悅
qǔyuè.

flattery n. 諂媚 chǎnmèi.

flaunt n. & v. 炫耀 xuànyào.

flavor n. 味道 wèidao. — v. 調
味 tiáowèi.

flaw n. ①裂縫 lièfèng (crack).
②缺點 quēdiǎn (defect),瑕疵
xiácī (blemish).

flax n. 亞麻 yàmá.

flea n. 跳蚤 tiàozǎo.

fleck n. 斑點 bāndiǎn.

flee v. 逃走 táozǒu (escape),
逃避 táobì (evade).

fleece n. 羊毛 yángmáo (wool).
— v. 剪羊毛 jiǎn yángmáo
(shear).

fleet n. 艦隊 jiànduì.

fleeting adj. 疾逝的 jíshì de.

flesh n. ①肉 ròu (meat). ②骨肉
gǔròu (one's own children).
~ and blood ①血肉之軀
xuèròu zhī qū / xiěròu zhī qū

(human beings). ②骨肉 gǔròu
(family). *in the ~* 本人 běnrén.

flexible adj. ①有彈性的 yǒu
tánxìng de (adjustable). ②易彎
曲的 yì wānqū de (bendable).

flick n. & v. 輕打 qīngdǎ,輕彈
qīngtán.

flicker v. 閃爍 shǎnshuò,
搖曳 yáoyè / yáoyì. — n. 閃動
shǎndòng.

flier n. ①飛行員 fēixíngyuán
(airman). ②傳單 chuándān
⟨advertisement⟩.

flight n. ①飛行 fēixíng (flying).
②航程 hángchéng (journey).

flimsy adj. 脆弱的 cuìruò de
(not strong),輕而薄的 qīng ér
báo de / qīng ér bó de (light
and thin).

flinch n. & v. 畏縮 wèisuō.

fling v. 投 tóu,擲 zhì / zhí
(throw).

flint n. 打火石 dǎhuǒshí,燧石
suìshí.

flip v. ①彈拋 tánpāo,輕彈
qīngtán ⟨into the air⟩. ②翻 fān
(turn over).

flippant adj. 無禮的 wúlǐ de.

flirt v. 調情 tiáoqíng. — n. 調
情者 tiáoqíngzhě,賣弄風騷
者 màinong fēngsāo zhě.

float v. 漂流 piāoliú,漂浮
piāofú (drift). — n. 浮標
fúbiāo (buoy).

flock n. 群 qún (group). — v.
群集 qúnjí.

flog v. 重打 zhòngdǎ,鞭笞
biānchī.

flood n. 洪水 hóngshuǐ,水災
shuǐzāi. — v. 氾濫 fànlàn,淹
沒 yānmò (overflow).

floor n. ①地板 dìbǎn (ground).
②樓層 lóucéng (story).

flop v. ①啪嗒地跳動 pādā de

tiàodòng (move clumsily).
②猛落 měngluò (fall). ③失敗
shībài (fail).

floppy adj. 鬆軟的 sōngruǎn
de. ~ *disk* 軟盤 ruǎnpán / 磁
片 cípiàn.

floral adj. 花的 huā de.

florist n. 花店 huādiàn ⟨store⟩.
花商 huāshāng ⟨person⟩.

flotilla n. 小艦隊 xiǎo jiànduì.

flounder v. 掙扎 zhēngzhá
(struggle). — n. 鰈魚 diéyú, 比
目魚 bǐmùyú.

flour n. 麵粉 miànfěn.

flourish v. ①繁盛 fánshèng
(prosper). ②興隆 xīnglóng
(thrive). ③揮動 huīdòng
(wave).

flout v. 輕視 qīngshì.

flow n. & v. 流動 liúdòng.

flowchart n. 流程圖
liúchéngtú.

flower n. 花 huā. — v. 開花
kāihuā.

flu n. 流行性感冒 liúxíngxìng
gǎnmào.

fluctuate v. 動搖 dòngyáo,
波動 bōdòng, 變動 biàndòng.

fluent adj. 流利的 liúlì de, 流
暢的 liúchàng de.

fluff n. 軟毛 ruǎnmáo, 絨毛
róngmáo (soft, feathery stuff).
— v. 使鬆軟 shǐ sōngruǎn.

fluid n. 液體 yètǐ / yìyǐ, 流體
liútǐ. — adj. ①流動的 liúdòng
de (flowing). ②易變的 yì biàn
de (easily changed).

flunk v. 不及格 bù jígé.

fluorescence n. 螢光
yíngguāng.

fluorescent adj. 螢光的
yíngguāng de.

flurry n. ①疾風 jífēng ⟨wind⟩.
②驟雨 zhòuyǔ / zòuyǔ ⟨rain⟩.

③小雪 xiǎoxuě ⟨snow⟩. ④騷動
sāodòng ⟨activity⟩.

flush v. ①發紅 fāhóng, 臉紅
liǎnhóng (blush). ②沖洗
chōngxǐ (wash out). ③驚起
jīngqǐ (drive out). — n. 同花
tónghuā ⟨cards⟩.

fluster v. 使慌亂 shǐ
huāngluàn.

flustered adj. 手忙腳亂的
shǒu-máng-jiǎo-luàn de.

flute n. 笛 dí.

flutter v. & n. 鼓翼 gǔyì, 拍翅
pāichì (flap).

fly v. ①飛 fēi, 飛行 fēixíng
(move through the air). ②搭飛
機 dā fēijī (go by airplane).
③空運 kōngyùn (transport by
air). ④飄揚 piāoyáng (flutter).
⑤飛奔 fēibēn (move quickly).
— n. 蒼蠅 cāngyíng (housefly).

foal n. ①小馬 xiǎomǎ ⟨horse⟩.
②小驢 xiǎolú ⟨ass⟩.

foam n. 泡沫 pàomò (bubble).
— v. 起泡 qǐpào.

focus n. 焦點 jiāodiǎn (focal
point or central point), 焦距
jiāojù (focal length). — v. 集中
焦點於⋯⋯ jízhōng jiāodiǎn
yú⋯.

fodder n. 芻料 chúliào.

foe n. 敵人 dírén, 仇人 chóurén.

fog n. 霧 wù (mist). — v. 使朦
朧 shǐ ménglóng, 變朦朧 biàn
ménglóng.

foggy adj. 有濃霧的 yǒu
nóngwù de.

foil v. 阻撓 zǔnáo (prevent), 打
敗 dǎbài (defeat). — n. ①箔 bó
⟨metal⟩. ②陪襯 péichèn
⟨contrast⟩.

fold n. & v. 摺疊 zhédié (bend).

folder n. 文件夾 wénjiànjiā /
wénjiànjiá.

foliage n. 樹葉 shùyè (leaves).

folk n. ①民族 mínzú (ethnic group). ②人們 rénmen (people). — adj. 民間的 mínjiān de.
~ customs 民俗 mínsú.
~ dance 土風舞 tǔfēngwǔ.
~ hero 民族英雄 mínzú yīngxióng. ~ song 民謠 mínyáo.

follow v. ①跟隨 gēnsuí, 跟著 gēnzhe (go after). ②接著 jiēzhe, 繼之而來 jì-zhī-ér-lái (succeed). ③遵循 zūnxún (obey). ④理解 lǐjiě (comprehend).

follower n. 追隨者 zhuīsuízhě, 門徒 méntú (pupil).

following n. 擁護者 yōnghùzhě / yǒnghùzhě. — adj. 下列的 xiàliè de (listed below), 下一(個) xià yī (ge) (next). ~ day 第二天 dì-èr tiān.

follow-up n. 追蹤調查 zhuīzōng diàochá (trace). — adj. 後續的 hòuxù de.

folly n. 愚笨 yúbèn.

fond adj. 喜愛的 xǐ'ài de (like).

fondle v. 愛撫 àifǔ.

font n. ①洗禮盆 xǐlǐpén ⟨baptismal⟩. ②字型 zìxíng ⟨type⟩.

food n. 食物 shíwù. ~ bank 食物賑貧站 shíwù zhěnpínzhàn.

foodie n. 美食家 měishíjiā.

fool n. ①愚人 yúrén (silly person). ②小丑 xiǎochǒu (clown). — v. 愚弄 yúnòng (trick), 欺騙 qīpiàn (cheat). ~ around ①開玩笑 kāi wánxiào (joke). ②鬼混 guǐhùn, 亂來 luànlái (mess around). ③玩弄 wánnòng (tease).

foolish adj. 愚蠢的 yúchǔn de, 笨的 bèn de.

foot n. ①足 zú, 腳 jiǎo ⟨of

person, animals⟩. ②呎 chǐ (measure of length). ③基部 jībù (base). on ~ 徒步 túbù, 步行 bùxíng.

football n. ①足球 zúqiú (soccer). ②美式足球 měishì zúqiú (American football).

footlights n. 腳燈 jiǎodēng.

footnote n. 註腳 zhùjiǎo, 註釋 zhùshì.

footpath n. 小徑 xiǎojìng, 人行道 rénxíngdào.

footprint n. 足跡 zújì, 腳印 jiǎoyìn.

footstep n. ①腳步聲 jiǎobùshēng ⟨sound⟩. ②步 bù (a step). ③足跡 zújì (footprint).

footstool n. 腳凳 jiǎodèng.

for prep. ①為 wèi, 為了 wèile (on behalf of). ②替 tì (in place of). ③因為 yīnwèi, 由於 yóuyú (because of). ④對 duì, 對……來說 duì...láishuō (with respect to). ⑤贊成 zànchéng (in favor of).

forage n. 飼料 sìliào. — v. 搜尋 sōuxún.

forbear v. 抑制 yìzhì, 忍住 rěnzhù (refrain).

forbid v. 禁止 jìnzhǐ (prohibit).

forbidden adj. 被禁止的 bèi jìnzhǐ de.

force n. ①力 lì, 力量 lìliang (strength). ②勢力 shìlì, 影響力 yǐngxiǎnglì (power). ③軍隊 jūnduì ⟨army⟩. — v. 強迫 qiǎngpò (compel).

forceps n. 鉗子 qiánzi, 鑷子 nièzi.

ford n. 淺灘 qiǎntān. — v. 涉過 shèguò.

forearm n. 前臂 qiánbì.

forecast n. & v. 預測 yùcè, 預告 yùgào.

forefather n. 祖先 zǔxiān.

F

forefinger n. 食指 shízhǐ.

forefront n. 最前部 zuì qiánbù.

foregoing adj. 之前的 zhīqián de.

foreground n. 前景 qiánjǐng.

forehead n. 前額 qián'é.

foreign adj. 外國的 wàiguó de (of another country), 外來的 wàilái de (coming from outside).

foreigner n. 外國人 wàiguórén.

foreman n. 工頭 gōngtóu, 領班 língbān.

foremost adj. ①最好的 zuì hǎo de (best). ②首要的 shǒuyào de (most important). ③最先的 zuì xiān de (first).

forerunner n. 先驅 xiānqū.

foresee v. 預知 yùzhī, 預見 yùjiàn.

foresight n. 先見之明 xiān-jiàn-zhī-míng, 遠見 yuǎnjiàn.

forest n. 森林 sēnlín.

forestall v. 先發制人地阻止 xiān-fā-zhì-rén de zǔzhǐ.

foretell v. 預言 yùyán.

forethought n. 深謀遠慮 shēnmóu-yuǎnlǜ.

forever adv. 永遠地 yǒngyuǎn de.

forewarn v. 預先警告 yùxiān jǐnggào.

foreword n. 前言 qiányán, 序 xù.

forfeit v. ①被沒收 bèi mòshōu (be taken away). ②喪失 sàngshī (lose). — n. 沒收物 mòshōuwù.

forge n. ①鐵工廠 tiěgōngchǎng (smithy). ②鍛鐵爐 duàntiělú (furnace). — v. ①鍛打 duàndǎ (hammer out). ②偽造 wěizào / wèizào, 假造 jiǎzào (counterfeit).

forget v. 忘記 wàngjì, 遺忘 yíwàng.

forgive v. 原諒 yuánliàng.

forgo v. 棄絕 qìjué, 放棄 fàngqì.

fork n. 叉 chā, 叉子 chāzi. — v. ①叉起 chāqǐ ⟨utensil⟩. ②分岔 fēnchà (split).

forlorn adj. ①被遺棄的 bèi yíqì de (deserted). ②可憐的 kělián de (pitiable). ③絕望的 juéwàng de (hopeless).

form n. ①形狀 xíngzhuàng (appearance). ②形式 xíngshì (shape). — v. ①形成 xíngchéng (take shape). ②組成 zǔchéng (make).

formal adj. 正式的 zhèngshì de.

formation n. ①形成 xíngchéng, 構成 gòuchéng (structure). ②排列 páiliè (order).

former adj. ①從前的 cóngqián de, 以前的 yǐqián de (earlier). ②前者的 qiánzhě de (previous).

formerly adv. 以前 yǐqián, 從前 cóngqián.

formidable adj. 令人畏懼的 lìng rén wèijù de.

formula n. ①公式 gōngshì (rule). ②配方 pèifāng ⟨substance⟩.

formulaic adj. 公式化的 gōngshìhuà de.

formulate v. 明確陳述 míngquè chénshù (express clearly).

forsake v. 遺棄 yíqì, 拋棄 pāoqì.

fort n. 堡壘 bǎolěi, 要塞 yàosài.

forth adv. ①向前 xiàng qián (forward). ②外出 wàichū (out).

forthcoming adj. ①即將出現的 jíjiāng chūxiàn de (imminent). ②現成的 xiànchéng de, 準備好的 zhǔnbèi hǎo de (ready). ③願意回答的 yuànyì huídá de (willing to answer).

forthwith adv. 立刻 lìkè.

fortieth n. & adj. 第四十 dì-sìshí.

fortification n. 堡壘 bǎolěi, 要塞 yàosài.

fortify v. ①設防 shèfáng (protect). ②加強 jiāqiáng (strengthen).

fortnight n. 兩星期 liǎng xīngqí / liǎng xīngqí, 雙週 shuāng zhōu.

fortress n. 堡壘 bǎolěi, 要塞 yàosài.

fortunate adj. 幸運的 xìngyùn de.

fortunately adv. 幸好 xìnghǎo, 好在 hǎozài.

fortune n. ①命運 mìngyùn (fate). ②幸運 xìngyùn (luck). ③財富 cáifù (wealth).

fortuneteller n. 算命者 suànmìngzhě.

forty n. & adj. 四十 sìshí.

forum n. ①座談會 zuòtánhuì (meeting). ②論壇 lùntán (open discussion).

forward adv. 向前 xiàng qián. — adj. 向前的 xiàng qián de (front). — v. ①轉送 zhuǎnsòng, 傳遞 chuándì (pass on). ②促進 cùjìn (advance). — n. 前鋒 qiánfēng (sports).

fossil n. 化石 huàshí (rock).

foster v. ①培養 péiyǎng (cultivate). ②助長 zhùzhǎng (promote). ③撫育 fǔyù (bring up).

foul adj. ①污穢的 wūhuì de (dirty). ②令人厭惡的 lìng rén yànwù de (disgusting). ③不正

的 bú zhèng de (unfair). ④犯規的 fànguī de (sports).

found v. 建立 jiànlì, 創設 chuàngshè.

foundation n. ①基礎 jīchǔ, 根基 gēnjī (basis). ②地基 dìjī (base). ③建立 jiànlì, 創辦 chuàngbàn (establishment). ④基金會 jījīnhuì (organization).

founder n. 創辦者 chuàngbànzhě, 建立者 jiànlìzhě.

foundry n. 鑄造廠 zhùzàochǎng.

fountain n. 噴水池 pēnshuǐchí.

four n. & adj. 四 sì, 四個 sì ge.

fourteen n. 十四 shísì.

fourteenth n. & adj. 第十四 dì-shísì.

fourth n. & adj. 第四 dì-sì.

fowl n. 禽類 qínlèi.

fox n. 狐狸 húlí (animal).

fraction n. ①部分 bùfen, 碎片 suìpiàn (piece). ②分數 fēnshù (mathematics).

fracture n. & v. ①破裂 pòliè, 折斷 zhéduàn (break). ②骨折 gǔzhé (medical).

fragile adj. 易碎的 yì suì de.

fragment n. 碎片 suìpiàn.

fragrant adj. 芳香的 fāngxiāng de.

frail adj. ①脆弱的 cuìruò de (flimsy). ②意志薄弱的 yìzhì bóruò de (wavering).

frame n. ①框 kuàng, 框架 kuàngjià (border). ②體格 tǐgé (shape). ③鏡頭 jìngtóu (film). ④骨架 gǔjià (skeleton). — v. ①架構 jiàgòu, 擬定 nǐdìng (plan). ②誣陷 wūxiàn (crime).

framework n. ①骨架 gǔjià (frame). ②組織 zǔzhī (organization), 體系 tǐxì (system). ③思想脈絡 sīxiǎng màiluò (frame of reference).

franchise n.①選舉權 xuǎnjǔquán (right to vote).②特權 tèquán (privilege).③經銷權 jīngxiāoquán (right to deal).④加盟體 jiāméngtǐ〈business〉.

frank adj. 坦白的 tǎnbái de, 率直的 shuàizhí de.

frantic adj. 發狂似的 fākuáng sì de.

fraternal adj.①兄弟的 xiōngdì de (having to do with brothers).②友善的 yǒushàn de (friendly).

fraternity n.①兄弟會 xiōngdìhuì (society of men).②手足之情 shǒuzú zhī qíng (brotherhood).

fraud n. 詐欺 zhàqī, 欺騙 qīpiàn.

fraught adj. 充滿的 chōngmǎn de (filled with).

fray n. 爭吵 zhēngchǎo, 喧嘩 xuānhuá (quarrel).

freak n. 怪物 guàiwù, 畸形 jīxíng (abnormal feature). — adj. 怪異的 guàiyì de.

freckle n. 雀斑 quèbān.

free adj.①自由的 zìyóu de (at liberty).②無拘束的 wú jūshù de (not bound).③免費的 miǎnfèi de (without charge).④空閒的 kòngxián de (unoccupied). ~ *speech* 言論自由 yánlùn zìyóu. ~ *will* 自由意志 zìyóu yìzhì. — v. 釋放 shìfàng, 使自由 shǐ zìyóu.

freedom n. 自由 zìyóu.

Freemason n. 共濟會會員 Gòngjìhuì huìyuán.

freeway n. 高速公路 gāosù gōnglù.

freewill adj. 自願的 zìyuàn de.

freeze v.①結冰 jiébīng (become ice).②凍僵 dòngjiāng (chill).③冷凍 lěngdòng (refrigerate).④凍結 dòngjié (fix).

freight n.①貨物 huòwù (cargo).②運費 yùnfèi〈money〉.

French n. & adj.①法國人 Fǎguórén / Fàguórén〈people〉.②法語 Fǎyǔ / Fàyǔ〈language〉. ~ *fries* 炸土豆條 zhá tǔdòutiáo / 薯條 shǔtiáo. ~ *kiss* 法式接吻 fǎshì jiēwěn / fàshì jiēwěn.

frenzy n. 狂亂 kuángluàn.

frequency n. 頻率 pínlǜ, 次數 cìshù.

frequent adj. 頻繁的 pínfán de,屢次的 lǚcì de.

fresco n. 壁畫 bìhuà.

fresh adj.①新鮮的 xīnxiān de〈food〉.②清新的 qīngxīn de〈air〉.③淡的 dàn de〈water〉.④新奇的 xīnqí de〈idea〉.

freshman n. 新生 xīnshēng〈student〉, 新鮮人 xīnxiānrén〈society〉.

fret v. 煩躁 fánzào.

friar n. 修道士 xiūdàoshì.

friction n.①摩擦 mócā (rubbing).②衝突 chōngtū / chōngtú, 不和 bùhé (conflict).

Friday n. 星期五 Xīngqíwǔ / Xīngqíwǔ.

fridge n. 冰箱 bīngxiāng.

friend n. 朋友 péngyou, 友人 yǒurén〈companion〉.

friendly adj. 友善的 yǒushàn de (well-disposed), 親切的 qīnqiè de (affectionate).

friendship n. 友誼 yǒuyì / yǒuyí, 友情 yǒuqíng.

fright n. 驚駭 jīnghài, 恐怖

F

kǒngbù.

frighten v. 驚嚇 jīngxià, 使害怕 shǐ hàipà.

frightful adj. 可怕的 kěpà de.

frigid adj. ①嚴寒的 yánhán de (very cold). ②冷淡的 lěngdàn de (unfriendly).

frill n. 褶邊 zhébiān 〈folds〉.

fringe n. ①縫 suì, 鬚邊 xūbiān (border). ②邊緣 biānyuán (edge).

frisk v. 搜身 sōushēn (search).

frisky adj. 歡躍的 huānyuè de.

fritter v. 慢慢耗費 mànmàn hàofèi (waste). — n. 油條 yóutiáo, 油煎餅 yóujiānbǐng.

frivolous adj. ①不重要的 bú zhòngyào de (unimportant). ②輕浮的 qīngfú de (not serious).

frock n. ①僧袍 sēngpáo 〈monk〉. ②長袍 chángpáo (gown).

frog n. 蛙 wā, 青蛙 qīngwā.

frolic n. & v. 嬉戲 xīxì, 作樂 zuòlè (play).

from prep. ①從 cóng, 自 zì 〈time, place〉. ②離 lí 〈distance〉.

front n. ①前部 qiánbù, 前面 qiánmian (forefront). ②前線 qiánxiàn 〈battle area〉. ③鋒面 fēngmiàn 〈weather〉. **in ~ of** 在……的前面 zài...de qiánmian.

frontage n. 正面 zhèngmiàn.

frontier n. 邊界 biānjiè, 邊境 biānjìng (border).

frost n. 霜 shuāng.

frostbite n. 凍傷 dòngshāng, 凍瘡 dòngchuāng.

froth n. 泡沫 pàomò (bubbles). — v. 起泡沫 qǐ pàomò.

frown n. & v. 皺眉 zhòuméi.

frozen adj. 結冰的 jiébīng de, 凍僵的 dòngjiāng de.

frozen embryo n. 冷凍胚胎 lěngdòng pēitāi.

frugal adj. 節儉的 jiéjiǎn de.

fruit n. 水果 shuǐguǒ, 果實 guǒshí.

fruitful adj. ①結果實的 jié guǒshí de, 豐收的 fēngshōu de (abundant). ②有成果的 yǒu chéngguǒ de, 有利的 yǒulì de (profitable).

fruitless adj. 無效的 wúxiào de (useless).

frustrate v. 使受挫 shǐ shòucuò (make frustrated), 使失敗 shǐ shībài (cause to fail).

frustrated adj. 有挫折感的 yǒu cuòzhégǎn de.

fry v. 油煎 yóujiān 〈skillet〉, 油炸 yóuzhá (deep fry), 炒 chǎo (stir-fry).

FTP 檔案傳輸協定 dàng'àn chuánshū xiédìng / dǎng'àn chuánshū xiédìng 〈computer〉.

fudge n. 牛奶軟糖 niúnǎi ruǎntáng.

fuel n. 燃料 ránliào.

fugitive n. 亡命之徒 wángmìng-zhī-tú, 逃亡者 táowángzhě 〈person〉. — adj. 逃亡的 táowáng de.

fulfil v. ①履行 lǚxíng, 完成 wánchéng (accomplish). ②滿足 mǎnzú (satisfy).

full adj. 滿的 mǎn de, 裝滿的 zhuāngmǎn de (filled). **~-figured** 豐滿的 fēngmǎn de. **~ moon** 滿月 mǎnyuè.

full-time adj. 全職的 quánzhí de, 專任的 zhuānrèn de.

fully adv. 完全地 wánquán de, 充分地 chōngfèn de (completely).

fumble n. & v. 笨拙地處理 bènzhuō de chǔlǐ / bènzhuó

de chǔlǐ (mishandle).

fume *n. (pl.)* 難聞的煙 nánwén de yān 〈smoke〉. — *v.* ①發出煙氣 fāchū yānqì (emit smoke). ②發怒 fānù (be angry).

fun *n.* 樂趣 lèqù (enjoyment). **make ~ of** 開……的玩笑 kāi...de wánxiào. — *adj.* 好玩 的 hǎowán de, 有趣的 yǒuqù de.

function *n.* ①作用 zuòyòng, 功能 gōngnéng (purpose). ②職責 zhízé (duty). — *v.* 運轉 yùnzhuǎn.

fund *n.* ①基金 jījīn, 專款 zhuānkuǎn 〈money〉. ②蘊藏 yùncáng 〈things〉.

fundamental *adj.* 基本的 jīběn de (basic), 重要的 zhòngyào de (important). — *n.* 基本原理 jīběn yuánlǐ, 基本 法則 jīběn fǎzé.

funeral *n.* 葬禮 zànglǐ, 喪禮 sānglǐ.

fungus *n.* 菌類 jūnlèi / jùnlèi.

funnel *n.* ①漏斗 lòudǒu 〈for liquids〉. ②煙囪 yāncōng 〈for gases〉.

funny *adj.* ①有趣的 yǒuqù de, 好玩的 hǎowán de (humorous). ②滑稽古怪的 huáji gǔguài de / huájī gǔguài de (strange). ③好笑的 hǎoxiào de (laughable).

fur *n.* 毛皮 máopí.

furious *adj.* 狂怒的 kuángnù de.

furl *v.* 捲起 juǎnqǐ.

furnace *n.* 火爐 huǒlú, 鎔爐

rónglú.

furnish *v.* ①提供 tígōng, 供應 gōngyìng (provide). ②家具 佈置 jiāju bùzhì 〈furniture〉.

furniture *n.* 家具 jiāju.

furrow *n.* 犁溝 lígōu.

furry *adj.* 毛皮製的 máopí zhì de.

further *adj.* 較遠的 jiào yuǎn de (more distant). — *adv.* 較遠 地 jiào yuǎn de (farther). — *v.* 促進 cùjìn, 推展 tuīzhǎn.

furthermore *adv.* 此外 cǐwài, 再者 zàizhě.

furtive *adj.* 鬼鬼祟祟的 guǐ-guǐ-suì-suì de.

fury *n.* 盛怒 shèngnù.

fuse *n.* ①保險絲 bǎoxiǎnsī 〈wire〉. ②導火線 dǎohuǒxiàn, 引信 yǐnxìn 〈bomb〉. **~ box** 電 源保險絲箱 diànyuán bǎoxiǎnsī xiāng. — *v.* 熔化 rónghuà.

fuselage *n.* 機身 jīshēn.

fusible *adj.* 易熔的 yì róng de.

fusion *n.* 熔合 rónghé, 融解 róngjiě.

fuss *n. & v.* ①大驚小怪 dà-jīng-xiǎo-guài, 小題大做 xiǎo-tí-dà-zuò. ②忙亂 mángluàn 〈hurry〉.

futile *adj.* 徒勞的 túláo de, 無用的 wúyòng de.

future *n.* 將來 jiānglái, 未來 wèilái. — *adj.* 未來的 wèilái de.

fuzz *n.* 絨毛 róngmáo, 細毛 xìmáo.

fuzzy logic 模糊理論 móhu lǐlùn, 模糊邏輯 móhu luóji.

F

G

G7 七大工業國 qī dà gōngyèguó.

gadget *n.* 小巧的機械 xiǎoqiǎo de jīxiè.

gag *v.* 塞住口 sāizhù kǒu (plug).

gaily *adv.* 歡樂地 huānlè de (happily).

gain *v.* ①獲得 huòdé (obtain). ②增加 zēngjiā (increase). ③促進 cùjìn, 進步 jìnbù (improve). — *n.* 利益 lìyì, 利潤 lìrùn (profit).

gait *n.* 步態 bùtài, 步法 bùfǎ.

gala *n.* 歡慶 huānqìng.

galaxy *n.* 銀河 yínhé.

gale *n.* 強風 qiángfēng (windstorm).

gallant *adj.* 英勇的 yīngyǒng de (brave).

gallery *n.* ①陳列館 chénlièguǎn, 畫廊 huàláng ⟨art⟩. ②觀眾 guānzhòng ⟨sports⟩.

gallon *n.* 加侖 jiālún.

gallop *n.* 飛跑 fēipǎo.

gamble *n. & v.* 賭博 dǔbó.

gambler *n.* 賭徒 dǔtú.

game *n.* ①遊戲 yóuxì (amusement). ②比賽 bǐsài (contest). ~ *plan* 行動計劃 xíngdòng jìhuà. ~ *show* 有獎遊戲節目 yǒu jiǎng yóuxì jiémù.

gang *n.* 一群 yì qún, 一幫 yì bāng (gangster).

gangster *n.* 歹徒 dǎitú.

gap *n.* 縫隙 fèngxì, 裂縫 lièfèng (break).

gape *n. & v.* 張嘴注視 zhāngzuǐ zhùshì (stare with an open mouth).

garage *n.* ①車庫 chēkù ⟨for parking⟩. ②修車廠 xiūchēchǎng ⟨for repairing⟩.

garbage *n.* 垃圾 lājí / lèsè. ~ *can* 垃圾箱 lājíxiāng / lèsèxiāng. ~ *truck* 垃圾車 lājíchē / lèsèchē.

garble *v.* 竄改 cuàngǎi.

garden *n.* 花園 huāyuán, 庭園 tíngyuán ⟨flower⟩.

gardener *n.* 園丁 yuándīng.

gargle *v.* 漱口 shùkǒu.

garish *adj.* 俗麗的 súlì de, 炫耀的 xuànyào de.

garlic *n.* 蒜 suàn, 大蒜 dàsuàn.

garment *n.* 衣服 yīfu.

garrulous *adj.* 愛說閒話的 ài shuō xiánhuà de (talkative).

gas *n.* ①氣體 qìtǐ (vapor). ②瓦斯 wǎsī ⟨fuel⟩. ~ *station* 加油站 jiāyóuzhàn.

gaseous *adj.* 氣體的 qìtǐ de.

gash *n.* 切痕 qiēhén, 傷痕 shānghén.

gasoline *n.* 汽油 qìyóu.

gasp *v.* 喘氣 chuǎnqì (breathe quickly).

gastric *adj.* 胃的 wèi de. ~ *ulcer* 胃潰瘍 wèikuìyáng.

gate *n.* ①門 mén, 大門 dàmén (door). ②登機門 dēngjīmén ⟨planes⟩.

gather *v.* ①聚集 jùjí, 集合 jíhé (assemble). ②採集 cǎijí (collect).

gathering *n.* 聚集 jùjí, 集合 jíhé.

gaudy *adj.* 俗麗的 súlì de.

gauge n. 計量器 jìliàngqì
(measuring tool). — v. 計量
jìliàng, 測量 cèliáng (measure).

gaunt adj. 瘦削的 shòuxuē de /
shòuxuè de (extremely thin).

gauze n. 紗布 shābù, 薄紗
báoshā / bóshā.

gay adj. ①愉快的 yúkuài de
(merry). ②同性戀的
tóngxìngliàn de (homosexual).
— n. 同性戀 tóngxìngliàn.

gaze n. & v. 凝視 níngshì, 注
視 zhùshì.

gear n. ①齒輪 chǐlún (wheel).
②工具 gōngjù, 用具 yòngjù
(tool).

geek n. 呆子 dāizi.

gelatin n. 膠 jiāo, 膠質 jiāozhì /
jiāozhí.

gem n. 寶石 bǎoshí, 珠寶
zhūbǎo (jewel).

Gemini 雙子座 Shuāngzǐzuò.

gender n. ①性別 xìngbié (sex).
②性 xìng (grammar).

gene n. 基因 jīyīn.

genealogy n. 系譜學 xìpǔxué
(study of family history).

general adj. ①一般的 yìbān
de (common). ②概括的 gàikuò
de, 總的 zǒng de (overall). — n.
將軍 jiāngjūn, 上將 shàngjiàng
(officer). ~ election 大選 dàxuǎn.

generalize v. 歸納 guīnà, 概
括 gàikuò (summarize).

generally adv. ①通常地
tōngcháng de (usually). ②廣
泛地 guǎngfàn de (widely).

generate v. 產生 chǎnshēng,
造成 zàochéng (cause).

generation n. ①一代 yí dài,
世代 shìdài (a stage in family
descent). ②同時代的人
tóngshídài de rén (people in
the same period). ~ gap 代溝
dàigōu.

generator n. 發電機 fādiànjī.

generic adj. 屬的 shǔ de,
類的 lèi de (of a genus).

generosity n. 慷慨 kāngkǎi,
寬大 kuāndà.

generous adj. 慷慨的 kāngkǎi
de, 大方的 dàfang de.

genetic engineering n. 基
因工程 jīyīn gōngchéng.

genetics n. 遺傳學
yíchuánxué.

genial adj. 和藹的 hé'ǎi de,
親切的 qīnqiè de.

genius n. 天才 tiāncái (talent),
天賦 tiānfù (gift).

genocide n. 大屠殺 dàtúshā.

gentle adj. 溫和的 wēnhé de,
文雅的 wényǎ de.

gentleman n. 紳士 shēnshì,
君子 jūnzǐ.

genuine adj. ①真正的
zhēnzhèng de (real). ②真誠
的 zhēnchéng de (sincere).

geography n. 地理學 dìlǐxué
⟨science⟩.

geology n. 地質學 dìzhìxué /
dìzhíxué.

geometric adj. 幾何學的
jǐhéxué de.

geometry n. 幾何學 jǐhéxué.

germ n. 細菌 xìjūn / xìjùn, 病
菌 bìngjūn / bìngjùn (bacteria).

German n. & adj. 德國人
Déguórén ⟨people⟩. ②德語
Déyǔ ⟨language⟩.

germinate v. 使發芽 shǐ
fāyá (sprout).

gesture n. 手勢 shǒushì.

get v. ①獲得 huòdé, 得到
dédào (obtain). ②拿到 nádào,
捉住 zhuōzhù (fetch). ③瞭解
liǎojiě, 明白 míngbai
(comprehend). ~ through 通過

G

G

tōngguò. ~ *together* 相聚 xiāngjù. ~ *up* 起床 qǐchuáng.

ghost n. 鬼 guǐ, 靈魂 línghún (spirit).

ghostbuster n. 驅鬼者 qūguǐzhě.

giant n. 巨人 jùrén (colossus). — *adj.* 巨大的 jùdà de (huge).

gift n. 禮物 lǐwù (present).

gifted adj. 有天賦的 yǒu tiānfù de (very talented).

gigantic adj. 巨大的 jùdà de.

giggle n. & v. 傻笑 shǎxiào, 吃吃地笑 chīchī de xiào.

gill n. 鰓 sāi (fish).

gimmick n. 花招 huāzhāo, 噱頭 xuétóu / juétóu.

gin n. 杜松子酒 dùsōngzǐjiǔ.

ginger n. 薑 jiāng (plant).

gingerly adj. & adv. 小心謹慎的 xiǎoxīn jǐnshèn de.

giraffe n. 長頸鹿 chángjǐnglù.

girl n. 女孩 nǚhái, 少女 shàonǚ.

girlfriend n. 女朋友 nǚpéngyou.

gist n. 要旨 yàozhǐ, 要點 yàodiǎn.

give v. ①給予 gěiyǔ (grant). ②供給 gōngjǐ (offer). ~ *in* 屈服 qūfú. ~ *up* 放棄 fàngqì.

glacier n. 冰河 bīnghé.

glad adj. 高興的 gāoxìng de, 快樂的 kuàilè de (pleased and happy).

gladiator n. 鬥士 dòushì.

glamour n. 魅力 mèilì (attractiveness).

glance n. 一瞥 yìpiē (look). — v. 瞥見 piējiàn (look).

gland n. 腺 xiàn.

glare n. & v. ①眩光 xuànguāng (strong light). ②怒視 nùshì (fierce look).

glass n. ①玻璃 bōli (substance). ②玻璃杯 bōlibēi (cup).

gleam n. & v. 閃光 shǎnguāng (flash).

glee n. 歡樂 huānlè (merriment).

glib adj. 油腔滑調的 yóu-qiāng-huá-diào de (smooth-spoken).

glide v. 滑行 huáxíng (slide).

glimmer n. 微光 wēiguāng / wéiguāng (gleam). — v. 發微光 fā wēiguāng / fā wéiguāng.

glimpse n. 一瞥 yìpiē. — v. 瞥見 piējiàn.

glitter n. & v. 閃爍 shǎnshuò.

gloat v. 洋洋得意地看著 yáng-yáng-déyì de kànzhe (brag).

global adj. 全球的 quánqiú de (universal). ~ *village* 地球村 dìqiúcūn.

globalization n. 全球化 quánqiúhuà.

globalize v. 全球化 quánqiúhuà.

globe n. 地球 dìqiú (the earth).

gloom n. 幽暗 yōu'àn, 陰暗 yīn'àn (semidarkness).

gloomy adj. 憂鬱的 yōuyù de (sad).

glorify v. ①讚美 zànměi (praise). ②加榮耀於 jiā róngyào yú (make glorious).

glorious adj. 光榮的 guāngróng de, 輝煌的 huīhuáng de (possessing glory).

glory n. ①光榮 guāngróng (honor). ②讚美 zànměi (adoration). ③壯麗 zhuànglì (great beauty).

gloss n. & v. 光澤 guāngzé.

glossary n. 字彙 zìhuì, 詞彙 cíhuì (vocabulary), 字彙表 zìhuìbiǎo, 詞彙表 cíhuìbiǎo (wordlist).

glove *n.* 手套 shǒutào.

glow *n. & v.* 容光煥發 róngguāng-huànfā (flush).

glucose *n.* 葡萄糖 pútaotáng.

glue *n.* 膠 jiāo。– *v.* 黏 nián.

go *v.* 去 qù, 行走 xíngzǒu (move).
~ *abroad* 出國 chūguó.
~ *ahead* 向前進 xiàng qián jìn, 做下去 zuòxiaqu。~ *into* 進入 jìnrù。~ *on* 繼續 jìxù。~ *out* 外出 wàichū。~ *through* 經歷 jīnglì.

goal *n.* ①目標 mùbiāo (target).
②球門 qiúmén〈football〉.

goat *n.* 山羊 shānyáng.

god *n.* 上帝 shàngdì, 神 shén (divine being).

goddess *n.* 女神 nǚshén.

godfather *n.* 教父 jiàofù 〈religion〉.

goggles *n.* 護目鏡 hùmùjìng, 擋風眼鏡 dǎngfēng yǎnjìng.

gold *n.* 金 jīn, 金黃 huángjīn.
~ *card* 金卡 jīnkǎ.

golden *adj.* ①黃金的 huángjīn de〈metal〉.②金色的 jīnsè de〈color〉.

golf *n.* 高爾夫球 gāo'ěrfūqiú.

gondola *n.* 平底船 píngdǐchuán〈boat〉.

gone *adj.* ①消失的 xiāoshī de (past).②死去的 sǐqù de (dead).

good *adj.* 好的 hǎo de (fine).
~ *afternoon* 午安 wǔ'ān.
~ *evening* 晚安 wǎn'ān.
~ *morning* 早安 zǎo'ān.
~ *night* 晚安 wǎn'ān.

good-bye *n. & interj.* 再見 zàijiàn.

good-for-nothing *adj.* 無用的 wúyòng de。– *n.* 無用之人 wúyòng zhī rén.

good-looking *adj.* 貌美的 màoměi de, 漂亮的 piàoliang

de.

good-natured *adj.* 和藹的 hé'ǎi de.

goodness *n.* 良善 liángshàn (quality of being good).

goods *n.* 貨物 huòwù, 商品 shāngpǐn, 東西 dōngxi (things).

goodwill *n.* 善意 shànyì, 好意 hǎoyì.

goose *n.* 鵝 é〈bird〉.

gorge *n.* 峽谷 xiágǔ。– *v.* 塞飽 sāibǎo, 狼吞虎嚥 láng-tūn-hǔ-yàn (stuff).

gorgeous *adj.* 華麗的 huálì de (splendid).

gorilla *n.* 猩猩 xīngxing.

gory *adj.* 染血的 rǎnxuè de / rǎnxiě de.

gosh *interj.* 天哪！ Tiānna! 哎呀！ Āiya!

gospel *n.* 福音 fúyīn.

gossip *n.* 閒話 xiánhuà (chatter)。– *v.* 說閒話 shuō xiánhuà.

gourmet *n.* 美食家 měishíjiā.

govern *v.* ①治理 zhìlǐ, 管理 guǎnlǐ (be in charge of).②控制 kòngzhì (control).

government *n.* ①政府 zhèngfǔ (administration).
②管理 guǎnlǐ (management).

governor *n.* 州長 zhōuzhǎng〈of a state〉.

gown *n. & v.* 長袍 chángpáo.

grab *n. & v.* 攫 jué, 掠奪 lüèduó (snatch).

grace *n.* 優雅 yōuyǎ (elegance).

graceful *adj.* ①優雅的 yōuyǎ de〈shape or movement〉.②溫文儒雅的 wēnwén rúyǎ de〈manner〉.

gracious *adj.* ①優雅的 yōuyǎ de (elegant).②仁慈的 réncí de

G

(merciful).

grade n. ①等級 děngjí (level). ②年級 niánjí (class). ③成績 chéngjī / chéngjì, 分數 fēnshù (mark).

gradient n. 坡度 pōdù, 斜度 xiédù.

gradual adj. 逐漸的 zhújiàn de.

graduate v. 畢業 bìyè (finish). — n. 畢業生 bìyèshēng.

graduate school n. 研究生 院 yánjiūshēngyuàn / yánjiùshēngyuàn.

graduation n. 畢業 bìyè.

grain n. 穀物 gǔwù, 穀類 gǔlèi (seed).

gram n. 克 kè (weight).

grammar n. 文法 wénfǎ.

granary n. 穀倉 gǔcāng.

grand adj. 宏偉的 hóngwěi de (magnificent), 重大的 zhòngdà de (enormous).
G- Canyon 大峽谷 Dàxiágǔ. ~ jury 大陪審團 dà péishěntuán. ~ piano 平台型鋼琴 píngtáixíng gāngqín.

grandchild n. 孫子 sūnzi.

granddaughter n. 孫女 sūnnǚ.

grandeur n. 宏偉壯麗 hóngwěi zhuànglì (spectacle).

grandfather n. 祖父 zǔfù.

grandiose adj. 浮華不實的 fúhuá bù shí de.

grandmother n. 祖母 zǔmǔ.

grandson n. 孫子 sūnzi.

grant v. ①授與 shòuyǔ, 贈與 zèngyǔ (give). ②允許 yǔnxǔ, 答應 dāyìng (allow).

grape n. 葡萄 pútao.

grapefruit n. 葡萄柚 pútaoyòu.

graph n. 圖表 túbiǎo.

graphic adj. ①生動的 shēngdòng de (vivid). ②繪畫 的 huìhuà de (drawing). ~ arts 平面藝術 píngmiàn yìshù.

grasp v. 緊握 jǐnwò, 抓住 zhuāzhù (catch).

grass n. 草 cǎo.

grasshopper n. 蚱蜢 zhàměng.

grateful adj. 感謝的 gǎnxiè de.

gratitude n. 感謝 gǎnxiè, 感激 gǎnjī.

gratuity n. 小費 xiǎofèi (tip).

gravel n. 碎石 suìshí.

gravestone n. 墓碑 mùbēi.

graveyard n. 墓地 mùdì.

gravity n. ①地心引力 dìxīn yǐnlì, 引力 yǐnlì, 重力 zhònglì (gravitation). ②嚴重 yánzhòng, 重大 zhòngdà (seriousness). ③嚴肅 yánsù, 莊重 zhuāngzhòng (solemnity).

gravy n. 肉湯 ròutāng, 滷汁 lǔzhī (sauce).

gray n. & adj. 灰色 huīsè.

graze v. ①吃青草 chī qīngcǎo (eat grass). ②擦過 cāguò (brush).

grease n. 油脂 yóuzhī.

great adj. ①大的 dà de (large). ②偉大的 wěidà de (remarkable). ③極好的 jí hǎo de (excellent).

greed n. 貪婪 tānlán.

greedy adj. 貪婪的 tānlán de (avaricious).

Greek n. & adj. ①希臘人 Xīlàrén (people). ②希臘文 Xīlàwén (language).

green n. & adj. 綠色 lǜsè. ~ bean 四季豆 sìjìdòu.

greenhouse n. 溫室 wēnshì. ~ effect 溫室效應 wēnshì

xiàoyìng.

greet v. 歡迎 huānyíng, 打招呼 dǎ zhāohu.

greeting n. 問候 wènhòu (regards).

greyhound n. ①靈堤 língtí ⟨animal⟩.②(G~) 灰狗巴士 huīgǒu bāshì ⟨bus⟩.

gregarious adj. 社交的 shèjiāo de, 好交際的 hào jiāojì de (sociable).

grenade n. 手榴彈 shǒuliúdàn.

grid n. 格子 gézi.

grief n. 悲傷 bēishāng.

grievance n. 委屈 wěiqu, 不平 bùpíng.

grieve v. 使悲傷 shǐ bēishāng, 痛苦 tòngkǔ.

grill n. ①烤架 kǎojià ⟨device⟩.②燒烤食品 shāokǎo shípǐn ⟨food⟩. – v. 燒 shāo, 烤 kǎo ⟨cook⟩.

grim adj. 嚴厲的 yánlì de.

grimace n. 愁眉苦臉 chóuméi-kǔ-liǎn, 鬼臉 guǐliǎn.

grime n. 污穢 wūhuì.

grin n. 露齒笑 lòu chǐ xiào.

grind v. 磨碎 mósuì, 研磨 yánmó ⟨crush⟩.

grip n. & v. 緊握 jǐnwò.

groan n. & v. 呻吟 shēnyín.

grocer n. 雜貨商 záhuòshāng.

grocery n. 雜貨店 záhuòdiàn.

groggy adj. ①眩暈虛弱的 xuànyūn xūruò de ⟨weak⟩.②不穩的 bù wěn de ⟨unsteady⟩.

groom n. 新郎 xīnláng ⟨bridegroom⟩.

groomsman n. 男儐相 nánbīnxiàng.

gross adj. ①總的 zǒng de ⟨total⟩.②重大錯誤的 zhòngdà cuòwù de ⟨extremely bad⟩. – n. 毛收入 máoshōurù

(income). – v. 總共賺入 zǒnggòng zhuàn rù.

grotesque adj. 古怪的 gǔguài de, 怪誕的 guàidàn de.

ground n. 地 dì, 土地 tǔdì (land).

groundless adj. 無根據的 wú gēnjù de.

group n. 群 qún, 組 zǔ, 團體 tuántǐ (set).

grow v. ①生長 shēngzhǎng, 成長 chéngzhǎng (develop).②增長 zēngzhǎng (increase).③種植 zhòngzhí ⟨plant⟩. **~ up** 長大 zhǎngdà.

growl v. 作低吠聲 zuò dīfèishēng.

grown-up n. 成人 chéngrén.

growth n. ①生長 shēngzhǎng (development).②增長 zēngzhǎng (increase).

gruesome adj. 毛骨悚然的 máogǔ-sǒngrán de (horrible).

grumble v. 發牢騷 fā láosāo.

grunt n. & v. 咕嚕聲 gūlūshēng.

guarantee n. & v. 保證 bǎozhèng.

guarantor n. 保證人 bǎozhèngrén.

guard v. 看守 kānshǒu. – n. ①守衛者 shǒuwèizhě, 衛兵 wèibīng (watchman).②警戒 jǐngjiè (lookout).

guardian n. 監護人 jiānhùrén.

guerrilla n. 游擊隊 yóujíduì / yóujíduì.

guess n. & v. 猜想 cāixiǎng.

guest n. 客人 kèrén, 旅客 lǚkè.

guidance n. 指導 zhǐdǎo / zhǐdǎo.

guide v. 引導 yǐndǎo, 指導

G

zhǐdǎo / zhídǎo (lead).

guidebook n. 旅遊指南 lǚyóu zhǐnán.

guilt n. 罪 zuì, 罪行 zuìxíng (guiltiness).

guilty adj. ①有罪的 yǒu zuì de (not innocent). ②有罪惡感 的 yǒu zuì'ègǎn de (ashamed).

guitar n. 吉他 jítā.

gulf n. 海灣 hǎiwān (bay).

gull n. 海鷗 hǎi'ōu (bird).

gulp v. 吞飲 tūnyǐn (swallow hastily).

gum n. ①樹膠 shùjiāo (tree). ②口香糖 kǒuxiāngtáng (for chewing).

gun n. 槍 qiāng.

gunpowder n. 火藥 huǒyào.

gust n. 一陣強風 yí zhèn qiángfēng.

guts n. ①內臟 nèizàng

(bowels). ②勇氣 yǒngqì (courage).

gutter n. 排水溝 páishuǐgōu.

guy n. 人 rén, 傢伙 jiāhuo.

guzzle v. 豪飲 háoyǐn.

gym n. 體育館 tǐyùguǎn (gymnasium).

gymnasium n. 健身房 jiànshēnfáng, 體育館 tǐyùguǎn.

gymnast n. 體育家 tǐyùjiā (expert), 體操運動員 tǐcāo yùndòngyuán (gymnastics).

gymnastics n. 體操 tǐcāo.

gynecology n. 婦科醫學 fùkē yīxué (medical).

gyrate v. 旋轉 xuánzhuǎn (revolve).

gyroscope n. 迴轉儀 huízhuǎnyí, 陀螺儀 tuóluóyí.

H

H

habit n. 習慣 xíguàn.

habitation n. ①居住 jūzhù (living in). ②住所 zhùsuǒ (place to live in).

habitual adj. 慣常的 guàncháng de.

hack v. 亂砍 luànkǎn, 劈 pī.

hacker n. 黑客 hēikè / 電腦 駭客 diànnǎo hàikè (computer).

hag n. 老醜婆 lǎo chǒu pó (ugly woman).

haggard adj. 憔悴的 qiáocuì de (person).

haggle n. & v. 討價還價 tǎo-jià-huán-jià (bargaining).

hail n. 冰雹 bīngbáo (frozen raindrops).

hair n. 髮 fà / fǎ, 頭髮 tóufa, 毛 máo, 毛髮 máofà / máofǎ.

haircut n. 理髮 lǐfà / lǐfǎ, 剪髮 jiǎnfà / jiǎnfǎ.

hairdo n. 髮型 fàxíng / fǎxíng.

hairdresser n. 理髮師 lǐfàshī / lǐfǎshī.

hairstyle n. 髮型 fàxíng / fǎxíng.

hairy adj. 多毛的 duō máo de.

halcyon adj. 平靜的 píngjìng de, 太平的 tàipíng de.

hale adj. 強壯的 qiángzhuàng

de.

half n. 一半 yíbàn, 二分之一 èr fēn zhī yī. — adj. 一半的 yíbàn de.

halfway adj. & adv. 半路的 bànlù de, 中途的 zhōngtú de.

hall n. ①會堂 huìtáng (auditorium). ②走廊 zǒuláng (corridor). ③大廳 dàtīng (large room).

Halloween n. 萬聖節前夕 Wànshèngjié qiánxī / Wànshèngjié qiánxì.

hallucination n. 幻覺 huànjué.

halt n. & v. ①中止 zhōngzhǐ (end). ②停止前進 tíngzhǐ qiánjìn (stop).

ham n. 火腿 huǒtuǐ.

hamburger n. 漢堡包 hànbǎobāo / 漢堡 hànbǎo.

hammer n. 鎚 chuí, 鐵鎚 tiěchuí. — n. 鎚打 chuídǎ.

hammock n. 吊床 diàochuáng.

hand n. 手 shǒu (fist). — v. 交給 jiāogěi, 傳遞 chuándì.

handbag n. 手提包 shǒutíbāo.

handbook n. 手冊 shǒucè (pamphlet), 指南 zhǐnán (guidebook).

handcuff n. 手銬 shǒukào.

handful n. 一撮 yì cuō, 一把 yì bǎ ⟨amount⟩.

handicap n. 障礙 zhàng'ài ⟨disability⟩.

handicraft n. 手藝 shǒuyì, 手工藝 shǒugōngyì.

handkerchief n. 手帕 shǒupà.

handle n. 把手 bǎshǒu ⟨part⟩. — v. 處理 chǔlǐ (take care of), 控制 kòngzhì (control).

handsome adj. ①好看的 hǎo

kàn de (good-looking). ②英俊 的 yīngjùn de ⟨man⟩.

handwriting n. 筆跡 bǐjī, 手 跡 shǒujī.

handy adj. 便利的 biànlì de (convenient).

hang v. ①掛 guà, 吊 diào ⟨place⟩. ②絞死 jiǎosǐ ⟨execute⟩.

hanger n. 掛鈎 guàgōu ⟨hook⟩, 衣架 yījià ⟨clothes⟩.

hangman n. 劊子手 guìzishǒu / kuàizishǒu.

haphazard n. 偶然 ǒurán.

happen v. 發生 fāshēng (take place).

happening n. 事件 shìjiàn.

happily adv. ①快樂地 kuàilè de, 幸福地 xìngfú de ⟨happy⟩. ②幸好 xìnghǎo, 幸運地 xìngyùn de (fortunately).

happiness n. 快樂 kuàilè, 幸 福 xìngfú.

happy adj. 快樂的 kuàilè de (good spirits), 幸福的 xìngfú de (contentment).

harass v. 騷擾 sāorǎo (disturb), 困擾 kùnrǎo (bother).

harassment n. 騷擾 sāorǎo.

harbor n. 港 gǎng, 港口 gǎngkǒu.

hard adj. ①堅硬的 jiānyìng de (solid). ②辛苦的 xīnkǔ de, 困 難的 kùnnán de (difficult). ③艱苦的 jiānkǔ de (painful). ④劇烈的 jùliè de (strong). ~ **disk** 硬盤 yìngpán / 硬碟 yìngdié.

harden v. 使堅硬 shǐ jiānyìng.

hardhearted adj. 無情的 wúqíng de.

hardly adv. 幾乎不 jīhū bù (almost not).

hardship n. 艱苦 jiānkǔ.

H

hardware n. ①武器 wǔqì (weapon). ②硬件 yìngjiàn / 硬體 yìngtǐ ‹computer›.

hardy adj. ①吃苦耐勞的 chīkǔ-nàiláo de ‹man›. ②耐寒的 nàihán de ‹plants›.

hare n. 野兔 yětù.

harm n. & v. 損害 sǔnhài (damage), 傷害 shānghài (hurt).

harmful adj. 有害的 yǒuhài de.

harmless adj. 無害的 wúhài de.

harmonica n. 口琴 kǒuqín.

harmonious adj. ①調和的 tiáohe de, 協調的 xiétiáo de (amicable). ②悅耳的 yuè'ěr de (melodious).

harmonize v. 調和 tiáohe, 和諧 héxié ‹balance›.

harmony n. ①調和 tiáohe, 和諧 héxié (balance). ②和聲 héshēng ‹music›.

harp n. 豎琴 shùqín.

harsh adj. ①粗糙的 cūcāo de (rough). ②刺耳的 cì'ěr de (croaking). ③刺眼的 cìyǎn de (dazzling). ④苛刻的 kēkè de (severe).

harvest n. ①收穫 shōuhuò (gathering in). ②結果 jiéguǒ (result). — v. 收穫 shōuhuò (gather).

haste n. 匆忙 cōngmáng, 急忙 jímáng ‹hurried›.

hasten v. 催促 cuīcù, 使趕快 shǐ gǎnkuài.

hasty adj. ①匆忙的 cōngmáng de (hurried). ②草率的 cǎoshuài de (rushed).

hat n. 帽子 màozi.

hatch v. ①孵 fū, 孵化 fūhuà (brood). ②計畫 jìhuà, 設計 shèjì (plan). — n. 艙口 cāngkǒu, 艙門 cāngmén ‹ship›.

hate n. & v. 憎惡 zēngwù, 痛恨 tònghèn (loathing). ~ **mail** 攻擊性信件 gōngjīxìng xìnjiàn / gōngjíxìng xìnjiàn, 黑函 hēihán.

hatred n. 憎惡 zēngwù, 痛恨 tònghèn (loathing).

haul v. 拖 tuō, 拉 lā (pull or drag). — n. 用力拖 yònglì tuō (dragging).

haunt v. 常去 chángqù (visit frequently).

have v. 有 yǒu, 具有 jùyǒu (possess). ~ **to** 不得不 bùdé bù.

haven n. 避難所 bìnànsuǒ ‹safe›.

hawk n. 隼 sǔn, 鷹 yīng ‹bird›.

hawker n. 小販 xiǎofàn.

hay n. 乾草 gāncǎo, 秣 mò.

hazard n. 冒險 màoxiǎn, 危險 wēixiǎn / wéixiǎn (danger).

hazardous adj. 冒險的 màoxiǎn de (dangerous).

haze n. 陰霾 yīnmái (thin mist).

hazel n. ①榛 zhēn ‹tree›. ②淡褐色 dànhèsè / dànhésè ‹color›.

hazy adj. 有霧的 yǒu wù de.

H-bomb n. 氫彈 qīngdàn.

he pron. 他 tā.

head n. ①頭 tóu, 頭部 tóubù ‹part of body›. ②領袖 lǐngxiù, 首長 shǒuzhǎng, 主管 zhǔguǎn (chief). — v. ①為首 wéishǒu, 領導 lǐngdǎo (be in charge of). ②朝……前進 cháo...qiánjìn (head for).

headache n. 頭痛 tóutòng.

heading n. 標題 biāotí.

head-hunt v. 獵人頭 liè réntóu.

headlight n. 前燈 qiándēng.

headline n. 標題 biāotí ⟨newspaper⟩.

headmaster n. 校長 xiàozhǎng.

headquarters n. 總部 zǒngbù.

headstrong adj. 頑固的 wángù de ⟨stubborn⟩.

headway n. 進步 jìnbù, 進展 jìnzhǎn ⟨progress⟩.

heal v. 治癒 zhìyù ⟨make well again⟩.

health n. 健康 jiànkāng ⟨body or mind⟩.

healthful adj. 有益健康的 yǒuyì jiànkāng de.

healthy adj. 健康的 jiànkāng de ⟨person⟩, 有益健康的 yǒuyì jiànkāng de ⟨food⟩.

heap n. ①堆 duī ⟨pile⟩. ②大量 dàliàng, 許多 xǔduō ⟨mass⟩. — v. 堆積 duījī.

hear v. 聽見 tīngjiàn, 聽到 tīngdào.

hearing n. 聽力 tīnglì, 聽覺 tīngjué ⟨ability to hear⟩. ~ **aid** 助聽器 zhùtīngqì.

hearsay n. 謠傳 yáochuán.

hearse n. 靈車 língchē.

heart n. ①心臟 xīnzàng ⟨part of body⟩. ②心 xīn, 感情 gǎnqíng ⟨feeling⟩. ③紅心 hóngxīn ⟨cards⟩.

heartbreak n. 傷心 shāngxīn, 悲痛 bēitòng.

hearth n. 爐床 lúchuáng.

hearty adj. ①熱誠的 rèchéng de ⟨warm⟩. ②強壯的 qiángzhuàng de ⟨strong⟩. ③豐盛的 fēngshèng de ⟨large⟩.

heat n. ①熱 rè ⟨hot⟩. ②暖氣 nuǎnqì ⟨warm air⟩. — v. 加熱 jiārè ⟨warm up⟩.

heater n. 加熱器 jiārèqì, 暖爐 nuǎnlú.

heave v. ①舉起 jǔqǐ ⟨lift⟩. ②投 tóu, 擲 zhì / zhí ⟨throw⟩.

heaven n. ①天堂 tiāntáng ⟨religion⟩. ②天空 tiānkōng ⟨sky⟩.

heavenly adj. ①美麗的 měilì de ⟨beautiful⟩. ②愉悅的 yúyuè de ⟨delightful⟩. ③天空的 tiānkōng de ⟨sky⟩.

heavy adj. ①重 zhòng ⟨weighty⟩. ②大量的 dàliàng de ⟨amount⟩. ~ **industry** 重工業 zhònggōngyè.

Hebrew n. & adj. ①希伯來人 Xībóláirén ⟨people⟩. ②希伯來 語 Xībóláiyǔ ⟨language⟩.

heckle v. 詰問 jiéwèn ⟨bother⟩.

hedge n. 樹籬 shùlí ⟨bushes⟩. — v. ①以樹籬圍 yǐ shùlí wéi ⟨garden⟩. ②騎牆 qíqiáng ⟨go with the tide⟩.

heed n. & v. 注意 zhùyì, 留意 liúyì.

heel n. 後跟 hòugēn.

height n. 高 gāo, 高度 gāodù.

heir n. 繼承人 jìchéngrén.

heirloom n. 祖傳物 zǔchuánwù, 傳家之寶 chuánjiā zhī bǎo.

helicopter n. 直升機 zhíshēngjī.

helium n. 氦 hài.

hell n. ①地獄 dìyù ⟨religion⟩. ②苦境 kǔjìng ⟨suffering⟩.

hello n. & v. & interj. 喂! Wèi! 哈囉! Hāluó!

helmet n. 頭盔 tóukuī.

help v. ①幫忙 bāngmáng, 幫助 bāngzhù ⟨aid⟩. ②減輕 jiǎnqīng, 減緩 jiǎnhuǎn ⟨lessen⟩. — n. 幫助 bāngzhù.

helper n. 助手 zhùshǒu.

helpful *adj.* 有幫助的 yǒu bāngzhù de.

helping *n.* 一份 yí fèn.

helpless *adj.* 無助的 wúzhù de,無能為力的 wú-néng-wéi-lì de.

hem *n.* 褶邊 zhébiān.

hemisphere *n.* 半球 bànqiú.

hemorrhoids *n.* 痔瘡 zhìchuāng.

hemp *n.* ①麻 má ⟨plant⟩. ②大麻 dàmá ⟨marijuana⟩.

hen *n.* 母雞 mǔjī ⟨chicken⟩.

hence *adv.* 因此 yīncǐ, 所以 suǒyǐ (therefore).

henceforth *adv.* 今後 jīnhòu, 從此 cóngcǐ.

henchman *n.* 親信 qīnxìn.

her *pron.* 她 tā, 她的 tā de.

herb *n.* 藥草 yàocǎo (medicine).

herd *n.* 獸群 shòuqún ⟨animals⟩. — *v.* 群集 qúnjí (group together).

here *adv.* 在這裡 zài zhèlǐ (in, at).

hereafter *adv.* 此後 cǐhòu (from now on). — *n.* 將來 jiānglái.

hereby *adv.* 藉此 jiècǐ.

hereditary *adj.* ①遺傳的 yíchuán de ⟨of body⟩. ②世襲的 shìxí de ⟨of position⟩.

heredity *n.* 遺傳 yíchuán.

herein *adv.* 在此 zài cǐ, 鑒於 jiàn yú.

hereof *adv.* 關於此點 guānyú cǐ diǎn.

heresy *n.* 異說 yìshuō.

heretic *n.* 異教徒 yìjiàotú.

heritage *n.* 遺產 yíchǎn.

hermit *n.* 隱者 yǐnzhě, 隱士 yǐnshì (recluse).

hernia *n.* 疝氣 shànqì

⟨medical⟩.

hero *n.* 英雄 yīngxióng (great man).

heroic *adj.* 英勇的 yīngyǒng de (very brave).

heroin *n.* 海洛因 hǎiluòyīn / 海洛英 hǎiluòyìng ⟨drug⟩.

heroism *n.* 英雄事蹟 yīngyǒng shìjì.

herpes *n.* 疱疹 pàozhěn ⟨medical⟩.

herring *n.* 鯡魚 fēiyú.

hers *pron.* 她的 tā de.

herself *pron.* 她自己 tā zìjǐ.

hesitant *adj.* 猶豫的 yóuyù de, 遲疑的 chíyí de ⟨uncertain⟩.

hesitate *v.* 猶豫 yóuyù, 遲疑 chíyí (undecided).

hesitation *n.* 躊躇 chóuchú, 遲疑 chíyí (state of hesitating).

heterogeneous *adj.* 異種的 yìzhǒng de, 不同類的 bù tónglèi de ⟨different⟩.

hexagon *n.* 六角形 liùjiǎoxíng.

hey *interj.* 喂！Wèi!

heyday *n.* 全盛時期 quánshèng shíqí / quánshèng shíqí.

hi *interj.* 喂！Wèi! 嗨！Hāi!

hibernate *v.* 冬眠 dōngmián.

hiccup *n. & v.* 打嗝 dǎgé.

hidden *adj.* ①隱藏的 yǐncáng de ⟨hide⟩. ②祕密的 mìmì de ⟨secret⟩.

hide *v.* ①隱藏 yǐncáng, 藏 cáng (keep out of sight). ②隱瞞 yǐnmán (keep secret). — *n.* 獸皮 shòupí (animal's skin).

hide-and-seek *n.* 捉迷藏 zhuōmícáng.

hideous *adj.* 醜惡的 chǒu'è de, 可憎的 kězēng de.

hierarchy *n.* ①階級組織 jiējí zǔzhī (organization). ②階級制

度 jiēfǐ zhìdù (system).

high adj. ①高的 gāo de (tall). ②主要的 zhǔyào de, 重大的 zhòngdà de (chief). — adv. 高 gāo, 高度地 gāodù de. ~ **blood pressure** 高血壓 gāoxuěyā / gāoxiěyā. ~ **school** 中學 zhōngxué.

highland n. 高地 gāodì, 高原 gāoyuán

highlight v. 使顯著 shǐ xiǎnzhù, 強調 qiángdiào (emphasize).

highly adv. 高度地 gāodù de, 非常 fēicháng (very).

Highness n. 殿下 diànxià (title).

high-pitched adj. 聲調高的 shēngdiào gāo de.

high-pressure adj. 高壓的 gāoyā de, 強迫的 qiǎngpò de.

high tech n. & adj. 高技術 gāojìshù / 高科技 gāokējì.

highway n. 公路 gōnglù.

hijack v. 劫持 jiéchí (airplane).

hike n. & v. 健行 jiànxíng, 遠足 yuǎnzú, 徒步旅行 túbù lǚxíng.

hiking n. 健行 jiànxíng, 遠足 yuǎnzú, 徒步旅行 túbù lǚxíng.

hilarious adj. ①歡樂的 huānlè de (happy). ②爆笑的 bàoxiào de (joke).

hill n. 丘陵 qiūlíng, 小山 xiǎoshān.

hillside n. 山坡 shānpō.

him pron. 他 tā.

himself pron. 他自己 tā zìjǐ.

hinder v. 妨礙 fáng'ài, 阻止 zǔzhǐ.

Hindu n. & adj. ①印度教教徒 Yìndùjiào jiàotú (of Hinduism). ②印度人 Yìndùrén (people).

Hinduism n. 印度教

Yìndùjiào.

hinge n. ①鉸鏈 jiǎoliàn (metal part). ②樞紐 shūniǔ (key).

hint n. & v. 暗示 ànshì, 提示 tíshì (indirect statement).

hip n. 臀 tún.

hippo n. 河馬 hémǎ.

hippopotamus n. 河馬 hémǎ.

hire v. ①租用 zūyòng (things). ②雇用 gùyòng (person).

his pron. 他的 tā de.

hiss v. ①發嘶嘶聲 fā sīsīshēng (sound). ②發噓聲 fā xūshēng (jeer).

historian n. 歷史學家 lìshǐxué jiā.

historic adj. 史上著名的 shǐshang zhùmíng de, 歷史性的 lìshǐxìng de.

historical adj. 歷史的 lìshǐ de, 基於歷史的 jīyú lìshǐ de.

history n. 歷史 lìshǐ.

hit v. ①擊中 jīzhòng / jízhòng, 打中 dǎzhòng (strike). ②打擊 dǎjí / dájí (affect). — n. ①打擊 dǎjí / dájí (blow). ②成功 chénggōng (success).

hitch v. 繫住 jìzhù (fasten). — n. 索結 suǒjié (knot).

hitchhike v. 搭便車 dā biànchē.

hive n. 蜂房 fēngfáng.

hoard v. 貯藏 zhùcáng / zhǔcáng. — n. 貯藏物 zhùcángwù / zhǔcángwù.

hoarse adj. 嘶啞的 sīyǎ de.

hoax n. 騙人的把戲 piànrén de bǎxì, 騙局 piànjú.

hobby n. 嗜好 shìhào.

hockey n. ①曲棍球 qūgùnqiú (field). ②冰上曲棍球 bīng shàng qūgùnqiú (ice).

hog n. ①豬 zhū (pig). ②貪婪者

tānlánzhě 〈person〉.

hoist v. ①舉起 jǔqǐ, 升高 shēnggāo (lift). — n. 起重機 qǐzhòngjī 〈apparatus〉.

hold v. ①握住 wòzhù, 抓住 zhuāzhù (grip). ②擁有 yōngyǒu / yǒngyǒu (possess). ③舉行 jǔxíng (take place). ④容納 róngnà, 裝 zhuāng (contain). ⑤保持 bǎochí (keep in). — n. ①握 wò, 持 chí (grip). ②掌握 zhǎngwò, 支配 zhīpèi (control).

holder n. 持有人 chíyǒurén.

holding n. ①所有物 suǒyǒuwù (belongings). ②持有股份 chíyǒu gǔfèn (shares in a business).

holdup n. ①耽擱 dānge (delay). ②攔路搶劫 lánlù qiǎngjié (rob).

hole n. 洞 dòng, 洞穴 dòngxué / dòngxuè (cavity).

holiday n. 假日 jiàrì, 休假 xiūjià. ~ center 渡假村 dùjiàcūn.

hollow adj. ①空的 kōng de (empty). ②空虛的 kōngxū de, 虛假的 xūjiǎ de (insubstantial). — n. 洞 dòng, 凹陷 āoxiàn.

Holocaust n. 大屠殺 Dàtúshā 〈World War II〉.

holy adj. ①神聖的 shénshèng de (regarded as sacred). ②聖潔的 shèngjié de (moral and pure).

homage n. 尊崇 zūnchóng, 敬意 jìngyì.

home n. ①家 jiā, 家庭 jiātíng (place where one lives). ②家鄉 jiāxiāng (native land). ~ shopping 電視購物 diànshì gòuwù.

homeless adj. 無家可歸的 wú-jiā-kě-guī de.

homely adj. 不漂亮的 bú piàoliang de (not pretty), 平凡的 píngfán de (plain).

homemade adj. 自製的 zìzhì de.

homepage n. 主網頁 zhǔwǎngyè, 首頁 shǒuyè 〈computer〉.

homesick adj. 思鄉的 sīxiāng de, 想家的 xiǎngjiā de.

homework n. 家庭作業 jiātíng zuòyè.

homosexual adj. 同性戀的 tóngxìngliàn de. — n. 同性戀者 tóngxìngliàn zhě.

honest adj. 誠實的 chéngshí de (truthful). 正直的 zhèngzhí de (not cheating).

honestly adv. 誠實地 chéngshí de, 坦白地 tǎnbái de.

honesty n. 誠實 chéngshí, 正直 zhèngzhí.

honey n. 蜂蜜 fēngmì (sweet substance).

honeymoon n. 蜜月 mìyuè. — v. 度蜜月 dù mìyuè.

honor n. ①榮幸 róngxìng (regard). ②榮譽 róngyù (reputation). — v. 使榮耀 shǐ róngyào (show great respect for).

honorable adj. 可敬的 kějìng de, 高尚的 gāoshàng de (admirable).

honorary adj. 名譽上的 míngyùshang de.

hood n. 頭巾 tóujīn 〈covering〉, 兜帽 dōumào 〈hat〉.

hoof n. 蹄 tí 〈animals〉.

hook n. 鉤 gōu, 釣鉤 diàogōu. — v. 鉤住 gōuzhù 〈hold〉.

hoop n. 箍 gū, 環箍 huángū (circular band). — v. 加箍於 jiā gū yú.

hop v. 單腳跳躍 dānjiǎo tiàoyuè. — n. 跳躍 tiàoyuè (short jump).

hope *n. & v.* 希望 xīwàng (wish).

hopeless *adj.* 沒有希望的 méiyǒu xīwàng de.

hopeful *adj.* 有希望的 yǒu xīwàng de.

horizon *n.* 地平線 dìpíngxiàn, 水平線 shuǐpíngxiàn.

horizontal *adj.* 地平的 dìpíng de, 水平的 shuǐpíng de.

hormone *n.* 荷爾蒙 hé'ěrméng.

horn *n.* ①角 jiǎo (antler). ②號角 hàojiǎo, 喇叭 lǎba ⟨instrument⟩.

horoscope *n.* 天宮圖 tiāngōngtú, 占星 zhānxīng.

horrible *adj.* 可怕的 kěpà de, 恐怖的 kǒngbù de (terrible).

horrid *adj.* 可怕的 kěpà de, 可厭的 kěyàn de.

horrify *v.* 使恐怖 shǐ kǒngbù, 使戰慄 shǐ zhànlì (terrify).

horror *n.* ①恐怖 kǒngbù, 恐懼 kǒngjù (fear). ②厭惡 yànwù (dislike).

horsepower *n.* 馬力 mǎlì.

horseshoe *n.* 蹄鐵 títiě.

horsewhip *n.* 馬鞭 mǎbiān.

hose *n.* ①長統襪 chángtǒngwà (stockings). ②橡皮管 xiàngpíguǎn, 軟管 ruǎnguǎn (tube).

hospitable *adj.* 好客的 hàokè de.

hospital *n.* 醫院 yīyuàn.

hospitality *n.* 好客 hàokè, 款待 kuǎndài.

host *n.* ①主人 zhǔrén ⟨of a group⟩. ②主持人 zhǔchírén ⟨of a show⟩.

hostage *n.* 人質 rénzhì ⟨person⟩.

hostel *n.* 旅社 lǚshè.

hostess *n.* 女主人 nǚzhǔrén.

hostile *adj.* 敵對的 díduì de, 懷敵意的 huái díyì de ⟨unfriendly⟩.

hostility *n.* 敵意 díyì, 敵對 díduì (being hostile).

hot *adj.* ①熱的 rè de (warm). ②辛辣的 xīnlà de (spicy). ③暴躁的 bàozào de (angry).

hotel *n.* 旅館 lǚguǎn.

hour *n.* 小時 xiǎoshí, 鐘頭 zhōngtóu ⟨time⟩.

house *n.* 房屋 fángwū, 住宅 zhùzhái ⟨building⟩. – *v.* 供給住所 gōngjǐ zhùsuǒ (provide accommodation).

household *adj.* 家庭的 jiātíng de, 家屬的 jiāshǔ de.

housekeeper *n.* 管家 guǎnjiā.

housemaid *n.* 女佣 nǚyōng.

housewife *n.* 主婦 zhǔfù.

housework *n.* 家事 jiāshì.

housing *n.* 供給住宅 gōngjǐ zhùzhái.

how *adv.* 如何 rúhé, 怎樣 zěnyàng (in what way).

however *adv.* 無論如何 wúlùn rúhé. – *conj.* 然而 rán'ér.

howl *v.* 嚎 háo, 咆哮 páoxiào / páoxiào.

Huanghe River 黃河 Huánghé.

hug *v.* 緊抱 jǐnbào, 擁抱 yǒngbào / yǒngbào (to hold close).

huge *adj.* 巨大的 jùdà de.

hum *v.* 嗡嗡叫 wēngwēngjiào. – *n.* 嗡嗡聲 wēngwēngshēng (indistinct murmur).

human *adj.* 人的 rén de, 人類的 rénlèi de. – *n.* 人 rén, 人類 rénlèi.

humane *adj.* 仁慈的 réncí de

(having kindness).

humanism *n.* 人文主義 rénwén zhǔyì, 人道主義 réndào zhǔyì.

humanity *n.* ①人性 rénxìng (human nature). ②人道 réndào (mercy).

humble *adj.* 謙虛的 qiānxū de.

humid *adj.* 潮濕的 cháoshī de.

humiliate *v.* 羞辱 xiūrǔ / xiūrù, 使丟臉 shǐ diūliǎn.

humility *n.* 謙恭 qiāngōng.

humor *n.* ①幽默 yōumò (sense of fun). ②情緒 qíngxù, 心情 xīnqíng (mood).

humorist *n.* 幽默作家 yōumò zuòjiā (writer).

humorous *adj.* 幽默的 yōumò de.

hump *n.* ①隆肉 lóngròu (lump). ②圓丘 yuánqiū (mound).

humpback *n.* 駝背 tuóbèi.

hundred *n. & adj.* 一百 yìbǎi.

hunger *n.* ①飢餓 jī'è (starvation). ②渴望 kěwàng (desire).

hungry *adj.* 飢餓的 jī'è de (starving).

hunt *n. & v.* ①狩獵 shòuliè (chase). ②搜索 sōusuǒ, 追捕 zhuībǔ (search for).

hunter *n.* 獵人 lièrén (people).

hurdle *n.* 欄 lán, 跳欄 tiàolán (athletics).

hurl *v.* 用力投擲 yònglì tóuzhí / yònglì tóuzhì (throw violently).

hurricane *n.* 颶風 jùfēng.

hurry *v.* 催促 cuīcù. — *n.* 匆忙 cōngmáng.

hurt *v.* 使疼痛 shǐ téngtòng (pain), 使受傷 shǐ shòushāng

(injury). — *n.* 疼痛 téngtòng (pain), 傷害 shānghài (injury).

husband *n.* 丈夫 zhàngfu.

hush *v.* 安靜 ānjìng.

husk *n.* 外殼 wàiké (grain). — *v.* 去殼 qùké.

husky *adj.* ①殼的 ké de (husk). ②沙啞的 shāyǎ de (sound).

hustle *v.* ①驅趕 qūgǎn, 催促 cuīcù (hurry). ②推擠 tuījǐ (push).

hut *n.* 小屋 xiǎowū, 茅舍 máoshè (small roughly-built house).

hutch *n.* 籠子 lóngzi (cage).

hybrid *n.* 雜種 zázhǒng, 混種 hùnzhǒng (parents of different species).

hydrant *n.* 消防栓 xiāofángshuān.

hydroelectric *adj.* 水力發電 的 shuǐlì fādiàn de.

hydrogen *n.* 氫 qīng (chemistry).

hygiene *n.* 衛生學 wèishēngxué.

hymn *n.* 讚美詩 zànměishī.

hypermedia *n.* 超媒體 chāoméitǐ.

hyphen *n.* 連字號 liánzìhào.

hypnosis *n.* 催眠 cuīmián.

hypnotism *n.* 催眠術 cuīmiánshù.

hypocrisy *n.* 偽善 wěishàn / wèishàn.

hypocrite *n.* 偽君子 wěijūnzǐ / wèijūnzǐ.

hypothesis *n.* 假說 jiǎshuō, 假設 jiǎshè.

hysteria *n.* 歇斯底里症 xiēsīdǐlǐ zhèng (wild uncontrollable emotion).

I

I *pron.* 我 wǒ.

ice *n.* 冰 bīng (frozen water).
~ *cream* 冰淇淋 bīngqílín.
~ *hockey* 冰上曲棍球
bīng shàng qūgùnqiú.
~ *skates* 冰鞋 bīngxié / 溜冰鞋
liūbīngxié.

iceberg *n.* 冰山 bīngshān.

icebox *n.* 冰箱 bīngxiāng.

icing *n.* 糖衣 tángyī (frosting).

icon *n.* ①聖像 shèngxiàng
⟨picture⟩. ②圖像 túxiàng, 圖標
túbiāo ⟨computer⟩.

icy *adj.* 冰的 bīng de (very cold).

idea *n.* 想法 xiǎngfǎ (thought),
觀念 guānniàn (concept), 主意
zhǔyi (plan).

ideal *n.* 理想 lǐxiǎng. — *adj.*
①理想的 lǐxiǎng de (perfect).
②想像中的 xiǎngxiàngzhōng
de (imaginary).

idealistic *adj.* 理想主義的
lǐxiǎng zhǔyì de.

idealize *v.* 理想化 lǐxiǎnghuà.

identical *adj.* 同一的 tóngyī
de (the same), 相同的
xiāngtóng de (exactly alike).

identification *n.* 認明
rènmíng, 識別 shíbié / shìbié.
~ *card* 身分證 shēnfēnzhèng.

identify *v.* 認明 rènmíng,
識別 shíbié / shìbié.

identity *n.* 身分 shēnfen.

ideology *n.* 意識形態 yìshí
xíngtài / yìshì xíngtài.

idiom *n.* 成語 chéngyǔ,
慣用語 guànyòngyǔ.

idiot *n.* 白癡 báichī, 傻瓜
shǎguā, 笨蛋 bèndàn.

idle *adj.* ①閒散的 xiánsǎn de
(not busy). ②懶惰的 lǎnduò
de (lazy).

idol *n.* 偶像 ǒuxiàng.

idolize *v.* 偶像化 ǒuxiànghuà.

if *conj.* 如果 rúguǒ, 假如 jiǎrú
(supposing).

ignite *v.* 點火 diǎnhuǒ, 著火
zháohuǒ.

ignorance *n.* 無知 wúzhī,
愚昧 yúmèi.

ignorant *adj.* 無知的 wúzhī
de, 愚昧的 yúmèi de.

ignore *v.* 忽視 hūshì (neglect).

ill *adj.* 生病的 shēngbìng de.

illegal *adj.* 違法的 wéifǎ de.

illegible *adj.* 難讀的 nándú
de, 難認的 nánrèn de
(difficult to read).

illegitimate *adj.* ①違法的
wéifǎ de (illegal). ②私生的
sīshēng de ⟨birth⟩.

illicit *adj.* 不法的 bùfǎ de,
被禁止的 bèi jìnzhǐ de
(unlawful).

illiteracy *n.* 文盲 wénmáng.

illiterate *adj.* 文盲的
wénmáng de.

illness *n.* 疾病 jíbìng.

illogical *adj.* 不合邏輯的 bù
hé luójí de.

illuminate *v.* ①照明
zhàomíng, 照耀 zhàoyào
(brighten). ②闡釋 chǎnshì
(clarify).

illusion *n.* 幻影 huànyǐng.

illustrate *v.* ①加插圖 jiā
chātú (picture). ②舉例說明 jǔlì
shuōmíng (explain).

I

illustration 132 imperative

illustration n. ①插圖 chātú, 圖解 tújiě (picture). ②實例 shílì (example).

illustrious adj. 著名的 zhùmíng de (famous).

image n. ①像 xiàng, 肖像 xiàoxiàng (statue). ②意象 yìxiàng, 形象 xíngxiàng (mental picture).

imaginable adj. 可想像的 kě xiǎngxiàng de.

imaginary adj. 想像的 xiǎngxiàng de.

imagination n. 想像力 xiǎngxiànglì 〈ability〉, 想像 xiǎngxiàng 〈act〉.

imagine v. 想像 xiǎngxiàng.

imbalance n. 不平衡 bù pínghéng.

imitate v. 模仿 mófǎng (mimic), 效法 xiàofǎ (be like).

imitation n. ①模仿 mófǎng (copy). ②仿造品 fǎngzàopǐn (duplicate).

immaculate adj. 純潔的 chúnjié de (pure).

immaterial adj. ①不重要的 bú zhòngyào de (insignificant). ②非物質的 fēi wùzhí de / fēi wùzhí de, 精神上的 jīngshenshang de (spiritual).

immature adj. 未成熟的 wèi chéngshú de.

immediate adj. ①立即的 lìjí de, 立刻的 lìkè de (instant). ②鄰近的 línjìn de (near).

immense adj. 巨大的 jùdà de, 廣大的 guǎngdà de.

immerse v. 使浸沒 shǐ jìnmò (sink).

immigrant n. 移民 yímín.

immigrate v. 移居入境 yíjū rùjìng.

immigration n. 移民 yímín.

imminent adj. 急迫的 jípò de, 危急的 wēijí de / wéijí de.

immobile adj. 不能移動的 bù néng yídòng de.

immoral adj. 不道德的 bú dàodé de.

immortal adj. 不死的 bù sǐ de, 不朽的 bùxiǔ de.

immovable adj. 不可移動的 bù kě yídòng de.

immune adj. 免疫的 miǎnyì de.

immunity n. 免疫性 miǎnyìxìng.

immunize v. 使免疫 shǐ miǎnyì.

impact n. ①衝擊 chōngjī / chōngjí (collision). ②影響 yǐngxiǎng (strong effect).

impair v. 損害 sǔnhài, 削弱 xuēruò / xuèruò.

impale v. 刺穿 cìchuān.

impartial adj. 公正的 gōngzhèng de.

impartiality n. 公正 gōngzhèng.

impassable adj. 不能通行的 bù néng tōngxíng de.

impassioned adj. 熱情的 rèqíng de (passionate).

impassive adj. 無感情的 wú gǎnqíng de (without emotion).

impatient adj. 不耐煩的 bú nàifán de.

impeach v. 彈劾 tánhé (accuse).

impede v. 妨礙 fáng'ài, 阻礙 zǔ'ài.

impel v. 推進 tuījìn (propel).

imperative adj. ①必要的 bìyào de (necessary). ②緊急的 jǐnjí de, 急迫的 jípò de (urgent). — n. 祈使法 qíshǐfǎ

⟨grammar⟩.

imperfect *adj.* 不完全的 bù wánquán de, 有缺點的 yǒu quēdiǎn de.

imperial *adj.* 帝國的 dìguó de, 皇帝的 huángdì de.

imperialism *n.* 帝國主義 dìguó zhǔyì.

impersonal *adj.* 不具人格的 bú jù réngé de.

impersonate *v.* 扮演 bànyǎn (pretend to be), 模仿 mófǎng (intentionally copy).

implant *v.* 灌輸 guànshū (put in deeply).

implement *n.* 器具 qìjù, 工具 gōngjù. — *v.* 實施 shíshí, 履行 lǚxíng (carry out).

implicate *v.* ①牽涉 qiānshè, 涉及 shèjí (involve). ②暗示 ànshì (imply).

implication *n.* ①牽涉 qiānshè, 涉及 shèjí (involvement). ②暗示 ànshì (hint).

implicit *adj.* 暗示的 ànshì de (implied).

imply *v.* 暗示 ànshì.

impolite *adj.* 無禮的 wúlǐ de, 不客氣的 bú kèqi de.

import *n. & v.* 輸入 shūrù, 進口 jìnkǒu.

importance *n.* 重要 zhòngyào, 重要性 zhòngyàoxìng.

important *adj.* 重要的 zhòngyào de, 重大的 zhòngdà de.

impose *v.* 把……強加於 bǎ... qiángjiā yú (place on).

imposition *n.* 負擔 fùdān (burden).

impossible *adj.* 不可能的 bù kěnéng de (not possible).

impostor *n.* 騙子 piànzi.

impotent *adj.* ①無力的 wúlì de, 衰弱的 shuāiruò de (weak). ②陽痿的 yángwěi de ⟨medical⟩.

impound *v.* 扣押 kòuyā, 充公 chōnggōng.

impoverish *v.* 使貧困 shǐ pínkùn (make poor).

impress *v.* 使印象深刻 shǐ yìnxiàng shēnkè (influence deeply).

impression *n.* 印象 yìnxiàng.

impressive *adj.* 印象深刻的 yìnxiàng shēnkè de.

imprint *v.* ①印跡 yìnjī, 印記 yìnjì (print). ②出版說明 chūbǎn shuōmíng ⟨publication⟩.

imprison *v.* 下獄 xiàyù, 禁錮 jìngù.

improbable *adj.* 未必然的 wèi bìrán de (not likely to happen).

impromptu *adj. & adv.* 臨時的 línshí de, 即席的 jíxí de. — *n.* 即席演說 jíxí yǎnshuō ⟨speech⟩.

improper *adj.* ①不適當的 bú shìdàng de (inappropriate). ②錯誤的 cuòwù de (incorrect).

improve *v.* 改善 gǎishàn, 改進 gǎijìn.

improvement *n.* 改善 gǎishàn, 改進 gǎijìn.

improvise *v.* 即席創作 jíxí chuàngzuò.

impulsive *adj.* 衝動的 chōngdòng de.

impure *adj.* 髒的 zāng de, 不純潔的 bù chúnjié de.

impurity *n.* 不潔 bùjié.

in *adv. & prep.* 在……內 zài... nèi, 在……情況下 zài...

qíngkuàng xià.

inability n. 無能力 wú nénglì, 無才能 wú cáinéng.

inaccessible adj. 難親近的 nán qīnjìn de, 難接近的 nán jiējìn de.

inaccuracy n. 錯誤 cuòwù (mistake).

inaccurate adj. 不準確的 bù zhǔnquè de, 錯誤的 cuòwù de.

inadequate adj. 不充分的 bù chōngfèn de (insufficient).

inanimate adj. ①無生命的 wú shēngmìng de (lifeless). ②無生氣的 wú shēngqì de (boring).

inapplicable adj. 不適用的 bú shìyòng de.

inappropriate adj. 不適宜 bú shìyí de.

inapt adj. 不恰當的 bú qiàdàng de (unsuitable).

inaudible adj. 聽不見的 tīngbùjiàn de.

inborn adj. 天生的 tiānshēng de.

incalculable adj. 數不盡的 shǔbùjìn de.

incapable adj. 無能力的 wú nénglì de.

incapacitate v. 使無能力 shǐ wú nénglì, 使無資格 shǐ wú zīgé (disable).

incarcerate v. 監禁 jiānjìn (shut in a prison).

incense n. 香 xiāng, 香料 xiāngliào. — v. 激怒 jīnù (make angry).

incentive n. 刺激 cìjī, 誘因 yòuyīn.

incessant adj. 不斷的 búduàn de, 繼續的 jìxù de.

incest n. 亂倫 luànlún.

inch n. 吋 cùn.

incident n. 事件 shìjiàn (event).

incidental adj. 附帶的 fùdài de (minor).

incinerate v. 燒成灰 shāo chéng huī, 焚化 fénhuà.

inclination n. 傾向 qīngxiàng.

incline v. 傾向於 qīngxiàng yú (tend towards). — n. 傾斜 qīngxié (slope).

include v. 包括 bāokuò, 包含 bāohán.

inclusive adj. 包括的 bāokuò de, 包含的 bāohán de.

incoherent adj. 無連貫的 wú liánguàn de.

income n. 收入 shōurù, 所得 suǒdé. ~ tax 所得稅 suǒdéshuì.

incomparable adj. 無比的 wúbǐ de, 不可比擬的 bù kě bǐnǐ de.

incompatible adj. 不相容的 bù xiāngróng de.

incompetent adj. 無能力的 wú nénglì de (not able), 不合格的 bù hégé de (not qualified).

incomplete adj. 不完全的 bù wánquán de.

incomprehensible adj. 不能理解的 bù néng lǐjiě de.

inconceivable adj. 難以想像的 nányǐ xiǎngxiàng de (can't be imagined).

inconclusive adj. 非決定性的 fēi juédìngxìng de.

inconsequential adj. 不重要的 bú zhòngyào de (of no significance).

inconsiderable adj. 不足道的 bù zú dào de (insignificant), 不重要的 bú zhòngyào de (unimportant).

inconsiderate adj. 不體貼的

bù tǐtiē de.

inconsistent adj. 矛盾的 máodùn de, 不一致的 bù yízhì de (not in harmony).

inconstant adj. 反覆無常的 fǎnfù-wúcháng de (changeable).

inconvenience n. 不便 búbiàn.

inconvenient adj. 不便的 búbiàn de.

inconvertible adj. 不能兌換的 bù néng duìhuàn de (currency).

incorporate v. 合併 hébìng, 併入 bìngrù (merge).

incorrect adj. 錯誤的 cuòwù de.

increase v. 增加 zēngjiā.

incredible adj. 難以置信的 nányí-zhìxìn de.

increment n. 增加 zēngjiā (increase).

incur v. 招致 zhāozhì, 招惹 zhāorě.

incurable adj. 無可救藥的 wú-kě-jiù-yào de, 不能治療的 bù néng zhìliáo de.

incursion n. 襲擊 xíjí / xíjí, 入侵 rùqīn (raid).

indebted adj. ①感激的 gǎnjī de (grateful). ②負債的 fùzhài de (money).

indecent adj. ①不適當的 bú shìdàng de (improper). ②不道德的 bú dàodé de (immodest).

indeed adv. 的確 díquè, 實在 shízài (really). — interj. 真的！ Zhēnde!

indefinite adj. ①不確定的 bú quèdìng de (unclear). ②無限制的 wú xiànzhì de (unlimited).

indemnify v. 使免於蒙受損失 shǐ miǎn yú méngshòu sǔnshī (protect).

indemnity n. 賠款 péikuǎn, 賠償 péicháng.

indent v. ①成鋸齒狀 chéng jùchǐzhuàng (make notches). ②縮排 suōpái (papers).

independence n. 獨立 dúlì, 自主 zìzhǔ.

independent adj. 獨立的 dúlì de, 自主的 zìzhǔ de.

indescribable adj. 難以形容的 nányí xíngróng de.

indestructible adj. 不能破壞的 bù néng pòhuài de.

index n. ①索引 suǒyǐn (alphabetical list). ②指標 zhǐbiāo (sign). ③食指 shízhǐ (finger).

Indian n. & adj. ①印度人 Yìndùrén (of India). ②印第安人 Yìndǐ'ānrén (American Indian). ③印第安語 Yìndǐ'ānyǔ (American Indian language). the ~ Ocean 印度洋 Yìndùyáng.

indicate v. 指示 zhǐshì, 指出 zhǐchū.

indication n. 指示 zhǐshì, 象徵 xiàngzhēng.

indicative adj. 指示的 zhǐshì de.

indicator n. 指示器 zhǐshìqì.

indict v. 起訴 qǐsù, 控告 kònggào (accuse).

indifference n. 不關心 bù guānxīn.

indifferent adj. 不關心的 bù guānxīn de, 沒興趣的 méi xìngqù de.

indigenous adj. 土著的 tǔzhù de, 本土的 běntǔ de.

indigestible adj. 難消化的 nán xiāohuà de.

indigestion n. 消化不良 xiāohuà bùliáng.

indignity n. 侮辱 wǔrǔ /

wǔrù, 輕蔑 qīngmiè.

indirect adj. 間接的 jiànjiē de.

indiscriminate adj. 未加區別的 wèijiā qūbié de.

indispensable adj. 不可缺的 bù kě quē de, 必要的 bìyào de.

indisputable adj. 不容爭辯的 bùróng zhēngbiàn de.

indissoluble adj. 不能溶解的 bù néng róngjiě de.

indistinct adj. 不清楚的 bù qīngchu de, 模糊的 móhu de (unclear).

individual n. 個人 gèrén, 個體 gètǐ. — adj. ①個別的 gèbié de, 個人的 gèrén de (personal). ②獨特的 dútè de (characteristic).

Indochina n. 中南半島 Zhōngnánbàndǎo.

indoor adj. 室內的 shìnèi de.

indoors adv. 在室內 zài shìnèi.

induce v. ①引誘 yǐnyòu, 勸誘 quànyòu (persuade). ②招致 zhāozhì (cause).

indulge v. 放任 fàngrèn, 縱容 zòngróng.

industrial adj. 工業的 gōngyè de.

industrialize v. 工業化 gōngyèhuà.

industrious adj. 勤勉的 qínmiǎn de.

industry n. ①工業 gōngyè (production). ②勤勉 qínmiǎn (diligence).

inebriate v. 使醉 shǐ zuì (make drunk). — n. 醉漢 zuìhàn, 酒鬼 jiǔguǐ (alcoholic).

ineffective adj. 無效的 wúxiào de.

ineffectual adj. 無效果的 wú xiàoguǒ de, 無益的 wúyì de (futile).

inefficient adj. 無效率的 wú xiàolǜ de.

inelegant adj. 不雅的 bùyǎ de.

ineligible adj. 沒有資格的 méiyǒu zīgé de.

inept adj. 不合適的 bù héshì de (unfit).

inequality n. 不平等 bù píngděng.

inevitable adj. 不可避免的 bù kě bìmiǎn de.

inexact adj. 不精確的 bù jīngquè de.

inexcusable adj. 不能原諒的 bù néng yuánliàng de.

inexpensive adj. 價廉的 jiàlián de.

inexperience n. 無經驗 wú jīngyàn.

infamous adj. 不名譽的 bù míngyù de.

infamy n. 不名譽 bù míngyù, 醜名 chǒumíng.

infancy n. 幼年 yòunián.

infant n. 嬰兒 yīng'ér. — adj. 嬰兒的 yīng'ér de.

infantry n. 步兵 bùbīng ⟨army⟩.

infatuate v. 使迷戀 shǐ míliàn.

infect v. 傳染 chuánrǎn, 感染 gǎnrǎn ⟨disease⟩.

infection n. 傳染 chuánrǎn, 傳染病 chuánrǎnbìng.

infectious adj. 傳染性的 chuánrǎnxìng de.

infer v. 推論 tuīlùn.

inferior adj. 下級的 xiàjí de (low in rank), 較低的 jiàodī de (lower).

inferiority n. 下級 xiàjí, 低劣 dīliè. ~ complex 自卑感 zìbēigǎn.

infest v. 擾亂 rǎoluàn, 蹂躪 róulìn ⟨pests⟩.

infinite adj. 無限的 wúxiàn de (without limits).

infinitive n. & adj. 不定詞 búdìngcí ⟨grammar⟩.

infinity n. 無限 wúxiàn, 無窮 wúqióng.

inflame v. ①激怒 jīnù, 煽動 shāndòng (provoke). ②發炎 fāyán, 紅腫 hóngzhǒng ⟨medical⟩.

inflammable adj. 易燃的 yìrán de (burnable).

inflammation n. 發炎 fāyán.

inflate v. 充氣 chōngqì (fill with air), 使膨脹 shǐ péngzhàng (swell).

inflation n. ①通貨膨脹 tōnghuò péngzhàng ⟨currency⟩. ②膨脹 péngzhàng (increase).

inflection n. ①音調變化 yīndiào biànhuà (tone). ②語尾變化 yǔwěi biànhuà ⟨grammar⟩.

inflexible adj. ①堅定的 jiāndìng de (uncompromising). ②不可彎曲的 bù kě wānqū de (unbending).

inflict v. 使遭受 shǐ zāoshòu, 施罰 shīfá.

infliction n. 施罰 shīfá.

inflow n. 流入 liúrù.

influence n. 影響 yǐngxiǎng, 勢力 shìlì.

influential adj. 有影響力的 yǒu yǐngxiǎnglì de.

influenza n. 流行性感冒 liúxíngxìng gǎnmào ⟨medical⟩.

inform v. 通知 tōngzhī, 通報 tōngbào (give information).

informal adj. 非正式的 fēi zhèngshì de.

information n. ①消息 xiāoxi (news). ②情報 qíngbào, 知識 zhīshi (data). ③信息 xìnxī / 資訊 zīxùn ⟨computer⟩.
~ **center** 問訊處 wènxùnchù / 詢問處 xúnwènchù.

infringe v. 侵犯 qīnfàn, 侵害 qīnhài.

infuriate v. 激怒 jīnù.

ingratitude n. 忘恩負義 wàng-ēn-fù-yì.

ingredient n. 成分 chéngfèn.

inhabit v. 居住於 jūzhù yú.

inhabitant n. 居民 jūmín.

inhale v. 吸入 xīrù.

inharmonious adj. 不和諧的 bù héxié de.

inherent adj. 與生俱來的 yǔ-shēng-jù-lái de.

inherit v. 繼承 jìchéng.

inheritance n. ①繼承 jìchéng (succession). ②遺產 yíchǎn (heritage).

inhibit v. 抑制 yìzhì, 阻止 zǔzhǐ.

inhospitable adj. 冷淡的 lěngdàn de, 不好客的 bú hàokè de (not friendly).

inhuman adj. 不人道的 bù réndào de, 殘忍的 cánrěn de (cruel).

inhumane adj. 不人道的 bù réndào de, 殘忍的 cánrěn de (cruel).

initial adj. 最初的 zuìchū de. — n. 起首字母 qǐshǒu zìmǔ.

initiate v. 創始 chuàngshǐ, 開始 kāishǐ.

initiative n. ①初步 chūbù (the first act). ②創造力 chuàngzàolì (inventiveness). ③創制權 chuàngzhìquán ⟨election⟩.

inject v. 注射 zhùshè (put into).

injunction n. 命令 mìnglìng, 禁止令 jìnzhǐlìng ⟨law⟩, 禁制令 jìnzhìlìng ⟨court⟩.

injure v. 傷害 shānghài, 損害 sǔnhài.

injury n. 傷害 shānghài, 損害 sǔnhài (harm).

injustice n. 不公正 bù gōngzhèng, 不公平 bù gōngping.

ink n. 墨水 mòshuǐ.
~ *jet printer* 噴墨打印機 pēnmò dǎyìnjī / 針孔噴墨印表機 zhēnkǒng pēnmò yìnbiǎojī 〈computer〉.

inland adj. 內陸的 nèilù de, 內地的 nèidì de (interior).

in-law n. 姻親 yīnqīn.

inlet n. 水灣 shuǐwān, 海口 hǎikǒu, 入口 rùkǒu.

in-line skates 滾軸溜冰鞋 gǔnzhóu liūbīngxié / 直排輪溜冰鞋 zhípáilún liūbīngxié.

inmate n. 被收容者 bèi shōuróng zhě.

inn n. 客棧 kèzhàn, 小酒館 xiǎo jiǔguǎn.

innate adj. 天生的 tiānshēng de.

inner adj. 內部的 nèibù de, 內在的 nèizài de.

inning n. 一局 yì jú 〈baseball〉.

innkeeper n. 旅館主人 lǚguǎn zhǔrén.

innocence n. 清白 qīngbái, 無罪 wúzuì 〈not guilty〉.

innocent adj. ①無罪的 wúzuì de (not guilty). ②天真的 tiānzhēn de (naive).

innovate v. 革新 géxīn, 創新 chuàngxīn, 改革 gǎigé.

innumerable adj. 無數的 wúshù de.

inopportune adj. 不合時宜 的 bùhé shíyí de.

inorganic adj. 無機的 wújī de 〈chemistry〉.

input n. 輸入 shūrù 〈computer〉.

inquire v. 詢問 xúnwèn, 查問 cháwèn.

inquiry n. ①詢問 xúnwèn, 查閱 cháyuè (inquiring). ②調查 diàochá (investigation).

inquisition n. 審訊 shěnxùn, 調查 diàochá.

inquisitive adj. 好問的 hàowèn de, 好奇的 hàoqí de.

insane adj. 患精神病的 huàn jīngshénbìng de, 發狂的 fākuáng de (mentally ill).

inscription n. 銘刻 míngkè, 刻字 kèzì.

insect n. 昆蟲 kūnchóng.

insecure adj. ①缺乏自信的 quēfá zìxìn de (not cofident). ②隨時不保的 suíshí bù bǎo de (lost). ③不安全的 bù ānquán de (not safe).

insensible adj. ①無知覺的 wú zhījué de (unconscious). ②未察覺的 wèi chájué de (unaware).

insensitive adj. 無感覺的 wú gǎnjué de (lack of feeling), 不敏感的 bù mǐngǎn de (obtuse).

inseparable adj. 不能分離的 bù néng fēnlí de.

insert v. 插入 chārù.

inside n. 內部 nèibù, 內側 nèicè. — adj. & adv. 在內部 zài nèibù, 在……裡面 zài...lǐmiàn.

insight n. 洞察 dòngchá, 見識 jiànshi.

insignificant adj. 不重要的 bú zhòngyào de.

insincere adj. 不誠懇的 bù chéngkěn de.

insinuate v. 暗指 ànzhǐ, 暗諷 ànfěng / ànfèng.

insipid adj. ①乏味的 fáwèi de (dull). ②無味的 wúwèi de (flavorless).

insist v. ①堅持 jiānchí (emphasize). ②主張 zhǔzhāng (declare).

insolent adj. 無禮的 wúlǐ de (rude), 傲慢的 àomàn de (arrogant).

insoluble adj. ①不能溶解的 bù néng róngjiě de (not able to dissolve). ②不能解決的 bù néng jiějué de (unsolvable).

insomnia n. 失眠 shīmián.

inspect v. 檢查 jiǎnchá, 視察 shìchá.

inspection n. 檢查 jiǎnchá.

inspector n. 檢查員 jiǎncháyuán.

inspiration n. ①靈感 línggǎn (creativity). ②激勵 jīlì (spur).

inspire v. ①激勵 jīlì, 鼓舞 gǔwǔ (animate). ②給靈感 gěi línggǎn (fill with creativity).

instability n. 不穩定 bù wěndìng.

install v. ①安裝 ānzhuāng, 設置 shèzhì (set up). ②使就職 shǐ jiùzhí (position). ③安置 ānzhì (place).

installment n. ①分期付款 fēnqí fùkuǎn / fēnqí fùkuǎn (payment). ②分冊 fēncè, 一冊 yí cè (book).

instance n. 例子 lìzi, 例證 lìzhèng. *for ~* 例如 lìrú.

instant n. 立即 lìjí. — adj. ①立刻的 lìkè de (immediate). ②緊急的 jǐnjí de (urgent). *~ noodles* 方便麵 fāngbiànmiàn / 速食麵 sùshímiàn, 泡麵 pàomiàn.

instantly adv. 立刻 lìkè.

instead adv. 代替 dàitì.

instep n. 腳背 jiǎobèi.

instinct n. 本能 běnnéng.

instinctive adj. 本能的 běnnéng de, 天生的 tiānshēng de.

institute v. 創立 chuànglì (establish). — n. 學會 xuéhuì, 研究所 yánjiūsuǒ / yánjiùsuǒ.

institution n. ①機構 jīgòu, 社團 shètuán (organization). ②慣例 guànlì (convention).

instruct v. ①教導 jiàodǎo, 教授 jiàoshòu / jiāoshòu (teach). ②指示 zhǐshì (command).

instruction n. ①指導 zhídǎo (leadership), 教導 jiàodǎo (teaching). ②指示 zhǐshì, 命令 mìnglìng (command).

instructive adj. 教育性的 jiàoyùxìng de.

instrument n. ①儀器 yíqì, 器具 qìjù (apparatus). ②樂器 yuèqì (music).

insufficient adj. 不充足的 bù chōngzú de.

insulate v. 隔離 gélí, 使孤立 shǐ gūlì (isolate).

insult n. & v. 侮辱 wǔrǔ / wǔrù.

insurance n. 保險 bǎoxiǎn (contract).

insure v. 保險 bǎoxiǎn.

intact adj. 未觸動的 wèi chùdòng de (untouched), 完整的 wánzhěng de (complete).

intake n. ①攝取量 shèqǔliàng (amount). ②入口 rùkǒu (opening).

integral adj. ①整體的 zhěngtǐ de, 完整的 wánzhěng de (whole). ②必要的 bìyào de, 關鍵的 guānjiàn de (key).

integrate v. 整合 zhěnghé, 結合 jiéhé, 合併 hébìng (combine).

integrity n. 完整 wánzhěng

(completeness).

intellect n. 智力 zhìlì, 理解力 lǐjiělì (intelligence).

intellectual adj. 智力的 zhìlì de (of the intellect). — n. 知識分子 zhīshì fènzǐ.

~ *property rights* 知識產權 zhīshì chǎnquán / 智慧財產權 zhìhuì cáichǎnquán.

intelligence n. ①智力 zhìlì, 理解力 lǐjiělì (intellect). ②情報 qíngbào, 消息 xiāoxi (information).

intelligent adj. 有才智的 yǒu cáizhì de, 有理解力的 yǒu lǐjiělì de.

intelligentsia n. 知識分子 zhīshì fènzǐ.

intelligible adj. 可理解的 kě lǐjiě de.

intend v. 意欲 yìyù, 想要 xiǎngyào, 企圖 qìtú / qǐtú.

intense adj. ①強烈的 qiángliè de (ardent). ②劇烈的 jùliè de (fierce).

intensify v. 使強烈 shǐ qiángliè.

intensity n. 強度 qiángdù (degree).

intensive adj. ①徹底的 chèdǐ de, 深入的 shēnrù de (thorough). ②密集的 mìjí de, 集中的 jízhōng de (concentrated).

intent n. 意向 yìxiàng (law).

intention n. 意圖 yìtú.

intentional adj. 有意的 yǒuyì de.

inter v. 埋葬 máizàng (bury).

interact v. 交互作用 jiāohù zuòyòng.

intercept v. ①中途攔截 zhōngtú lánjié (stop). ②截斷 jiéduàn (cut off).

intercession n. 代人求情 dài rén qiúqíng.

interchange v. 交換 jiāohuàn, 更換 gēnghuàn, 替換 tìhuàn (exchange). — n. 立交橋 lìjiāoqiáo / 交流道 jiāoliúdào (highway).

interchangeable adj. 可交換的 kě jiāohuàn de.

intercom n. 對講機 duìjiǎngjī.

intercourse n. ①交際 jiāojì, 交流 jiāoliú (exchange). ②性交 xìngjiāo (sex).

interest n. ①關心 guānxīn (attention). ②興趣 xìngqù, 嗜好 shìhào (hobby). ③利息 lìxī / lìxí (money). ~ *group* 利益團體 lìyì tuántǐ. ~ *rates* 利率 lìlǜ. — v. 使感興趣 shǐ gǎn xìngqù, 引起興趣 yǐnqǐ xìngqù.

interested adj. 感興趣的 gǎn xìngqù de.

interesting adj. 有趣的 yǒuqù de.

interfere v. 妨礙 fáng'ài, 干涉 gānshè.

interference n. 妨礙 fáng'ài, 干涉 gānshè, 干擾 gānrǎo.

interior n. 內部 nèibù. — adj. 內部的 nèibù de.

interject v. 突然插入 tūrán chārù / 插入 chārù.

interjection n. 感歎詞 gǎntàncí (grammar).

interlock v. 互相連結 hùxiāng liánjié.

intermediary n. 中間人 zhōngjiānrén, 調解者 tiáojiězhě (mediator). — adj. 中間的 zhōngjiān de, 調解的 tiáojiě de.

intermediate adj. ①中間的 zhōngjiān de (middle). ②中級的 zhōngjí de (level).

intermission n. 間歇 jiànxiē.

intern n. 實習醫生 shíxí yīshēng ⟨doctor⟩, 實習者 shíxízhě ⟨other professions⟩.

internal adj. 內部的 nèibù de.

international adj. 國際的 guójì de.

Internet n. 因特網 Yīntèwǎng, 國際互聯網 guójì hùlánwǎng / 網際網路 Wǎngjì wǎnglù ⟨computer⟩.

Internet café 網吧 Wǎngbā / 網路咖啡店 Wǎnglù kāfēidiàn, 網咖 Wǎngkā.

interpret v. ①解釋 jiěshì, 闡明 chǎnmíng ⟨explain⟩. ②口譯 kǒuyì ⟨translate orally⟩.

interpretation n. ①解釋 jiěshì ⟨explanation⟩. ②口譯 kǒuyì ⟨translation⟩.

interpreter n. 傳譯員 chuányìyuán.

interrogate v. 審問 shěnwèn, 訊問 xùnwèn.

interrogative adj. 疑問的 yíwèn de. — n. 疑問詞 yíwèncí ⟨grammar⟩.

interrupt v. ①中斷 zhōngduàn, 打斷 dǎduàn ⟨break in⟩. ②妨礙 fáng'ài ⟨obstruct⟩.

intersect v. 交叉 jiāochā ⟨cross⟩.

intersection n. 交叉點 jiāochādiǎn, 交叉 jiāochā.

interval n. 間隔 jiàngé.

intervene v. 干涉 gānshè, 調停 tiáotíng.

interview n. & v. 會見 huìjiàn, 面談 miàntán ⟨meeting⟩.

intestine n. 腸 cháng.

intimacy n. 親密 qīnmì, 親近 qīnjìn.

intimate adj. ①親密的 qīnmì de, 親近的 qīnjìn de ⟨close⟩.

②詳細的 xiángxì de ⟨detailed⟩. — v. 暗示 ànshì ⟨imply⟩.

intimidate v. 恐嚇 kǒnghè, 脅迫 xiépò ⟨threaten⟩.

into prep. 進入……之內 jìnrù...zhī nèi ⟨inside⟩.

intolerable adj. 無法忍受的 wúfǎ rěnshòu de ⟨unbearable⟩.

intolerant adj. 不容忍的 bù róngrěn de.

intonation n. 語調 yǔdiào, 音調 yīndiào ⟨voice⟩.

intoxicate v. ①使醉 shǐ zuì ⟨cause to be drunk⟩. ②使興奮 shǐ xīngfèn ⟨excite⟩.

intranet n. 內聯網 nèiliánwǎng / 內部網路 nèibù wǎnglù ⟨computer⟩.

intricate adj. 錯綜複雜的 cuòzōng-fùzá de / cuòzòng-fùzá de.

intrigue n. 陰謀 yīnmóu, 密謀 mìmóu. — v. ①密謀 mìmóu ⟨plot⟩. ②引起興趣 yǐnqǐ xìngqù ⟨interest⟩.

introduce v. ①介紹 jièshào ⟨acquaint⟩. ②引進 yǐnjìn ⟨bring in⟩.

introduction n. ①介紹 jièshào ⟨acquaint⟩. ②前言 qiányán, 緒論 xùlùn ⟨preface⟩.

introductory adj. 導引的 dǎoyǐn de.

intuition n. 直覺 zhíjué, 第六感 dìliùgǎn.

intuitive adj. 直覺的 zhíjué de.

invade v. 侵略 qīnlüè, 入侵 rùqīn ⟨attack⟩.

invalid n. 病弱者 bìngruòzhě, 病人 bìngrén ⟨weak person⟩. — adj. 無效的 wúxiào de, 無用的 wúyòng de ⟨not vaild⟩.

invaluable adj. 無價的 wújià

de, 極珍貴的 jí zhēnguì de.
invariable adj. 不變的 búbiàn de.
invasion n. 侵入 qīnrù, 侵犯 qīnfàn.
invent v. 發明 fāmíng (create or design).
invention n. 發明 fāmíng (creation).
inventory n. ①目錄 mùlù, 貨物清單 huòwù qīngdān (list). ②存貨 cúnhuò (goods).
inverse adj. 倒轉的 dàozhuǎn de, 顛倒的 diāndǎo de.
invert v. 倒轉 dàozhuǎn, 顛倒 diāndǎo (reverse).
invertebrate n. 無脊椎動物 wú jǐzhuī dòngwù.
invest v. 投資 tóuzī.
investigate v. 調查 diàochá (examine), 研究 yánjiū / yánjiù (research).
investigation n. 調查 diàochá (examination), 研究 yánjiū / yánjiù (research).
investment n. 投資 tóuzī.
invigorate v. 賦與活力 fùyǔ huólì, 鼓舞 gǔwǔ.
invincible adj. 難以征服的 nányǐ zhēngfú de.
invisible adj. 看不見的 kànbùjiàn de.
invitation n. 邀請 yāoqǐng (request).
invite v. ①邀請 yāoqǐng (ask). ②招致 zhāozhì, 引來 yǐnlái (attract).
invocation n. 祈求 qíqiú (prayer).
invoice n. & v. 發票 fāpiào.
involuntary adj. 非自願的 fēi zìyuàn de.
involve v. ①包括 bāokuò, 包含 bāohán (contain). ②牽涉

qiānshè, 涉及 shèjí (embroil).
inward adj. & adv. 向內的 xiàng nèi de, 在內的 zài nèi de.
iodine n. 碘 diǎn, 碘酒 diǎnjiǔ (chemistry).
IQ, I.Q. 智商數 zhìf)*)... 智商 zhìshāng (intelligence quotient).
irate adj. 發怒的 fānù de.
iris n. ①虹膜 hóngmó / hóngmó (eyes). ②鳶尾 yuānwěi (plant).
Irish n. & adj. ①愛爾蘭人 Ài'ěrlánrén (people). ②愛爾蘭語 Ài'ěrlányǔ (language).
iron n. ①鐵 tiě (metal). ②熨斗 yùndǒu (for clothes). — adj. 鐵的 tiě de. — v. 熨平 yùnpíng.
ironic adj. 諷刺的 fěngcì de / fèngcì de.
irony n. 諷刺 fěngcì / fèngcì.
irrational adj. 無理性的 wú lǐxìng de (unreasonable), 不合理的 bù héli de (absurd).
irregular adj. 不規則的 bù guīzé de.
irrelevant adj. 不相關的 bù xiāngguān de.
irreligious adj. 反宗教的 fǎn zōngjiào de.
irreparable adj. 不能修補的 bù néng xiūbǔ de.
irreplaceable adj. 不能替換的 bù néng tìhuàn de.
irresistible adj. 不可抵抗的 bù kě dǐkàng de.
irresolute adj. 優柔寡斷的 yōuróu-guǎduàn de.
irrespective adj. 不顧的 búgù de, 不論的 búlùn de.
irresponsible adj. 不負責任的 bú fù zérèn de.
irreverent adj. 不敬的 bújìng

de.
irrevocable adj. 不能撤回的 bù néng chèhuí de.
irrigate v. 灌溉 guàngài (supply with water).
irritable adj. 易怒的 yì nù de.
irritate v. 激怒 jīnù (make angry).
is v. 是 shì.
Islam n. ①回教 Huíjiào 〈religion〉. ②回教徒 Huíjiàotú (Muslims). ③回教世界 Huíjiào shìjiè (Muslim world).
island n. 島 dǎo, 島嶼 dǎoyǔ.
islander n. 島民 dǎomín.
isolate v. 孤立 gūlì, 隔離 gélí.
issue v. 發行 fāxíng (publish). — n. ①發行 fāxíng (publication). ②事項 shìxiàng, 要項 yàoxiàng (affair). ③結果 jiéguǒ (result). ④爭論點

zhēnglùndiǎn (point).
it pron. 它 tā, 牠 tā.
Italian n. & adj. ①意大利人 Yìdàlìrén / 義大利人 Yìdàlìrén 〈people〉. ②意大利語 Yìdàlìyǔ / 義大利語 Yìdàlìyǔ 〈language〉.
italic adj. 斜體的 xiétǐ de. — n. 斜體字 xiétǐzì.
itch n. 癢 yǎng 〈skin〉. — v. 發癢 fāyǎng 〈scratch〉.
item n. 項目 xiàngmù, 條 tiáo, 款 kuǎn.
itinerary n. 旅行記錄 lǚxíng jìlù, 旅行計畫 lǚxíng jìhuà 〈language〉.
its pron. 它的 tā de, 牠的 tā de.
itself pron. 它自己 tā zìjǐ.
ivory n. 象牙 xiàngyá (elephant's tusk).
ivy n. 常春藤 chángchūnténg.

J

jab n. & v. 刺 cì, 戳 chuō.
jabber v. 含糊地說 hánhu de shuō. — n. 含糊不清的話 hánhu bù qīng de huà.
jack n. 千斤頂 qiānjīndǐng 〈device〉.
jacket n. 夾克 jiākè / jiákè, 外套 wàitào.
jade n. 翡翠 fěicuì, 玉 yù.
jagged adj. 鋸齒狀的 jùchǐzhuàng de.
jaguar n. 美洲虎 měizhōuhǔ.
jail n. 監獄 jiānyù, 監牢 jiānláo.
jam v. ①推擠 tuǐjǐ (crowd). ②擁塞 yōngsè / yǒngsè

(block). — n. 果醬 guǒjiàng (jelly).
janitor n. 管理員 guǎnlǐyuán.
January n. 一月 Yīyuè.
Japanese n. & adj. ①日本人 Rìběnrén 〈people〉. ②日語 Rìyǔ 〈language〉.
jar n. 瓶 píng, 瓶子 píngzi, 罐子 guànzi 〈bottle〉.
jargon n. 術語 shùyǔ, 行話 hánghuà.
jasmine n. 茉莉 mòlì.
jaundice n. 黃疸病 huángdǎnbìng 〈medical〉.
jaunt n. & v. 遊覽 yóulǎn.

javelin n. 標槍 biāoqiāng.

jaw n. 顎 è.

jazz n. 爵士樂 juéshìyuè ⟨music⟩.

jealous adj. 嫉妒的 jídù de (unhappy and angry).

jeans n. 牛仔褲 niúzǎikù.

jeep n. 吉普車 jípǔchē.

jeer n. & v. 嘲弄 cháonòng, 嘲笑 cháoxiào.

jelly n. ①果醬 guǒjiàng ⟨spread on bread⟩. ②果凍 guǒdòng ⟨solid⟩.

jellyfish n. 水母 shuǐmǔ, 海蜇 hǎizhé.

jeopardize v. 使危險 shǐ wēixiǎn / shǐ wéixiǎn, 危害 wēihài / wéihài.

jeopardy n. 危險 wēixiǎn / wéixiǎn.

jerk n. ①急拉 jílā (pull). ②抽動 chōudòng (twitch). ③混蛋 húndàn (idiot). — v. 急拉 jílā (pull suddenly).

jest n. 笑柄 xiàobǐng. — v. 嘲弄 cháonòng, 取笑 qǔxiào.

Jesus n. 耶穌 Yēsū, 上帝 Shàngdì.

jet n. ①噴射 pēnshè (spout). ②噴口 pēnkǒu (nozzle). ③噴氣式飛機 pēnqìshì fēijī / 噴射機 pēnshèjī ⟨aircraft⟩. — v. 噴射 pēnshè, 噴出 pēnchū (gush).

Jew n. 猶太人 Yóutàirén.

Jewish adj. 猶太的 Yóutài de.

jewel n. 珠寶 zhūbǎo, 寶石 bǎoshí (gem).

jewelry n. 珠寶 zhūbǎo.

jiffy n. 一瞬間 yíshùnjiān, 馬上 mǎshàng (in a moment).

jigsaw n. 拼圖玩具 pīntú wánjù ⟨puzzle⟩.

jingle n. & v. 叮噹響 dīngdāngxiǎng.

jinx v. 使倒霉 shǐ dǎoméi (give bad luck).

job n. 工作 gōngzuò, 職業 zhíyè (regular paid employment).

jockey n. 騎師 qíshī / jìshī.

jog v. ①輕推 qīngtuī, 輕觸 qīngchù (push slightly). ②喚起 huànqǐ (recall). ③慢跑 mànpǎo (run slowly). — n. 輕推 qīngtuī, 輕觸 qīngchù.

join v. ①連接 liánjiē (connect). ②會合 huìhé (meet). ③加入 jiārù (participate in).

joint n. ①接頭 jiētóu (place joined). ②關節 guānjié ⟨bones⟩. —adj. 共同的 gòngtóng de, 共有的 gòngyǒu de.

joke n. 笑話 xiàohuà, 玩笑 wánxiào. — v. ①說笑話 shuō xiàohuà, 開玩笑 kāi wánxiào ⟨humor⟩. ②取笑 qǔxiào (tease).

jolly adj. 愉快的 yúkuài de (cheerful).

jostle n. & v. 推撞 tuīzhuàng.

jot n. 少量 shǎoliàng. ~ down 摘要記下 zhāiyào jìxià.

journal n. ①日記 rìjì, 日誌 rìzhì (diary). ②期刊 qīkān / qíkān (periodical).

journalism n. 新聞業 xīnwényè.

journalist n. 新聞工作者 xīnwén gōngzuò zhě, 新聞記者 xīnwén jìzhě.

journey n. 旅行 lǚxíng (trip), 旅程 lǚchéng (itinerary). — v. 旅行 lǚxíng.

jowl n. 顎 è, 下顎 xià'è.

joy n. 歡樂 huānlè, 喜悅 xǐyuè (great happiness).

joyful adj. 歡喜的 huānxǐ de, 喜悅的 xǐyuè de.

J

jubilant *adj.* 喜洋洋的 xǐyángyáng de (delighted).

Judaism *n.* 猶太教 Yóutàijiào.

judge *n.* ①法官 fǎguān (court). ②裁判 cáipàn (contest). — *v.* ①裁判 cáipàn (decide). ②審判 shěnpàn (convict). ③判斷 pànduàn (evaluate).

judgment *n.* ①判決 pànjué (conviction). ②判斷 pànduàn, 判斷力 pànduànlì (discretion).

judicial *adj.* 司法的 sīfǎ de.

judicious *adj.* 明智的 míngzhì de (wise), 深思遠慮 的 shēnsī-yuǎnlǜ de (well-considered).

judo *n.* 柔道 róudào.

jug *n.* 壺 hú, 水罐 shuǐguàn (pitcher).

juggle *v.* 變戲法 biàn xìfǎ, 耍把戲 shuǎ bǎxì.

juice *n.* 汁 zhī, 液 yè.

juicy *adj.* 多汁的 duōzhī de (having much juice).

jukebox *n.* 自動唱機 zìdòng diǎnchàngjī.

July *n.* 七月 Qīyuè.

jumble *v.* 混雜 hùnzá, 混合 hùnhé (mix). — *n.* 一團糟 yìtuánzāo, 混雜 hùnzá ⟨mixed up⟩.

jumbo *adj.* 巨大的 jùdà de.

jump *v.* ①跳 tiào, 跳躍 tiàoyuè (leap). ②暴漲 bàozhǎng (rise). ③跳過 tiàoguo, 越過 yuèguo (hurdle).

jumper *n.* 跳躍者 tiàoyuèzhě ⟨person⟩.

jumpy *adj.* 神經質的 shénjīngzhì de / shénjīngzhí de (nervous).

junction *n.* 交叉點 jiāochādiǎn (intersection), 連接處 liánjiēchù (connection).

June *n.* 六月 Liùyuè.

jungle *n.* 叢林 cónglín (a thick tropical forest).

junior *adj.* ①年幼的 niányòu de (younger). ②資淺的 zīqiǎn de (lower). — *n.* 年幼者 niányòuzhě, 少年 shàonián. ~ *high school* 初級中學 chūjí-zhōngxué.

junk *n.* 破爛 pòlàn, 廢物 fèiwù (unwanted things). ~ *food* 垃圾食物 lājī shíwù / lèsè shíwù, 零食 língshí. ~ *mail* 垃圾郵件 lājī yóujiàn / lèsè yóujiàn.

junkie *n.* 有毒癮者 yǒu dúyǐn zhě, 毒蟲 dúchóng.

juridical *adj.* 法律上的 fǎlùshang de, 審判上的 shěnpànshang de.

jurisdiction *n.* 司法權 sīfǎquán ⟨law⟩, 管轄權 guǎnxiáquán ⟨area of control⟩.

juror *n.* 陪審員 péishěnyuán.

jury *n.* 陪審團 péishěntuán (group of jurors).

just *adj.* 公正的 gōngzhèng de, 公平的 gōngping de (fair). — *adv.* ①正好 zhènghǎo, 正要 zhèngyào (exactly). ②剛才 gāngcái (very recently). ③只是 zhǐshì (only).

justice *n.* 公平 gōngping, 正義 zhèngyì (fairness).

justifiable *adj.* 有理由的 yǒu lǐyóu de.

justify *v.* 證明正當 zhèngmíng zhèngdàng, 為⋯ ⋯辯護 wèi...biànhù (give a good reason for).

juvenile *adj.* 少年的 shàonián de (young). — *n.* 少年 shàonián (youth).

J

K

kale *n.* 甘藍 gānlán.

kaleidoscope *n.* 萬花筒 wànhuātǒng ⟨tube⟩.

kangaroo *n.* 袋鼠 dàishǔ.

karaoke *n.* 卡拉 OK kǎlā OK.

karate *n.* 空手道 kōngshǒudào.

keel *n.* 龍骨 lónggǔ ⟨bar⟩. — *v.* 傾倒 qīngdǎo (fall over sideways).

keen *adj.* ①鋒利的 fēnglì de, 尖銳的 jiānruì de (sharp). ②敏銳的 mǐnruì de (perceptive).

keep *v.* ①保存 bǎocún, 保持 bǎochí (hold). ②持續 chíxù (continue). ③維持 wéichí (maintain). ④照顧 zhàogu, 保管 bǎoguǎn (care for). ⑤保留 bǎoliú (retain).

keepsake *n.* 紀念品 jìniànpǐn.

keg *n.* 小桶 xiǎo tǒng.

kennel *n.* 狗屋 gǒuwū, 狗窩 gǒuwō (house for dog).

kerchief *n.* 頭巾 tóujīn.

kernel *n.* ①核仁 hérén (core). ②核心 héxīn, 要點 yàodiǎn (point).

ketchup *n.* 番茄醬 fānqiéjiàng.

kettle *n.* 壺 hú, 鍋 guō (a metal container).

key *n.* ①鑰匙 yàoshi (opener). ②解答 jiědá (answer), 關鍵 guānjiàn (essential point). ③鍵 jiàn ⟨piano⟩. ~ word 關鍵語 guānjiànyǔ.

keyboard *n.* 鍵盤 jiànpán.

keyhole *n.* 鑰匙孔 yàoshikǒng.

khaki *n. & adj.* ①卡其布 kǎqíbù ⟨cloth⟩. ②卡其色 kǎqísè ⟨color⟩.

kick *n. & v.* 踢 tī (strike with the foot).

kid *n.* ①小孩 xiǎohái, 孩子 háizi (child). ②小山羊 xiǎo shānyáng (goat). — *v.* 戲弄 xìnòng (deceive).

kidnap *v.* 綁架 bǎngjià.

kidney *n.* 腎 shèn.

kill *v.* ①殺 shā, 殺死 shāsǐ (slaughter). ②摧毀 cuīhuǐ, 破壞 pòhuài (destroy). ③消磨 xiāomó ⟨time⟩.

kilogram *n.* 公斤 gōngjīn.

kilometer *n.* 公里 gōnglǐ.

kilowatt *n.* 千瓦 qiānwǎ.

kilt *n.* 褶式短裙 zhéshì duǎnqún.

kimono *n.* ①和服 héfú (coat-like garment worn in Japan). ②晨服 chénfú (loose dressing gown).

kin *n.* 家族 jiāzú (family), 親屬 qīnshǔ (relatives).

kind *adj.* 親切的 qīnqiè de (friendly), 仁慈的 réncí de (nice). — *n.* 種 zhǒng, 類 lèi (type).

kindergarten *n.* 幼兒園 yòu'éryuán / 幼稚園 yòuzhìyuán.

kindhearted *adj.* 仁慈的 réncí de.

kindle *v.* 點燃 diǎnrán, 燃燒 ránshāo.

kindly *adj.* 親切的 qīnqiè de (friendly), 仁慈的 réncí de (nice).

kindness *n.* 親切 qīnqiè (friendliness), 仁慈 réncí

⟨behavior⟩.

kindred *n.* 家族 jiāzú ⟨family⟩, 親屬 qīnshǔ ⟨one's relatives⟩.

king *n.* 國王 guówáng ⟨monarchy⟩, 君主 jūnzhǔ ⟨ruler⟩.

kingdom *n.* 王國 wángguó ⟨empire⟩.

king-size(d) *adj.* 特大的 tè dà de (bigger than usual).

kink *n.* 扭結 niǔjié (twist).

kiosk *n.* ①販賣亭 fànmàitíng ⟨stand⟩. ②電話亭 diànhuàtíng ⟨telephone booth⟩.

kiss *n.* & *v.* 吻 wěn, 接吻 jiēwěn.

kit *n.* 一套用具 yí tào yòngjù (a set of tools).

kitchen *n.* 廚房 chúfáng.

kite *n.* 風箏 fēngzheng ⟨toy⟩.

kitten *n.* 小貓 xiǎomāo.

kiwi *n.* 獼猴桃 míhóutáo / 奇異果 qíyìguǒ ⟨fruit⟩.

knack *n.* 竅門 qiàomén, 技巧 jìqiǎo (skill).

knapsack *n.* 背包 bèibāo / bēibāo, 背袋 bēidài.

knead *v.* ①揉 róu ⟨clay⟩. ②按 摩 ànmó ⟨muscle⟩.

knee *n.* 膝 xī.

kneel *v.* 跪下 guìxià, 屈膝 qūxī.

knell *n.* 喪鐘聲 sāngzhōngshēng.

knickknack *n.* 小衣飾 xiǎo

yīshì.

knife *n.* 刀 dāo, 小刀 xiǎodāo ⟨cutting blade⟩. — *v.* 用刀切 yòng dāo qiē.

knight *n.* ①騎士 qíshì ⟨soldier⟩. ②爵士 juéshì ⟨title⟩.

knit *v.* 編織 biānzhī.

knob *n.* ①把手 bǎshou ⟨handle⟩. ②節 jié, 瘤 liú (protuberance).

knock *v.* ①敲 qiāo ⟨door⟩, 撞 zhuàng (hit hard). — *n.* 敲打聲 qiāodǎshēng (a pounding noise).

knockout *n.* ①打敗 dǎbài, 擊 倒 jīdǎo / jídǎo.

knot *n.* 結 jié ⟨rope⟩. — *v.* 打結 dǎjié (tie in a knot).

know *v.* ①知道 zhīdao (have learned). ②認識 rènshi (be familiar with).

knowledge *n.* 知識 zhīshi, 學 識 xuéshí / xuéshì (learning).

knuckle *n.* 指關節 zhǐ guānjié (finger joint).

koala *n.* 樹袋熊 shùdàixióng / 無尾熊 wúwěixióng.

Korean *n.* & *adj.* ①韓國人 Hánguórén ⟨people⟩. ②韓國語 Hánguóyǔ ⟨language⟩.

kowtow *v.* 磕頭 kētóu.

kungfu *n.* 中國功夫 Zhōngguó gōngfu, 中國武術 Zhōngguó wǔshù.

L

lab *n.* 實驗室 shíyànshì.

label *n.* 標籤 biāoqiān. — *v.* 貼

標籤 tiē biāoqiān, 標記 biāojì (tag).

labor *n.* ①勞力 láolì (manual work), 工作 gōngzuò (work). ②勞工 láogōng (workers).

laboratory *n.* 實驗室 shíyànshì.

laborer *n.* 勞工 láogōng.

laborious *adj.* 辛勞的 xīnláo de (tiresome), 艱難的 jiānnán de (difficult).

lack *n. & v.* 缺乏 quēfá, 不足 bùzú.

lad *n.* 少年 shàonián (youth).

ladder *n.* 梯 tī (stairs).

laden *adj.* 載滿的 zàimǎn de.

ladle *n.* 長柄杓 chángbǐngsháo.

lady *n.* 夫人 fūren, 貴婦 guìfù (women), 淑女 shūnǚ / shúnǚ (well-bred).

lag *v.* 落後 luòhòu, 延遲 yánchí (delay).

lagoon *n.* 潟湖 xìhú (shallow).

lair *n.* 巢穴 cháoxué / cháoxuè.

laity *n.* ①一般信徒 yìbān xìntú (region). ②外行人 wàihángrén, 門外漢 ménwàihàn (nonprofessional).

lake *n.* 湖 hú.

lama *n.* 喇嘛 lǎma.

lamb *n.* 羔羊 gāoyáng.

lame *adj.* 跛足的 bǒzú de (crippled). — *v.* 使跛 shǐ bǒ.

lament *v.* 哀悼 āidào. — *n.* ①哀悼 āidào (wailing). ②哀歌 āigē, 輓詩 wǎnshī (dirge).

lamp *n.* 燈 dēng.

land *n.* ①陸地 lùdì (earth). ②田地 tiándì (farm). ③國土 guótǔ (country). — *v.* 使著陸 shǐ zhuólù, 降落 jiàngluò (alight).

landing *n.* 登陸 dēnglù, 降落 jiàngluò (alighting).

landlady *n.* 女房東 nǚ fángdōng.

landlord *n.* ①房東 fángdōng

(house). ②地主 dìzhǔ (land). ③主人 zhǔrén (hotel).

landmark *n.* 陸標 lùbiāo, 界標 jièbiāo (building).

landscape *n.* ①風景 fēngjǐng (scenery). ②風景畫 fēngjǐnghuà (picture).

landslide *n.* 山崩 shānbēng.

lane *n.* 小路 xiǎo lù, 小徑 xiǎo jìng, 巷道 xiàngdào (path).

language *n.* ①語言 yǔyán (speech). ②術語 shùyǔ (jargon).

lank *adj.* 細直的 xìzhí de (thin and straight).

lanky *adj.* 瘦長的 shòucháng de (thin).

lantern *n.* 燈籠 dēnglong (container).

lap *n.* 大腿上側 dàtuǐ shàngcè. — *v.* 舐食 shìshí (lick).

lapidary *n.* 寶石匠 bǎoshíjiàng.

lapse *n. & v.* ①失誤 shīwù, 差錯 chācuò (error). ②墮落 duòluò (backsliding).

laptop *n.* 膝上型計算機 xīshuàngxíng jìsuànjī, 筆記本電腦 bǐjìběn diànnǎo / 筆記型電腦 bǐjìxíng diànnǎo.

larceny *n.* 竊盜 qièdào.

lard *n.* 豬油 zhūyóu.

large *adj.* 大的 dà de (big).

largely *adv.* 主要地 zhǔyào de (mainly), 大部分地 dà bùfen de (mostly).

lark *n.* ①雲雀 yúnquè (bird). ②玩樂 wánlè (for fun).

larva *n.* 幼蟲 yòuchóng.

laryngitis *n.* 喉炎 hóuyán.

laser *n.* 激光 jīguāng / 雷射 léishè (physics). ~ *printer* 激光打印機 jīguāng dǎyìnjī / 雷射印表機 léishè yìnbiǎojī.

lash *n.* ①皮條 pítiáo (whip).

②鞭打 biāndǎ (whipping). ③睫毛 jiémáo (eyelash). — v. ①鞭打 biāndǎ (whip). ②抨擊 pēngjí / pēngjǐ (criticize).

lass n. 少女 shàonǚ (girl).

last adj. ①最後的 zuìhòu de (final). ②上次的 shàngcì de (most recent). ~ *name* 姓 xìng. — adv. 最後地 zuìhòu de (finally). — v. ①延續 yánxù, 持續 chíxù (continue).

lasting adj. 持久的 chíjiǔ de, 永久的 yǒngjiǔ de (enduring).

latch n. 門閂 ménshuān (bar). — v. 栓上 shuānshàng.

late adj. ①遲到的 chídào de, 晚的 wǎn de (delayed). ②已故的 yǐgù de (dead). ~ *movie* 夜場電影 yèchǎng diànyǐng / 午夜場 wǔyèchǎng.

lately adv. 近來 jìnlái, 最近 zuìjìn.

latent adj. 潛在的 qiánzài de, 潛伏的 qiánfú de.

later adj. 更遲的 gèng chí de, 更後的 gèng hòu de.

latest adj. 最遲的 zuì chí de, 最新的 zuì xīn de.

lathe n. 車床 chēchuáng.

lather n. 肥皂泡沫 féizào pàomò ⟨soap⟩.

Latin n. & adj. 拉丁文 Lādīngwén. ~ *America* 拉丁美洲 Lādīng Měizhōu.

latitude n. 緯度 wěidù.

latter adj. 後者的 hòuzhě de, 後半的 hòubàn de (later).

lattice n. 格子 gézi.

laud v. 讚美 zànměi.

laugh n. & v. 笑 xiào.

laughter n. 笑 xiào, 笑聲 xiàoshēng.

launch v. ①下水 xiàshuǐ (set off). ②發射 fāshè (blast off).

③開始 kāishǐ, 展開 zhǎnkāi (begin). — n. ①下水 xiàshuǐ ⟨ship⟩. ②發射 fāshè ⟨rocket⟩.

launder v. 洗滌 xǐdí (wash).

laundry n. ①洗衣店 xǐyīdiàn ⟨store⟩. ②待洗衣物 dài xǐ yīwù (washing).

laureate n. 桂冠詩人 guìguān shīrén (poet laureate).

laurel n. ①月桂樹 yuèguìshù ⟨tree⟩. ②榮譽 róngyù (honor).

lava n. 熔岩 róngyán.

lavatory n. 洗手間 xǐshǒujiān, 廁所 cèsuǒ.

lavender n. 薰衣草 xūnyīcǎo ⟨plant⟩.

lavish adj. ①豐富的 fēngfù de (bountiful). ②浪費的 làngfèi de (wasteful). — v. 浪費 làngfèi.

law n. 法律 fǎlǜ (rule).

lawful adj. 合法的 héfǎ de (legal).

lawmaker n. 立法者 lìfǎzhě.

lawn n. 草地 cǎodì (grass).

lawsuit n. 訴訟 sùsòng.

lawyer n. 律師 lǜshī.

lax adj. ①寬鬆的 kuānsōng de (loose). ②散漫的 sǎnmàn de / sànmàn de (careless).

laxative adj. 通便的 tōngbiàn de. — n. 瀉藥 xièyào.

lay v. ①置放 zhìfàng, 安放 ānfàng (put down). ②鋪設 pūshè ⟨cover⟩. ③產卵 chǎnluǎn ⟨eggs⟩. — adj. ①世俗的 shìsú de ⟨religion⟩. ②外行的 wàiháng de (amateur).

layer n. 層 céng (thickness).

layman n. ①俗人 súrén ⟨religion⟩. ②外行人 wàihángrén (amateur).

layout n. 設計 shèjì (design).

lazy adj. 懶惰的 lǎnduò de

(indolent).

lead v. ①引導 yǐndǎo (conduct). ②率領 shuàilǐng (command). ③領先 língxiān (head). — n. 鉛 qiān (metal).

leader n. 領袖 lǐngxiù (chief).

leadership n. ①領導地位 lǐngdǎo dìwèi (status). ②領導能力 lǐngdǎo nénglì (ability).

leading adj. 主要的 zhǔyào de, 一流的 yīliú de.

leaf n. ①葉 yè (plant). ②書頁 shūyè (paper).

leaflet n. ①小葉 xiǎo yè (small leaf). ②傳單 chuándān (printed sheet).

league n. 聯合 liánhé, 同盟 tóngméng (group), 聯盟 liánméng (confederation).

leak n. 漏洞 lòudòng, 漏隙 lòuxì (hole). — v. ①漏出 lòuchū, 滲漏 shènlòu (drip). ②洩露 xièlòu (make known).

leakage n. 漏 lòu.

lean v. ①傾斜 qīngxié (incline). ②靠 kào, 倚靠 yǐkào (support). ③依靠 yīkào (rely for support).

leap v. 跳躍 tiàoyuè (jump).

learn v. ①學習 xuéxí (be taught). ②得知 dézhī (find out).

learning n. 學識 xuéshí / xuéshì, 學問 xuéwen (knowledge).

lease n. 租約 zūyuē (contract). — v. 租用 zūyòng (rent).

leash n. 皮帶 pídài.

least adj. & pron. 最小的 zuì xiǎo de, 最少的 zuì shǎo de. — adv. 最少 zuì shǎo.

leather n. 皮革 pígé (hide).

leave v. ①離開 líkāi (go away). ②遺留 yíliú, 留下 liúxià (bequeath). ③辭去 cíqù (quit). ④保留 bǎoliú (remain). — n. ①

許可 xǔkě (permission). ②請假 qǐngjià (absence).

leaven n. 酵母 jiàomǔ / xiàomǔ (yeast). — v. 使發酵 shǐ fājiào / shǐ fāxiào (ferment).

lecture n. & v. ①演講 yǎnjiǎng, 講演 jiǎngkè (speech). ②訓誡 xùnjiè (reprimand).

ledge n. 架 jià, 檯 tái (a narrow flat shelf).

leech n. 水蛭 shuǐzhì. — v. 榨取 zhàqǔ.

leek n. 韭葱 jiǔcōng.

leer n. & v. ①斜視 xiéshì, 睨視 nìshì (sideways look). ②色瞇瞇地看 sèmīmī de kàn (thought of sex).

left adj. 左方的 zuǒfāng de. — n. 左方 zuǒfāng, 左側 zuǒcè (side). — adv. 向左 xiàng zuǒ.

leftist n. 左派 zuǒpài.

leg n. 腿 tuǐ, 腳 jiǎo (limb).

legacy n. 遺產 yíchǎn (law).

legal adj. ①法律的 fǎlù de (judicial). ②合法的 héfǎ de (lawful).

legalize v. 使合法 shǐ héfǎ, 合法化 héfǎhuà.

legend n. 傳說 chuánshuō, 傳奇 chuánqí (myth).

legible adj. 可辨讀的 kě biàn dú de (readable).

legislate v. 立法 lìfǎ.

legislation n. 立法 lìfǎ (lawmaking).

legislative adj. 立法的 lìfǎ de.

legislator n. 立法者 lìfǎzhě.

legislature n. 立法機關 lìfǎ jīguān, 議會 yìhuì.

legitimate adj. 合法的 héfǎ de (legal), 正當的 zhèngdàng de (upright).

leisure n. & adj. 閒暇 xiánxiá, 空閒 kòngxián.

leisurely adj. & adv. 閒暇的 xiánxiá de.

lemon n. 檸檬 níngméng 〈fruit〉.

lemonade n. 檸檬水 níngméngshuǐ.

lend v. 借出 jièchū, 借與 jièyǔ 〈loan〉.

length n. 長度 chángdù, 長 cháng 〈measurement〉.

lengthen v. 加長 jiācháng, 變 長 biàncháng.

lengthy adj. 長的 cháng de.

lenient adj. 寬大的 kuāndà de 〈generous〉, 溫和的 wēnhé de 〈easy-going〉.

lens n. ①透鏡 tòujìng 〈glass〉. ②水晶體 shuǐjīngtǐ 〈eye〉.

Lent n. 四旬齋 Sìxúnzhāi.

Leo 獅子座 Shīzizuò.

leopard n. 豹 bào.

leper n. 癩瘋病人 máfēngbìng rén 〈someone who has leprosy〉.

leprosy n. 癩瘋病 máfēngbìng.

lesbian n. & adj. 女同性戀 nǚ tóngxìngliàn.

less adj. 較少的 jiào shǎo de 〈amount〉, 較小的 jiào xiǎo de 〈size, degree〉. — adv. 較少 jiào shǎo 〈amount〉, 較小 jiào xiǎo 〈amount〉.

lessen v. 減少 jiǎnshǎo, 縮小 suōxiǎo.

lesser adj. 較少的 jiào shǎo de 〈amount〉, 較小的 jiào xiǎo de 〈size, degree〉.

lesson n. ①課業 kèyè, 課 kè 〈class〉. ②教訓 jiàoxun 〈reprimand〉.

lest conj. 唯恐 wéikǒng, 以免 yǐmiǎn 〈for fear that〉.

let v. ①讓 ràng 〈allow〉. ②出租 chūzū 〈rent〉.

lethal adj. 致命的 zhìmìng de.

letter n. ①字母 zìmǔ 〈character〉. ②書信 shūxìn 〈message〉. ~ of credit 信用證 xìnyòngzhèng / 信用狀 xìnyòngzhuàng.

lettuce n. 萵苣 wōju.

leukemia n. 血癌 xuè'ái / xiě'ái, 白血病 báixuèbìng / báixiěbìng.

levee n. 堤防 dīfáng / tífáng.

level adj. ①水平的 shuǐpíng de 〈flat〉. ②同等的 tóngděng de, 平等的 píngděng de 〈equal〉. — n. ①水平 shuǐpíng / 水準 shuǐzhǔn 〈standard〉. ②水 平面 shuǐpíngmiàn 〈height〉. ③等級 děngjí 〈degree〉. ④程度 chéngdù 〈grade〉. ⑤樓 lóu, 層 céng 〈floor〉.

lever n. 槓桿 gànggǎn.

levy n. & v. 徵稅 zhēngshuì 〈tax〉.

lewd adj. 淫蕩的 yíndàng de, 好色的 hàosè de 〈suggesting thoughts of sex〉.

lexicon n. 辭典 cídiǎn, 字典 zìdiǎn 〈dictionary〉.

liable adj. ①易患的 yì huàn de 〈likely〉. ②應負責的 yīng fùzé de 〈responsible〉.

liaison n. ①聯絡 liánluò 〈communication〉. ②外遇 wàiyù 〈affair〉.

liar n. 說謊者 shuōhuǎngzhě.

libel n. 誹謗 fěibàng 〈law〉.

liberal adj. ①慷慨的 kāngkǎi de 〈bountiful〉. ②寬厚的 kuānhòu de 〈broad-minded〉. ③自由主義的 zìyóu zhǔyì de 〈politics〉. — n. 自由主義者 zìyóu zhǔyì zhě 〈person〉.

liberate v. 釋放 shìfàng 〈set free〉.

liberty n. 自由 zìyóu (freedom).

librarian n. 圖書館員 túshūguǎn yuán.

library n. 圖書館 túshūguǎn.

license n. ①執照 zhízhào (certificate). ②許可 xǔkě (permission). — v. 許可 xǔkě, 特許 tèxǔ (give permission).

lick n. & v. 舐 shì.

licorice n. ①甘草 gāncǎo 〈herb〉. ②甘草糖 gāncǎotáng 〈candy〉.

lid n. ①蓋子 gàizi (cover). ②眼皮 yǎnpí (eyelid).

lie n. 謊言 huǎngyán (untrue statement). — v. ①說謊 shuō huǎng, 撒謊 sā huǎng (falsify). ②臥 wò, 躺 tǎng (recline).

lieutenant n. ①中尉 zhōngwèi 〈army〉. ②上尉 shàngwèi 〈navy〉.

life n. ①生命 shēngmìng (being). ②一生 yìshēng (all one's life). ~ insurance 人壽保險 rénshòu bǎoxiǎn. ~ style 生活方式 shēnghuó fāngshì.

lifeboat n. 救生艇 jiùshēngtǐng.

lifeguard n. 救生人員 jiùshēng rényuán.

lifeless adj. 無生命的 wú shēngmìng de (dead).

lifelong adj. 終身的 zhōngshēn de.

lifetime n. 一生 yìshēng, 終身 zhōngshēn.

lift v. 舉起 jǔqǐ (raise). — n. ①舉起 jǔqǐ (lifting). ②電梯 diàntī (elevator).

ligament n. 韌帶 rèndài.

light n. ①光 guāng, 光線 guāngxiàn (ray). ②燈 dēng (lamp). — v. ①點燃 diǎnrán (ignite). ②使明亮 shǐ míngliàng (brighten). — adj. 輕的 qīng de 〈weight〉.

lighten v. ①使光明 shǐ guāngmíng, 照亮 zhàoliàng (brighten). ②使輕 shǐ qīng 〈weight〉.

lighter n. 打火機 dǎhuǒjī 〈cigarette〉.

lighthouse n. 燈塔 dēngtǎ.

lightning n. 閃電 shǎndiàn. ~ bug 螢火蟲 yínghuǒchóng. ~ rod 避雷針 bìléizhēn.

likable adj. 可愛的 kě'ài de (cute), 受人喜歡的 shòu rén xǐhuan de (friendly).

like prep. 像……一樣 xiàng... yíyàng (similar to). — adj. 同樣的 tóngyàng de, 相似的 xiàngsì de. — v. 喜歡 xǐhuan (enjoy).

likelihood n. 可能性 kěnéngxìng.

likely adj. 可能的 kěnéng de (possible). — adv. 大概 dàgài, 也許 yěxǔ.

liken v. 比喻 bǐyù.

likeness n. 相似 xiàngsì (resemblance).

likewise adv. 同樣地 tóngyàng de (similarly).

liking n. 愛好 àihào.

lilac n. 紫丁香 zǐdīngxiāng. — adj. 淡紫色的 dànzǐsè de.

lily n. 百合花 bǎihéhuā.

limb n. ①四肢 sìzhī 〈body〉. ②大枝 dà zhī 〈tree〉.

limber adj. 柔軟的 róuruǎn de. — v. 變柔軟 biàn róuruǎn.

lime n. ①石灰 shíhuī 〈substance〉. ②酸橙 suānchéng / 萊姆 láimǔ 〈fruit〉.

limit n. ①界限 jièxiàn (boundary). ②極限 jíxiàn (maximum). — v. 限制 xiànzhì (confine).

L

limitation n. 限制 xiànzhì, 有限 yǒuxiàn (confinement).

limited adj. 有限的 yǒuxiàn de (confined).

limousine n. 高級轎車 gāojí jiàochē ⟨car⟩.

limp adj. ①柔軟的 róuruǎn de (soft). ②沒有勁的 méiyǒu jìn de (weak).

linden n. 菩提樹 pútíshù.

line n. ①線 xiàn, 直線 zhíxiàn (long narrow mark). ②列 liè, 排 pái (row). ③路線 lùxiàn (route). — v. 畫線 huàxiàn (mark with lines). ~ *up* 排隊 páiduì (form rows).

lineage n. 家系 jiāxì, 血統 xuètǒng / xiětǒng.

lineal adj. 直系的 zhíxì de, 正統的 zhèngtǒng de (in direct descending line).

linear adj. 線的 xiàn de (aligned).

linen n. 亞麻布 yàmábù ⟨cloth⟩.

liner n. 班輪 bānlún, 郵輪 yóulún ⟨ship⟩.

linger v. 徘徊 páihuái, 逗留 dòuliú (tarry).

linguist n. 語言學家 yǔyánxuéjiā (philologist).

linguistic adj. 語言的 yǔyán de, 語言學的 yǔyánxué de.

lining n. 襯裡 chènlǐ.

link v. 連結 liánjié (connect).

links n. 高爾夫球場 gāo'ěrfū qiúchǎng (golf course).

linoleum n. 油氈 yóuzhān, 油布 yóubù.

lion n. 獅子 shīzi.

lip n. 唇 chún ⟨mouth⟩.

lipstick n. 唇膏 chúngāo, 口紅 kǒuhóng.

liquefy v. 液化 yèhuà.

liquid n. 液體 yètǐ (fluid). — adj. 液體的 yètǐ de (fluid). ~ *crystal display* 液晶顯示器 yèjīng xiǎnshìqì.

liquidate v. 償付 chángfù, 清算 qīngsuàn (pay).

liquor n. 酒 jiǔ, 酒類 jiǔlèi (alcohol).

lisp n. 口齒不清的發音 kǒuchǐ bù qīng de fāyīn (unclear speech). — v. 含糊發音 hánhu fāyīn.

list n. 一覽表 yìlǎnbiǎo. — v. 列表 lièbiǎo ⟨catalog⟩.

listen v. 傾聽 qīngtīng, 聽 tīng (hear).

listless adj. 無精打采的 wú-jīng-dǎ-cǎi de (languid).

liter n. 公升 gōngshēng.

literacy n. 識字 shízì / shìzì.

literal adj. 文字上的 wénzìshang de (verbatim).

literary adj. 文學的 wénxué de (of literature).

literate adj. ①能讀寫的 néng dúxiě de, 識字的 shízì de / shìzì de (able to read). ②受過良好教育的 shòuguo liánghǎo jiàoyù de (well-educated).

literature n. 文學 wénxué (writings).

litigate v. 訴訟 sùsòng (contest in law).

litter n. 廢棄物 fèiqì wù, 垃圾 lājī / lèsè (rubbish). — v. 使雜亂 shǐ záluàn, 弄亂 nòngluàn (scatter).

little adj. 少的 shǎo de ⟨amount⟩, 小的 xiǎo de ⟨size⟩. — adv. 很少 hěn shǎo (rarely). — n. 少許 shǎoxǔ.

live v. ①居住 jūzhù (dwell). ②活 huó, 生存 shēngcún (stay

alive). ③生活 shēnghuó
(remain alive). — *adj.* ①活的
huó de,有生命的 yǒu
shēngmìng de (living). ②當前
的 dāngqián de (current).

livelihood *n.* 生計 shēngjì.

lively *adj.* ①活潑的 huópo de
(vigorous). ②有生氣的
shēngqì de,生動的 shēngdòng
de (active). ③輕快的 qīngkuài
de (spirited).

liver *n.* 肝臟 gānzàng ⟨organ⟩.

livestock *n.* 家畜 jiāchù
⟨animals⟩.

livid *adj.* ①青黑色的
qīnghēisè de (black and blue).
②憤怒的 fènnù de (very angry).

living *adj.* ①活的 huó de
(alive). ②現存的 xiàncún de
(existing). ③逼真的 bīzhēn de
(lifelike). — *n.* 生計 shēngjì,
生存 shēngcún (livelihood).
earn one's ~ 謀生 móushēng.

lizard *n.* ①蜥蜴 xīyì ⟨reptile⟩.
②壁虎 bìhǔ ⟨gecko⟩.

llama *n.* 駱馬 luòmǎ.

load *n.* 負荷 fùhè,載量
zàiliàng (weight). — *v.* 裝載
zhuāngzài (pack).

loaf *n.* 一條麵包 yì tiáo
miànbāo ⟨bread⟩. — *v.* 游手
好閒 yóu-shǒu-hào-xián.

loan *n.* ①貸款 dàikuǎn
⟨money⟩. ②借出 jièchū
⟨lending⟩.

loath *adj.* ①厭惡的 yànwù de
(of hateful). ②極不願意的 jí bú
yuànyì de (unwilling).

loathe *v.* 厭惡 yànwù.

lobby *n.* 大廳 dàtīng,接待室
jiēdàishì (hall). — *v.* 遊說
yóushuì.

lobe *n.* 耳垂 ěrchuí (earlobe).

lobster *n.* 龍蝦 lóngxiā.

local *adj.* ①地方的 dìfang de,
本地的 běndì de ⟨district⟩. ②
局部的 júbù de ⟨part⟩. — *n.* 本
地居民 běndì jūmín.

locality *n.* 所在地 suǒzàidì,
現場 xiànchǎng.

locate *v.* 位於 wèiyú (situate).

location *n.* 位置 wèizhì,場所
chǎngsuǒ (place).

lock *n.* ①鎖 suǒ ⟨door⟩. ②水閘
shuǐzhá ⟨water⟩. — *v.* 鎖 suǒ
(latch).

locker *n.* 櫥櫃 chúguì.

locomotion *n.* 移動 yídòng
(movement).

locomotive *n.* 火車頭
huǒchētóu. — *adj.* 移動的
yídòng de (moving).

locust *n.* 蝗蟲 huángchóng.

lodge *v.* ①提供住宿 tígōng
zhùsù (shelter). ②住宿 zhùsù
(stay). — *n.* 小旅館 xiǎo
lǚguǎn (hotel).

lodging *n.* 寄宿處 jìsùchù
(place to stay).

loft *n.* 頂樓 dǐnglóu (attic).

lofty *adj.* 高的 gāo de,高聳的
gāosǒng de (high).

log *n.* ①圓木 yuánmù ⟨wood⟩.
②航海日誌 hánghǎi rìzhì
⟨record⟩.

logic *n.* 邏輯 luójí ⟨process⟩,理
則學 lízéxué ⟨field of study⟩.

logo *n.* 商標 shāngbiāo.

loin *n.* ①(*pl.*) 腰部 yāobù
(waist). ②腰肉 yāoròu ⟨meat⟩.
③恥骨區 chǐgǔqū ⟨sex organs⟩.

loiter *v.* 閒蕩 xiándàng,徘徊
páihuái (hang around).

lollipop *n.* 棒糖 bàngtáng /
棒棒糖 bàngbàngtáng.

lone *adj.* 孤寂的 gūjì de / gūjí
de (alone).

lonely *adj.* 孤單的 gūdān de,

寂寞的 jìmò de / jímò de.

lonesome *adj.* 寂寞的 jìmò de / jímò de.

long *adj.* ①長的 cháng de (lengthy). ②長久的 chángjiǔ de (lasting). — *adv.* 長久地 chángjiǔ de.

long-distance *adj.* 長途的 chángtú de.

longevity *n.* 長壽 chángshòu (long life).

longing *n. & adj.* 渴望 kěwàng.

longitude *n.* 經度 jīngdù.

look *v.* ①看 kàn (see). ②看似 kànsì (seem). ③面向 miànxiàng (face). ~ *after* 照料 zhàoliào. ~ *down on* 瞧不起 qiáobuqǐ. ~ *for* 尋找 xúnzhǎo. ~ *out* 當心 dāngxīn. — *n.* ①看 kàn (glance). ②表情 biǎoqíng (expression). ③容貌 róngmào (appearance).

loom *n.* 織布機 zhībùjī.

loop *n.* 圈環 quānhuán (circle). — *v.* 使成圈環 shǐ chéng quānhuán (make into a loop).

loophole *n.* 漏洞 lòudòng.

loose *adj.* ①鬆的 sōng de (loosened). ②自由的 zìyóu de (free). ③寬鬆的 kuānsōng de (slack). ④散漫的 sǎnmàn de / sànmàn de, 不精確的 bù jīngquè de (ill-defined).

loosen *v.* ①解開 jiěkāi (release). ②鬆開 sōngkāi (become loose).

loot *n.* 掠奪品 lüèduópǐn (spoil). — *v.* 掠奪 lüèduó.

lop *v.* 砍伐 kǎnfá.

Lord *n.* 上帝 Shàngdì (God).

lord *n.* 貴族 guìzú (noble).

lore *n.* 學問 xuéwen, 傳說的知識 chuánshuō de zhīshì (tale).

lorry *n.* 卡車 kǎchē.

lose *v.* ①失去 shīqù, 遺失 yíshī (fail to find). ②損失 sǔnshī (waste). ③輸掉 shūdiào (be defeated). ④迷失 míshī (be lost).

loss *n.* 損失 sǔnshī (gone from one's possession).

lost *adj.* ①失去的 shīqù de (forfeited). ②迷路的 mílù de (disorientated).

lot *n.* ①許多 xǔduō, 很多 hěn duō (many). ②一塊地 yí kuài dì (piece of land). ③籤 qiān ⟨decision by chance⟩. ④命運 mìngyùn, 運氣 yùnqi (fortune).

lottery *n.* 彩券 cǎiquàn (raffle).

lotto *n.* 樂透 lètòu.

lotus *n.* 蓮花 liánhuā ⟨flower⟩.

loud *adj.* 大聲的 dàshēng de, 吵鬧的 chǎonào de (noisy).

loudspeaker *n.* 擴音器 kuòyīnqì ⟨apparatus⟩.

lounge *v.* 閒散度日 xiánsǎn dùrì (pass time idly). — *n.* 會客室 huìkèshì.

louse *n.* 蝨 shī ⟨insect⟩.

lousy *adj.* ①糟透的 zāotòu de (bad). ②多蝨的 duō shī de (lice-infested).

lout *n.* 粗鄙之人 cūbǐ zhī rén.

lovable *adj.* 可愛的 kě'ài de.

love *n.* ①愛 ài, 愛情 àiqíng (fondness). ②愛人 àirén, 情人 qíngrén (lover). ~ *affair* 戀情 liànqíng. — *v.* 愛 ài (adore).

lovely *adj.* 可愛的 kě'ài de (charming).

lover *n.* 愛人 àirén, 情人 qíngrén (love).

low *adj.* ①低的 dī de (not high). ②微賤的 wēijiàn de / wéijiàn de (abject). ③低級的 dījí de (vulgar).

lower *v.* 降低 jiàngdī, 降下

jiāngxià (reduce).

lowly *adj*. 低的 dī de, 卑下的 bēixià de (humble).

loyal *adj*. 忠誠的 zhōngchéng de, 忠實的 zhōngshí de.

loyalty *n*. 忠誠 zhōngchéng.

lozenge *n*. ①菱形 língxíng ⟨shape⟩. ②藥片 yàopiàn ⟨medicine⟩.

lubricant *n*. 潤滑油 rùnhuáyóu.

lubricate *v*. 加潤滑油 jiā rùnhuáyóu, 潤滑 rùnhuá.

lucid *adj*. 明白的 míngbai de, 清楚的 qīngchu de.

Lucifer *n*. 金星 Jīnxīng (Venus).

luck *n*. 運氣 yùnqi, 幸運 xìngyùn.

lucky *adj*. 幸運的 xìngyùn de (fortunate).

lucrative *adj*. 可獲利的 kě huòlì de (profitable).

ludicrous *adj*. 可笑的 kěxiào de (laughable), 滑稽的 huájī de / huáji de (ridiculous).

lug *v*. 猛拉 měnglā, 拖拉 tuōlā (drag).

luggage *n*. 行李 xíngli.

lukewarm *adj*. 溫熱的 wēnrè de (slightly warm).

lull *v*. 使平靜 shǐ píngjìng, 使緩和 shǐ huǎnhé (soothe). — *n*. 間歇 jiànxiē (break).

lullaby *n*. 搖籃曲 yáolánqǔ, 催眠曲 cuīmiánqǔ.

lumber *n*. 木材 mùcái (wood).

luminous *adj*. 發光的 fāguāng de (bright).

lump *n*. ①小塊 xiǎo kuài (mass). ②腫塊 zhǒngkuài (bulge). — *v*. ①使結成塊狀 shǐ jiéchéng kuàizhuàng (form into lumps). ②混為一談

hùn-wéi-yì-tán ⟨place together⟩.

lunacy *n*. 瘋癲 fēngdiān (madness).

lunar *adj*. ①月亮的 yuèliang de ⟨moon⟩. ②陰曆的 yīnlì de ⟨calendar⟩.

lunatic *n*. 瘋子 fēngzi, 精神病者 jīngshénbìng zhě. — *adj*. 瘋狂的 fēngkuáng de.

lunch *n*. 午餐 wǔcān (midday meal). ~ **box** 盒飯 héfàn / 便當 biàndāng. — *v*. 吃午餐 chī wǔcān.

luncheon *n*. 午餐 wǔcān.

lung *n*. 肺 fèi.

lunge *n*. ①刺 cì (stab). ②前衝 qiánchōng (rush).

lurch *n. & v*. 傾斜 qīngxié, 搖晃 yáohuang (stumble).

lure *n*. ①魅力 mèilì, 誘惑力 yòuhuòlì (attraction). ②誘餌 yòu'ěr (bait). — *v*. 誘惑 yòuhuò.

lurid *adj*. ①色彩濃烈的 sècǎi nóngliè de (strongly colored). ②驚人的 jīngrén de, 駭人的 hàirén de (sensational).

lurk *v*. 潛伏 qiánfú (hide).

lush *adj*. ①茂盛的 màoshèng de (luxuriant). ②奢侈的 shēchǐ de (luxurious).

lust *n*. 色慾 sèyù, 慾望 yùwàng (desire). — *v*. 渴望 kěwàng (desire).

luster *n*. 光彩 guāngcǎi, 光澤 guāngzé (brightness).

lute *n*. 琵琶 pípa.

luxuriant *adj*. 茂盛的 màoshèng de, 肥沃的 féiwò de (fertile).

luxurious *adj*. 奢侈的 shēchǐ de (wasteful), 豪華的 háohuá de (very fine and expensive).

luxury *n*. 奢侈 shēchǐ

(extravagance).

lying *n.* 說謊 shuōhuǎng.

lymph *n.* 淋巴 línbā 〈physiology〉.

lyric *n.* ①抒情詩 shūqíngshī 〈poem〉. ②*(pl.)* 歌詞 gēcí 〈words〉. — *adj.* 抒情的 shūqíng de.

M

macabre *adj.* 陰森的 yīnsēn de, 可怕的 kěpà de.

macaroni *n.* 通心粉 tōngxīnfěn, 通心麵 tōngxīnmiàn.

mace *n.* 權杖 quánzhàng 〈staff〉.

machine *n.* 機械 jīxiè, 機器 jīqì.

machinery *n.* 機器 jīqì.

mackerel *n.* 鯖魚 qīngyú.

mad *adj.* ①瘋狂的 fēngkuáng de, 精神異常的 jīngshén yìcháng de 〈insane〉. ②憤怒的 fènnù de 〈angry〉. ③狂熱的 kuángrè de 〈enthusiastic〉.

madam *n.* 女士 nǚshì, 夫人 fūren.

madden *v.* ①使發狂 shǐ fākuáng 〈craze〉. ②使憤怒 shǐ fènnù 〈anger〉.

madness *n.* 瘋狂 fēngkuáng 〈crazy〉, 精神錯亂 jīngshén cuòluàn 〈lunacy〉.

Madonna *n.* 聖母瑪利亞 Shèngmǔ Mǎlìyà / Shèngmǔ Mǎlìyà.

madrigal *n.* 抒情短詩 shūqíng duǎnshī 〈short love poem〉.

Mafia *n.* 黑手黨 Hēishǒudǎng.

mag *n.* 雜誌 zázhì 〈magazine〉.

magazine *n.* ①雜誌 zázhì 〈journal〉. ②火藥庫 huǒyàokù 〈ammunition〉.

magenta *n.* 紫紅色 zǐhóngsè 〈color〉.

maggot *n.* 蛆 qū 〈larva〉.

magic *n.* ①魔法 mófǎ 〈by witches〉. ②魔術 móshù 〈by conjurors〉. — *adj.* 魔術的 móshù de.

magician *n.* 魔術師 móshùshī.

magnate *n.* 鉅子 jùzǐ, 大亨 dàhēng.

magnet *n.* 磁鐵 cítiě 〈lodestone〉.

magnetic *adj.* ①有吸引力的 yǒu xīyǐnlì de 〈attractive〉. ②有磁性的 yǒu cíxìng de 〈magnet〉.

magnetism *n.* 磁性 cíxìng.

magnificent *adj.* 壯麗的 zhuànglì de, 宏偉的 hóngwěi de.

magnify *v.* ①放大 fàngdà 〈enlarge〉. ②誇張 kuāzhāng 〈exaggerate〉.

magnitude *n.* ①大小 dàxiǎo 〈size〉. ②重要性 zhòngyàoxìng 〈importance〉.

magpie *n.* ①鵲 què 〈bird〉. ②饒舌者 ráoshézhě 〈person〉.

mahogany *n.* 桃花心木

M

táohuāxīn mù ⟨wood⟩.②紅褐色 hónghèsè / hónghésè ⟨color⟩.

maid n. 女僕 nǚpú ⟨servant⟩.

maiden n. 未婚少女 wèihūn shàonǚ. — adj. 未婚的 wèihūn de ⟨unmarried⟩.

mail n. 郵件 yóujiàn, 信件 xìnjiàn ⟨letters⟩. — v. 郵寄 yóujì.

mailbox n. 信箱 xìnxiāng, 郵 筒 yóutǒng.

mailman n. 郵差 yóuchāi.

maim v. 使殘廢 shǐ cánfèi.

main adj. 主要的 zhǔyào de, 重要的 zhòngyào de ⟨chief⟩. — n. 主幹線 zhǔgànxiàn, 總管道 zǒngguǎndào ⟨chief pipe⟩. *in the ~* 大致上 dàzhìshang.

mainland n. 大陸 dàlù.

mainly adv. 主要地 zhǔyào de, 大部分 dàbùfen ⟨chiefly⟩.

maintain v. ①維持 wéichí, 保持 bǎochí ⟨keep up⟩.②保養 bǎoyǎng ⟨keep in good condition⟩.③供養 gōngyǎng / gòngyàng ⟨support⟩.④堅持 jiānchí ⟨insist⟩.

maintenance n. 維持 wéichí, 保養 bǎoyǎng ⟨preservation⟩.

maize n. 玉蜀黍 yùshǔshǔ.

majestic adj. 莊嚴的 zhuāngyán de.

majesty n. ①莊嚴 zhuāngyán, 威嚴 wēiyán ⟨stateliness⟩.②高貴 gāoguì ⟨nobility⟩.③陛下 bìxià ⟨royalty⟩.

major adj. ①較大的 jiào dà de ⟨bigger⟩.②較多的 jiào duō de ⟨greater⟩.③主要的 zhǔyào de ⟨chief⟩. — n. ①主修科 zhǔxiūkē ⟨subject⟩.②少校 shàoxiào ⟨army⟩.

majority n. 多數 duōshù, 大部分 dàbùfen ⟨the bulk⟩.

make v. ①做 zuò, 製造 zhìzào ⟨produce⟩.②使 shǐ ⟨oblige⟩.③獲得 huòdé, 賺 zhuàn ⟨gain⟩. *~ up* ①組成 zǔchéng ⟨constitute⟩.②捏造 niēzào ⟨fabricate⟩.③化妝 huàzhuāng ⟨with cosmetics⟩.

maker n. 製造者 zhìzàozhě ⟨manufacturer⟩.

make-up n. ①化妝品 huàzhuāngpǐn ⟨cosmetics⟩.②組成 zǔchéng ⟨composition⟩.

malady n. 疾病 jíbìng ⟨disease⟩.

malaria n. 瘧疾 nüèjí ⟨medical⟩.

male n. ①男人 nánrén ⟨man⟩.②雄性 xióngxìng ⟨animal⟩. — adj. ①男性的 nánxìng de ⟨of men⟩.②雄性的 xióngxìng de ⟨animal⟩.

malevolence n. 惡意 èyì.

malfunction n. 故障 gùzhàng.

malice n. 惡意 èyì, 怨恨 yuànhèn ⟨spite⟩.

malicious adj. 惡意的 èyì de.

malignant adj. ①致命的 zhìmìng de, 惡性的 èxìng de ⟨fatal⟩.②懷惡意的 huái èyì de ⟨malevolent⟩.

malleable adj. 可鍛的 kě duàn de ⟨moldable⟩.

mallet n. 木槌 mùchuí ⟨hammer⟩.

malnutrition n. 營養不良 yíngyǎng bùliáng.

malt n. 麥芽 màiyá ⟨grain⟩.

maltreat v. 虐待 nüèdài ⟨torture⟩, 苛待 kēdài ⟨treat poorly⟩.

mama n. 媽媽 māma.

mammal n. 哺乳動物 bǔrǔ

dòngwù.

mammoth n. 長毛巨象 chángmáo jùxiàng. — adj. 巨大的 jùdà de (enormous).

man n. ①人 rén (human being). ②男人 nánrén (male).

manacle n. 手銬 shǒukào. — v. 上手銬 shàng shǒukào (handcuff), 束縛 shùfù / shùfú (fetter).

manage v. ①管理 guǎnlǐ, 經營 jīngyíng (administer). ②處理 chǔlǐ (handle). ③完成 wánchéng (accomplish).

management n. ①管理 guǎnlǐ, 經營 jīngyíng (administering). ②管理人員 guǎnlǐ rényuán (administrator), 資方 zīfāng ⟨as opposed to labor⟩.

manager n. 經理 jīnglǐ.

Mandarin n. 漢語 Hànyǔ (Chinese).

mandate n. ①命令 mìnglìng, 訓令 xùnlìng (order). ②委任 wěirèn, 委託 wěituō (authorization).

mandolin n. 曼陀林琴 màntuólíngín.

mane n. 鬃 zōng.

maneuver n. & v. ①策略 cèlüè, 計謀 jìmóu (plan). ②調動 diàodòng (move). ③演習 yǎnxí ⟨military⟩.

manger n. 馬槽 mǎcáo.

mangle v. 撕裂 sīliè (destroy).

mango n. 芒果 mángguǒ.

manhood n. 成年 chéngnián (adulthood).

mania n. ①癲狂 diānkuáng (insanity). ②狂熱 kuángrè, 熱中 rèzhōng (enthusiasm).

manicure n. & v. 修指甲 xiū zhǐjiǎ / xiū zhǐjiá.

manifest v. ①顯示 xiǎnshì,

表明 biǎomíng (show clearly). ②顯露 xiǎnlù (reveal). — n. 載貨清單 zàihuò qīngdān (checklist).

manifesto n. 宣言 xuānyán.

manifold adj. 多種的 duō zhǒng de, 多方面的 duō fāngmiàn de (various). — v. 複寫 fùxiě.

manipulate v. ①把持 bǎchí, 操縱 cāozòng (control). ②應付 yìngfu (handle), 使用 shǐyòng (manage).

mankind n. 人類 rénlèi (humanity).

manly adj. ①勇敢的 yǒnggǎn de (brave). ②男子漢的 nánzǐhàn de (masculine).

man-made adj. 人造的 rénzào de.

manner n. ①方法 fāngfǎ, 方式 fāngshì (way). ②態度 tàidu (attitude). ③禮貌 lǐmào (politeness). ④習俗 xísú (custom). ⑤種類 zhǒnglèi (kind).

mannerism n. 獨特風格 dútè fēnggé ⟨style⟩.

mansion n. 大廈 dàshà / dàxià, 宅邸 zháidǐ (residence).

manslaughter n. 殺人 shārén.

mantis n. 螳螂 tángláng.

mantle n. 斗篷 dǒupeng, 披風 pīfēng (cloak).

manual adj. ①手的 shǒu de ⟨hands⟩. ②手工的 shǒugōng de (done by hand). — n. 手冊 shǒucè, 簡介 jiǎnjiè (handbook).

manufacture v. 製造 zhìzào, 生產 shēngchǎn (make). — n. ①製造 zhìzào (making). ②製造品 zhìzàopǐn (product).

manufacturer n. 製造商

M

zhìzàoshāng.

manure n. 肥料 féiliào, 糞肥 fènféi.

manuscript n. 手稿 shǒugǎo, 原稿 yuángǎo.

many adj. 許多的 xǔduō de.

map n. 地圖 dìtú (chart). — v. 繪地圖 huì dìtú.

maple n. ①楓樹 fēngshù 〈tree〉. ②楓木 fēngmù 〈wood〉.

mar v. 損毀 sǔnhuǐ (damage), 傷害 shānghài (hurt).

marathon n. 馬拉松 mǎlāsōng.

maraud v. 搶掠 qiǎnglüè.

marble n. 大理石 dàlǐshí 〈limestone〉.

march v. 行軍 xíngjūn, 行進 xíngjìn (parade). — n. ①行軍 xíngjūn 〈troops〉. ②進行曲 jìnxíngqǔ 〈music〉.

March n. 三月 Sānyuè.

mare n. 母馬 mǔmǎ.

margarine n. 人造奶油 rénzào nǎiyóu.

margin n. ①邊 biān, 邊界 biānjiè (edge). ②頁邊 yèbiān, 空白 kòngbái (space). ③餘地 yúdì (extra).

marigold n. 金盞花 jīnzhǎnhuā.

marijuana n. 大麻 dàmá.

marina n. 遊艇港 yóutínggǎng.

marine adj. ①海的 hǎi de (of the sea). ②海軍的 hǎijūn de 〈navy〉. — n. ①水兵 shuǐbīng (soldier). ②船隻 chuánzhī (ship). ③艦隊 jiànduì (fleet).

mariner n. 水手 shuǐshǒu, 船員 chuányuán.

marital adj. 婚姻的 hūnyīn de.

maritime adj. ①海的 hǎi de (of the sea). ②沿海的 yánhǎi de (near the sea).

mark n. ①符號 fúhào, 記號 jìhào (sign). ②污點 wūdiǎn, 痕跡 hénjī (stain). ③標誌 biāozhì, 特徵 tèzhēng (figure). ④分數 fēnshù (grade). — v. ①做記號 zuò jìhào (put a mark on). ②標示 biāoshì (indicate). ③評分 píngfēn (grade).

marker n. 麥克筆 màikèbǐ 〈pen〉.

market n. 市場 shìchǎng, 商場 shāngchǎng (mart). — v. 在市場上買賣 zài shìchǎng shàng mǎimai, 交易 jiāoyì.

marketing n. 買賣 mǎimai (sales), 行銷 xíngxiāo (promotion).

marketplace n. 市場 shìchǎng, 市集 shìjí.

marksman n. 射手 shèshǒu.

marmalade n. 柑橘果醬 gānjú guǒjiàng.

maroon n. & adj. 栗色 lìsè, 茶色 chásè (brownish red).

marquis n. 侯爵 hóujué.

marriage n. ①婚姻 hūnyīn, 結婚 jiéhūn (matrimony). ②婚禮 hūnlǐ (wedding).

marrow n. 骨髓 gǔsuǐ 〈bone〉.

marry v. ①結婚 jiéhūn 〈matrimony〉. ②使結合 shǐ jiéhé (join).

Mars n. 火星 Huǒxīng.

marsh n. 沼澤 zhǎozé, 濕地 shīdì.

marshal n. ①高級軍官 gāojí jūnguān 〈official〉. ②司儀 sīyí 〈for public events〉. — v. 整理 zhěnglǐ, 使排列 shǐ páiliè (arrange).

M

marten *n.* 貂 diāo.

martial *adj.* ①戰爭的 zhànzhēng de (of war). ②軍事的 jūnshì de (of military). ③好戰的 hàozhàn de (warlike). ~ *art* 武術 wǔshù. ~ *law* 戒嚴令 jièyánlìng.

martyr *n.* 殉道者 xùndàozhě, 烈士 lièshì (victim).

marvel *n.* 驚異之事物 jīngyì zhī shìwù (remarkable thing). — *v.* 驚異 jīngyì.

Marxism *n.* 馬克思主義 Mǎkèsī zhǔyì / 馬克斯主義 Mǎkèsī zhǔyì.

mascara *n.* 睫毛膏 jiémáo gāo.

mascot *n.* 吉人 jírén, 福星 fúxīng.

masculine *adj.* ①男性的 nánxìng de (male). ②有男子氣概的 yǒu nánzǐ qìgài de (manly).

mask *n.* 面具 miànjù (disguise). — *v.* 戴面具 dài miànjù.

masochism *n.* 受虐狂 shòunüèkuáng.

mason *n.* 泥水匠 níshuǐjiàng.

masquerade *n.* 化裝舞會 huàzhuāng wǔhuì (masked ball). — *v.* 偽裝 wěizhuāng / wèizhuāng.

mass *n.* ①塊 kuài, 團 tuán (bulk). ②大量 dàliàng, 多數 duōshù (lot). ~ *media* 大眾媒體 dàzhòng méitǐ. ~ *transportation* 公交 gōngjiāo / 大眾運輸 dàzhòng yùnshū.

Mass *n.* 彌撒 Mísa.

massacre *n. & v.* 大屠殺 dàtúshā.

massage *n. & v.* 按摩 ànmó.

masseur *n.* 按摩師 ànmóshī.

massive *adj.* 又大又重的 yòu dà yòu zhòng de (large and heavy).

mast *n.* 桅 wéi ⟨boat⟩.

master *n.* ①主人 zhǔrén (owner). ②男教師 nán jiàoshī (teacher). ③船長 chuánzhǎng (captain). — *v.* 精通 jīngtōng.

Master Card *n.* 萬事達卡 Wànshìdákǎ.

masterful *adj.* 專橫的 zhuānhèng de (imperious).

masterly *adj.* 巧妙的 qiǎomiào de.

masterpiece *n.* 傑作 jiézuò, 名著 míngzhù.

mastery *n.* ①支配 zhīpèi, 控制 kòngzhì (control). ②精通 jīngtōng (great skill).

mat *n.* 蓆子 xízi, 墊子 diànzi (cushion).

matador *n.* 鬥牛士 dòuniúshì.

match *n.* ①火柴 huǒchái ⟨fire⟩. ②相配 xiāngpèi (fit).

matchmaker *n.* 媒人 méirén.

mate *n.* ①配偶 pèi'ǒu (spouse). ②伙伴 huǒbàn (companion).

material *n.* ①材料 cáiliào, 原料 yuánliào (substance). ②料子 liàozi ⟨cloth⟩. ③資料 zīliào (information). — *adj.* ①物質的 wùzhì de / wùzhí de (of substance). ②肉體的 ròutǐ de (of the body).

materialism *n.* 唯物論 wéiwùlùn.

materialize *v.* 具體化 jùtǐhuà (make concrete).

maternal *adj.* 母親的 mǔqīn de, 母系的 mǔxì de.

maternity *n.* 母性 mǔxìng.

math *n.* 數學 shùxué.

mathematical *adj.* 數學的 shùxué de.

mathematician *n.* 數學家 shùxuéjiā.

mathematics *n.* 數學 shùxué.

matriculate *v.* 准許入學 zhǔnxǔ rùxué.

matrimony *n.* 結婚 jiéhūn, 婚姻 hūnyīn.

matron *n.* ①已婚婦女 yǐhūn fùnǚ (married woman). ②女舍監 nǚ shèjiān ⟨of dormitory⟩. ③護士長 hùshizhǎng (nursing officer).

matter *n.* ①事情 shìqing (affair). ②物質 wùzhí / wùzhì (material). *as a ~ of fact* 事實上 shìshíshang. *no ~* 無論 wúlùn. — *v.* 關係重要 guānxi zhòngyào.

matting *n.* 蓆 xí.

mattress *n.* 床墊 chuángdiàn.

mature *adj.* ①成熟的 chéngshú de (full-grown). ②到期的 dàoqí de / dàoqí de (due).

mauve *n. & adj.* 淡紫色 dànzǐsè.

maxim *n.* 格言 géyán (proverb).

maximize *v.* 使達最大限度 shǐ dá zuì dà xiàndù.

maximum *n.* 最大限度 zuì dà xiàndù ⟨level⟩, 最大量 zuì dàliàng ⟨amount⟩. — *adj.* 最高的 zuì gāo de, 最大的 zuì dà de.

may *aux. v.* ①可能 kěnéng (might). ②可以 kěyǐ (can).

May *n.* 五月 Wǔyuè.

maybe *adv.* 可能 kěnéng, 大概 dàgài.

mayonnaise *n.* 蛋黃醬 dànhuángjiàng, 美乃滋 měinǎizī.

mayor *n.* 市長 shìzhǎng.

maze *n.* ①迷宮 mígōng (labyrinth). ②迷惘 míwǎng (confusion).

me *pron.* 我 wǒ.

meadow *n.* 草地 cǎodì, 草原 cǎoyuán (grassland).

meager *adj.* ①瘦的 shòu de (thin). ②貧弱的 pínruò de (scanty).

meal *v.* 餐 cān, 食物 shíwù.

mean *v.* ①意謂 yìwèi (symbolize). ②打算 dǎsuan, 意欲 yìyù (intend). — *adj.* ①低劣的 dīliè de (lowly). ②吝嗇的 lìnsè de, 自私的 zìsī de (self-ish). ③卑賤的 bēijiàn de (poor). ④中庸的 zhōngyōng de, 平均的 píngjūn de (average).

meander *v.* 蜿蜒而流 wānyán ér liú (wander).

meaning *n.* 意義 yìyì. — *adj.* 有意義的 yǒu yìyì de.

meantime *adv.* 同時 tóngshí.

meanwhile *n. & adv.* 同時 tóngshí.

measles *n.* 麻疹 mázhěn.

measure *v.* 量 liáng, 測 cè (calculate). — *n.* ①標準 biāozhǔn, 單位 dānwèi (standard). ②議案 yì'àn (bill).

measurement *n.* 量度 liàngdù.

meat *n.* 肉 ròu, 肉類 ròulèi (flesh).

mechanic *n.* 機匠 jījiàng, 技師 jìshī.

mechanical *adj.* 機械的 jīxiè de, 機械製的 jīxiè zhì de (of machinery).

mechanism *n.* 機械裝置

jīxiè zhuāngzhì (machine part).

mechanize v. 機械化 jīxièhuà.

medal n. 獎牌 jiǎngpái, 獎章 jiǎngzhāng.

meddle v. 干預 gānyù.

media n. 媒體 méitǐ, 媒介 méijiè.

mediate v. 仲裁 zhòngcái, 調停 tiáotíng.

medical adj. 醫學的 yīxué de, 醫藥的 yīyào de.

medicate v. 以藥物治療 yǐ yàowù zhìliáo.

medicinal adj. 有藥效的 yǒu yàoxiào de.

medicine n. ①藥 yào, 藥物 yàowù (medication). ②醫學 yīxué (healing).

medieval adj. 中世紀的 zhōngshìjì de.

mediocre adj. 平凡的 píngfán de (average).

meditate v. 沈思 chénsī (reflect), 冥思 míngsī ⟨religion⟩.

Mediterranean Sea 地中海 Dìzhōnghǎi.

medium adj. 中間的 zhōngjiān de, 中庸的 zhōngyōng de. — n. ①中間 zhōngjiān, 中庸 zhōngyōng (average). ②媒介物 méijièwù, 媒體 méitǐ (media).

meek adj. 溫順的 wēnshùn de, 謙和的 qiānhé de (humble).

meet v. ①遇到 yùdào (encounter), 會面 huìmiàn (see in person). ②迎接 yíngjiē (pick up). ③會合 huìhé (gather). ④交會 jiāohuì (cross). ⑤滿足 mǎnzú (satisfy).

meeting n. ①會議 huìyì (assembly). ②碰上 pèngshang (encounter). ③約會 yuēhuì

(appointment). ④交會 jiāohuì (crossing).

megaphone n. 擴音器 kuòyīnqì.

melancholia n. 憂鬱症 yōuyùzhèng.

melancholy n. & adj. 憂鬱 yōuyù.

mellow adj. 柔和的 róuhé de (soft).

melodious adj. 悅耳的 yuè'ěr de.

melodrama n. 通俗劇 tōngsújù ⟨play⟩.

melody n. 旋律 xuánlǜ.

melon n. 瓜 guā.

melt v. 融化 rónghuà, 溶解 róngjiě (dissolve).

member n. ①會員 huìyuán, 社員 shèyuán (associate). ②肢體 zhītǐ (limb).

membership n. 會員資格 huìyuán zīgé (admission).

membrane n. 膜 mó / mò, 薄膜 bómó / bómò.

memento n. 紀念品 jìniànpǐn.

memo n. 備忘錄 bèiwànglù.

memoir n. 傳記 zhuànjì (biography).

memorable adj. 值得紀念的 zhíde jìniàn de.

memorandum n. 備忘錄 bèiwànglù (note).

memorial n. 紀念物 jìniànwù (monument). — adj. 紀念的 jìniàn de, 追悼的 zhuīdào de.

memorize v. 記憶 jìyì, 背誦 bèisòng.

memory n. ①記憶 jìyì (remembrance). ②懷念 huáiniàn (recollection).

men n. 男人們 nánrénmen.

menace n. & v. 威嚇 wēihè, 脅迫 xiépò.

M

mend v. ①修補 xiūbǔ, 修理 xiūlǐ (repair). ②改進 gǎijìn, 改善 gǎishàn (improve).

menial n. 奴僕 núpú, 傭人 yōngrén.

menopause n. 停經期 tíngjīngqī / tíngjīngqí, 更年期 gēngniánqī / gēngniánqí.

menses n. 月經 yuèjīng.

mental adj. ①心理的 xīnlǐ de (psychological). ②智力的 zhìlì de (intellectual).

mentality n. ①智力 zhìlì (intelligence). ②心理狀態 xīnlǐ zhuàngtài (attitude).

mention n. & v. 提及 tíjí, 談起 tánqǐ. Don't ~ it. 不客氣 bú kèqi.

menu n. 菜單 càidān (bill of fare).

mercantile adj. 商業的 shāngyè de.

mercenary n. 傭兵 yōngbīng.

merchandise n. 商品 shāngpǐn, 貨物 huòwù. — v. 交易 jiāoyì, 買賣 mǎimai (deal).

merchant n. 商人 shāngrén.

merciful adj. 仁慈的 réncí de.

merciless adj. 殘忍的 cánrěn de.

mercury n. ①水銀 shuǐyín, 汞 gǒng (quicksilver). ②(M-) 水星 Shuǐxīng (planet).

mercy n. 慈悲 cíbēi, 憐憫 liánmǐn (kindness).

mere adj. 祇 zhǐ, 僅僅 jǐnjǐn, 不過是 búguòshì.

merely adv. 僅僅 jǐnjǐn.

merge v. 合併 hébìng.

meridian n. 子午線 zǐwǔxiàn (longitude).

merit n. 優點 yōudiǎn (good point), 功績 gōngjì / gōngjī

(reward).

mermaid n. 人魚 rényú, 美人魚 měirényú.

merry adj. 快樂的 kuàilè de, 愉快的 yúkuài de.

merry-go-round n. 旋轉木馬 xuánzhuǎn mùmǎ.

mesh n. 網孔 wǎngkǒng. — v. 以網捕捉 yǐ wǎng bǔzhuō (snare).

mess n. 亂七八糟 luàn-qī-bā-zāo (untidy objects). — v. 使紊亂 shǐ wěnluàn, 弄髒 nòngzāo (clutter). ~ up 弄亂 nòngluàn, 弄糟 nòngzāo.

message n. ①消息 xiāoxi, 音訊 yīnxùn (information). ②含意 hányì (significance).

messenger n. 信差 xìnchāi, 使者 shǐzhě.

metabolism n. 新陳代謝 xīn-chén-dàixiè.

metal n. 金屬 jīnshǔ (substance).

metallic adj. 金屬的 jīnshǔ de.

metaphor n. 隱喻 yǐnyù, 暗喻 ànyù.

meteor n. 流星 liúxīng.

meteorite n. 隕石 yǔnshí.

meteorology n. 氣象學 qìxiàngxué.

meter n. 公尺 gōngchǐ, 米 mǐ (measure).

method n. ①方法 fāngfǎ (way). ②條理 tiáolǐ, 順序 shùnxù (orderliness).

methodical adj. 有條理的 yǒu tiáolǐ de, 有秩序的 yǒu zhìxù de.

methodology n. 方法論 fāngfǎlùn.

metropolis n. ①大都市 dàdūshì, 都會 dūhuì (city). ②首都 shǒudū, 首府 shǒufǔ (capital).

metropolitan adj. ①大都市的 dàdūshì de (of a city). ②首都的 shǒudū de (of a capital). — n. 都會居民 dūhuì jūmín.

Mexican n. & adj. ①墨西哥人 Mòxīgērén ⟨people⟩. ②墨西哥語 Mòxīgēyǔ ⟨language⟩.

mica n. 雲母 yúnmǔ.

microbe n. 微生物 wēishēngwù / wéishēngwù, 細菌 xìjūn / xíjūn ⟨bacterium⟩.

microbiology n. 微生物學 wēishēngwùxué / wéishēngwùxué.

microchip n. 微晶片 wēijīngpiàn / wéijīngpiàn ⟨electricity⟩.

microcircuit n. 積體電路 jītǐ diànlù.

microcomputer n. 微電腦 wēidiànnǎo / wéidiànnǎo.

microcosm n. 小宇宙 xiǎo yǔzhòu, 縮影 suōyǐng.

microfilm n. 縮影膠捲 suōyǐng jiāojuǎn.

microorganism n. 微生物 wēishēngwù / wéishēngwù.

microphone n. 麥克風 màikèfēng.

microscope n. 顯微鏡 xiǎnwēijìng / xiǎnwéijìng.

mid adj. 中間的 zhōngjiān de, 中央的 zhōngyāng de.

midday n. & adj. 正午 zhèngwǔ.

middle adj. 中間的 zhōngjiān de (central). — n. 中間 zhōngjiān (center). **the M- East** 中東 Zhōngdōng.

middle-aged adj. 中年的 zhōngnián de.

middle-class adj. 中產階級的 zhōngchǎn jiējí de.

midge n. 小蟲 xiǎochóng.

midget n. 侏儒 zhūrú, 矮人 ǎirén.

midland n. & adj. 內陸 nèilù.

mid-life crisis 中年危機 zhōngnián wēijī / zhōngnián wēijī.

midnight n. & adj. 午夜 wǔyè. **~ snack** 夜餐 yècān / 宵夜 xiāoyè.

midst n. 中間 zhōngjiān.

midsummer n. 仲夏 zhòngxià.

midterm adj. 學期中的 xuéqī zhōng de / xuéqí zhōng de. **~ exam** 期中考試 qī zhōng kǎoshì / qí zhōng kǎoshì (test).

midway adj. & adv. 中途的 zhōngtú de.

midwife n. 助產士 zhùchǎnshì, 接生婆 jiēshēngpó.

mien n. 風采 fēngcǎi, 態度 tàidu.

might aux. v. 可能 kěnéng (be able). — n. 力氣 lìqi, 力量 lìliang (strength).

mighty adj. ①強有力的 qiáng yǒulì de (strong). ②巨大的 jùdà de (enormous).

migraine n. 偏頭痛 piāntóutòng.

migrant n. 候鳥 hòuniǎo ⟨bird⟩, 遷居者 qiānjūzhě ⟨people⟩.

migrate v. 遷移 qiānyí, 移居 yíjū.

migration n. 遷移 qiānyí, 移動 yídòng.

mild adj. ①溫和的 wēnhé de, 寬大的 kuāndà de (gentle). ②溫暖的 wēnnuǎn de (warm). ③適口的 shìkǒu de ⟨taste⟩.

mildew n. 霉 méi, 黴 méi.

M

mile n. 哩 lǐ, 英里 yīnglǐ.

mileage n. 哩數 lǐshù, 哩程 lǐchéng.

milestone n. 哩程標 lǐchéngbiāo.

militant adj. 好戰的 hàozhàn de, 好鬥爭的 hào dòuzhēng de.

militarism n. 軍國主義 jūnguó zhǔyì.

military adj. 軍事的 jūnshì de. — n. ①軍隊 jūnduì (troops). ②軍人 jūnrén (soldier).

militia n. 民兵部隊 mínbīng bùduì, 國民兵 guómínbīng.

milk n. 牛奶 niúnǎi. — v. 擠乳 jǐ rǔ.

milky adj. 乳白色的 rǔbáisè de.

mill n. ①碾磨機 niǎnmójī 〈machine〉. ②製造廠 zhìzàochǎng 〈factory〉.

millennium n. ①千禧年 qiānxǐnián 〈the Bible〉. ②一千年 yìqiān nián 〈period〉.

millet n. 粟 sù, 稷 jì.

million n. 百萬 bǎiwàn (1,000,000).

millionaire n. 百萬富翁 bǎiwàn fùwēng.

mime n. 啞劇 yǎjù / 默劇 mòjù (pantomime).

mimeograph n. 油印機 yóuyìnjī.

mimic v. 模仿 mófǎng 〈copy〉.

mimosa n. 含羞草 hánxiūcǎo 〈plant〉.

mince v. 切碎 qiēsuì, 剁碎 duòsuì 〈chop〉.

mind n. ①腦力 nǎolì, 理解力 lǐjiělì 〈brain〉. ②心 xīn, 心意 xīnyì, 想法 xiǎngfa 〈opinion〉. *make up one's ~* 決心 juéxīn. — v. 注意 zhùyì, 留心 liúxīn

(notice).

minded adj. 有意的 yǒuyì de.

mindful adj. 注意的 zhùyì de, 留意的 liúyì de.

mindless adj. 不留心的 bù liúxīn de 〈heedless〉.

mine pron. 我的 wǒ de. — n. ①礦 kuàng, 礦坑 kuàngkēng 〈coal〉. ②地雷 dìléi 〈weapon〉.

miner n. 礦工 kuànggōng 〈worker〉.

mineral n. 礦物 kuàngwù 〈substance〉. ~ *water* 礦泉水 kuàngquánshuǐ.

mineralogy n. 礦物學 kuàngwùxué.

mingle v. 混合 hùnhé.

mini n. 迷你 mínǐ, 小型 xiǎoxíng (miniature).

miniature n. 小模型 xiǎo móxíng. — adj. 小型的 xiǎoxíng de.

minimize v. 極小化 jíxiǎohuà 〈reduce〉.

minimum n. 最低限度 zuì dī xiàndù, 最小量 zuì xiǎoliàng. — adj. 最小的 zuì xiǎo de, 最低的 zuì dī de (least).

mining n. 採礦 cǎikuàng 〈mine〉.

minister n. ①牧師 mùshi 〈clergyman〉. ②部長 bùzhǎng 〈head〉. ③公使 gōngshǐ 〈ambassador〉.

ministry n. ①部 bù 〈government〉. ②內閣 nèigé 〈cabinet〉. ③牧師 mùshi 〈clergyman〉.

mink n. ①貂 diāo 〈animal〉. ②貂皮 diāopí 〈fur skin〉.

minor adj. 較小的 jiào xiǎo de, 較次要的 jiào cìyào de 〈smaller〉. — n. ①未成年者 wèichéngnián zhě 〈of age〉.

M

②副修科目 fùxiū kēmù 〈subject〉.

minority n. ①少數 shǎoshù (smaller number). ②未成年 wèichéngnián 〈age〉. ③少數民族 shǎoshù mínzú 〈nationality〉.

minstrel n. 吟遊詩人 yínyóu shīrén.

mint n. ①薄荷 bòhe 〈plant〉. ②造幣廠 zàobìchǎng 〈coin〉. — v. 鑄幣 zhùbì 〈coin〉.

minus adj. 減的 jiǎn de, 負的 fù de. — n. 負數 fùshù.

minute n. 分 fēn, 分鐘 fēnzhōng 〈time〉. — adj. 細微的 xìwēi de / xìwéi de.

miracle n. 奇蹟 qíjī 〈wonder〉.

mirage n. 海市蜃樓 hǎi-shì-shèn-lóu.

mire n. 泥濘 nínìng, 泥沼 nízhǎo. — v. 陷入泥濘 xiànrù nínìng (bog).

mirror n. 鏡子 jìngzi. — v. 反映 fǎnyìng.

mirth n. 歡樂 huānlè, 歡笑 huānxiào.

misadventure n. 不幸 búxìng.

misappropriate v. 侵占 qīnzhàn, 盜用 dàoyòng.

misbehave v. 行為不端 xíngwéi bù duān.

miscalculate v. 誤算 wùsuàn.

miscarriage n. 流產 liúchǎn 〈pregnancy〉.

miscarry v. 流產 liúchǎn 〈pregnancy〉.

miscellaneous adj. 繁雜的 fánzá de, 各種的 gè zhǒng de.

miscellany n. 混雜 hùnzá

(mixture).

mischance n. 不幸 búxìng, 惡運 èyùn.

mischief n. ①傷害 shānghài, 危害 wēihài / wéihài (damage). ②惡作劇 èzuòjù, 戲謔 xìxuè / xìnuè (foolish).

mischievous adj. 有害的 yǒuhài de (harmful).

misconceive v. 誤解 wùjiě.

misconduct n. 行為不檢 xíngwéi bù jiǎn (misbehavior).

misdeed n. 惡行 èxíng.

miser n. 守財奴 shǒucáinú, 吝嗇鬼 lìnsèguǐ.

miserable adj. 悲慘的 bēicǎn de, 痛苦的 tòngkǔ de (wretched).

misery n. 悲慘 bēicǎn, 痛苦 tòngkǔ.

misfire n. & v. ①失敗 shībài 〈plan〉. ②不著火 bù zháohuǒ, 不發火 bù fāhuǒ 〈gun or engine〉.

misfit n. 不適應者 bú shìyìng zhě.

misfortune n. 不幸 búxìng.

misgiving n. 疑慮 yílǜ, 不安 bù'ān.

misguided adj. 被誤導的 bèi wùdǎo de.

mishap n. 災禍 zāihuò.

misjudge v. 誤判 wùpàn.

mislead v. 誤導 wùdǎo.

mismanage v. 處置失當 chǔzhì shīdàng.

misprint n. & v. 印錯 yìncuò, 誤印 wùyìn.

misquote v. 誤引 wùyǐn.

misrepresent v. 誤傳 wùchuán, 誤述 wùshù.

miss v. ①錯失 lòushī, 錯過 cuòguò (lose). ②失誤 shīwù, 不中 bú zhòng (fail). ③想念 xiǎngniàn, 懷念 huáiniàn

M

(long for). — n. 錯失 cuòshī,
未中 wèizhòng (failure to hit)

Miss n. 小姐 xiǎojiě (maiden).

missile n. 飛彈 fēidàn (projectile).

missing adj. 不見的 bújiàn
de, 失蹤的 shīzōng de (lost).

mission n. ①使命 shǐmìng,
任務 rènwu (task). ②使節團
shǐjiétuán, 代表團
dàibiǎotuán (representatives).

missionary n. 傳教士
chuánjiàoshì. — adj. 傳教的
chuánjiào de (religion).

misspell v. 拼錯 pīncuò.

misspend v. 虛度 xūdù, 浪費
làngfèi.

mist n. 霧 wù. — v. 起霧 qǐ wù.

mistake n. 錯誤 cuòwù, 誤會
wùhuì. — v. 誤會 wùhuì, 弄錯
nòngcuò.

mister n. ……先生
...xiānsheng.

mistress n. 情婦 qíngfù
(lover).

mistrust n. & v. 懷疑 huáiyí.

misty adj. 有霧的 yǒu wù de.

misunderstand v. 誤解
wùjiě.

misuse n. & v. ①誤用
wùyòng, 濫用 lànyòng
(careless use). ②虐待 nüèdài
(abuse).

mitigate v. 減輕 jiǎnqīng,
使緩和 shǐ huǎnhé.

mitt n. 棒球手套 bàngqiú
shǒutào (glove).

mix n. & v. 混合 hùnhé
(combination).

mixed adj. 混合的 hùnhé de
(mingled).

mixture n. 混合物 hùnhéwù.

moan n. & v. 呻吟 shēnyín
(groan).

moat n. 壕溝 háogōu.

mob n. ①群眾 qúnzhòng, 民眾
mínzhòng (crowd). ②暴徒
bàotú, 暴民 bàomín (rioter).

mobile adj. 移動的 yídòng de
(movable).

mobilize v. 動員 dòngyuán.

mock n. & v. 嘲弄 cháonòng,
嘲笑 cháoxiào (ridicule).

mockery n. 嘲弄 cháonòng
(ridicule).

mode n. ①方式 fāngshì (way).
②樣式 yàngshì (form).

model n. ①模型 móxíng
(scale). ②模範 mófàn (example). ③款式 kuǎnshì (style).

moderate adj. 適度的 shìdù
de, 有節制的 yǒu jiézhì de
(restrained).

moderator n. 仲裁者
zhòngcáizhě, 調停者
tiáotíngzhě (mediator).

modern adj. 現代的 xiàndài
de (present). — n. 現代人
xiàndàirén.

modernism n. 現代主義
xiàndài zhǔyì.

modernize v. 現代化
xiàndàihuà.

modest adj. ①謙虛的 qiānxū
de (humble). ②高雅的 gāoyǎ
de (decent).

modesty n. 謙虛 qiānxū, 謙遜
qiānxùn (unobtrusiveness).

modify v. 修改 xiūgǎi, 修正
xiūzhèng (change).

modulate v. 調節 tiáojié
(adjust).

mohair n. 毛海 máohǎi,
安哥拉羊毛 āngēlā
shānyángmáo.

moist adj. 潮濕的 cháoshī de
(wet).

moisten v. 使潮濕 shǐ

cháoshī, 弄濕 nòngshī.

moisture n. 濕氣 shīqì (humidity).

molar n. 臼齒 jiùchǐ.

mold n. ①模型 móxíng, 模子 mózi / múzi (shape). ② 霉 méi (spore). — v. 模鑄 mózhù (shape into).

molder v. 崩壞 bēnghuài.

moldy adj. 發霉的 fāméi de.

mole n. ① 痣 zhì (spot). ② 鼴鼠 yǎnshǔ (animal).

molecule n. 分子 fēnzǐ (particle).

molest v. 干擾 gānrǎo, 妨害 fánghài (disturb), 騷擾 sāorǎo (harass).

mollify v. 安慰 ānwèi, 緩和 huǎnhé (soothe).

molt n. & v. 換毛 huànmáo, 蛻 皮 tuìpí.

mom n. 媽媽 māma.

moment n. ①瞬間 shùnjiān, 片刻 piànkè (time). ② 重要 zhòngyào (importance).

momentary adj. 瞬間的 shùnjiān de.

momentous adj. 極重要的 jí zhòngyào de.

momentum n. 動量 dòngliàng, 動力 dònglì (physics).

monarch n. 君主 jūnzhǔ, 國王 guówáng.

monarchic adj. 君主的 jūnzhǔ de.

monarchy n. 君主政體 jūnzhǔ zhèngtǐ (empire).

monastery n. 修道院 xiūdàoyuàn, 僧院 sēngyuàn.

monastic adj. 修道院的 xiūdàoyuàn de (of monasteries).

Monday n. 星期一 Xīngqīyī /

Xīngqíyī.

monetary adj. 貨幣的 huòbì de.

money n. 金錢 jīnqián, 貨幣 huòbì (currency). *make* ~ 賺錢 zhuànqián.

Mongolian n. ①蒙古人 Ménggǔrén (people). ②蒙古語 Ménggǔyǔ (language).

mongoos(e) n. u méng.

mongrel n. 雜種狗 zázhǒnggǒu (dogs). — adj. 雜種的 zázhǒng de.

monitor n. ①班長 bānzhǎng (of school). ②監視員 jiānshìyuán, 監聽員 jiāntīngyuán (person). ③監視器 jiānshìqì, 監聽器 jiāntīngqì (machine). — v. 監視 jiānshì (watch), 監聽 jiāntīng (listen to).

monk n. 修道士 xiūdàoshì (Christianity), 僧侶 sēnglǚ (Buddhism).

monkey n. 猴子 hóuzi, 猿 yuán (simian).

monogamy n. 一夫一妻 yì fū yì qī.

monologue n. 獨白 dúbái (soliloquy).

monopolize v. 壟斷 lǒngduàn.

monopoly n. ①獨占 dúzhàn (sole possession). ②專賣 zhuānmài (sole right to trade).

monorail n. 單軌 dānguǐ.

monosyllable n. 單音節字 dān yīnjié zì.

monotheism n. 一神論 yìshénlùn.

monotone n. 單調 dāndiào.

monotonous adj. 單調的 dāndiào de (boring).

monsoon n. 季風 jìfēng (wind).

M

monster n. 怪物 guàiwù ⟨creature⟩.

monstrous adj. ①巨大的 jùdà de ⟨huge⟩. ②恐怖的 kǒngbù de, 兇惡的 xiōng'è de ⟨horrible⟩.

month n. 月 yuè.

monthly adj. 每月的 měi yuè de. — n. 月刊 yuèkān.

monument n. 紀念碑 jìniànbēi ⟨memorial⟩.

mood n. 心情 xīnqíng, 情緒 qíngxù.

moody adj. 心情不定的 xīnqíng bú dìng de ⟨uneven emotions⟩, 憂鬱的 yōuyù de ⟨gloomy⟩.

moon n. 月亮 yuèliang ⟨heavenly body⟩. ~ cake 中秋月餅 zhōngqiū yuèbǐng.

moonlight n. & adj. 月光 yuèguāng.

moor n. 曠野 kuàngyě, 荒地 huāngdì ⟨wilderness⟩.

moose n. 麋 mí.

mop n. 拖把 tuōbǎ ⟨for cleaning⟩. — v. 洗擦 xǐcā ⟨scrub⟩.

mope v. 抑鬱不樂 yìyù bú lè.

moral adj. ①道德的 dàodé de ⟨ethical⟩. ②有道德的 yǒu dàodé de ⟨virtuous⟩. — n. ①教訓 jiàoxùn, 寓意 yùyì ⟨lesson⟩. ②道德 dàodé ⟨ethic⟩.

morale n. 士氣 shìqì.

morality n. 道德 dàodé, 美德 měidé ⟨virtue⟩.

morass n. 沼地 zhǎodì, 泥沼 nízhǎo ⟨marsh⟩.

morbid adj. ①疾病的 jíbìng de, 病態的 bìngtài de ⟨sick⟩. ②不健康的 bú jiànkāng de, 不正常的 bú zhèngcháng de ⟨unhealthy⟩.

more adj. & adv. & pron. 更多的 gèng duō de ⟨quantity⟩, 更大的 gèng dà de ⟨size⟩.

moreover adv. 而且 érqiě, 此外 cǐwài.

morgue n. 陳屍所 chénshīsuǒ ⟨mortuary⟩.

Mormon n. 摩門教徒 Móménjiàotú.

morning n. 早晨 zǎochén, 上午 shàngwǔ.

morning-glory n. 牽牛花 qiānniúhuā.

moron n. 低能者 dīnéngzhě.

morose adj. 憂鬱的 yōuyù de ⟨gloomy⟩.

morphia n. 嗎啡 mǎfēi.

morphine n. 嗎啡 mǎfēi.

morrow n. 翌日 yìrì, 明天 míngtiān ⟨the next day⟩.

morsel n. ①一口 yì kǒu ⟨bite⟩. ②少量 shǎoliàng ⟨small amount⟩.

mortal adj. ①人類的 rénlèi de, 凡人的 fánrén de ⟨human⟩. ②會死的 huì sǐ de ⟨human⟩. ③致命的 zhìmìng de ⟨fatal⟩.

mortar n. ①灰泥 huīní ⟨cement⟩. ②迫擊砲 pòjīpào, 砲擊砲 pòjīpào ⟨gun⟩.

mortgage n. & v. 抵押 dǐyā ⟨deposit⟩.

mortify v. 使屈辱 shǐ qūrù, 使屈辱 shǐ qūrù ⟨cause shame⟩.

mortuary n. 停屍間 tíngshījiān, 太平間 tàipíngjiān.

mosaic n. 鑲嵌 xiāngqiàn, 鑲嵌 xiāngqiàn, 嵌工 qiàngōng, 嵌工 qiàngōng ⟨inlay⟩.

mosque n. 回教寺院 Huíjiào sìyuàn.

mosquito n. 蚊子 wénzi.

moss n. 苔 tái, 蘚 xiǎn.

most adj. & pron. ①最多的

M

zuì duō de, 最大的 zuì dà de (greatest in number). ②大多數的 dàduōshù de (majority). — adv. 最 zuì.

mostly adv. ①主要地 zhǔyào de (mainly). ②通常 tōngcháng de (usually).

motel n. 汽車旅館 qìchē lǚguǎn.

moth n. 蛾 é ⟨insect⟩.

mothball n. 樟腦丸 zhāngnǎowán.

motherboard n. 主機板 zhǔjībǎn ⟨computer⟩.

mother n. 母親 mǔqīn, 媽媽 māma (female parent). ~ country 祖國 zǔguó. ~ tongue 母語 mǔyǔ.

mother-in-law n. 婆婆 pópo (husband's mother), 岳母 yuèmǔ (wife's mother).

Mother's Day n. 母親節 Mǔqīnjié.

motif n. 主題 zhǔtí, 主旨 zhǔzhǐ.

motion n. ①動作 dòngzuò (movement). ②動議 dòngyì (proposal). — v. 示意 shìyì.

motivate v. 引起動機 yǐnqǐ dòngjī (encourage), 激發 jīfā (inspire).

motive n. 動機 dòngjī (intention).

motor n. ①馬達 mǎdá, 發動機 fādòngjī ⟨machine⟩. ②汽車 qìchē (car).

motorbike n. 輕型機車 qīngxíng jīchē.

motorcycle n. 機車 jīchē.

motto n. 箴言 zhēnyán, 座右銘 zuòyòumíng (maxim).

mound n. 土堆 tǔduī, 堤 dī / tí ⟨dike⟩.

mount v. ①登上 dēngshang

(ascend). ②騎乘 qíchéng (ride). — n. 山 shān (mountain).

mountain n. 山 shān, 山脈 shānmài (peak).

mountaineer n. 登山者 dēngshānzhě (climber).

mourn v. 哀悼 āidào, 悲傷 bēishāng (feel sorrow).

mournful adj. 哀悼的 āidào de, 悲傷的 bēishāng de.

mourning n. 哀悼 āidào, 悲傷 bēishāng ⟨grief⟩.

mouse n. ①鼠 shǔ (rat). ②膽小者 dǎnxiǎozhě (timid person). ③鼠標 shǔbiāo / 滑鼠 huáshǔ ⟨computer⟩.

mousse n. ①慕絲 mùsī ⟨hair⟩. ②奶油凍甜點 nǎiyóudòng tiándiǎn ⟨dessert⟩.

mouth n. ①嘴 zuǐ, 口 kǒu ⟨face⟩. ②出入口 chūrùkǒu ⟨opening⟩. ③河口 hékǒu ⟨river⟩.

mouthful n. 一口 yì kǒu, 少量 shǎoliàng ⟨quantity⟩.

moveable adj. 可移動的 kě yídòng de (mobile).

move v. ①移動 yídòng (change position). ②感動 gǎndòng (affect the emotions). ③搬家 bānjiā, 遷動 qiāndòng (change residence). ④提議 tíyì (suggest).

movement n. ①行動 xíngdòng, 活動 huódòng ⟨action⟩. ②運動 yùndòng ⟨by group⟩.

movie n. 電影 diànyǐng, 影片 yǐngpiàn (film).

mow v. 割 gē, 刈 yì (cut).

MP3 電腦壓縮檔案 diànnǎo yāsuō dàng'àn / 電腦壓縮檔案 yāsuō dǎng'àn.

Mr. n. 先生 xiānsheng. ~ Right 如意郎君 rúyì lángjūn.

M

Mrs. *n.* 太太 tàitai, 夫人 fūrén.

Ms. *n.* 女士 nǚshì.

Mt. Everest 埃弗勒斯峰 Āifúlèsīfēng.

much *adj.* 很多的 hěn duō de (a large quantity). — *adv.* ①多 duō, 極 jí (more). ②非常 fēicháng (greatly).

muck *n.* 糞肥 fènféi.

mucus *n.* 黏液 niányè.

mud *n.* 泥 ní (mire).

muddle *n. & v.* 混亂 hùnluàn / hǔnluàn.

muddy *adj.* 泥濘的 nínìng de (miry).

mudguard *n.* 擋泥板 dǎngníbǎn.

muff *n.* 暖手筒 nuǎnshǒutǒng 〈warm material〉.

muffin *n.* 鬆餅 sōngbǐng.

muffle *v.* 裹 guǒ, 包 bāo 〈wrap〉, 蒙住 méngzhù 〈silence〉.

mug *n.* 馬克杯 mǎkèbēi 〈beaker〉.

Muhammad *n.* 穆罕默德 Mùhǎnmòdé.

mulberry *n.* 桑樹 sāngshù 〈tree〉, 桑椹 sāngshèn 〈fruit〉.

mule *n.* 騾 luó 〈animal〉.

mull *v.* 仔細考慮 zǐxì kǎolǜ.

multifarious *adj.* 多種的 duōzhǒng de, 各式各樣的 gè shì gè yàng de.

multilateral *adj.* 多邊的 duōbiān de (involving two or more participants). ~ **trade** 多邊 貿易 duōbiān màoyì.

multimedia *n.* 多介質 duōjièzhì / 多媒體 duōméitǐ.

multiple *adj.* 複合的 fùhé de, 複式的 fùshì de (numerous). — *n.* 倍數 bèishù 〈mathematics〉.

multiplication *n.* ①增多 zēngduō, 倍加 bèijiā (multiplying). ②乘法 chéngfǎ 〈mathematics〉.

multiply *v.* ①增加 zēngjiā (increase). ②乘 chéng 〈mathematics〉.

multitude *n.* ①眾多 zhòngduō (large number). ②群 眾 qúnzhòng (crowd).

mum *adj.* 沈默的 chénmò de.

mumble *v.* 喃喃自語 nánnán-zì-yǔ (murmur).

mummy *n.* 木乃伊 mùnǎiyī.

mumps *n.* 腮腺炎 sāixiànyán.

munch *v.* 用力咀嚼 yònglì jǔjué.

mundane *adj.* 世俗的 shìsú de, 現世的 xiànshì de (secular).

municipal *adj.* 都市的 dūshì de, 市政的 shìzhèng de (civic).

munition *n.* 軍火 jūnhuǒ, 軍 需品 jūnxūpǐn.

mural *n.* 壁畫 bìhuà.

murder *n. & v.* 謀殺 móushā.

murderer *n.* 兇手 xiōngshǒu, 謀殺犯 móushāfàn.

murky *adj.* 黑暗的 hēi'àn de, 陰暗的 yīn'àn de (dark).

murmur *n.* ①潺潺聲 chánchánshēng 〈of stream〉. ②呢喃聲 nínánshēng 〈of words〉.

muscle *n.* 肌肉 jīròu 〈tissue〉.

muscular *adj.* 肌肉的 jīròu de (of muscles).

muse *v.* 沈思 chénsī, 冥想 míngxiǎng.

museum *n.* 博物館 bówùguǎn.

mushroom *n.* 蘑菇 mógu, 蕈 xùn (fungus).

music *n.* 音樂 yīnyuè 〈sound〉, 樂曲 yuèqǔ 〈composition〉.

musical *adj.* 音樂的 yīnyuè de (of music). — *n.* 音樂劇 yīnyuèjù.

musician *n.* 音樂家 yīnyuèjiā 〈person〉.

musk *n.* 麝香 shèxiāng.

muskrat *n.* 麝鼠 shèshǔ.

Muslim *n.* & *adj.* 回教徒 Huíjiàotú.

muslin *n.* 薄棉布 bómiánbù.

must *aux. v.* 必須 bìxū.

mustache *n.* 髭 zī, 鬚 xū.

mustard *n.* ①芥菜 jiècài 〈plant〉. ②芥末 jièmo 〈condiment〉.

muster *n.* & *v.* 集合 jíhé, 召集 zhàojí (gathering).

musty *adj.* 發霉的 fāméi de, 陳腐的 chénfǔ de (moldy).

mutation *n.* ①變化 biànhuà (change). ②突變 tūbiàn / túbiàn 〈genes〉.

mute *adj.* ①沈默的 chénmò de (silent). ②啞的 yǎ de (dumb). — *n.* 啞巴 yǎba (person unable to speak).

mutilate *v.* 使殘廢 shǐ cánfèi.

mutiny *n.* & *v.* 叛變 pànbiàn, 兵變 bīngbiàn.

mutter *v.* 喃喃低語 nánnán-dīyǔ.

mutton *n.* 羊肉 yángròu.

mutual *adj.* 相互的 xiānghù de, 共同的 gòngtóng de (reciprocal). ~ *fund* 共同基金 gòngtóng jījīn.

muzzle *n.* ①口鼻 kǒubí 〈animal〉. ②槍口 qiāngkǒu, 砲口 pàokǒu 〈gun〉. — *v.* 封口 fēngkǒu.

my *pron.* 我的 wǒ de.

myopia *n.* 近視 jìnshì 〈medical〉.

myriad *n.* 無數 wúshù (extremely large number).

myself *pron.* 我自己 wǒ zìjǐ.

mystery *n.* 神祕 shénmì, 奧妙 àomiào (secret).

mystic *n.* 神祕主義者 shénmì zhǔyì zhě.

mystify *v.* 使迷惑 shǐ míhuo.

myth *n.* ①神話 shénhuà (legend). ②虛構故事 xūgòu gùshì (fiction).

mythology *n.* 神話學 shénhuàxué.

N

nag *v.* 嘮叨 láodao.

nail *n.* ①指甲 zhǐjia / zhǐjiǎ 〈finger〉. ②釘子 dīngzi (stud). — *v.* 釘牢 dìngláo.

naive *adj.* 天真的 tiānzhēn de.

naked *adj.* 赤裸的 chìluǒ de.

name *n.* ①名字 míngzi (given name). ②名稱 míngchēng (title). ③姓名 xìngmíng (full name). — *v.* 命名 mìngmíng, 取名 qǔmíng.

namely *adv.* 就是 jiùshì, 即 jí.

nanny *n.* 奶媽 nǎimā, 保姆 bǎomǔ.

nap *n.* & *v.* 小睡 xiǎoshuì.

nape *n.* 頸背 jǐngbèi.

napkin *n.* 餐巾 cānjīn.

N

narcissus n. 水仙花 shuǐxiānhuā.

narcotic n. 麻醉劑 mázuìjì. — adj. 麻醉的 mázuì de.

narrate v. ①敘述 xùshù (relate). ②說明 shuōmíng (explain).

narration n. 記敘文 jìxùwén.

narrative n. ①故事 gùshi (story). ②敘述 xùshù (storytelling).

narrow adj. 窄的 zhǎi de. — v. 變窄 biànzhǎi, 使狹小 shǐ xiáxiǎo.

narrow-minded adj. 氣量小的 qìliàng xiǎo de, 小心眼的 xiǎoxīnyǎn de.

nasal adj. ①鼻的 bí de (of nose). ②鼻音的 bíyīn de (of sound). — n. 鼻音 bíyīn (sound).

nasty adj. ①為難的 wéinán de (mean). ②骯髒的 āngzāng de (dirty).

nation n. ①國家 guójiā (country). ②國民 guómín (citizens). ③民族 mínzú (ethnicity).

national adj. ①國家的 guójiā de (country). ②國民的 guómín de (citizens). ③民族的 mínzú de (ethnicity).

nationalism n. 國家主義 guójiā zhǔyì, 愛國主義 àiguó zhǔyì.

nationality n. 國籍 guójí (citizenship).

nationalize v. ①使國有 shǐ guóyǒu (owned by state). ②國家化 guójiāhuà (become a country).

nationalized adj. 國有的 guóyǒu de (property).

native n. 本地人 běndìrén. — adj. 本地的 běndì de, 本土的 běntǔ de (local).

nativity n. 誕生 dànshēng (birth).

natural adj. ①自然的 zìrán de (to be expected). ②天賦的 tiānfù de (inherent). ③天然的 tiānrán de (not artificial).

naturally adv. ①自然地 zìrán de (of its own accord). ②天然地 tiānrán de (not artificially).

nature n. ①自然 zìrán (wildlife). ②天性 tiānxìng, 特質 tèzhì / tèzhí (characteristics).

naughty adj. 頑皮的 wánpí de.

nausea n. 作嘔 zuò'ǒu.

nauseous adj. 噁心的 ěxīn de.

nautical adj. 船舶的 chuánbó de (of ships), 航海的 hánghǎi de (of navigation).

naval adj. 海軍的 hǎijūn de.

navel n. 肚臍 dùqí.

navigate v. 航行 hángxíng (sail).

navigation n. 航海 hánghǎi, 航行 hángxíng.

navy n. 海軍 hǎijūn. ~ blue 深藍色 shēnlánsè.

near adv. 近 jìn. — adj. ①近的 jìn de (close), 離……很近 lí... hěn jìn (close to...). ②親密的 qīnmì de (intimate). — prep. 接近 jiējìn. — v. 靠近 kàojìn, 接近 jiējìn.

nearby adj. 附近的 fùjìn de.

nearly adv. 幾乎 jīhū, 差不多 chàbuduō (almost).

nearsighted adj. 近視的 jìnshì de.

neat adj. 整潔的 zhěngjié de (clean).

necessarily adv. 必定 bìdìng, 必然 bìrán.

necessary adj. 必要的 bìyào de.

necessitate v. 使必要 shǐ bìyào.

necessity n. 必要 bìyào (requirement), 急需 jíxū (urgent need).

neck n. 頸 jǐng, 脖子 bózi ⟨body⟩.

necklace n. 項鍊 xiàngliàn.

necktie n. 領帶 lǐngdài.

need n. 需要 xūyào. — v. 需要 xūyào.

needle n. 針 zhēn.

needless adj. 不需要的 bù xūyào de.

needy adj. 貧窮的 pínqióng de.

negation n. 否定 fǒudìng.

negative adj. ①否定的 fǒudìng de (contrary). ②消極的 xiāojí de (pessimistic). ③負面的 fùmiàn de (the bad side of something).

neglect v. 忽略 hūlüè, 疏忽 shūhu.

negligence n. 疏忽 shūhu.

negligible adj. 微不足道的 wēi-bù-zú-dào de / wéi-bù-zú-dào de.

negotiable adj. 可磋商的 kě cuōshāng de.

negotiate v. 磋商 cuōshāng, 協商 xiéshāng (discuss), 談判 tánpàn, 交涉 jiāoshè ⟨diplomacy, trade, etc⟩.

negotiation n. 磋商 cuōshāng, 協商 xiéshāng (discussion), 談判 tánpàn, 交涉 jiāoshè ⟨diplomacy, trade, etc⟩.

neighbor n. 鄰居 línjū.

neighborhood n. 附近 fùjìn, 鄰近 línjìn.

neighboring adj. 附近的 fùjìn de, 鄰近的 línjìn de.

neither adv. 既不……也不… …

… jìbù…yěbù….

neon n. ①氖 nǎi ⟨gas⟩. ②霓虹燈 níhóngdēng ⟨light⟩.

nephew n. 姪兒 zhí'ér (brother's son), 外甥 wàisheng (sister's son).

nepotism n. 裙帶關係 qúndài guānxi.

nerve n. ①神經 shénjīng (part of body). ②勇氣 yǒngqì, 膽量 dǎnliàng (courage).

nervous adj. ①緊張的 jǐnzhāng de (anxious). ②神經的 shénjīng de (neural).

nest n. 窠 kē (burrow). — v. 築巢 zhùcháo / zhúcháo.

nestle v. ①舒適地躺下 shūshì de tǎngxià (lie down). ②依偎 yīwēi (cuddle).

net n. 網 wǎng, 網狀物 wǎngzhuàngwù (netting). — v. 用網捕 yòng wǎng bǔ. — adj. 淨值的 jìngzhí de. ~ *price* 實價 shíjià. ~ *profit* 淨利 jìnglì. ~ *weight* 淨重 jìngzhòng.

nettle n. 蕁麻 xúnmá ⟨plant⟩. — *rash* 蕁麻疹 xúnmázhěn.

network n. 網狀組織 wǎngzhuàng zǔzhī, 網絡 wǎngluò.

neurology n. 神經學 shénjīngxué.

neurosis n. 神經病 shénjīngbìng.

neurotic adj. 神經病的 shénjīngbìng de (crazy), 神經過敏的 shénjīng guòmǐn de (overly sensitive). — n. 神經病患 shénjīngbìng huàn.

neuter adj. ①無性的 wúxìng de ⟨gender⟩. ②中性的 zhōngxìng de ⟨grammar⟩. — v. 去勢 qùshì, 閹割 yāngē.

N

neutral *adj.* 中立的 zhōnglì de.

neutron *n.* 中子 zhōngzǐ.

never *adv.* 從未 cóng wèi (never yet), 永不 yǒng bù, 決不 jué bù (at no time).

nevertheless *adv.* 儘管如此 jǐnguǎn rúcǐ, 然而 rán'ér.

new *adj.* 新的 xīn de. *N- Year* 新年 xīnnián. *N- Year's Day* 元旦 Yuándàn. *N- Year's Eve* 除夕 chúxī / chúxì.

newborn *adj.* 剛出生的 gāng chūshēng de, 新生的 xīnshēng de.

news *n.* ①新聞 xīnwén (report). ②消息 xiāoxi (information).

newscast *n.* 新聞廣播 xīnwén guǎngbō / xīnwén guǎngbò.

newsgroup *n.* 討論群組 tǎolùn qúnzǔ.

newsletter *n.* 簡訊 jiǎnxùn, 通訊 tōngxùn.

newspaper *n.* 報紙 bàozhǐ.

newsstand *n.* 書報攤 shūbàotān.

next *adj.* ①下一個 xià yí ge (next one). ②其次的 qícì de (in a list). — *adv.* 接下來 jiēxialai / jiēxiàlái (afterwards), 下次 xiàcì (next time). — *prep.* 在……旁邊 zài...pángbiān.

nibble *n. & v.* 一點一點地吃 yìdiǎn yìdiǎn de chī.

nice *adj.* ①好的 hǎo de (good). ②友善的 yǒushàn de (friendly). ③優雅的 yōuyǎ de (elegant).

niche *n.* ①壁龕 bìkān (alcove). ②適合之處 shìhé zhī chù (suitable place).

nick *n.* 刻痕 kèhén (small cut).

nickel *n.* ①鎳 niè (Ni). ②鎳幣

nièbì (coin).

nickname *n.* 綽號 chuòhào, 暱稱 nìchēng.

nicotine *n.* 尼古丁 nígǔdīng.

niece *n.* 姪女 zhínǚ (brother's daughter), 外甥女 wàishengnǚ (sister's daughter).

niggard *n.* 小氣鬼 xiǎoqìguǐ. — *adj.* 吝嗇的 lìnsè de, 小氣的 xiǎoqì de (stingy).

night *n.* 夜晚 yèwǎn. *~ blindness* 夜盲 yèmáng. *~ school* 夜校 yèxiào.

nightcap *n.* ①睡帽 shuìmào (hat). ②睡前酒 shuìqiánjiǔ (drink).

nightclub *n.* 夜總會 yèzǒnghuì.

nightgown *n.* 長睡衣 cháng shuìyī, 睡袍 shuìpáo.

nightingale *n.* 夜鶯 yèyīng (bird).

nightlife *n.* 夜生活 yèshēnghuó.

nightmare *n.* 夢魘 mèngyǎn, 惡夢 èmèng.

nil *n.* 無 wú, 零 líng.

nimble *adj.* 敏捷的 mǐnjié de, 輕快的 qīngkuài de (agile).

nine *n. & adj.* 九 jiǔ.

nineteen *n. & adj.* 十九 shíjiǔ.

nineteenth *n. & adj.* 第十九 dì-shíjiǔ.

ninetieth *n. & adj.* 第九十 dì-jiǔshí.

ninety *n. & adj.* 九十 jiǔshí.

ninja *n.* 忍者 rěnzhě.

ninth *n. & adj.* 第九 dì-jiǔ.

nip *v.* ①咬 yǎo (bite). ②刺骨 cìgǔ (chill).

nipple *n.* 乳頭 rǔtóu (teat).

nit *n.* 卵 luǎn.

nitrogen *n.* 氮 dàn

nitwit n. 蠢人 chǔnrén (fool).

no adj. ①沒有 méiyǒu (lack). ②不 bù, 不是 bú shì 〈disagreement〉.

nobility n. ①高貴 gāoguì (dignity). ②貴族 guìzú (nobleman).

noble adj. ①貴族的 guìzú de (royal). ②高貴的 gāoguì de (dignified). ③高尚的 gāoshàng de, 偉大的 wěidà de (heroic).

nobleman n. 貴族 guìzú.

nobody pron. 無人 wú rén. —n. 平凡的人 píngfán de rén, 小人物 xiǎorénwù.

nocturnal adj. 夜間的 yèjiān de (nightly).

nod n. & v. ①點頭 diǎntóu (bow). ②打盹 dǎdǔn (doze).

noise n. 噪音 zàoyīn, 吵鬧聲 chǎonàoshēng (unpleasant sound).

noisy adj. 吵鬧的 chǎonào de.

nomad n. 遊牧民族 yóumù mínzú 〈people〉, 流浪者 liúlàngzhě (wanderer).

nominal adj. ①名義上的 míngyìshang de, 掛名的 guàmíng de (in name only). ②極微薄的 jí wēibó de / jí wéibó de (small).

nominate v. 提名 tímíng (propose).

nomination n. 提名 tímíng.

nominee n. 被提名者 bèi tímíng zhě.

noncommissioned adj. 無任命狀的 wú rènmìngzhuàng de.

none pron. ①毫無 háowú (not any). ②無一人 wú yì rén (no one).

nonentity n. 小人物 xiǎorénwù (unimportant person).

nonprofit adj. 非營利的 fēi yínglì de.

nonsense n. 無意義的話 wú yìyì de huà, 廢話 fèihuà 〈meaningless〉, 胡說 húshuō (untrue).

nonsmoking adj. 禁煙的 jìnyān de.

nonstop adj. & adv. 直達的 zhídá de.

noodle n. ①麵條 miàntiáo 〈food〉. ②傻瓜 shǎguā (person).

nook n. ①角落 jiǎoluò (corner). ②隱蔽處 yǐnbìchù (sheltered spot).

noon n. 中午 zhōngwǔ, 正午 zhèngwǔ. —adj. 中午的 zhōngwǔ de.

noose n. 活結 huójié (slipknot).

nor conj. 也不 yě bù.

norm n. 標準 biāozhǔn, 規範 guīfàn.

normal adj. 正常的 zhèngcháng de, 一般的 yìbān de, 標準的 biāozhǔn de.

normalization n. 正常化 zhèngchánghuà, 標準化 biāozhǔnhuà.

north n. ①北方 běi 〈direction〉. ②北方 běifāng (northern region). ③北邊 běibiān, 北部 běibù (northern part). —adv. 北 běi, 向北 xiàng běi, 往北 wǎng běi. —adj. ①北 běi (of the north). ②北方的 běifāng de (of the northern region). ③北部的 běibù de (of the northern part).

North America 北美洲 Běiměizhōu.

North Pole 北極 Běijí.

northern adj. 北方的 běifāng de. ~ *hemisphere* 北半球

N

běibànqiú.

northward *adv.* 向北地 xiàng běi de.

nose *n.* 鼻子 bízi 〈organ〉.

nostalgia *n.* ①鄉愁 xiāngchóu (homesickness). ②懷舊 huáijiù (long for the past).

nostril *n.* 鼻孔 bíkǒng.

nosy *adj.* 好管閒事的 hào guǎn xiánshì de.

not *adv.* 不 bù.

notable *adj.* ①值得注意的 zhíde zhùyì de, 顯著的 xiǎnzhù de (remarkable). ②著名的 zhùmíng de (well-known).

notary *n.* 公證人 gōngzhèngrén.

note *n.* ①備忘錄 bèiwànglù, 筆記 bǐjì (memo). ②註釋 zhùshì (annotation). ③音符 yīnfú 〈music〉. — *v.* ①注意 zhùyì (notice). ②記錄 jìlù, 寫下 xiěxià (write down).

notebook *n.* ①筆記本 bǐjìběn (book). ②筆記本電腦 bǐjìběn diànnǎo / 筆記型電腦 bǐjìxíng diànnǎo 〈computer〉.

noted *adj.* 著名的 zhùmíng de, 顯著的 xiǎnzhù de (famous).

nothing *n.* 什麼都沒有 shénme dōu méiyǒu, 無 wú.

notice *n. & v.* ①注意 zhùyì (attention). ②通知 tōngzhī (information).

notify *v.* 通知 tōngzhī.

notion *n.* ①觀念 guānniàn, 概念 gàiniàn (concept). ②意見 yìjiàn, 想法 xiǎngfa (idea).

notoriety *n.* 惡名 èmíng.

notorious *adj.* 惡名昭彰的 èmíng-zhāozhāng de.

notwithstanding *conj.* 雖然

suīrán.

nougat *n.* 牛軋糖 niúzhátáng 〈candy〉.

noun *n.* 名詞 míngcí 〈grammar〉.

nourish *v.* ①滋養 zīyǎng (provide nutrition). ②培養 péiyǎng (develop).

novel *adj.* 新奇的 xīnqí de. — *n.* 小說 xiǎoshuō.

novelist *n.* 小說家 xiǎoshuōjiā.

novelty *n.* 新奇 xīnqí (newness).

November *n.* 十一月 Shíyīyuè.

novice *n.* 生手 shēngshǒu, 初學者 chūxuézhě (beginner).

now *adv.* 現在 xiànzài, 目前 mùqián.

nowadays *n. & adv.* 現今 xiànjīn, 時下 shíxià.

nowhere *adv.* 無處 wúchù.

noxious *adj.* ①有毒的 yǒu dú de (poisonous). ②有害的 yǒu hài de (harmful).

nozzle *n.* 管嘴 guǎnzuǐ 〈opening〉, 噴氣口 pēnqìkǒu 〈spout〉.

nuance *n.* 細微差異 xìwēi chāyì / xìwéi chāyì.

nuclear *adj.* 核的 hé de.
~ *energy* 核能 hénéng.
~ *power station* 核電站 hédiànzhàn / 核能電廠 hénéng diànchǎng.

nucleus *n.* 核心 héxīn, 中心 zhōngxīn.

nude *adj.* 裸體的 luǒtǐ de (naked). — *n.* 裸體畫像 luǒtǐ huàxiàng 〈arts〉.

nudge *v.* 輕推 qīngtuī.

nudity *n.* 裸體 luǒtǐ.

nuisance *n.* 討厭的人或事

tǎoyàn de rén huò shì.

null adj. 無效的 wúxiào de (of no effect).

numb adj. 麻木的 mámù de. — v. 使麻木 shǐ mámù.

number n. ①數 shù, 數字 shùzì (numeral). ②號碼 hàomǎ (serial number). ③一期 yì qī / yì qí (publications). ④數目 shùmù (amount). *phone ~* 電話號碼 diànhuà hàomǎ.

numeral n. & adj. 數字 shùzì.

numerous adj. 極多的 jí duō de, 無數的 wúshù de.

nun n. 修女 xiūnǚ (Catholic), 尼姑 nígū (Buddhist).

nunnery n. 女修道院 nǚxiūdàoyuàn (Catholic), 尼姑庵 nígū'ān (Buddhist).

nurse n. ①護士 hùshi (hospital). ②保姆 bǎomǔ (nanny). — v. ①看護 kānhù, 照

顧 zhàogu (look after). ②哺乳 bǔrǔ (breastfeed).

nursery n. ①育兒室 yù'érshì 〈children〉. ②苗圃 miáopǔ 〈plant〉.

nurture n. & v. 養育 yǎngyù, 教養 jiàoyǎng (bringing-up).

nut n. ①核果 héguǒ, 堅果 jiānguǒ (food). ②瘋子 fēngzi 〈person〉.

nutcracker n. 胡桃鉗 hútáoqián 〈tool〉.

nutmeg n. 荳蔻 dòukòu.

nutrient n. 營養素 yíngyǎngsù.

nutrition n. 營養 yíngyǎng.

nutritious adj. 營養的 yíngyǎng de.

nuts adj. 瘋的 fēng de, 笨的 bèn de.

nylon n. 尼龍 nílóng 〈fiber〉.

O

oak n. 橡樹 xiàngshù.

oar n. 槳 jiǎng.

oasis n. 綠洲 lùzhōu.

oath n. 誓約 shìyuē, 誓言 shìyán (promise). *take an ~* 發誓 fāshì.

oatmeal n. 麥片 màipiàn.

obedience n. 順從 shùncóng, 服從 fúcóng.

obedient adj. 順從的 shùncóng de, 聽話的 tīnghuà de.

obese adj. 非常胖的 fēicháng pàng de.

obey v. 順從 shùncóng, 服從

fúcóng.

obituary n. 訃聞 fùwén.

object n. ①東西 dōngxi (thing). ②目的 mùdì (goal). ③對象 duìxiàng (recipient). ④受詞 shòucí 〈grammar〉. — v. 反對 fǎnduì (protest).

objection n. 反對 fǎnduì.

objective n. 目標 mùbiāo, 目的 mùdì (goal). — adj. 客觀的 kèguān de (unbiased).

obligation n. 義務 yìwù (duty), 責任 zérèn (responsibility).

obligatory *adj.* ①義務的 yìwù de (required). ②必要的 bìyào de (necessary).

oblige *v.* ①強制 qiángzhì / qiǎngzhì, 逼迫 bīpò (force). ②施予恩惠 shīyǔ ēnhuì (do a favor).

oblique *adj.* ①斜的 xié de (slanting). ②間接的 jiànjiē de (indirect).

obliterate *v.* 消滅 xiāomiè (eliminate), 塗掉 túdiào (erase).

oblivious *adj.* 不在意的 bú zàiyì de

oblong *n. & adj.* 長方形 chángfāngxíng

obnoxious *adj.* 使人討厭的 shǐ rén tǎoyàn de

oboe *n.* 雙簧管 shuānghuángguǎn

obscene *adj.* 猥褻的 wěixiè de

obscure *adj.* ①不清楚的 bù qīngchu de (unclear), 朦朧的 ménglóng de (vague). ②無名的 wúmíng de (unknown). ③曖昧的 àimèi de (ambiguous), 難解的 nánjiě de (complex).

obsequious *adj.* 諂媚的 chǎnmèi de.

observant *adj.* 善於觀察的 shànyú guānchá de.

observation *n.* ①觀察 guānchá (notice). ②評論 pínglùn (comment).

observatory *n.* 天文臺 tiānwéntái ⟨astronomy⟩, 氣象臺 qìxiàngtái ⟨weather⟩.

observe *v.* ①觀察 guānchá (notice). ②評論 pínglùn (remark). ③慶祝 qìngzhù, 紀念 jìniàn (celebrate). ④遵守 zūnshǒu (obey).

observer *n.* 觀察者 guāncházhě.

obsess *v.* 常縈繞於心中 cháng yíngrào yú xīnzhōng, 著迷 zháomí.

obsolete *adj.* 作廢的 zuòfèi de (useless), 被取代的 bèi qǔdài de (replaced).

obstacle *n.* 障礙 zhàng'ài.

obstetrics *n.* 產科醫學 chǎnkē yīxué.

obstinate *adj.* 頑固的 wángù de, 固執的 gùzhí de.

obstruct *v.* 阻礙 zǔ'ài, 妨礙 fáng'ài.

obtain *v.* 得到 dédào, 獲得 huòdé (get).

obtuse *adj.* ①鈍的 dùn de, 遲鈍的 chídùn de (stupid). ②鈍角的 dùnjiǎo de ⟨geometry⟩.

obvious *adj.* 顯然的 xiǎnrán de, 明顯的 míngxiǎn de.

occasion *n.* ①場合 chǎnghé (a time and place). ②大事 dàshì (important event). ③時機 shíjī (chance). ④理由 lǐyóu (excuse).

occasionally *adv.* 偶爾 ǒu'ěr, 有時候 yǒushíhou.

occupant *n.* ①占有者 zhànyǒuzhě (possession). ②居住者 jūzhùzhě, 居民 jūmín (residence).

occupation *n.* ①占有 zhànyǒu (possession). ②職業 zhíyè (job).

occupational *adj.* 職業的 zhíyè de (vocational). ~ *disease* 行業病 hángyèbìng / 職業病 zhíyèbìng.

occupy *v.* ①占有 zhànyǒu, 占據 zhànjù (possess). ②居住於 jūzhù yú (live in). *be ~ied with* 忙著 mángzhe.

O

occur v. 發生 fāshēng (happen), 出現 chūxiàn (appear).

occurrence n. ①事情 shìqing, 事件 shìjiàn (event). ②發生 fāshēng (happening).

ocean n. 海洋 hǎiyáng.

Oceania 大洋洲 Dàyángzhōu.

oceanography n. 海洋學 hǎiyángxué.

o'clock adv. 點鐘 diǎnzhōng.

octagon n. 八角形 bājiǎoxíng.

October n. 十月 Shíyuè.

octopus n. 章魚 zhāngyú.

odd adj. ①奇數的 jīshù de ⟨numbers⟩. ②古怪的 gǔguài de (abnormal).

oddity n. 古怪 gǔguài ⟨situation⟩, 怪物 guàiwù ⟨thing or person⟩.

odds n. 可能性 kěnéngxìng (probability).

odious adj. 可惡的 kěwù de.

odor n. 氣味 qìwèi, 味道 wèidao.

of prep. ……的 ...de.

off adj. 關的 guān de ⟨machine⟩.
get ~ 下 xià ⟨disembark⟩.
on and ~ 斷斷續續地 duànduàn-xùxù de (intermittently). take ~ 脫 tuō, 脫下 tuōxià ⟨clothing⟩.
take something ~ 拿掉 nádiào (remove from).
turn something ~ 關 guān ⟨machine⟩

offend v. ①冒犯 màofàn (annoy). ②犯法 fànfǎ (transgress).

offender n. 違犯者 wéifànzhě.

offense n. ①犯罪 fànzuì (crime). ②冒犯 màofàn (annoyance). ③攻擊 gōngjī / gōngjí (attack).

offensive adj. 冒犯的 màofàn de (annoying).

offer v. ①提供 tígōng (provide). ②奉獻 fèngxiàn (present). ③出價 chūjià (price).

office n. ①辦公室 bàngōngshì ⟨room⟩. ②職務 zhíwù (duty).

officer n. ①軍官 jūnguān ⟨military⟩. ②官員 guānyuán (official). ③警官 jǐngguān (policeman).

official n. 官員 guānyuán, 公務員 gōngwùyuán. — adj. 公務的 gōngwù de, 職務的 zhíwù de (authorized).

officially adv. 官方地 guānfāng de ⟨government⟩, 正式地 zhèngshì de (formal).

offshore adj. 近海的 jìnhǎi de.

offspring n. 子孫 zǐsūn.

often adv. 常常 chángcháng.

oil n. ①油 yóu (fat). ②石油 shíyóu (petroleum).

oily adj. 油的 yóu de (fat).

ointment n. 軟膏 ruǎngāo, 油膏 yóugāo.

OK adj. & adv. 好 hǎo, 可以 kěyǐ.

old adj. ①老的 lǎo de ⟨person⟩. ②舊的 jiù de ⟨thing⟩. ③古老的 gǔlǎo de ⟨era⟩.

old-fashioned adj. 過時的 guòshí de, 舊式的 jiùshì de.

olive n. 橄欖 gǎnlǎn ⟨fruit⟩.
~ oil 橄欖油 gǎnlǎnyóu.
— adj. 橄欖色的 gǎnlǎnsè de ⟨color⟩.

Olympic Games 奧林匹克 運動會 Àolínpǐkè Yùndònghuì / Àolínpǐkè Yùndònghuì.

Olympics n. 奧運會 Àoyùnhuì.

omelet n. 煎蛋捲 jiān dànjuǎn.

O

omen n. 徵兆 zhēngzhào, 預示 yùshì.

ominous adj. 惡兆的 èzhào de, 不吉的 bù jí de.

omit v. 省略 shěnglüè (leave out), 刪除 shānchú (eliminate).

on prep. 在……之上 zài...zhī shàng. — adj. 開的 kāi de ⟨machine⟩.

once adv. ①一次 yí cì (one time). ②曾經 céngjīng (in the past). — n. 一次 yí cì. at ~ 立刻 lìkè. — conj. 一旦……就 yídàn... jiù (as soon as).

one n. 一 yī. ~ another 互相 hùxiāng. ~ by ~ 一個一個的 yí ge yí ge de. — adj. 單一的 dānyī de (single), 某一的 mǒu yī de (some one).

onerous adj. 討厭的 tǎoyàn de, 可惡的 kěwù de.

one's pron. ①某人的 mǒu rén de (someone's). ②自己的 zìjǐ de (one's own).

oneself pron. 自己 zìjǐ.

ongoing adj. ①繼續中的 jìxù zhōng de, 進行中的 jìnxíng zhōng de (in process). ②長期 chángqí / chángqī (long-term).

onion n. 洋蔥 yángcōng.

onlooker n. 旁觀者 pángguānzhě.

only adj. 唯一的 wéiyī de (sole). — adv. 唯一 wéiyī (solely). not ~ but also 不但……而且 búdàn...érqiě. — conj. 不過 búguò, 只 zhǐ ⟨whereas⟩.

onset n. 剛開始 gāng kāishǐ (the very beginning).

onshore adj. & adv. 向陸地 xiàng lùdì.

onslaught n. 猛攻 měnggōng.

on-the-spot adj. 現場的 xiànchǎng de.

onto prep. 到……之上 dào...zhī shàng.

onward adv. 向前 xiàng qián.

ooze v. 滲出 shènchū (leak). — n. 淤泥 yūní, 稀泥 xīní (slimy mud).

opaque adj. ①不透明的 bú tòumíng de ⟨visual⟩. ②不清楚 的 bù qīngchu de, 曖昧的 àimèi de ⟨situation⟩.

open adj. ①打開的 dǎkāi de (not closed). ②公開的 gōngkāi de (public). — n. 戶外 hùwài (outdoors). — v. 打開 dǎkāi (unclose).

opening n. ①洞 dòng, 開口 kāikǒu (hole). ②開始 kāishǐ (beginning). ③空缺 kòngquē (vacancy).

openly adv. ①公開地 gōngkāi de (publicly). ②公然地 gōngrán de (without disguise).

open-minded adj. 無偏見的 wú piānjiàn de (unprejudiced).

opera n. 歌劇 gējù.

operate v. ①運轉 yùnzhuǎn ⟨machine⟩. ②操作 cāozuò (use). ③動手術 dòng shǒushù ⟨surgery⟩.

operation n. ①運轉 yùnzhuǎn (working). ②操作 cāozuò (action). ③手術 shǒushù (surgery). ④軍事行動 jūnshì xíngdòng ⟨military⟩.

operator n. ①操作員 cāozuòyuán ⟨machine⟩. ②接線生 jiēxiànshēng ⟨telephone⟩.

opinion n. 意見 yìjiàn, 看法 kànfa. in my ~ 在我看來 zài wǒ kàn lái.

opium n. 鴉片 yāpiàn.

opponent n. 對手 duìshǒu,

反對者 fǎnduìzhě.

opportune adj. 合時宜的 hé shíyí de.

opportunity n. 機會 jīhuì.

oppose v. 反對 fǎnduì, 與……對立 yǔ...duìlì.

opposite adj. ①反對的 xiāngfǎn de (opposed). ②相對 的 xiāngduì de (contrasting). — n. 相對事物 xiāngduì shìwù.

opposition n. ①反對 fǎnduì (disapproval). ②反對黨 fǎnduìdǎng ⟨political party⟩. ③對手 duìshǒu (opponent).

oppress v. 壓迫 yāpò (repress).

oppression n. 壓迫 yāpò.

optical adj. ①眼的 yǎn de ⟨eyes⟩. ②光學的 guāngxué de ⟨vision⟩.

optics n. 光學 guāngxué.

optimism n. 樂觀主義 lèguān zhǔyì.

optimist n. 樂觀主義者 lèguān zhǔyì zhě.

optimistic adj. 樂觀的 lèguān de.

option n. 選擇 xuǎnzé (choice).

optional adj. ①可選擇的 kě xuǎnzé de (can be chosen). ②不必要的 bú bìyào de (not required).

opulence n. 富裕 fùyù, 豐富 fēngfù.

opus n. 作品 zuòpǐn (a work).

or conj. ①或者 huòzhě. ②還是 háishi. ~ **else** 否則 fǒuzé, 要不 然 yàobùrán.

oral adj. ①口頭的 kǒutóu de, 口語的 kǒuyǔ de (spoken). ②口腔的 kǒuqiāng de ⟨regarding the mouth⟩.

orange n. 柳橙 liǔchéng

⟨fruit⟩. ②橘色 júsè, 橙色 chéngsè ⟨color⟩.

orator n. 演說者 yǎnshuōzhě.

orbit n. 軌道 guǐdào (circuit).

orchard n. 果園 guǒyuán.

orchestra n. 管絃樂隊 guǎnxián yuèduì.

orchid n. 蘭花 lánhuā.

ordain v. 任命神職 rènmìng shénzhí ⟨priest⟩.

ordeal n. 嚴酷考驗 yánkù kǎoyàn (trial).

order n. ①順序 shùnxù, 次序 cìxù (sequence). ②命令 mìnglìng (command). ③秩序 zhìxù, 規律 guīlǜ (rules). **an ~ for goods** 訂單 dìngdān. **in ~ to** 為了…… wèile.... — v. 命令 mìnglìng (command). ~ **food** 點菜 diǎn cài. ~ **goods** 訂購 dìnggòu, 訂 貨 dìnghuò.

orderly adj. ①有秩序的 yǒu zhìxù de (organized). ②順從的 shùncóng de (controlled).

ordinal adj. 順序的 shùnxù de (showing order in series).

ordinary adj. 普通的 pǔtōng de, 一般的 yìbān de.

organ n. ①器官 qìguān ⟨of body⟩. ②風琴 fēngqín ⟨instrument⟩.

organic adj. 有機的 yǒujī de (living). ~ **food** 有機食品 yǒujī shípǐn.

organism n. 有機體 yǒujītǐ (a living being).

organization n. 機構 jīgòu, 組織 zǔzhī (institution).

organize v. 組織 zǔzhī (form).

orgy n. 性派對 xìng pàiduì.

orient v. 定方位 dìng fāngwèi

(orientate).

Orient n. 東方 Dōngfāng.

Oriental adj. 東方的 Dōngfāng de.

Oriental n. 東方人 Dōngfāngrén.

orientation n. ①方向 fāngxiàng (direction). ②新人輔導 xīnrén fǔdǎo ⟨instruction⟩.

orifice n. 穴 xué / xuè, 洞 dòng.

origin n. ①起源 qǐyuán (beginning). ②出身 chūshēn (ancestry).

original adj. ①最初的 zuìchū de (earliest). ②有創作性的 yǒu chuàngzuòxìng de (creative). ③原創的 yuánchuàng de (genuine). — n. ①原物 yuánwù, 原作品 yuánzuòpǐn ⟨object⟩. ②原文 yuánwén ⟨writing⟩.

originality n. 創造力 chuàngzàolì.

originally adv. 原來 yuánlái, 最初 zuìchū (initially).

originate v. 創始 chuàngshǐ, 發明 fāmíng. — from 來自 láizì.

ornament n. 裝飾品 zhuāngshìpǐn.

ornamental adj. 裝飾的 zhuāngshì de.

orphan n. 孤兒 gū'ér.

orphanage n. 孤兒院 gū'éryuàn.

orthodox adj. ①正教的 zhèngjiào de ⟨religion⟩. ②公認的 gōngrèn de (approved).

orthopedics n. 整形手術 zhěng xíng shǒushù.

oscillate v. 擺動 bǎidòng, 振盪 zhèndàng (vibrate).

ostensible adj. ①表面的

biǎomiàn de (seeming). ②所謂的 suǒwèi de (so-called).

ostentatious adj. 炫耀的 xuànyào de.

osteoporosis n. 骨質疏鬆症 gǔzhì shūsōngzhèng / gǔzhí shūsōngzhèng.

ostrich n. 鴕鳥 tuóniǎo.

other adj. 其他的 qítā de, 別的 bié de.

otherwise adv. 用別的方法 yòng bié de fāngfǎ (using other means), 在其他方面 zài qítā fāngmiàn ⟨differently⟩. — conj. 否則 fǒuzé, 要不然 yàoburán.

otter n. 水獺 shuǐtǎ / shuǐtà.

ought aux. v. 應該 yīnggāi (should).

ounce n. 盎斯 àngsī.

our pron. 我們的 wǒmen de.

ours pron. 我們的 wǒmen de.

ourselves pron. 我們自己 wǒmen zìjǐ ⟨reflexive⟩.

oust v. ①逐出 zhúchū (expel). ②免職 miǎnzhí (unseat).

out adj. 在外 zài wài. to be ~ 不在 bú zài (not present). — adv. 外出 wàichū. — prep. 在……外 zài...wài. ~ of something 在……之外 zài...zhī wài.

outbid v. 出高價 chū gāojià.

outbreak n. 爆發 bàofā (outburst).

outburst n. 爆發 bàofā, 迸發 bèngfā.

outcast n. 被逐出者 bèi zhúchū zhě.

outcome n. 結果 jiéguǒ.

outdo v. 勝過 shèngguo.

outdoor adj. 戶外的 hùwài de.

outdoors adv. 在戶外 zài

hùwài. 在外面 **zài wàimian.**
— n. 戶外 **hùwài.**

outer adj. 外面的 **wàimian de.**
~ **space** 外層空間 **wàicéng
kōngjiān** / 外太空 **wàitàikōng.**

outfit n. 全套裝備 **quántào
zhuāngbèi.**

outgoing adj. ①友善的
yǒushàn de (friendly). ②外出
的 **wàichū de,** 離去的 **líqù de**
(going out).

outgrow v. 長得較大 **zhǎng
de jiào dà.**

outing n. 遠足 **yuǎnzú.**

outlandish adj. 奇異的 **qíyì
de** (strange).

outlaw n. 不法之徒 **bùfǎ zhī
tú,** 歹徒 **dǎitú** (criminal).

outlet n. ①出口 **chūkǒu** (way
out). ②發洩方法 **fāxiè fāngfǎ**
(emotional release).

outline n. 輪廓 **lúnkuò**
(silhouette). 大綱 **dàgāng**
(summary). — v. 概括 **gàikuò.**

outlook n. ①觀點 **guāndiǎn**
(viewpoint). ②展望 **zhǎnwàng**
(future prospect).

outlying adj. 偏僻的 **piānpì
de** (remote).

out-of-date adj. 過時的
guòshí de.

outpatient adj. 門診的
ménzhěn de.

outpost n. 前哨 **qiánshào.**

output n. 輸出 **shūchū,** 產量
chǎnliàng (production).

outrage n. ①粗暴 **cūbào**
(atrocity). ②憤怒 **fènnù** (anger).

outrageous adj. ①粗暴的
cūbào de (atrocious). ②荒謬的
huāngmiù de (ridiculous).

outright adv. ①率直地
shuàizhí de (openly). ②直接
的 **zhíjiē de,** 乾脆 **gāncuì**

(straightforward).

outside n. 外面 **wàimian,** 外側
wàicè. — adj. 在外面的 **zài
wàimian de.** — adv. 在外 **zài
wài.**

outsider n. 局外人 **júwàirén.**

outsize n. 特大號 **tèdàhào.**

outskirts n. 郊外 **jiāowài.**

outspoken adj. 直言的
zhíyán de.

outstanding adj. ①傑出的
jiéchū de, 引人注目的 **yǐn rén
zhùmù de** (great). ②未付的
wèifù de (unpaid).

outstretched adj. ①伸開的
shēnkāi de ⟨thing⟩. ②直躺的
zhítǎng de ⟨person⟩.

outstrip v. 超越 **chāoyuè,**
勝過 **shèngguo.**

outward(s) adj. 向外的
xiàng wài de. — adv. 向外
xiàng wài.

outweigh v. 比……重 **bǐ...
zhòng.**

outwit v. 智取 **zhìqǔ.**

oval n. & adj. 卵形 **luǎnxíng,**
橢圓形 **tuǒyuánxíng.**

ovation n. 熱烈喝采 **rèliè
hècǎi.**

oven n. 烤爐 **kǎolú,** 烤箱
kǎoxiāng.

over adv. & prep. 在……之上
zài...zhī shàng (above). — adj.
結束的 **jiéshù de** (finished).

overall adj. ①全面的
quánmiàn de, 全部的 **quánbù
de** (complete). ②大體上
dàtǐshang (in general).

overboard adv. 落水 **luòshuǐ.**

overcast adj. 陰暗的 **yīn'àn de.**

overcharge v. 索價過高
suǒjià guò gāo.

overcoat n. 大衣 **dàyī,** 外套
wàitào.

O

overcome v. 克服 kèfú (conquer).

overdo v. ①過分 guòfèn, 過火 guòhuǒ (do excessively). ②煮太久 zhǔ tài jiǔ (overcook).

overdraft n. 透支 tòuzhī.

overdraw v. 透支 tòuzhī (make an overdraft).

overdue adj. 過期的 guòqí de / guòqí de.

overgrown adj. 成長過度的 chéngzhǎng guòdù de (having grown too large), 長滿的 zhǎng mǎn de (covered).

overhang n. 突出物 tūchūwù / túchūwù.

overhaul v. 修改 xiūgǎi.

overhead adv. 在上面 zài shàngmian de. — adj. 上面的 shàngmian de — n. 支出 zhīchū (expense).

overhear v. 無意中聽到 wúyìzhōng tīngdào.

overheat v. 過度加熱 guòdù jiārè.

overlap v. 重疊 chóngdié, 重複 chóngfù.

overload v. 超負載 chāo fùzài (overburden).

overlook v. ①看漏 kànlòu, 忽略 hūlüè (ignore). ②俯視 fǔshì, 俯瞰 fǔkàn (look on to).

overnight adj. 夜間的 yèjiān de. — adv. ①一夜之間 yí yè zhījiān (in a short time). ②整夜地 zhěngyè de (for the night).

overpower v. 打敗 dǎbài, 壓倒 yādǎo (overcome).

overrate v. 高估 gāogū.

override v. 藐視 miǎoshì (ignore), 否決 fǒujué (do the opposite of).

overrule v. 推翻 tuīfān, 駁回 bóhuí (disallow).

overrun v. ①蔓延 mànyán (spread over). ②侵占 qīnzhàn, 蹂躪 róulìn (invade).

oversea(s) adv. 在海外 zài hǎiwài, 在外國 zài wàiguó.

oversee v. 監督 jiāndū.

overseer n. 監督者 jiāndūzhě.

oversight n. ①疏忽 shūhu, 失察 shīchá (neglect). ②監督權 jiāndūquán (right to oversee).

oversleep v. 睡過頭 shuìguòtóu.

overstep v. 超越 chāoyuè.

overt adj. 公開的 gōngkāi de.

overtake v. 趕上 gǎnshang, 追及 zhuījí (catch).

overthrow v. 推翻 tuīfān (overturn).

overtime n. 加班時間 jiābān shíjiān.

overture n. ①提議 tíyì (proposal). ②序曲 xùqǔ 〈music〉.

overturn v. 傾覆 qīngfù, 推翻 tuīfān.

overweight adj. 超重的 chāozhòng de. — n. 超重 chāozhòng.

overwhelm v. 壓倒 yādǎo.

overwork v. 工作過度 gōngzuò guòdù.

overwrought adj. 過度緊張的 guòdù jǐnzhāng de (too nervous).

ovum n. 卵 luǎn, 卵細胞 luǎnxìbāo.

owe v. 欠 qiàn, 欠債 qiànzhài.

owing adj. 虧欠的 kuīqiàn de (unpaid).

owl n. 貓頭鷹 māotóuyīng.

own adj. 自己的 zìjǐ de (belonging to oneself). — v. 擁

有 yōngyǒu / yǒngyǒu
(possess).
owner n. 所有者 suǒyǒuzhě.
ownership n. 所有權
suǒyǒuquán.
ox n. 公牛 gōngniú.

oxygen n. 氧氣 yǎngqì.
oyster n. 牡蠣 mǔlì, 蠔 háo.
ozone n. 臭氧 chòuyǎng.
　~ layer 臭氧層
chòuyǎngcéng.

P

pace n. ①步 bù (step). ②速度
sùdù (rate). ③步調 bùdiào
(tempo).
Pacific Ocean 太平洋
Tàipíngyáng.
pacifism n. 和平主義 hépíng
zhǔyì.
pacify v. 撫慰 fǔwèi (comfort),
使平靜 shǐ píngjìng (calm).
pack n. ①包裹 bāoguǒ
(bundle). ②背包 bèibāo /
bēibāo (bag). ③一群 yì qún
(group). － v. ①包裝
bāozhuāng, 打包 dǎbāo (bun-
dle). ②塞滿 sāimǎn (cram).
package n. 包裹 bāoguǒ
(parcel).
packed adj. 擁擠的 yōngjǐ de /
yǒngjǐ de.
packing n. 包裝材料
bāozhuāng cáiliào, 填料
tiánliào (wadding).
pact n. 協定 xiédìng (agreement), 公約 gōngyuē (accord).
pad n. ①墊 diàn, 軟墊
ruǎndiàn (cushion). ②便條紙
biàntiáozhǐ, 拍紙簿 pāizhǐbù
(notebook). － v. 填塞 tiánsāi
(stuff).
paddle v. ①用槳划 yòng jiǎng

huá (row). ②拍打 pāidǎ (hit).
paddock n. 小牧場 xiǎo
mùchǎng, 圍場 wéichǎng.
paddy n. ①水稻 shuǐdào
(rice). ②稻田 dàotián (field).
padlock n. 掛鎖 guàsuǒ.
pagan n. 異教徒 yìjiàotú.
　－ adj. 異教的 yìjiào de.
page n. 頁 yè.
pageant n. ①歷史劇 lìshǐjù
(historical play). ②遊行
yóuxíng, 慶典 qìngdiǎn
(celebration).
pagoda n. 寶塔 bǎotǎ, 浮屠
fútú.
pail n. 桶 tǒng.
pain n. ①痛苦 tòngkǔ, 疼痛
téngtòng (ache). ②辛苦 xīnkǔ
(trouble).
painful adj. 痛苦的 tòngkǔ
de.
painkiller n. 止痛藥
zhǐtòngyào.
paint n. 油漆 yóuqī (for walls),
顏料 yánliào (pigment). － v.
①油漆 yóuqī (wall). ②繪畫
huìhuà (picture).
painter n. ①畫家 huàjiā
(artist). ②油漆匠 yóuqījiàng
(workman).

painting n. 畫 huà, 繪畫 huìhuà.

pair n. 一對 yí duì ⟨living things⟩, 一雙 yì shuāng ⟨inanimate objects⟩.

pajamas n. 睡衣 shuìyī.

pal n. 朋友 péngyou, 夥伴 huǒbàn.

palace n. 宮殿 gōngdiàn, 皇宮 huánggōng.

palatable adj. 可口的 kěkǒu de, 味美的 wèiměi de ⟨delicious⟩.

pale adj. ①蒼白的 cāngbái de ⟨bloodless⟩. ②暗淡的 àndàn de ⟨dim⟩.

palette n. 調色盤 tiáosèpán.

pall n. ①柩衣 jiùyī ⟨mantle⟩. ② 幕罩 mùzhào ⟨covering⟩.

pallid adj. 蒼白的 cāngbái de ⟨pale⟩.

palm n. ①手掌 shǒuzhǎng ⟨hand⟩. ②棕櫚 zōnglǘ ⟨tree⟩.

palmistry n. 手相術 shǒuxiàngshù.

palpable adj. 可觸知的 kě chùzhī de ⟨tangible⟩, 明顯的 míngxiǎn de ⟨clear⟩.

palpitate v. 悸動 jìdòng, 跳動 tiàodòng.

palpitation n. 心悸 xīnjì.

paltry adj. 無價值的 wú jiàzhí de, 微不足道的 wēi-bù-zú-dào de / wéi-bù-zú-dào de ⟨trifling⟩.

pamper v. 縱容 zòngróng.

pamphlet n. 小冊子 xiǎocèzi.

pan n. 平底鍋 píngdǐguō.

panacea n. 萬靈藥 wànlíngyào.

pancake n. 薄煎餅 báojiānbǐng / bójiānbǐng.

pancreas n. 胰臟 yízàng.

panda n. 貓熊 māoxióng.

pandemonium n. 大混亂 dà hùnluàn / dà hǔnluàn ⟨chaos⟩.

pane n. 窗玻璃 chuāngbōli.

panel n. ①方格 fānggé ⟨oblong piece⟩. ②討論小組 tǎolùn xiǎozǔ, 座談小組 zuòtán xiǎozǔ ⟨group⟩.

pang n. 劇痛 jùtòng.

panic n. 恐慌 kǒnghuāng. — adj. 恐慌的 kǒnghuāng de. — v. 使恐慌 shǐ kǒnghuāng.

panorama n. 全景 quánjǐng.

pansy n. 三色菫 sānsèjǐn.

pant n. 喘息 chuǎnxī / chuǎnxí, 喘氣 chuǎnqì. — v. 喘息 chuǎnxī / chuǎnxí, 喘氣 chuǎnqì ⟨gasp⟩.

panther n. 豹 bào.

panties n. 短襯褲 duǎn chènkù.

pantomime n. 啞劇 yǎjù / 默劇 mòjù.

pantry n. ①餐具室 cānjùshì ⟨dishes⟩. ②食品室 shípǐnshì ⟨food⟩.

pants n. 褲子 kùzi.

paparazzo n. 狗仔隊 gǒuzǎiduì.

paper n. ①紙 zhǐ ⟨material⟩. ②(pl.) 文件 wénjiàn ⟨document⟩. ③報紙 bàozhǐ ⟨newspaper⟩. ④論文 lùnwén ⟨thesis⟩, 報告 bàogào ⟨report⟩. — v. 糊紙 hú zhǐ.

paperback n. 平裝本 píngzhuāngběn.

paperweight n. 書鎮 shūzhèn.

paperwork n. 文書工作 wénshū gōngzuò.

paprika n. ①乾辣椒 gānlàjiāo ⟨pepper⟩. ②辣椒粉 làjiāofěn ⟨powder⟩.

par n. ①標準 biāozhǔn, 常態

chángtài (average). ②同等
tóngděng, 同價 tóngjià
(parity). ③標準桿數 biāozhǔn
gǎnshù 〈golf〉.

parable n. 寓言 yùyán, 譬語
pìyù.

parachute n. 降落傘
jiàngluòsǎn.

parachutist n. 傘兵 sǎnbīng.

parade n. ①遊行 yóuxíng
(procession). ②閱兵 yuèbīng
〈military〉. — v. ①遊行 yóuxíng
(march). ②誇耀 kuāyào
(display).

paradigm n. 模範 mófàn, 範
典 fàndiǎn.

paradise n. 天堂 tiāntáng
(heaven), 樂園 lèyuán (fantasy
land).

paradox n. 似非而是的議論
sì fēi ér shì de yìlùn, 自相矛
盾的話 zì xiāng máodùn de
huà.

paraffin n. 石蠟 shílà.

paragraph n. 段 duàn, 節 jié,
段落 duànluò.

parallel adj. 平行的 píngxíng
de. — v. 與……平行 yǔ...
píngxíng.

paralysis n. 麻痺 mábì, 癱瘓
tānhuàn.

paralytic adj. 麻痺的 mábì
de, 癱瘓的 tānhuàn de.

paralyze v. 使麻痺 shǐ mábì,
使癱瘓 shǐ tānhuàn.

paramount adj. 最高的 zuì
gāo de, 卓越的 zhuóyuè de /
zhuóyuè de.

paranoia n. 偏執狂
piānzhíkuáng, 妄想症
wàngxiǎngzhèng.

paranoid adj. 偏執狂的
piānzhíkuáng de. — n. 偏執狂
患者 piānzhíkuáng huànzhě.

paraphernalia n. 小用品
xiǎo yòngpǐn, 小用具 xiǎo
yòngjù (article).

paraphrase n. & v. 意譯 yìyì.

parasite n. 寄生蟲
jìshēngchóng.

parasol n. 陽傘 yángsǎn 〈um-
brella〉.

paratrooper n. 傘兵
sǎnbīng.

paratroops n. 傘兵部隊
sǎnbīng bùduì.

parcel n. 包裹 bāoguǒ, 小包
xiǎobāo (package). — v. 分配
fēnpèi.

parch v. 烘乾 hōnggān, 烤乾
kǎogān (toast under dry heat).

parchment n. 羊皮紙
yángpízhǐ.

pardon n. & v. ①寬恕
kuānshù, 原諒 yuánliàng
(forgiveness). ②赦免 shèmiǎn
(absolution).

pare v. ①剝 bāo, 削皮 xiāopí
(peel). ②削減 xuējiǎn /
xuējiǎn (cut).

parent n. 父或母 fù huò mǔ.

parents n. 父母親 fùmǔqīn,
雙親 shuāngqīn (father and
mother).

parentage n. 出身 chūshēn,
家世 jiāshì.

parenthesis n. 括弧 kuòhú /
guāhú.

parish n. 教區 jiàoqū.

park n. ①公園 gōngyuán
(public garden). ②運動場
yùndòngchǎng (sports ground).
— v. 停車 tíngchē.

parking n. 停車 tíngchē 〈car〉.
~ *lot* 停車場 tíngchēchǎng.

parley n. & v. 談判 tánpàn.

parliament n. 國會 guóhuì,
議院 yìyuàn.

parlor *n.* 客廳 kètīng, 會客室 huìkèshì.

parody *n.* 諷刺詩文 fěngcì shīwén / fèngcì shīwén.

parole *n.* & *v.* 假釋 jiǎshì.

parrot *n.* 鸚鵡 yīngwǔ.

parry *v.* 避開 bìkāi, 擋開 dǎngkāi.

parse *v.* 分析 fēnxī.

parsimonious *adj.* 吝嗇的 lìnsè de.

parsley *n.* 荷蘭芹 hélánqín, 西洋芹 xīyángqín.

parson *n.* 教區牧師 jiàoqū mùshi.

part *n.* ①部分 bùfen (portion). ②角色 juésè (role). ③臺詞 táicí (lines). ④地區 dìqū (area). — *v.* 分開 fēnkāi (separate from).

partake *v.* ①參與 cānyù (participate). ②分擔 fēndān, 分享 fēnxiǎng (share).

partial *adj.* ①部分的 bùfen de (incomplete). ②偏袒的 piāntǎn de (not fair). ③偏愛的 piān'ài de (favoring).

partially *adv.* ①部分地 bùfen de (partly). ②偏袒地 piāntǎn de (prejudicially).

participant *n.* 參與者 cānyùzhě.

participate *v.* 參與 cānyù (take part), 參加 cānjiā (join).

participle *n.* 分詞 fēncí.

particle *n.* ①微粒 wēilì / wéilì, 粒子 lìzi (small grains), 分子 fēnzǐ (small piece). ②質詞 zhìcí / zhící, 冠詞 guàncí 〈grammar〉.

particular *adj.* ①獨特的 dútè de (distinct). ②特別的 tèbié de (special). ③挑剔的 tiāoti de (choosy). — *n.* 細節

xìjié (detail).

particularly *adv.* 特別地 tèbié de.

partisan *n.* 有偏見的 yǒu piānjiàn de.

partition *n.* 分割 fēngē, 瓜分 guāfēn (separation).

partly *adv.* 部分地 bùfen de.

partner *n.* 夥伴 huǒbàn (companion), 合夥人 héhuǒrén 〈business〉.

partnership *n.* 合夥 héhuǒ.

partridge *n.* 山鶉 shānchún, 鷓鴣 zhègū.

part-time *adj.* 兼任的 jiānrèn de.

party *n.* ①聚會 jùhuì, 宴會 yànhuì (social gathering). ②政黨 zhèngdǎng 〈politics〉.

pass *v.* ①經過 jīngguò, 通過 tōngguò (go by). ②傳給 chuángěi (hand over). ③及格 jígé (approve). — *n.* 通行證 tōngxíngzhèng (permit).

passable *adj.* ①可接受的 kě jiēshòu de (acceptable). ②可通過的 kě tōngguò de (unblocked).

passage *n.* ①通道 tōngdào, 走廊 zǒuláng (hallway). ②航行 hángxíng (voyage).

passenger *n.* 乘客 chéngkè, 旅客 lǚkè.

passion *n.* 熱情 rèqíng.

passionate *adj.* 熱情的 rèqíng de.

passive *adj.* 被動的 bèidòng de.

passport *n.* 護照 hùzhào.

password *n.* ①密碼 mìmǎ 〈machine〉. ②口令 kǒulìng (secret word).

past *adj.* 過去的 guòqù de (past time).

pasta *n.* 麵糰 miàntuán.

paste *n.* 漿糊 jiànghu.

pastel *n.* 蠟筆 làbǐ.

pastime *n.* 娛樂 yúlè, 消遣 xiāoqiǎn.

pastor *n.* 牧師 mùshi.

pastry *n.* 糕餅 gāobǐng.

pasture *n.* 牧場 mùchǎng, 牧草地 mùcǎodì.

pasty *adj.* ①糊狀的 húzhuàng de (like paste). ②蒼白的 cāngbái de (pale).

pat *v.* 輕拍 qīngpāi.

patch *n.* 補綻 bǔzhàn. — *v.* 補綴 bǔzhuì.

patent *adj.* 專利的 zhuānlì de. — *n.* 專利 zhuānlì. — *v.* 取得專利 qǔdé zhuānlì.

paternal *adj.* 父親的 fùqīn de, 父系的 fùxì de.

paternity *n.* 父系 fùxì. ~ *leave* 陪產假 péichǎnjià.

path *n.* 小徑 xiǎojìng, 小路 xiǎolù.

pathetic *adj.* 悲慘的 bēicǎn de.

pathology *n.* 病理學 bìnglǐxué.

pathos *n.* 悲哀 bēi'āi.

patience *n.* 耐心 nàixīn.

patient *adj.* 有耐心的 yǒu nàixīn de. — *n.* 病人 bìngrén.

patriarch *n.* 元老 yuánlǎo, 族長 zúzhǎng.

patriot *n.* 愛國者 àiguózhě.

patriotic *adj.* 愛國的 àiguó de.

patriotism *n.* 愛國心 àiguóxīn.

patrol *n.* ①巡邏 xúnluó (watch). ②巡邏者 xúnluózhě (watch-man). — *v.* 巡邏 xúnluó.

patron *n.* ①資助人 zīzhùrén (sponsor). ②顧客 gùkè (cus-tomer).

patronize *v.* ①光顧 guānggù, 惠顧 huìgù ⟨shop⟩. ②高高在上 gāogāo-zài-shàng (talk down to). ③資助 zīzhù, 贊助 zànzhù (support).

patter *n.* 急速輕拍聲 jísù qīngpāishēng.

pattern *n.* ①花樣 huāyàng, 樣式 yàngshì (design). ②模範 mófàn, 樣本 yàngběn (model).

paunch *n.* 大肚子 dà dùzi.

pause *n.* 中止 zhōngzhǐ.

pave *v.* 鋪 pū.

pavement *n.* 人行道 rénxíngdào.

pavilion *n.* 亭 tíng, 閣 gé.

paw *n.* 足掌 zúzhǎng, 爪 zhuǎ.

pawn *v.* 典當 diǎndàng, 質押 zhìyā.

pawnshop *n.* 當鋪 dàngpù.

pay *v.* 付 fù, 支付 zhīfù. — *n.* 報酬 bàochóu.

payable *adj.* ①可支付的 kě zhīfù de (may be paid). ②應支付的 yīng zhīfù de (must be paid).

payday *n.* 發薪日 fāxīnrì.

payee *n.* 收款人 shōukuǎnrén.

payer *n.* 付款人 fùkuǎnrén.

payment *n.* ①支付 zhīfù (paying). ②支付金額 zhīfù jīn'é (amount of money).

PC 個人機 gèrénjī / 個人電腦 gèrén diànnǎo (personal computer).

PDA 個人電腦助理 gèrén diànnǎo zhùlǐ / 個人數位助理 gèrén shùwèi zhùlǐ (personal digital assistant).

pea *n.* 豌豆 wāndòu.

peace *n.* 和平 hépíng.

peaceful *adj.* 和平的 hépíng de.

peacemaker n. 調停人 tiáotíngrén.

peach n. ①桃子 táozi ⟨fruit⟩. ②桃樹 táoshù ⟨tree⟩.

peacock n. 孔雀 kǒngquè.

peak n. 山頂 shāndǐng, 山峰 shānfēng.

peanut n. 花生 huāshēng.

pear n. ①梨 lí ⟨fruit⟩. ②梨樹 líshù ⟨tree⟩.

pearl n. 珍珠 zhēnzhū.

peasant n. 農夫 nóngfū, 佃農 diànnóng.

peasantry n. 農夫 nóngfū.

peat n. 泥煤 níméi (turf).

pebble n. 小圓石 xiǎo yuánshí, 卵石 luǎnshí.

peck v. 啄 zhuó.

peculiar adj. ①特有的 tèyǒu de (special). ②奇怪的 qíguài de, 奇異的 qíyì de (strange).

peculiarity n. ①特性 tèxìng, 特色 tèsè (characteristic). ②怪癖 guàipǐ, 怪異 guàiyì (oddity).

pecuniary adj. 金錢上的 jīnqiánshang de.

pedagogy n. 教育學 jiàoyùxué.

pedal n. 踏板 tàbǎn.

pedant n. 迂腐學儒 yūfǔ xuérú.

pedantic adj. 迂儒的 yūrú de, 賣弄學問的 màinong xuéwèn de.

peddle v. 沿街叫賣 yánjiē jiàomài (hawk).

peddler n. 小販 xiǎofàn.

pedestal n. 基座 jīzuò.

pedestrian n. 步行者 bùxíngzhě, 行人 xíngrén.

pediatrics n. 小兒科 xiǎo'érkē.

pedigree n. 系譜 xìpǔ, 家系 jiāxì.

peek n. & v. 偷看 tōukàn.

peel n. 果皮 guǒpí. — v. 剝皮 bāopí.

peep n. & v. 偷看 tōukàn, 窺視 kuīshì (peek).

peer n. 同輩 tóngbèi, 同儕 tóngchái. ~ pressure 同儕壓力 tóngchái yālì. — v. 凝視 níngshì.

peevish adj. 脾氣暴躁的 píqì bàozào de.

peg n. 木釘 mùdìng. — v. 釘住 dìngzhù.

pelican n. 鵜鶘 tíhú.

pellet n. ①小球 xiǎoqiú (small ball). ②小彈丸 xiǎo dànwán ⟨gun⟩. ③藥丸 yàowán (pill).

pelt n. 毛皮 máopí.

pelvis n. 骨盆 gǔpén.

pen n. 筆 bǐ. ~ pal 筆友 bǐyǒu.

penal adj. 刑罰的 xíngfá de.

penalize v. 處罰 chǔfá.

penalty n. ①刑罰 xíngfá (punishment). ②罰金 fájīn (fine). ③判罰 pànfá ⟨sports⟩.

penance n. 懺悔 chànhuǐ, 贖罪 shúzuì.

pencil n. 鉛筆 qiānbǐ.

pendant n. 垂飾 chuíshì.

pending adj. ①未決定的 wèi juédìng de (not yet decided). ②待解決的 dài jiějué de (not yet settled).

pendulum n. 鐘擺 zhōngbǎi.

penetrate v. ①穿透 chuāntòu (bore through). ②滲透 shèntòu (spread through). ③洞察 dòngchá (see through). ④滲入 shènrù (infiltrate).

penguin n. 企鵝 qǐ'é / qǐé.

penicillin n. 盤尼西林 pánníxīlín.

peninsula n. 半島 bàndǎo.

penis n. 陰莖 yīnjīng.

penitence n. 懺悔 chànhuǐ.

penknife n. 小刀 xiǎodāo.

penniless adj. 身無分文的 shēn-wú-fēn-wén de.

penny n. ①便士 biànshì 〈British coin〉.②一分 yì fēn (cent).

pension n. 養老金 yǎnglǎojīn (subsidy), 退休金 tuìxiūjīn (retirement pay).

pensive adj. 沈思的 chénsī de.

pentagon n. 五角形 wǔjiǎoxíng.

penthouse n. 閣樓 gélóu, 頂樓公寓 dǐnglóu gōngyù.

people n. ①人們 rénmen (persons).②民族 mínzú (race).

pepper n. 胡椒 hújiāo.

peppermint n. 薄荷 bòhe.

per prep. 每 měi.

perceive v. 感覺 gǎnjué (feel), 察覺 chájué (see).

percent n. 百分比 bǎifēnbǐ.

percentage n. 百分率 bǎifēnlǜ.

perceptible adj. ①可察覺的 kě chájué de (noticeable).②明顯的 míngxiǎn de.

perception n. 感覺 gǎnjué, 知覺 zhījué.

perceptive adj. 知覺的 zhījué de.

perch n. 棲木 qīmù 〈branch〉. — v. 棲息 qīxí / qíxí (rest).

percolate v. 過濾 guòlǜ.

percussion n. 衝擊 chōngjí / chōngjí, 碰撞 pèngzhuàng.

perdition n. 地獄 dìyù (hell).

perennial adj. 永久的 yǒngjiǔ de. — n. 多年生植物 duōniánshēng zhíwù.

perfect adj. ①完美的 wánměi

de, 理想的 lǐxiǎng de (faultless).②完全的 wánquán de (complete).

perfection n. ①完美 wánměi (faultlessness).②完全 wánquán (completeness).

perfectly adv. 完全地 wánquán de (completely).

perforate v. 穿孔 chuānkǒng, 打洞 dǎdòng.

perform v. ①實行 shíxíng, 履行 lǚxíng (carry out).②表演 biǎoyǎn (act).

performance n. ①表演 biǎoyǎn (acting).②實行 shíxíng, 履行 lǚxíng (carrying out).

performer n. 表演者 biǎoyǎnzhě, 演出者 yǎnchūzhě.

perfume n. ①香味 xiāngwèi (fragrant smell).②香水 xiāngshuǐ 〈liquid〉.

perhaps adv. 或許 huòxǔ, 可能 kěnéng.

peril n. 危險 wēixiǎn / wéixiǎn.

perimeter n. 周邊 zhōubiān, 周圍 zhōuwéi (periphery).

period n. ①時期 shíqí / shíqí, 期間 qíjiān / qíjiān 〈time〉. ②句點 jùdiǎn (full stop).

periodical n. 期刊 qíkān / qíkān. — adj. 定期的 dìngqí de / dìngqí de.

periphery n. 周圍 zhōuwéi.

periscope n. 潛望鏡 qiánwàngjìng.

perish v. 死 sǐ, 死亡 sǐwáng (die).

peritonitis n. 腹膜炎 fùmóyán / fùmòyán.

perjure v. 做偽證 zuò wěizhèng / zuò wēizhèng 〈law〉.

perm n. & v. 燙髮 tàngfà / tàngfǎ.

permanence n. 永恆 yǒnghéng, 永久 yǒngjiǔ.

permanent adj. 永久的 yǒngjiǔ de.

permeate v. 瀰漫 mímàn, 滲透 shèntòu.

permissible adj. 可容許的 kě róngxǔ de.

permission n. 許可 xǔkě, 允許 yǔnxǔ.

permissive adj. ①縱容的 zòngróng de (allowing too much freedom). ②准許的 zhǔnxǔ de (permissible).

permit v. 允許 yǔnxǔ, 准許 zhǔnxǔ. — n. 許可證 xǔkězhèng.

pernicious adj. 有害的 yǒuhài de.

perpendicular adj. ①垂直的 chuízhí de (vertical). ②成直角的 chéng zhíjiǎo de (angle). — n. 垂直線 chuízhíxiàn.

perpetrate v. 犯罪 fànzuì, 作惡 zuò'è.

perpetual adj. ①不斷的 búduàn de (continual). ②永久的 yǒngjiǔ de (permanent).

perpetuate v. 使永久 shǐ yǒngjiǔ.

perpetuity n. 永久 yǒngjiǔ (eternity).

perplex v. 使迷惑 shǐ míhuo.

persecute v. 迫害 pòhài.

perseverance n. 堅忍 jiānrěn.

persevere v. 堅忍 jiānrěn, 堅持 jiānchí.

persimmon n. ①柿子 shìzi (fruit). ②柿子樹 shìzishù (tree).

persist v. 堅持 jiānchí, 固執 gùzhí.

persistent adj. 堅持的 jiānchí

de (persevering), 固執的 gùzhí de (stubborn).

person n. 人 rén.

personal adj. ①個人的 gèrén de, 私人的 sīrén de (private). ②本人的 běnrén de, 親自的 qīnzì de (in person).
~ computer 個人機 gèrénjī / 個人電腦 gèrén diànnǎo.

personality n. ①個性 gèxìng, 性格 xìnggé (character). ②名人 míngrén (celebrity).

personally adv. 親自地 qīnzì de.

personify v. 擬人化 nǐrénhuà.

personnel n. (pl.) 全體人員 quántǐ rényuán.

perspective n. ①透視法 tòushìfǎ (art). ②遠景 yuǎnjǐng (outlook).

perspire v. 流汗 liúhàn.

persuade v. 說服 shuōfú / shuìfú, 勸服 quànfú.

persuasion n. ①說服 shuōfú / shuìfú (persuading). ②確信 quèxìn (belief).

persuasive adj. 有說服力的 yǒu shuōfúlì de / yǒu shuìfúlì de.

pert adj. ①冒失的 màoshī de, 魯莽的 lǔmǎng de (impertinent). ②活潑的 huópo de (lively).

pertain v. ①有關 yǒuguān (be connected with). ②屬於 shǔyú (belong to).

pertinent adj. ①有關的 yǒuguān de (relevant to). ②適切的 shìqiè de (to the point).

perturb v. 擾亂 rǎoluàn, 使不安 shǐ bù'ān.

pervade v. 瀰漫 mímàn, 遍及 biànjí.

perverse adj. 乖張的

guāizhāng de, 倔強的
juéjiàng de.

perversion n. ①曲解 qūjiě
(distortion). ②倒錯 dǎocuò /
dàocuò (abnormality).

perversity n. 乖僻 guāipì, 倔
強 juéjiàng.

pervert v. ①曲解 qūjiě (distort). ②使墮落 shǐ duòluò (go
astray). — n. 變態 biàntài.

pessimism n. 悲觀 bēiguān.

pessimist n. 悲觀者
bēiguānzhě.

pest n. ①令人討厭者 lìng rén
tǎoyàn zhě (annoyance). ②害
蟲 hàichóng (insect).

pester v. 煩擾 fánrǎo.

pesticide n. 殺蟲劑
shāchóngjì.

pet n. 伴侶動物 bànlǚ
dòngwù, 安慰動物 ānwèi
dòngwù / 寵物 chǒngwù
(animal). — v. 愛撫 àifǔ.

petal n. 花瓣 huābàn.

petition n. 請願 qǐngyuàn, 陳情
chénqíng.

petrify v. ①使石化 shǐ shíhuà
(change into stone). ②嚇呆
xiàdāi (terrify).

petrol n. 汽油 qìyóu.

petroleum n. 石油 shíyóu.

petticoat n. 襯裙 chènqún.

petty adj. ①不重要的 bú
zhòngyào de (unimportant).
②心胸狹窄的 xīnxiōng
xiázhǎi de (small-minded).

petulant adj. 易怒的 yìnù de.

pew n. 教堂長凳 jiàotáng
chángdèng.

phantom n. ①幽靈 yōulíng
(ghost). ②幻影 huànyǐng
(illusion).

Pharaoh n. 法老 Fǎlǎo.

pharmacology n. 藥物學

yàowùxué.

pharmacy n. 藥房 yàofáng.

phase n. 階段 jiēduàn, 時期
shíqí / shíqí (stage).

pheasant n. 雉 zhì.

phenomenal adj. 驚人的
jīngrén de (extraordinary).

phenomenon n. ①現象
xiànxiàng (event). ②特殊的人
tèshū de rén (very unusual
person).

philosopher n. 哲學家
zhéxuéjiā.

philosophical adj. ①哲學的
zhéxué de (of philosophy).
②冷靜的 lěngjìng de (calm).

philosophy n. 哲學 zhéxué,
哲理 zhélǐ.

phlegm n. 痰 tán.

phlegmatic adj. 遲鈍的
chídùn de.

phobia n. 恐懼 kǒngjù.

phone n. 電話 diànhuà. ~ card
電話磁卡 diànhuà cíkǎ / 電話
卡 diànhuàkǎ. — v. 打電話
dǎdiànhuà.

phone booth n. 公共電話亭
gōnggòng diànhuàtíng.

phoneme n. 音素 yīnsù.

phonetic adj. 語音的 yǔyīn
de.

phonetics n. 語音學
yǔyīnxué.

phoney adj. 假的 jiǎ de (fake),
偽造的 wěizào de / wèizào
de (false). — n. 贋品 yànpǐn.

phosphorescence n. 磷光
línguāng.

phosphorus n. 磷 lín.

photo n. 照片 zhàopiàn, 相片
xiàngpiàn.

photocopy n. 影印本
yǐngyìnběn. — v. 影印 yǐngyìn.

photogenic adj. 上鏡頭的

shàng jìngtóu de.
photograph n. 照片 zhàopiàn, 相片 xiàngpiàn.
— v. 照相 zhàoxiàng ⟨still⟩, 攝影 shèyǐng ⟨movies⟩.
photographer n. 攝影家 shèyǐngjiā.
photography n. 攝影術 shèyǐngshù.
phrase n. ①片語 piànyǔ ⟨grammar⟩. ②措辭 cuòcí ⟨expression⟩.
physical adj. ①身體的 shēntǐ de (bodily). ②物質的 wùzhì de / wùzhí de (material).
physician n. 內科醫生 nèikē yīshēng.
physicist n. 物理學家 wùlǐxué jiā.
physics n. 物理學 wùlǐxué.
physiology n. 生理學 shēnglǐxué.
physique n. 體格 tǐgé.
pianist n. 鋼琴家 gāngqínjiā, 鋼琴師 gāngqínshī.
piano n. 鋼琴 gāngqín.
pick v. ①挑選 tiāoxuǎn (select). ②採, 摘 cǎi, zhāi (pluck).
picket n. ①尖椿 jiānzhuāng (stake). ②哨兵 shàobīng, 步哨 bùshào ⟨soldier⟩. — v. 站哨 糾察 zhànshào jiūchá (demonstrate).
pickle n. 醃汁 yānzhī (brine). — v. 醃 yān.
pickpocket n. 扒手 páshǒu.
picnic n. 野餐 yěcān.
pictorial adj. 圖畫的 túhuà de.
picture n. ①畫 huà, 圖畫 túhuà (painting). ②照片 zhàopiàn (photograph). — v. ①描繪 miáohuì (portray). ②想像 xiǎngxiàng (imagine).

picturesque adj. 如畫的 rúhuà de (charming).
pidgin n. 洋涇濱語 yángjīngbāngyǔ / yángjīngbīnyǔ.
pie n. 餡餅 xiànbǐng, 派 pài.
piece n. ①片 piàn (slice), 塊 kuài (chip). ②部分 bùfen (part). ③一首 yì shǒu ⟨music⟩. ④一篇 yì piān ⟨article⟩.
piecemeal adv. ①逐漸地 zhújiàn de (little by little). ②零碎地 língsuì de, 片斷地 piànduàn de (piece by piece).
pier n. 碼頭 mǎtou.
pierce v. 戳入 chuōrù, 刺 cì (penetrate).
piety n. 虔敬 qiánjìng, 虔誠 qiánchéng.
pig n. 豬 zhū.
pigeon n. 鴿子 gēzi.
pigment n. ①顏料 yánliào ⟨colored powder⟩. ②色素 sèsù ⟨natural coloring matter⟩.
pike n. 矛 máo (long-handled spear).
pile n. ①一堆 yì duī (heap). ②椿 zhuāng (post). — v. 堆積 duījī, 堆起 duīqǐ (heap).
pilfer v. 扒竊 páqiè, 偷竊 tōuqiè.
pilgrim n. 朝聖者 cháoshèngzhě.
pilgrimage n. 朝聖旅程 cháoshèng lǚchéng.
pill n. 藥丸 yàowán.
pillage n. & v. 掠奪 lüèduó, 劫掠 jiélüè.
pillar n. 柱子 zhùzi (staff).
pillow n. 枕頭 zhěntou.
pillowcase n. 枕頭套 zhěntoutào.
pilot n. ①駕駛員 jiàshǐyuán (airman). ②領航員 lǐnghángyuán (navigator). — v.

pimple n. 粉刺 fěncì, 青春痘 qīngchūndòu.

pin n. 大頭針 dàtóuzhēn, 別針 biézhēn (tack).

pincers n. (pl.) 鉗子 qiánzi (pliers).

pinch n. 捏 niē, 夾 jiā / jiá (nip).

pine n. ①松樹 sōngshù (tree). ②松木 sōngmù (wood).

pineapple n. 鳳梨 fènglí.

pinhole n. 針孔 zhēnkǒng.

pinion n. 翼 yì, 翅膀 chìbǎng (wing). — v. 束縛 shùfù / shùfú.

pink n. & adj. 粉紅色 fěnhóngsè.

pinnacle n. ①尖頂 jiāndǐng, 尖峰 jiānfēng (peak). ②尖塔 jiāntǎ (spire).

pinpoint n. 針尖 zhēnjiān (point of a pin).

pint n. 品脫 pǐntuō.

pioneer n. 拓荒者 tuòhuāngzhě (first settler), 先鋒 xiānfēng (forerunner). — v. 開拓 kāituò, 作先鋒 zuò xiānfēng.

pious adj. 虔誠的 qiánchéng de.

pipe n. ①管 guǎn (tube). ②煙斗 yāndǒu (for smoking).

piquant adj. ①開胃的 kāiwèi de (tasty). ②辛辣的 xīnlà de (spicy). ③有趣的 yǒuqù de (interesting).

piracy n. ①海上搶劫 hǎi shàng qiǎngjié (ships). ②盜版 dàobǎn (software).

pirate n. 海盜 hǎidào (freebooter). — v. 盜印 dàoyìn (print illegally), 侵害著作權 qīnhài zhùzuòquán (infringe on copyright).

Pisces n. 雙魚座 Shuāngyúzuò.

pistol n. 手槍 shǒuqiāng.

piston n. 活塞 huósāi.

pit n. 坑 kēng (hole).

pitch v. ①紮營 zháyíng / zháyíng (tent). ②投擲 tóuzhì / tóuzhí (throw). — n. ①投擲 tóuzhì / tóuzhí (throwing). ②傾斜度 qīngxiédù (slope).

pitcher n. ①水罐 shuǐguàn (jug). ②投手 tóushǒu (baseball).

piteous adj. 可憐的 kělián de.

pitfall n. 陷阱 xiànjǐng, 圈套 quāntào (trap).

pith n. 髓 suǐ.

pitiable adj. 可憐的 kělián de.

pitiful adj. 可憐的 kělián de.

pitiless adj. 無情的 wúqíng de, 無憐憫心的 wú liánmǐnxīn de.

pittance n. 微薄收入 wēibó shōurù / wéibó shōurù.

pity n. 憐憫 liánmǐn, 同情 tóngqíng.

pivot n. 旋軸 xuánzhóu, 樞軸 shūzhóu (swivel). — v. 以軸為中心旋轉 yǐ zhóu wéi zhōngxīn xuánzhuǎn.

pixy n. 小精靈 xiǎo jīnglíng.

pizza n. 皮雜餅 pízábǐng / 披薩 pīsà, 義大利薄餡餅 yìdàlì bó xiànbǐng.

placard n. 招貼 zhāotiē.

placate v. 撫慰 fǔwèi.

place n. ①地方 dìfang (area), 場所 chǎngsuǒ (location). ②地點 dìdiǎn (point). — v. 放 fàng, 置放 zhìfàng (put).

placenta n. 胎盤 tāipán.

placid adj. ①平靜的 píngjìng de (calm). ②溫和的 wēnhé de (even-tempered).

plague n. 瘟疫 wēnyì.

plaid n. 格子呢 gézíní.

plain adj. ①清楚的 qīngchu

P

de, 明白的 míngbai de (clear).
②平淡的 píngdàn de, 簡單的
jiǎndān de (ordinary).

plaint n. 悲歎 bēitàn, 訴苦
sùkǔ (lament).

plaintiff n. 原告 yuángào.

plait n. 髮辮 fàbiàn / fàbiàn
(braid). — v. 編成辮
biānchéng biàn (braid).

plan n. ①計畫 jìhuà, 方案
fāng'àn (project). ②設計圖
shèjìtú (diagram). — v. ①計畫
jìhuà, 打算 dǎsuan (intend).
②設計 shèjì (design).

plane n. ①飛機 fēijī (airplane).
②平面 píngmiàn (level).

planet n. 行星 xíngxīng.

planetarium n. 天文館
tiānwénguǎn (building).

plank n. 厚板 hòubǎn (board).

plankton n. 浮游生物 fúfóu
shēngwù.

plant n. ①植物 zhíwù (living).
②工廠 gōngchǎng (factory).
— v. 栽種 zāizhòng, 種植
zhòngzhí (sow).

plantation n. ①農場
nóngchǎng (farm). ②植林地
zhílíndì (for trees).

plaque n. 匾額 biǎn'é, 牌匾
páibiǎn.

plaster n. 灰泥 huīní.

plastic adj. 塑料的 sùliào de /
塑膠的 sùjiāo de. — n. 塑料
sùliào / 塑膠 sùjiāo.

plate n. 盤 pán, 碟 dié (dish).

plateau n. 高原 gāoyuán, 高
地 gāodì (tableland).

platform n. ①講臺 jiǎngtái
(podium). ②月台 yuètái (station).

platinum n. 白金 báijīn.
— adj. 白金的 báijīn de.

platitude n. 陳腔濫調

chénqiāng-làndiào.

platoon n. 排 pái, 小隊
xiǎoduì.

plausible adj. 似合理的 sì
hélǐ de (reasonable).

play n. ①遊戲 yóuxì, 遊玩
yóuwán (amusement). ②戲劇
xìjù (drama). — v. ①玩 wán
(have fun). ②扮演 bànyǎn
(act). ③彈奏 tánzòu, 演奏
yǎnzòu (perform). ④比賽 bǐsài
(compete).

playboy n. 花花公子 huāhuā
gōngzǐ.

playful adj. 好嬉戲的 hào
xīxì de.

playground n. 遊樂場
yóulèchǎng.

playmate n. 玩伴 wánbàn,
遊伴 yóubàn.

plea n. ①辯解 biànjiě, 抗辯
kàngbiàn (appeal). ②懇求
kěnqiú (request).

plead v. ①辯護 biànhù
(appeal). ②懇求 kěnqiú
(request).

pleasant adj. 愉快的 yúkuài
de.

pleasantry n. 幽默 yōumò,
詼諧 huīxié (humorous
remark).

please v. ①使高興 shǐ
gāoxìng, 取悅 qǔyuè (amuse).
②請 qǐng (request politely).

pleasure n. ①快樂 kuàilè
(enjoyment). ②樂趣 lèqù
(amusement).

pleat n. 褶 zhé. — v. 打褶
dǎzhé.

pledge n. ①抵押品 dǐyāpǐn
(surety). ②誓言 shìyán, 誓約
shìyuē (vow). — v. 發誓 fāshì,
保證 bǎozhèng (guarantee).

plentiful adj. 豐富的 fēngfù

plenty n. 豐富 fēngfù, 充分 chōngfèn de, 充分的 chōngfèn de.

plenty n. 豐富 fēngfù, 充分 chōngfèn (fullness).

pliable adj. ①易曲的 yì qū de (bendable). ②易受影響的 yì shòu yǐngxiǎng de (easily led).

pliers n. 鉗子 qiánzi.

plight n. 處境 chǔjìng, 情況 qíngkuàng.

plod v. ①蹣跚而行 pánshān ér xíng, 重步行走 zhòngbù xíngzǒu (trudge). ②孜孜從事 zīzī cóngshì (work).

plot n. ①陰謀 yīnmóu (plan). ②情節 qíngjié (story). ③小塊地 xiǎo kuài dì (small piece of land). — v. ①圖謀 túmóu, 密謀 mìmóu (collude). ②製……之圖 zhī tú (chart).

plow n. 犁 lí.

ploy n. 策略 cèlüè.

pluck v. ①摘 zhāi, 採 cǎi (pick). ②拉 lā (pull).

plug n. ①塞子 sāizi (stopper). ②插頭 chātóu ‹electrical›. — v. 塞住 sāizhù ‹block›.

plum n. ①李樹 lǐshù, 梅樹 méishù ‹tree›. ②李子 lǐzi, 梅子 méizi ‹fruit›.

plumage n. 羽毛 yǔmáo (feathers).

plumb n. 鉛錘 qiānchuí. — adj. ①垂直的 chuízhí de (vertical). ②完全的 wánquán de (absolute).

plumber n. 鉛管工人 qiānguǎn gōngrén.

plummet n. 鉛錘 qiānchuí. — v. 垂直落下 chuízhí luòxià.

plump adj. 圓胖的 yuánpàng de.

plunder v. 掠奪 lüèduó. — n. 掠奪物 lüèduówù.

plunge v. ①跳進 tiàojìn (fall into). ②投入 tóurù, 陷入 xiànrù (put into).

plural adj. 複數的 fùshù de. — n. 複數 fùshù ‹grammar›.

plus prep. 加 jiā, 加上 jiāshang.

plush n. 絲絨 sīróng.

plutonium n. 鈽 bù.

ply v. ①定期來回 dìngqī láihuí / dìngqí láihuí (go back and forth regularly). ②經營 jīngyíng, 從事 cóngshì (work).

plywood n. 三夾板 sānjiābǎn / sānjiábǎn, 合板 hébǎn.

p.m., P.M. adj. & adv. 下午 xiàwǔ, 午後 wǔhòu.

pneumonia n. 肺炎 fèiyán.

pock n. 痘痕 dòuhén, 麻子 mázi, 痘疱 dòupào.

pocket n. 口袋 kǒudài, 衣袋 yīdài.

pod n. 豆莢 dòujiá (beans).

poem n. 詩 shī, 韻文 yùnwén.

poet n. 詩人 shīrén. ~ **laureate** 桂冠詩人 guìguān shīrén.

poetic adj. 詩的 shī de, 詩意的 shīyì de.

poetry n. 詩 shī, 詩歌 shīgē.

poignant adj. ①痛切的 tòngqiè de (painful). ②深刻的 shēnkè de (deeply moving).

point n. ①尖端 jiānduān (sharp end). ②點 diǎn (dot). ③地點 dìdiǎn (place). ④要點 yàodiǎn (main idea). ⑤特點 tèdiǎn (quality). ~ **of view** 見解 jiànjiě, 看法 kànfǎ. — v. 指 zhǐ, 指出 zhǐchū (indicate).

point-blank adj. & adv. ①近距離射擊的 jìn jùlí shèjí de / jìn jùlí shèjí de ‹shot›. ②率直的 shuàizhí de (direct).

pointed adj. ①尖的 jiān de (sharp). ②尖銳的 jiānruì de

(biting).

pointer n. ①指示棒 zhǐshìbàng (stick). ②指針 zhǐzhēn (indicator).

pointless adj. 無意義的 wú yìyì de (meaningless).

poise n. 鎮定 zhèndìng (calmness).

poison n. 毒物 dúwù, 毒藥 dúyào. — v. 下毒 xiàdú, 毒害 dúhài.

poisonous adj. 有毒的 yǒudú de.

poke v. 刺 cì, 戳 chuō (thrust).

poker n. 撲克牌戲 pūkèpáixì. ~ *face* 撲克臉 pūkèliǎn.

polar adj. ①近北極的 jìn běijí de (north). ②近南極的 jìn nánjí de (south).

pole n. ①北極 běijí (north). ②南極 nánjí (south). ③磁極 cíjí (magnet). ④電極 diànjí (electrical). ⑤竿 gān, 柱 zhù, 桿 gǎn (long stick).

police n. 警察 jǐngchá. ~ *officer* 警員 jǐngyuán, 警官 jǐngguān.

policeman n. 警察 jǐngchá.

policewoman n. 女警 nǚjǐng.

policy n. ①政策 zhèngcè (strategy). ②保險單 bǎoxiǎndān (insurance).

polish v. 擦亮 cāliàng (rubbing), 磨光 móguāng (grinding). — n. ①光澤 guāngzé, 光滑 guānghuá (brightness). ②優雅 yōuyǎ (elegance).

Polish adj. 波蘭的 Bōlán de. — n. 波蘭語 Bōlányǔ.

polite adj. 有禮貌的 yǒu lǐmào de.

political adj. 政治的 zhèngzhì de.

politician n. 政治家 zhèngzhìjiā (profession), 政客

zhèngkè (negative connotation).

politics n. ①政治 zhèngzhì (art). ②政治學 zhèngzhìxué (science). ③政見 zhèngjiàn (views).

polka n. 波卡舞 bōkǎwǔ.

poll n. ①投票 tóupiào (ballot). ②民意調查 mínyì diàochá (survey).

pollen n. 花粉 huāfěn.

pollute v. 污染 wūrǎn.

pollution n. 污染 wūrǎn.

polo n. 馬球 mǎqiú.

polygamy n. 一夫多妻 yī fū duō qī.

polygon n. 多角形 duōjiǎoxíng, 多邊形 duōbiānxíng.

polytheism n. 多神論 duōshénlùn.

pomade n. 髮油 fàyóu / fǎyóu.

pomegranate n. 石榴 shíliu.

pompous adj. 自大的 zìdà de.

poncho n. 斗篷 dǒupeng.

pond n. 池塘 chítáng.

ponder v. 仔細考慮 zǐxì kǎolǜ, 沈思 chénsī.

ponderous adj. ①笨重的 bènzhòng de (heavy). ②慢吞吞的 màntūntūn de (slow).

pony n. 小馬 xiǎomǎ.

ponytail n. 馬尾 mǎwěi.

pool n. ①池 chí, 水塘 shuǐtáng (pond). ②游泳池 yóuyǒngchí (swimming pool). ③總賭注 zǒngdǔzhù (gambling).

poolroom n. 撞球場 zhuàngqiúchǎng.

poor adj. ①貧窮的 pínqióng de (having no money). ②可憐的 kělián de (pathetic). ③壞的 huài de, 差的 chà de (bad).

④貧瘠的 pínjí de (barren).

pop v. 發短促爆裂聲 fā
duǎncù bàolièshēng (explode
lightly). — n. 短促爆裂聲
duǎncù bàolièshēng 〈sound〉.
— adj. 流行的 liúxíng de.
~ art 普普藝術 pǔpǔ yìshù.

popcorn n. 爆米花
bàomǐhuā.

pope n. 教皇 jiàohuáng / 教宗
jiàozōng.

poplar n. 白楊 báiyáng.

poppy n. 罌粟 yīngsù.

populace n. 平民 píngmín, 民
眾 mínzhòng (common
people).

popular adj. ①受歡迎的
shòu huānyíng de (accepted).
②流行的 liúxíng de (fashion-
able).

popularity n. 流行程度
liúxíng chéngdù.

popularize v. 使流行 shǐ
liúxíng (make fashionable), 使
普遍 shǐ pǔbiàn (broaden
appeal of).

populate v. 居住於 jūzhù yú.

population n. 人口 rénkǒu.

populous adj. 人口稠密的
rénkǒu chóumì de.

porcelain n. 瓷器 cíqì.

porch n. 門廊 ménláng.

pore n. 毛孔 máokǒng.

pork n. 豬肉 zhūròu.

pornography n. 色情文字
sèqíng wénzì 〈writing〉, 色情
照片 sèqíng zhàopiàn
〈picture〉.

porous adj. 多孔的 duō kǒng
de, 有細孔的 yǒu xìkǒng de.

porpoise n. 海豚 hǎitún.

porridge n. 麥片粥
màipiànzhōu.

port n. 港口 gǎngkǒu, 埠 bù.

portable adj. 可攜帶的 kě
xīdài de.

portal n. 入口 rùkǒu (door).

portend v. 預示 yùshì.

porter n. ①搬運工
bānyùngōng, 挑夫 tiāofū
(carrier). ②門房 ménfáng
(door-keeper).

portfolio n. ①公事包
gōngshìbāo, 檔案夾
dàng'ànjiá / dǎng'ànjiá
(holder). ②檔案文件 dàng'àn
wénjiàn / dǎng'àn wénjiàn
(folder).

porthole n. 舷窗 xiánchuāng.

portico n. 門廊 ménláng.

portion n. 部分 bùfen. — v.
分配 fēnpèi.

portly adj. 壯碩的
zhuàngshuò de.

portrait n. ①肖像 xiàoxiàng
(drawing). ②描寫 miáoxiě
(description).

portray v. 描繪 miáohuì, 描
寫 miáoxiě (represent).

Portuguese n. & adj. ①葡萄
牙人 Pútáoyárén 〈people〉.
②葡萄牙語 Pútáoyáyǔ
〈language〉.

pose n. ①姿勢 zīshì (posture).
②裝模作樣 zhuāng-mú-zuò-
yàng 〈act〉. — v. ①擺姿勢
zīshì 〈model〉. ②提出 tíchū (ask).

posh adj. 豪華的 háohuá de.

position n. ①位置 wèizhì
(location). ②工作 gōngzuò,
職位 zhíwèi (job). ③地位
dìwèi (rank). ④姿勢 zīshì
(pose).

positive adj. ①確定的
quèdìng de, 確實的 quèshí de
(affirmative). ②明確的
míngquè de (explicit). ③積極的
jījí de, 有助益的 yǒu zhùyì de

(beneficial). — n. ①陽極 yángjí 〈electricity〉. ②正數 zhèngshù 〈mathematics〉.

possess v. 擁有 yōngyǒu / yǒngyǒu.

possession n. 所有物 suǒyǒuwù.

possessive adj. ①有占有慾的 yǒu zhànyǒuyù de (domineering). ②所有格的 suǒyǒugé de 〈grammar〉.

possibility n. 可能 kěnéng (option), 可能性 kěnéngxìng (probability).

possible adj. 可能的 kěnéng de.

possibly adv. 或許 huòxǔ.

post n. ①郵件 yóujiàn (mail). ②郵政 yóuzhèng (postal service). ③柱 zhù, 樁 zhuāng (pole). ④哨站 shàozhàn, 崗位 gǎngwèi (sentry). ⑤職位 zhíwèi, 工作 gōngzuò (job). ~ *office* 郵局 yóujú. — v. ①郵寄 yóujì (mail). ②張貼 zhāngtiē (stick up). ③公告 gōnggào, 公布 gōngbù (announce).

postage n. 郵資 yóuzī.

postcard n. 明信片 míngxìnpiàn.

poster n. 海報 hǎibào, 大幅廣告 dàfú guǎnggào (placard).

posterior adj. 在後的 zài hòu de. — n. 臀部 túnbù.

posterity n. 後代 hòudài.

postgraduate n. 研究生 yánjiūshēng / yánjiùshēng.

posthumous adj. 死後的 sǐ hòu de.

postman n. 郵差 yóuchāi.

postmark n. 郵戳 yóuchuō.

postmaster n. 郵政局長 yóuzhèng júzhǎng.

postmodernism n. 後現代主義 hòuxiàndài zhǔyì.

postmortem adj. 死後的 sǐ hòu de. — n. 驗屍 yànshī.

postpone v. 延期 yánqí / yánqí.

postscript n. 附筆 fùbǐ, 後記 hòujì.

posture n. ①姿勢 zīshì 〈physical〉. ②態度 tàidu 〈mental〉. — v. 擺出姿勢 bǎichū zīshì.

postwar adj. 戰後的 zhànhòu de.

pot n. 壺 hú 〈tea〉, 盆 pén 〈flowers〉, 鍋 guō 〈cooking〉.

potassium n. 鉀 jiǎ.

potato n. 土豆 tǔdòu / 馬鈴薯 mǎlíngshǔ, 洋芋 yángyù.

potent adj. ①有效的 yǒuxiào de (effective). ②有力的 yǒulì de (powerful).

potential adj. 有可能性的 yǒu kěnéngxìng de, 潛在的 qiánzài de.

potter n. 陶工 táogōng.

pottery n. 陶器 táoqì.

pouch n. 小袋 xiǎodài.

poultice n. 膏藥 gāoyào.

poultry n. 家禽 jiāqín.

pounce v. 撲過去 pūguòqù.

pound n. ①磅 bàng 〈weight〉. ②鎊 bàng 〈money〉. ③獸欄 shòulán (enclosure). — v. 連續重擊 liánxù zhòngjí / liánxù zhòngjí (strike).

pour v. 倒 dào, 灌 guàn.

poverty n. 貧窮 pínqióng (state of being poor).

powder n. 粉 fěn, 粉末 fěnmò. — v. ①使成粉 shǐ chéng fěn (reduce to powder). ②撒粉 sǎfěn (put powder on).

power n. ①力 lì, 力量 lìliang (strength). ②能力 nénglì

P

(ability). ③權力 quánlì, 勢力 shìlì (authority).

powerboat n. 汽艇 qìtǐng.

powerful adj. 有力的 yǒulì de, 強的 qiáng de.

powerless adj. ①無力的 wúlì de 〈strength〉. ②無權的 wúquán de 〈without authority〉.

practical adj. ①實際的 shíjì de (realistic). ②實用的 shíyòng de (useful). ③應用的 yìngyòng de (applied). ~ joke 惡作劇 èzuòjù.

practically adv. ①實際上 shíjìshang, 事實上 shìshíshang (virtually). ②幾乎 jīhū (almost).

practice n. ①練習 liànxí (exercise). ②習慣 xíguàn (habit). ③實行 shíxíng (application). — v. ①練習 liànxí, 訓練 xùnliàn (exercise). ②實行 shíxíng (carry out).

pragmatic adj. 實用主義的 shíyòng zhǔyì de (practical).

pragmatics n. 語用學 yǔyòngxué.

prairie n. 大草原 dà cǎoyuán (plain).

praise n. & v. 讚美 zànměi, 稱讚 chēngzàn.

praiseworthy adj. 值得讚美 的 zhíde zànměi de.

prank n. 惡作劇 èzuòjù.

prattle v. 閒談 xiántán (chatter).

pray v. 祈禱 qídǎo 〈hope〉, 禱告 dǎogào 〈religion〉.

prayer n. 祈禱 qídǎo.

preach v. 傳教 chuánjiào, 講道 jiǎngdào 〈in church〉.

preacher n. 傳道者 chuándàozhě.

precarious adj. ①危險的

wēixiǎn de / wéixiǎn de (dangerous). ②不確定的 bú quèdìng de (uncertain).

precaution n. 預防 yùfáng.

precede v. 在前 zài qián.

precedence n. ①在先 zài xiān 〈time〉. ②上位 shàngwèi, 優先權 yōuxiānquán 〈of importance〉.

precedent n. 先例 xiānlì.

preceding adj. 在前的 zài qián de, 在先的 zài xiān de.

precept n. 箴言 zhēnyán.

precinct n. 區域 qūyù (district).

precious adj. 珍貴的 zhēnguì de (valuable).

precipice n. 懸崖 xuányá / xuányái.

precipitate v. ①突然引起 túrán yǐnqǐ / túrán yǐnqǐ (cause). ②加速…… 發生 jiāsù...fāshēng (hasten).

precis n. 大綱 dàgāng, 摘要 zhāiyào.

precise adj. ①精確的 jīngquè de (accurate). ②嚴謹的 yánjǐn de (careful).

precision n. & adj. 精密 jīngmì.

preclude v. 阻止 zǔzhǐ, 排除 páichú (exclude).

precocious adj. 早熟的 zǎoshú de.

predatory adj. 掠奪的 lüèduó de.

predecessor n. ①前任 qiánrèn 〈position〉. ②祖先 zǔxiān (ancestor).

predicament n. 苦境 kǔjìng.

predicate n. 述語 shùyǔ 〈grammar〉.

predict v. 預言 yùyán, 預料 yùliào.

P

prediction n. 預言 yùyán.

predilection n. 偏愛 piān'ài, 偏好 piānhào.

predispose v. 偏向於 piānxiàng yú (incline to).

predominant adj. ①有優勢的 yǒu yōushì de (prevailing). ②主要的 zhǔyào de (chief).

predominate v. 支配 zhīpèi, 控制 kòngzhì, 佔優勢 zhàn yōushì.

preeminent adj. 卓越的 zhuōyuè de / zhuóyuè de.

prefabricate v. 預製 yùzhì.

preface n. 序言 xùyán.

prefect n. 長官 zhǎngguān.

prefecture n. 縣 xiàn.

prefer v. 較喜歡 jiào xǐhuan, 偏好 piānhào (favor).

preferable adj. 較合意的 jiào héyì de.

preference n. 偏好 piānhào (favoritism).

preferential adj. ①優先的 yōuxiān de (privileged). ②優惠的 yōuhuì de (favorable).

prefix n. 字首 zìshǒu.

pregnancy n. 懷孕 huáiyùn.

prehistoric adj. 史前的 shǐqián de.

prejudge v. 貿然判斷 màorán pànduàn.

prejudice n. 偏見 piānjiàn. — v. 使存偏見 shǐ cún piānjiàn (influence unfairly).

preliminary adj. 初步的 chūbù de.

prelude n. 前奏曲 qiánzòuqǔ, 序曲 xùqǔ (music).

premarital adj. 婚前的 hūnqián de.

premature adj. 過早的 guòzǎo de (too early), 未成熟的 wèi chéngshú de (not mature).

premeditate v. 預謀 yùmóu.

premier n. 內閣總理 nèigé zǒnglǐ, 首相 shǒuxiàng. — adj. 首要的 shǒuyào de, 第一的 dì-yī de.

premiere n. 首演 shǒuyǎn.

premise n. 前提 qiántí.

premium n. ①額外費用 éwài fèiyòng (additional payment). ②保險費 bǎoxiǎnfèi (insurance).

premonition n. 預感 yùgǎn.

preoccupation n. 全神貫注 quánshén-guànzhù, 專心 zhuānxīn (concentration).

preparation n. 準備 zhǔnbèi, 預備 yùbèi (preparing).

preparatory adj. 預備的 yùbèi de. ~ school 大學預科 dàxué yùkē.

prepare v. ①預備 yùbèi, 準備 zhǔnbèi (arrange). ②為……鋪路 wèi...pūlù (smooth the way for).

preposition n. 介系詞 jièxìcí.

preposterous adj. 荒謬的 huāngmiù de (absurd).

prescribe v. ①開藥方 kāi yàofāng (medicine). ②規定 guīdìng, 指定 zhǐdìng (assign).

prescription n. 藥方 yàofāng, 處方 chǔfāng.

prescriptive adj. 規定的 guīdìng de.

presence n. ①在場出席 zàichǎng chūxí (attendance). ②風采 fēngcǎi (personality).

present v. ①給 gěi, 贈 zèng (give). ②介紹 jièshào (introduce). — n. 禮物 lǐwù. — adj. ①在場的 zàichǎng de (in attendance). ②現在的

xiànzài de (current).

presentation *n.* ①介紹 jièshào (introducing). ②演出 yǎnchū (acting).

presently *adv.* ①不久地 bùjiǔ de (soon). ②現在 xiànzài, 目前 mùqián de (now).

preservation *n.* 保存 bǎocún.

preservative *n.* 防腐劑 fángfǔjì.

preserve *v.* 保存 bǎocún 〈food〉, 保持 bǎochí (maintain), 保護 bǎohù (protect). — *n.* ①自然保護區 zìrán bǎohùqū 〈place〉. ②(pl.) 果醬 guǒjiàng (jam).

preside *v.* ①主持 zhǔchí, 當主席 dāng zhǔxí (be in charge). ②管理 guǎnlǐ (govern).

presidency *n.* ①職位 zhíwèi (position). ②任期 rènqí / rènqí (term).

president *n.* ①總統 zǒngtǒng 〈of country〉. ②主席 zhǔxí, 會長 huìzhǎng 〈of a group〉. ③總裁 zǒngcái, 董事長 dǒngshìzhǎng 〈of a company〉.

press *v.* ①按 àn (push). ②熨燙 yùntàng (iron). ③迫 pò, 逼 bī (force). ④催促 cuīcù (urge). — *n.* ①壓榨機 yāzhàjī 〈machine〉. ②印刷 yìnshuā (printing). ③新聞界 xīnwénjiè 〈newspapers〉. ~ **conference** 記者會 jìzhěhuì.

pressure *n.* 壓力 yālì.

prestige *n.* 聲望 shēngwàng.

presumable *adj.* 可假定的 kě jiǎdìng de.

presume *v.* 推測 tuīcè, 假定 jiǎdìng (suppose).

presumption *n.* 推測 tuīcè, 假定 jiǎdìng (supposition).

presuppose *v.* ①事先推定 shìxiān tuīdìng (assume). ②以……為前提 yǐ...wéi qiántí (prerequisite).

pretend *v.* 假裝 jiǎzhuāng.

pretension *n.* ①主張 zhǔzhāng (claim). ②自負 zìfù (conceit).

pretentious *adj.* ①自負的 zìfù de (pompous). ②炫耀的 xuànyào de (ostentation).

pretext *n.* 藉口 jièkǒu.

pretty *adj.* 漂亮的 piàoliang de (beautiful). — *adv.* 相當 xiāngdāng.

prevail *v.* ①盛行 shèngxíng (be widespread). ②戰勝 zhànshèng (win).

prevailing *adj.* 盛行的 shèngxíng de (prevalent).

prevalent *adj.* 流行的 liúxíng de, 普遍的 pǔbiàn de.

prevent *v.* ①防止 fángzhǐ, 預防 yùfáng (avoid). ②阻礙 zǔài (hinder).

prevention *n.* 預防 yùfáng.

preventive *adj.* 預防的 yùfáng de.

preview *n.* 試映 shìyìng (see ahead of time), 預告片 yùgàopiàn (trailer).

previous *adj.* 在前的 zài qián de, 先前的 xiānqián de (prior).

prey *n.* 被捕食的動物 bèi bǔshí de dòngwù.

price *n.* 價格 jiàgé (amount of money), 代價 dàijià (other cost). — *v.* 定價 dìngjià (set the cost).

priceless *adj.* 無價的 wújià de.

prick *n.* 尖刺 jiāncì. — *v.* 刺 cì (stab). ②刺痛 cìtòng (hurt).

pride *n.* ①自尊 zìzūn (dignity). ②驕傲 jiāo'ào (arrogance).

priest *n.* 教士 jiàoshì, 牧師 mùshī.

primarily *adv.* 主要地 zhǔyào de.

primary *adj.* 首要的 shǒuyào de, 主要的 zhǔyào de.
~ *school* 小學 xiǎoxué.

prime *adj.* ①主要的 zhǔyào de, 首要的 shǒuyào de (primary). ②最上等的 zuì shàngděng de (best).

primer *n.* 入門書 rùménshū ⟨book⟩.

primitive *adj.* ①原始的 yuánshǐ de (ancient). ②最初的 zuìchū de (basic).

prince *n.* 王子 wángzǐ.

princess *n.* 公主 gōngzhǔ.

principal *adj.* 主要的 zhǔyào de ⟨chief⟩. — *n.* 校長 xiàozhǎng.

principle *n.* ①原則 yuánzé (rule). ②原理 yuánlǐ (basics). ③主義 zhǔyì (belief).

print *v.* ①印刷 yìnshuā ⟨on paper⟩. ②出版 chūbǎn (publish). — *n.* ①印刷 yìnshuā (printing). ②痕跡 hénjì (imprint). ③印刷字體 yìnshuā zìtǐ ⟨characters⟩. *out of* ~ 絕版 juébǎn.

printer *n.* ①印刷業者 yìnshuāyè zhě ⟨firm⟩. ②排版工人 páibǎn gōngrén ⟨worker⟩. ③印刷機 yìnshuājī ⟨machine⟩. ④打印機 dǎyìnjī / 印表機 yìnbiǎojī ⟨for computers⟩.

printing *n.* ①印刷 yìnshuā ⟨act of printing⟩. ②印刷物 yìnshuāwù ⟨books⟩.

prior *adj.* 在前的 zài qián de.

priority *n.* 優先權 yōuxiānquán.

prism *n.* ①稜鏡 léngjìng ⟨glass⟩. ②稜柱體 léngzhùtǐ ⟨shape⟩.

prison *n.* 監獄 jiānyù, 牢房 láofáng.

prisoner *n.* 囚犯 qiúfàn, 犯人 fànrén.

privacy *n.* ①隱私權 yǐnsīquán, 隱私 yǐnsī (secrecy). ②獨處 dúchǔ (being alone).

private *adj.* ①私人的 sīrén de (not public), 私有的 sīyǒu de (personal). ②祕密的 mìmì de (secret). — *n.* 士兵 shìbīng ⟨soldier⟩.

privilege *n.* 特權 tèquán.

prize *n.* 獎品 jiǎngpǐn (reward). — *v.* 珍視 zhēnshì (value).

prizefight *n.* 職業拳賽 zhíyè quánsài (boxing match).

pro *adv.* 贊成地 zànchéng de. — *n.* ①贊成者 zànchéngzhě (supporter). ②專業人員 zhuānyè rényuán (professional).

probability *n.* 可能性 kěnéngxìng.

probably *adv.* 可能 kěnéng, 大概 dàgài.

probation *n.* ①試用期 shìyòngqí / shìyòngqí (trial period). ②緩刑 huǎnxíng ⟨law⟩.

probe *v.* ①探查 tànchá (examine). ②探求 tànqiú (investigate).

problem *n.* 問題 wèntí.

procedure *n.* 程序 chéngxù.

proceed *v.* ①繼續進行 jìxù jìnxíng (continue). ②開始進行 kāishǐ jìnxíng, 著手 zhuóshǒu (start doing).

proceeding *n.* ①(*pl.*) 記錄 jìlù (records). ②(*pl.*) 訴訟程序 sùsòng chéngxù ⟨lawsuit⟩.

proceeds *n.* 營業額 yíngyè'é, 收益 shōuyì.

process n. ①過程 guòchéng (course). ②方法 fāngfǎ (method). ③進展 jìnzhǎn (progress). – v. 加工 jiāgōng (treat).

proclaim v. 宣布 xuānbù.

proclamation n. 宣布 xuānbù, 聲明 shēngmíng (announcement).

proclivity n. 傾向 qīngxiàng, 癖性 pǐxìng.

procrastinate v. 拖延 tuōyán, 耽擱 dāngē.

prod v. 刺 cì, 戳 chuō (poke).

prodigal adj. 浪費的 làngfèi de.

prodigious adj. ①龐大的 pángdà de (enormous). ②驚人的 jīngrén de (amazing).

prodigy n. ①奇才 qícái (genius). ②神童 shéntóng ⟨child⟩.

produce v. ①生產 shēngchǎn (make). ②拿出 náchū (bring out).

producer n. ①生產者 shēngchǎnzhě (manufacturer). ②製作人 zhìzuòrén ⟨film⟩.

product n. ①產品 chǎnpǐn, 產物 chǎnwù (goods). ②結果 jiéguǒ (result).

production n. ①生產 shēngchǎn (producing). ②產量 chǎnliàng (quantity). ~ line 流水線 liúshuǐxiàn / 生產線 shēngchǎnxiàn.

productive adj. ①生產的 shēngchǎn de, 肥沃的 féiwò de (fertile). ②產生利益的 chǎnshēng lìyì de (beneficial).

profane adj. 褻瀆的 xièdú de (blasphemous).

profanity n. 褻瀆 xièdú.

profess v. 聲稱 shēngchēng.

profession n. 職業 zhíyè (occupation).

professional adj. 專業的 zhuānyè de. – n. ①專家 zhuānjiā, 專業人員 zhuānyè rényuán (expert). ②職業選手 zhíyè xuǎnshǒu ⟨sports⟩.

professor n. 教授 jiàoshòu.

proficient adj. 熟練的 shúliàn de (well-practiced), 精通的 jīngtōng de (knowing well).

profile n. ①側面像 cèmiànxiàng (side view). ②輪廓 lúnkuò (outline). ③人物簡介 rénwù jiǎnjiè (biography).

profit n. 利益 lìyì, 利潤 lìrùn. – v. ①對……有利 duì……yǒulì (benefit). ②獲利 huòlì (earn money).

profitable adj. 有利益的 yǒu lìyì de.

profligate adj. ①浪費的 làngfèi de (wasteful). ②放蕩的 fàngdàng de (shamelessly immoral).

profound adj. ①深的 shēn de ⟨depth⟩. ②深刻的 shēnkè de ⟨knowledge⟩.

profuse adj. 豐富的 fēngfù de (plentiful).

program n. ①節目 jiémù ⟨performance⟩. ②計畫 jìhuà (plan). ③程式 chéngshì ⟨computer⟩.

progress n. ①進步 jìnbù (advance). ②前進 qiánjìn (forward movement).

progression n. 進展 jìnzhǎn (the action of progressing).

progressive adj. ①進步的 jìnbù de (advancing). ②前進的 qiánjìn de (moving forward).

prohibit v. ①禁止 jìnzhǐ (forbid). ②阻止 zǔzhǐ (prevent).

prohibitive adj. ①禁止的 jìnzhǐ de (not allowed). ②高昂

的 gāo'áng de 〈of price〉.
project n. 計畫 jìhuà, 方案 fāng'àn. — v. 投射 tóushè 〈cause a shadow〉.
projectile n. 發射物 fāshèwù.
projection n. 投射 tóushè, 放映 fàngyìng 〈projecting〉.
projector n. 放映機 fàngyìngjī.
proletariat n. 無產階級 wúchǎnjiējí.
proliferate v. 繁殖 fánzhí 〈multiply〉.
prolific adj. 多產的 duōchǎn de 〈fruitful〉.
prologue n. 序言 xùyán, 開場白 kāichǎngbái.
prolong v. 延長 yáncháng.
prom n. 舞會 wǔhuì.
prominent adj. ①卓越的 zhuóyuè de / zhuóyuè de 〈distinguished〉. ②突起的 tūqǐ de / túqǐ de 〈jutting out〉.
promiscuous adj. 濫交的 lànjiāo de 〈sex〉.
promise n. ①諾言 nuòyán 〈assurance〉. ②前途 qiántú 〈potential〉. — v. ①承諾 chéngnuò 〈assure〉. ②有……希望 yǒu...xīwàng, 有可能 yǒu kěnéng 〈give hope〉.
promote v. ①擢升 zhuóshēng, 提升 tíshēng 〈elevate〉. ②促進 cùjìn 〈move something forward〉. ③宣傳促銷 xuānchuán cùxiāo 〈market〉.
promotion n. ①升遷 shēngqiān 〈elevation〉. ②促進 cùjìn 〈move something forward〉. ③促銷 cùxiāo 〈marketing〉.
prompt adj. ①立刻的 lìkè de 〈immediate〉. ②迅速的 xùnsù de 〈quick〉.
prone adj. ①易於……的 yì

yú...de 〈inclined〉. ②俯臥的 fǔwò de 〈face down〉.
pronoun n. 代名詞 dàimíngcí.
pronounce v. ①發音 fāyīn 〈utter〉. ②宣稱 xuānchēng 〈announce〉.
pronunciation n. 發音 fāyīn.
proof n. 證明 zhèngmíng.
proofread v. 校對 jiàoduì.
prop v. 支撐 zhīcheng, 支持 zhīchí. — n. 支撐物 zhīchengwù.
propaganda n. 宣傳 xuānchuán.
propagate v. ①繁殖 fánzhí 〈reproduce〉. ②傳播 chuánbō / chuánbò, 宣傳 xuānchuán 〈spread〉.
propel v. 推進 tuījìn.
propeller n. 推進器 tuījìnqì.
proper adj. ①適當的 shìdàng de 〈appropriate〉. ②得體的 détǐ de 〈acceptable〉.
properly adv. 適當地 shìdàng de.
property n. ①財產 cáichǎn 〈possessions〉. ②特性 tèxìng 〈quality〉.
prophecy n. 預言 yùyán.
prophesy v. 預言 yùyán, 預告 yùgào.
prophet n. 預言家 yùyánjiā, 先知 xiānzhī.
proportion n. ①比例 bǐlì 〈ratio〉. ②部分 bùfen 〈part〉. ③均衡 jūnhéng 〈balance〉.
proportionate adj. 成比例的 chéng bǐlì de.
proposal n. ①建議 jiànyì, 提議 tíyì 〈suggestion〉. ②求婚 qiúhūn 〈offer of marriage〉.
propose v. ①提議 tíyì, 建議 jiànyì 〈suggest〉. ②求婚 qiúhūn

⟨marriage⟩.

proposition *n.* 提議 tíyì.

proprietor *n.* 所有者 suǒyǒuzhě.

propriety *n.* ①適當 shìdàng (appropriateness). ②得體 détǐ (good manners).

proscribe *v.* 禁止 jìnzhǐ (forbid).

prose *n.* 散文 sǎnwén.

prosecute *v.* 因……而起訴 yīn...ér qǐsù, 控告 kònggào (accuse).

prosecution *n.* 起訴 qǐsù, 控告 kònggào.

prosecutor *n.* 檢察官 jiǎncháguān ⟨official⟩.

prospect *n.* ①展望 zhǎnwàng (expectation). ②景象 jǐngxiàng (scene).

prospective *adj.* 預期的 yùqī de / yùqí de.

prospectus *n.* 說明書 shuōmíngshū.

prosper *v.* 繁榮 fánróng.

prosperity *n.* 繁榮 fánróng.

prosperous *adj.* 繁盛的 fánshèng de.

prostitute *n.* 娼妓 chāngjì.

prostitution *n.* 賣淫 màiyín.

prostrate *v.* 使……倒下 shǐ...dǎoxià. — *adj.* ①俯臥的 fǔwò de (prone). ②被征服的 bèi zhēngfú de (overcome).

protagonist *n.* ①主角 zhǔjué (chief character). ②倡導者 chàngdǎozhě (leader).

protect *v.* 保護 bǎohù.

protection *n.* 保護 bǎohù.

protective *adj.* 保護的 bǎohù de.

protector *n.* 保護者 bǎohùzhě.

protectorate *n.* 保護國

bǎohùguó.

protein *n.* 蛋白質 dànbáizhì / dànbáizhí.

protest *n.* 抗議 kàngyì (demonstration), 反對 fǎnduì (objection). — *v.* 抗議 kàngyì.

Protestant *n. & adj.* 新教徒 Xīnjiàotú.

protocol *n.* ①議定書 yìdìngshū (agreement). ②外交禮節 wàijiāo lǐjié (etiquette).

proton *n.* 質子 zhìzǐ / zhízǐ.

prototype *n.* 原型 yuánxíng.

protract *v.* 延長 yáncháng.

protrude *v.* 伸出 shēnchū, 凸出 tūchū / túchū.

protuberant *adj.* 隆起的 lóngqǐ de, 凸出的 tūchū de / túchū de (bulging).

proud *adj.* ①以……為榮 yǐ...wéiróng (satisfied with). ②驕傲的 jiāo'ào de (arrogant).

prove *v.* 證明 zhèngmíng (show to be true).

proverb *n.* 諺語 yànyǔ, 格言 géyán.

provide *v.* 提供 tígōng, 供給 gōngjǐ (supply).

provided *conj.* 假若 jiǎruò.

providence *n.* 天意 tiānyì (destiny).

provident *adj.* 有先見的 yǒu xiānjiàn de (far-sighted).

providential *adj.* 幸運的 xìngyùn de (lucky).

province *n.* 省 shěng.

provincial *adj.* 省的 shěng de.

provision *n.* ①準備 zhǔnbèi (preparation). ②(*pl.*) 糧食 liángshí (food). ③條款 tiáokuǎn ⟨law⟩.

provisional *adj.* 臨時的 línshí de.

proviso n. 但書 dànshū, 條件 tiáojiàn.

provocation n. 激怒 jīnù.

provocative adj. 挑撥性的 tiǎobōxìng de, 煽動的 shāndòng de.

provoke v. ①激怒 jīnù (make angry). ②引起 yǐnqǐ (arouse).

prowl v. 潛行 qiánxíng.

proximity n. 接近 jiējìn.

proxy n. ①代理 dàilǐ 〈authority〉. ②代理人 dàilǐrén (deputy). ③委託書 wěituōshū 〈document〉.

prude n. 故作拘謹的人 gùzuò jūjǐn de rén.

prudent adj. 謹慎的 jǐnshèn de.

prune v. 修剪 xiūjiǎn. — n. 乾梅子 gān méizi.

psalm n. 讚美歌 zànměigē.

pseudonym n. 假名 jiǎmíng (false name), 筆名 bǐmíng (pen name).

psychedelic adj. 產生幻覺的 chǎnshēng huànjué de.

psychiatry n. 精神醫學 jīngshén yīxué.

psychoanalysis n. 精神分析 jīngshén fēnxī.

psychological adj. 心理的 xīnlǐ de.

psychologist n. 心理學家 xīnlǐxué jiā.

psychology n. 心理學 xīnlǐxué.

psychotherapy n. 心理療法 xīnlǐ liáofǎ.

pub n. 酒館 jiǔguǎn.

puberty n. 青春期 qīngchūnqī / qīngchūnqí.

public adj. ①公眾的 gōngzhòng de (of people in general). ②公開的 gōngkāi de

(open). — n. 大眾 dàzhòng (populace).

publication n. ①出版 chūbǎn (issuing). ②出版品 chūbǎnpǐn (book).

publicity n. 宣傳 xuānchuán.

publicly adv. 公開地 gōngkāi de.

publish v. ①出版 chūbǎn 〈printing〉. ②發表 fābiǎo, 公開 gōngkāi (make publicly known).

pucker n. 皺 zhòu, 褶 zhé.

pudding n. 布丁 bùdīng.

puddle n. 水坑 shuǐkēng.

puff v. ①吹氣 chuīqì, 噴 pēn (blow). ②喘息 chuǎnxí / chuǎnxí (pant). ③膨脹 péngzhàng (inflate). — n. ①吹 chuī, 噴 pēn 〈breath or wind〉. ②粉撲 fěnpū 〈powder〉.

pull v. ①拉 lā, 拖 tuō (drag). ②拔 bá (pull out). — n. 拉 lā (tug).

pulley n. 滑輪 huálún.

pullover n. 套頭毛衣 tàotóu máoyī.

pulp n. ①果肉 guǒròu 〈fruit〉. ②紙漿 zhǐjiāng 〈for making paper〉.

pulpit n. 講壇 jiǎngtán.

pulsate v. 脈動 màidòng, 跳動 tiàodòng (beat).

pulse n. ①脈搏 màibó (beat). ②拍子 pāizi (rhythm).

pulverize v. 磨成粉 mó chéng fěn, 搗碎 dǎosuì.

puma n. 美洲獅 měizhōushī.

pump n. 唧筒 jītǒng / jítǒng, 抽水機 chōushuǐjī. — v. 用抽水機汲水 yòng chōushuǐjī jíshuǐ (drain).

pumpkin n. 南瓜 nánguā.

pun n. 雙關語 shuāngguānyǔ.

punch v. ①以拳擊 yǐ quán jī / yǐ quán jí (hit with the fist). ②打洞 dǎdòng (pierce). — n. ①打孔器 dǎkǒngqì 〈tool〉. ②擊打 jī / jí, 打 dǎ (strike).

punctual adj. 守時的 shǒushí de.

punctuate v. ①加標點於 jiā biāodiǎn yú (put punctuation marks). ②打斷 dǎduàn (interrupt).

punctuation n. 標點 biāodiǎn. ~ **marks** 標點符號 biāodiǎn fúhào.

puncture n. 孔 kǒng. — v. 穿孔 chuānkǒng (pierce).

pungent adj. 刺激性的 cìjīxìng de, 辛辣的 xīnlà de.

punish v. 處罰 chǔfá, 懲罰 chéngfá.

punishment n. ①罰 fá, 刑罰 xíngfá (penalty). ②嚴厲的對待 yánlì de duìdài (rough treatment).

punt n. 平底小船 píngdǐ xiǎochuán.

puny adj. 弱的 ruò de.

pup n. 小狗 xiǎogǒu (puppy).

pupil n. 學生 xuésheng.

puppet n. ①木偶 mùǒu 〈doll〉. ②傀儡 kuǐlěi 〈person or group〉.

puppy n. 小狗 xiǎogǒu.

purchase v. 購買 gòumǎi (buy). — n. 購買 gòumǎi.

pure adj. ①純粹的 chúncuì de (neat). ②純淨的 chúnjìng de (clean). ③純潔的 chúnjié de (innocent). ④完全的 wánquán de (complete).

purely adv. ①完全地 wánquán de (completely). ②純粹地 chúncuì de (merely).

purgative n. 瀉藥 xièyào.

purgatory n. 煉獄 liànyù.

purge v. ①清除 qīngchú (expel). ②洗滌 xǐdí (clean).

purify v. ①使清淨 shǐ qīngjìng (clean). ②純化 chúnhuà (clarify).

purity n. 純潔 chúnjié.

purple n. 紫色 zǐsè. — adj. 紫色的 zǐsè de.

purpose n. ①目的 mùdì (intention). ②決心 juéxīn (determination).

purse n. 錢袋 qiándài, 錢包 qiánbāo.

pursue v. ①追捕 zhuībǔ, 追趕 zhuīgǎn (chase). ②追求 zhuīqiú (aim for).

pursuit n. ①追捕 zhuībǔ (chase). ②追求 zhuīqiú (going for). ③消遣 xiāoqiǎn (interest).

purvey v. 供應 gōngyìng.

pus n. 膿 nóng.

push v. ①推 tuī (press). ②催促 cuīcù (urge on).

pussy n. 貓咪 māomī (cat).

put v. ①放 fàng, 安置 ānzhì (place). ②提出 tíchū (express). ~ **down** 放下 fàngxià. ~ **on** 穿 chuān 〈clothes〉, 戴 dài 〈accessory〉.

putrefy v. 使腐敗 shǐ fǔbài.

putrid adj. 腐爛的 fǔlàn de (rotten).

putty n. 油灰 yóuhuī.

puzzle n. ①難題 nántí (question). ②謎 mí (riddle). — v. ①困惑 kùnhuò (confuse). ②苦思 kǔsī (think).

pylon n. ①鐵塔 tiětǎ 〈for power cable〉. ②指示塔 zhǐshìtǎ 〈in airports〉.

pyramid n. ①金字塔 jīnzìtǎ 〈Egypt〉. ②角錐 jiǎozhuī 〈shape〉.

python n. 蟒 mǎng, 巨蛇 jùshé.

Q

quack n. 鴨叫聲 yājiàoshēng 〈sound〉. — v. 鴨叫 yājiào.

quadrangle n. 四邊形 sìbiānxíng, 方形 fāngxíng 〈shape〉.

quadrille n. 方塊舞 fāngkuàiwǔ.

quadruple adj. 四倍的 sì bèi de (four times).

quagmire n. ①泥沼 nízhǎo (bog). ②困境 kùnjìng (difficulty).

quail n. 鵪鶉 ānchún 〈bird〉.

quaint adj. 古怪的 gǔguài de.

quake v. 震動 zhèndòng, 戰慄 zhànlì.

qualification n. ①資格 zīgé (competence). ②限制 xiànzhì (limitation).

qualified adj. ①有資格的 yǒu zīgé de (appropriate). ②受限制的 shòu xiànzhì de (limited).

qualify v. ①給與……的資格 gěiyǔ...de zīgé (authorize). ②取得……的資格 qǔdé...de zīgé (become eligible). ③限制 xiànzhì (limit).

quality n. ①品質 pǐnzhì / pǐnzhí (goodness). ②特質 tèzhì / tèzhí (characteristic).

qualm n. 不安 bù'ān, 疑懼 yíjù (uncertainty).

quandary n. 困惑 kùnhuò, 窘境 jiǒngjìng.

quantitative adj. 可量化的 kě liànghuà de.

quantity n. 量 liàng.

quarantine n. & v. 隔離檢疫 gélí jiǎnyì.

quarrel n. 爭吵 zhēngchǎo, 口角 kǒujiǎo. — v. 爭吵 zhēngchǎo (argue).

quarrelsome adj. 愛爭吵的 ài zhēngchǎo de.

quarry n. 採石場 cǎishíchǎng 〈place〉. — v. 採石 cǎishí.

quart n. 夸脫 kuātuō.

quarter n. ①四分之一 sì fēn zhī yī (¼). ②一刻鐘 yí kè zhōng (15 minutes). ③二角五分 èr jiǎo wǔ fēn (25 cents). ④區域 qūyù (area).

quarterly adj. 每季的 měi jì de. — adv. 每季地 měi jì de. — n. 季刊 jìkān.

quartet n. 四重唱 sìchóngchàng 〈singers〉, 四重奏 sìchóngzòu 〈instruments〉.

quartz n. 石英石 shíyīngshí.

quash v. 鎮壓 zhènyā (suppress).

quaver v. 震顫 zhènchàn.

quay n. 碼頭 mǎtou.

queasy adj. 作嘔的 zuò'ǒu de, 不舒服的 bù shūfu de.

queen n. 女王 nǚwáng, 皇后 huánghòu.

queer adj. ①奇怪的 qíguài de, 古怪的 gǔguài de (bizarre). ②可疑的 kěyí de (suspicious). — n. 同性戀者 tóngxìngliàn zhě.

quell v. 壓服 yāfú.

quench v. ①熄滅 xīmiè / xímiè (extinguish). ②解渴 jiěkě (relieve thirst).

query n. 問題 wèntí. — v. 質

問 zhìwèn / zhíwèn, 詢問 xúnwèn (question).

quest n. 探尋 tànxún.

question n. 疑問 yíwèn, 問題 wèntí. ~ *mark* 問號 wènhào. — v. 質問 zhìwèn / zhíwèn.

questionable adj. 有問題的 yǒu wèntí de, 可疑的 kěyí de.

questionnaire n. 問卷 wènjuàn.

queue n. 一行隊伍 yì háng duìwǔ.

quick adj. ①迅速的 xùnsù de (fast). ②即刻的 jíkè de (immediate). ③機伶的 jīling de (clever).

quicken v. 加速 jiāsù.

quickly adv. 快地 kuài de, 迅速地 xùnsù de.

quicksand n. 流沙 liúshā ⟨sand⟩.

quicksilver n. 水銀 shuǐyín, 汞 gǒng.

quiet adj. ①安靜的 ānjìng de (noiseless). ②平靜的 píngjìng de (calm). ③溫和的 wēnhé de (soft). — v. 使安靜 shǐ ānjìng.

quietly adv. 安靜地 ānjìng de.

quilt n. 棉被 miánbèi.

quinine n. 奎寧 kuíníng.

quintet n. 五重唱 wǔchóngchàng ⟨singers⟩, 五重奏 wǔchóngzòu ⟨instruments⟩.

quip n. 妙語 miàoyǔ, 警語 jǐngyǔ.

quit v. ①離去 líqù (leave). ②辭去 cíqù (resign).

quite adv. ①完全 wánquán (entirely). ②相當 xiāngdāng (fairly).

quiver n. & v. 顫抖 chàndǒu.

quiz n. 對…測驗 duì... cèyàn, 考試 kǎoshì. — n. 小考 xiǎokǎo.

quota n. 配額 pèi'é, 限額 xiàn'é.

quotation n. ①引用文 yǐnyòngwén (citation). ②估價 gūjià (estimated price). ~ *marks* 引號 yǐnhào.

quote v. ①引用 yǐnyòng (cite). ②報（價）bào (jià) (offer a price).

quotient n. 商數 shāngshù.

R

rabbit n. 兔子 tùzi.

rabble n. 暴民 bàomín (disorderly crowd).

rabid adj. ①狂暴的 kuángbào de (furious). ②患狂犬病的 huàn kuángquǎnbìng de.

rabies n. 狂犬病 kuángquǎnbìng.

raccoon n. 浣熊 huànxióng / wǎnxióng.

race n. ①競賽 jìngsài (contest). ②種族 zhǒngzú (people).

racial adj. 種族的 zhǒngzú de.

racism n. 種族歧視 zhǒngzú qíshì.

rack n. 掛物架 guàwùjià.

racket n. ①球拍 qiúpāi ⟨tennis⟩. ②喧嘩 xuānhuá (noise). ③詐

R

騙 zhàpiàn (swindle).

radar n. 雷達 léidá.

radiance n. 光輝 guānghuī、光亮 guāngliàng.

radiant adj. ①光亮的 guāngliàng de (bright). ②容光煥發的 róngguāng-huànfā de (happy).

radiate v. 發射 fāshè.

radiation n. 輻射 fúshè.

radiator n. ①電熱器 diànrèqì (heater). ②冷卻器 lěngquèqì 〈engine〉.

radical adj. ①根本的 gēnběn de (fundamental). ②激進的 jījìn de (extreme). — n. 激進分子 jījìn fènzǐ.

radio n. ①無線電廣播 wúxiàndiàn guǎngbō / wúxiàndiàn guǎngbò (broadcasting). ②收音機 shōuyīnjī 〈device〉. ~ **station** 無線電臺 wúxiàn diàntái.

radioactive adj. 放射性的 fàngshèxìng de.

radioactivity n. 放射性 fàngshèxìng.

radish n. 蘿蔔 luóbo.

radium n. 鐳 léi.

radius n. 半徑 bànjìng.

raffle n. & v. 抽獎 chōujiǎng.

raft n. 筏 fá.

rag n. 破布 pòbù.

rage n. 盛怒 shèngnù. — v. 發怒 fānù.

ragged adj. ①襤褸的 lánlǚ de、破爛的 pòlàn de (tattered). ②凹凸不平的 āotū bùpíng de / āotú bùpíng de (uneven).

raid n. & v. 襲擊 xíjī / xíjí (attack).

rail n. ①鐵軌 tiěguǐ (track). ②欄杆 lángān (fence).

railing n. 欄杆 lángān.

railroad n. 鐵路 tiělù、鐵道 tiědào.

rain n. 雨 yǔ. — v. 下雨 xiàyǔ.

rainbow n. 彩虹 cǎihóng.

raincoat n. 雨衣 yǔyī.

rainfall n. 降雨量 jiàngyǔliàng.

rainy adj. 多雨的 duōyǔ de.

raise v. ①舉起 jǔqǐ (lift up). ②提高 tígāo (make higher). ③擢升 zhuóshēng (promote). ④養育 yǎngyù (bring up). ⑤招募 zhāomù (collect).

raisin n. 葡萄乾 pútaogān 〈food〉.

rake n. 耙子 pázi. — v. 耙 pá.

rally v. ①召集 zhàojí (assemble). ②重振 chóngzhèn (recover). — n. 集會 jíhuì (meeting).

ram n. 公羊 gōngyáng. — v. 撞 zhuàng、撞入 zhuàngrù (crash into).

ramble v. ①漫步 mànbù (stroll). ②漫談 màntán (wander).

rambling adj. ①雜亂的 záluàn de (straggling). ②漫談的 màntán de 〈aimless〉.

ramp n. 坡道 pōdào (slope).

rampage v. 亂衝 luànchōng.

rampant adj. 猖獗的 chāngjué de (widespread).

rampart n. 堡壘 bǎolěi、壁壘 bìlěi (defensive wall).

ramshackle adj. 要倒塌的 yào dǎotā de (almost collapsing).

ranch n. 大牧場 dà mùchǎng、大農場 dà nóngchǎng.

rancid adj. 腐臭的 fǔchòu de.

random adj. 無目的的 wú mùdì de、隨便的 suíbiàn de.

range n. ①範圍 fànwéi (extent). ②射程 shèchéng

rank n. ③靶場 bǎchǎng (shooting practice area). ④分布地區 fēnbù dìqū ⟨area⟩. — 在……範圍之內 zài...fànwéi zhī nèi (be within).

rank n. ①階級 jiējí (class). ②行列 hángliè (row). ③排列 shǐ páiliè (line). ④位居 wèijū..., 列於…… liè yú... (place in order). — adj. 惡臭的 èchòu de (smelling).

rankle v. 使人心痛 shǐ rén xīntòng.

ransack v. ①遍搜 biànsōu (search). ②洗劫 xǐjié (rob).

ransom n. 贖金 shújīn.

rant v. 怒吼 nùhǒu, 咆哮 páoxiāo / páoxiāo.

rap v. 輕敲 qīngqiāo (knock). — n. ①敲擊 qiāojí / qiāojí (knocking). ②饒舌音樂 ráoshé yīnyuè ⟨music⟩.

rape n. & v. 強姦 qiángjiān, 強暴 qiángbào.

rapid adj. 迅速的 xùnsù de, 快的 kuài de (fast). — n. 急流 jíliú.

rapt adj. 全神貫注的 quánshén-guànzhù de, 入神的 rùshén de (deep in thought).

rapture n. 欣喜若狂 xīnxǐ-ruò-kuáng.

rare adj. 罕有的 hǎnyǒu de (uncommon). ~ animal 珍稀動物 zhēnxī dòngwù / 稀有動物 xīyǒu dòngwù.

rarity n. 罕有的事物 hǎnyǒu de shìwù.

rascal n. 流氓 liúmáng, 惡棍 ègùn.

rash adj. 鹵莽的 lǔmǎng de, 輕率的 qīngshuài de. — n. 疹 zhěn.

raspberry n. 覆盆子 fùpénzi.

rat n. ①鼠 shǔ (mouse). ②卑鄙小人 bēibǐ xiǎorén (despicable person). ③叛徒 pàntú (betrayer). — v. 背叛 bèipàn (betray).

rate n. ①比率 bǐlǜ (ratio). ②速度 sùdù (speed). — v. 評估 pínggū (evaluate).

rather adv. 寧可 nìngkě / níngkě.

ratify v. ①批准 pīzhǔn (approve). ②確認 quèrèn (confirm).

rating n. 等級 děngjí (ranking).

ratio n. 比率 bǐlǜ ⟨mathematics⟩.

ration n. 配給量 pèijǐliàng, 配額 pèi'é (allotted quantity). — v. 配給 pèijǐ.

rational adj. ①理智的 lǐzhì de (sensible). ②合理的 hélǐ de (reasonable).

rationalism n. 理性主義 lǐxìng zhǔyì.

rationalize v. 合理化 hélǐhuà.

rattle v. 發嘎嘎聲 fā gāgāshēng (make short, sharp sounds). — n. 嘎嘎聲 gāgāshēng ⟨noise⟩.

raucous adj. ①沙啞的 shāyǎ de (hoarse). ②吵鬧的 chǎonào de (noisy).

ravage n. & v. ①毀壞 huǐhuài (destruction). ②掠奪 lüèduó (robbery).

rave v. ①咆哮 páoxiāo / páoxiāo, 怒吼 nùhǒu (roar). ②過度讚揚 guòdù zànyáng (praise). — n. ①狂歡聚會 kuánghuān jùhuì (party). ②激賞 jīshǎng (praise).

raven n. 渡鳥 dùniǎo ⟨bird⟩.

ravenous adj. 飢餓的 jī'è de (very hungry), 貪婪的 tānlán

de (greedy).

ravine n. 峽谷 xiágǔ.

ravish v. ①迷住 mízhù (charm).
②強姦 qiángjiān (rape).

raw adj. ①生的 shēng de
(uncooked). ②未加工的
wèi jiāgōng de (untreated).
③擦破皮的 cā pòpí de
(chafed).

ray n. ①光線 guāngxiàn
(beam). ②射線 shèxiàn
(radiant light).

rayon n. 人造絲 rénzàosī.

razor n. 剃刀 tìdāo, 剃鬚刀
tìxūdāo / 刮鬍刀 guāhúdāo.

reach v. ①到達 dàodá (arrive
at). ②與……連絡 yǔ...liánluò
(contact).

react v. 反應 fǎnyìng (act).

reaction n. 反應 fǎnyìng.

reactor n. 原子爐 yuánzǐlú,
反應爐 fǎnyìnglú.

read v. ①讀 dú, 閱讀 yuèdú
(study). ②朗讀 lǎngdú (read
aloud).

reader n. ①讀者 dúzhě
〈person〉. ②讀本 dúběn 〈book〉.

readily adj. ①簡單地 jiǎndān
de (easily). ②欣然 xīnrán
(willingly).

reading n. ①讀物 dúwù
〈book〉. ②見解 jiànjiě, 解讀
jiědú (interpretation).

ready adj. ①預備好的 yùbèi
hǎo de (prepared). ②願意的
yuànyì de (willing).

ready-made adj. 現成的
xiànchéng de.

real adj. ①真的 zhēn de,
真實的 zhēnshí de (genuine).
②實際的 shíjì de (actual).
~ *estate* 不動產 búdòngchǎn.

really adv. 真實地 zhēnshí
de, 真正地 zhēnzhèng de.

realism n. 現實主義 xiànshí
zhǔyì, 寫實主義 xiěshí zhǔyì.

realistic adj. ①逼真的 bīzhēn
de, 寫實的 xiěshí de (lifelike).
②實際的 shíjì de (practical).

reality n. 真實 zhēnshí.

realize v. ①了解 liǎojiě
(comprehend). ②實現 shíxiàn
(accomplish).

realm n. ①王國 wángguó
(kingdom). ②領域 lǐngyù
(field).

reap v. ①收割 shōugē (cut).
②獲得 huòdé (get).

rear n. 後方 hòufāng, 背後
bèihòu. — adj. 後部的 hòubù
de. — v. ①養育 yǎngyù (bring
up). ②飼養 sìyǎng (feed).

reason n. ①理由 lǐyóu, 原因
yuányīn (cause). ②理性 lǐxìng
(reasonableness).

reasonable adj. ①講道理的
jiǎng dàolǐ de (sensible). ②合
理的 hélǐ de (acceptable).
③公道的 gōngdào de (fair).

reassure v. 使安心 shǐ ānxīn.

rebate n. 折扣 zhékòu. — v.
給折扣 gěi zhékòu.

rebel n. 叛徒 pàntú, 謀反者
móufǎnzhě. — v. 反叛 fǎnpàn,
謀反 móufǎn.

rebellion n. 叛亂 pànluàn,
反叛 fǎnpàn.

rebirth n. 再生 zàishēng, 復
活 fùhuó.

rebound n. & v. 彈回 tánhuí,
跳 tiào.

rebuff n. & v. 斷然拒絕
duànrán jùjué.

rebuke v. 指責 zhǐzé, 譴責
qiǎnzé.

recall v. ①召回 zhàohuí (call
back). ②憶起 yìqǐ, 回憶 huíyì
(remember).

recant v. 撤回 chèhuí, 取消 qǔxiāo.

recede v. 後退 hòutuì.

receipt n. 收據 shōujù.

receive v. ①收到 shōudào, 接受 jiēshòu (get). ②款待 kuǎndài (greet).

receiver n. ①收受者 shōushòuzhě (person). ②聽筒 tīngtǒng (of telephone).

recent adj. 最近的 zuìjìn de.

recently adv. 近來 jìnlái.

receptacle n. 容器 róngqì.

reception n. ①接待 jiēdài (greeting). ②歡迎會 huānyínghuì (party).

receptionist n. 接待員 jiēdàiyuán.

receptive adj. 能接納的 néng jiēnà de.

recess n. ①休會期 xiūhuìqī / xiūhuìqí, 休業期 xiūyèqī / xiūyèqí (adjournment). ②壁凹 bì'āo (alcove).

recession n. 蕭條 xiāotiáo, 衰退 shuāituì (economy).

recipe n. 食譜 shípǔ (cooking).

recipient n. 接受者 jiēshòuzhě.

reciprocal adj. 相互的 xiānghù de, 互惠的 hùhuì de.

recital n. 獨奏會 dúzòuhuì (concert).

recitation n. 朗誦 lǎngsòng (declamation).

recite v. 朗誦 lǎngsòng.

reckless adj. 鹵莽的 lǔmǎng de, 不顧後果的 bú gù hòuguǒ de.

reckon v. 計算 jìsuàn.

reclaim v. ①要求歸還 yāoqiú guīhuán, 收回 shōuhuí (recover). ②開墾 kāikěn (make usable).

recline v. 斜倚 xiéyǐ.

recluse n. 隱士 yǐnshì.

recognition n. ①認得 rènde, 認出 rènchū, 辨認 biànrèn (identification). ②承認 chéngrèn (admition).

recognize v. ①認得 rènde, 認出 rènchū, 辨認 biànrèn (identify). ②承認 chéngrèn (admit).

recoil v. 退卻 tuìquè, 退縮 tuìsuō (draw back).

recollect v. 記起 jìqǐ, 憶起 yìqǐ.

recommend v. ①推薦 tuījiàn (speak in favor). ②勸告 quàngào (advise).

recommendation n. ①推薦 tuījiàn (act). ②推薦書 tuījiànshū (statement).

recompense v. ①賠償 péicháng (make up for). ②報答 bàodá (reward).

reconcile v. 調解 tiáojiě.

reconnaissance n. 偵察 zhēnchá.

reconstruct v. 重建 chóngjiàn.

record v. ①紀錄 jìlù (write down). ②錄存 lùcún (preserve). — n. ①記錄 jìlù (written statement). ②唱片 chàngpiàn (album). ③紀錄 jìlù (performance).

recorder n. 錄音機 lùyīnjī.

recount v. ①重數 chóngshǔ, 重新計算 chóngxīn jìsuàn (count again). ②描述 miáoshù (describe).

recoup v. 補償 bǔcháng (make up).

recourse n. 求助 qiúzhù.

recover v. ①恢復 huīfù (get back). ②復元 fùyuán (get well

again).

recovery n. ①恢復 huīfù (restoration). ②復元 fùyuán (healing).

recreation n. 娛樂 yúlè, 消遣 xiāoqiǎn.

recriminate v. 反控 fǎnkòng.

recruit n. ①新兵 xīnbīng (soldier). ②新加入者 xīn jiārù zhě (new member). — v. 招募 zhāomù.

rectangle n. 長方形 chángfāngxíng.

rectify v. 改正 gǎizhèng, 糾正 jiūzhèng (put right).

rectitude n. 正直 zhèngzhí (honesty).

rectum n. 直腸 zhícháng.

recuperate v. 恢復健康 huīfù jiànkāng (recover from illness).

recur v. 重現 chóngxiàn (happen again).

recycle v. 循環利用 xúnhuán lìyòng, 再使用 zài shǐyòng.

red n. & adj. 紅色 hóngsè.

redeem v. ①贖回 shúhuí (buy back). ②挽回 wǎnhuí, 彌補 míbǔ (get back).

redemption n. ①贖回 shúhuí (buying back). ②救贖 jiùshú (rescue).

red-hot adj. 熾熱的 chìrè de.

redress v. 改正 gǎizhèng, 糾正 jiūzhèng.

reduce v. ①減少 jiǎnshǎo, 降低 jiàngdī (decrease). ②濃縮 nóngsuō (condense).

reduction n. 減少 jiǎnshǎo 〈quantity〉, 降低 jiàngdī 〈level〉.

redundant adj. 多餘的 duōyú de, 冗贅的 rǒngzhuì de.

reed n. 蘆葦 lúwěi.

reef n. 暗礁 ànjiāo.

reek n. ①惡臭 èchòu 〈smell〉. ②濃煙 nóngyān 〈thick smoke〉. — v. 發出強烈臭氣 fāchū qiángliè chòuqì.

reel n. ①紡車 fǎngchē, 捲軸 juǎnzhóu (bobbin). ②一卷 yì juǎn 〈for a film〉. — v. 繞 rào (move).

reelect v. 重選 chóngxuǎn.

reestablish v. 重建 chóngjiàn.

referee n. ①仲裁者 zhòngcáizhě (arbitrator). ②裁判員 cáipànyuán (judge in a game).

reference n. ①參考 cānkǎo (something to consult). ②參考書 cānkǎoshū 〈book〉.

referendum n. 公民投票 gōngmín tóupiào.

refer to 提到 tídào, 談到 tándào (speak of).

refill v. 再注滿 zài zhùmǎn.

refine v. ①精製 jīngzhì, 提煉 tíliàn (purify). ②使文雅 shǐ wényǎ (cultivate).

reflect v. ①反射 fǎnshè (throw back). ②反映 fǎnyìng (echo).

reflection n. ①反射 fǎnshè 〈image〉. ②反映 fǎnyìng (echo).

reflex adj. 反射的 fǎnshè de. — n. 反射作用 fǎnshè zuòyòng.

reform v. 改革 gǎigé.

reformation n. 改革 gǎigé, 改良 gǎiliáng.

refract v. 使光屈折 shǐ guāng qūzhé.

refrain v. 抑制 yìzhì (control), 避免 bìmiǎn (avoid).

refresh v. ①提神 tíshén (energize). ②喚起 huànqǐ (remind).

refreshing adj. 提神的 tíshén de.

refreshment n. ①提神 tíshén 〈refresh〉.②點心 diǎnxīn 〈food or drink〉.

refrigerate v. 冷藏 lěngcáng, 冷凍 lěngdòng.

refrigerator n. 冰箱 bīngxiāng.

refuge n. 避難所 bìnànsuǒ.

refugee n. 逃難者 táonànzhě.

refund n. & v. 退款 tuìkuǎn, 償還 chánghuán.

refusal n. 拒絕 jùjué 〈rejection〉.

refuse v. 拒絕 jùjué. — n. 垃圾 lājī / lèsè.

regain v. 復得 fùdé 〈get back〉, 恢復 huīfù 〈recover〉.

regard v. ①視……為…… shì...wéi... 〈consider〉.②注視 zhùshì 〈look at〉.

regardless adj. & adv. 無論如何 wúlùn rúhé.

regency n. 攝政 shèzhèng.

regenerate v. 改造 gǎizào, 革新 géxīn. — adj. 改造過的 gǎizàoguo de.

regent n. 攝政者 shèzhèngzhě.

regime n. 政體 zhèngtǐ.

regiment n. 軍團 jūntuán.

region n. 地區 dìqū, 區域 qūyù.

register n. 登記簿 dēngjìbù. — v. 登記 dēngjì 〈hotel〉, 註冊 zhùcè 〈classes〉.

registrar n. 註冊員 zhùcèyuán.

registry n. 登記處 dēngjìchù, 註冊處 zhùcèchù.

regret n. & v. ①抱歉 bàoqiàn 〈regretfulness〉.②遺憾 yíhàn

〈pity〉.

regular adj. ①定期的 dìngqī de / dìngqí de, 有規律的 yǒu guīlǜ de 〈consistent〉.②有條理 的 yǒu tiáolǐ de 〈orderly〉.

regulate v. ①管制 guǎnzhì 〈control〉.②調節 tiáojié 〈adjust〉.

regulation n. 規定 guīdìng, 規則 guīzé.

rehabilitate v. ①恢復 huīfù, 修復 xiūfù 〈restore〉.②復職 fùzhí, 復權 fùquán 〈help recover〉.

rehearsal n. 排演 páiyǎn 〈practice〉.

rehearse v. 排演 páiyǎn 〈practice〉.

reign n. ①朝代 cháodài, 王朝 wángcháo 〈dynasty〉.②統治 tǒngzhì 〈rule〉. — v. 統治 tǒngzhì 〈rule〉.

reimburse v. 償還 chánghuán.

rein n. 韁繩 jiāngsheng / jiāngshéng 〈strap〉. — v. 駕馭 jiàyù, 控制 kòngzhì.

reindeer n. 馴鹿 xúnlù.

reinforce v. 增強 zēngqiáng 〈strengthen〉, 增援 zēngyuán 〈troops〉, 強調 qiángdiào 〈emphasize〉.

reinstate v. 復職 fùzhí 〈position〉, 復權 fùquán 〈power〉.

reiterate v. 反覆地說 fǎnfù de shuō.

reject v. ①拒絕 jùjué 〈refuse〉.②駁回 bóhuí 〈repel〉.

rejoice v. 欣喜 xīnxǐ, 高興 gāoxìng.

rejuvenate v. 恢復青春 huīfù qīngchūn, 返老還童 fǎn-lǎo-huán-tóng.

relapse v. 惡化 èhuà, 復發

fùfā.

relate v. ①敘述 xùshù (narrate). ②有關係 yǒu guānxi (be relevant).

related adj. 有關的 yǒuguān de.

relation n. ①關係 guānxi (connection). ②親戚 qīnqi (relative).

relationship n. 關係 guānxi.

relative n. 親戚 qīnqi.

relax v. 放鬆 fàngsōng.

relay n. ①接替人員 jiētì rényuán 〈shift〉. ②轉播 zhuǎnbō / zhuǎnbò 〈broadcast〉. ③接力賽跑 jiēlì sàipǎo 〈race〉. — v. 傳遞 chuándì (transmit).

release n. & v. ①釋放 shìfàng 〈set free〉. ②准許發表 zhǔnxǔ fābiǎo 〈make available〉.

relegate v. ①降級 jiàngjí, 貶黜 biǎnchù (demote). ②移交 yíjiāo (hand over).

relent v. 變溫和 biàn wēnhé.

relevant adj. 有關的 yǒuguān de.

reliable adj. 可靠的 kěkào de, 可信賴的 kě xìnlài de.

reliance n. 信賴 xìnlài, 信任 xìnrèn.

relic n. 遺物 yíwù, 遺跡 yíjī.

relief n. ①減輕 jiǎnqīng (alleviation). ②救濟 jiùjì (aid).

relieve v. ①減輕 jiǎnqīng (lessen). ②解救 jiějiù, 援助 yuánzhù (aid).

religion n. 宗教 zōngjiào.

religious adj. 宗教的 zōngjiào de.

relinquish v. ①放棄 fàngqì (give up). ②放手 fàngshǒu (release).

relish n. ①嗜好 shìhào (liking). ②調味料 tiáowèiliào 〈sauce〉, 開胃菜 kāiwèicài 〈pickle〉. — v. 享受 xiǎngshòu, 喜好 xǐhào.

reluctant adj. 不甘願的 bù gānyuàn de, 勉強的 miǎnqiǎng de.

rely v. 依賴 yīlài.

remain v. ①留下 liúxià (stay). ②剩下 shèngxià (be left).

remainder n. 殘餘 cányú.

remark n. ①評論 pínglùn (comment). ②注意 zhùyì (notice).

remarkable adj. 值得注意的 zhíde zhùyì de (worth noticing), 非凡的 fēifán de (extraordinary).

remedy v. ①治療 zhìliáo (cure). ②糾正 jiūzhèng (correct). — n. 治療 zhìliáo.

remember v. 記得 jìde.

remembrance n. ①記憶 jìyì (memory). ②紀念物 jìniànwù (souvenir).

remind v. 提醒 tíxǐng.

reminisce v. 追憶 zhuīyì.

reminiscence n. 追憶 zhuīyì (recall).

remiss adj. 疏忽的 shūhu de.

remission n. ①寬恕 kuānshù (forgiveness). ②和緩 héhuǎn (lessening).

remit v. 匯寄 huìjì 〈money〉.

remittance n. 匯款 huìkuǎn.

remnant n. 殘餘 cányú.

remonstrate v. 抗議 kàngyì (protest).

remorse n. 懊悔 àohuǐ, 悔恨 huǐhèn.

remote adj. ①遙遠的 yáoyuǎn de (distant). ②冷淡的 lěngdàn de (aloof).

removal n. ①搬移 bānyí (transfer). ②免職 miǎnzhí (dismissal).

remove v. ①除去 chúqù (get rid of). ②移動 yídòng (transfer).

remunerate v. 報酬 bàochóu, 酬勞 chóuláo.

renaissance n. 新生 xīnshēng, 復興 fùxīng. **the R-** 文藝復興 Wényì fùxīng.

render v. ①給與 gěiyǔ, 報答 bàodá (give). ②演出 yǎnchū (perform). ③使……成為 shǐ... chéngwéi (make). ④翻譯 fānyì (translate).

rendezvous n. ①約會 yuēhuì (appointment). ②會合地 huìhédì (place to meet).

rendition n. 演出 yǎnchū, 演奏 yǎnzòu (performance).

renegade n. 變節者 biànjiézhě, 叛徒 pàntú.

renew v. 更新 gēngxīn (update), 再開始 zài kāishǐ (start again).

renounce v. ①放棄 fàngqì (give up). ②與……斷絕關係 yǔ...duànjué guānxi (refuse to associate with).

renovate v. 革新 géxīn, 變新 biànxīn (make new again).

renown n. 名望 míngwàng, 聲譽 shēngyù.

rent n. 租金 zūjīn (rental).

renunciation n. 放棄 fàngqì (giving up).

reorganize v. 改組 gǎizǔ, 重組 chóngzǔ.

repair n. & v. ①修理 xiūlǐ (fix). ②修補 xiūbǔ (sew up).

reparation n. ①補償 bǔcháng 〈damage〉. ②賠償 péicháng 〈war damages〉.

repatriate v. 遣返 qiǎnfǎn.

repay v. ①付還 fùhuán (pay back). ②報答 bàodá (reward).

repeal n. & v. ①撤銷 chèxiāo (withdrawal). ②廢止 fèizhǐ (cancellation).

repeat v. ①覆述 fùshù (say again). ②重複 chóngfù (do again).

repeatedly adv. 重複地 chóngfù de.

repel v. ①逐退 zhútuì (drive away). ②使不悅 shǐ búyuè (offend). ③排斥 páichì (keep out).

repent v. 後悔 hòuhuǐ.

repercussion n. 影響 yǐngxiǎng (effect).

repertoire n. 戲目 xìmù 〈drama〉, 曲目 qǔmù 〈music〉.

repertory n. 戲目 xìmù, 曲目 qǔmù.

repetition n. 重複 chóngfù, 反覆 fǎnfù.

replace v. ①放回原處 fànghuí yuánchù (put back). ②代替 dàitì (take the place of).

replenish v. 再裝滿 zài zhuāngmǎn (refill), 補充 bǔchōng (recharge).

replica n. 複製品 fùzhìpǐn.

reply n. & v. 回答 huídá, 答覆 dáfù.

report n. ①報導 bàodǎo 〈account〉. ②報告 bàogào 〈written〉. — v. ①報告 bàogào (give an account of). ②報到 bàodào (go to somebody). ③揭發 jiēfā (complain).

reporter n. 記者 jìzhě.

repose n. ①休息 xiūxi (rest). ②安靜 ānjìng (quietness). — v. 休息 xiūxi.

represent v. ①表示 biǎoshì,

R

象徵 xiàngzhēng (embody).
②代表 dàibiǎo (speak on behalf).

representation n. 代表
dàibiǎo.

representative n. 代表
dàibiǎo.

repress v. 壓制 yāzhì, 壓抑
yāyì.

reprieve n. & v. 延緩處決
yánhuǎn chǔjué.

reprimand n. & v. 懲戒
chéngjiè, 嚴斥 yánchì.

reprisal n. 報復 bàofù.

reproach n. & v. 譴責
qiǎnzé, 斥責 chìzé.

reproduce v. ①複製 fùzhì
(copy). ②生殖 shēngzhí
(procreate).

reproduction n. ①複製 fùzhì
(copying), 複製品 fùzhìpǐn (a
copy). ②生殖 shēngzhí
(procreation).

reprove v. 譴責 qiǎnzé.

reptile n. 爬行動物 páxíng
dòngwù.

republic n. 共和國
gònghéguó.

republican adj. 共和國的
gònghéguó de (of a republic).
— n. 共和黨黨員 gònghédǎng
dǎngyuán (party member).

repudiate v. 拒絕 jùjué
(refuse).

repulse v. 驅逐 qūzhú.

reputation n. 名譽 míngyù,
聲望 shēngwàng.

repute n. 名譽 míngyù.

request n. & v. 請求 qǐngqiú,
要求 yāoqiú.

require v. ①需要 xūyào
(need). ②要求 yāoqiú
(demand).

requirement n. 必要事物
bìyào shìwù ⟨thing⟩, 必備條件
bìbèi tiáojiàn ⟨qualification⟩.

requisite adj. 需要的 xūyào
de, 必要的 bìyào de.

requite v. 回報 huíbào, 報答
bàodá (repay).

rescind v. 廢止 fèizhǐ.

rescue n. & v. 解救 jiějiù, 救
出 jiùchū, 救援 jiùyuán.

research n. 研究 yánjiū /
yánjiù.

resemblance n. 相似
xiāngsì.

resemble v. 相似 xiāngsì.

resent v. 憤恨 fènhèn.

reservation n. ①預訂 yùdìng
(booking). ②保留 bǎoliú
(doubt). ③保留地 bǎoliúdì
(protected area).

reserve v. ①留下 liúxià (keep).
②預約 yùyuē (book). — n.
①貯藏 zhùcáng / zhǔcáng
(stores). ②保留地 bǎoliúdì
(protected area).

reservoir n. 貯水池
zhùshuǐchí / zhǔshuǐchí, 水庫
shuǐkù.

reside v. 居住 jūzhù (live).

residence n. 住宅 zhùzhái,
住處 zhùchù (dwelling).

resident n. 居民 jūmín.

residential adj. 住宅的
zhùzhái de.

residual adj. 殘餘的 cányú de.

residue n. 殘餘 cányú.

resign v. 辭職 cízhí (quit).

resignation n. ①辭職 cízhí
(resigning). ②辭呈 cíchéng
(letter to resign).

resin n. 樹脂 shùzhī, 松脂
sōngzhī.

resist v. ①抵抗 dǐkàng
(oppose). ②防止 fángzhǐ
(prevent).

resistance n. 抵抗 dǐkàng

(opposition). 抵抗力 dǐkànglì ⟨force⟩.

resistor n. 電阻器 diànzǔqì.

resolute adj. 堅決的 jiānjué de, 斷然的 duànrán de.

resolution n. ①決心 juéxīn, 堅決 jiānjué (determination). ②決議 juéyì (decision).

resolve v. ①決定 juédìng, 下決心 xià juéxīn (decide). ②解決 jiějué (have an answer to).

resonance n. 回響 huíxiǎng, 共鳴 gòngmíng.

resort n. 度假勝地 dùjià shèngdì. — v. 採取 cǎiqǔ, 訴諸 sùzhū (adopt).

resound v. 回響 huíxiǎng, 共鳴 gòngmíng (echo).

resource n. (pl.) 資源 zīyuán.

respect n. ①尊敬 zūnjìng, 尊重 zūnzhòng (admiration). ②方面 fāngmiàn (aspect).

respectable adj. ①高尚的 gāoshàng de (decent). ②可觀的 kěguān de (considerable). ③端莊的 duānzhuāng de (modest).

respectful adj. 恭敬的 gōngjìng de.

respective adj. 個別的 gèbié de.

respectively adv. 個別地 gèbié de, 各自地 gèzì de.

respiration n. 呼吸 hūxī.

respite n. 休息 xiūxi (rest), 中止 zhōngzhǐ (pause).

resplendent adj. 燦爛的 cànlàn de, 華麗的 huálì de.

respond v. ①回答 huídá (answer). ②回應 huíyìng (act in answer).

response n. 回答 huídá (answer), 回應 huíyìng (reaction).

responsibility n. 責任 zérèn ⟨general⟩, 職責 zhízé ⟨work⟩.

responsible adj. 負責任的 fù zérèn de.

responsive adj. 有反應的 yǒu fǎnyìng de.

rest n. 休息 xiūxi (break). ~ *room* 廁所 cèsuǒ, 洗手間 xǐshǒujiān. ~ *stop* 休息站 xiūxizhàn. — v. 休息 xiūxi.

restaurant n. 餐廳 cāntīng, 餐館 cānguǎn, 飯店 fàndiàn.

restless adj. ①不安靜的 bù ānjìng de, 好動的 hàodòng de (agitated). ②無法休息的 wúfǎ xiūxi de (sleepless).

restoration n. ①修復 xiūfù (restoring). ②恢復 huīfù (bringing back).

restore v. ①修復 xiūfù (fix). ②歸還 guīhuán (give back). ③恢復 huīfù (put in original condition).

restrain v. 克制 kèzhì, 抑制 yìzhì.

restraint n. 克制 kèzhì, 抑制 yìzhì.

restrict v. 限制 xiànzhì.

restriction n. 限制 xiànzhì.

result n. 結果 jiéguǒ ⟨effect⟩.

resume v. 再開始 zài kāishǐ (start again), 繼續 jìxù (continue).

résumé n. 履歷 lǚlì.

resurrect v. ①使復活 shǐ fùhuó (bring back to life). ②復興 fùxīng (revive).

retail n. & v. 零售 língshòu.

retailer n. 零售商 língshòushāng.

retain v. ①保持 bǎochí (hold), 保留 bǎoliú (keep). ②記得 jìde (remember).

retaliate v. 報復 bàofù.

retard v. 延遲 yánchí.

retarded *adj.* 智能遲緩的 zhìnéng chíhuǎn de.

retention *n.* 保留 bǎoliú (retaining).

reticent *adj.* 沈默的 chénmò de.

retina *n.* 視網膜 shìwǎngmó / shìwǎngmò.

retire *v.* 退休 tuìxiū (stop working).

retirement *n.* 退休 tuìxiū.

retort *v.* 回嘴 huízuǐ (answer back), 反駁 fǎnbó (refute).

retrace *v.* 折回 zhéhuí (go back over).

retract *v.* ①縮回 suōhuí (pull back). ②收回 shōuhuí (withdraw).

retreat *n.* & *v.* 撤退 chètuì (withdrawal).

retribution *n.* 報應 bàoyìng.

retrieve *v.* 尋回 xúnhuí.

retrogressive *adj.* 後退的 hòutuì de, 退化的 tuìhuà de.

retrospect *n.* 回顧 huígù, 回溯 huísù.

return *v.* ①回來 huílai (come back). ②回歸 huíguī (go back). ③歸還 guīhuán (give back). — *n.* ①回來 huílai (coming back). ②盈利 yínglì (profit).

reunion *n.* 重聚 chóngjù (get together again), 團圓 tuányuán ⟨of family, friends, etc.⟩.

reveal *v.* ①顯露 xiǎnlù (display). ②洩露 xièlòu (make known).

revelation *n.* 洩露 xièlòu.

revenge *n.* & *v.* 報仇 bàochóu, 報復 bàofù (vengeance).

revenue *n.* 收入 shōurù (income), 歲收 suìshōu ⟨taxes⟩.

revere *v.* 尊敬 zūnjìng.

reverence *n.* 尊敬 zūnjìng.

reversal *n.* 反轉 fǎnzhuǎn, 逆轉 nìzhuǎn.

reverse *v.* 反轉 fǎnzhuǎn (go back), 顛倒 diāndǎo (turn over). — *adj.* 相反的 xiāngfǎn de. — *v.* ①反轉 fǎnzhuǎn, 顛倒 diāndǎo (turn round). ②逆行 nìxíng (go backwards). ③取消 qǔxiāo (cancel).

revert *v.* 恢復原狀 huīfù yuánzhuàng.

review *v.* ①復習 fùxí ⟨of school work⟩. ②評論 pínglùn ⟨for publication⟩. ③覆審 fùshěn (re-examine).

revise *v.* 修訂 xiūdìng, 校訂 jiàodìng.

revision *n.* 修訂 xiūdìng, 校訂 jiàodìng.

revival *n.* 振興 zhènxīng.

revive *v.* 振興 zhènxīng.

revoke *v.* 取消 qǔxiāo.

revolt *v.* ①背叛 bèipàn (rebel). ②使厭惡 shǐ yànwù (disgust). — *n.* 背叛 bèipàn (rebellion).

revolution *n.* ①革命 gémìng (reformation). ②週期 zhōuqí / zhōuqí (circuit).

revolutionary *adj.* 革命性的 gémìngxìng de.

revolve *v.* 旋轉 xuánzhuǎn (go around in a circle).

revolver *n.* 左輪手槍 zuǒlún shǒuqiāng.

reward *n.* & *v.* 報酬 bàochóu.

rewrite *v.* 重寫 chóngxiě (write again), 改寫 gǎixiě (correct).

rhapsody *n.* 狂想曲 kuángxiǎngqǔ.

rhetoric n. 修辭學 xiūcíxué.

rheumatism n. 風濕症 fēngshīzhèng.

rhinoceros n. 犀牛 xīniú.

rhyme v. 押韻 yāyùn. — n. ①韻 yùn (rhythm). ②詩 shī, 韻文 yùnwén (poem).

rhythm n. 韻律 yùnlǜ, 節奏 jiézòu.

rib n. 肋骨 lèigǔ / lèigǔ ⟨bone⟩.

ribbon n. 絲帶 sīdài (long, narrow strip).

rice n. 米 mǐ ⟨uncooked⟩, 飯 fàn ⟨cooked⟩.

rich adj. ①有錢的 yǒuqián de, 富有的 fùyǒu de (wealthy). ②富足的 fùzú de (abundant). ③肥沃的 féiwò de (fruitful).

rickets n. 佝僂病 yǔlóubìng / yǔlóubìng.

rid v. 免除 miǎnchú.

riddance n. 除去 chúqù.

riddle n. 謎語 míyǔ, 謎 mí.

ride v. 騎 qí ⟨bike, horse⟩, 乘 chéng ⟨be carried on⟩. — n. 乘坐 chéngzuò.

rider n. ①騎乘者 qíchéngzhě ⟨person⟩. ②附文 fùwén, 附件 fùjiàn ⟨statement⟩.

ridge n. ①山脊 shānjǐ ⟨hill⟩. ②屋脊 wūjǐ ⟨house⟩.

ridicule n. & v. 訕笑 shànxiào, 嘲弄 cháonòng.

ridiculous adj. 荒謬的 huāngmiù de.

rife adj. ①流行的 liúxíng de (widespread). ②眾多的 zhòngduō de (full of).

rifle n. 來福槍 láifúqiāng, 步槍 bùqiāng.

rig n. ①裝備 zhuāngbèi (equipment). ②服裝 fúzhuāng (clothing). — v. 裝索具於 zhuāng suǒjù yú.

right adj. ①正確的 zhèngquè de (correct). ②公正的 gōngzhèng de (just). ③右方的 yòufāng de (right-hand). ~ **wing** 右派 yòupài. — n. 權利 quánlì.

righteous adj. 正義的 zhèngyì de (morally right).

rigid adj. ①僵硬的 jiāngyìng de (stiff). ②嚴格的 yángé de (strict).

rim n. 邊緣 biānyuán.

rind n. ①樹皮 shùpí ⟨of trees⟩. ②果皮 guǒpí ⟨of fruits⟩.

ring n. ①環 huán, 圈 quān (circle). ②戒指 jièzhǐ ⟨for finger⟩. ③鈴聲 língshēng ⟨sound⟩. — v. 響 xiǎng ⟨sound⟩.

rink n. 旱冰場 hànbīngchǎng / 溜冰場 liūbīngchǎng.

rinse v. 清洗 qīngxǐ, 洗濯 xǐzhuó.

riot n. 暴動 bàodòng (violent disturbance). — v. 暴動 bàodòng, 騷動 sāodòng.

rip v. 撕開 sīkāi, 扯裂 chěliè.

ripe adj. 成熟的 chéngshú de.

ripen v. 使成熟 shǐ chéngshú.

ripple n. 漣漪 liányī (very small wave). — v. 起漣漪 qǐ liányī.

rise v. ①站起 zhànqǐ (stand up). ②升起 shēngqǐ (advance in rank). ③起床 qǐchuáng (get up). ④上升 shàngshēng, 漲 zhǎng (increase). — n. ①往上 的斜坡 wǎng shàng de xiépō (ascent). ②上升 shàngshēng, 增高 zēnggāo (increase).

risk n. 危險 wēixiǎn / wéixiǎn. — v. 冒……危險 mào... wēixiǎn / mào...wéixiǎn.

risky adj. 冒險的 màoxiǎn de.

rite n. 儀式 yíshì.

R

ritual *n.* 儀式 yíshì.

rival *n.* 競爭者 jìngzhēngzhě (competitor), 對手 duìshǒu (opponent), 敵手 díshǒu (enemy). — *v.* 與……競爭 yǔ...jìngzhēng.

river *n.* 河 hé, 江 jiāng.

rivet *n.* 鉚釘 mǎodīng.

rivulet *n.* 溪流 xīliú, 小河 xiǎohé.

road *n.* 路 lù, 道路 dàolù.

roam *v.* 閒逛 xiánguàng, 漫遊 mànyóu.

roar *v.* 吼叫 hǒujiào. — *n.* 吼 hǒu.

roast *v.* 烤 kǎo (grill). — *n.* 烤肉 kǎoròu (meat). — *adj.* 烘烤的 hōngkǎo de.

rob *v.* 搶劫 qiǎngjié.

robber *n.* 強盜 qiángdào.

robbery *n.* 搶劫 qiǎngjié.

robe *n.* 長外袍 chángwàipáo.

robin *n.* 知更鳥 zhīgēngniǎo.

robot *n.* 機器人 jīqìrén.

robust *adj.* 強壯的 qiángzhuàng de.

rock *n.* 岩石 yánshí, 石塊 shíkuài (stone). — *v.* 搖擺 yáobǎi, 搖動 yáodòng (sway). ~ *and roll* 搖滾樂 yáogǔnyuè.

rocket *n.* 火箭 huǒjiàn. — *v.* 向上直衝 xiàng shàng zhíchōng.

rocky *adj.* 多岩石的 duō yánshí de.

rod *n.* 桿 gǎn, 棒 bàng.

rogue *n.* 流氓 liúmáng, 惡棍 ègùn.

role *n.* 角色 juésè (character).

roll *v.* ①滾 gǔn, 轉 zhuǎn (move round). ②捲 juǎn (curl). ③輾平 niǎnpíng (flatten). — *n.* ①一捲 yì juǎn (scroll). ②名冊 míngcè, 名單 míngdān (list).

roller *n.* 滾軸 gǔnzhóu (cylinder), 滾輪 gǔnlún (wheel). ~ *coaster* 雲霄飛車 yúnxiāo fēichē. ~ *skate* 旱冰鞋 hànbīngxié / 溜冰鞋 liūbīngxié.

romance *n.* ①愛情故事 àiqíng gùshi (story). ②傳奇小說 chuánqí xiǎoshuō (adventure). ③情事 qíngshì (love interest).

romantic *adj.* ①浪漫的 làngmàn de (dream-like). ②浪漫派的 làngmànpài de (of art, music, etc.).

roof *n.* 屋頂 wūdǐng (building), 頂部 dǐngbù (top).

rookie *n.* 生手 shēngshǒu, 新手 xīnshǒu (beginner), 新兵 xīnbīng (recruit).

room *n.* ①房間 fángjiān (in a house). ②空間 kōngjiān (space).

roommate *n.* 同屋 tóngwū / 室友 shìyǒu.

roost *v.* 棲息 qīxī / qíxī. — *n.* 棲木 qīmù.

rooster *n.* 公雞 gōngjī.

root *n.* ①根 gēn, 根部 gēnbù (plant). ②根源 gēnyuán (source). ③字根 zìgēn (grammar). ④根數 gēnshù (mathematics).

rope *n.* 繩 shéng.

rosary *n.* 念珠 niànzhū.

rose *n.* ①玫瑰 méiguī (flower). ②玫瑰色 méiguìsè (color).

rostrum *n.* 講壇 jiǎngtán.

rosy *adj.* ①玫瑰色的 méiguìsè de (reddish). ②光明的 guāngmíng de (bright).

rot *v.* 腐爛 fǔlàn, 腐壞 fǔhuài (decay). — *n.* 腐爛 fǔlàn, 腐壞 fǔhuài (rottenness).

rotary adj. 旋轉的 xuánzhuǎn de.

rotate v. ①旋轉 xuánzhuǎn (turn). ②循環 xúnhuán (recur in order).

rotation n. ①旋轉 xuánzhuǎn (revolution). ②輪流 lúnliú (taking turns).

rotten adj. ①腐爛的 fǔlàn de 〈food〉. ②腐朽的 fǔxiǔ de 〈wood〉. ③壞的 huài de (bad).

rough adj. ①粗糙的 cūcāo de (coarse), 凹凸不平的 āotū bù píng de / āotú bù píng de (not even). ②粗魯的 cūlǔ de (impolite). ③概略的 gàilüè de (approximate). ④粗厲的 cūlì de (rasping). ⑤艱苦的 jiānkǔ de (difficult).

roughen v. 使崎嶇不平 shǐ qíqū bù píng / shǐ qíqū bù píng, 變粗糙 biàn cūcāo.

roughly adv. 概略地 gàilüè de.

round adj. 圓的 yuán de (circular). — n. 回合 huíhé, 局 jú 〈game〉.

rouse v. 喚醒 huànxǐng (waken).

rout v. 擊潰 jīkuì / jíkuì (defeat completely). — n. 潰敗 kuìbài.

route n. 路線 lùxiàn.

routine n. & adj. 例行公事 lìxíng gōngshì, 慣例 guànlì (regular activity).

rove v. 漫遊 mànyóu.

row n. 列 liè, 排 pái (line). — v. 划船 huáchuán.

rowdy adj. 粗暴的 cūbào de.

royal adj. 王室的 wángshì de, 皇家的 huángjiā de.

royalty n. 皇族 huángzú, 皇室 huángshì (royal family).

R.S.V.P. 敬請答覆 jìngqǐng dáfù.

rub v. 摩擦 mócā.

rubber n. 橡膠 xiàngjiāo, 橡皮 xiàngpí 〈substance〉. ~ **band** 橡皮筋 xiàngpíjīn.

rubbish n. ①廢物 fèiwù, 垃圾 lājī / lèsè (waste). ②廢話 fèihuà (nonsense).

rubble n. 碎石 suìshí, 瓦礫 wǎlì.

ruby n. ①紅寶石 hóngbǎoshí 〈stone〉. ②深紅色 shēnhóngsè 〈color〉.

rudder n. 船舵 chuánduò.

ruddy adj. 紅潤的 hóngrùn de.

rude adj. ①無禮貌的 wú lǐmào de, 粗魯的 cūlǔ de (impolite). ②粗暴的 cūbào de, 猛烈的 měngliè de (violent).

rudimentary adj. 初期的 chūqī de / chūqí de (elementary).

rue v. 悔恨 huǐhèn.

ruffian n. 凶漢 xiōnghàn, 惡棍 ègùn.

ruffle v. ①使皺 shǐ zhòu (ripple). ②弄亂 nòngluàn (mess up). ③惹……生氣 rě...shēngqì (annoy).

rug n. 地毯 dìtǎn (thick floor mat).

rugby n. 橄欖球 gǎnlǎnqiú.

rugged adj. 崎嶇的 qíqū de / qíqú de (rocky).

ruin n. ①毀滅 huǐmiè (collapse). ②廢墟 fèixū (debris). — v. 摧毀 cuīhuǐ, 破壞 pòhuài (destroy).

rule n. ①規則 guīzé (regulation). ②統治 tǒngzhì (government), 管理 guǎnlǐ (management). ③慣例 guànlì (habit). — v. 統治 tǒngzhì (govern).

ruler n. ①統治者 tǒngzhìzhě

R

(governor). ②尺 chǐ 〈for measuring〉.

rum n. 萊姆酒 láimǔjiǔ.

rumble n. & v. 隆隆聲 lónglóngshēng 〈sound〉.

rumor n. 謠言 yáoyán (gossip). — v. 謠傳 yáochuán.

rump n. 臀部 túnbù.

run v. ①跑 pǎo (race). ②行駛 xíngshǐ 〈car〉. ③運轉 yùnzhuǎn (work). ④流 liú (flow). ⑤經營 jīngyíng 〈business〉. — n. 跑 pǎo (race).

runaway n. 逃亡者 táowángzhě.

runner n. 奔跑者 bēnpǎozhě (someone who runs).

running adj. ①連續的 liánxù de (consecutive). ②流動的 liúdòng de (flowing).

runway n. 跑道 pǎodào (air strip).

rupture n. & v. 破裂 pòliè (burst), 決裂 juéliè (breaking).

rural adj. 鄉村的 xiāngcūn de.

rush v. ①衝進 chōngjìn (bolt). ②急促行事 jícù xíngshì (act quickly). — n. ①匆促 cōngcù (haste). ②衝進 chōngjìn (act of rushing).

Russian n. & adj. ①俄國人 Éguórén / Èguórén 〈people〉. ②俄語 Éyǔ / Èyǔ 〈language〉.

rust n. 銹 xiù. — v. 生銹 shēngxiù (get rusty).

rustic adj. ①鄉村的 xiāngcūn de (rural). ②單純的 dānchún de (simple).

rustle n. & v. 沙沙聲 shāshāshēng 〈sound〉.

rusty adj. ①生銹的 shēngxiù de (oxidized). ②荒疏的 huāngshū de (unused).

rut n. 車轍 chēzhé (track made by wheels).

ruthless adj. 無情的 wúqíng de (cold), 殘忍的 cánrěn de (cruel).

rye n. 裸麥 luǒmài, 黑麥 hēimài.

S

Sabbath n. 安息日 Ānxīrì / Ānxírì.

saber n. 軍刀 jūndāo.

sable n. 貂 diāo.

sabotage n. & v. 陰謀破壞 yīnmóu pòhuài.

sachet n. 香囊 xiāngnáng.

sack n. 袋子 dàizi. — v. ①解雇 jiěgù (fire). ②劫掠 jiélüè (plunder).

sacrament n. 聖禮 shènglǐ. *S~* 聖餐 Shèngcān (Communion).

sacred adj. 神聖的 shénshèng de.

sacrifice n. ①祭品 jìpǐn (offering). ②犧牲 xīshēng (giving up). — v. ①祭祀 jìsì (offer). ②犧牲 xīshēng (give up).

sacrilege n. 褻瀆 xièdú, 瀆神 dúshén.

sad adj. ①悲傷的 bēishāng de, 難過的 nánguò de (sorrowful). ②令人悲傷的 lìng rén bēishāng de (distressing).

sadden v. 使悲傷 shǐ bēishāng.

saddle n. 鞍 ān. — v. 給⋯⋯裝鞍 gěi...zhuāng'ān.

sadness n. 悲傷 bēishāng, 難過 nánguò.

safe adj. ①安全的 ānquán de (secure). ②平安的 píng'ān de (peaceful). ③小心的 xiǎoxīn de (cautious).

safeguard n. & v. 保護 bǎohù, 防護 fánghù.

safety n. 安全 ānquán (security). ~ *belt* 安全帶 ānquándài.

sag v. 壓陷 yāxiàn, 下墜 xiàzhuì.

saga n. ①長篇故事 chángpiān gùshì (long story). ②英勇事蹟 yīngyǒng shìjī (hero's journey).

sage adj. 賢明的 xiánmíng de. — n. 聖人 shèngrén.

Sagittarius 射手座 Shèshǒuzuò.

Sahara 撒哈拉沙漠 Sāhālā shāmò.

sail n. ①帆 fān / fán (foresail). ②航行 hángxíng (voyage). — v. ①航行 hángxíng (travel). ②駕駛 jiàshǐ (navigate).

sailboat n. 帆船 fánchuán.

sailing n. ①航行 hángxíng (voyage). ②航海術 hánghǎishù (skill).

sailor n. ①船員 chuányuán (crew). ②水手 shuǐshǒu (seaman).

saint n. ①聖徒 shèngtú

(religion). ②聖人 shèngrén (sage).

sake n. 緣故 yuángù. *for the* ~ *of*⋯ 為了⋯⋯ wèile....

salad n. 沙拉 shālā, 生菜食品 shēngcài shípǐn.

salary n. 薪資 xīnzī.

sale n. 銷售 xiāoshòu, 銷路 xiāolù. *for* ~ 出售 chūshòu. *on* ~ 打折 dǎzhé.

salesman n. 推銷員 tuīxiāoyuán, 業務員 yèwùyuán, 售貨員 shòuhuòyuán.

saliva n. 唾液 tuòyè.

sallow adj. 病黃色的 bìnghuángsè de (sickly yellow), 氣色差的 qìsè chà de (looking unwell).

salmon n. 鮭魚 guīyú.

salon n. ①會客廳 huìkètīng (room). ②美術展覽會 měishù zhǎnlǎnhuì, 畫廊 huàláng (art gallery). ③藝文聚會 yìwén jùhuì (artistic gathering). ④美髮沙龍 měifà shālóng / měifǎ shālóng (hair).

saloon n. 酒館 jiǔguǎn, 酒吧 jiǔbā (bar).

salt n. 鹽 yán.

salty adj. 鹹的 xián de.

salubrious adj. 有益健康的 yǒuyì jiànkāng de, 怡人的 yírén de.

salutary adj. ①有益的 yǒuyì de (beneficial). ②健康的 jiànkāng de (healthy).

salutation n. 致意 zhìyì, 招呼 zhāohu.

salute v. ①致敬 zhìjìng, 敬禮 jìnglǐ (show honor). ②致意 zhìyì, 招呼 zhāohu (greet).

salvage n. 災難救援 zāinàn jiùyuán. — v. ①災難救援

zāinàn jiùyuán 〈damaged building〉. ②挽救 wǎnjiù 〈failed situation〉.

salvation n. ①拯救 zhěngjiù 〈redemption〉. ②救助 jiùzhù 〈help〉. *the S- Army* 救世軍 Jiùshìjūn.

salve n. 軟膏 ruǎngāo, 藥膏 yàogāo 〈ointment〉.

same adj. 相同的 xiāngtóng de, 同樣的 tóngyàng de.

sample n. 樣本 yàngběn, 樣品 yàngpǐn.

sanatorium n. 療養院 liáoyǎngyuàn.

sanction n. & v. ①認可 rènkě, 批准 pīzhǔn 〈permission〉. ②制裁 zhìcái 〈penalty〉.

sanctity n. 神聖 shénshèng.

sanctuary n. ①聖所 shèngsuǒ 〈holy place〉. ②保護區 bǎohùqū 〈wildlife reserve〉. ③避難所 bìnànsuǒ 〈shelter〉.

sand n. 沙 shā.

sandal n. 涼鞋 liángxié.

sandglass n. 沙漏 shālòu.

sandwich n. 三明治 sānmíngzhì.

sandy adj. 含沙的 hánshā de.

sane adj. ①神志清醒的 shénzhì qīngxǐng de 〈not mad〉. ②明智的 míngzhì de 〈sensible〉.

sanguine adj. 樂天的 lètiān de 〈optimistic〉.

sanitary adj. 衛生的 wèishēng de. ~ *napkin* 衛生棉 wèishēngmián.

sanitation n. ①衛生 wèishēng, 公共衛生 gōnggòng wèishēng 〈hygiene〉. ②衛生設備 wèishēng shèbèi 〈equipment〉.

sanity n. 心智健全 xīnzhì jiànquán, 神志清醒 shénzhì qīngxǐng.

Santa Claus n. 聖誕老人 Shèngdàn Lǎorén.

sap n. 樹液 shùyè 〈plant〉. — v. 削弱 xuēruò / xuèruò, 耗竭 hàojié.

sapphire n. 藍寶石 lánbǎoshí.

sarcasm n. 諷刺 fěngcì / fèngcì, 譏諷 jīfěng / jīfèng.

sarcastic adj. 諷刺的 fěngcì de / fèngcì de, 譏諷的 jīfěng de / jīfèng de.

sardine n. 沙丁魚 shādīngyú.

sash n. ①帶 dài, 飾帶 shìdài 〈clothing〉. ②窗框 chuāngkuàng 〈window〉.

Satan n. 撒旦 Sādàn, 惡魔 Èmó.

satchel n. 小皮包 xiǎo píbāo, 小書包 xiǎo shūbāo.

satellite n. ①衛星 wèixīng 〈planet〉. ②人造衛星 rénzào wèixīng 〈man-made device〉. ~ *television* 衛星電視 wèixīng diànshì.

satin n. 緞 duàn.

satire n. 諷刺詩文 fěngcì shīwén / fèngcì shīwén.

satisfaction n. 滿足 mǎnzú, 滿意 mǎnyì.

satisfactory adj. 令人滿意的 lìng rén mǎnyì de.

satisfied adj. 滿足的 mǎnzú de, 滿意的 mǎnyì de.

satisfy v. 使滿足 shǐ mǎnzú, 使滿意 shǐ mǎnyì.

saturate v. ①浸透 jìntòu 〈drench〉. ②飽和 bǎohé 〈fill completely〉.

Saturday n. 星期六 Xīngqīliù / Xīngqíliù.

Saturn n. 土星 Tǔxīng.

sauce n. 調味汁 tiáowèizhī, 調味醬 tiáowèijiàng.

saucepan n. 燉鍋 dùnguō.

saucer n. 茶盤 chápán, 碟子 diézi.

sauna n. 桑拿浴 sāngnáyù / 三溫暖 sānwēnnuǎn.

saunter n. 閒逛 xiánguàng, 漫步 mànbù.

sausage n. 臘腸 làcháng, 香腸 xiāngcháng.

savage adj. ①野蠻的 yěmán de (barbaric). ②殘酷的 cánkù de (cruel), 兇猛的 xiōngměng de (fierce). — n. 野蠻人 yěmánrén.

savannah n. 大草原 dà cǎoyuán.

save v. ①拯救 zhěngjiù, 援救 yuánjiù (rescue). ②儲蓄 chǔxù / chúxù, 存 cún (collect). ③節省 jiéshěng (lessen).

saving n. 節省 jiéshěng (amount saved). ②(pl.) 儲蓄 chǔxù / chúxù (money saved up).

savior n. 拯救者 zhěngjiùzhě.

savor v. ①享受 xiǎngshòu (enjoy). ②品嘗 pǐncháng (flavor).

savory adj. 美味的 měiwèi de, 可口的 kěkǒu de (pleasant to taste).

saw n. 鋸子 jùzi. — v. 鋸開 jùkāi.

saxophone n. 薩克管 sàkèguǎn / 薩克斯風 sàkèsīfēng.

say v. 說 shuō, 講 jiǎng.

saying n. 諺語 yànyǔ, 格言 géyán.

scab n. 疤 bā, 痂 jiā.

scabbard n. 劍鞘 jiànqiào.

scaffold n. ①鷹架 yīngjià (for building). ②斷頭臺 duàntóutái, 絞臺 jiǎotái (gallows).

scaffolding n. 鷹架 yīngjià.

scald v. 燙傷 tàngshāng.

scale n. ①天秤 tiānchèng (balance). ②鱗 lín (fish). ③比例 尺 bǐlìchǐ (map). ④刻度 kèdù (marks for measuring). ⑤音階 yīnjiē (music).

scallop n. 扇貝 shànbèi.

scalp n. 頭皮 tóupí. — v. 剝頭 皮 bō tóupí.

scamper v. 蹦蹦跳跳地跑 bèngbèng-tiàotiào de pǎo.

scan v. ①細察 xìchá, 審視 shěnshì (examine). ②瀏覽 liúlǎn (glance at). ③掃描 sǎomiáo (copy).

scandal n. ①醜聞 chǒuwén (disgrace). ②誹謗 fěibàng (slander).

scanner n. 掃瞄器 sǎomiáoqì.

scanty adj. 不足的 bùzú de, 少量的 shǎoliàng de.

scapegoat n. 代罪羔羊 dàizuì gāoyáng.

scar n. 傷痕 shānghén, 疤 bā. — v. 留下傷痕 liú xià shānghén.

scarce adj. 缺乏的 quēfá de, 不足的 bùzú de.

scarcely adv. 幾乎不 jīhū bù, 僅僅 jǐnjǐn.

scarcity n. 缺乏 quēfá, 不足 bùzú.

scare v. 驚嚇 jīngxià, 驚恐 jīngkǒng. — n. 驚恐 jīngkǒng.

scared adj. 受驚的 shòujīng de, 害怕的 hàipà de.

scarecrow n. 稻草人 dàocǎorén.

scarf n. 圍巾 wéijīn.

scarlet n. 深紅 shēnhóng. — adj. 深紅的 shēnhóng de.

~ *fever* 猩紅熱 xīnghóngrè.

scathing adj. 嚴苛的 yánkē
de (severe).

scatter v. ①驅散 qūsàn
(dispel). ②散播 sànbō / sànbò
(spread).

scavenger n. 清道夫
qīngdàofū.

scenario n. 劇情 jùqíng, 劇本
jùběn.

scene n. ①現場 xiànchǎng
〈location〉. ②風景 fēngjǐng, 景
色 jǐngsè (landscape). ③一幕 yí
mù (episode). ④場景 chǎngjǐng,
佈景 bùjǐng (backdrop).

scenery n. ①風景 fēngjǐng,
景色 jǐngsè (landscape). ②舞
臺佈景 wǔtái bùjǐng (back-
drop).

scent n. ①香味 xiāngwèi
(fragrance). ②氣味 qìwèi
(smell). ③香水 xiāngshuǐ
(perfume). — v. 嗅出 xiùchū
(smell).

schedule n. 表 biǎo, 時刻表
shíkèbiǎo (timetable), 行程表
xíngchéngbiǎo (agenda). — v.
將……列表 jiāng...lièbiǎo
(put in schedule), 安排 ānpái
(arrange).

scheme n. ①計畫 jìhuà (plan).
②陰謀 yīnmóu (conspiracy).
③圖表 túbiǎo (diagram).
④設計 shèjì (design). — v. 計
畫 jìhuà (plan), 圖謀 túmóu
(connive).

schizophrenia n. 精神分裂
症 jīngshén fēnliè zhèng.

scholar n. 學者 xuézhě
(learned person).

scholarship n. ①獎學金
jiǎngxuéjīn (award). ②學識
xuéshí / xuéshì, 學問 xuéwèn
(knowledge).

school n. 學校 xuéxiào
〈institution〉. ~ *bus* 校車
xiàochē. ~ *of thought* 學派
xuépài.

schooling n. 學校教育
xuéxiào jiàoyù.

schoolmate n. 同學 tóngxué.

schoolteacher n. 教師
jiàoshī.

sciatica n. 坐骨神經痛 zuògǔ
shénjīng tòng.

science n. 科學 kēxué.
~ *fiction* 科幻小說 kēhuàn
xiǎoshuō. ~ *park* 科學園區
kēxué yuánqū.

scientific adj. 科學的 kēxué
de.

scientist n. 科學家 kēxuéjiā.

scintillate v. 發出火花 fāchū
huǒhuā, 閃爍 shǎnshuò
(twinkle).

scissors n. 剪刀 jiǎndāo.

scoff n. & v. 嘲笑 cháoxiào.

scold v. 責罵 zémà.

scoop n. ①杓子 sháozi (ladle).
②獨家新聞 dújiā xīnwén
〈news〉. — v. 鏟起 chǎnqǐ, 舀出
yǎochū.

scooter n. 摩托車 mótuōchē
(motor scooter).

scope n. ①範圍 fànwéi (range).
②眼界 yǎnjiè, 視野 shìyě
(outlook).

scorch v. 燒焦 shāojiāo.

score n. ①得分 défēn (number
of points). ②畫線 huàxiàn, 記
號 jìhào (mark). ③帳 zhàng,
欠款 qiànkuǎn (debt). ④分數
fēnshù, 成績 chéngjī (grade).
— v. ①得分 défēn (gain
points). ②畫線 huàxiàn, 作記
號 zuò jìhào (mark).

scorn n. & v. 輕視 qīngshì,
輕蔑 qīngmiè, 蔑視 mièshì.

S

scornful *adj.* 輕蔑的 qīngmiè de, 不屑的 búxiè de.

Scorpio 天蠍座 Tiānxiēzuò.

scorpion *n.* 蠍子 xiēzi.

scoundrel *n.* 無賴 wúlài, 惡漢 èhàn.

scour *v.* ① 擦亮 cāliàng (rub). ② 洗滌 xǐdí (clean). ③ 遍尋 biànxún (search).

scourge *n.* ① 鞭 biān (whip). ② 天譴 tiānqiǎn ⟨suffering⟩. — *v.* ① 鞭笞 biānchī (whip). ② 懲罰 chéngfá (punish).

scout *n.* 偵察兵 zhēnchábīng (lookout). *Boy S~s* 童子軍 Tóngzǐjūn. — *v.* 偵察 zhēnchá.

scowl *n. & v.* 皺眉表示 zhòuméi biǎoshì.

scramble *v.* ① 攀緣 pānyuán, 爬行 páxíng (climb). ② 爭奪 zhēngduó (compete). *~d eggs* 炒蛋 chǎodàn. — *n.* ① 攀緣 pānyuán, 爬行 páxíng (climb). ② 爭奪 zhēngduó (struggle).

scrap *n.* ① 小片 xiǎo piàn, 小塊 xiǎo kuài (piece). ② 廢物 fèiwù (waste). — *v.* 丟棄 diūqì (throw away), 放棄 fàngqì (abandon).

scrape *v.* ① 擦傷 cāshāng ⟨injure⟩. ② 擦淨 cājìng (clean). — *n.* ① 摩擦聲 mócāshēng ⟨sound⟩. ② 麻煩 máfan (trouble).

scratch *v.* 抓 zhuā, 搔 sāo. — *n.* ① 刮痕 guāhén (mark). ② 抓傷 zhuāshāng (graze).

scrawl *n. & v.* 潦草書寫 liáocǎo shūxiě, 塗鴉 túyā.

scream *n. & v.* 尖聲叫喊 jiānshēng jiàohǎn.

screech *n.* 尖叫聲 jiānjiàoshēng. — *v.* 尖叫 jiānjiào (cry out).

screen *n.* ① 幕 mù, 屏 píng, 簾 lián, 帳 zhàng (curtain). ② 銀幕 yínmù ⟨movies⟩. ③ 屏幕 píngmù, 螢屏 yíngpíng / 螢幕 yíngmù ⟨TV⟩. — *v.* ① 遮蔽 zhēbì, 掩護 yǎnhù (protect). ② 審查 shěnchá (examine).

screenplay *n.* 電影腳本 diànyǐng jiǎoběn.

screw *n.* ① 螺絲釘 luósīdīng (nail). ② 螺旋槳 luóxuánjiǎng (propeller). — *v.* ① 釘住 dìngzhù (fasten). ② 扭轉 niǔzhuǎn, 旋轉 xuánzhuǎn (twist).

screwdriver *n.* 螺絲起子 luósīqǐzi.

scribble *n. & v.* ① 潦草書寫 liáocǎo shūxiě ⟨writing⟩. ② 塗鴉 túyā ⟨drawing⟩.

script *n.* ① 筆跡 bǐjī, 手跡 shǒujī ⟨handwriting⟩. ② 腳本 jiǎoběn (screenplay).

scripture *n.* ① 經典 jīngdiǎn ⟨religion⟩. ② 聖經 shèngjīng (Bible).

scroll *n.* 紙卷 zhǐjuàn, 卷軸 juànzhóu.

scrub *v.* 擦洗 cāxǐ. — *n.* 灌木叢 guànmùcóng ⟨bushes⟩.

scruff *n.* 頸背 jǐngbèi.

scruple *n.* 顧忌 gùjì.

scrupulous *adj.* 多慮的 duōlǜ de, 小心翼翼的 xiǎoxīn-yìyì de.

scrutiny *n.* 細察 xìchá, 詳審 xiángshěn.

scuba *n.* 水肺 shuǐfèi.

scuffle *n. & v.* 混戰 hùnzhàn, 扭打 niǔdǎ.

sculpt *v.* 雕刻 diāokè.

sculptor *n.* 雕刻家 diāokèjiā.

sculpture *n.* ① 雕刻 diāokè ⟨art form⟩. ② 雕像 diāoxiàng

S

〈art object〉.

scum n. 泡沫 pàomò, 浮渣 fúzhā.

scurrilous adj. 謾罵的 mànmà de, 辱罵的 rǔmà de / rùmà de.

scurry v. 急促奔走 jícù bēnzǒu.

scurvy n. 壞血症病 huàixuèzhèng / huàixiězhèng.

scythe n. 大鐮刀 dà liándāo.

sea n. 海 hǎi, 海洋 hǎiyáng.

seacoast n. 海岸 hǎi'àn.

seal n. ①海豹 hǎibào 〈animal〉. ②印章 yìnzhāng 〈stamp〉, 印信 yìnxìn 〈confirmation〉. ③封印 fēngyìn 〈attached to an envelope〉. — v. ①封住 fēngzhù 〈fasten〉. ②蓋印於 gàiyìn yú 〈stamp〉.

seam n. 接縫 jiēfèng.

seaman n. 船員 chuányuán.

seamstress n. 女裁縫 nǚ cáiféng.

search n. & v. 尋覓 xúnmì, 搜索 sōusuǒ 〈looking for〉.

searchlight n. 探照燈 tànzhàodēng.

seashore n. 海岸 hǎi'àn.

seaside n. 海邊 hǎibiān.

season n. 季 jì, 季節 jìjié.

seasoning n. 調味品 tiáowèipǐn.

seat n. 座 zuò, 座位 zuòwèi. ~ *belt* 安全帶 ānquándài.

seaweed n. 海藻 hǎizǎo.

secede v. 退出 tuìchū.

seclude v. 退隱 tuìyǐn, 隔離 gélí.

seclusion n. 退隱 tuìyǐn, 隔離 gélí.

second adj. 第二的 dì-èr de. — n. ①第二 dì-èr 〈after the first〉. ②秒 miǎo 〈time〉.

secondary adj. 其次的

qícì de, 第二的 dì-èr de.

~ *school* 中等學校 zhōngděng xuéxiào.

secondhand adj. 二手的 èrshǒu de, 用過的 yòngguo de. ~ *smoke* 二手煙 èrshǒuyān.

secret adj. 祕密的 mìmì de. — n. 祕密 mìmì.

secretary n. ①祕書 mìshū, 書記 shūjì 〈employee〉. ②大臣 dàchén, 部長 bùzhǎng 〈minister〉.

secrete v. 分泌 fēnmì 〈produce〉.

secretly adv. 祕密地 mìmì de.

sect n. 宗派 zōngpài.

section n. ①段 duàn, 片段 piànduàn, 部分 bùfen 〈part〉. ②區域 qūyù 〈area〉. ③部門 bùmén 〈department〉.

sector n. ①區域 qūyù 〈area〉. ②扇形 shànxíng 〈geometry〉.

secular adj. 世俗的 shìsú de.

secure adj. ①安全的 ānquán de 〈safe〉. ②牢固的 láogù de 〈fixed〉. ③穩定的 wěndìng de 〈stable〉. — v. ①獲得 huòdé 〈obtain〉. ②使安全 shǐ ānquán 〈make safe〉. ③緊閉 jǐnbì, 關緊 guānjǐn 〈fasten〉.

security n. ①安全 ānquán 〈safety〉. ②安全措施 ānquán cuòshī 〈measures〉. ~ *deposit* 抵押品 dǐyāpǐn.

sedate adj. 靜肅的 jìngsù de.

sedative adj. 鎮定劑 zhèndìngjì.

sedentary adj. 慣坐的 guànzuò de, 久坐的 jiǔzuò de.

sediment n. 沈澱物 chéndiànwù.

seduce v. 誘惑 yòuhuò.

seduction n. 引誘 yǐnyòu, 誘

惑 yòuhuò.

see v. ①看見 kànjiàn (behold).
②了解 liǎojiě (comprehend).
③會面 huìmiàn (meet). ④考慮
kǎolǜ, 想想 xiǎngxiang (consider).

seed n. 種子 zhǒngzǐ.

seek v. 尋找 xúnzhǎo, 追尋
zhuīxún.

seem v. 似乎 sìhu, 看似 kànsì.

seemly adj. 適當的 shìdàng
de, 端莊的 duānzhuāng de.

seep v. 滲出 shènchū.

seesaw n. 蹺蹺板
qiāoqiāobǎn.

seethe v. 激昂 jī'áng, 激動
jīdòng (excite).

segment n. 部分 bùfen, 片斷
piànduàn.

segregate v. 隔離 gélí.

seismic adj. 地震的 dìzhèn
de.

seize v. ①抓住 zhuāzhù, 握住
wòzhù (grab). ②捕獲 bǔhuò,
捉住 zhuōzhù (capture). ③攻
佔 gōngzhàn (invade). ④扣押
kòuyā, 沒收 mòshōu (confis-
cate). ⑤奪取 duóqǔ (take).

seizure n. ①扣押 kòuyā, 沒收
mòshōu (confiscation). ②發作
fāzuò (illness). ③奪取 duóqǔ
(taking).

seldom adv. 很少 hěn shǎo,
不常 bùcháng.

select v. 選擇 xuǎnzé, 挑選
tiāoxuǎn.

selection n. 選擇 xuǎnzé, 挑
選 tiāoxuǎn.

self n. 自身 zìshēn, 自己 zìjǐ.

self-aware adj. 自覺的 zìjué
de.

self-conscious adj. ①忸怩的
niǔní de, 不自然的 bú zìrán
de (shy). ②自覺的 zìjué de

⟨self-aware⟩.

self-contained adj. ①寡言的
guǎyán de (reserved). ②配備
齊全的 pèibèi qíquán de
⟨complete⟩. ③獨立的 dúlì de
(independent), 自足的 zìzú de
(self-sufficient).

self-control n. 自制 zìzhì.

self-denial n. 自制 zìzhì.

selfish adj. 自私的 zìsī de.

self-respect n. 自重 zìzhòng,
自尊 zìzūn.

self-service n. 自助 zìzhù.

self-sufficient adj. 自足的
zìzú de.

sell v. 賣 mài, 出售 chūshòu.

seller n. 賣方 màifāng, 售者
shòuzhě.

semantic adj. 語意的 yǔyì de.

semantics n. 語意學 yǔyìxué.

semblance n. ①外觀
wàiguān, 外表 wàibiǎo
(appearance). ②類似 lèisì
(resemblance).

semen n. 精液 jīngyè.

semester n. 學期 xuéqī /
xuéqí.

semicolon n. 分號 fēnhào.

seminar n. 研討會 yántǎohuì,
講習會 jiǎngxíhuì.

semiofficial adj. 半官方的
bànguānfāng de.

senate n. 上議院
shàngyìyuàn, 參議院
cānyìyuàn.

senator n. 參議員 cānyìyuán.

send v. ①寄送 jìsòng (mail).
②派 pài, 遣 qiǎn (dispatch).
③發出 fāchū (emit), 發射
fāshè (discharge).

senile adj. 衰老的 shuāilǎo de.

senior adj. ①年長的 niánzhǎng
de (older). ②前輩的 qiánbèi
de, 資深的 zīshēn de (superior).

S

seniority *n.* 工齡 gōnglíng / 年資 niánzī.

sensation *n.* ①感覺 gǎnjué, 知覺 zhījué. ②轟動 hōngdòng (excitement).

sense *n.* ①意義 yìyì (meaning). ②感覺 gǎnjué, 知覺 zhījué (feeling). ③理智 lǐzhì (judgment). ④意識 yìshí / yìshì, 概念 gàiniàn (understanding). ~ *of humor* 幽默感 yōumògǎn. *common* ~ 常識 chángshí / chángshì. *make* ~ 合理 hélǐ, 有道理 yǒu dàolǐ. — *v.* 感覺 gǎnjué, 意識到 yìshí dào / yìshì dào.

senseless *adj.* ①無知覺的 wú zhījué de (unconscious). ②無意義的 wú yìyì de (meaningless). ③愚蠢的 yúchǔn de (foolish).

sensible *adj.* ①明智的 míngzhì de, 有理性的 yǒu lǐxìng de (reasonable). ②可察覺的 kě chájué de (perceptible).

sensitive *adj.* 敏感的 mǐngǎn de.

sensitivity *n.* ①敏感度 mǐngǎndù, 靈敏度 língmǐndù 〈person〉. ②感光度 gǎnguāngdù 〈film〉.

sensual *adj.* 肉慾的 ròuyù de.

sensuous *adj.* 感官的 gǎnguān de.

sentence *n.* ①句 jù, 句子 jùzi 〈language〉. ②判決 pànjué, 宣判 xuānpàn 〈law〉. — *v.* 宣判 xuānpàn.

sentiment *n.* ①感情 gǎnqíng (feeling). ②意見 yìjiàn, 觀點 guāndiǎn (opinion). ③傷感 shānggǎn (tender feelings).

sentimental *adj.* 多愁善感的 duō-chóu-shàn-gǎn de, 多情的 duōqíng de.

sentry *n.* 哨兵 shàobīng.

separate *v.* 分離 fēnlí, 分開 fēnkāi. — *adj.* 分開的 fēnkāi de.

separation *n.* 分離 fēnlí, 分開 fēnkāi.

September *n.* 九月 Jiǔyuè.

sequel *n.* ①續集 xùjí, 續篇 xùpiān (continuation). ②結果 jiéguǒ, 結局 jiéjú (outcome).

sequence *n.* ①順序 shùnxù (order). ②連續 liánxù (succession).

serenade *n.* 小夜曲 xiǎoyèqǔ.

serene *adj.* 寧靜的 níngjìng de.

serf *n.* 農奴 nóngnú.

sergeant *n.* ①中士 zhōngshì, 士官 shìguān 〈military〉. ②巡佐 xúnzuǒ, 警官 jǐngguān 〈police〉.

serial *n.* 連載作品 liánzǎi zuòpǐn. — *adj.* 連續的 liánxù de.

series *n.* ①系列 xìliè, 一連串 yìliánchuàn (succession). ②連續劇 liánxùjù (soap opera).

serious *adj.* ①嚴肅的 yánsù de (stern). ②認真的 rènzhēn de (earnest). ③嚴重的 yánzhòng de (severe).

sermon *n.* 說教 shuōjiào, 訓誡 xùnjiè, 講道 jiǎngdào.

serpent *n.* 蛇 shé.

serum *n.* 血漿 xuèjiāng / xiějiāng, 血清 xuèqīng / xiěqīng.

servant *n.* 僕人 púrén. *civil* ~ 公務員 gōngwùyuán.

serve *v.* ①服務 fúwù (assist).

②任職 rènzhí〈job〉,服役 fúyì〈military〉.③把……端上桌 bǎ...duānshang zhuō〈food etc.〉.

server n.①服務器 fúwùqì／伺服器 sìfúqì〈computer〉.②服務者 fúwùzhě〈person〉.

service n.①服務 fúwù (something done for others).②勤務 qínwù (public duties),兵役 bīngyì (military duties).③公職 gōngzhí (government employment).④公共事業 gōnggòng shìyè (public business).⑤禮拜式 lǐbàishì,儀式 yíshì (ceremony).⑥保養 bǎoyǎng (maintenance).

servile adj.屈從的 qūcóng de.

session n.①會議 huìyì (meeting).②會期 huìqī／huìqì (period).

set v.①放置 fàngzhì (put).②調整 tiáozhěng (adjust).③訂定 dìngdìng (fix).④沈落 chénluò (go down).⑤凝固 nínggù (become solid).⑥固定 gùdìng (make firm).~ *about* 著手 zhuóshǒu,開始 kāishǐ.~ *up* 設定 shèdìng,設立 shèlì,創立 chuànglì.

setback n.挫折 cuòzhé.

settee n.長椅 chángyǐ.

setting n.①環境 huánjìng (environment).②布景 bùjǐng (backdrop).③沈落 chénluò (going down).④置放 zhìfàng (putting).

settle v.①安置 ānzhì (place).②安頓 āndùn (set up home).③安坐 ānzuò (sit down).④平息 píngxī／píngxí,平靜 píngjìng (calm down).⑤解決 jiějué (resolve).⑥付清 fùqìng (pay).⑦沈落 chénluò (sink).

settlement n.①殖民地 zhímíndì (colony).②殖民 zhímín (colonists).③解決 jiějué (settling).④清償 qīngcháng〈debt etc.〉.

settler n.殖民者 zhímínzhě (colonist),移居者 yíjūzhě (immigrant).

seven n. & adj.七 qī.

seventeen n. & adj.十七 shíqī.

seventeenth n. & adj.第十七 dì-shíqī.

seventh n. & adj.第七 dì-qī.

seventieth n. & adj.第七十 dì-qīshí.

seventy n. & adj.七十 qīshí.

sever v.切斷 qiēduàn.

several adj.幾個的 jǐ ge de.

severe adj.①嚴厲的 yánlì de (strict).②劇烈的 jùliè de (violent).③艱難的 jiānnán de (harsh).

sew v.縫合 fénghé,縫紉 féngrèn.

sewage n.污水 wūshuǐ.

sewer n.下水道 xiàshuǐdào,陰溝 yīngōu (drain).

sewerage n.下水道設備 xiàshuǐdào shèbèi.

sewing n.縫紉 féngrèn.

sex n.①性 xìng,性別 xìngbié (gender).②性行為 xìngxíngwéi (sexual activity).*have* ~ 做愛 zuò'ài,有性行為 yǒu xìngxíngwéi.

sexual adj.性的 xìng de.~ *harassment* 性騷擾 xìngsāorǎo.

sexy adj.性感的 xìnggǎn de.

shabby adj.①襤褸的 lánlǚ de,破舊的 pòjiù de (in poor condition).②卑鄙的 bēibǐ de (mean).

shack n. 小木屋 xiǎo mùwū.

shackle n. 手銬 shǒukào, 腳鐐 jiǎoliáo / jiǎoliáo.

shade n. ①陰 yìn,陰 yīn (shadow). ②遮陽 zhēyáng, 蔽日物 bìrìwù (covering). ③色度 sèdù ⟨color⟩. — v. ①遮蔽 zhēbì (conceal). ②使暗 shǐ àn (darken).

shadow n. 影子 yǐngzi,陰影 yīnyǐng (shade). — v. ①使陰暗 shǐ yīn'àn,投影於……上 tóuyǐng yú...shàng (darken). ②跟蹤 gēnzōng (follow).

shadowy adj. 陰影的 yīnyǐng de.

shady adj. ①陰涼的 yìnliáng de,多陰影的 duō yīnyǐng de (cool). ②可疑的 kěyí de (suspicious).

shaft n. ①箭幹 jiàngàn, 矛柄 máobǐng (arrow). ②光線 guāngxiàn (beam).

shaggy adj. 毛茸茸的 máoróngróng de / máoróngróng de.

shake v. ①搖動 yáodòng (move). ②動搖 dòngyáo (weaken). ~ hands 握手 wòshǒu. — n. 搖動 yáodòng, 震動 zhèndòng.

shaky adj. 搖動的 yáodòng de,不穩的 bù wěn de.

shall aux. v. ①將 jiāng (will). ②應該 yīnggāi (ought to).

shallow adj. ①淺的 qiǎn de ⟨water⟩. ②膚淺的 fūqiǎn de (superficial).

sham n. ①假裝 jiǎzhuāng (pretence). ②贗品 yànpǐn (fake). — adj. 假的 jiǎ de, 假裝的 jiǎzhuāng de.

shamble v. 蹣跚而行 pánshān ér xíng.

shambles n. 凌亂 língluàn.

shame n. 恥辱 chǐrǔ / chǐrù, 羞愧 xiūkuì.

shameful adj. 可恥的 kěchǐ de.

shameless adj. 無恥的 wúchǐ de.

shampoo v. 洗髮 xǐfà / xǐfǎ. — n. 洗髮精 xǐfàjīng / xǐfǎjīng ⟨soap⟩.

shank n. 脛 jìng, 脛骨 jìnggǔ, 小腿 xiǎotuǐ.

shanty n. 簡陋小屋 jiǎnlòu xiǎo wū.

shape n. 形狀 xíngzhuàng (form),樣子 yàngzi (appearance). — v. 使成形 shǐ chéngxíng.

share n. ①部分 bùfen, 份 fèn (portion). ②股份 gǔfèn (stock). — v. ①分享 fēnxiǎng (enjoy together), 分擔 fēndān (divide a burden). ②共有 gòngyǒu (jointly own).

shareholder n. 股東 gǔdōng.

shark n. 鯊 shā, 鮫 jiāo.

sharp adj. ①銳利的 ruìlì de (cutting). ②急轉的 jízhuǎn de ⟨direction⟩. ③劇烈的 jùliè de (severe). ④敏銳的 mǐnruì de (sensitive). ⑤精明的 jīngmíng de (clever). ⑥鮮明的 xiānmíng de (clear).

sharpen v. 使尖銳 shǐ jiānruì, 削 xiāo.

shatter v. 粉碎 fěnsuì.

shave v. 刮鬍子 guā húzi, 剃 tì.

shawl n. 披肩 pījiān, 圍巾 wéijīn.

she pron. 她 tā.

sheaf n. 束 shù, 捆 kǔn.

shear v. 修剪 xiūjiǎn (cut).

shears n. 大剪刀 dà jiǎndāo.

sheath n. 鞘 qiào.

shed n. 小屋 xiǎo wū 〈storing〉,
家畜棚 jiāchùpéng 〈cattle〉.
— v. 脫落 tuōluò 〈fur〉.

sheep n. 綿羊 miányáng.

sheer adj. ①純粹的 chúncuì
de, 全然的 quánrán de 〈pure〉.
②透明的 tòumíng de 〈transparent〉.

sheet n. 被單 bèidān, 床單
chuángdān.

shelf n. 架子 jiàzi.

shell n. ①殼 ké 〈outer〉. ②砲彈
pàodàn 〈ammunition〉.

shellfish n. 貝殼類 bèiké lèi.

shelter n. ①避難所 bìnànsuǒ
〈refuge〉, 遮蔽物 zhēbìwù 〈covering〉. ②庇護 bìhù, 遮蔽 zhēbì
〈protection〉. — v. ①庇護 bìhù
〈protect〉. ②掩護 yǎnhù
〈accommodate〉.

shelve v. ①放在架上 fàng zài
jià shàng 〈put on〉. ②擱置
gēzhì 〈put off〉.

shepherd n. 牧羊人
mùyángrén. — v. ①帶領
dàilíng, 引導 yǐndǎo 〈lead〉.
②看守 kānshǒu 〈watch〉.

sheriff n. 警長 jǐngzhǎng.

sherry n. 雪利酒 xuělìjiǔ.

shield n. ①盾 dùn 〈buckler〉.
②防禦物 fángyùwù
〈protection〉. — v. 保護 bǎohù,
防護 fánghù.

shift v. 變換 biànhuàn. — n.
①變換 biànhuàn 〈change〉.
②輪值 lúnzhí, 換班 huànbān
〈work〉.

shimmer v. 閃閃發光
shǎnshǎn fāguāng. — n. 閃光
shǎnguāng.

shine v. ①發光 fāguāng, 發亮
fāliàng 〈give off light〉. ②擦亮
cāliàng 〈polish〉. — n. ①光亮
guāngliàng 〈brightness〉. ②擦亮

cāliàng 〈polished appearance〉.

shiny adj. 發光的 fāguāng de.

ship n. 船 chuán. — v. 以船運
送 yǐ chuán yùnsòng.

shipper n. 裝運貨物者
zhuāngyùn huòwù zhě.

shipping n. 船運 chuányùn
〈transporting〉.

shipwreck n. 船難
chuánnàn, 海難 hǎinàn.

shipyard n. 造船廠
zàochuánchǎng.

shirt n. 襯衫 chènshān.

shiver n. & v. 顫抖 chàndǒu /
zhàndǒu.

shoal n. ①魚群 yúqún 〈school
of fish〉. ②淺灘 qiǎntān, 沙洲
shāzhōu 〈sandbank〉.

shock n. ①震驚 zhènjīng
〈surprising〉. ②震動 zhèndòng
〈disturbance〉. ③衝擊 chōngjī /
chōngjí 〈impact〉. ④休克 xiūkè
〈medical〉. — v. ①驚人 jīngrén,
震驚 zhènjīng 〈surprise〉. ②震
動 zhèndòng 〈shake up〉. ③觸
電 chùdiàn 〈electrical〉.

shocking adj. ①驚人的
jīngrén de 〈surprising〉. ②糟糕
的 zāogāo de, 很壞的 hěn
huài de 〈in a terrible state〉.

shoe n. 鞋 xié.

shoemaker n. 鞋匠 xiéjiang.

shoestring n. 鞋帶 xiédài.

shoot v. ①射擊 shejī / shèjí, 發
射 fāshè 〈fire〉. ②射殺 shèshā
〈kill〉. ③芽 yá, 嫩枝 nènzhī
〈plant〉.

shop n. ①店 diàn, 店鋪 diànpù
〈store〉. ②工廠 gōngchǎng
〈workshop〉. ③買東西 mǎi
dōngxi, 購物 gòuwù 〈buy〉.

shopkeeper n. 店主 diànzhǔ.

shoplifter n. 扒手 páshǒu,
竊物者 qièwùzhě.

S

shopper n. 購物者 gòuwùzhě.

shopping n. 購物 gòuwù.
~ **mall** 購物商場 gòuwù shāngchǎng.

shore n. 岸 àn ⟨land⟩, 海岸 hǎi'àn ⟨sea⟩, 河岸 hé'àn ⟨river⟩.

short adj. ①短的 duǎn de (not long). ②矮的 ǎi de (not tall). ③簡短的 jiǎnduǎn de (brief). ④不足的 bùzú de (lacking).

shortage n. 缺乏 quēfá, 不足 bùzú.

shortcoming n. 缺點 quēdiǎn, 短處 duǎnchù.

shortcut n. 捷徑 jiéjìng.

shorten v. 使短 shǐ duǎn, 縮短 suōduǎn.

shorthand n. 速記法 sùjìfǎ.

short-handed adj. 人手不足 的 rénshǒu bùzú de.

shortly adv. ①不久 bùjiǔ (soon). ②簡略地 jiǎnlüè de (briefly).

shortsighted adj. ①短視的 duǎnshì de ⟨opinion⟩. ②近視 的 jìnshì de ⟨eyes⟩.

shot n. ①子彈 zǐdàn, 砲彈 pàodàn (bullet). ②射手 shèshǒu (marksman). ③發射 fāshè, 射擊 shèjī / shèjí (firing). **give it a** ~ 嘗試 chángshì.

should aux. v. 應該 yīnggāi.

shoulder n. 肩 jiān, 肩膀 jiānbǎng. ~ **pad** 墊肩 diànjiān. — v. 肩負 jiānfù.

shout n. & v. 喊 hǎn, 叫 jiào.

shove n. & v. 推擠 tuījǐ.

shovel n. 鏟 chǎn. — v. 鏟起 chǎnqǐ.

show v. ①展示 zhǎnshì (exhibit). ②顯露 xiǎnlù (make visible). ③指出 zhǐchū (point out). ④證明 zhèngmíng

(prove). ⑤做給……看 zuògěi...kàn (demonstrate). ~ **off** 誇耀 kuāyào. ~ **up** 出現 chūxiàn. — n. ①節目 jiémù (program). ②展覽 zhǎnlǎn (exhibition). ③演出 yǎnchū, 表演 biǎoyǎn (performance). ④展現 zhǎnxiàn, 表示 biǎoshì (expression).

shower n. ①淋浴 línyù ⟨bath⟩. ②陣雨 zhènyǔ ⟨rain⟩. — v. ①淋浴 línyù (bathe). ②下陣雨 xià zhènyǔ (rain).

showroom n. 展示室 zhǎnshìshì.

shred n. 碎片 suìpiàn, 細條 xìtiáo. — v. 撕成碎片 sī chéng suìpiàn, 切成細條 qiē chéng xìtiáo.

shrewd adj. 精明的 jīngmíng de.

shriek n. & v. 尖叫 jiānjiào.

shrill adj. 尖聲的 jiānshēng de.

shrimp n. 蝦 xiā.

shrine n. ①聖殿 shèngdiàn, 祠堂 cítáng ⟨holy place⟩. ②神 龕 shénkān ⟨tomb or casket⟩.

shrink n. & v. 縮小 suōxiǎo, 收縮 shōusuō (becoming smaller). ~ **back** 畏縮 wèisuō.

shroud n. 壽衣 shòuyī (burial garment).

shrub n. 灌木 guànmù.

shrug n. & v. 聳肩 sǒngjiān.

shudder n. & v. 戰慄 zhànlì, 發抖 fādǒu.

shuffle v. ①曳足而行 yèzú ér xíng / yìzú ér xíng ⟨walk⟩. ②洗 牌 xǐpái ⟨card⟩.

shun v. ①避開 bìkāi (avoid). ②排斥 páichì (ostracize).

shunt v. 轉軌 zhuǎnguǐ ⟨train⟩.

shut v. 閉 bì, 關閉 guānbì.

~ off 關掉 guāndiào. **~ up** 住口 zhùkǒu, 閉嘴 bìzuǐ.

shutter n. ①百葉窗 bǎiyèchuāng ⟨window⟩. ②快門 kuàimén ⟨camera⟩.

shuttle n. 梭 suō. — v. 往返移動 wǎngfǎn yídòng.

shuttlecock n. 羽毛球 yǔmáoqiú.

shy adj. 害羞的 hàixiū de, 羞怯的 xiūqiè de / xiūquè de.

sibling n. 手足 shǒuzú, 兄弟姊妹 xiōngdì zǐmèi / xiōngdì jiěmèi.

sick adj. ①有病的 yǒubìng de, 不舒服的 bù shūfu de (ill). ②作嘔的 zuò'ǒu de (nauseous). ③厭惡的 yànwù de (upset by). **~ of something** 厭煩 yànfán.

sickle n. 鐮刀 liándāo.

sickly adj. ①多病的 duōbìng de, 不健康的 bú jiànkāng de (often ill). ②蒼白的 cāngbái de, 憔悴的 qiáocuì de (pale). ③令人作嘔的 lìng rén zuò'ǒu de (nauseating).

sickness n. 患病 huànbìng.

side n. ①面 miàn (face). ②邊 biān (border). ③方面 fāngmiàn (aspect).

sideboard n. 餐具櫥 cānjùchú.

sidewalk n. 人行道 rénxíngdào.

siege n. & v. 圍攻 wéigōng.

sieve n. 篩 shāi.

sift v. 篩 shāi, 過濾 guòlǜ.

sigh n. & v. 歎息 tànxī / tànxì.

sight n. ①視力 shìlì (eyesight). ②視野 shìyě (view). ③風景 fēngjǐng, 名勝 míngshèng (scenery).

sightsee v. 觀光 guānguāng.

sightseer n. 觀光客 guānguāngkè.

sign n. ①記號 jìhào, 符號 fúhào (mark). ②手勢 shǒushì (gesture). ③跡象 jīxiàng, 徵兆 zhēngzhào (forewarning). ④告示 gàoshì, 標誌 biāozhì (notice). — v. ①簽字 qiānzì, 簽名 qiānmíng (endorse). ②以手勢示意 yǐ shǒushì shìyì ⟨gesture⟩.

signal n. 信號 xìnhào. — v. 發信號 fā xìnhào. — adj. 顯著的 xiǎnzhù de.

signatory n. 簽名者 qiānmíngzhě.

signature n. 簽字 qiānzì, 簽名 qiānmíng, 署名 shǔmíng / shǔmíng.

significance n. ①意義 yìyì (meaning). ②重要(性) zhòngyào (xìng) (importance).

significant adj. ①有意義的 yǒu yìyì de (meaningful). ②重要的 zhòngyào de (important).

signify v. 表示 biǎoshì (mean).

silence n. ①寂靜 jìjìng / jíjìng (stillness). ②沈默 chénmò (muteness). — v. 使沈默 shǐ chénmò.

silent adj. ①寂靜的 jìjìng de / jíjìng de, 無聲的 wúshēng de (still). ②沈默的 chénmò de (mute).

silicon n. 硅 guī / 矽 xì. **S~ Valley** 硅谷 Guīgǔ / 矽谷 Xìgǔ.

silk n. 絲 sī, 蠶絲 cánsī.

silly adj. 愚蠢的 yúchǔn de.

silt n. 淤泥 yūní.

silver n. 銀 yín ⟨metal⟩. **~ ware** 銀器 yínqì.

silversmith n. 銀匠 yínjiàng.

similar adj. 類似的 lèisì de, 同樣的 tóngyàng de.

similarity n. 類似 lèisì, 相似

xiāngsì.

similarly *adv.* 類似地 lèisì de.

simile *n.* 直喻 zhíyù，明喻 míngyù.

simmer *v.* 慢煮 mànzhǔ，燉 dùn.

simper *v.* 假笑 jiǎxiào ‹not sincere›，傻笑 shǎxiào ‹silly›.

simple *adj.* ①簡單的 jiǎndān de (not complicated). ②樸實的 púshí de (plain). ③單純的 dānchún de (innocent).

simplicity *n.* ①簡單 jiǎndān (being simple). ②純真 chúnzhēn (innocence).

simplify *v.* 使簡化 shǐ jiǎnhuà (make easier)，使單純 shǐ dānchún (make less complicated).

simply *adv.* ①簡單地 jiǎndān de (in a simple way). ②簡直 jiǎnzhí (really). ③僅 jǐn (just).

simulate *v.* ①模仿 mófǎng (imitate). ②假裝 jiǎzhuāng (pretend)，偽裝 wěizhuāng / wèizhuāng (fake).

simulator *n.* 模擬裝置 mónǐ zhuāngzhì.

simultaneous *adj.* 同時發生的 tóngshí fāshēng de.

sin *n.* 罪 zuì，罪惡 zuì'è.

since *prep.* 從 cóng (from)，自⋯⋯以後 zì...yǐhòu. — *conj.* ①自⋯⋯以後 zì... yǐhòu (after). ②既然 jìrán (as). ③因為 yīnwèi (because).

sincere *adj.* ①真實的 zhēnshí de，誠實的 chéngshí de (honest). ②誠摯的 chéngzhì de (genuine).

sincerity *n.* 真實 zhēnshí，誠懇 chéngkěn.

sinew *n.* 腱 jiàn.

sing *v.* 唱 chàng，歌唱

gēchàng.

singer *n.* 歌手 gēshǒu.

single *adj.* ①單一的 dānyī de (one)，惟一的 wéiyī de (only). ②單身的 dānshēn de (not married). ③單人用的 dānrén yòng de (used for one person). ~ *parent* 單親 dānqīn. ~ *parent family* 半邊家庭 bànbiān jiātíng / 單親家庭 dānqīn jiātíng. ~ *room* 單人房 dānrénfáng.

singular *adj.* ①單數的 dānshù de ‹grammar›. ②奇特的 qítè de (uncommon). — *n.* 單數 dānshù.

sinister *adj.* ①有惡意的 yǒu èyì de (malevolent). ②邪惡的 xié'è de (evil). ③不祥的 bùxiáng de (inauspicious).

sink *v.* ①沉落 chénluò (go down). ②沈沒 chénmò (founder). ③下降 xiàjiàng (become lower).

sinner *n.* 罪人 zuìrén.

sip *v.* 啜飲 chuòyǐn.

siphon *n.* 虹吸管 hóngxīguǎn.

sir *n.* 先生 xiānsheng (mister).

siren *n.* 海妖 hǎiyāo.

sister *n.* ①姊姊 jiějie ‹elder›. ②妹妹 mèimei ‹younger›. ③修女 xiūnǚ (nun). ~s 姊妹 jiěmèi (female siblings).

sit *v.* 坐 zuò.

site *n.* 位置 wèizhi，地點 dìdiǎn.

situated *adj.* 坐落於⋯⋯的 zuòluò yú...de.

situation *n.* ①情形 qíngxing，情況 qíngkuàng (condition). ②職位 zhíwèi (employment). ③場所 chǎngsuǒ (location).

six *n. & adj.* 六 liù.

sixteen *n. & adj.* 十六 shíliù.

sixteenth *n. & adj.* 第十六

dì-shíliù.

sixth n. & adj. 第六 dì-liù.

sixtieth n. & adj. 第六十 dì-liùshí.

sixty n. & adj. 六十 liùshí.

size n. 大小 dàxiǎo, 尺寸 chǐcùn. ~ *up* 估量 gūliang.

sizzle n. & v. 嘶嘶聲 sīsīshēng.

skate n. 冰刀 bīngdāo.
roller ~ 旱冰鞋 hànbīngxié / 溜冰鞋 liūbīngxié. *ice* ~ 冰鞋 bīngxié / 溜冰鞋 liūbīngxié. — v. 溜冰 liūbīng.

skateboard n. 滑板 huábǎn.

skeleton n. 骨骼 gǔgé.

sketch n. ①草圖 cǎotú, 素描 sùmiáo 〈drawing〉. ②短劇 duǎnjù 〈short play〉. — v. ①素描 sùmiáo 〈draw〉. ②記述……的概略 jìshù...de gàilüè 〈outline〉.

ski n. 滑雪板 huáxuěbǎn. — v. 滑雪 huáxuě.

skid v. 滑向一側 huá xiàng yí cè.

skiff n. 小艇 xiǎotǐng.

skillful adj. 熟練的 shúliàn de, 有技巧的 yǒu jìqiǎo de.

skill n. 技巧 jìqiǎo, 技能 jìnéng.

skim v. ①略讀 lüèdú 〈read quickly〉. ②掠過 lüèguò 〈move lightly〉.

skin n. ①皮膚 pífū 〈human〉. ②毛皮 máopí 〈animal〉. — v. 剝皮 bāopí.

skip v. ①跳躍 tiàoyuè 〈jump〉. ②略過 lüèguò 〈pass over〉. ③跳讀 tiàodú 〈reading〉.

skirt n. 裙子 qúnzi.

skunk n. 臭鼬 chòuyòu.

sky n. 天空 tiānkōng, 天 tiān.

skylark n. 雲雀 yúnquè.

skylight n. 天窗 tiānchuāng.

skyscraper n. 摩天樓 mótiānlóu.

slab n. 厚板 hòubǎn.

slack adj. ①鬆弛的 sōngchí de 〈loose〉. ②懈怠的 xièdài de 〈idle〉. ③不活躍的 bù huóyuè de 〈inactive〉.

slacken v. ①使鬆弛 shǐ sōngchí 〈make looser〉. ②使緩慢 shǐ huǎnmàn 〈make slower〉.

slam v. 砰然關閉 pēngrán guānbì 〈shut〉. — n. 砰然聲 pēngránshēng.

slander n. & v. 誹謗 fěibàng.

slang n. 俚語 lǐyǔ.

slant n. 傾斜 qīngxié.

slap n. 掌擊 zhǎngjī / zhǎngjí, 摑 guó. — v. 掌摑 zhǎngguó, 打……巴掌 dǎ...bāzhǎng.

slat n. 細長薄板 xìcháng báobǎn / xìcháng bóbǎn.

slate n. 石板 shíbǎn 〈rock〉.

slaughter n. & v. 屠殺 túshā, 殺戮 shālù.

slave n. 奴隸 núlì.

slavery n. ①奴役 núyì 〈enslavement〉. ②奴隸身分 núlì shēnfen 〈being a slave〉.

slavish adj. 奴性的 núxìng de.

slay v. 殺戮 shālù 〈kill violently〉.

sled n. 雪橇 xuěqiāo, 雪車 xuěchē. — v. 乘雪橇 chéng xuěqiāo.

sleep v. 睡 shuì. — n. 睡眠 shuìmián.

sleepy adj. ①睏的 kùn de, 想睡的 xiǎngshuì de 〈ready to sleep〉. ②不活潑的 bù huópo de 〈inactive〉.

sleet n. 霰 xiàn. — v. 降霰 jiàngxiàn.

sleeve n. 袖 xiù.

sleigh n. 雪車 xuěchē, 雪橇

xuěqiāo. — v. 乘雪橇 chéng
xuěqiāo.

slender *adj.* ①纖細的 xiānxì
de (slight). ②薄弱的 bóruò de
(feeble).

slice *n.* 片 piàn, 薄片 báopiàn /
bópiàn.

slick *adj.* 光滑的 guānghuá de
(slippery).

slide *v.* 滑行 huáxíng, 滑動
huádòng. — *n.* ①溜滑梯
liūhuátī (chute). ②幻燈片
huàndēngpiàn 〈film〉.

slight *adj.* ①少許的 shǎoxǔ
de, 微小的 wēixiǎo de /
wéixiǎo de (imperceptible).
②瘦弱的 shòuruò de (thin).

slightly *adv.* 輕微地 qīngwēi
de / qīngwéi de, 稍微
shāowēi / shāowéi.

slim *adj.* ①苗條的 miáotiao
de, 細長的 xìcháng de
(slender). ②微少的 wēishǎo de
/ wéishǎo de (small).

slime *n.* 黏土 niántǔ.

sling *n.* 吊索 diàosuǒ, 吊帶
diàodài. — *v.* 投擲 tóuzhì /
tóuzhí.

slink *v.* 潛行 qiánxíng, 潛逃
qiántáo.

slip *v.* ①滑倒 huádǎo (fall).
②犯錯 fàncuò (make a mis-
take). ~ *away* 溜走 liūzǒu.

slipper *n.* 拖鞋 tuōxié.

slippery *adj.* ①滑的 huá de
〈surface〉. ②狡猾的 jiǎohuá de
(devious).

slit *v.* 割裂 gēliè. — *n.* 裂縫
lièfèng.

slither *v.* 滑動 huádòng.

slogan *n.* 標語 biāoyǔ, 口號
kǒuhào.

slope *v.* 傾斜 qīngxié. — *n.* 傾
斜 qīngxié, 斜坡 xiépō.

sloppy *adj.* ①邋遢的 lāta de /
láta de (slovenly). ②泥濘
nínìng de (muddy).

slot *n.* ①狹縫 xiáfèng (narrow
opening). ②投幣口 tóubìkǒu
〈coin〉.

sloth *n.* 怠惰 dàiduò.

slouch *v.* 彎腰駝背地走
wānyāo tuóbèi de zǒu.

slovenly *adj.* & *adv.* 邋遢的
lāta de / láta de.

slow *adj.* ①緩慢的 huǎnmàn
de (not fast). ②遲鈍的 chídùn
de (obtuse).

slowly *adv.* 緩慢地 huǎnmàn de.

sludge *n.* 污泥 wūní.

slug *n.* 蛞蝓 kuòyú 〈animal〉.

sluggish *adj.* 行動遲緩的
xíngdòng chíhuǎn de (slow
moving).

sluice *n.* ①水門 shuǐmén
(gate). ②排水道 páishuǐdào
(channel).

slum *n.* 貧民窟 pínmínkū.

slumber *n.* 睡眠 shuìmián.
— *v.* 安睡 ānshuì.

slump *v.* ①猛然落下 měngrán
luòxià (drop heavily). ②暴跌
bàodiē / bàodié 〈price〉.

slur *v.* 含糊說出 hánhu
shuōchū (pronounce unclearly).

slut *n.* 放蕩女子 fàngdàng
nǚzǐ.

sly *adj.* ①狡猾的 jiǎohuá de,
詭秘的 guǐmì de (deceitful).
②頑皮的 wánpí de, 淘氣的
táoqì de (mischievous).

small *adj.* 小的 xiǎo de.

smart *v.* 感到劇痛 gǎndào
jùtòng 〈hurt〉. — *adj.* ①聰明的
cōngming de (clever). ②輕快
的 qīngkuài de (quick).

smash *v.* ①搗碎 dǎosuì,
使破碎 shǐ pòsuì (break).

②碰撞 pèngzhuàng (hit).

smear v. ①塗 tú, 敷 fū (cover with). ②弄髒 nòngzāng, 塗污 túwū (make dirty).

smell v. ①聞 wén, 嗅 xiù (scent). ②發出氣味 fāchū qìwèi (stink). — n. 味道 wèidao.

smile n. & v. 微笑 wēixiào / wéixiào.

smirk n. & v. 冷笑 lěngxiào, 得意地笑 déyì de xiào.

smock n. 罩衫 zhàoshān.

smog n. 煙霧 yānwù.

smoke n. 煙 yān, 煙霧 yānwù (fumes). — v. ①吸煙 xīyān 〈cigarette〉. ②冒煙 màoyān (fume).

smooth adj. ①平滑的 pínghuá de (flat). ②平靜的 píngjìng de (calm). ③流暢的 liúchàng de (flowing). — v. ①使平滑 shǐ pínghuá (flatten). ②使平順 shǐ píngshùn (make steady).

smother v. ①使窒息 shǐ zhìxí / shǐ zhìxì (choke). ②悶熄 mēnxī / mènxí 〈fire〉.

smudge n. 污點 wūdiǎn, 污跡 wūjī.

smug adj. 沾沾自喜的 zhānzhān-zì-xǐ de.

smuggle v. 走私 zǒusī.

smut n. 猥褻書刊 wěixiè shūkān (pornographic materials).

snack n. 點心 diǎnxin, 小吃 xiǎochī.

snail n. 蝸牛 wōniú / guāniú.

snake n. 蛇 shé.

snap v. ①啪一聲折斷 pā yì shēng zhéduàn (crack). ②咬 yǎo (bite). — adj. 突然的 túrán de / túrán de (sudden).

snapshot n. 快照 kuàizhào.

snare n. 羅網 luówǎng, 陷阱 xiànjǐng (trap). — v. 誘捕 yòubǔ.

snarl v. 咆哮 páoxiāo, 怒吼 nùhǒu (growl).

snatch v. 搶去 qiǎngqù, 奪去 duóqù.

sneak v. 偷偷進入 tōutōu jìnrù, 潛行 qiánxíng (go stealthily).

sneakily adv. 偷偷地 tōutōu de.

sneer v. 輕蔑 qīngmiè, 嘲笑 cháoxiào.

sneeze v. 打噴嚏 dǎ pēntì. — n. 噴嚏 pēntì.

snicker n. & v. 暗笑 ànxiào, 竊笑 qièxiào.

sniff v. ①聞 wén, 嗅 xiù (smell). ②以鼻吸氣 yǐ bí xīqì (breathe in noisily).

snigger n. & v. 暗笑 ànxiào, 竊笑 qièxiào.

snip v. 剪斷 jiǎnduàn.

snipe n. 鷸 yù 〈bird〉. — v. 伏擊 fújí / fújí, 狙擊 jūjí / jújí.

snippet n. 片段 piànduàn.

snivel v. 啜泣 chuòqì.

snob n. 勢利小人 shìlì xiǎorén.

snoop v. 窺察 kuīchá.

snooze n. & v. 小睡 xiǎoshuì.

snore v. 打鼾 dǎhān. — n. 鼾聲 hānshēng.

snort v. 噴之以鼻 chī-zhī-yǐ-bí.

snow n. 雪 xuě. — v. 下雪 xiàxuě.

snowboard n. 滑雪板 huáxuěbǎn.

snowflake n. 雪花 xuěhuā.

snowstorm n. 暴風雪 bàofēngxuě.

snow-white adj. 雪白的 xuěbái de / xuěbái de.

snowy *adj.* 多雪的 duōxuě de.

snub *n. & v.* 怠慢 dàimàn, 冷落 lěngluò.

snuff *v.* 用鼻吸 yòng bí xī. — *n.* 鼻煙 bíyān.

snug *adj.* 舒適的 shūshì de, 溫暖的 wēnnuǎn de (comfortable).

so *adv.* 如此 rúcǐ. — *conj.* 所以 suǒyǐ.

soak *v.* 浸濕 jìnshī, 浸透 jìntòu.

soap *n.* 肥皂 féizào.

soar *v.* 高飛 gāofēi.

sob *v.* 啜泣 chuòqì.

sober *adj.* ①清醒的 qīngxǐng de (clear-headed). ②有節制的 yǒu jiézhì de (abstemious). ③嚴肅的 yánsù de (solemn).

so-called *adj.* 所謂的 suǒwèi de.

soccer *n.* 足球 zúqiú.

sociable *adj.* 好交際的 hào jiāojì de, 社交的 shèjiāo de.

social *adj.* ①群居的 qúnjū de ⟨group⟩. ②社會的 shèhuì de ⟨community⟩. — *n.* 聯誼會 liányíhuì.

socialism *n.* 社會主義 shèhuì zhǔyì.

socialist *n.* 社會主義者 shèhuì zhǔyì zhě.

society *n.* 社會 shèhuì.

sociology *n.* 社會學 shèhuìxué.

sock *n.* 短襪 duǎnwà.

socket *n.* 插座 chāzuò.

soda *n.* 蘇打水 sūdǎshuǐ / sūdǎshuǐ, 汽水 qìshuǐ.

sodium *n.* 鈉 nà.

sofa *n.* 沙發 shāfā.

soft *adj.* ①柔軟的 róuruǎn de (not hard). ②溫和的 wēnhé de (mild). ③柔和的 róuhé de ⟨of light⟩.

softball *n.* 壘球 lěiqiú.

soften *v.* 使柔軟 shǐ róuruǎn.

software *n.* 軟件 ruǎnjiàn / 軟體 ruǎntǐ. ~ *package* 軟件包 ruǎnjiànbāo / 套裝軟體 tàozhuāng ruǎntǐ.

soggy *adj.* 濕透的 shītòu de.

soil *n.* 土壤 tǔrǎng, 土 tǔ.

solar *adj.* 太陽的 tàiyáng de.

solder *n.* 焊料 hànliào. — *v.* 焊接 hànjiē.

soldier *n.* 軍人 jūnrén, 士兵 shìbīng.

sole *adj.* 唯一的 wéiyī de.

solely *adv.* ①獨一地 dúyī de (alone). ②僅僅 jǐnjǐn (only).

solemn *adj.* 嚴肅的 yánsù de (serious), 莊重的 zhuāngzhòng de (grand).

solicit *v.* 懇求 kěnqiú, 請求 qǐngqiú.

solicitor *n.* 律師 lǜshī.

solid *adj.* ①堅實的 jiānshí de (dense). ②立體的 lìtǐ de (cubic). ③切實的 qièshí de (concrete). ④固體的 gùtǐ de (form).

solidify *v.* ①使凝固 shǐ nínggù (harden). ②使團結 shǐ tuánjié (become united).

solitary *adj.* ①唯一的 wéiyī de (only). ②僻遠的 pìyuǎn de (remote). ③孤獨的 gūdú de (alone).

solitude *n.* ①孤獨 gūdú (loneliness). ②荒僻 huāngpì (remoteness).

solo *n.* 獨唱 dúchàng ⟨singing⟩, 獨奏 dúzòu ⟨performance⟩. — *adj.* 單獨的 dāndú de.

soluble *adj.* 可溶解的 kě róngjiě de.

solution *n.* ①解決 jiějué, 解答 jiědá (resolution). ②溶解

rôngjiě (mixture).

solve v. 解答 jiědá, 解決 jiějué.

solvent adj. ①能償債的 néng chángzhài de ⟨credit⟩. ②有溶解力的 yǒu róngjiěli de (able to dissolve).

somber adj. ①幽暗的 yōu'àn de (dark). ②憂鬱的 yōuyù de (cheerless).

some adj. 一些 yìxiē.

somebody pron. 某人 mǒurén.

someday adv. 有一天 yǒu yì tiān.

somehow adv. 以某種方法 yǐ mǒu zhǒng fāngfǎ.

someone pron. 某人 mǒurén.

somersault n. 觔斗 jīndǒu. — v. 翻觔斗 fānjīndǒu.

something pron. 某事 mǒushì, 某物 mǒuwù.

sometime adv. 某時 mǒushí.

sometimes adv. 有時 yǒushí.

somewhat adv. & pron. 稍微 shāowēi / shāowéi.

somewhere adv. 在某處 zài mǒuchù.

son n. 兒子 érzi.

sonar n. 聲納 shēngnà.

sonata n. 奏鳴曲 zòumíngqǔ.

song n. 歌 gē, 歌曲 gēqǔ.

sonnet n. 十四行詩 shísìhángshī.

soon adv. ①不久 bùjiǔ (not long). ②早 zǎo, 快 kuài (early).

soot n. 煤煙 méiyān.

soothe v. 安慰 ānwèi, 撫慰 fǔwèi.

sophisticated adj. 世故的 shìgù de, 老練的 lǎoliàn de.

sophomore n. 二年級學生 èr niánjí xuésheng.

soppy adj. 浸透的 jìntòu de, 濕透的 shītòu de (very wet).

soprano n. 女高音 nǚ gāoyīn.

sorcerer n. 男巫 nánwū.

sorcery n. 巫術 wūshù.

sordid adj. ①污穢的 wūhuì de (dirty). ②卑鄙的 bēibǐ de (contemptible).

sore adj. ①疼痛的 téngtòng de (painful). ②傷心的 shāngxīn de (sorrowful). — n. 痛處 tòngchù.

sorrow n. 悲傷 bēishāng.

sorrowful adj. 悲傷的 bēishāng de.

sorry adj. ①感到抱歉的 gǎndào bàoqiàn de (pitiful). ②難過的 nánguò de (grieved).

sort n. 種 zhǒng, 類 lèi. — v. 分類 fēnlèi.

so-so adj. & adv. 馬馬虎虎 mǎmǎ-hūhū / mǎma-hūhū.

soul n. 靈魂 línghún.

sound n. 聲音 shēngyīn. — v. ①發出聲音 fāchū shēngyīn (make sound). ②聽起來 tīngqilai (seem when heard).

soundproof adj. 隔音的 géyīn de.

soup n. 湯 tāng, 羹 gēng.

sour adj. ①酸的 suān de (acidic). ②乖戾的 guāilì de (bad-tempered).

source n. ①來源 láiyuán (origin). ②水源 shuǐyuán ⟨water⟩.

south n. ①南 nán ⟨direction⟩. ②南方 nánfāng (southern region). ③南邊 nánbiān, 南部 nánbù (southern part). — adv. 南 nán, 向南 xiàng nán, 往南 wǎng nán. — adj. ①南的 nán de (of the south). ②南方的 nánfāng de (of the southern region). ③南部的 nánbù de (of the southern part).

S

South America 南美洲 Nán Měizhōu.

southeast adj. 東南的 dōngnán de.

southern adj. 南方的 nánfāng de.

South Pole n. 南極 Nánjí.

southward adj. & adv. 向南的 xiàng nán de.

southwest adj. 西南的 xīnán de.

souvenir n. 紀念品 jìniànpǐn.

sovereign n. 元首 yuánshǒu, 統治者 tǒngzhìzhě (king or queen). — adj. ①最高的 zuì gāo de (supreme). ②有主權的 yǒu zhǔquán de (self-governing).

sow v. 播種 bōzhǒng / bòzhǒng. — n. 母豬 mǔzhū.

soybean n. 大豆 dàdòu, 黃豆 huángdòu.

soy sauce n. 醬油 jiàngyóu.

spa n. 溫泉 wēnquán, 礦泉 kuàngquán.

space n. ①太空 tàikōng ⟨astronomy⟩. ②空間 kōngjiān (emptiness). ~ **station** 宇宙站 yǔzhòuzhàn, 航天站 hángtiānzhàn / 太空站 tàikōngzhàn.

spaceship n. 宇宙飛船 yǔzhòu fēichuán / 太空船 tàikōngchuán.

spacious adj. 廣闊的 guǎngkuò de.

spade n. ①鏟子 chǎnzi ⟨tool⟩. ②黑桃 hēitáo ⟨cards⟩. — v. 鏟 chǎn.

spaghetti n. 意大利麵 yìdàlìmiàn / 義大利麵 yìdàlìmiàn.

span n. ①一掌距 yì zhǎngjù ⟨distance⟩. ②一段時間 yíduàn shíjiān ⟨time⟩.

Spanish n. & adj. ①西班牙人 Xībānyárén ⟨people⟩. ②西班牙語 Xībānyáyǔ ⟨language⟩.

spank v. 拍打 pāidǎ.

spanner n. 螺旋鉗 luóxuánqián, 扳手 bānshǒu.

spar v. 拳鬥 quándòu.

spare v. ①赦免 shèmiǎn, 饒恕 ráoshù (forgive). ②節省使用 jiéshěng shǐyòng (use in small quantities). — adj. ①剩餘的 shèngyú de, 多餘的 duōyú de (additional). ②備用的 bèiyòng de (in reserve).

spark n. 火花 huǒhuā, 火星 huǒxīng. — v. ①發出火花 fāchū huǒhuā ⟨fire⟩. ②引發 yǐnfā (set off).

sparkle v. 發出火花 fāchū huǒhuā, 閃爍 shǎnshuò. — n. 火花 huǒhuā, 閃爍 shǎnshuò.

sparrow n. 麻雀 máquè.

sparse adj. 稀少的 xīshǎo de.

spasm n. 痙攣 jìngluán / jìnglüán.

spawn n. 卵 luǎn. — v. 產卵 chǎnluǎn.

speak v. 說話 shuōhuà, 講 jiǎng.

speaker n. 說話者 shuōhuàzhě.

spear n. 矛 máo, 槍 qiāng.

special adj. 特殊的 tèshū de, 特別的 tèbié de.

specialist n. 專家 zhuānjiā.

specialty n. ①專長 zhuāncháng (expertise). ②特性 tèxìng (quality).

species n. 種 zhǒng, 種類 zhǒnglèi.

specific adj. ①明確的 míngquè de (definite). ②特定

的 tèdìng de (particular).

specification n. 詳述 xiángshù.

specify v. 列舉 lièjǔ.

specimen n. 樣品 yàngpǐn (sample), 標本 biāoběn (example).

speck n. 斑點 bāndiǎn, 瑕疵 xiácī.

speckle n. 小點 xiǎodiǎn, 斑點 bāndiǎn.

spectacle n. ①奇觀 qíguān, 景象 jǐngxiàng (sight). ②展覽物 zhǎnlǎnwù ⟨display⟩.

spectacular adj. 壯觀的 zhuàngguān de.

spectator n. 觀眾 guānzhòng, 旁觀者 pángguānzhě.

spectrum n. 光譜 guāngpǔ.

speculate v. ①推測 tuīcè (make a guess). ②投機 tóujī ⟨stocks⟩.

speculation n. ①推測 tuīcè (making guesses). ②投機買賣 tóujī mǎimài ⟨of stocks⟩.

speech n. 演說 yǎnshuō.

speed n. 速度 sùdù. — v. 加速前進 jiāsù qiánjìn.

spell v. 拼字 pīnzì. — n. 符咒 fúzhòu ⟨magic⟩.

spelling n. 拼字 pīnzì.

spend v. ①花費 huāfèi ⟨money⟩. ②度過 dùguò ⟨time⟩.

sperm n. 精液 jīngyè.

sphere n. ①球 qiú, 球形 qiúxíng ⟨shape⟩. ②範圍 fànwéi, 領域 lǐngyù ⟨range⟩.

spice n. 香料 xiāngliào, 調味品 tiáowèipǐn.

spicy adj. 辛辣的 xīnlà de.

spider n. 蜘蛛 zhīzhū.

spike n. 長釘 chángdīng, 大釘 dàdīng. — v. ①以大釘釘牢 yǐ dàdīng dìngláo (nail). ②暗加

毒物於……中 àn jiā dúwù yú…zhōng (add drugs).

spill v. 潑出 pōchū, 溢出 yìchū.

spin v. ①紡織 fǎngzhī ⟨thread⟩. ②旋轉 xuánzhuǎn (rotate).

spinach n. 菠菜 bōcài.

spindle n. ①紡錘 fǎngchuí (rod). ②軸 zhóu ⟨pin⟩.

spine n. 脊椎骨 jǐzhuīgǔ.

spinster n. 年長的未婚女性 niánzhǎng de wèihūn nǚxìng.

spiral n. & adj. 螺旋形 luóxuánxíng.

spire n. 塔尖 tǎjiān.

spirit n. ①精神 jīngshén, 心靈 xīnlíng (mind). ②靈魂 línghún (soul). ③幽靈 yōulíng, 精靈 jīnglíng (ghost). ④元氣 yuánqì (liveliness).

spiritual adj. 精神上的 jīngshénshang de.

spit v. 吐唾液 tǔ tuòyè. — n. 唾液 tuòyè.

spite n. 惡意 èyì.

splash v. 濺 jiàn, 潑水 pōshuǐ. — n. 激濺聲 jījiànshēng.

splendid adj. ①壯麗的 zhuànglì de, 輝煌的 huīhuáng de (glorious). ②很好的 hěnhǎo de (excellent).

splendor n. 壯麗 zhuànglì, 輝煌 huīhuáng.

splint n. 夾板 jiābǎn / jiábǎn.

split v. ①劈開 pīkāi, 裂開 lièkāi (break). ②分開 fēnkāi, 分裂 fēnliè (divide). — n. ①裂開 lièkāi (break). ②分裂 fēnliè (division).

spoil v. ①破壞 pòhuài (ruin). ②寵壞 chǒnghuài (coddle). ③腐壞 fǔhuài (rot).

spoken adj. 口頭的 kǒutóu de.

spokesman n. 發言人

S

sponge *n.* 海綿 hǎimián. — *v.*
用海綿吸乾 yòng hǎimián
xīgān.

sponsor *n.* ①保證人
bǎozhèngrén (guarantor).
②贊助人 zànzhùrén
(supporter). — *v.* 贊助 zànzhù.

spontaneous *adj.* 自然的
zìrán de, 自發的 zìfā de.

spool *n.* 線軸 xiànzhóu.

spoon *n.* 匙 chí, 調羹
tiáogēng.

sporadic *adj.* 零星的 língxīng
de, 偶爾的 ǒu'ěr de.

spore *n.* 孢子 bāozǐ.

sport *n.* 運動 yùndòng, 戶外
活動 hùwài huódòng.

sportsman *n.* 運動員
yùndòngyuán.

spot *n.* ①污點 wūdiǎn (stain).
②斑點 bāndiǎn 〈mark〉. ③地點
dìdiǎn (place).

spotlight *n.* 聚光燈
jùguāngdēng.

spouse *n.* 配偶 pèi'ǒu.

spout *v.* ①噴出 pēnchū (erupt).
②滔滔不絕地說 tāotāo-bùjué
de shuō (speak). — *n.* 管嘴
guǎnzuǐ, 噴水口 pēnshuǐkǒu.

sprain *n. & v.* 扭傷 niǔshāng.

sprawl *v.* ①伸開手足而臥或
坐 shēnkāi shǒuzú ér wò huò
zuò 〈lie〉. ②蔓延 mànyán,
展開 zhǎnkāi (spread).

spray *n.* ①水沫 shuǐmò
〈water〉. ②噴霧器 pēnwùqì
〈paint〉. — *v.* 噴灑 pēnsǎ.

spread *v.* ①鋪 pū, 展開
zhǎnkāi (lay out). ②塗敷 túfū
(apply). ③延伸 yánshēn, 擴散
kuòsàn (broaden). ④散布
sànbù, 傳播 chuánbó /
chuánbò (scatter).

spring *v.* 跳躍 tiàoyuè (jump).
— *n.* ①春季 chūnjì / 春天
chūntiān 〈season〉. ②彈簧
tánhuáng, 發條 fātiáo 〈device〉.
③跳躍 tiàoyuè 〈movement〉.
④泉源 quányuán 〈water〉.

sprinkle *v.* 灑 sǎ, 撒 sǎ. — *n.*
毛毛雨 máomáoyǔ.

sprint *v.* 全速衝刺 quánsù
chōngcì.

sprout *v.* 發芽 fāyá. — *n.* 芽 yá.

spur *n.* ①激勵 jīlì (encouragement). ②刺馬釘 cìmǎdīng
〈horse〉. — *v.* ①激勵 jīlì
(encourage). ②以刺馬釘刺 yǐ
cìmǎdīng cì 〈horse〉.

spurious *adj.* 偽造的 wěizào
de / wèizào de, 假的 jiǎ de
(not genuine).

spurn *v.* 不屑地趕走 búxiè de
gǎnzǒu.

spurt *v.* 噴出 pēnchū, 湧出
yǒngchū.

spy *n.* 間諜 jiàndié. — *v.* ①偵
察 zhēnchá, 暗中調查
ànzhōng diàochá (be a spy).
②發現 fāxiàn (discover).

squabble *n. & v.* 小爭吵
xiǎozhēngchǎo.

squad *n.* 小隊 xiǎoduì
〈people〉, 班 bān 〈soldiers〉.

squadron *n.* ①騎兵中隊
qíbīng zhōngduì / jíbīng
zhōngduì 〈cavalry〉. ②中隊
zhōngduì 〈military〉.

squalid *adj.* 污穢的 wūhuì de.

squall *v.* 大哭 dàkū, 大叫
dàjiào. — *n.* ①狂風
kuángfēng 〈wind〉. ②大哭
dàkū, 大叫 dàjiào 〈cry〉.

squander *v.* 浪費 làngfèi.

square *n.* ①正方形
zhèngfāngxíng 〈shape〉. ②廣場
guǎngchǎng (plaza). — *adj.*

①正方形的 zhèngfāngxíng de 〈shape〉. ②直角的 zhíjiǎo de (right-angled). ③公平的 gōngping de, 正直的 zhèngzhí de (honest). — v. 成方形 shǐ chéng fāngxíng.

squash v. ①壓爛 yālàn, 壓碎 yāsuì (crush). ②擠入 jǐrù (crowd). ③鎮壓 zhènyā (repress). — n. ①壓碎聲 yāsuìshēng 〈sound〉. ②南瓜 nánguā (gourd).

squat v. 蹲踞 dūnjù.

squawk n. & v. 咯咯叫聲 gēgē jiàoshēng / gégé jiàoshēng 〈bird〉.

squeak n. & v. 尖銳聲 jiānruìshēng.

squeal n. & v. 尖叫聲 jiānjiàoshēng.

squeamish adj. 有潔癖的 yǒu jiépǐ de.

squeeze v. 壓榨 yāzhà, 擠壓 jǐyā.

squid n. 烏賊 wūzéi, 魷魚 yóuyú.

squirm v. 蠕動 rúdòng, 扭曲 niǔqū.

squirrel n. 松鼠 sōngshǔ.

squirt v. 噴出 pēnchū.

stab n. & v. 刺 cì, 戳 chuō, 刺傷 cìshāng.

stability n. 穩定 wěndìng, 穩固 wěngù.

stabilize v. 使穩定 shǐ wěndìng.

stable adj. 穩定的 wěndìng de.

stack n. 堆 duī (pile).

stadium n. 體育場 tǐyùchǎng.

staff n. ①棒 bàng, 杖 zhàng (stick). ②竿 gān (pole). ③全體職員 quántǐ zhíyuán (assistants).

stag n. 雄鹿 xiónglù (male deer).

stage n. ①舞臺 wǔtái (platform). ②階段 jiēduàn (period).

stagger v. ①蹣跚 pánshān, 搖晃 yáohuang (falter). ②使吃驚 shǐ chījīng (amaze).

stagnant adj. 不流動的 bù liúdòng de.

stagnate v. 停滯 tíngzhì.

staid adj. 沈著的 chénzhuó de.

stain n. 污點 wūdiǎn, 瑕疵 xiácī (blemish). — v. 染污 rǎnwū (blemish).

stair n. 樓梯 lóutī, 階梯 jiētī.

staircase n. 樓梯 lóutī.

stake n. ①樁 zhuāng (stick). ②賭注 dǔzhù (bet).

stale adj. 不新鮮的 bù xīnxiān de (no longer fresh).

stalk n. 莖 jīng. — v. 潛行 qiánxíng.

stall n. ①廄 jiù 〈compartment〉. ②貨攤 huòtān (stand). — v. ①失速 shīsù 〈speed〉. ②拖延 tuōyán (delay).

stammer v. 口吃 kǒuchī / kǒují, 結巴地說 jiēba de shuō. — n. 口吃 kǒuchī / kǒují.

stamp v. ①跺 duò, 踏 tà 〈foot〉. ②蓋印於 gàiyìn yú (imprint). — n. ①印章 yìnzhāng (seal). ②郵票 yóupiào (letter).

stance n. ①姿勢 zīshì (posture). ②態度 tàidu (attitude). ③立場 lìchǎng (position).

stand v. ①站立 zhànlì (rise). ②豎起 shùqǐ (erect). ③不變 búbiàn (remain valid). ④忍受 rěnshòu (endure). — n. ①臺架 táijià (support). ②攤 tān (stall).

standard n. 標準 biāozhǔn 〈level〉. — adj. 標準的 biāozhǔn de.

standing n. ①身分 shēnfen,

S

地位 dìwèi (position). ②持續 chíxù (continuance). — adj. 持續的 chíxù de (continuing).

standpoint n. 立場 lìchǎng, 觀點 guāndiǎn.

stanza n. 一節 yì jié.

staple n. ①釘書針 dìngshūzhēn ⟨stapler⟩. ②主要 物產 zhǔyào wùchǎn ⟨product⟩.

stapler n. 釘書機 dìngshūjī.

star n. ①星 xīng ⟨astronomy⟩. ②星形 xīngxíng ⟨pentagram⟩. ③明星 míngxīng ⟨performer⟩.

starch n. ①澱粉 diànfěn ⟨carbohydrate⟩. ②漿 jiāng ⟨clothes⟩.

stare v. 凝視 níngshì, 瞪眼 dèngyǎn.

starfish n. 海星 hǎixīng.

stark adj. ①僵硬的 jiāngyìng de (stiff). ②全然的 quánrán de (complete).

starry adj. 多星的 duōxīng de.

start v. 開始 kāishǐ (begin). ~ out 出發 chūfā (depart). — n. 開始 kāishǐ, 著手 zhuóshǒu.

startle v. 使吃驚 shǐ chījīng.

startling adj. 令人吃驚的 lìng rén chījīng de.

starvation n. 饑餓 jī'è.

starve v. 饑餓 jī'è, 使挨餓 shǐ ái'è.

state n. ①狀態 zhuàngtài, 情形 qíngxing (condition). ②國家 guójiā (country). ③州 zhōu (political unit). — v. 述說 shùshuō.

stately adj. 莊嚴的 zhuāngyán de.

statement n. 陳述 chénshù, 聲明 shēngmíng.

statesman n. 政治家 zhèngzhìjiā.

static adj. 靜止的 jìngzhǐ de, 靜態的 jìngtài de. — n. 靜電 jìngdiàn.

station n. ①崗位 gǎngwèi (position). ②署 shǔ, 局 jú (office). ③車站 chēzhàn (stopping-place). ④電臺 diàntái (channel).

stationary adj. 不動的 bú dòng de, 固定的 gùdìng de.

stationery n. 文具 wénjù.

statistics n. 統計 tǒngjì.

statue n. 雕像 diāoxiàng.

stature n. ①身高 shēngāo, 身材 shēncái ⟨physical⟩. ②地位 dìwèi ⟨status⟩.

status n. ①地位 dìwèi, 身分 shēnfen (position). ②狀態 zhuàngtài (condition).

statute n. 法規 fǎguī, 法令 fǎlìng.

stay v. ①停留 tíngliú (remain). ②居住 jūzhù (be housed). ③延緩 yánhuǎn (postpone).

STD 性傳播疾病 xìng chuánbō jíbìng / 性病 xìngbìng (Sexually Transmitted Disease).

steadfast adj. 堅定的 jiāndìng de, 不變的 búbiàn de.

steadily adv. 穩健地 wěnjiàn de.

steady adj. ①穩定的 wěndìng de (stable). ②有規律的 yǒu guīlǜ de (unvarying).

steak n. 牛排 niúpái, 肉片 ròupiàn.

steal v. 偷 tōu, 竊取 qièqǔ.

steam n. 蒸氣 zhēngqì, 水氣 shuǐqì. — v. 蒸 zhēng.

steamboat n. 汽船 qìchuán.

steel n. 鋼 gāng.

steep adj. ①陡峭的 dǒuqiào

de (precipitous). ②過分的 guòfèn de (exorbitant). — v. 浸漬於 jìnzì yú.

steeple n. 尖塔 jiāntǎ.

steer v. 駕駛 jiàshǐ, 掌舵 zhǎngduò.

stem n. 莖 jīng (stalk).

stench n. 臭氣 chòuqì, 惡臭 èchòu.

step n. ①步 bù, 一步 yí bù (pace). ②步驟 bùzòu (stage). — v. 踏 tà.

stepfather n. 繼父 jìfù.

stepmother n. 繼母 jìmǔ.

stereo n. 音響 yīnxiǎng.

stereotype n. ①刻板形象 kèbǎn xíngxiàng (common perception), 老套 lǎotào (fixed in form). ②鉛版印刷 qiānbǎn yìnshuā (printing).

sterile adj. ①不肥沃的 bù féiwò de, 貧瘠的 pínjí de (barren). ②無菌的 wújūn de / wújùn de (germ-free).

sterilization n. 結紮 jiézā.

sterilize v. ①殺菌 shājūn / shājùn (clean). ②使不育 shǐ búyù (castrate).

stern adj. ①嚴格的 yángé de (strict). ②嚴厲的 yánlì de (severe). — n. 船尾 chuánwěi.

stethoscope n. 聽診器 tīngzhěnqì.

stew v. 燉 dùn, 燜 mèn. — n. 燉菜 dùncài.

steward n. ①服務員 fúwùyuán (attendant). ②管家 guǎnjiā, 執事 zhíshì ⟨of a large house⟩.

stewardess n. ①女服務員 nǚ fúwùyuán (attendant). ②女管家 nǚ guǎnjiā ⟨of a house⟩.

stick n. ①棒 bàng, 棍 gùn (bar). ②木條 mùtiáo, 柴枝

cháizhī (branch). — v. ①刺 cì, 戳 chuō (dig). ②黏貼 niántiē (adhere).

sticker n. 黏貼標籤 niántiē biāoqiān, 貼紙 tiēzhǐ ⟨paper⟩.

sticky adj. ①黏的 nián de (adhesive). ②濕熱的 shīrè de (damp).

stiff adj. ①硬的 yìng de (firm). ②緊的 jǐn de (tight). ③困難的 kùnnán de, 棘手的 jíshǒu de (difficult). ④生硬的 shēngyìng de, 呆板的 áibǎn de (clumsy). ⑤嚴厲的 yánlì de (strict).

stiffen v. ①變硬 biànyìng (harden). ②使堅強 shǐ jiānqiáng (become strong).

stifle v. ①使窒息 shǐ zhìxī / shǐ zhìxí (smother). ②抑制 yìzhì (repress).

still adj. ①靜寂的 jìngjì de / jìngjí de (noiseless). ②不動的 bú dòng de (unmoving). ③不起泡的 bù qǐpào de (calm). — v. 使安靜 shǐ ānjìng. — adv. 仍 réng, 仍然 réngrán, 還 hái (even so).

stimulant n. 興奮劑 xīngfènjì ⟨drug⟩. ②刺激物 cìjīwù (stimulus).

stimulate v. 刺激 cìjī, 鼓舞 gǔwǔ.

stimulus n. 刺激 cìjī, 激勵 jīlì.

sting n. & v. ①刺 cì (prick). ②刺痛 cìtòng (stab).

stingy adj. 吝嗇的 lìnsè de, 小氣的 xiǎoqi de (miserly).

stink n. 臭味 chòuwèi. — v. 發臭味 fā chòuwèi (give a strong bad smell).

stipulate v. 規定 guīdìng, 約定 yuēdìng.

stipulation n. 條件 tiáojiàn (condition).

S

stir v. ①攪拌 jiǎobàn (mix). ②移動 yídòng (move). ③激發 jīfā (inspire).

stitch n. 一針 yì zhēn. — v. 縫 féng.

stock n. ①股票 gǔpiào, 公債 gōngzhài (shares). ②貯存 zhùcún / zhùcún, 積蓄 jīxù (hoard). ③存貨 cúnhuò, 現貨 xiànhuò (goods). ④家畜 jiāchù (animals). — v. 備置 bèizhì, 採辦 cǎibàn (keep a stock of).

stockbroker n. 證券經紀人 zhèngquàn jīngjìrén.

stocking n. 長襪 chángwà.

stoke v. 加燃料於 jiā ránliào yú (fill with coal).

stomach n. 胃 wèi.

stone n. ①石頭 shítou, 石 shí (rock). ②紀念碑 jìniànbēi (memorial). ③寶石 bǎoshí (gem).

stony adj. ①石的 shí de (rocky). ②鐵石心腸的 tiě-shí-xīncháng de (heartless).

stool n. 凳 dèng, 凳子 dèngzi.

stoop v. 彎腰 wānyāo, 俯身 fǔshēn (lean over).

stop v. ①使停止 shǐ tíngzhǐ (cease). ②停止 tíngzhǐ (come to rest). ③阻止 zǔzhǐ (block). ④塞住 sāizhù (plug). ⑤停留 tíngliú (stay). — n. ①停止 tíngzhǐ (halt). ②停留處 tíngliúchù (resting-place). ③停留 tíngliú (stay). ④車站 chēzhàn (station).

stopper n. 塞子 sāizi, 阻塞物 zǔsèwù.

storage n. ①倉庫 cāngkù (warehouse). ②貯藏 zhùcáng / zhùcáng (storing).

store n. ①商店 shāngdiàn (shop). ②貯藏 zhùcáng / zhǔcáng (accumulation).

storehouse n. 倉庫 cāngkù.

storekeeper n. 店主 diànzhǔ.

stork n. 鸛 guàn.

storm n. ①暴風雨 bàofēngyǔ 〈weather〉. ②騷動 sāodòng (outburst). — v. ①起風暴 qǐ fēngbào 〈weather〉. ②猛攻 měnggōng.

stormy adj. 有暴風的 yǒu bàofēng de 〈weather〉.

story n. ①故事 gùshi (tale). ②新聞報導 xīnwén bàodǎo (report). ③層 céng, 樓 lóu (floor).

stout adj. ①堅決的 jiānjué de (fearless). ②粗壯的 cūzhuàng de, 結實的 jiēshi de (thick).

stove n. 火爐 huǒlú, 暖爐 nuǎnlú.

stow v. 存放 cúnfàng, 堆置 duīzhì.

straight adj. ①直的 zhí de (aligned). ②整齊的 zhěngqí de (neat). ③連續的 liánxù de (continuous). ④坦白的 tǎnbái de, 正直的 zhèngzhí de (honest).

straighten v. 使直 shǐ zhí, 變直 biànzhí.

straightforward adj. 正直的 zhèngzhí de.

strain v. ①拉緊 lājǐn (pull). ②盡全力 jìn quánlì (endeavor). ③過勞 guòláo (exhaust). ④曲解 qūjiě (twist from the truth). ⑤過濾 guòlǜ (filter). — n. ①過度負擔 guòdù fùdān, 辛苦 xīnkǔ (hardship). ②拉緊 lājǐn (being stretched).

strait n. 海峽 hǎixiá.

strand n. ①繩股 shénggǔ (rope). ②濱 bīn, 岸 àn (shore).

— v. 擱淺 gēqiǎn (run aground).

strange adj. ①奇異的 qíyì de, 奇怪的 qíguài de (abnormal). ②陌生的 mòshēng de (unfamiliar).

stranger n. 陌生人 mòshēngrén.

strangle v. 勒死 lēisǐ, 使窒息 shǐ zhìxí / shǐ zhìxí.

strap n. 帶 dài, 皮帶 pídài (strip). — v. 用帶綑 yòng dài kǔn (bind).

strategic adj. 戰略上的 zhànlüèshang de.

strategy n. 策略 cèlüè, 戰略 zhànlüè.

stratum n. 地層 dìcéng, 岩層 yáncéng (rock).

straw n. ①稻草 dàocǎo (dry grass). ②吸管 xīguǎn ⟨for drinking⟩.

strawberry n. 草莓 cǎoméi.

stray v. ①迷路 mílù (get lost). ②遊蕩 yóudàng (wander).

streak n. ①條紋 tiáowén (line). ②性情 xìngqíng (quality).

stream n. ①溪 xī (river). ②流 動 liúdòng (flow).

street n. 街 jiē, 街道 jiēdào.

strength n. 力 lì, 力量 lìliang.

strengthen v. 加強 jiāqiáng, 變強 biànqiáng.

strenuous adj. 費力的 fèilì de (exhausting).

stress n. ①壓力 yālì, 壓迫 yāpò (tension). ②強調 qiángdiào (emphasis). ③重音 zhòngyīn (accent). — v. ①強調 qiángdiào, 著重 zhuózhòng (emphasize). ②重讀 zhòngdú ⟨words⟩. ③加壓力於 jiā yālì yú ⟨pressure⟩.

stretch n. & v. 伸展 shēnzhǎn, 延伸 yánshēn (extension).

stretcher n. 擔架 dānjià.

stricken adj. 受侵襲的 shòu qīnxí de.

strict adj. ①嚴格的 yángé de, 嚴厲的 yánlì de (firm). ②精確 的 jīngquè de (accurate).

stride v. 大步行走 dàbù xíngzǒu. — n. 大步 dàbù.

strike v. ①打 dǎ, 擊 jí / jí, 敲 qiāo (hit). ②敲響 qiāoxiǎng (chime). ③罷工 bàgōng (stop work). ④取下 qǔxià (take down). — n. ①罷工 bàgōng (stopping of work). ②好球 hǎoqiú ⟨ball⟩.

striking adj. 顯著的 xiǎnzhù de, 引人注意的 yǐn rén zhùyì de (attracting attention).

string n. ①線 xiàn, 細繩 xìshéng (cord). ②一串 yí chuàn, 一列 yí liè (series). ③弦 xián ⟨instrument⟩.

strip v. ①剝去 bōqù, 脫去 tuōqù (take off). ②奪去 duóqù (take away). ③裸露 luǒlù / luǒlòu (bare yourself). — n. 狹 長片條 xiácháng piàntiáo.

stripe n. 條紋 tiáowén.

striped adj. 有條紋的 yǒu tiáowén de.

strive v. ①努力 nǔlì, 奮鬥 fèndòu (try). ②鬥爭 dòuzhēng (struggle).

stroke n. ①打擊 dǎjí / dǎjí (hit). ②筆畫 bǐhuà ⟨writing⟩. ③中風 zhòngfēng ⟨sickness⟩. ④一動 yídòng (single movement).

stroll n. & v. 漫步 mànbù, 遨遊 áoyóu (ramble).

strong adj. ①強的 qiáng de, 強壯的 qiángzhuàng de ⟨power⟩. ②濃的 nóng de ⟨taste⟩. ③有力的 yǒulì de (cogent).

structure n. ①構造 gòuzào,

結構 jiégòu (organization).
②建築物 jiànzhùwù /
jiànzhúwù (building).

struggle *n. & v.* ①挣扎
zhēngzhá (strive). ②努力 nǔlì
(endeavor).

strut *v.* 高視闊步 gāo shì
kuòbù. 一 *n.* 支柱 zhīzhù,
撐木 chēngmù.

stubble *n.* ①殘株 cánzhū
(butt). ②短鬚 duǎnxū (beard).

stubborn *adj.* 頑固的 wángù
de, 固執的 gùzhí de
(determined).

stud *n.* ①飾釘 shìdīng (nail).
②種馬 zhǒngmǎ (horse).

student *n.* 學生 xuésheng.

studio *n.* ①畫室 huàshì, 工作
室 gōngzuòshì (workroom).
②攝影棚 shèyǐngpéng
(filming). ③播音室 bōyīnshì /
bòyīnshì (broadcast). ④公寓套
房 gōngyù tàofáng (apartment).

studious *adj.* 用功的
yònggōng de, 好學的 hàoxué
de (fond of studying).

study *n. & v.* 讀書 dúshū, 研
究 yánjiū / yánjiù, 學習 xuéxí.

stuff *n.* 材料 cáiliào, 原料
yuánliào. 一 *v.* 填塞 tiánsāi.

stuffing *n.* 填塞物 tiánsàiwù.

stuffy *adj.* 通風不良的
tōngfēng bù liáng de.

stumble *v.* ①絆倒 bàndǎo
(blunder). ②結巴 jiēba
(stammer).

stump *n.* 殘幹 cángàn (tree).
一 *v.* 困惑 kùnhuò, 難倒
nándǎo (baffle).

stun *v.* ①使昏暈 shǐ hūnyūn
(daze). ②目瞪口呆 shǐ mù-
dèng-kǒu-dāi, 使吃驚 shǐ
chījīng (shock).

stunt *v.* 阻礙生長 zǔ'ài

shēngzhǎng. 一 *n.* ①特技 tèjì
(skill). ②惡作劇 èzuòjù (trick).

stupendous *adj.* 驚人的
jīngrén de.

stupid *adj.* 愚蠢的 yúchǔn de.

stupor *n.* 昏迷 hūnmí, 恍惚
huǎnghū.

sturdy *adj.* 強健的 qiángjiàn
de (strong), 堅決的 jiānjué de
(firm).

stutter *v.* 口吃 kǒuchī / kǒují,
結巴 jiēba.

style *n.* ①風格 fēnggé
(idiosyncrasy). ②樣式 yàngshì
(type). ③優雅 yōuyǎ (elegance).
④文體 wéntǐ (manner of
writing).

stylish *adj.* 優雅的 yōuyǎ de
(elegant), 時髦的 shímáo de
(fashionable).

Styrofoam *n.* 保麗龍
Bǎolílóng.

subconscious *n. & adj.* 潛意
識 qiányìshì / qiányìshì, 下意
識 xiàyìshì / xiàyìshì.

subdivide *v.* 再分 zàifēn, 細
分 xìfēn.

subdue *v.* ①克服 kèfú, 征服
zhēngfú (overcome). ②抑制
yìzhì, 克制 kèzhì (repress).

subject *n.* ①主題 zhǔtí
(theme). ②科目 kēmù (course).
一 *adj.* 受制於……的
shòuzhì yú...de (captive). ~ *to*
易患……的 yìhuàn...de.
一 *v.* 使蒙受 shǐ méngshòu
(expose).

subjective *adj.* ①主觀的
zhǔguān de (emotional). ②主
詞的 zhǔcí de (grammar).

sublime *adj.* 崇高的 chónggāo
de, 高尚的 gāoshàng de
(extremely good).

submarine *n.* 潛水艇

S

qiánshuǐtǐng.

submerge v. 浸入水中 jìnrù shuǐzhōng.

submission n. 服從 fúcóng, 屈服 qūfú (obedience).

submit v. ①服從 fúcóng (surrender). ②提出 tíchū (give in). ③主張 zhǔzhāng, 建議 jiànyì (suggest).

subordinate adj. 下級的 xiàjí de 〈rank〉, 次要的 cìyào de (less important). — n. 屬下 shǔxià.

subscribe v. ①捐助 juānzhù, 認捐 rènjuān (pay money regularly). ②訂閱 dìngyuè (buy regularly). ③同意 tóngyì (agree with).

subscription n. ①捐助款 juānzhùkuǎn (contribution). ②訂閱金 dìngyuèjīn (fee).

subsequent adj. 隨後的 suíhòu de, 接下來的 jiēxialai de / jiēxiàlái de.

subservient adj. 阿諛的 ēyú de.

subside v. ①退落 tuìluò, 消退 xiāotuì (decline). ②下沈 xiàchén, 下陷 xiàxiàn (sink).

subsidiary adj. ①輔助的 fǔzhù de, 次要的 cìyào de (ancillary). ②附屬的 fùshǔ de (affiliated).

subsidize v. 補助 bǔzhù, 津貼 jīntiē.

subsidy n. 補助金 bǔzhùjīn, 津貼 jīntiē.

substance n. ①物質 wùzhí / wùzhì (material). ②實質 shízhí, 意義 yìyì (meaning).

substantial adj. ①堅固的 jiāngù de (solid). ②相當大的 xiāngdāng dà de (considerable). ③有實體的 yǒu shítǐ de (real).

substantiate v. ①使具體化 shǐ jùtǐhuà (make concrete). ②證實 zhèngshí, 證明 zhèngmíng (prove).

substitute n. 代理人 dàilǐrén 〈person〉, 代替物 dàitìwù 〈thing〉. — v. 代替 dàitì.

subterranean adj. 地下的 dìxià de (under the ground).

subtitle n. ①副標題 fùbiāotí (secondary title). ②字幕 zìmù (caption).

subtle adj. ①精緻的 jīngzhì de, 微妙的 wēimiào de / wéimiào de (delicate). ②敏銳的 mǐnruì de (clever). ③淡薄的 dànbó de (mild).

subtract v. 減去 jiǎnqù.

suburb n. 市郊 shìjiāo, 郊區 jiāoqū.

subvert v. 顛覆 diānfù, 毀滅 huǐmiè.

subway n. 地下鐵 dìxiàtiě.

succeed v. ①成功 chénggōng (be successful). ②完成 wánchéng (complete). ③繼承 jìchéng, 繼任 jìrèn (come after).

success n. ①成功 chénggōng (accomplishment). ②成功者 chénggōngzhě 〈person〉. ③成功的事物 chénggōng de shìwù 〈thing〉.

successful adj. 成功的 chénggōng de.

succession n. ①連續 liánxù (continuity). ②繼承 jìchéng 〈property〉.

successive adj. 連續的 liánxù de.

successor n. 繼任者 jìrènzhě, 後繼者 hòujìzhě.

succinct adj. 簡明的 jiǎnmíng de.

S

succulent *adj.* 多汁液的 duō zhīyè de (juicy).

succumb *v.* ①屈從 qūcóng (yield). ②死 sǐ (die).

such *adj.* 如此的 rúcǐ de, 這樣的 zhèyàng de (of an extreme degree). ~ **as** 諸如…… zhūrú ....

suck *v.* ①吸入 xīrù (draw up). ②吸吮 xīshǔn (hold in the mouth). ③吸收 xīshōu (absorb).

suckle *v.* 哺乳 bǔrǔ, 餵奶 wèinǎi.

sudden *adj.* 突然的 tūrán de / túrán de, 忽然的 hūrán de.

suddenly *adv.* 突然地 tūrán de / túrán de.

suds *n.* 肥皂泡沫 féizào pàomò.

sue *v.* ①起訴 qǐsù, 控告 kònggào (indict). ②請求 qǐngqiú (beg).

suffer *v.* ①忍受 rěnshòu (bear). ②遭受 zāoshòu (experience). ③受懲罰 shòu chéngfá (be punished). ④受苦 shòukǔ (feel pain).

suffering *n.* 痛苦 tòngkǔ, 苦難 kǔnàn (pain).

suffice *v.* 足夠 zúgòu (to be enough).

sufficient *adj.* 足夠的 zúgòu de, 充分的 chōngfèn de.

suffix *n.* 字尾 zìwěi, 語尾詞 yǔwěicí.

suffocate *v.* 窒息 zhìxī / zhìxí, 悶死 mēnsǐ.

sugar *n.* 糖 táng.

suggest *v.* ①提議 tíyì, 建議 jiànyì (propose). ②暗示 ànshì (hint).

suggestion *n.* 建議 jiànyì.

suicide *n.* ①自殺 zìshā ⟨act⟩. ②自殺者 zìshāzhě ⟨person⟩.

suit *n.* ①一套 yí tào ⟨clothes⟩. ②一副 yí fù ⟨card⟩. ③訴訟 sùsòng ⟨law⟩. — *v.* ①適合於 shìhé yú (be a good match). ②合身 héshēn (fit in).

suitable *adj.* 適合的 shìhé de, 恰當的 qiàdàng de.

suitcase *n.* 手提箱 shǒutíxiāng.

suite *n.* 套房 tàofáng.

sulfur *n.* 硫磺 liúhuáng.

sulk *v.* 慍怒 yùnnù, 不高興 bù gāoxìng.

sullen *adj.* ①悶悶不樂的 mènmèn-bú-lè de (cheerless). ②陰沉的 yīnchén de (dark).

sultry *adj.* 悶熱的 mēnrè de (hot and humid).

sum *n.* ①合計 héjì, 總合 zǒnghé (total amount). ②金額 jīn'é (amount of money). — *v.* 總計 zǒngjì.

summarize *v.* 摘要 zhāiyào, 概述 gàishù.

summary *n.* 摘要 zhāiyào. — *adj.* ①簡明的 jiǎnmíng de (brief). ②迅速的 xùnsù de (hasty).

summer *n.* 夏季 xiàjì, 夏天 xiàtiān.

summit *n.* ①頂點 dǐngdiǎn, 巔峰 diānfēng (top). ②高層會議 gāocéng huìyì (meeting).

summon *v.* ①傳喚 chuánhuàn, 召喚 zhàohuàn (command). ②召集 zhàojí (assemble).

summons *n.* 傳票 chuánpiào.

sumo *n.* 相撲 xiāngpū.

sun *n.* 日 rì, 太陽 tàiyáng ⟨star⟩. ~ **block** 防曬乳 fángshàirǔ.

sunburn *n.* 曬傷 shàishāng ⟨sore⟩.

Sunday *n.* 星期日 Xīngqírì /

Xīngqírì.

sunken adj. 下陷的 xiàxiàn de.

sunlight n. 日光 rìguāng.

sunny adj. ①陽光充足的 yángguāng chōngzú de (bright). ②愉快的 yúkuài de, 開朗的 kāilǎng de (cheerful).

sunrise n. 日出 rìchū.

sunset n. 日落 rìluò.

sunshine n. 陽光 yángguāng.

sunstroke n. 中暑 zhòngshǔ.

suntan n. 日曬的膚色 rìshài de fūsè.

superb adj. ①宏偉的 hóngwěi de (grand). ②極好的 jí hǎo de, 第一流的 dì-yī liú de (wonderful).

superficial adj. ①表面的 biǎomiàn de, 外表的 wàibiǎo de (on the surface). ②膚淺的 fūqiǎn de (without depth).

superfluous adj. 多餘的 duōyú de, 不必要的 bú bìyào de.

superior adj. ①上級的 shàngjí de (senior). ②優良的 yōuliáng de (better). ③有優越感的 yǒu yōuyuègǎn de (arrogant). — n. 上司 shàngsī, 長官 zhǎngguān.

superiority n. 優越 yōuyuè.

superlative adj. ①最高的 zuì gāo de (the highest degree). ②最高級的 zuì gāojí de 〈grammar〉.

superman n. 超人 chāorén.

supermarket n. 超級市場 chāojí shìchǎng.

supernatural adj. 超自然的 chāozìrán de.

supersede v. 替代 tìdài, 代換 dàihuàn.

supersonic adj. 超音速的 chāoyīnsù de. ~ waves

超聲波 chāoshēngbō/超音波 chāoyīnbō.

superstition n. 迷信 míxìn.

superstitious adj. 迷信的 míxìn de.

supervise v. 監督 jiāndū, 管理 guǎnlǐ.

supervisor n. 監督者 jiāndūzhě, 管理者 guǎnlǐzhě.

supper n. 晚餐 wǎncān.

supplement n. 附錄 fùlù, 補充 bǔchōng.

supplementary adj. 補充的 bǔchōng de, 附加的 fùjiā de.

supplicate v. 懇求 kěnqiú.

supply v. 供給 gōngjǐ (provide for). — n. 供應品 gōngyìngpǐn.

support n. & v. ①支持 zhīchí (hold up). ②維持 wéichí (maintenance), 撫養 fǔyǎng (bringing-up). ③支援 zhīyuán (aid).

suppose v. ①假定 jiǎdìng, 認為 rènwéi (assume). ②想像 xiǎngxiàng (imagine).

suppress v. ①鎮壓 zhènyā, 抑制 yìzhì (repress). ②壓抑 yāyì (restrain). ③隱瞞 yǐnmán (conceal).

supreme adj. 至高的 zhìgāo de, 無上的 wúshàng de.

surcharge n. 額外索價 éwài suǒjià.

sure adj. ①確信的 quèxìn de (assured). ②必定會的 bìdìng huì de (certain). ③確實的 quèshí de (accurate). — adv. 確實地 quèshí de, 的確 díquè, 當然 dāngrán.

surely adv. 確實地 quèshí de.

surf v. 衝浪 chōnglàng. — n. 碎浪 suìlàng.

surface n. 表面 biǎomiàn, 外表 wàibiǎo. — v. ①浮出水面

fúchū shuǐmiàn (rise). ②出現 chūxiàn (appear).

surge v. ①洶湧而至 xiōngyǒng ér zhì 〈waves〉. ②蜂擁而來 fēngyǒng ér lái / fēngyǒng ér lái 〈people〉. — n. ①巨浪 jùlàng, 波濤 bōtāo / bōtáo 〈waves〉. ②洶湧 xiōngyǒng (rush).

surgeon n. 外科醫生 wàikē yīshēng.

surgery n. ①外科手術 wàikē shǒushù (operation). ②手術室 shǒushùshì (operating room).

surly adj. 乖戾的 guāilì de, 粗暴的 cūbào de.

surmise n. & v. 臆測 yìcè, 推測 tuīcè.

surname n. 姓 xìng.

surpass v. 超越 chāoyuè, 凌駕 língjià, 勝過 shèngguò.

surplus n. 剩餘 shèngyú, 盈餘 yíngyú.

surprise n. 驚奇 jīngqí, 驚訝 jīngyà (astonishment). — v. 使驚奇 shǐ jīngqí, 使驚訝 shǐ jīngyà (cause shock to).

surprising adj. 令人驚奇地 lìng rén jīngqí de, 令人吃驚的 lìng rén chījīng de.

surrender v. ①投降 tóuxiáng 〈war〉. ②放棄 fàngqì (give up). — n. ①投降 tóuxiáng (capitulation). ②放棄 fàngqì (giving up).

surreptitious adj. 祕密的 mìmì de, 偷偷的 tōutōu de (done secretly).

surround v. 環繞 huánrào, 包圍 bāowéi.

surroundings n. 環境 huánjìng.

survey v. ①調查 diàochá (investigate). ②測量 cèliáng (measure).

survival n. 生存 shēngcún, 存活 cúnhuó, 繼續存在 jìxù cúnzài.

survive v. 存活 cúnhuó, 生存 shēngcún.

survivor n. 生還者 shēnghuánzhě, 生存者 shēngcúnzhě.

susceptible adj. 敏感的 mǐngǎn de (sensitive), 易受影響的 yì shòu yǐngxiǎng de (impressionable).

suspect v. 猜想 cāixiǎng, 懷疑 huáiyí (distrust). — n. 嫌疑犯 xiányífàn. — adj. 可疑的 kěyí de.

suspend v. ①懸掛 xuánguà (hang). ②使暫停 shǐ zhàntíng (adjourn).

suspenders n. 吊褲帶 diàokùdài 〈trousers〉.

suspense n. 懸而未決 xuán-ér-wèi-jué (indecisiveness).

suspicion n. 懷疑 huáiyí (doubt), 嫌疑 xiányí (mistrust).

suspicious adj. 可疑的 kěyí de (doubtful). ②猜疑的 cāiyí de (suspected).

sustain v. ①支持 zhīchí, 維持 wéichí (support). ②蒙受 méngshòu (suffer). ③認可 rènkě (agree with).

sustenance n. 食物 shíwù (food).

swab n. ①拖把 tuōbǎ (mop). ②棉花棒 miánhuābàng 〈Q-tip〉. — v. 擦淨 cājìng (clean).

swagger n. & v. 昂首闊步 ángshǒu-kuòbù 〈walk〉.

swallow v. 吞 tūn, 嚥 yàn. — n. 燕子 yànzi.

swamp n. 沼澤 zhǎozé.

swan n. 天鵝 tiān'é.

swarm n. 群 qún. — v. 群集 qúnjí.

swarthy adj. 黝黑的 yǒuhēi de.

sway v. 搖擺 yáobǎi (swing from side to side).

swear v. 發誓 fāshì, 宣誓 xuānshì.

sweat n. 汗 hàn, 出汗 chūhàn. — v. 出汗 chūhàn.

sweater n. 毛衣 máoyī.

sweep v. ①掃 sǎo, 打掃 dǎsǎo (clean). ②掠過 lüèguo (move quickly).

sweet adj. ①甜的 tián de (sugary). ②柔和的 róuhé de (harmonious). ③甜美的 tiánměi de, 吸引人的 xīyǐn rén de (lovable). — n. 甜食 tiánshí (candy).

sweeten v. 變甜 biàntián.

sweetheart n. 戀人 liànrén, 愛人 àirén (lover).

swell v. 膨脹 péngzhàng (expand), 增大 zēngdà (increase). — n. 大浪 dàlàng (waves).

swerve v. 突然轉向 tūrán zhuǎnxiàng / túrán zhuǎnxiàng.

swift adj. & adv. ①迅速的 xùnsù de (quick). ②即刻的 jíkè de (prompt).

swim v. 游泳 yóuyǒng.

swindle n. & v. 欺騙 qīpiàn.

swing v. ①搖擺 yáobǎi (sway). ②回轉 huízhuǎn (turn around). ③盪鞦韆 dàng qiūqiān (swing on). — n. ①搖擺 yáobǎi (sway). ②鞦韆 qiūqiān (seat held by ropes).

swirl v. 打漩渦 dǎ xuánwō (spin). — n. 漩渦 xuánwō (water).

switch n. ①開關 kāiguān (electric circuit). ②轉變 zhuǎnbiàn (shift).

switchboard n. ①配電盤 pèidiànpán (electrical). ②電話總機 diànhuà zǒngjī (telephone).

swivel n. 轉環 zhuǎnhuán.

swollen adj. 腫的 zhǒng de, 脹的 zhàng de.

swoon n. 昏厥 hūnjué, 暈倒 yūndǎo (faint).

sword n. 劍 jiàn, 刀 dāo.

sworn adj. 宣誓過的 xuānshìguo de.

sycamore n. 大楓樹 dàfēngshù.

syllable n. 音節 yīnjié.

syllabus n. 大綱 dàgāng.

symbol n. ①象徵 xiàngzhēng (sign). ②符號 fúhào (mark).

symbolic adj. ①象徵(性)的 xiàngzhēng(xìng) de (sign). ②符號的 fúhào de (mark).

symbolize v. 象徵 xiàngzhēng.

symmetry n. 對稱 duìchèn / duìchèng, 勻稱 yúnchèn / yúnchèng.

sympathetic adj. 同情心的 yǒu tóngqíngxīn de.

sympathize v. 同情 tóngqíng.

sympathy n. 同情 tóngqíng.

symphony n. 交響樂團 jiāoxiǎngyuètuán (orchestra), 交響曲 jiāoxiǎngqǔ (music).

symposium n. 專題論文會 zhuāntí lùnwénhuì.

symptom n. 徵候 zhēnghòu, 徵兆 zhēngzhào.

synagogue n. 猶太教的會堂 yóutàijiào de huìtáng.

synonym n. 同義字 tóngyìzì.

相似字 xiāngsìzì.

synonymous *adj.* 同義的 tóngyì de.

syntax *n.* 句法 jùfǎ.

synthesis *n.* 綜合 zōnghé / zònghé, 合成 héchéng.

syringe *n.* 注射器 zhùshèqì.

syrup *n.* 糖漿 tángjiāng.

system *n.* ①系統 xìtǒng (network). ②制度 zhìdù (principles). ③方法 fāngfǎ (method).

systematic *adj.* 有系統的 yǒu xìtǒng de.

T

tab *n.* ①垂飾 chuíshì (small strip). ②帳單 zhàngdān (bill).

table *n.* ①桌子 zhuōzi, 餐桌 cānzhuō 〈furniture〉. ②表 biǎo (list).

tablecloth *n.* 桌布 zhuōbù.

tablespoon *n.* 大湯匙 dà tāngchí.

tablet *n.* ①藥片 yàopiàn (pill). ②碑 bēi 〈stone〉.

taboo *n.* 禁忌 jìnjì.

tacit *adj.* 心照不宣的 xīn-zhào-bù-xuān de.
~ *agreement* 默契 mòqì.

tack *n.* ①圖釘 túdīng, 大頭釘 dàtóudīng (nail). ②方向 fāngxiàng, 方針 fāngzhēn (direction). — *v.* 以大頭釘釘住 yǐ dàtóudīng dìngzhù (nail). ~ *on* 加上 jiāshang, 附上 fùshang.

tackle *n.* 用具 yòngjù (equipment). *fishing* ~ 漁具 yújù. — *v.* ①抱住 bàozhù (seize). ②搶球 qiǎngqiú 〈football〉. ③處理 chǔlǐ (take care of).

tact *n.* 得體 détǐ.

tactic *n.* 策略 cèlüè, 戰略 zhànlüè.

tactical *adj.* 戰術的 zhànshù de.

tactics *n.* 戰術 zhànshù 〈battle〉.

tadpole *n.* 蝌蚪 kēdǒu.

tag *n.* 標籤 biāoqiān (label). — *v.* 加上標籤 jiāshang biāoqiān.

tail *n.* 尾巴 wěiba 〈animal〉, 後部 hòubù (tail-end). — *v.* 尾隨 wěisuí (follow).

taillight *n.* 尾燈 wěidēng.

tailor *n.* 裁縫師 cáifengshī.

take *v.* ①拿 ná (hold), 握 wò (grasp), 取 qǔ (attain). ②捕捉 bǔ, 捉 zhuō (capture). ③帶 dài (bring). ④吃 chī, 喝 hē, 服用 fúyòng (eat or drink). ⑤乘 chéng, 坐 zuò 〈transportation〉. ⑥接受 jiēshòu (accept). ⑦採用 cǎiyòng (use). ⑧選修 xuǎnxiū 〈course〉. ⑨選擇 xuǎnzé (choose).

tale *n.* 故事 gùshì (story or report).

talent *n.* 才能 cáinéng (capability), 天份 tiānfèn (natural ability).

talented *adj.* 有才能的 yǒu

cáinéng de. 有天份的 yǒu
tiānfèn de.

talk *n.* 演講 yǎnjiǎng (speech).
— *v.* ①說話 shuōhuà, 講話
jiǎnghuà (speak). ②閒聊
xiánliáo, 閒談 xiántán (chat).
③討論 tǎolùn (discuss).

talkative *adj.* 好說話的 hào
shuōhuà de, 多嘴的 duōzuǐ
de.

tall *adj.* 高的 gāo de.

talon *n.* 爪 zhuǎ.

tame *v.* ①馴服 xúnfú ⟨animal⟩.
②克服 kèfú ⟨difficult⟩. — *adj.*
①馴服的 xúnfú de ⟨domesti-
cated⟩. ②單調的 dāndiào de,
乏味的 fáwèi de (boring).

tamper *v.* 干預 gānyù (interfere with something).

tan *v.* 曬黑 shàihēi (get a
suntan). — *adj.* 黃褐色的
huánghèsè de / huánghésè
de.

tang *n.* 強烈的味道 qiángliè
de wèidao (sharp taste).

tangerine *n.* 柑橘 gānjú.

tangible *adj.* ①可觸的 kěchù
de (touchable). ②明確的
míngquè de (definite).

tangle *n. & v.* 纏結 chánjié.

tango *n.* 探戈舞 tàngēwǔ.

tank *n.* ①槽 cáo (container).
②戰車 zhànchē, 坦克車
tǎnkèchē (armored vehicle).

tankard *n.* 大酒杯 dà jiǔbēi.

tanker *n.* ①油輪 yóulún
⟨ship⟩. ②油罐車 yóuguànchē
⟨vehicle⟩.

tanner *n.* 製革者 zhìgézhě.

tantalize *v.* 吊胃口 diào
wèikǒu, 逗惑 dòuhuò.

tantrum *n.* 發脾氣 fā píqi.

Taoism *n.* 道教 Dàojiào.

tap *v.* 輕敲 qīngqiāo, 輕拍

qīngpāi. — *n.* ①水龍頭
shuǐlóngtóu (faucet). ②輕敲
qīngqiāo, 輕拍 qīngpāi (a light
touch).

tape *n.* ①帶子 dàizi, 膠帶
jiāodài (band). ②錄音帶
lùyīndài ⟨audio⟩. ③錄像帶
lùxiàngdài / 錄影帶
lùyǐngdài ⟨video⟩. — *v.* ①捆
住 kǔnzhù (tie). ②錄音 lùyīn
⟨audio⟩. ③錄像 lùxiàng / 錄影
lùyǐng ⟨video⟩.

tapestry *n.* 繡帷 xiùwéi.

tar *n.* 柏油 bóyóu, 瀝青 lìqīng.

tardy *adj.* ①緩慢的 huǎnmàn
de (slow). ②晚到的 wǎndào
de (late).

target *n.* ①靶 bǎ, 目標
mùbiāo (goal). ②對象
duìxiàng (object).

tariff *n.* ①關稅 guānshuì
(customs). ②價目表 jiàmùbiǎo
(price list).

tarnish *v.* 失去光澤 shīqù
guāngzé.

taro *n.* 芋 yù, 芋頭 yùtóu.

tarpaulin *n.* 防水布
fángshuǐbù (waterproof canvas).

tart *n.* 果子餡餅 guǒzi
xiànbǐng ⟨food⟩. — *adj.* 酸的
suān de (sour).

tartan *n.* 格子呢 gézíní.

task *n.* 工作 gōngzuò (work),
任務 rènwu (responsibility).

tassel *n.* 流蘇 liúsū, 穗 suì.

taste *n.* ①味道 wèidao (flavor).
②味覺 wèijué ⟨sensory⟩. ③品味
pǐnwèi ⟨appreciation⟩. — *v.* 品
嘗 pǐncháng.

tasty *adj.* 味美的 wèiměi de
(delicious).

tattoo *n.* ①紋身 wénshēn, 刺
青 cìqīng (image on skin). ②歸
營號 guīyínghào (military

T

signal).

taunt *n. & v.* 嘲笑 cháoxiào (tease), 嘲罵 cháomà (insult).

Taurus *n.* 金牛座 Jīnniúzuò.

taut *adj.* ①拉緊的 lājǐn de (tight). ②緊張的 jǐnzhāng de (tense).

tavern *n.* 酒店 jiǔdiàn (pub), 客棧 kèzhàn (inn).

tawny *adj.* 黃褐色的 huánghèsè de / huánghèsè de.

tax *n.* 稅 shuì ⟨money⟩. — *v.* 課稅 kèshuì (require to pay tax).

taxation *n.* ①稅制 shuìzhì ⟨legal system⟩. ②稅收 shuìshōu (tax revenue).

taxi *n.* 出租車 chūzūchē / 計程車 jìchéngchē.

tea *n.* ①茶 chá ⟨drink⟩. ②茶葉 cháyè ⟨leaves⟩. ③下午茶 xiàwǔchá ⟨meal⟩.

teach *v.* 教 jiāo, 教書 jiāoshū.

teacher *n.* 教師 jiàoshī.

teaching *n.* ①教書 jiāoshū (instruction). ②教義 jiàoyì, 教訓 jiàoxun (doctrine).

teak *n.* 柚木 yòumù.

team *n.* 隊 duì, 組 zǔ.

tear *n.* 淚 lèi, 眼淚 yǎnlèi ⟨weeping⟩. — *v.* 撕 sī, 撕裂 sīliè (rip).

tease *v.* 揶揄 yéyú, 嘲弄 cháonòng.

teaspoon *n.* 茶匙 cháchí.

teat *n.* 乳頭 rǔtou.

technical *adj.* ①工藝的 gōngyì de ⟨craft⟩, 技術的 jìshùshang de ⟨skill⟩. ②專門的 zhuānmén de (specialized).

technician *n.* 技術人員 jìshù rényuán, 技工 jìgōng.

technique *n.* 技術 jìshù, 技巧 jìqiǎo (skill).

technology *n.* 科技 kējì

⟨science⟩, 工業技術 gōngyè jìshù ⟨industry⟩.

tedious *adj.* 冗長乏味的 rǒngcháng fáwèi de.

teenage *adj.* 十幾歲的 shíjǐsuì de.

teenager *n.* 青少年 qīngshàonián.

teens *n.* 十幾歲的年齡 shíjǐsuì de niánlíng.

teeth *n.* 牙齒 yáchǐ.
brush the ~ 刷牙 shuāyá.

teetotalism *n.* 禁酒主義 jìnjiǔ zhǔyì.

telegram *n.* 電報 diànbào.

telegraph *n.* ①電報機 diànbàojī ⟨apparatus⟩. ②電報 diànbào (telegram). — *v.* 發電報 fā diànbào.

telephone *n.* 電話 diànhuà. — *v.* 打電話 (給) dǎdiànhuà (gěi).

telescope *n.* 望遠鏡 wàngyuǎnjìng.

televise *v.* 由電視播送 yóu diànshì bōsòng / yóu diànshì bòsòng.

television *n.* 電視 diànshì (TV).

telex *n.* 電報 diànbào. — *v.* 電傳聯繫 diànchuán liánxì.

tell *v.* ①告訴 gàosu (advise). ②分辨 fēnbiàn, 辨別 biànbié (distinguish).

temper *n.* ①脾氣 píqi, 性情 xìngqíng (disposition). ②心情 xìngqíng (mood). ③硬度 yìngdù (degree of hardness). — *v.* 緩和 huǎnhé (alleviate), 調節 tiáojié (adjust).

temperament *n.* 氣質 qìzhì / qìzhí, 性情 xìngqíng (disposition).

temperate *adj.* ①有節制的

yǒu jiézhì de (moderate). ②溫
和的 wēnhé de ⟨climate⟩.

temperature n. ①溫度
wēndù (degree of heat). ②體溫
tǐwēn ⟨body⟩. *take one's* ~ 量體
溫 liáng tǐwēn.

tempest n. 暴風雨
bàofēngyǔ.

temple n. 廟 miào, 寺 sì, 神殿
shéndiàn ⟨non-Christian reli-
gions⟩.

tempo n. 拍子 pāizi ⟨music⟩,
速度 sùdù (speed).

temporal adj. 世俗的 shìsú
de (worldly).

temporary adj. 暫時的
zhànshí de.

tempt v. 引誘 yǐnyòu (arouse a
desire).

tempter n. 引誘者 yǐnyòuzhě.

ten n. & adj. 十 shí.

tenable adj. ①可防守的 kě
fángshǒu de (defensible).
②合理的 hélǐ de (reasonable).

tenancy n. 租賃 zūlìn.

tenant n. 房客 fángkè, 承租者
chéngzūzhě.

tend v. 傾向 qīngxiàng, 朝向
cháoxiàng.

tendency n. 傾向 qīngxiàng,
趨勢 qūshì (trend).

tender adj. ①柔嫩的 róunèn
de (meat). ②柔軟的 róuruǎn
de (soft). ③溫柔的 wēnróu de
(gentle). ④柔和的 róuhé de
(mild). — v. ①提出 tíchū, 提供
tígōng (offer). ②投標 tóubiāo
(bid on).

tendon n. 腱 jiàn.

tennis n. 網球 wǎngqiú.

tenor n. ①男高音 nán gāoyīn
⟨music⟩. ②要旨 yàozhǐ (drift).
③風格 fēnggé (style).

tense adj. ①拉緊的 lājǐn de

(tight). ②緊張的 jǐnzhāng de
(nervous). — n. 時式 shíshì, 時
態 shítài.

tension n. ①拉緊 lājǐn (tight-
ness). ②緊張 jǐnzhāng
(nervousness).

tent n. 帳蓬 zhàngpeng, 帷幕
wéimù.

tentacle n. 觸角 chùjiǎo, 觸鬚
chùxū ⟨animal⟩.

tentative adj. 試驗性質的
shìyàn xìngzhì de / shìyàn
xìngzhì de.

tenth n. & adj. 第十 dì-shí.

tepid adj. ①微熱的 wēirè de /
wéirè de (lukewarm). ②不大熱
烈的 bú dà rèliè de (apathetic).

term n. ①期間 qījiān / qíjiān
(duration). ②學期 xuéqī /
xuéqí (semester). ③術語 shùyǔ
(technical name). ④條件
tiáojiàn (condition). ⑤措辭
cuòcí (words).

terminal adj. 最終的
zuìzhōng de (last). — n. ①終
端機 zhōngduānjī ⟨computer⟩.
②航站 hángzhàn ⟨airport⟩.

terminate v. 終結 zhōngjié,
結束 jiéshù.

terminology n. 術語 shùyǔ,
專門名詞 zhuānmén míngcí.

terminus n. 終點 zhōngdiǎn
(the end), 終站 zhōngzhàn
⟨station⟩.

termite n. 白蟻 báiyǐ.

terrace n. 平台 píngtái
⟨house⟩.

terrain n. 地域 dìyù ⟨region⟩,
地形 dìxíng (topography).

terrestrial adj. 地球上的
dìqiú shàng de ⟨of the Earth⟩,
陸地的 lùdì de ⟨of the land⟩.

terrible adj. ①可怕的 kěpà
de, 令人恐懼的 lìng rén

kǒngjù de (frightening). ②精糕
的 zāogāo de (very bad).

terribly adv. ①非常地
fēicháng de (extremely). ②糟
糕地 zāogāo de (in a very
bad way).

terrific adj. ①極好的 jí hǎo
de (very good). ②非常的
fēicháng de (extreme).

terrify v. 使害怕 shǐ hàipà,
使恐怖 shǐ kǒngbù.

territorial adj. 領土的 lǐngtǔ
de.

territory n. 領土 lǐngtǔ
(possessed land), 地域 dìyù
(area).

terror n. 恐懼 kǒngjù.

terrorism n. 恐怖主義
kǒngbù zhǔyì.

terrorist n. 恐怖份子 kǒngbù
fènzǐ.

terse adj. 簡潔的 jiǎnjié de.

test n. ①考驗 kǎoyàn (trial).
②測驗 cèyàn, 考試 kǎoshì
(school). ③試驗 shìyàn (experiment). — v. 試驗 shìyàn, 考驗
kǎoyàn (experiment), 檢驗
jiǎnyàn (medical purposes).

testament n. ①證明
zhèngmíng (proof). ②遺囑
yízhǔ (will).

testicle n. 睪丸 gāowán.

testify v. 作證 zuòzhèng.

testimonial n. ①證明書
zhèngmíngshū (prove). ②推薦
書 tuījiànshū (reference).

testimony n. ①證言
zhèngyán (statement). ②證據
zhèngjù (evidence).

test tube n. 試管 shìguǎn.

text n. 本文 běnwén (piece of
writing), 原文 yuánwén
(original version).

textbook n. 教科書

jiàokēshū, 課本 kèběn.

textile n. 織物 zhīwù.

texture n. 質地 zhìdì / zhídì
(surface).

than conj. 比…… bǐ...
(comparison).

thank v. 感謝 gǎnxiè, 道謝
dàoxiè.

thankful adj. 感謝的 gǎnxiè
de.

Thanksgiving n. 感恩節
Gǎn'ēnjié.

that adj. & pron. 那 nà, 那個
nàge. — adv. 那麼 nàme.

thaw n. & v. 融解 róngjiě.

the def. art. 這 zhè (this), 那 nà
(that).

theater n. ①戲院 xìyuàn, 劇
場 jùchǎng (building). ②戲劇
xìjù (drama).

their pron. 他們的 tāmen de.

theirs pron. 他們的 tāmen de.

theism n. 有神論 yǒushénlùn.

them pron. 他們 tāmen.

thematic adj. 主題的 zhǔtí
de.

theme n. 主題 zhǔtí, 題目
tímù.

themselves pron. 他們自己
tāmen zìjǐ.

then adv. ①當時 dāngshí (at
that time). ②然後 ránhòu
(afterward). ③那麼 nàme
(therefore). ④並且 bìngqiě
(also).

theology n. 神學 shénxué.

theoretical adj. 理論的 lǐlùn
de.

theoretically adv. 理論上
lǐlùnshang (in principle).

theory n. 學說 xuéshuō, 理論
lǐlùn.

therapist n. 心理醫生 xīnlǐ
yīshēng.

therapy n. 療法 liáofǎ, 治療 zhìliáo (cure).

there adv. 那裡 nàli.

thereafter adv. 從此 cóngcǐ, 其後 qíhòu.

thereby adv. 藉以 jièyǐ.

therefore adv. 所以 suǒyǐ, 因此 yīncǐ.

thermal adj. 熱的 rè de (hot).

thermometer n. 溫度計 wēndùjì, 寒暑表 hánshǔbiǎo.

thermos n. 熱水瓶 rèshuǐpíng.

these adj. & pron. 這些 zhèxiē.

thesis n. ①論點 lùndiǎn (argument). ②論文 lùnwén (treatise).

they pron. 他們 tāmen.

thick adj. ①厚的 hòu de (not thin). ②密集的 mìjí de (dense). ③濃稠的 nóngchóu de (heavy).

thicken v. 變厚 biàn hòu.

thicket n. 灌木叢 guànmùcóng.

thickness n. 厚度 hòudù.

thief n. 賊 zéi, 小偷 xiǎotōu.

thigh n. 大腿 dàtuǐ.

thimble n. 頂針 dǐngzhēn.

thin adj. ①薄的 báo de / bó de (not thick). ②瘦的 shòu de (slim). ③稀薄的 xībó de〈air〉. ④淡的 dàn de (weak).

thing n. ①東西 dōngxi (object). ②事情 shìqing (affair).

think v. ①思索 sīsuǒ, 想 xiǎng, 考慮 kǎolǜ (consider). ②認為 rènwéi (be of the opinion that), 覺得 juéde (feel).

thinking adj. 有思考力的 yǒu sīkǎolì de (thoughtful). — n. 思想 sīxiǎng, 思考 sīkǎo (thoughts), 見解 jiànjiě (opinion).

third n. & adj. 第三 dì-sān.

thirst n. 口渴 kǒukě.

thirsty adj. 口渴的 kǒukě de.

thirteen n. & adj. 十三 shísān.

thirteenth n. & adj. 第十三 dì-shísān.

thirtieth n. & adj. 第三十 dì-sānshí.

thirty n. & adj. 三十 sānshí.

this pron. 這 zhè, 這個 zhège.

thistle n. 薊 jì.

thong n. 皮條 pítiáo, 皮帶 pídài.

thorn n. 荊棘 jīngjí.

thorough adj. 完全的 wánquán de, 徹底的 chèdǐ de.

thoroughfare n. 通道 tōngdào.

those adj. & pron. 那些 nàxiē.

thou pron. 你 nǐ.

though conj. 雖然 suīrán, 縱使 zòngshǐ.

thought n. ①看法 kànfa, 想法 xiǎngfa (opinion). ②主意 zhǔyì (idea). ③思想 sīxiǎng (philosophy). ④思考 sīkǎo (thinking).

thoughtful adj. 深思的 shēnsī de (thinking deeply).

thoughtless adj. ①不關心他人的 bù guānxīn tārén de, 不體貼的 bù tǐtiē de (inconsiderate). ②欠考慮的 qiàn kǎolǜ de, 輕率的 qīngshuài de (careless).

thousand n. & adj. 千 qiān.

thrash v. ①打穀 dǎgǔ (thresh). ②鞭打 biāndǎ (beat). ③擊敗 jíbài / jíbài (defeat).

thread n. 線 xiàn (sewing).

threat n. 恐嚇 kǒnghè, 威脅 wēixié.

three n. & adj. 三 sān.

T

thresh v. 打穀 dǎgǔ.

threshold n. 門檻 ménkǎn.

thrift n. 節儉 jiéjiǎn.

thrifty adj. 節儉的 jiéjiǎn de.

thrill n. & v. 震顫 zhènchàn
(tremor).

thrive v. 繁盛 fánshèng, 興盛
xīngshèng.

throat n. 喉嚨 hóulóng.

throb n. & v. 跳動 tiàodòng.

throes n. 陣痛 zhèntòng.

throne n. 王位 wángwèi
⟨political position⟩, 寶座
bǎozuò ⟨seat⟩.

throng n. 群眾 qúnzhòng.
— v. 蜂擁 fēngyōng /
fēngyǒng, 擠滿 jǐmǎn.

throttle n. 節流閥 jiéliúfá
⟨valve⟩. — v. 勒死 lēisǐ
(strangle).

through prep. ①經過 jīngguò,
通過 tōngguò (pass by). ②遍
及 biànjí (throughout). ③藉 jiè,
由 yóu (by means of). ④從頭到
尾 cóng-tóu-dào-wěi (from
beginning to end).

throughout prep. 遍及 biànjí.

throw v. 投 tóu, 擲 zhì / zhí.

thrush n. 畫眉鳥 huàméiniǎo.

thrust v. 用力推 yònglì tuī
(push strongly). ~ into 插入
chārù.

thud n. 重擊聲 zhòngjīshēng /
zhòngjíshēng (sound).

thug n. 惡棍 ègùn, 兇徒
xiōngtú.

thumb n. 拇指 mǔzhǐ.

thump n. 重擊 zhòngjī /
zhòngjí (beat heavily).

thunder n. 雷 léi (lightning),
雷聲 léishēng ⟨sound⟩. — v.
打雷 dǎléi.

thunderbolt n. 雷電 léidiàn.

thunderclap n. 雷響 léixiǎng

(crash of thunder).

Thursday n. 星期四 Xīngqīsì
/ Xīngqísì.

thus adv. 如此 rúcǐ, 於是
yúshì.

thwart v. 阻撓 zǔnáo.

thyme n. 百里香 bǎilǐxiāng.

tick n. 滴答聲 dīdāshēng
⟨sound⟩. — v. 滴答響 dīdā
xiǎng.

ticket n. ①票 piào, 車票
chēpiào ⟨transportation⟩. ②入
場券 rùchǎngquàn, 門票
ménpiào ⟨entertainment⟩.

tickle v. ①呵癢 hēyǎng (touch
or stroke). ②逗樂 dòulè, 使高
興 shǐ gāoxìng ⟨fun⟩.

ticklish adj. 怕癢的 pàyǎng
de.

tide n. 潮 cháo, 潮汐 cháoxī /
cháoxì.

tidings n. 消息 xiāoxi.

tidy adj. 整潔的 zhěngjié de.
— v. 使整潔 shǐ zhěngjié.

tie v. ①繫 jì, 綁 bǎng (fasten).
②與……得同分 yǔ…dé
tóngfēn (be equal). — n. 領帶
lǐngdài ⟨clothing⟩.

tiger n. 虎 hǔ, 老虎 lǎohǔ.

tight adj. ①緊的 jǐn de (fixed).
②緊密的 jǐnmì de (inflexible).
— adv. 緊緊地 jǐnjǐn de.

tighten v. 變緊 biàn jǐn.

tights n. 緊身衣 jǐnshēnyī.

tile n. 瓦 wǎ, 瓷磚 cízhuān.

till prep. & conj. 直到 zhídào.
— v. 耕種 gēngzhòng.

tilt v. 傾斜 qīngxié (slant).

timber n. 木材 mùcái (wood).

time n. ①時間 shíjiān ⟨hour⟩.
②時代 shídài (era). ③次數
cìshù (occasion). — v. 計時
jìshí.

timely adj. 適時的 shìshí de.

timer n. ①計時器 jìshíqì 〈device〉. ②計時員 jìshíyuán 〈person〉.

timetable n. 時刻表 shíkèbiǎo.

timid adj. 膽小的 dǎnxiǎo de, 膽怯的 dǎnqiè de / dǎnquè de.

tin n. 錫 xī / xí.

tincture n. 酊 dīng.

tinfoil n. 錫箔 xībó / xíbó.

tingle v. 感到刺痛 gǎndào cìtòng. — n. 刺痛 cìtòng.

tinkle v. 發叮璫聲 fā dīngdāngshēng. — n. 叮璫聲 dīngdāngshēng.

tint n. 色澤 sèzé 〈color〉, 濃淡 nóngdàn 〈hue〉. — v. 著色 zhuósè.

tiny adj. 極小的 jí xiǎo de.

tip n. ①尖 jiān, 尖端 jiānduān 〈sharp end〉. ②頂端 dǐngduān 〈top〉. ③小費 xiǎofèi 〈money〉. ④指示 zhǐshì, 暗示 ànshì 〈hint〉. — v. ①傾斜 qīngxié 〈incline〉. ②給小費 gěi xiǎofèi 〈money〉. ③給暗示 gěi ànshì 〈hint〉.

tipsy adj. 微醺的 wēixūn de / wéixūn de.

tiptoe n. 腳尖 jiǎojiān. — v. 踮著腳走 diǎnzhejiǎo zǒu / diànzhejiǎo zǒu.

tire v. 疲倦 píjuàn, 厭倦 yànjuàn. — n. 輪胎 lúntāi.

tired adj. 疲倦的 píjuàn de 〈energy〉, 厭倦的 yànjuàn de 〈interest〉.

tiresome adj. 令人厭倦的 lìng rén yànjuàn de 〈tedious〉, 無聊的 wúliáo de 〈boring〉.

tissue n. ①組織 zǔzhī 〈biology〉. ②薄紙 báozhǐ / bózhǐ, 面紙 miànzhǐ 〈tissue-paper〉.

title n. ①標題 biāotí, 名稱 míngchēng 〈name〉. ②頭銜 tóuxián 〈position〉.

titter n. & v. 竊笑 qièxiào.

to prep. ①向 xiàng, 對 duì, 往 wǎng 〈in the direction of〉. ②到 dào, 達 dá 〈towards a destination〉.

toad n. 蟾蜍 chánchú 〈frog〉.

toast n. 烤土司 kǎo tǔsī. — v. ①烤 kǎo 〈grill〉. ②舉杯祝賀 jǔbēi zhùhè 〈drink a toast to〉.

tobacco n. 煙草 yāncǎo.

today n. & adv. 今天 jīntiān.

toddle v. 蹣跚行走 pánshān xíngzǒu.

toddler n. 剛學走路的幼兒 gāng xué zǒulù de yòu'ér.

toe n. 腳趾 jiǎozhǐ.

together adv. 一起 yìqǐ, 共同 gòngtóng.

toil n. & v. 辛勞 xīnláo, 辛苦工作 xīnkǔ gōngzuò.

toilet n. ①浴室 yùshì 〈bathroom〉. ②盥洗室 guànxǐshì, 廁所 cèsuǒ 〈lavatory〉. ③馬桶 mǎtǒng 〈structure〉.

token n. ①表徵 biǎozhēng, 象徵 xiàngzhēng 〈symbol〉. ②代幣 dàibì 〈coin〉.

tolerance n. 寬容 kuānróng 〈acceptance〉, 容忍度 róngrěndù 〈endurance〉.

tolerant adj. 寬容的 kuānróng de, 容忍的 róngrěn de.

tolerate v. 容忍 róngrěn.

toleration n. 容忍 róngrěn.

toll v. 鳴鐘 míng zhōng 〈ring〉. — n. 通行費 tōngxíngfèi 〈charge〉.

tollway n. 收費高速公路 shōufèi gāosù gōnglù.

tomato n. 西紅柿 xīhóngshì / 番茄 fānqié.

tomb n. 墳墓 fénmù.

tomboy *n.* 行為似男孩的女孩 xíngwéi sì nánhái de nǚhái, 男人婆 nánrénpó.

tomcat *n.* 雄貓 xióngmāo.

tomorrow *n. & adv.* 明天 míngtiān.

ton *n.* 噸 dùn.

tone *n.* ①聲音 shēngyīn, 音調 yīndiào (sound). ②氣氛 qìfēn (atmosphere). ③色調 sèdiào (color). ④語調 yǔdiào, 語氣 yǔqì (manner).

tongs *n.* 鉗 qián.

tongue *n.* ①舌 shé, 舌頭 shétou ⟨organ⟩. ②語言 yǔyán (language).

tonic *n.* 滋補品 zībǔpǐn, 補藥 bǔyào ⟨medicine⟩.

tonight *n. & adv.* 今夜 jīnyè, 今晚 jīnwǎn.

tonnage *n.* 噸位 dùnwèi.

tonsil *n.* 扁桃腺 biǎntáoxiàn.

too *adv.* ①也 yě (also). ②太 tài, 過於 guòyú (overly).

tool *n.* 工具 gōngjù, 器具 qìjù.

tooth *n.* 牙齒 yáchǐ.

toothache *n.* 牙痛 yátòng.

toothbrush *n.* 牙刷 yáshuā.

toothpaste *n.* 牙膏 yágāo.

toothpick *n.* 牙籤 yáqiān.

top *n.* 頂 dǐng, 最高點 zuì gāodiǎn, 上端 shàngduān. — *adj.* ①最高的 zuì gāo de (tallest). ②最好的 zuì hǎo de (best).

topic *n.* 話題 huàtí, 題目 tímù.

topple *v.* ①翻倒 fāndǎo (fall over), 搖搖欲墜 yáoyáo-yù-zhuì (be unsteady and fall). ②推翻 tuīfān ⟨power⟩.

torch *n.* 火炬 huǒjù, 火把 huǒbǎ.

torment *v.* 使痛苦 shǐ tòngkǔ. — *n.* 痛苦 tòngkǔ.

tornado *n.* 龍捲風 lóngjuǎnfēng.

torpedo *n.* 魚雷 yúléi.

torpid *adj.* 麻痺的 mábì de (paralytic).

torpor *n.* 麻痺 mábì.

torrent *n.* 急流 jíliú.

torrid *adj.* ①炎熱的 yánrè de (hot). ②激情的 jīqíng de (passionate).

tortoise *n.* 龜 guī, 烏龜 wūguī.

torture *n. & v.* 拷問 kǎowèn, 折磨 zhémo.

toss *v.* ①擲 zhì / zhí, 拋 pāo (cast). ②搖盪 yáodàng (swing).

total *adj.* ①全部的 quánbù de, 總的 zǒng de (entire). ②完全的 wánquán de (complete). — *n.* 合計 héjì, 總數 zǒngshù.

totalitarian *n.* 極權主義者 jíquánzhǔyìzhě.

totality *n.* 總數 zǒngshù (sum).

totally *adv.* 完全地 wánquán de.

totter *v.* 蹣跚 pánshān, 搖搖欲墜 yáoyáo-yù-zhuì (stagger).

touch *v.* ①觸摸 chùmō, 觸及 chùjí ⟨emotion⟩. ②感動 gǎndòng (move). ③達到 dádào (reach). — *n.* ①接觸 jiēchù (contact). ②觸覺 chùjué ⟨sense⟩.

touching *adj.* 動人的 dòngrén de, 令人感動的 lìng rén gǎndòng de.

touch screen *n.* 觸摸式螢幕 chùmōshì yíngmù.

tough *adj.* ①堅韌的 jiānrèn de (firm). ②困難的 kùnnán de, 棘手的 jíshǒu de (difficult). ③粗暴的 cūbào de (violent).

tour *n. & v.* 旅行 lǚxíng

(journey).

tourism n. ①觀光 guānguāng (sightseeing). ②觀光事業 guānguāng shìyè 〈business〉.

tourist n. 觀光客 guānguāngkè, 遊客 yóukè.

tournament n. 比賽 bǐsài, 競賽 jìngsài.

town n. & v. 拖 tuō, 曳 yè / yì.

toward prep. 向 xiàng, 對 duì, 向著 xiàngzhe (in the direction of).

towel n. 毛巾 máojīn.

tower n. 塔 tǎ (tall narrow structure).

town n. 城鎮 chéngzhèn, 市鎮 shìzhèn.

toxic adj. 有毒的 yǒudú de.

toxin n. 毒素 dúsù.

toy n. 玩具 wánjù.

trace n. ①痕跡 hénjī, 蹤跡 zōngjī (vestige). ②微量 wēiliàng / wéiliàng (little bit). — v. ①追蹤 zhuīzōng (track). ②追溯 zhuīsù (seek out). ③描繪 miáohuì (sketch).

trachoma n. 砂眼 shāyǎn.

track n. ①痕跡 hénjī (vestige). ②路徑 lùjìng (path). ③軌道 guǐdào (rail). ④徑賽運動 jìngsài yùndòng (racetrack). — v. 追蹤 zhuīzōng (follow).

tract n. ①區域 qūyù (area). ②小冊子 xiǎocèzi 〈written work〉.

traction n. 牽引 qiānyǐn, 拖曳 tuōyè / tuōyì.

tractor n. 牽引機 qiānyǐnjī.

trade n. ①貿易 màoyì (commerce). ②職業 zhíyè (profession). — v. 交易 jiāoyì, 做生意 zuò shēngyi.

trademark n. 商標 shāngbiāo.

trader n. 商人 shāngrén.

tradition n. 傳統 chuántǒng, 慣例 guànlì (convention).

traffic n. 交通 jiāotōng, 運輸 yùnshū 〈vehicles〉. ~ light 紅綠燈 hónglùdēng.

tragedy n. 悲劇 bēijù.

tragic adj. 悲劇的 bēijù de.

trail v. ①拖 tuō, 拉 lā (drag). ②尾隨 wěisuí (follow). — n. ①痕跡 hénjī, 蹤跡 zōngjī (vestige). ②道路 dàolù, 小徑 xiǎojìng (path).

trailer n. 拖車 tuōchē 〈truck〉.

train n. ①火車 huǒchē (railway). ②連續 liánxù (sequence). ③行列 hángliè (row). — v. ①訓練 xùnliàn (instruct). ②瞄準 miáozhǔn (aim). ③練習 liànxí (exercise).

trainer n. 訓練者 xùnliànzhě.

training n. 訓練 xùnliàn.

trait n. 特性 tèxìng, 特色 tèsè.

traitor n. 叛徒 pàntú, 反叛者 fǎnpànzhě.

tram n. 電車 diànchē (public passenger vehicle).

tramp v. ①沈重地行走 chénzhòng de xíngzǒu (walk with heavy steps). ②步行 bùxíng (walk). — n. ①徒步旅行 túbù lǚxíng (long walk). ②飄泊者 piāobózhě (wanderer).

trample v. 踐踏 jiàntà, 蹂躪 róulìn.

trampoline n. 跳床 tiàochuáng.

trance n. ①恍惚 huǎnghū (dreamy state). ②電子舞曲 diànzǐ wǔqǔ 〈dance music〉.

tranquil adj. 平靜的 píngjìng de, 寧靜的 níngjìng de.

tranquilize v. 使寧靜 shǐ

níngjìng.

transact v. ①辦理 bànlǐ, 處理 chǔlǐ.

transaction n. ①辦理 bànlǐ (conduct). ②交易 jiāoyì (deal).

transcend v. ①超越 chāoyuè (surpass). ②勝過 shèngguò (be better than).

transcribe v. ①謄寫 téngxiě, 抄寫 chāoxiě (copy). ②錄製 lùzhì (record).

transcript n. ①副本 fùběn, 謄本 téngběn. ②成績單 chéngjīdān / chéngjìdān 〈student〉.

transfer v. ①移動 yídòng, 調動 diàodòng (move). ②讓渡 ràngdù, 轉讓 zhuǎnràng 〈hand over〉. ③調任 diàorèn 〈job〉.

transform v. 使變形 shǐ biànxíng, 使改觀 shǐ gǎiguān (change shape).

transformation n. ①變形 biànxíng, 改觀 gǎiguān (transfiguration). ②變壓 biànyā 〈electrical〉.

transformer n. 變壓器 biànyāqì.

transfuse v. 輸血 shūxuè / shūxiě 〈blood〉.

transgress v. ①踰越 yúyuè (go beyond). ②違犯 wéifàn 〈law〉.

transistor n. 電晶體 diànjīngtǐ 〈electricity〉.

transit n. ①運送 yùnsòng (transport). ②通過 tōngguò (traveling through).

transition n. 轉移 zhuǎnyí, 變遷 biànqiān (change).

transitive adj. 及物的 jíwù de 〈grammar〉.

translate v. 翻譯 fānyì.

translation n. ①翻譯 fānyì (translating). ②譯文 yìwén, 譯本 yìběn (translated version).

translator n. 翻譯家 fānyìjiā, 譯者 yìzhě.

transmission n. ①傳送 chuánsòng, 傳達 chuándá (conveyance). ②播送 bōsòng / bòsòng (broadcast). ③傳動系統 chuándòng xìtǒng 〈engine〉.

transmit v. ①傳送 chuánsòng, 傳達 chuándá (move). ②傳導 chuándǎo (communicate). ③傳染 chuánrǎn (infect).

transparent adj. ①透明的 tòumíng de (clear). ②顯然的 xiǎnrán de (obvious).

transplant v. ①移植 yízhí 〈organs, plant〉. ②遷移 qiānyí (move).

transport v. 運輸 yùnshū, 運送 yùnsòng.

transportation n. 運輸 yùnshū.

transpose v. 更換位置 gēnghuàn wèizhi (change places).

transverse adj. 橫互的 hénggèn de, 橫斷的 héngduàn de.

trap n. 陷阱 xiànjǐng 〈device〉, 圈套 quāntào 〈plan〉. — v. 誘捕 yòubǔ, 設陷阱 shè xiànjǐng, 計陷 jìxiàn.

trash n. 垃圾 lājī / lèsè, 廢物 fèiwù.

trauma n. ①外傷 wàishāng, 創傷 chuāngshāng (external injury). ②精神創傷 jīngshén chuāngshāng (emotional injury).

travel n. & v. 旅行 lǚxíng, 旅

遊 lǚyóu.

traveler n. 旅行者 lǚxíngzhě
⟨tourist⟩.

traverse v. ①橫過 héngguò,
橫亙 hénggèn ⟨extend across⟩.
②穿過 chuānguò ⟨travel across⟩.

trawl n. 拖網 tuōwǎng
⟨large net⟩. — v. 以拖網捕魚
yǐ tuōwǎng bǔyú.

tray n. 盤 pán, 碟 dié.

treacherous adj. 不忠的
bùzhōng de ⟨disloyal⟩, 叛逆的
pànnì de ⟨traitorous⟩.

treacle n. 糖蜜 tángmì.

tread v. ①行走 xíngzǒu ⟨walk⟩,
踩踏 cǎità ⟨step⟩. ②踐踏 jiàntà
⟨trample⟩.

treadle n. 踏板 tàbǎn.

treason n. 叛逆 pànnì ⟨ruler⟩,
叛國 pànguó ⟨country⟩.

treasure n. 財寶 cáibǎo, 貴重
品 guìzhòngpǐn. — v. 珍愛
zhēn'ài ⟨cherish⟩, 珍惜
zhēnxī / zhēnxí ⟨value⟩, 重視
zhòngshì ⟨see as important⟩.

treasurer n. 會計 kuàijì.

treasury n. ①金庫 jīnkù, 寶庫
bǎokù ⟨location⟩. ②基金 jījīn
⟨fund⟩. ③(T~) 財政部
cáizhèngbù ⟨government⟩.

treat v. ①對待 duìdài ⟨behave
toward⟩. ②視為 shìwéi
⟨consider⟩. ③治療 zhìliáo
⟨cure⟩. ④款待 kuǎndài, 請客
qǐngkè ⟨pay for⟩. ⑤處理 chǔlǐ
⟨deal with⟩.

treatise n. 論文 lùnwén.

treatment n. ①看待 kàndài,
對待 duìdài ⟨dealing with⟩.
②治療 zhìliáo ⟨cure⟩. ③療法
liáofǎ ⟨way⟩.

treaty n. 條約 tiáoyuē ⟨written
agreement⟩.

treble adj. 三倍的 sān bèi de

⟨three times⟩. — n. 最高音部
zuì gāoyīn bù ⟨music⟩.

tree n. 樹 shù, 樹木 shùmù.

tremble n. & v. 戰慄 zhànlì,
發抖 fādǒu ⟨quiver⟩.

tremendous adj. ①驚人的
jīngrén de ⟨surprising⟩. ②巨大
的 jùdà de ⟨big⟩. ③很棒的 hěn
bàng de ⟨excellent⟩.

tremor n. 顫抖 chàndǒu /
zhàndǒu ⟨slight shaking⟩.

trench n. 戰壕 zhànháo, 溝
gōu.

trend n. & v. 趨勢 qūshì, 傾向
qīngxiàng.

trepidation n. 驚恐 jīngkǒng
⟨great fear⟩.

trespass v. 侵入 qīnrù ⟨intrude⟩,
侵犯 qīnfàn ⟨violate⟩.

trestle n. 支架 zhījià ⟨table-
top⟩.

trial n. ①審判 shěnpàn
⟨court⟩. ②試驗 shìyàn, 考驗
kǎoyàn ⟨test⟩. ③試用 shìyòng
⟨job⟩.

triangle n. 三角形
sānjiǎoxíng ⟨geometry⟩.

triangular adj. 三角形的
sānjiǎoxíng de.

tribe n. 種族 zhǒngzú ⟨race⟩,
部落 bùluò ⟨clan⟩.

tribunal n. 法庭 fǎtíng
⟨court⟩.

tributary n. & adj. 支流
zhīliú ⟨river⟩.

tribute n. ①貢品 gòngpǐn
⟨contribution⟩. ②讚辭 zàncí
⟨commendation⟩.

trick n. ①詭計 guǐjì, 欺詐
qīzhà ⟨trickery⟩. ②把戲 bǎxì,
戲法 xìfǎ ⟨conjuring magic⟩.
③惡作劇 èzuòjù ⟨joke⟩.
— v. 欺騙 qīpiàn ⟨deceive⟩.

trickery n. 欺騙 qīpiàn.

T

trickle v. 滴流 dīliú, 慢慢地流 mànmàn de liú. — n. 細流 xìliú 〈flow〉.

tricycle n. 三輪車 sānlúnchē.

trifle n. ①瑣事 suǒshì 〈thing〉. ②少量 shǎoliàng 〈amount〉.

trigger n. 扳機 bānjī 〈gun〉.

trill v. 以顫音唱 yǐ chànyīn chàng 〈sing〉. — n. 顫音 chànyīn 〈musical effect〉.

trillion n. 兆 zhào (a million million).

trilogy n. 三部曲 sānbùqǔ.

trim v. 修整 xiūzhěng 〈cut〉. — adj. 整齊的 zhěngqí de (neat and tidy).

trinity n. 三合一 sān hé yī. *the T~* 三位一體 Sān wèi yìtǐ.

trinket n. 小飾物 xiǎo shìwù (small ornament).

trip n. 旅行 lǚxíng, 遠足 yuǎnzú (journey). — v. 跌倒 diēdǎo / diédǎo (fall).

triple n. & adj. 三倍 sān bèi (three times).

triplicate n. 一式三份 yí shì sān fèn 〈document〉.

tripod n. 三腳架 sānjiǎojià.

triumph n. 勝利 shènglì. — v. 獲勝 huòshèng.

triumphant adj. 勝利的 shènglì de (victorious), 成功的 chénggōng de (successful).

trivial adj. ①不重要的 bú zhòngyào de (unimportant). ②瑣碎的 suǒsuì de (trifling).

trolley n. ①電車 diànchē (tram). ②手推車 shǒutuīchē (handcart).

trombone n. 伸縮喇叭 shēnsuō lǎba.

troop n. ①群 qún (group). ②軍隊 jūnduì (military).

trophy n. 戰利品 zhànlìpǐn

〈hunting, war〉.

tropic n. ①回歸線 huíguīxiàn 〈line〉. ②熱帶 rèdài 〈area〉.

tropical adj. 熱帶的 rèdài de.

trot v. 快步走 kuàibùzǒu, 小跑 xiǎopǎo. — n. 疾走 jízǒu.

trouble n. 麻煩 máfan, 使煩惱 shǐ fánnǎo. — n. ①麻煩 máfan (bother). ②煩惱 fánnǎo (worry).

troublesome adj. 麻煩的 máfan de, 使人苦惱的 shǐ rén kǔnǎo de.

trough n. ①飼料槽 sìliàocáo 〈food〉. ②水槽 shuǐcáo 〈liquid〉.

troupe n. 班 bān, 團 tuán.

trousers n. 褲子 kùzi.

trout n. 鱒魚 zūnyú.

trowel n. ①鏝子 mànzi 〈flat-bladed〉. ②小鏟子 xiǎo chǎnzi 〈scoop〉.

truant n. 逃學者 táoxuézhě 〈school〉.

truce n. 休戰 xiūzhàn 〈war〉.

truck n. 卡車 kǎchē, 貨車 huòchē 〈carrying goods〉.

truculent adj. 兇猛的 xiōngměng de, 好鬥的 hàodòu de.

true adj. ①真實的 zhēnshí de (real). ②真正的 zhēnzhèng de (actual). ③忠實的 zhōngshí de (faithful).

truly adv. ①真實地 zhēnshí de (really). ②誠心地 chéngxīn de (sincerely). ③事實上 shìshíshàng (actually).

trump n. 王牌 wángpái 〈card games〉. — v. 出王牌獲勝 chū wángpái huòshèng 〈beat〉.

trumpet n. 喇叭 lǎba 〈instrument〉.

trunk n. ①樹幹 shùgàn 〈tree〉. ②身軀 shēnqū 〈body〉. ③象鼻

trust n. ①信賴 xìnlài (reliance). ②信託 xìntuō ⟨legal relation⟩. ③責任 zérèn (responsibility). ④托拉斯 tuōlāsī ⟨firm⟩. — v. ①信賴 xìnlài, 信任 xìnrèn (rely on). ②委託 wěituō (entrust).

trustee n. 受託人 shòutuōrén.

trustworthy adj. 可信賴的 kě xìnlài de, 可靠的 kěkào de.

truth n. ①真實 zhēnshí (facts). ②真實性 zhēnshíxìng (accuracy). ③真理 zhēnlǐ (reality).

try v. ①嘗試 chángshì (attempt). ②試驗 shìyàn (examine). ③審問 shěnwèn ⟨law⟩.

tub n. 桶 tǒng, 盆 pén.

tubby adj. 圓胖的 yuánpàng de (short and fat).

tube n. ①管 guǎn, 筒 tǒng (pipe). ②(T~) 地下鐵道 dìxià tiědào ⟨subway⟩. ③真空管 zhēnkōngguǎn (valve).

tuberculosis n. 結核病 jiéhébìng, 肺結核 fèijiéhé.

tuck v. 摺起 zhéqǐ, 捲起 juǎnqǐ (fold). — n. 褶 zhě / zhé, 襇 jiǎn ⟨skirt⟩.

Tuesday n. 星期二 Xīngqí'èr / Xīngqí'èr.

tuft n. 一束 yí shù, 一簇 yí cù (bunch).

tug v. 用力拉 yònglì lā, 拖曳 tuōyè / tuōyì (pull).

tuition n. 學費 xuéfèi ⟨fee⟩.

tulip n. 鬱金香 yùjīnxiāng.

tumble v. ①跌倒 diēdǎo / diédǎo, 跌落 diēluò / diéluò (fall). ②使跌倒 shǐ diēdǎo / shǐ diédǎo, 使跌落 shǐ diēluò / shǐ diéluò (cause to fall).

tumbler n. ①平底玻璃杯 píngdǐ bōlibēi (glass). ②雜技演員 zájì yǎnyuán (acrobat).

tumor n. 腫瘤 zhǒngliú.

tumult n. 喧囂 xuānxiāo, 騷動 sāodòng.

tuna n. 鮪魚 wěiyú.

tune n. 曲調 qǔdiào (melody). — v. 調音 tiáoyīn ⟨adjust⟩.

tunnel n. 隧道 suìdào, 地道 dìdào (underground passage).

turbine n. 渦輪機 wōlúnjī.

turbot n. 比目魚 bǐmùyú, 鰈魚 diéyú.

turbulence n. 亂流 luànliú ⟨air⟩.

turbulent adj. ①狂暴的 kuángbào de (violent). ②混亂的 hùnluàn de / hǔnluàn de (disorderly). ③騷動的 sāodòng de (riotous).

turf n. ①草地 cǎodì, 草皮 cǎopí ⟨grass⟩. ②地盤 dìpán.

turkey n. 火雞 huǒjī.

turmoil n. 混亂 hùnluàn / hǔnluàn, 騷動 sāodòng.

turn v. ①旋轉 xuánzhuàn (rotate). ②轉向 zhuǎnxiàng (change direction). ③轉動 zhuǎndòng (twist). ④變成 biànchéng (become). ~ off 關閉 guānbì。~ on 打開 dǎkāi.

turning n. 轉彎處 zhuǎnwānchù. ~ point 轉捩點 zhuǎnzhédiǎn / 轉捩點 zhuǎnlièdiǎn.

turnip n. 蘿蔔 luóbo.

turnover n. 營業額 yíngyè'é ⟨business⟩.

turnstile n. 十字旋轉門 shízì xuánzhuǎnmén.

turpentine n. 松節油 sōngjiéyóu.

turquoise n. ①綠寶石

lǔbǎoshí 〈stone〉. ②青綠色
qīnglǜsè 〈color〉.

turret n. ①砲塔 pàotǎ 〈gun〉.
②小塔 xiǎotǎ, 角樓 jiǎolóu
(small tower).

turtle n. 龜 guī, 海龜 hǎiguī.

tusk n. 長牙 chángyá.

tut n. & interj. 噓! xū, 嘖! zé.

tutor n. ①家庭教師 jiātíng
jiàoshī 〈home〉. ②個人導師
gèrén dǎoshī 〈school〉.

twang n. ①弦聲 xiánshēng
〈instrument〉. ②鼻音 bíyīn
〈speaking〉.

tweak n. & v. 擰 nǐng, 扭 niǔ.

tweed n. 呢料 níliào.

tweezers n. 鑷子 nièzi.

twelfth n. & adj. 第十二
dì-shí'èr.

twelve n. & adj. 十二 shí'èr.

twentieth n. & adj. 第二十
dì-èrshí.

twenty n. & adj. 二十 èrshí.

twice adv. 兩次 liǎngcì
〈number〉, 兩倍 liǎngbèi
〈amount〉.

twig n. 小枝 xiǎozhī, 嫩枝
nènzhī.

twilight n. ①曙光 shǔguāng /
shùguāng 〈before sunrise〉.
②薄暮 bómù 〈before sunset〉.

twill n. 斜紋布 xiéwénbù
(cotton).

twin n. 攣生子之一
luánshēngzǐ zhī yī /
lüánshēngzǐ zhī yī. — adj. 攣
生的 luánshēng de /
lüánshēng de 〈pair of
children〉.

twins n. 雙胞胎
shuāngbāotāi.

twine n. 細繩 xìshéng 〈string〉.

twinkle n. & v. 閃爍
shǎnshuò 〈flash〉.

twirl n. & v. ①旋轉
xuánzhuǎn (spin). ②扭轉
niǔzhuǎn (twist).

twist v. ①搓 cuō, 捻 niǎn, 編
biān (coil). ②纏繞 chánrào
(entangle). ③扭 niǔ, 擰 nǐng
(wrench). ④曲解 qūjiě (alter).
— n. ①扭 niǔ, 擰 nǐng
(wrench). ②曲折 qūzhé (bend).

twitch v. 抽動 chōudòng, 痙
攣 jìngluán / jìngluán (jerk).

twitter n. & v. 鳥鳴 niǎomíng,
吱吱地叫 zhīzhī de jiào (chirp).

two n. & adj. 二 èr.

tycoon n. 鉅子 jùzǐ, 大亨
dàhēng.

tympanitis n. 中耳炎
zhōng'ěryán.

type n. ①型 xíng, 類型 lèixíng,
種類 zhǒnglèi (kind). ②典型
diǎnxíng (example). ③字體 zìtǐ
(font). — v. 打字 dǎzì.

typewriter n. 打字機 dǎzìjī.

typhoid n. & adj. 傷寒
shānghán.

typhoon n. 颱風 táifēng.

typhus n. 斑疹傷寒
bānzhěn shānghán.

typical adj. 典型的 diǎnxíng
de.

typically adv. 典型地
diǎnxíng de.

typist n. 打字員 dǎzìyuán.

tyrannical adj. 暴虐的
bàonüè de.

tyranny n. 暴政 bàozhèng
〈government〉.

tyrant n. 暴君 bàojūn.

U

udder *n.* 乳房 rǔfáng.

UFO *n.* 不明飛行物體 bù míng fēixíng wùtǐ, 幽浮 yōufú, 飛碟 fēidié.

ugly *adj.* 難看的 nánkàn de, 醜陋的 chǒulòu de.

ulcer *n.* 潰瘍 kuìyáng.

ultimate *adj.* ①最後的 zuìhòu de, 終極的 zhōngjí de (final). ②根本的 gēnběn de (basic).

ultimatum *n.* 最後通牒 zuìhòu tōngdié.

ultrafiche *n.* 超微縮膠片 chāowéisuō jiāopiàn / chāowéisuō jiāopiàn.

ultraviolet *adj.* 紫外線的 zǐwàixiàn de.

umbrella *n.* 傘 sǎn, 雨傘 yǔsǎn.

umpire *n.* 裁判 cáipàn, 仲裁者 zhòngcáizhě.

unable *adj.* 不能的 bù néng de.

unaccountable *adj.* 無法解釋的 wúfǎ jiěshì de (inexplicable).

unaffected *adj.* ①未受影響的 wèi shòu yǐngxiǎng de (not influenced). ②無矯飾的 wú jiǎoshì de (natural).

unanimous *adj.* 全體一致的 quántǐ yízhì de.

unarmed *adj.* 無武裝的 wú wǔzhuāng de.

unassuming *adj.* 謙虛的 qiānxū de.

unattended *adj.* ①無伴的 wúbàn de (unaccompanied). ②無人照料的 wú rén zhàoliào de (not taken care of).

unavoidable *adj.* 不得已的 bùdéyǐ de, 無可避免的 wú kě bìmiǎn de.

unaware *adj.* 未察覺的 wèi chájué de, 不知不覺的 bù-zhī-bù-jué de.

unbearable *adj.* 無法忍受的 wúfǎ rěnshòu de.

unbelief *n.* 不信 búxìn.

unbelievable *adj.* ①難以置信的 nányǐ zhì xìn de (hard to believe). ②不可思議的 bù-kě-sī-yì de (outrageous).

unbroken *adj.* 未破損的 wèi pòsǔn de.

uncalled-for *adj.* ①不必要的 bú bìyào de (unnecessary). ②不當的 búdàng de (improper).

uncanny *adj.* ①神秘的 shénmì de (mysterious). ②怪異的 guàiyì de (unnatural).

uncertain *adj.* ①不確定的 bú quèdìng de (not ascertained). ②不清楚的 bù qīngchu de (unclear).

unchangeable *adj.* 不變的 búbiàn de.

uncharitable *adj.* 不慈悲的 bù cíbēi de.

uncle *n.* ①叔叔 shūshu / shúshu, 叔父 shūfù / shúfù (father's younger brother). ②伯父 bófù, 伯伯 bóbo (father's older brother). ③舅父 jiùfù, 舅舅 jiùjiu (mother's brother).

uncomfortable *adj.* 不舒服的 bù shūfu de.

uncommon adj. 稀有的 xīyǒu de, 不尋常的 bù xúncháng de.

uncompromising adj. 不妥協的 bù tuǒxié de.

unconcerned adj. 不關心的 bù guānxīn de.

unconscious adj. 不知不覺的 bù-zhī-bù-jué de, 無意識的 wú yìshí de / wú yìshì de.

uncouth adj. ①粗魯的 cūlǔ de (rude). ②笨拙的 bènzhuō de / bènzhuó de (awkward).

uncover v. 打開覆蓋 dǎkāi fùgài.

undecided adj. 未決定的 wèi juédìng de.

undeniable adj. 無可否認的 wú kě fǒurèn de.

under prep. ①在……之下 zài...zhī xià (below). ②少於 shǎo yú (less than). — adv. 在下面 zài xiàmian.

underbid v. 喊價低於 hǎnjià dī yú.

underclothes n. 內衣褲 nèiyīkù.

undercurrent n. 潛流 qiánliú, 暗流 ànliú.

underdog n. 居劣勢者 jū lièshì zhě.

underestimate v. 低估 dīgū.

undergo v. 遭受 zāoshòu.

undergraduate n. 大學生 dàxuésheng.

underground adj. & adv. 在地下的 zài dìxià de (below the surface). — n. 地下鐵 dìxiàtiě (subway).

undergrowth n. 矮樹叢 ǎishùcóng.

underline v. ①在下面畫線 zài xiàmian huà xiàn (draw a line under). ②強調 qiángdiào

(emphasize).

undermine v. 逐漸損壞 zhújiàn sǔnhuài (weaken).

underneath prep. 在……的下面 zài...de xiàmian. — adv. 在下面 zài xiàmian.

underpass n. 地下道 dìxiàdào 〈underground〉, 下層道 xiàcéng dào 〈lower level〉.

undersell v. 低價出售 dījià chūshòu.

understand v. 懂 dǒng, 了解 liǎojiě.

understanding n. ①理解力 lǐjiělì 〈ability〉. ②諒解 liàngjiě 〈sympathy〉. ③協議 xiéyì 〈agreement〉.

understudy n. 候補演員 hòubǔ yǎnyuán.

undertake v. ①承擔 chéngdān, 擔負 dānfù (accept responsibility for). ②從事 cóngshì (participate in), 著手 zhuóshǒu (start).

undertaker n. 殯葬業者 bìnzàngyè zhě.

undertaking n. 事業 shìyè (enterprise).

undervalue v. 低估 dīgū.

underwear n. 內褲 nèikù.

underworld n. ①地獄 dìyù (hell). ②地下社會 dìxià shèhuì 〈organized crime〉.

undeveloped adj. 未開發的 wèi kāifā de 〈land〉.
~ countries 不發達國家 bù fādá guójiā / 未開發國家 wèi kāifā guójiā.

undo v. ①解開 jiěkāi (unfasten). ②破壞 pòhuài (destroy). ③恢復原狀 huīfù yuánzhuàng 〈reverse〉.

undoubted adj. 無疑的 wúyí de.

undress v. 脫去衣服 tuōqù yīfu.

undue adj. 不當的 búdàng de (inappropriate), 過分的 guòfèn de (excessive).

uneasy adj. ①不舒適的 bù shūshì de (uncomfortable). ②不自在的 bú zìzài de (awkward). ③不安的 bù'ān de (anxious).

unemployed adj. 失業的 shīyè de.

unemployment n. 失業 shīyè. ~ **rate** 失業率 shīyèlǜ.

unequal adj. 不相等的 bù xiāngděng de, 不平等的 bù píngděng de.

uneven adj. ①不平坦的 bù píngtǎn de (not smooth). ②參差不齊的 cēncī-bù-qí de (unbalanced).

unexpected adj. 意外的 yìwài de.

unfair adj. 不公平的 bù gōngping de.

unfaithful adj. 不忠實的 bù zhōngshí de.

unfamiliar adj. 不熟悉的 bù shúxī de. ~ **with...** 跟…… 不熟悉 gēn...bù shúxī.

unfasten v. 解開 jiěkāi.

unfavorable adj. 不利的 búlì de.

unfinished adj. 未完成的 wèi wánchéng de.

unfit adj. 不合適的 bù héshì de.

unfold v. ①打開 dǎkāi (open), 展開 zhǎnkāi (unfurl). ②表明 biǎomíng (reveal).

unforeseen adj. 預料不到的 yùliào bú dào de, 出乎意料的 chū-hū-yìliào de.

unforgettable adj. 難忘的 nánwàng de.

unfortunate adj. 不幸的 búxìng de.

unfriendly adj. 不友善的 bù yǒushàn de.

unfurl v. 展開 zhǎnkāi.

unfurnished adj. 不附家具的 bú fù jiāju de.

ungrateful adj. 忘恩負義的 wàng-ēn-fù-yì de.

unhappy adj. 不快樂的 bú kuàilè de.

unhealthy adj. 不健康的 bú jiànkāng de.

unicorn n. 獨角獸 dújiǎoshòu.

uniform adj. 相同的 xiāngtóng de (the same), 不變的 búbiàn de (unchanging). — n. 制服 zhìfú.

uniformity n. 一致性 yízhìxìng, 均一性 jūnyīxìng.

unify v. 統一 tǒngyī (combine), 使一致 shǐ yízhì (make uniform).

unilateral adj. 單方的 dānfāng de, 片面的 piànmiàn de.

unimportant adj. 不重要的 bú zhòngyào de.

union n. ①工會 gōnghuì (labor association). ②聯合 liánhé, 結合 jiéhé (joining). ③婚姻 hūnyīn (marriage). ④同盟 tóngméng (alliance).

unique adj. 獨特的 dútè de, 獨一無二的 dú-yī-wú-èr de.

unit n. ①單位 dānwèi 〈measurement〉. ②部隊 bùduì 〈troop〉.

unite v. ①結合 jiéhé, 合併 hébìng, 聯合 liánhé (combine). ②團結 tuánjié (cooperate).

united adj. ①聯合的 liánhé

de (joint). ②團結的 tuánjié de
(cooperating).

unity n. ①單一 dānyī, 統一
tǒngyī (being united). ②和諧
héxié (agreement).

universal adj. ①全世界的
quán shìjiè de (world-wide).
②普遍的 pǔbiàn de
(common). ③宇宙的 yǔzhòu
de (cosmic).

universe n. 宇宙 yǔzhòu.

university n. 大學 dàxué.

unjust adj. 不公正的
bù gōngzhèng de.

unkind adj. 不厚道的 bú
hòudào de.

unknown adj. 未知的
wèizhī de.

unlace v. 解開 jiěkāi.

unlawful adj. 不合法的 bù
héfǎ de, 違法的 wéifǎ de.

unless conj. 除非 chúfēi.

unlike adj. 不相似的 bù
xiāngsì de.

unlikely adj. ①不像是真的
bú xiàng shì zhēn de
(questionable). ②未必是的
wèibì shì de (not probable).

unlimited adj. 無限的
wúxiàn de.

unload v. 卸載 xièzài.

unlock v. 開鎖 kāisuǒ.

unlucky adj. 不幸的 búxìng
de.

unmarried adj. 未婚的
wèihūn de, 單身的 dānshēn
de.

unmentionable adj. 不可提
及的 bù kě tíjí de.

unmoved adj. 冷靜的
lěngjìng de.

unnatural adj. ①不自然的
bú zìrán de (not natural). ②離
譜的 lípǔ de, 誇張的

kuāzhāng de (stilted). ③邪惡
的 xié'è de (evil).

unnecessary adj. 不必要的
bú bìyào de.

unnerve v. 使膽怯 shǐ dǎnqiè
/ shǐ dǎnquè.

unoccupied adj. ①空的 kōng
de (vacant). ②空閒的
kòngxián de (free).

unofficial adj. 非正式的 fēi
zhèngshì de (not formal), 非官
方的 fēi guānfāng de (not
authoritative).

unpack v. 拆箱 chāixiāng, 拆
開 chāikāi.

unparalleled adj. 無比的
wúbǐ de, 無以匹敵的 wú-yǐ-
pǐdí de.

unpleasant adj. ①使人不快
的 shǐ rén búkuài de
〈situation〉. ②不友善的 bù
yǒushàn de (unfriendly). ③令
人討厭的 lìng rén tǎoyàn de
(annoying).

unpopular adj. ①不受歡迎
bú shòu huānyíng de
(disliked). ②不流行的 bù
liúxíng de (unfashionable).

unprecedented adj. 空前的
kōngqián de.

unpredictable adj. 不可預
測的 bù kě yùcè de.

unprepared adj. 沒有準備的
méiyǒu zhǔnbèi de.

unproductive adj. 無生產力
的 wú shēngchǎnlì de.

unprofitable adj. 無利益的
wú lìyì de.

unqualified adj. 不合格的
bù hégé de.

unquestionable adj. 無疑的
wúyí de, 確定的 quèdìng de.

unravel v. 解開 jiěkāi.

unreal adj. ①不真實的 bù

zhēnshí de (not real). ②不可
思議的 bù-kě-sī-yì de
(surprising).

unreasonable *adj.* 不合理的
bù héli de.

unrelenting *adj.* 無情的
wúqíng de, 嚴峻的 yánjùn de.

unreliable *adj.* 不可靠的 bù
kěkào de, 不可信賴的 bù kě
xìnlài de.

unreserved *adj.* ①未預訂的
wèi yùdìng de 〈seat〉.②坦率的
tǎnshuài de (open).

unrest *n.* 不安 bù'ān, 不寧
bùníng.

unripe *adj.* 未成熟的 wèi
chéngshú de.

unruly *adj.* ①難控制的 nán
kòngzhì de (hard to control).
②頑皮的 wánpí de (naughty).

unsatisfactory *adj.* ①不能
令人滿意的 bù néng lìng rén
mǎnyì de (not satisfying).
②不合格的 bù hégé de (not
good enough).

unscathed *adj.* 未受傷害的
wèi shòu shānghài de.

unscrupulous *adj.* 不道德的
bú dàodé de, 無良知的 wú
liángzhī de.

unseasonable *adj.* 不合季節
的 bùhé jìjié de.

unseat *v.* 罷免 bàmiǎn, 去職
qùzhí.

unseen *adj.* 看不見的
kànbujiàn de.

unselfish *adj.* 不自私的 bú
zìsī de.

unsettle *v.* 使不安 shǐ bù'ān
(make anxious), 使動搖 shǐ
dòngyáo (make unstable).

unsightly *adj.* 難看的
nánkàn de.

unsociable *adj.* 不善交際的

búshàn jiāojì de.

unsound *adj.* 不健康的 bú
jiànkāng de (unhealthy).

unspeakable *adj.* 無法形容
的 wúfǎ xíngróng de, 無法言
喻的 wúfǎ-yányù de, 說不出
的 shuōbuchū de.

unstable *adj.* 不穩定的 bù
wěndìng de.

unsteady *adj.* 不堅定的 bù
jiāndìng de.

unsuccessful *adj.* 未成功的
wèi chénggōng de.

unsuitable *adj.* 不合適的 bù
héshì de.

unthinkable *adj.* 無法想像
的 wúfǎ xiǎngxiàng de.

untidy *adj.* 邋遢的 lāta de /
láta de, 凌亂的 língluàn de.

untie *v.* 解開 jiěkāi.

until *prep. & conj.* 直到
zhídào.

untimely *adj. & adv.* 不合時
宜的 bùhé shíyí de.

untold *adj.* ①未說出的 wèi
shuōchū de (kept secret).
②數不清的 shǔbuqīng de
(countless).

untrue *adj.* 不真實的 bù
zhēnshí de.

unusual *adj.* 異常的 yìcháng
de.

unveil *v.* ①揭幕 jiēmù
(inaugurate).②揭露 jiēlù
(reveal).

unwilling *adj.* 不願意的 bú
yuànyì de.

unwise *adj.* 不明智的 bù
míngzhì de.

unworthy *adj.* 不值得的
bù zhídé de.

unwrap *v.* 解開 jiěkāi, 打開
dǎkāi.

up *adv.* 往上 wǎng shàng, 向上

xiàng shàng. — *prep.* 朝上 cháo shàng (facing upward), 在……上面 zài...shàngmian (above). — *adj.* 上揚的 shàngyáng de.

update *v.* 成為最新的 chéngwéi zuì xīn de, 使更新 的 shǐ gēngxīn de. — *n.* 最新 消息 zuì xīn xiāoxi.

upgrade *v.* 使……升級 shǐ... shēngjí.

uphill *adj.* ①上坡的 shàngpō de (ascending). ②困難的 kùnnán de (difficult). — *adv.* 上坡地 shàngpō de, 向上地 xiàng shàng de.

uphold *v.* 支持 zhīchí (support), 贊成 zànchéng (approve of).

upholstery *n.* ①室內裝潢業 shìnèi zhuānghuángyè 〈business〉. ②室內裝潢品 shìnèi zhuānghuángpǐn 〈materials〉.

uplift *v.* 使振奮 shǐ zhènfèn (encourage).

upon *prep.* 在上 zài shàng.

upper *adj.* ①在上面的 zài shàngmian de (higher). ②上級的 shàngjí de (superior).

upright *adj.* ①直立的 zhílì de (vertical). ②誠實的 chéngshí de (honest), 有道德的 yǒu dàodé de (moral).

uproar *n.* 喧囂 xuānxiāo, 騷動 sāodòng.

uproot *v.* 連根拔起 lián gēn bá qǐ 〈plant〉.

upset *v.* ①打翻 dǎfān (overturn). ②使混亂 shǐ hùnluàn / shǐ hǔnluàn (disrupt). ③使煩惱 shǐ fánnǎo (annoy). ④使悲傷 shǐ bēishāng (sadden).

upshot *n.* 結局 jiéjú, 結果

jiéguǒ.

upside-down *adv.* ①倒置地 dàozhì de (on its head). ②混亂 地 hùnluàn de / hǔnluàn de (disorderly).

upstairs *adv.* 在樓上 zài lóushàng. — *n.* 樓上 lóushàng.

upstart *n.* 暴發戶 bàofāhù.

up-to-date *adj.* 最新的 zuì xīn de.

upward *adj. & adv.* 向上的 xiàng shàng de.

upwards *adv.* 向上地 xiàng shàng de.

uranium *n.* 鈾 yóu.

Uranus *n.* 天王星 Tiānwángxīng.

urban *adj.* 都市的 dūshì de.

urbane *adj.* 有禮貌的 yǒu lǐmào de (polite).

urge *v.* ①驅策 qūcè (compel). ②催促 cuīcù (hurry), 力勸 lìquàn (persuade). ~ *on* 驅策 qūcè (encourage). — *n.* 欲望 yùwàng (desire).

urgent *adj.* 緊急的 jǐnjí de, 急迫的 jípò de.

urinate *v.* 小便 xiǎobiàn, 尿尿 niàoniào.

urine *n.* 尿 niào, 小便 xiǎobiàn.

urn *n.* ①骨灰罈 gǔhuītán 〈cremation〉. ②甕 wèng (vase).

usage *n.* ①使用 shǐyòng, 用法 yòngfǎ (use). ②習慣 xíguàn, 慣例 guànlì (custom).

use *v.* 使用 shǐyòng, 利用 lìyòng (utilize).

used *adj.* ①慣於 guànyú (accustomed). ②用過的 yòngguo de, 二手的 èrshǒu de (second-hand).

useful *adj.* 有用的 yǒuyòng

de.

useless *adj.* 無用的 wúyòng de.

usher *n.* 招待員 zhāodàiyuán.

usual *adj.* 通常的 tōngcháng de.

usually *adv.* 通常 tōngcháng.

usurer *n.* 放高利貸者 fàng gāolìdài zhě.

utensil *n.* 器皿 qìmǐn, 用具 yòngjù.

uterus *n.* 子宮 zǐgōng.

utility *n.* 效用 xiàoyòng (usefulness).

utilize *v.* 利用 lìyòng.

utmost *adj.* 最大的 zuì dà de (biggest), 極度的 jídù de (extreme). *do one's ~* 盡力而為 jìnlì-ér-wéi.

Utopia *n.* 烏托邦 wūtuōbāng, 理想國 lǐxiǎngguó.

utter *adj.* 完全的 wánquán de (complete). — *v.* 說出 shuōchū (make a sound).

utterly *adv.* 完全地 wánquán de.

UV 紫外線 zǐwàixiàn (ultraviolet).

V

vacancy *n.* ①空缺 kòngquē ⟨job⟩. ②空房間 kōng fángjiān ⟨room⟩.

vacant *adj.* ①空的 kōng de (empty). ②空虛的 kōngxū de, 茫然的 mángrán de (absent-minded).

vacate *v.* ①空出 kòngchū (leave empty). ②搬出 bānchū ⟨dwelling⟩. ③讓出 ràngchū ⟨seat⟩.

vacation *n.* 假期 jiàqī / jiàqí, 休假 xiūjià (holiday).

vaccinate *v.* 種痘 zhòngdòu, 接種疫苗 jiēzhòng yìmiáo.

vaccine *n.* 痘苗 dòumiáo, 疫苗 yìmiáo.

vacillate *v.* 猶疑不決 yóuyí-bùjué (waver).

vacuum *n.* 真空 zhēnkōng. *~ cleaner* 除塵器 chúchénqì / 吸塵器 xīchénqì. *~ tube* 真空

管 zhēnkōngguǎn.

vacuum-packed *adj.* 真空包裝的 zhēnkōng bāozhuāng de.

vagabond *n.* 流浪者 liúlàngzhě, 漂泊者 piāobózhě (tramp). — *adj.* 流浪的 liúlàng de, 漂泊的 piāobó de.

vagary *n.* 異想天開 yì-xiǎng-tiān-kāi ⟨thought⟩, 變幻莫測 biànhuàn-mò-cè ⟨change⟩.

vagrant *n.* 流浪者 liúlàngzhě. — *adj.* 流浪的 liúlàng de, 遊蕩的 yóudàng de.

vague *adj.* ①模糊的 móhu de, 含混的 hánhùn de (dim). ②不明確的 bù míngquè de (uncertain).

vain *adj.* ①徒然的 túrán de, 無效的 wúxiào de (ineffectual). ②自負的 zìfù de (conceited).

valet *n.* 男僕 nánpú, 服務生

fúwùshēng.

valid *adj.* 有效的 yǒuxiào de (effective).

validity *n.* 有效性 yǒuxiàoxìng.

valley *n.* 谷 gǔ, 山谷 shāngǔ ⟨mountains⟩.

valor *n.* 英勇 yīngyǒng.

valuable *adj.* 有價值的 yǒu jiàzhí de, 貴重的 guìzhòng de. — *n.* 貴重物品 guìzhòng wùpǐn.

valuation *n.* 評價 píngjià, 估價 gūjià.

value *n.* 價值 jiàzhí ⟨worth⟩. — *v.* ①估價 gūjià ⟨estimate⟩. ②重視 zhòngshì ⟨care for⟩.

valve *n.* ①活門 huómén, 閥 fá (tap). ②瓣膜 bànmó / bànmò ⟨in the heart⟩.

vampire *n.* 吸血鬼 xīxuèguǐ / xīxiěguǐ.

van *n.* 有蓋貨車 yǒu gài huòchē.

vanilla *n.* 香草 xiāngcǎo.

vanish *v.* 消失 xiāoshī.

vanity *n.* 自負 zìfù, 虛榮心 xūróngxīn.

vanquish *v.* 征服 zhēngfú, 擊敗 jībài / jíbài.

vantage *n.* 優勢 yōushì (superiority). **~ point** ①有利位置 yǒulì wèizhì ⟨position⟩. ②觀點 guāndiǎn ⟨viewpoint⟩.

vapor *n.* 蒸氣 zhēngqì, 煙霧 yānwù.

vaporize *v.* 蒸發 zhēngfā.

variable *adj.* 易變的 yìbiàn de, 可變的 kěbiàn de. — *n.* ①因素 yīnsù (factor). ②變數 biànshù ⟨mathematics⟩.

variant *adj.* 不同的 bùtóng de, 差異的 chāyì de. — *n.* 變體 biàntǐ, 異體 yìtǐ.

variation *n.* 變化 biànhuà, 改變 gǎibiàn (the act of varying).

varied *adj.* ①各樣的 gèyàng de (diverse). ②富於變化的 fù yú biànhuà de (changing).

variety *n.* 變化 biànhuà (change), 多樣 duōyàng (diversity).

various *adj.* ①各樣的 gèyàng de (diverse), 不同的 bùtóng de (different).

vary *v.* 改變 gǎibiàn, 變化 biànhuà.

vase *n.* 花瓶 huāpíng.

Vaseline *n.* 凡士林 fánshìlín.

vassal *n.* 家臣 jiāchén.

vast *adj.* 巨大的 jùdà de, 廣大的 guǎngdà de.

vat *n.* 大桶 dàtǒng.

vault *n.* ①拱形圓屋頂 gǒngxíng yuánwūdǐng (arched roof). ②保險庫 bǎoxiǎnkù ⟨safekeeping⟩. ③地下靈室 dìxià língshì ⟨underground room⟩. ④跳過 tiàoguo ⟨jump⟩. — *v.* 跳過 tiàoguo ⟨jump⟩. *pole ~* 撐竿跳 chēnggāntiào.

vaunt *v.* 誇耀 kuāyào.

VCR 錄放影機 lùfàngyǐngjī (video cassette recorder).

veal *n.* 小牛肉 xiǎoniúròu.

vegetable *n.* 蔬菜 shūcài. — *adj.* 蔬菜的 shūcài de.

vegetarian *n.* 素食者 sùshízhě. — *adj.* 吃素的 chīsù de.

vegetation *n.* 植物 zhíwù.

vehement *adj.* 熱烈的 rèliè de, 激烈的 jīliè de.

vehicle *n.* 車輛 chēliàng (car), 交通工具 jiāotōng gōngjù (transportation).

V

veil n. 面紗 miànshā, 面罩 miànzhào. — v. 以面罩遮掩 yǐ miànzhào zhēyǎn.

vein n. 靜脈 jìngmài.

velocity n. 速度 sùdù.

velvet n. 天鵝絨 tiān'éróng 〈material〉. — adj. 天鵝絨般的 tiān'éróng bān de.

vend v. 兜售 dōushòu, 叫賣 jiàomài.

vendor n. 小販 xiǎofàn (peddler), 兜售者 dōushòuzhě (seller).

venerable adj. 可敬的 kějìng de.

venerate v. 尊敬 zūnjìng.

venereal adj. ①性交的 xìngjiāo de 〈sexual〉. ②性病的 xìngbìng de 〈disease〉.
~ disease 性病 xìngbìng.

vengeance n. 復仇 fùchóu, 報復 bàofù.

vengeful adj. 報復的 bàofù de.

venison n. 鹿肉 lùròu.

venom n. ①毒液 dúyè (poison). ②惡意 èyì (spite).

venomous adj. ①有毒的 yǒudú de (poisonous). ②惡毒的 èdú de (spiteful).

vent n. 出口 chūkǒu, 通氣孔 tōngqìkǒng (outlet). — v. 發洩 fāxiè (relieve).

ventilate v. 使通風 shǐ tōngfēng 〈air〉.

ventilation n. 通風 tōngfēng 〈air〉.

venture n. & v. 冒險 màoxiǎn.

venturesome adj. 冒險的 màoxiǎn de.

Venus n. 金星 Jīnxīng.

veranda n. 走廊 zǒuláng.

verb n. 動詞 dòngcí.

verbal adj. ①言辭的 yáncí de (lexical). ②口頭的 kǒutóu de

(oral).

verbose adj. 冗長的 rǒngcháng de (wordy).

verdict n. ①陪審員的裁決 péishěnyuán de cáijué 〈jury〉. ②判斷 pànduàn, 定論 dìnglùn (judgment).

verge n. 邊緣 biānyuán (edge).

verify v. ①證實 zhèngshí (confirm). ②鑑定 jiàndìng (ascertain).

verification n. 證實 zhèngshí.

veritable adj. 真正的 zhēnzhèng de, 確實的 quèshí de.

verity n. 真實性 zhēnshíxìng (truth).

vermilion adj. 朱紅的 zhūhóng de. — n. 朱紅色 zhūhóngsè.

vermin n. ①害蟲 hàichóng 〈insect〉. ②害獸 hàishòu 〈small animal〉.

versatile adj. ①多才多藝的 duō-cái-duō-yì de 〈skill〉. ②多用途的 duō yòngtú de 〈uses〉.

verse n. ①詩 shī, 韻文 yùnwén (poetry, poem). ②詩節 shíjié (stanza).

versed adj. 精通的 jīngtōng de.

version n. ①譯文 yìwén, 譯本 yìběn (translation). ②說法 shuōfa (description). ③版本 bǎnběn (form). ④形式 xíngshì (style).

versus prep. ……對…… ...duì....

vertebra n. 脊椎 jǐzhuī.

vertebrate n. 脊椎動物 jǐzhuī dòngwù.

vertical adj. 垂直的 chuízhí de. — n. 垂直線 chuízhíxiàn

⟨line⟩.

very *adv.* 很 hěn, 極 jí (extremely). — *adj.* 真正的 zhēnzhèng de (actual).

vessel *n.* ①容器 róngqì (container). ②船 chuán (ship).

vest *n.* 背心 bèixīn (waistcoat).

vestige *n.* 痕跡 hénjī.

veteran *n.* ①退伍軍人 tuìwǔ jūnrén, 老兵 lǎobīng (ex-serviceman). ②老手 lǎoshǒu (old hand).

veterinarian *n.* 獸醫 shòuyī.

veterinary *adj.* 獸醫的 shòuyī de.

veto *n.* ①否決權 fǒujuéquán (right). ②否決 fǒujué (refusal).

vex *v.* 使苦惱 shǐ kǔnǎo (trouble).

vexation *n.* 苦惱 kǔnǎo.

via *prep.* 經由 jīngyóu (through), 藉 jiè (by).

viaduct *n.* 陸橋 lùqiáo, 高架橋 gāojiàqiáo.

vial *n.* 小瓶子 xiǎopíngzi.

vibrate *v.* 震動 zhèndòng.

vibration *n.* 震動 zhèndòng.

vice *n.* ①惡行 èxíng (wickedness). ②缺點 quēdiǎn (fault). ③壞習慣 huài xíguàn (bad habit).

vice versa *adv.* 反之亦然 fǎn-zhī-yì-rán.

vicinity *n.* 附近 fùjìn, 接近 jiējìn.

vicious *adj.* ①惡意的 èyì de (spiteful). ②有惡習的 yǒu èxí de (having bad habits). ③邪惡的 xié'è de (evil). ~ *circle* 惡性循環 èxìng xúnhuán. ~ *game* 電動玩具遊戲 diàndòngwánjù yóuxì.

victim *n.* ①受害者 shòuhàizhě (one harmed). ②犧牲者 xīshēngzhě (casualty).

victor *n.* 勝利者 shènglìzhě.

victorious *adj.* 勝利的 shènglì de.

victory *n.* 勝利 shènglì.

video *n.* 電視 diànshì. — *adj.* 影像的 yǐngxiàng de.

videotape *n.* 錄像帶 lùxiàngdài / 錄影帶 lùyǐngdài. — *v.* 錄像 lùxiàng / 錄影 lùyǐng.

vie *v.* 競爭 jìngzhēng.

view *n.* ①景色 jǐngsè (scene). ②視野 shìyě, 眼界 yǎnjiè (range of sight). ③意見 yìjiàn (opinion). — *v.* ①觀看 guānkàn (behold). ②把……看成 bǎ... kànchéng (regard as).

viewpoint *n.* 觀點 guāndiǎn.

vigil *n.* 徹夜不眠 chèyè bù mián (sleeplessness).

vigilance *n.* 警戒 jǐngjiè.

vigor *n.* 活力 huólì, 精力 jīnglì (energy).

vigorous *adj.* 精力充沛的 jīnglì chōngpèi de (energetic).

vile *adj.* 惡劣的 èliè de (evil), 可恥的 kěchǐ de (shameful).

villa *n.* 別墅 biéshù.

village *n.* 村莊 cūnzhuāng.

villager *n.* 村民 cūnmín.

villain *n.* 惡徒 ètú (scoundrel).

vindicate *v.* 辯證 biànzhèng, 澄清 chéngqīng.

vindictive *adj.* 有復仇心的 yǒu fùchóuxīn de (vengeful).

vine *n.* 藤蔓植物 téngmàn zhíwù.

vinegar *n.* 醋 cù.

vineyard *n.* 葡萄園 pútaoyuán.

viola *n.* 中音提琴 zhōngyīntíqín.

violate v. ①違犯 wéifàn
(transgress). ②侵害 qīnhài
(injure). ③破壞 pòhuài
(destroy). ④強暴 qiángbào
(rape). ⑤褻瀆 xièdú (dis-
respect).

violation n. 違犯 wéifàn
(transgression).

violence n. ①猛烈 měngliè,
激烈 jīliè (vehemence). ②暴行
bàoxíng, 暴力 bàolì ⟨physical
harm⟩.

violent adj. ①猛烈的 měngliè
de, 劇烈的 jùliè de (vehement).
②暴力的 bàolì de (harmful).

violet n. 紫羅蘭 zǐluólán
⟨plant⟩.

violin n. 小提琴 xiǎotíqín.

viper n. 毒蛇 dúshé.

virgin n. 處女 chǔnǚ. — adj.
處女的 chǔnǚ de (vestal).

virginity n. 童貞 tóngzhēn
(chastity).

Virgo 處女座 Chǔnǚzuò.

virtual adj. 實際上的
shíjìshang de (actual).
~ reality 虛擬真實 xūnǐ
zhēnshí / 虛擬實境 xūnǐ
shíjìng.

virtue n. 德行 déxíng / déxìng,
美德 měidé (goodness).

virtuous adj. 美德的 měidé
de.

virulent adj. ①有毒的 yǒudú
de (poisonous). ②惡毒的 èdú
de (spiteful).

virus n. 濾過性病毒
lǜguòxìng bìngdú.

visa n. 簽證 qiānzhèng.

Visa Card 威士卡 Wēishìkǎ.

visage n. 面貌 miànmào.

vise n. 老虎鉗 lǎohǔqián.

visible adj. 可見的 kějiàn de
(can be seen).

vision n. ①視力 shìlì
(eyesight). ②遠見 yuǎnjiàn
(foresight). ③幻影 huànyǐng,
幻像 huànxiàng (illusion). ④想
像 xiǎngxiàng (imagination).

visionary adj. ①有遠見的
yǒu yuǎnjiàn de (foresighted).
②幻想的 huànxiǎng de
(illusory). — n. ①有遠見者
yǒu yuǎnjiàn zhě ⟨foresight⟩.
②空想者 kōngxiǎngzhě
⟨lack reality⟩.

visit n. & v. 拜訪 bàifǎng,
訪問 fǎngwèn (call on), 參觀
cānguān (tour).

visitor n. ①訪客 fǎngkè
(guest). ②觀光客
guānguāngkè (tourist).

visor n. 帽舌 màoshé ⟨hat⟩.

vista n. 遠景 yuǎnjǐng
(prospect).

visual adj. 視覺的 shìjué de
(ocular), 看得見的 kàndejiàn
de (visible).

vital adj. 生命的 shēngmìng
de, 維持生命必需的 wéichí
shēngmìng bìxū de ⟨necessary⟩.

vitality n. 生命力 shēngmìnglì,
活力 huólì (energy).

vitalize v. 賦以生命力
fù yǐ shēngmìnglì.

vitamin n. 維他命 wéitāmìng.

vivacious adj. 活潑愉快的
huópo yúkuài de.

vivid adj. ①鮮明的 xiānmíng
de (bright). ②生動的
shēngdòng de (lifelike).

vocabulary n. 詞彙 cíhuì
(lexicon).

vocal adj. 聲音的 shēngyīn de
(of the voice), 有聲音的 yǒu
shēngyīn de (voiced).

vocalist n. 聲樂家
shēngyuèjiā, 歌手 gēshǒu.

vocation n. 職業 zhíyè (occupation).

vocational adj. 職業的 zhíyè de. ~ **school** 技校 jìxiào / 職業學校 zhíyè xuéxiào.

vociferous adj. 吵鬧的 chǎonào de.

vogue n. 流行 liúxíng, 時尚 shíshàng (fashion).

voice n. 聲音 shēngyīn (sound). ~ **mail** 語音信箱 yǔyīn xìnxiāng.

void adj. ①無效的 wúxiào de (ineffectual). ②空的 kōng de, 空虛的 kōngxū de (empty).

volatile adj. ①揮發性的 huīfāxìng de (liquid). ②易變的 yìbiàn de (person).

volcano n. 火山 huǒshān.

volley n. 齊發 qífā, 連發 liánfā (missile).

volleyball n. 排球 páiqiú.

volt n. 伏特 fútè.

voltage n. 電壓 diànyā.

voltmeter n. 伏特計 fútèjì, 電壓表 diànyābiǎo.

volume n. ①卷 juàn, 冊 cè (book). ②體積 tǐjī (capacity). ③音量 yīnliàng (sound).

voluminous adj. ①龐大的 pángdà de (large). ②大部頭的 dàbùtóu de (book).

voluntary adj. 自願的 zìyuàn de.

volunteer n. 志願者 zhìyuànzhě, 義工 yìgōng. — v. 自願做 zìyuàn zuò.

voluptuous adj. ①耽迷肉慾的 dānmí ròuyù de (sexual pleasure). ②肉感的 ròugǎn de (sexually attractive).

vomit v. 嘔吐 ǒutù.

vote n. & v. 投票 tóupiào.

voter n. 投票者 tóupiàozhě.

vouch v. 擔保 dānbǎo (guarantee).

voucher n. 收據 shōujù, 憑單 píngdān (receipt).

vow n. 誓言 shìyán. — v. 發誓 fāshì.

vowel n. 母音 mǔyīn.

voyage n. 航海 hánghǎi, 航行 hángxíng.

vulgar adj. ①粗俗的 cūsú de (impolite). ②通俗的 tōngsú de (common).

vulnerable adj. 易受傷害的 yì shòu shānghài de (weak).

vulture n. 兀鷹 wùyīng (bird).

W

wad n. 一捲 yì juǎn (roll), 小塊 xiǎokuài (small piece).

wadding n. 填料 tiánliào, 填塞物 tiánsāiwù.

waddle n. & v. 蹣跚地走 pánshān de zǒu.

wade v. 跋涉 báshè, 步行渡過 bùxíng dùguo.

waffle n. 鬆餅 sōngbǐng.

waft v. 飄浮 piāofú.

wag v. 搖擺 yáobǎi, 擺動 bǎidòng.

wage n. 工資 gōngzī (pay).
— v. 從事 cóngshì (engage in),
進行 jìnxíng (conduct). ~ *war*
打仗 dǎzhàng.

wager n. & v. 打賭 dǎdǔ.

wagon n. ①馬車 mǎchē
(horse-drawn carriage). ②運貨
車 yùnhuòchē (delivery
vehicle).

wail n. & v. ①哭泣 kūqì (cry).
②悲嘆 bēitàn (moan).

waist n. 腰 yāo.

waistband n. 腰帶 yāodài.

wait v. ①等 děng, 等待 děngdài,
等候 děnghòu (halt). ②服侍
fúshì (serve). ~ *a minute* 等一
下 děng yíxià.

waiter n. 侍者 shìzhě, 服務生
fúwùshēng.

waiting room n. 候車室
hòuchēshì.

waitress n. 女侍 nǚshì, 女服
務生 nǚ fúwùshēng.

wake v. ①醒來 xǐnglái, 喚醒
huànxǐng.

wakeful adj. 醒著的 xǐngzhe
de.

waken v. 醒來 xǐnglái, 喚醒
huànxǐng.

walk v. ①行走 xíngzǒu (on
foot). ②散步 sànbù (take a
stroll). — n. 散步 sànbù.

wall n. 牆 qiáng, 壁 bì.

wallet n. 皮夾 píjiá, 錢包
qiánbāo.

wallow v. 打滾 dǎgǔn.

wallpaper n. 壁紙 bìzhǐ.

walnut n. ①胡桃 hútáo ⟨nut⟩.
②胡桃木 hútáomù ⟨wood⟩.

walrus n. 海象 hǎixiàng.

waltz n. 華爾茲舞 huá'ěrzīwǔ.

wand n. ①棒 bàng, 短杖
duǎnzhàng (stick). ②魔杖
mózhàng ⟨conjurer⟩.

wander v. ①漫遊 mànyóu
(roam freely). ②徘徊 páihuái
(roam aimlessly).

wane n. & v. ①虧 kuī, 缺 quē
⟨moon⟩. ②減弱 jiǎnruò
(decrease).

want v. ①想要 xiǎngyào
(desire). ②需要 xūyào (need).
— n. ①需要 xūyào (need). ②缺
乏 quēfá (lack).

war n. 戰爭 zhànzhēng.

ward n. ①病房 bìngfáng
⟨hospital⟩. ②監房 jiānfáng
⟨prison⟩. ③被監護者 bèi jiānhù
zhě (protected person).

warden n. 監護人 jiānhùrén,
管理人 guǎnlǐrén.

wardrobe n. ①衣櫃 yīguì
(closet). ②衣服 yīfu (clothing).

warehouse n. 倉庫 cāngkù.

wares n. 商品 shāngpǐn.

warfare n. 戰爭 zhànzhēng.

warlike adj. 好戰的 hàozhàn
de (fond of war).

warm adj. 溫暖的 wēnnuǎn
de. — v. 使溫暖 shǐ wēnnuǎn.

warmth n. 溫暖 wēnnuǎn
⟨temperature⟩, 熱情 rèqíng
⟨emotion⟩.

warn v. 警告 jǐnggào (caution).

warning n. 警告 jǐnggào.

warp v. ①彎翹 wānqiào, 歪曲
wāiqū (twist).

warrant n. ①令狀 lìngzhuàng
⟨document⟩. ②正當理由
zhèngdàng lǐyóu (justification).
— v. ①保證 bǎozhèng (guar-
antee). ②使有正當性 shǐ yǒu
zhèngdàngxìng (appear right).
③認為 rènwéi (think that).

warranted adj. 有道理的
yǒu dàolǐ de (sensible), 有正
當理由的 yǒu zhèngdàng
lǐyóu de (justified).

warrior n. 戰士 zhànshì.

wart n. 疣 yóu.

wash n. & v. 洗 xǐ, 洗滌 xǐdí.

washer n. 洗衣機 xǐyījī.

washing n. 洗滌 xǐdí.
~ *machine* 洗衣機 xǐyījī.

washroom n. 廁所 cèsuǒ, 洗手間 xǐshǒujiān.

wasp n. 黃蜂 huángfēng.

wastage n. ①消耗 xiāohào (loss). ②消耗量 xiāohàoliàng (amount).

waste v. 浪費 làngfèi. — n. ①浪費 làngfèi (wasting). ②廢物 fèiwù (trash). — adj. ①廢棄的 fèiqì de (unwanted). ②荒蕪的 huāngwú de (barren).

wastebasket n. 廢紙簍 fèizhǐlǒu.

wasteful adj. 浪費的 làngfèi de.

watch v. ①看 kàn, 觀看 guānkàn (look at). ②看守 kānshǒu (guard). ~ *after* 照顧 zhàogu (care for). ~ *out* 小心 xiǎoxīn. — n. ①錶 biǎo (timer). ②看守 kānshǒu (act of watching).

watchful adj. 注意的 zhùyì de, 警戒的 jǐngjiè de.

watchmaker n. 錶匠 biǎojiàng.

watchman n. 看守者 kānshǒuzhě.

watchword n. 口令 kǒulìng (password).

water n. 水 shuǐ. — v. 灑水 sǎshuǐ, 澆水 jiāoshuǐ (pour water on).

waterfall n. 瀑布 pùbù.

watermelon n. 西瓜 xīguā.

waterproof adj. 防水的 fángshuǐ de, 不透水的 bú tòushuǐ de.

watery adj. ①含水的 hánshuǐ de (containing water). ②淡的 dàn de (diluted-tasting). ③水汪汪的 shuǐwāngwāng de (tearful).

watt n. 瓦特 wǎtè.

wave n. ①波 bō, 波浪 bōlàng 〈water〉. ②波動 bōdòng (wave-like movement). ③波紋 bōwén, 波浪形 bōlàngxíng (curve). — v. ①波動 bōdòng (move). ②彎曲 quánqū (curve). ③揮手 huīshǒu 〈hand〉.

waver v. ①搖曳 yáoyè / yáoyì (move unsteadily). ②猶豫 yóuyù (hesitate).

wax n. 蠟 là. — v. ①增大 zēngdà (increase). ②漸滿 jiànmǎn 〈moon〉.

way n. ①路 lù (route). ②方向 fāngxiàng (direction). ③方法 fāngfǎ (method). ④風氣 fēngqì (custom). *on the* ~ 在路上 zài lù shàng.

waylay v. 攔截 lánjié (intercept).

wayside n. & adj. 路邊 lùbiān.

wayward adj. ①任性的 rènxìng de, 不負責任的 bú fù zérèn de (irresponsible). ②捉摸不定的 zuōmō-bú-dìng de (unpredictable).

we pron. 我們 wǒmen.

weak adj. ①虛弱的 xūruò de 〈physical trait〉. ②懦弱的 nuòruò de 〈personality trait〉. ③弱的 ruò de, 無力的 wúlì de (powerless). ④淡的 dàn de (watery).

weaken v. 使虛弱 shǐ xūruò, 變弱 biànruò.

weakness n. ①弱點 ruòdiǎn (defect). ②虛弱 xūruò (being weak). ③偏好 piānhào (fondness for).

wealth n. 財富 cáifù.

wealthy adj. 有錢的 yǒu qián de, 富裕的 fùyù de.

wean v. 使斷乳 shǐ duànrǔ 〈baby〉.

weapon n. 武器 wǔqì.

wear v. ①穿 chuān 〈clothing〉, 佩戴 pèidài 〈jewelry, hat, etc〉. ②磨損 mósǔn (damage). — n. ①穿著 chuānzhuó, 佩戴 pèidài 〈clothing〉. ②磨損 mósǔn (damage).

weary adj. ①疲倦的 píjuàn de (tired). ②令人厭煩的 lìng rén yànfán de (tiresome). — v. ①使疲倦 shǐ píjuàn (tire out). ②使厭煩 shǐ yànfán (annoy).

weasel n. 鼬 yòu.

weather n. 天氣 tiānqì.

weather-beaten adj. 風吹雨打的 fēng-chuī-yǔ-dǎ de.

weathercock n. 風標 fēngbiāo, 風信雞 fēngxìnjī.

weave v. 編織 biānzhī.

weaver n. 織者 zhīzhě.

web n. 網 wǎng, 網狀物 wǎngzhuàngwù (net).
~ *browser* 全球信息網絡瀏覽器 quánqiú xìnxī wǎngluò liúlǎnqì / 全球資訊網路瀏覽器 quánqiú zīxùn wǎnglù liúlǎnqì. ~ *page* 網頁 wǎngyè.

website n. 網站 wǎngzhàn.

wed v. 跟……結婚 gēn... jiéhūn (get married to), 嫁給 jiàgěi 〈said of a woman〉, 娶 qǔ 〈said of a man〉.

wedding n. 婚禮 hūnlǐ.

wedge n. 楔 xiē (V-shaped piece of wood). — v. 以楔固定 yǐ xiē gùdìng.

wedlock n. 婚姻生活 hūnyīn shēnghuó (married life).

Wednesday n. 星期三 Xīngqīsān / Xīngqísān.

weed n. 雜草 zácǎo (unwanted wild plant). — v. 除雜草 chú zácǎo.

week n. 星期 xīngqī / xīngqí, 週 zhōu.

weekday n. 平日 píngrì, 工作日 gōngzuòrì.

weekend n. 週末 zhōumò.

weekly adj. & adv. 每週的 měi zhōu de. — n. 週刊 zhōukān.

weep v. 哭泣 kūqì, 流淚 liúlèi.

weigh v. ①稱重 chēngzhòng 〈measure〉. ②考慮 kǎolǜ, 斟酌 zhēnzhuó (consider). ③具有重要性 jùyǒu zhòngyàoxìng, 有份量 yǒu fènliang (be important).

weight n. ①重 zhòng, 重量 zhòngliàng (heaviness). ②重要性 zhòngyàoxìng (importance). — v. 加重 jiāzhòng.

weighty adj. 重要的 zhòngyào de.

weird adj. 怪異的 guàiyì de.

welcome n. & interj. 歡迎 huānyíng. — adj. 受歡迎的 shòu huānyíng de.

weld v. 焊接 hànjiē (solder).

welfare n. 幸福 xìngfú (well-being), 福利 fúlì (benefits).
social ~ 社會福利 shèhuì fúlì.

well adv. 很好 hěn hǎo (in a good way). — adj. 健康的 jiànkāng de (healthy). — n. ①井 jǐng 〈water〉. ②油井 yóujǐng 〈oil〉.

well-being n. 幸福 xìngfú.

well-bred adj. 有教養的 yǒu jiàoyǎng de (of good upbringing), 客氣的 kèqì de (polite).

well-done adj. 完全煮熟的

W

wánquán zhǔshú de / wánquán zhǔshóu de 〈cook〉.

well-known adj. 著名的 zhùmíng de.

were v. 是 shì.

west n. ①西 xī 〈direction〉. ②西方 xīfāng (western region). ③西邊 xībiān, 西部 xībù (western part). — adv. 西 xī, 向西 xiàng xī, 往西 wǎng xī. — adj. ①西 xī (of the west). ②西方的 xīfāng de (of the western region). ③西部的 xībù de (of the western part).

western adj. 西方的 xīfāng de.

westward adj. 西方的 xīfāng de. — adv. 向西方 xiàng xīfāng.

wet adj. 濕的 shī de (not dry). — n. 濕氣 shīqì (humid weather), 雨天 yǔtiān (rainy day).

whale n. 鯨 jīng.

whaling n. 捕鯨 bǔ jīng.

wharf n. 碼頭 mǎtou.

what adj. & pron. 甚麼 shénme.

whatever adj. & pron. 不論甚麼 búlùn shénme (no matter what).

wheat n. 小麥 xiǎomài.

wheel n. 輪 lún, 車輪 chēlún.

wheelchair n. 輪椅 lúnyǐ.

wheeze v. 喘息 chuǎnxī / chuǎnxí.

when adv. 何時 héshí, 甚麼時候 shénme shíhou. — conj. 當……時 dāng...shí (at some time).

whenever conj. 無論何時 wúlùn héshí (at whatever time). — adv. 隨時都可以 suíshí dōu kěyǐ (anytime is good).

where adv. 哪裡 nǎli, 何處

héchù (at what place).

whereabouts adv. 靠近何處 kàojìn héchù, 在哪裡附近 zài nǎli fùjìn (near what place). — n. 所在 suǒzài, 下落 xiàluò.

whereas conj. ①然而 rán'ér (although). ②鑑於 jiànyú, 茲因 zīyīn (because of the fact that).

wherever adv. 無論何處 wúlùn héchù.

whether conj. 是否 shìfǒu, 抑或 yìhuò (if).

which adj. & pron. 哪一個 nǎ yí ge.

whichever adj. & pron. 任何一個 rènhé yí ge.

whiff n. 一陣 yí zhèn.

while n. 短暫時間 duǎnzhàn shíjiān, 一會兒 yìhuǐr (short time). — conj. 當……的時候 dāng...de shíhou (during the time that).

whim n. 突然的念頭 tūrán de niàntou / túrán de niàntóu.

whimper v. 啜泣 chuòqì, 嗚咽 wūyè.

whimsical adj. 異想天開的 yì-xiǎng-tiān-kāi de.

whine v. 哀泣 āiqì. — n. 哀泣聲 āiqìshēng.

whinny n. 馬嘶聲 mǎsīshēng. — v. 發出馬嘶聲 fāchū mǎsīshēng.

whip n. 鞭 biān. — v. 鞭打 biāndǎ.

whirl n. & v. 旋轉 xuánzhuǎn.

whirlpool n. 漩渦 xuánwō.

whirlwind n. 旋風 xuànfēng.

whisker n. 頰鬚 jiáxū, 鬚 xū.

whisky n. 威士忌酒 wēishìjìjiǔ.

whisper n. & v. 低語 dīyǔ, 耳語 ěryǔ.

W

whistle v. ①吹口哨 chuī kǒushào ⟨mouth⟩. ②鳴笛 míng dí ⟨blow⟩. ③吹笛子 chuī dízi ⟨flute⟩. — n. ①口哨聲 kǒushàoshēng ⟨sound of whistling⟩. ②哨子 shàozi, 笛 dí ⟨instrument⟩. ③鳴笛聲 míngdíshēng ⟨sound of whistle blowing⟩.

white n. & adj. 白色 báisè.

whitewash v. ①粉刷 fěnshuā ⟨paint⟩. ②粉飾 fěnshì ⟨cover up⟩. — n. 石灰水 shíhuīshuǐ ⟨liquid⟩.

who pron. 誰 shuí / shéi.

whoever pron. 不論誰 búlùn shuí / búlùn shéi (no matter who).

whole adj. ①全部的 quánbù de, 整個的 zhěnggè de. — n. 全體 quántǐ.

wholesale n. 批銷 pīxiāo, 批發 pīfā. — adj. 批銷的 pīxiāo de, 批發的 pīfā de.

wholesome adj. ①衛生的 wèishēng de (sanitary). ②有益健康的 yǒuyì jiànkāng de (healthy).

whom pron. 誰 shuí / shéi.

whoop n. 呼喊聲 hūhǎnshēng. — v. 呼喊 hūhǎn.

whore n. ①娼妓 chāngjì, 妓女 jìnǚ ⟨female⟩. ②男妓 nánjì ⟨male⟩.

whose pron. 誰的 shuí de / shéi de.

why adv. 為甚麼 wèishénme.

wick n. 芯 xīn.

wicked adj. 邪惡的 xié'è de, 壞心腸的 huàixīnyān de.

wicker n. 柳條 liǔtiáo.

wide adj. 寬的 kuān de, 廣闊的 guǎngkuò de.

widely adv. ①廣大地 guǎngdà de, 廣泛地 guǎngfàn de (generally). ②相當地 xiāngdāng de (to a great extent).

widen v. 使……變寬 shǐ... biànkuān.

widespread adj. 流傳廣的 liúchuán guǎng de.

widow n. 寡婦 guǎfù.

widower n. 鰥夫 guānfū.

width n. 寬度 kuāndù.

wife n. 妻子 qīzi, 太太 tàitai.

wig n. 假髮 jiǎfà / jiǎfǎ.

wiggle v. 扭動 niǔdòng, 擺動 bǎidòng.

wild adj. ①野生的 yěshēng de (undomesticated). ②野蠻的 yěmán de (barbaric). ③未開化的 wèi kāihuà de (uncivilized). ④粗暴的 cūbào de (riotous). ⑤無人煙的 wú rényān de (uninhabited). ⑥狂暴的 kuángbào de (turbulent). ⑦瘋狂的 fēngkuáng de (crazy). — adv. 粗暴地 cūbào de. — n. 荒野 huāngyě.

wilderness n. 荒野 huāngyě.

wiles n. (pl.) 詭計 guǐjì.

will aux. v. ①將 jiāng (be going to). ②想要 xiǎngyào (wish). — n. ①意志 yìzhì (determination). ②遺囑 yízhǔ (testament).

willful adj. ①任性的 rènxìng de, 剛愎的 gāngbì de (strong-willed). ②故意的 gùyì de (done on purpose).

willing adj. 願意的 yuànyì de, 情願的 qíngyuàn de (of one's own accord), 樂意的 lèyì de ⟨happily⟩.

willingly adv. 願意地 yuànyì de.

willow n. 柳樹 liǔshù.

wilt v. 枯萎 kūwěi / kūwēi,

凋謝 diāoxiè.

wily *adj.* 狡猾的 jiǎohuá de.

win *v.* 贏 yíng, 獲勝 huòshèng. — *n.* 勝利 shènglì.

wince *v.* 畏縮 wèisuō.

winch *n.* 絞盤 jiǎopán, 絞車 jiǎochē.

wind *n.* ①風 fēng (air-current). ②氣味 qìwèi (scent). ③脹氣 zhàngqì (flatulence). — *v.* ①蜿蜒 wānyán ⟨road⟩. ②纏繞 chánrào ⟨thread⟩.

windmill *n.* 風車 fēngchē.

window *n.* 窗 chuāng, 窗戶 chuānghù.

windshield *n.* 擋風玻璃 dǎngfēng bōli.

windy *adj.* ①多風的 duōfēng de (breezy). ②迎風的 yíngfēng de (wind-swept).

wine *n.* ①酒 jiǔ (alcoholic drink). ②葡萄酒 pútaojiǔ (grape wine).

wing *n.* ①翼 yì, 翅 chì, 翅膀 chìbǎng.

wink *v.* ①眨眼 zhǎyǎn ⟨eye⟩. ②閃爍 shǎnshuò (flash).

winner *n.* 勝利者 shènglìzhě.

winning *adj.* ①勝利的 shènglì de (triumphant). ②迷人的 mírén de (charming).

winnings *n.* 贏得的獎金 yíngdé de jiǎngjīn.

winter *n.* 冬季 dōngjì, 冬天 dōngtiān.

wintry *adj.* 冬的 dōng de.

wipe *n. & v.* 擦 cā, 拭 shì.

wire *n.* ①金屬線 jīnshǔxiàn, 鐵絲 tiěsī ⟨metal⟩. ②電纜 diànlǎn (cable). ③電報 diànbào (telegram). — *v.* ①用鐵絲固定 yòng tiěsī gùdìng (fasten). ②裝電線 zhuāng diànxiàn ⟨install⟩. ③拍電報 pāi diànbào (telegram).

wireless *adj.* 無線的 wúxiàn de. — *n.* 無線電 wúxiàndiàn.

wiring *n.* 架線 jiàxiàn, 配線 pèixiàn.

wisdom *n.* 智慧 zhìhuì (understanding), 知識 zhīshi (knowledge).

wise *adj.* 有智慧的 yǒu zhìhuì de, 明智的 míngzhì de.

wish *v.* 意欲 yìyù (want), 希望 xīwàng (hope). — *n.* 願望 yuànwàng.

wisp *n.* 小束 xiǎoshù ⟨hair, hay, etc.⟩.

wistful *adj.* ①企盼的 qǐpàn de / qìpàn de ⟨wish⟩. ②傷感的 shānggǎn de ⟨sad⟩.

wit *n.* ①機智 jīzhì, 智力 zhìlì (understanding). ②幽默感 yōumògǎn (sense of humor).

witch *n.* 女巫 nǚwū, 巫婆 wūpó.

witchcraft *n.* 巫術 wūshù.

with *prep.* ①跟 gēn, 與 yǔ (accompanied by). ②具有 jùyǒu (having). ③用 yòng (by means of).

withdraw *v.* ①撤回 chèhuí (take back). ②撤退 chètuì (retreat). ③退出 tuìchū (leave). ④提取 tíqǔ (take out).

withdrawn *adj.* 孤獨的 gūdú de (solitary).

wither *v.* 凋謝 diāoxiè, 枯萎 kūwěi / kūwēi.

withhold *v.* ①制止 zhìzhǐ (prevent). ②扣留 kòuliú (hold).

within *prep.* 在……之內 zài...zhīnèi. — *adv.* 在內部 zài nèibù.

without *prep.* 沒有 méiyǒu, 無 wú (lacking). — *adv.* 在外部 zài wàibù.

withstand v. ①抵抗 dǐkàng, 反抗 fǎnkàng (resist). ②耐 nài, 禁得起 jīndeqǐ〈weather〉.

witness n. ①目擊者 mùjízhě / mùjízhě, 證人 zhèngrén〈person〉. ②證據 zhèngjù (evidence). — v. ①目擊 mùjí / mùjí, 目睹 mùdǔ.

witticism n. 詼諧語 huīxiéyǔ, 雋語 juànyǔ.

witty adj. 幽默的 yōumò de, 詼諧的 huīxié de.

wizard n. 男巫 nánwū.

woe n. 悲哀 bēi'āi, 悲痛 bēitòng.

wolf n. 狼 láng.

woman n. 女性 nǚxìng, 女人 nǚrén, 婦女 fùnǚ.

womb n. 子宮 zǐgōng.

wonder n. ①驚奇 jīngqí (amazement). ②奇觀 qíguān (spectacle), 奇蹟 qíjī (marvel). — v. ①想知道 xiǎng zhīdao (would like to know). ②感到好奇 gǎndào hàoqí (feel curious).

wonderful adj. 極好的 jí hǎo de (excellent).

wonderland n. 奇境 qíjìng, 仙境 xiānjìng.

wondrous adj. 令人驚奇的 lìng rén jīngqí de.

woo v. 求愛 qiú'ài (court).

wood n. ①木材 mùcái (timber). ②樹林 shùlín (forest).

woodcut n. 木刻 mùkè.

woodcutter n. 樵夫 qiáofū.

wooden adj. ①木製的 mùzhì de (made of wood). ②不自然的 bú zìrán de, 死板的 sǐbǎn de (stilted).

woodland n. 森林地區 sēnlín dìqū.

woodpecker n. 啄木鳥 zhuómùniǎo.

wool n. 羊毛 yángmáo.

woolen adj. 羊毛製的 yángmáo zhì de.

woolly adj. ①羊毛的 yángmáo de (of wool), 羊毛似的 yángmáo sì de (like wool). ②毛茸茸的 máorōngrōng de / máoróngróng de (fuzzy). ③不清楚的 bù qīngchu de (unclear).

word n. ①字 zì, 詞 cí (term). ②話 huà, 言辭 yáncí (utterance). ③消息 xiāoxi (news). ④諾言 nuòyán (promise), 保證 bǎozhèng (guarantee). ⑤命令 mìnglìng (command).

work n. ①工作 gōngzuò〈job〉. ②職業 zhíyè (profession). ③作品 zuòpǐn (artistic product). — v. ①工作 gōngzuò, 做事 zuòshì〈labor〉. ②運轉 yùnzhuǎn (function). ③有效 yǒuxiào (be effective), 有用 yǒuyòng (be useful).

worker n. 工作者 gōngzuòzhě, 工人 gōngrén.

working n. 作用 zuòyòng (function). ~ girl 娼妓 chāngjì (prostitute). ②職業婦女 zhíyè fùnǚ (woman who works). ~ mother 在職媽媽 zàizhí māma.

workman n. 勞工 láogōng.

workmanship n. 手藝 shǒuyì, 技藝 jìyì.

workshop n. ①工廠 gōngchǎng (factory). ②研討會 yántǎohuì, 工作坊 gōngzuòfāng〈seminar〉.

world n. ①世界 shìjiè (universe). ②界 jiè (group).

worldly adj. ①世俗的 shìsú de (temporal). ②物質的 wùzhì

de / wùzhì de (material).

world-wide *adj*. 全世界的
quánshìjiè de.

worm *n*. 蟲 chóng, 蠕蟲
rúchóng. — *v*. 蠕行 rúxíng.

worn *adj*. 磨破的 mópò de
〈damaged〉.

worn-out *adj*. ①磨破的 mópò
de (damaged). ②精疲力盡的
jīng-pí-lì-jìn de (exhausted).

worried *adj*. 擔心的 dānxīn
de.

worry *v*. ①困擾 kùnrǎo (cause
anxiety). ②擔心 dānxīn (feel
anxious). — *n*. 問題 wèntí
(problem), 煩惱的事 fánnǎo
de shì (annoyance).

worse *adj. & adv*. 更壞的
gèng huài de.

worsen *v*. 惡化 èhuà (become
worse), 變壞 biànhuài (become
bad).

worship *n*. ①崇拜 chóngbài,
尊敬 zūnjìng (reverence). ②禮
拜 lǐbài 〈ceremony〉. — *v*. 崇拜
chóngbài.

worst *adj. & adv*. 最壞的 zuì
huài de.

worth *prep*. ①值得 zhíde
(deserving of). ②值 zhí (of the
value of). — *n*. 價值 jiàzhí.

worthless *adj*. 無價值的 wú
jiàzhí de.

worthwhile *adj*. 值得的
zhíde de.

worthy *adj*. ①值得的 zhíde
de (worthwhile). ②可敬的
kějìng de (respectable).

wound *n*. 傷口 shāngkǒu, 創
傷 chuāngshāng. — *v*. 傷害
shānghài.

wrangle *n. & v*. 爭吵
zhēngchǎo, 口角 kǒujiǎo.

wrap *v*. 包 bāo, 裹 guǒ. — *n*. 披

肩 pījiān.

wrath *n*. 憤怒 fènnù.

wreath *n*. 花圈 huāquān, 花
冠 huāguān.

wreck *n*. ①毀壞 huǐhuài (ruin).
②船難 chuánnàn (shipwreck).

wrench *n*. ①猛扭 měngniǔ,
扭轉 niǔzhuǎn (twist). ②扳手
bānshou 〈tool〉. — *v*. 扭 niǔ, 擰
níng (twist).

wrestle *n. & v*. 摔角 shuāijiǎo.

wrestling *n*. 摔角 shuāijiǎo.

wretch *n*. ①可憐的人 kělián
de rén, 苦命人 kǔmìngrén
(pitiable person). ②惡劣的人
èliè de rén, 壞小子 huài
xiǎozi (vile person).

wretched *adj*. ①可憐的
kělián de, 悲慘的 bēicǎn de
(pitiable). ②惡劣的 èliè de
(vile).

wriggle *v*. 蠕動 rúdòng.

wring *v*. ①絞 jiǎo, 擰 níng
(squeeze). ②緊握 jǐnwò (grip).

wrinkle *n*. 皺紋 zhòuwén
(furrow). — *v*. 使起皺紋 shǐ qǐ
zhòuwén.

wrist *n*. 腕 wàn.

writ *n*. 令狀 lìngzhuàng 〈law〉.

write *v*. 書寫 shūxiě, 寫字
xiězì.

writer *n*. 作者 zuòzhě, 作家
zuòjiā.

writhe *v*. 扭動 niǔdòng.

writing *n*. ①書寫 shūxiě
(activity of writing). ②筆跡 bǐjī
(handwriting). ③寫作 xiězuò
(composition).

written *adj*. 書寫的 shūxiě
de.

wrong *adj*. ①錯誤的 cuòwù
de, 不正確的 bú zhèngquè
de, 不對的 bú duì de
(incorrect). ②不正當的 bú

zhèngdàng de (improper).
wrongdoing *n.* 犯罪 fànzuì,
罪行 zuìxíng.
WTO 世界貿易組織 Shìjiè
Màoyì Zǔzhī (World Trade

Organization).
WWW 萬維網 wànwéiwǎng,
環球網 huánqiúwǎng /
全球資訊網 quánqiú
zīxùnwǎng (World Wide Web).

X

Xmas *n.* 聖誕節 Shèngdànjié.
X-rated *adj.* X 級的 X jí de,
色情的 sèqíng de (obscene).

X ray *n.* X 光線 X guāngxiàn.
xylophone *n.* 木琴 mùqín.

Y

yacht *n.* 遊艇 yóutǐng, 快艇
kuàitǐng.
yak *n.* 犛牛 máoniú.
yam *n.* 甘薯 gānshǔ.
Yangtze River 長江
Chángjiāng.
yap *v.* 犬吠 quǎnfèi (bark).
yard *n.* ①庭院 tíngyuàn
(garden). ②碼 mǎ ⟨measure-
ment⟩.
yarn *n.* 紗 shā, 線 xiàn
(thread).
yawn *v.* 打呵欠 dǎ hēqiàn.
— *n.* 呵欠 hēqiàn.
yeah *adv.* 是 shì.
year *n.* ①年 nián ⟨time⟩. ②歲
suì ⟨age⟩.
yearly *adj.* 每年一次的 měi
nián yí cì de. — *adv.* 一年一度
yì nián yí dù, 每年 měi nián.

yearn *v.* 渴望 kěwàng, 嚮往
xiàngwǎng (long).
yeast *n.* 酵母 jiàomǔ / xiàomǔ.
yell *v.* 嘶喊 sīhǎn, 大聲叫
dàshēngjiào.
yellow *n.* 黃色 huángsè.
— *adj.* 黃色的 huángsè de.
Yellow River 黃河
Huánghé.
yes *adv.* 是 shì, 對 duì.
yesterday *n. & adv.* 昨天
zuótiān.
yet *adv.* 還 hái, 尚 shàng, 迄今
qìjīn (still). — *conj.* 然而
rán'ér, 但是 dànshì.
yew *n.* 紫杉 zǐshān.
yield *v.* ①出產 chūchǎn, 生產
shēngchǎn (produce). ②屈服
qūfú, 投降 tóuxiáng
(surrender to). — *n.* ①生產

shēngchǎn. 生產量 shēngchǎnliàng (product). ②收益 shōuyì (profit).

yoga *n.* 瑜伽 yújiā.

yogurt *n.* 酸牛奶 suānniúnǎi / 優酪乳 yōulùorǔ (curds).

yoke *n.* ①軛 è (harness). ②束縛 shùfù / shùfù (burden). — *v.* 駕以軛 jià yǐ è (harness).

yolk *n.* 蛋黃 dànhuáng.

yonder *adv.* 在那邊 zài nàbiān.

you *pron.* ①你 nǐ (singular, familiar). 您 nín (singular, respectful). ②你們 nǐmen (plural, familiar). 您們 nínmen (plural, respectful).

young *adj.* 年輕的 niánqīng de (youthful).

youngster *n.* 兒童 értóng (child). 少年 shàonián (youth).

your *pron.* ①你的 nǐ de (singular, familiar). 您的 nín de (singular, respectful). ②你們的 nǐmen de (plural, familiar). 您們的 nínmen de (plural, respectful).

yours *pron.* ①你的 nǐ de (singular, familiar). 您的 nín de (singular, respectful). ②你們的 nǐmen de (plural, familiar). 您們的 nínmen de (plural, respectful).

yourself *pron.* ①你自己 nǐ zìjǐ (singular, familiar). 您自己 nín zìjǐ (singular, respectful). ②你們自己 nǐmen zìjǐ (plural, familiar). 您們自己 nínmen zìjǐ (plural, respectful).

youth *n.* ①年輕 niánqīng, 青春 qīngchūn (being young). ②青春時期 qīngchūn shíqí / qīngchūn shíqí (adolescence).

youthful *adj.* 年輕的 niánqīng de, 青春的 qīngchūn de.

yo-yo *n.* 溜溜球 liūliūqiú (toy).

yummy *adj.* 好吃的 hǎochī de (delicious).

yuppie *n.* 雅皮士 yǎpíshì / 雅痞 yǎpǐ.

Z

zany *n.* ①丑角 chǒujué (clown). ②笨蛋 bèndàn (fool).

zapper *n.* ①遙控器 yáokòngqì (remote control). ②電蚊拍 diànwénpāi (insects).

zeal *n.* 熱心 rèxīn, 熱誠 rèchéng.

zealous *adj.* 熱心的 rèxīn de, 熱誠的 rèchéng de.

zebra *n.* 斑馬 bānmǎ.

zenith *n.* ①天頂 tiāndǐng (highest point). ②頂點 dǐngdiǎn (top).

zero *n.* 零 líng.

zest *n.* ①強烈的興趣 qiánglièdexìngqù (enthusiasm). ②風味 fēngwèi, 滋味 zīwèi (flavor). ③趣味 qùwèi (enjoyment).

zigzag *v.* 作鋸齒形 zuò jùchǐxíng. — *n.* 鋸齒形

jùchǐxíng.

zinc *n.* 鋅 xīn.

zip *n.* 颼颼聲 sōusōushēng
⟨sound⟩. *~ up* 拉上 lāshang.

zipper *n.* 拉鍊 lāliàn.

zone *n.* 地帶 dìdài, 地區 dìqū.

zoo *n.* 動物園 dòngwùyuán.

zoology *n.* 動物學
dòngwùxué.

zoom *v.* ①放大 fàngdà (zoom
in). ②縮小 suōxiǎo (zoom out).
③陡升 dǒushēng (go upward).
~ lens 變焦鏡頭 biànjiāo
jìngtóu.

Z

Appendices

附　　錄

fùlù

Appendix I 附錄一
Chinese Festivals
中國節日
Zhōngguó jiérì

Chinese New Year	春節	Chūnjié
Double Ninth Festival	重陽節	Chóngyángjié
Dragon Boat Festival	端午節	Duānwǔjié
Ghost Festival	中元節	Zhōngyuánjié
Lantern Festival	元宵節	Yuánxiāojié
Mid-Autumn Festival (Moon Festival)	中秋節	Zhōngqiūjié
New Year's Eve	除夕	Chúxī / Chúxì
Tomb Sweeping Day	清明節	Qīngmíngjié

Afghanistan	阿富汗 Āfùhàn
Africa	非洲 Fēizhōu
Albania	阿爾巴尼亞 Ā'ěrbāníyà / Ā'ěrbāníyǎ
Algeria	阿爾及利亞 Ā'ěrjílìyà / Ā'ěrjílìyǎ
America	美洲 Měizhōu
Amsterdam	阿姆斯特丹 Āmǔsītèdān
Angola	安哥拉 Āngēlā
Antarctic	南極洲 Nánjízhōu
Argentina	阿根廷 Āgēntíng
Armenia	亞美尼亞 Yàměiníyà / Yǎměiníyǎ
Asia	亞洲 Yàzhōu / Yǎzhōu
Athens	雅典 Yǎdiǎn
Auckland	奧克蘭 Àokèlán
Australia	澳大利亞 Àodàlìyà / Àodàlìyǎ, 澳洲 Àozhōu
Austria	奧地利 Àodìlì
Azerbaijan	亞塞拜然 Yàsàibàirán / Yǎsàibàirán
Baghdad	巴格達 Bāgédá
Bahamas	巴哈馬 Bāhāmǎ
Bahrain	巴林 Bālín
Bangkok	曼谷 Màngǔ
Bangladesh	孟加拉國 Mèngjiālāguó / 孟加拉 Mèngjiālā
Barcelona	巴塞羅那 Bāsàiluónà / 巴塞隆納 Bāsàilóngnà
Beijing	北京 Běijīng
Beirut	貝魯特 Bèilǔtè
Belarus	白俄羅斯 Bái'éluósī / Bái'èluósī
Belgium	比利時 Bǐlìshí
Belize	伯利茲 Bólìzī / 貝里斯 Bèilǐsī
Berlin	柏林 Bólín

Bermuda	百慕大 Bǎimùdà / 百慕達 Bǎimùdá
Berne	伯爾尼 Bó'ěrní / 伯恩 Bó'ēn
Bhutan	不丹 Bùdān
Bolivia	玻利維亞 Bōlìwéiyà / 玻利維亞 Bōlìwéiyǎ
Bonn	波恩 Bō'ēn / 波昂 Bō'áng
Bosnia	波士尼亞 Bōshìníyà / 波士尼亞 Bōshìníyǎ
Brazil	巴西 Bāxī
Britain	英國 Yīngguó
Brunei	文萊 Wénlái / 汶萊 Wènlái
Budapest	布達佩斯 Bùdápèisī
Buenos Aires	布宜諾斯艾利斯 Bùyínuòsī'àilìsī
Bulgaria	保加利亞 Bǎojiālìyà / 保加利亞 Bǎojiālìyǎ
Burundi	布隆迪 Bùlóngdí / 蒲隆地 Púlóngdì
Cairo	開羅 Kāiluó
Cambodia	柬埔寨 Jiǎnpǔzhài
Cameroon	喀麥隆 Kèmàilóng
Canada	加拿大 Jiānádà
Central African Republic	中非共和國 Zhōngfēi Gònghéguó
Chad	乍得 Zhàdé / 查德 Chádé
Chicago	芝加哥 Zhījiāgē
Chile	智利 Zhìlì
China	中國 Zhōngguó
Colombia	哥倫比亞 Gēlúnbǐyà / 哥倫比亞 Gēlúnbǐyǎ
Congo	剛果 Gāngguǒ
Copenhagen	哥本哈根 Gēběnhāgēn
Costa Rica	哥斯達黎加 Gēsīdálíjiā / 哥斯大黎加 Gēsīdàlíjiā
Croatia	克羅埃西亞 Kèluó'āixīyà / 克羅埃西亞 Kèluó'āixīyǎ
Cuba	古巴 Gǔbā
Cyprus	塞浦路斯 Sàipǔlùsī / 塞普勒斯 Sàipǔlèsī
Czech Republic	捷克 Jiékè
Denmark	丹麥 Dānmài
Dominican Republic	多米尼加 Duōmǐníjiā / 多明尼加 Duōmíngníjiā

Dublin	都柏林 Dūbólín
East Timor	東帝汶 Dōngdìwèn
Ecuador	厄瓜多爾 Èguāduō'ěr / 厄瓜多 Èguāduō
Egypt	埃及 Āijí
El Salvador	薩爾瓦多 Sà'ěrwǎduō
Estonia	愛沙尼亞 Àishāníyà / Àishāníyǎ
Ethiopia	埃塞俄比亞 Āisài'ébǐyà / 衣索比亞 Yīsuǒbǐyǎ
Europe	歐洲 Ōuzhōu
Fiji	斐濟 Fěijì
Finland	芬蘭 Fēnlán
France	法國 Fǎguó / Fàguó
Gabon	加蓬 Jiāpéng / 加彭 Jiāpéng
Gambia	岡比亞 Gāngbǐyà / 甘比亞 Gānbǐyǎ
Georgia	喬治亞 Qiáozhìyà / Qiáozhìyǎ
Germany	德國 Déguó
Ghana	加納 Jiānà / 迦納 Jiānà
Greece	希臘 Xīlà
Greenland	格陵蘭 Gélínglán
Grenada	格林納達 Gélínnàdá / 格瑞納達 Géruìnàdá
Guam	關島 Guāndǎo
Guangzhou	廣州 Guǎngzhōu
Guatemala	危地馬拉 Wēidìmǎlā / 瓜地馬拉 Guādìmǎlā
Guinea	幾內亞 Jǐnèiyà / Jǐnèiyǎ
Guyana	圭亞那 Guīyànà / 蓋亞納 Gàiyǎnà
Hague	海牙 Hǎiyá
Haiti	海地 Hǎidì
Hanoi	河內 Hénèi
Helsinki	赫爾辛基 Hè'ěrxīnjī
Ho Chi Minh City	胡志明市 Húzhìmíngshì
Holland	荷蘭 Hélán
Holy See	教廷 Jiàotíng
Honduras	洪都拉斯 Hóngdūlāsī / 宏都拉斯

	Hóngdūlāsī
Hong Kong	香港 Xiānggǎng
Hungary	匈牙利 Xiōngyálì
Iceland	冰島 Bīngdǎo
India	印度 Yìndù
Indonesia	印度尼西亞 Yìndùníxīyà / 印尼 Yìnní
Iran	伊朗 Yīlǎng
Iraq	伊拉克 Yīlākè
Ireland	愛爾蘭 Ài'ěrlán
Israel	以色列 Yǐsèliè
Italy	意大利 Yìdàlì / 義大利 Yìdàlì
Ivory Coast	象牙海岸 Xiàngyáhǎi'àn
Jakarta	雅加達 Yǎjiādá
Jamaica	牙買加 Yámǎijiā
Japan	日本 Rìběn
Java	爪哇 Zhǎowā
Jordan	約旦 Yuēdàn
Kaohsiung	高雄 Gāoxióng
Kashmir	克什米爾 Kèshímǐ'ěr / 喀什米爾 Kèshímǐ'ěr
Kazakhstan	哈薩克 Hāsàkè
Kenya	肯尼亞 Kěnníyà / 肯亞 Kěnyà
Kuala Lumpur	吉隆坡 Jílóngpō
Kuwait	科威特 Kēwēitè
Kyoto	京都 Jīngdū
Kyrgyz	吉爾吉斯 Jí'ěrjísī
Laos	老撾 Lǎowō / 寮國 Liáoguó
Latvia	拉脫維亞 Lātuōwéiyà / Lātuōwéiyǎ
Lebanon	黎巴嫩 Líbānèn
Lesotho	萊索托 Láisuǒtuō / 賴索托 Làisuǒtuō
Liberia	利比里亞 Lìbǐlǐyà / 賴比瑞亞 Làibǐruìyà
Libya	利比亞 Lìbǐyà / Lìbǐyǎ
Liechtenstein	列支敦士登 Lièzhīdūnshìdēng / 列支敦斯登 Lièzhīdūnsīdēng
Lithuania	立陶宛 Lìtáowǎn

London	倫敦 Lúndūn
Los Angeles	洛杉磯 Luòshānjī
Luxemburg	盧森堡 Lúsēnbǎo
Macao	澳門 Àomén
Macedonia	馬其頓 Mǎqídùn
Madagascar	馬達加斯加 Mǎdájiāsījiā
Madrid	馬德里 Mǎdélǐ
Malawi	馬拉維 Mǎlāwéi / 馬拉威 Mǎlāwēi
Malaysia	馬來西亞 Mǎláixīyà / Mǎláixīyà
Maldives	馬爾代夫 Mǎ'ěrdàifu / 馬爾地夫 Mǎ'ěrdìfū
Malta	馬耳他 Mǎ'ěrtā / 馬爾他 Mǎ'ěrtā
Manila	馬尼拉 Mǎnílā
Marshall Islands	馬紹爾群島 Mǎshào'ěrqúndǎo
Mauritania	毛里塔尼亞 Máolǐtǎníyà / 茅利塔尼亞 Máolìtǎníyà
Mauritius	毛里求斯 Máolǐqiúsī / 模里西斯 Mólǐxīsī
Melbourne	墨爾本 Mò'ěrběn
Mexico	墨西哥 Mòxīgē
Moldova	摩爾多瓦 Mó'ěrduōwǎ
Monaco	摩納哥 Mónàgē
Mongolia	蒙古 Ménggǔ
Morocco	摩洛哥 Móluògē
Moscow	莫斯科 Mòsīkē
Mozambique	莫桑比克 Mòsāngbǐkè / 莫三比克 Mòsānbǐkè
Myanmar	緬甸 Miǎndiàn
Namibia	納米比亞 Nàmǐbǐyà / 那米比亞 Nàmǐbǐyà
Nanjing	南京 Nánjīng
Nauru	瑙魯 Nǎolǔ / 諾魯 Nuòlǔ
Nepal	尼泊爾 Níbó'ěr
Netherlands	荷蘭 Hélán
New Delhi	新德里 Xīndélǐ
New York	紐約 Niǔyuē
New Zealand	新西蘭 Xīnxīlán / 紐西蘭 Niǔxīlán

Nicaragua	尼加拉瓜 Níjiālāguā
Niger	尼日爾 Nírì'ěr / 尼日 Nírì
Nigeria	尼日利亞 Nírìlìyà / 奈及利亞 Nàijílìyǎ
North America	北美洲 Běiměizhōu
North Korea	朝鮮 Cháoxiān / 北韓 Běihán
Norway	挪威 Nuówēi
Oceania	大洋洲 Dàyángzhōu
Oman	阿曼 Āmàn
Osaka	大阪 Dàbǎn
Oslo	奧斯陸 Àosīlù
Pakistan	巴基斯坦 Bājīsītǎn
Palau	帛琉 Bóliú
Palestine	巴勒斯坦 Bālèsītǎn
Panama	巴拿馬 Bānámǎ
Papua New Guinea	巴布亞新幾內亞 Bābùyàxīnjǐnèiyà / 巴布亞紐幾內亞 Bābùyǎniǔjǐnèiyà
Paraguay	巴拉圭 Bālāguī
Paris	巴黎 Bālí
Peru	秘魯 Bìlǔ / Mìlǔ
Philippines	菲律賓 Fēilǜbīn
Poland	波蘭 Bōlán
Polynesia	波利尼西亞 Bōlìníxīyà / 玻里尼西亞 Bōlǐníxīyà
Portugal	葡萄牙 Pútáoyá
Prague	布拉格 Bùlāgé
Puerto Rico	波多黎各 Bōduōlígè
Pyongyang	平壤 Píngrǎng
Qatar	卡塔爾 Kǎtǎ'ěr / 卡達 Kǎdá
Rio de Janeiro	里約熱內盧 Lǐyuē Rènèilú
Romania	羅馬尼亞 Luómǎníyà / Luómǎníyà
Rome	羅馬 Luómǎ
Russia	俄羅斯 Éluósī / Èluósī
Rwanda	盧旺達 Lúwàngdá / 盧安達 Lú'āndá
San Francisco	舊金山 Jiùjīnshān
San Marino	聖馬力諾 Shèngmǎlìnuò / 聖馬利諾

	Shèngmǎiìnuò
Saudi Arabia	沙特阿拉伯 Shātè Ālābó / 沙烏地阿拉伯 Shāwūdì Ālābó
Senegal	塞內加爾 Sàinèijiā'ěr
Seoul	漢城 Hànchéng
Shanghai	上海 Shànghǎi
Sierra Leone	塞拉利昂 Sàilālì'áng / 獅子山 Shīzishān
Sikkim	錫金 Xījīn / Xíjīn
Singapore	新加坡 Xīnjiāpō
Slovakia	斯洛伐克 Sīluòfákè
Slovenia	斯洛維尼亞 Sīluòwéiníyà / Sīluòwéiníyà
Solomon Islands	所羅門群島 Suǒluóménqúndǎo / 索羅門群島 Suǒluóménqúndǎo
Somalia	索馬里 Suǒmǎlǐ / 索馬利亞 Suǒmǎlìyà
South Africa	南非 Nánfēi
South America	南美洲 Nánměizhōu
South Korea	南朝鮮 Náncháoxiān / 大韓國 Dàhán Mínguó
Spain	西班牙 Xībānyá
Sri Lanka	斯里蘭卡 Sīlǐlánkǎ
Stockholm	斯德哥爾摩 Sīdégē'ěrmó
St. Petersburg	聖彼得堡 Shèngbǐdébǎo
Sudan	蘇丹 Sūdān
Suriname	蘇里南 Sūlǐnán / 蘇利南 Sūlìnán
Swaziland	斯威士蘭 Sīwēishìlán / 史瓦濟蘭 Shǐwǎjìlán
Sweden	瑞典 Ruìdiǎn
Switzerland	瑞士 Ruìshì
Sydney	悉尼 Xīní / 雪梨 Xuělí
Syria	敘利亞 Xùlìyà / Xùlìyà
Taichung	台中 Táizhōng
Taipei	台北 Táiběi
Taiwan	台灣 Táiwān
Tajikistan	塔吉克 Tǎjíkè
Tanzania	坦桑尼亞 Tǎnsāngníyà / 坦尚尼亞

	Tǎnshàngníyǎ
Thailand	泰國 Tàiguó
Tibet	西藏 Xīzàng
Tokyo	東京 Dōngjīng
Tonga	湯加 Tāngjiā / 東加 Dōngjiā
Tunisia	突尼斯 Tūnísī / 突尼西亞 Túníxīyǎ
Turkey	土耳其 Tǔ'ěrqí
Turkmenistan	土庫曼 Tǔkùmàn
Uganda	烏干達 Wūgāndá
Ukraine	烏克蘭 Wūkèlán
United Arab Emirates	阿拉伯聯合酋長國 Ālābó Liánhé Qiúzhǎngguó / 阿拉伯聯合大公國 Ālābó Liánhé Dàgōngguó
United States of America	美國 Měiguó
Uruguay	烏拉圭 Wūlāguī
Uzbekistan	烏茲別克 Wūzībiékè
Vancouver	溫哥華 Wēngēhuá
Vanuatu	萬那杜 Wànnàdù
Vatican	梵蒂岡 Fàndìgāng
Venezuela	委內瑞拉 Wěinèiruìlā
Vienna	維也納 Wéiyěnà
Vietnam	越南 Yuènán
Warsaw	華沙 Huáshā
Washington	華盛頓 Huáshèngdùn
Western Samoa	西薩摩亞 Xīsàmóyà / Xīsàmóyǎ
Yemen	也門 Yěmén / 葉門 Yèmén
Zaire	扎伊爾 Zhāyī'ěr / 薩伊 Sàyī
Zambia	贊比亞 Zànbǐyà / 尚比亞 Shàngbǐyà
Zimbabwe	津巴布韋 Jīnbābùwéi / 辛巴威 Xīnbāwēi

Appendix III 附錄三
Practical Daily Usage
日常實用語句

Rìcháng Shíyòng Yǔjù

● Asking for Directions 問路 wènlù   312

● Bank 銀行 yínháng   312

● Communication 溝通 gōutōng   313

● Congratulations 祝賀 zhùhè   315

● Greetings 招呼 zhāohu   315

● Health 健康 jiànkāng   316

● Hotel 住宿 zhùsù   318

● Restaurants 餐廳 cāntīng   319

● Shopping 買東西 mǎi dōngxi   321

● Telephoning 打電話 dǎdiànhuà   323

● Transportation 交通 jiāotōng   325

Asking for Directions 問路 wènlù

Excuse me, where is the railway station?
請問，火車站在哪裡？
Qǐngwèn, huǒchēzhàn zài nǎli?

Excuse me, which direction is China Hotel?
請問，中國飯店怎麼走？
Qǐngwèn, Zhōngguó Fàndiàn zěnme zǒu?

I'm lost.
我迷路了。
Wǒ mílù le.

Is there a post office near here?
這附近有郵局嗎？
Zhè fùjìn yǒu yóujú ma?

Is this Zhong Shan North Road?
這裡是中山北路嗎？
Zhèlǐ shì Zhōngshān Běi Lù ma?

Bank 銀行 yínháng

Can I withdraw cash using this credit card?
我能用這張信用卡領錢嗎？
Wǒ néng yòng zhè zhāng xìnyòngkǎ lǐngqián ma?

Can I exchange foreign currency (personal checks) here?
這裡能兌換外幣(私人支票)嗎？
Zhèlǐ néng duìhuàn wàibì (sīrén zhīpiào) ma?

Could you (please) tell me when the bank is open?
請告訴我銀行的營業時間。
Qǐng gàosu wǒ yínháng de yíngyè shíjiān.

How much commission do you charge?
你們收多少手續費？
Nǐmen shōu duōshao shǒuxùfèi?

I would like to change some money.
我想兌換點兒錢。
Wǒ xiǎng duìhuàn diǎnr qián.

What is the exchange rate?
匯率是多少？
Huìlǜ shì duōshao?

Where are the ATMs?
哪裡有自動提款機？
Nǎli yǒu zìdòng tíkuǎnjī?

Communication 溝通 gōutōng

Can you translate this for me?
你能為我翻譯一下嗎？
Nǐ néng wèi wǒ fānyì yíxià ma?

Could you speak more slowly, please?
請你說慢一點兒。
Qǐng nǐ shuō màn yìdiǎnr.

Do you speak English?
你會說英語嗎？
Nǐ huì shuō Yīngyǔ ma?

Do you understand?
你懂了嗎？
Nǐ dǒngle ma?

Does anyone here speak English?
這兒有人會說英語嗎？
Zhèr yǒu rén huì shuō Yīngyǔ ma?

How long have you been here?
你來多久了？
Nǐ lái duōjiǔ le?

I don't speak Chinese.
我不會說中文。
Wǒ bú huì shuō Zhōngwén.

I don't understand.
我不懂。
Wǒ bù dǒng.

I only speak a little Chinese.
我只會說一點兒中文。
Wǒ zhǐ huì shuō yìdiǎnr Zhōngwén.

Never mind.
沒關係。
Méi guānxi.

No problem.
沒問題。
Méi wèntí.

Not at all!
不客氣！
Bú kèqi!

Please give me a hand.
請你幫我個忙。
Qǐng nǐ bāng wǒ ge máng.

Please write it down.
請你寫下來。
Qǐng nǐ xiě xiàlai.

Sorry, could you please say that again?
對不起，請你再說一遍。
Duìbuqǐ, qǐng nǐ zài shuō yí biàn.

Thank you.
謝謝。
Xièxie.

What is today's date?
今天幾月幾號？
Jīntiān jǐ yuè jǐ hào?

What day is today?
今天星期幾？
Jīntiān xīngqī jǐ?

What does this mean?
這是甚麼意思？
Zhè shì shénme yìsi?

What time is it?
現在幾點？
Xiànzài jǐ diǎn?

Congratulations 祝賀 zhùhè

Congratulations!
恭喜！
Gōngxǐ!

Happy Birthday!
生日快樂！
Shēngrì kuàilè!

Happy New Year!
新年快樂！
Xīnnián kuàilè!

Have a nice weekend!
週末愉快！
Zhōumò yúkuài!

Have a safe trip!
一路順風！
Yí-lù-shùn-fēng!

I hope you have a good time!
祝你玩得愉快！
Zhù nǐ wán de yúkuài!

Greetings 招呼 zhāohu

Good-bye!
再見！
Zàijiàn!

Good morning!
早安！
Zǎo'ān!

Good night!
晚安！
Wǎn'ān!

Hello!
你好！
Nǐhǎo!

Here's my name card.
這是我的名片。
Zhè shì wǒ de míngpiàn.

How have you been recently?
最近怎麼樣?
Zuìjìn zěnmeyàng?

It's nice to see you again.
很高興再見到你。
Hěn gāoxìng zài jiàn dào nǐ.

I've heard so much about you.
久仰。
Jiǔyǎng.

Long time no see!
好久不見!
Hǎo jiǔ bú jiàn!

Pleased to meet you.
很高興認識你。
Hěn gāoxìng rènshi nǐ.

See you next time.
下次見。
Xià cì jiàn.

Health 健康 jiànkāng

Can I have a medical certificate?
請給我開診斷書。
Qǐng gěi wǒ kāi zhěnduànshū.

Do you have anything for a cold?
我要治感冒的藥。
Wǒ yào zhì gǎnmào de yào.

How do I take the medicine?
這個藥怎麼服用?
Zhège yào zěnme fúyòng?

I caught a cold.
我感冒了。
Wǒ gǎnmào le.

I'd like to see an English-speaking doctor.
我要找個會說英語的醫生。
Wǒ yào zhǎoge huì shuō Yīngyǔ de yīshēng.

I don't feel well.
我覺得不舒服。
Wǒ juéde bù shūfu.

I feel dizzy.
我頭暈。
Wǒ tóuyūn.

I feel sick.
我覺得想吐。
Wǒ juéde xiǎng tù.

I have a diarrhea.
我拉肚子。
Wǒ lā dùzi.

I have a fever.
我發燒了。
Wǒ fāshāo le.

I have a pain here.
我這兒痛。
Wǒ zhèr tòng.

I have a sore throat (toothache).
我喉嚨痛(牙痛)。
Wǒ hóulongtòng (yátòng).

I have allergies to medicine.
我對藥過敏。
Wǒ duì yào guòmǐn.

I want to register to see the doctor.
我要掛號。
Wǒ yào guàhào.

I've become ill.
我生病了。
Wǒ shēngbìng le.

I've been bitten by an insect.
我被蟲子咬了。
Wǒ bèi chóngzi yǎo le.

Please explain what is wrong with me.

請告訴我是甚麼病。

Qǐng gàosu wǒ shì shénme bìng.

Where can I buy this medicine?

哪裡能買到這個藥？

Nǎli néng mǎi dào zhège yào?

Hotel 住宿 zhùsù

Are there any others?

還有沒有別的房間？

Hái yǒu méiyǒu bié de fángjiān?

Could you have my baggage brought up?

請幫我把行李送來好嗎？

Qǐng bāng wǒ bǎ xíngli sòng lái hǎo ma?

Do you accept credit cards or traveler's checks?

可以使用信用卡或旅行支票嗎？

Kěyǐ shǐyòng xìnyòngkǎ huò lǚxíng zhīpiào ma?

Do you give a discount for students?

學生有沒有優惠？

Xuésheng yǒu méiyǒu yōuhuì?

Do you have a room available tonight?

今天晚上有沒有房間？

Jīntiān wǎnshang yǒu méiyǒu fángjiān?

Do you have any off-season discount rate?

有沒有淡季優惠？

Yǒu méiyǒu dànjì yōuhuì?

How much is it per night?

住一晚多少錢？

Zhù yì wǎn duōshao qián?

I'd like a wake-up call.

早上請打電話叫醒我。

Zǎoshang qǐng dǎdiànhuà jiàoxǐng wǒ.

I'd like a pot of mineral water.

我要礦泉水。

Wǒ yào kuàngquánshuǐ.

I'd like a single room (double room).

我要一間單人房(雙人房)。

Wǒ yào yì jiān dānrénfáng (shuāngrénfáng).

I'd like to change to another room.

我想換一個房間。

Wǒ xiǎng huàn yí ge fángjiān.

I'd like to stay an extra night.

我想再住一晚。

Wǒ xiǎng zài zhù yì wǎn.

Is there a dining room?

這兒有沒有餐廳？

Zhèr yǒu méiyǒu cāntīng?

Is there another hotel nearby?

附近還有其他旅館嗎？

Fùjìn hái yǒu qítā lǚguǎn ma?

May I see the room, please?

我可以看一看房間嗎？

Wǒ kěyǐ kànyikàn fángjiān ma?

Please bring me some ice cubes and water.

請送冰塊和水給我。

Qǐng sòng bīngkuài hé shuǐ gěi wǒ.

When is breakfast?

幾點吃早餐？

Jǐ diǎn chī zǎocān?

Restaurants 餐廳 cāntīng

Can you recommend any dishes?

你可以推薦幾道菜嗎？

Nǐ kěyǐ tuījiàn jǐ dào cài ma?

Do you have an English menu?

你有英文菜單嗎？

Nǐ yǒu Yīngwén càidān ma?

Don't add too much seasoning.

味道不要太重。

Wèidao bú yào tài zhòng.

How much longer will our food be?
我們點的菜還要等多久？
Wǒmen diǎn de cài hái yào děng duōjiǔ?

I am a vegetarian.
我是吃素的。
Wǒ shì chīsù de.

I can't use chopsticks.
我不會用筷子。
Wǒ bú huì yòng kuàizi.

I like to eat Chinese food.
我喜歡吃中國菜。
Wǒ xǐhuan chī Zhōngguó cài.

It's all together.
我們的帳一起算。
Wǒmen de zhàng yìqǐ suàn.

It's my treat.
我請你吃飯。
Wǒ qǐng nǐ chīfàn.

Just a cup of tea, please.
請給我一杯茶就好。
Qǐng gěi wǒ yì bēi chá jiù hǎo.

May I have the menu?
請給我菜單。
Qǐng gěi wǒ càidān.

No MSG, please.
請不要放味精。
Qǐng bú yào fàng wèijīng.

This restaurant is full.
這家餐廳客滿了。
Zhè jiā cāntīng kèmǎn le.

Please don't make it spicy.
不要放辣。
Bú yào fàng là.

Please give me a knife and fork.
請給我刀子和叉子。
Qǐng gěi wǒ dāozi hé chāzi.

That's not what I ordered.
我點的不是這個菜。
Wǒ diǎn de bú shì zhège cài.

The check, please.
請給我帳單。
Qǐng gěi wǒ zhàngdān.

The service in this restaurant is excellent.
這家餐廳的服務很好。
Zhè jiā cāntīng de fúwù hěn hǎo.

We'd like a table in the nonsmoking section.
我們要非吸煙區的位子。
Wǒmen yào fēi xīyānqū de wèizi.

We'd like to pay separately.
我們要各付各的。
Wǒmen yào gè fù gè de.

What is this dish made of ?
這道菜是用甚麼做的？
Zhè dào cài shì yòng shénme zuò de?

Do we need to leave a tip here?
要不要給小費？
Yào bú yào gěi xiǎofèi?

Would you like to make a reservation?
要不要訂位？
Yào bú yào dìngwèi?

Shopping 買東西 mǎi dōngxi

Are you open in the evening?
你們晚上營業嗎？
Nǐmen wǎnshang yíngyè ma?

Can I try it on?
我可以試穿嗎？
Wǒ kěyǐ shìchuān ma?

Can you give me a discount?
能打折扣嗎？
Néng dǎ zhékòu ma?

Can you reduce the price?
能便宜一點兒嗎？
Néng piányi yìdiǎnr ma?

Could I have a receipt, please?
請給我收據。
Qǐng gěi wǒ shōujù.

Could you wrap it for me?
你能不能幫我包起來？
Nǐ néng bù néng bāng wǒ bāoqilai?

Do you accept credit cards?
可以用信用卡嗎？
Kěyǐ yòng xìnyòngkǎ ma?

Do you accept traveler's checks?
你們收不收旅行支票？
Nǐmen shōu bù shōu lǚxíng zhīpiào?

Do you have another color (style)?
還有別的顏色(樣式)嗎？
Hái yǒu bié de yánsè (yàngshì) ma?

Do you have anything larger (smaller)?
有大(小)一點兒的嗎？
Yǒu dà (xiǎo) yìdiǎnr de ma?

Do you have anything less expensive?
還有更便宜的嗎？
Hái yǒu gèng piányi de ma?

How much is this?
這個多少錢？
Zhège duōshao qián?

I'd like to change this, please.
我想要換這個。
Wǒ xiǎngyào huàn zhège.

I'd like to think about it.
我再考慮一下。
Wǒ zài kǎolǜ yíxià.

I'm just looking.
我只是看看。
Wǒ zhǐshì kànkan.

It's too expensive.
太貴了。
Tài guì le.

Let's go shopping.
我們去逛街吧。
Wǒmen qù guàngjiē ba.

Welcome!
歡迎光臨！
Huānyíng guānglín!

Where do I pay?
在哪兒付款？
Zài nǎr fùkuǎn?

Telephoning 打電話 dǎdiànhuà

Can I have your telephone number?
請告訴我你的電話號碼。
Qǐng gàosu wǒ nǐ de diànhuà hàomǎ.

Can I make an international call from here?
這裡能不能打國際電話？
Zhèlǐ néng bù néng dǎ guójì diànhuà?

Could you ask him to call me back?
你可以請他回電嗎？
Nǐ kěyǐ qǐng tā huídiàn ma?

Extension 123, please.
請轉分機 123 。
Qǐng zhuǎn fēnjī 123.

He is not in now.
他現在不在。
Tā xiànzài bú zài.

Hold the line, please.
請不要掛電話。
Qǐng bú yào guà diànhuà.

I can't hear you.
我聽不清楚。
Wǒ tīng bù qīngchu.

I'd like a phone card, please.
請給我一張電話卡。
Qǐng gěi wǒ yì zhāng diànhuàkǎ.

I'll call back later.
我過一會兒再打。
Wǒ guò yìhuǐr zài dǎ.

I would like to make a collect call.
我要打對方付費電話。
Wǒ yào dǎ duìfāng fùfèi diànhuà.

Just a minute, please.
請稍候。
Qǐng shāohòu.

May I speak to Mr. Chen?
請問，陳先生在嗎？
Qǐngwèn, Chén xiānsheng zài ma?

May I take your message?
你要留話嗎？
Nǐ yào liúhuà ma?

Please call me.
請打電話給我。
Qǐng dǎdiànhuà gěi wǒ.

Please say it again. (Pardon?)
請你再說一次。
Qǐng nǐ zài shuō yí cì.

Please speak slowly.
請說慢一點兒。
Qǐng shuō màn yìdiǎnr.

Sorry, wrong number.
對不起，打錯了。
Duìbuqǐ, dǎcuò le.

Speaking.
我就是。
Wǒ jiù shì.

Thank you, I'll phone back.
謝謝，我再打過來。
Xièxie, wǒ zài dǎ guòlai.

This is the Far East Company.

這裡是遠東公司。

Zhèlǐ shì Yuǎn Dōng Gōngsī.

When will he be back?

他甚麼時候回來？

Tā shénme shíhou huílai?

Where is the nearest phone booth?

最近的電話亭在哪兒？

Zuì jìn de diànhuàtíng zài nǎr?

Who is speaking, please?

請問你是哪一位？

Qǐngwèn nǐ shì nǎ yí wèi?

Transportation 交通 jiāotōng

Are taxis expensive?

搭出租車(計程車)貴不貴？

Dā chūzūchē (jìchéngchē) guì bú guì?

Are there any seats left in the nonsmoking section?

禁煙區還有座位嗎？

Jìnyānqū hái yǒu zuòwèi ma?

Are there any ships leaving for Shanghai tomorrow?

明天有開往上海的船班嗎？

Míngtiān yǒu kāi wǎng Shànghǎi de chuánbān ma?

Could you call a taxi for me?

請幫我叫一輛出租車(計程車)。

Qǐng bāng wǒ jiào yí liàng chūzūchē (jìchéngchē).

How do I switch lines (buses)?

我應該怎麼換車？

Wǒ yīnggāi zěnme huàn chē?

How long does it take to get to the Taipei Main Station?

到台北車站要多久？

Dào Táiběi Chēzhàn yào duōjiǔ?

How long until the next bus?

下一班巴士(公車)要多久？

Xià yì bān bāshì (gōngchē) yào duōjiǔ?

How much is one ticket?

一張票多少錢？

Yī zhāng piào duōshao qián?

I would like to buy a round-trip ticket.

我要買來回票。

Wǒ yào mǎi láihuípiào.

I'd like a window seat, please.

我想要靠窗的座位。

Wǒ xiǎngyào kàochuāng de zuòwèi.

I'm going to take a plane there.

我會搭飛機去。

Wǒ huì dā fēijī qù.

Is there anyone sitting here?

這個座位有人嗎？

Zhège zuòwèi yǒu rén ma?

Is there food for sale on the train?

火車上販賣餐點嗎？

Huǒchē shàng fànmài cāndiǎn ma?

Please take me to the National Palace Museum.

請到故宮。

Qǐng dào Gùgōng.

Where can I buy a ticket?

到哪裡買票？

Dào nǎli mǎi piào?

Where is the nearest subway station?

最近的地鐵站在哪裡？

Zuì jìn de dìtiězhàn zài nǎli?

Which stop is Tiananmen Square?

天安門是第幾站？

Tiān'ānmén shì dì jǐ zhàn?

Which track is my train on?

在第幾月台搭車？

Zài dì jǐ yuètái dā chē?

Appendix IV　附錄四　Hanyu Pinyin Table

Finals		b	p	m	f	d	t	n	l	g	k	h	j	q	x	zh	ch	sh	r	z	c	s
a	a	ba	pa	ma	fa	da	ta	na	la	ga	ka	ha				zha	cha	sha		za	ca	sa
o	o	bo	po	mo	fo																	
e	e					de	te	ne	le	ge	ke	he				zhe	che	she	re	ze	ce	se
ê	ê																					
ai	ai	bai	pai	mai		dai	tai	nai	lai	gai	kai	hai				zhai	chai	shai		zai	cai	sai
ei	ei	bei	pei	mei	fei	dei		nei	lei	gei	kei	hei				zhei		shei		zei		
ao	ao	bao	pao	mao		dao	tao	nao	lao	gao	kao	hao				zhao	chao	shao	rao	zao	cao	sao
ou	ou		pou	mou	fou	dou	tou	nou	lou	gou	kou	hou				zhou	chou	shou	rou	zou	cou	sou
an	an	ban	pan	man	fan	dan	tan	nan	lan	gan	kan	han				zhan	chan	shan	ran	zan	can	san
en	en	ben	pen	men	fen			nen		gen	ken	hen				zhen	chen	shen	ren	zen	cen	sen
ang	ang	bang	pang	mang	fang	dang	tang	nang	lang	gang	kang	hang				zhang	chang	shang	rang	zang	cang	sang
eng	eng	beng	peng	meng	feng	deng	teng	neng	leng	geng	keng	heng				zheng	cheng	sheng	reng	zeng	ceng	seng
er	er																					
-i																zhi	chi	shi	ri	zi	ci	si
i	yi	bi	pi	mi		di	ti	ni	li				ji	qi	xi							
ia	ya								lia				jia	qia	xia							
io	yo																					
ie	ye	bie	pie	mie		die	tie	nie	lie				jie	qie	xie							
iai	yai																					
iao	yao	biao	piao	miao		diao	tiao	niao	liao				jiao	qiao	xiao							
iu	you			miu		diu		niu	liu				jiu	qiu	xiu							
ian	yan	bian	pian	mian		dian	tian	nian	lian				jian	qian	xian							
in	yin	bin	pin	min				nin	lin				jin	qin	xin							
iang	yang							niang	liang				jiang	qiang	xiang							
ing	ying	bing	ping	ming		ding	ting	ning	ling				jing	qing	xing							
u	wu	bu	pu	mu	fu	du	tu	nu	lu	gu	ku	hu				zhu	chu	shu	ru	zu	cu	su
ua	wa									gua	kua	hua				zhua	chua	shua				
uo	wo					duo	tuo	nuo	luo	guo	kuo	huo				zhuo	chuo	shuo	ruo	zuo	cuo	suo
uai	wai									guai	kuai	huai				zhuai	chuai	shuai				
ui	wei					dui	tui			gui	kui	hui				zhui	chui	shui	rui	zui	cui	sui
uan	wan					duan	tuan	nuan	luan	guan	kuan	huan				zhuan	chuan	shuan	ruan	zuan	cuan	suan
un	wen					dun	tun		lun	gun	kun	hun				zhun	chun	shun	run	zun	cun	sun
uang	wang									guang	kuang	huang				zhuang	chuang	shuang				
ong	weng					dong	tong	nong	long	gong	kong	hong				zhong	chong		rong	zong	cong	song
ü	yu					nü		lü					ju	qu	xu							
üe	yue					nüe		lüe					jue	que	xue							
üan	yuan							lüan					juan	quan	xuan							
ün	yun												jun	qun	xun							
iong	yong												jiong	qiong	xiong							

國家圖書館出版品預行編目資料

遠東拼音英漢辭典 = Far East English-Chinese
Pinyin Dictionary / 遠東圖書公司
編審委員會編輯.---初版.---臺北市 :
遠東, 2004 [民93]
　　面;　　公分
ISBN 957-612-674-6(48K平裝)
ISBN 957-612-678-9(60K平裝)
1.英國語言－字典, 辭典－中國語言
805.132　　　　　　　　　　　　93003579

Far East
English-Chinese Pinyin Dictionary
遠東英漢拼音辭典

60K 道林紙本　　2007年版

編　輯　者 / 遠 東 圖 書 公 司 編 審 委 員 會
發 行 人 / 浦　　　永　　　強
印　刷　者 / 遠 東 圖 書 股 份 有 限 公 司
發　行　所 / 遠 東 圖 書 股 份 有 限 公 司
地　　　址 / 台 北 市 重 慶 南 路 一 段 66 號
電 話 總 機 / (02)23118740 傳 真/(02)23114184
郵 政 劃 撥 / 00056691
美 國 發 行 所 / U.S. 國際出版公司
　　　　　　　U.S. International Publishing Inc.
　　　　　　　www.usipusa.com
登　記　證 / 局版台業字第0820號